S0-BNC-252

Lend Me Your Ears

Lend Me Your Ears

Oxford Dictionary of Political Quotations

FOURTH EDITION

Edited by Antony Jay

RECEIVED

MAY 19 2011

MINNESOTA STATE UNIVERSITY
MANKATO, MN 56002-8419

OXFORD
UNIVERSITY PRESS

OXFORD
UNIVERSITY PRESS

Great Clarendon Street, Oxford OX2 6DP

Oxford University Press is a department of the University of Oxford.
It furthers the University's objective of excellence in research, scholarship,
and education by publishing worldwide in

Oxford New York

Auckland Cape Town Dar es Salaam Hong Kong Karachi
Kuala Lumpur Madrid Melbourne Mexico City Nairobi
New Delhi Shanghai Taipei Toronto

With offices in

Argentina Austria Brazil Chile Czech Republic France Greece
Guatemala Hungary Italy Japan Poland Portugal Singapore
South Korea Switzerland Thailand Turkey Ukraine Vietnam

Oxford is a registered trade mark of Oxford University Press
in the UK and in certain other countries

Published in the United States
by Oxford University Press Inc., New York

© Oxford University Press 2010

Selection and arrangement © Antony Jay,
Oxford University Press 1996, 2001, 2006, 2010
Introduction © Antony Jay 1996, 2010
From Rhetoric to Sound Bites © Matthew Parris 2010

The moral rights of the authors have been asserted
Database right Oxford University Press (maker)

First published 1996
Second edition 2001
Third edition 2006
Fourth edition 2010
Previous editions published as *Oxford Dictionary of Political Quotations*

All rights reserved. No part of this publication may be reproduced, stored in a retrieval
system, or transmitted, in any form or by any means, without the prior permission in writing
of Oxford University Press, or as expressly permitted by law, or under terms agreed with the
appropriate reprographics rights organization. Enquiries concerning reproduction outside
the scope of the above should be sent to the Rights Department, Oxford University Press,
at the address above

You must not circulate this book in any other binding or cover
and you must impose the same condition on any acquirer

British Library Cataloguing in Publication Data

Data available
Library of Congress Cataloging in Publication Data

Data available
Library of Congress Control Number: 2010923325
Typeset by Datagrafix, Inc.
Printed in Great Britain
on acid-free paper by
Clays Ltd., St Ives plc

ISBN 978-0-19-957267-0

10 9 8 7 6 5 4 3 2 1

Ref.
PN
6084
.P6
O94
2010

Contents

Project Team

Commissioning Editors	Ben Harris
	Joanna Harris
Associate Editor	Susan Ratcliffe
Reading Programme	Jean Harker
	Verity Mason
Research	Ralph Bates
Data Capture	Susanne Charlett
Proofreading	Kim Allen

Introduction to the Fourth Edition

This ought to be the great age of quotations; never in the history of human communication has so much been written by so many at such length. A decline in printing costs has produced a significant increase in books, magazines, and newspapers, digital broadcasting has led to a massive increase in the number of radio and television channels, and the internet has poured millions of words into blogs, twitters, and websites. If words memorably quoted were in direct proportion to words produced, this dictionary would need at least twenty-four volumes. But in fact we have found that one volume still does very nicely.

Why should this be? One reason surely is that it has never been easier to write for public consumption and, as Sheridan pointed out, 'Easy writing's vile hard reading'. There was a time when writing involved physical as well as mental effort: carving words in marble or pressing them in clay or wax forced the writer to restrict himself to what was worth inscribing, and to express it as economically as possible. Even pen and ink, even manual typesetting, gave a motive for selection and compression. But today those disciplines and restraints have been abolished by the universal keyboard and the computer screen. The result is that this fourth edition of the dictionary has not been engulfed in a tsunami of the quoted and the quotable: the new candidates which meet our high criteria for inclusion have been no more numerous than for the previous three editions—although curiously the number of new entries from earlier years is as large as ever, if not larger.

Another reason is that we rarely include quotations that cannot be verified. In the past, this meant excluding those that had not appeared in print—or, very occasionally, on national radio or television, and even these usually found their way into print in the course of time. This is not due to lexicographical Luddism; it is because many electronic reference locations are unstable and capable of being changed or withdrawn at short notice. However, more and more websites are acquiring a reliability and permanence that suggest that by the next edition some of them may earn a place in their own right without adoption by a source printed on paper. (In passing it is perhaps worth recording that 2009 saw the first instance of one of the dictionary's quotations being physically stolen: the inscription 'Arbeit macht frei' was taken by thieves from the entrance to Auschwitz, though later recovered.)

There is certainly a need for a new edition: the world has seen many changes since the third edition was published in the spring of 2006, not least the most spectacular financial collapse for at least eighty years. Amongst its myriad effects has been its contribution of a classic observation by Warren Buffet to the fourth edition ('It's only when the tide goes out that you learn who's been swimming naked'). We have also seen the United States elect its first black president, who has already supplied a number of entries to this edition ('We will extend a hand if you are willing to unclench your fist', 'I am who the media says I am') and is likely to supply more to the next. And in Europe we have witnessed the installation of two unelected leaders: the first president of the European Community and a Prime Minister of the United Kingdom. Another newcomer has been the first entry in the dictionary from that literary masterpiece The Sale of Goods Act 1979, which passed into the language of political communication when the Home Secretary described the immigration system as 'not fit for purpose'. Among others, Hillary Clinton assured us that 'If I misspoke that was just a misstatement', Hazel Blears commented 'YouTube if you want to', and Vince Cable noted 'the Prime Minister's remarkable transformation in the last few weeks from Stalin to Mr Bean'.

Two groups of people became national news by virtue (if that is the right word) of the money they made while the rest of the country were being forced to tighten their belts. Bankers' bonuses were rarely out of the headlines, recalling Joe Hyman's observation 'There are three kinds of banks, and in descending order of integrity they are High Street banks, mountebanks, and merchant banks' though this did not stop Lord Mandelson assuring us that New Labour was 'intensely relaxed about people getting filthy rich', and MPs' expenses provoked national outrage with successive revelations of claims that included bath plugs, moat cleaning, and a duck house, even though Peter Viggers MP said 'I paid for it myself and in fact it was never liked by the ducks' and Anthony Steen asking 'What right does the public have to interfere with my private life? None'.

This all seems a world away from the first edition, when John Major was Prime Minister and Bill Clinton was still in his first term as president. Since then the Blair years have come and gone, and the troubles in Iraq have still not ended. We have had a general election (which has its own box on p. 445), a hung parliament, and the first peacetime coalition to be formed since 1931—and anyone who voted then would be at least 100 years old this year. There has however been one unchanging factor throughout the fifteen years in which I have been allowed to edit the dictionary, and that is the wise judgement, indefatigable research, and scholarly rigour of the editorial team at the Oxford University Press, and I would like to record my special gratitude to Joanna Harris, Ben Harris, and Susan Ratcliffe for their invaluable contributions to this edition. I was also fortunate enough to enlist the help and pick the brains of a distinguished panel of experts who read through the new quotations and provided excellent comments and suggestions, and I welcome this opportunity to record my grateful appreciation to Dr Simon Heffer, Professor Peter Hennessy, Elizabeth Knowles, and Andrew Roberts.

ANTONY JAY

Somerset, December 2009

Introduction to the First Edition

'The hard pressed writer in turning over these pages may find and note many excellent phrases, whether to give a pleasing touch of erudition or to save the trouble of thinking for himself.' Bernard Darwin's words in his introduction to the first *Oxford Dictionary of Quotations* are as true today as they were fifty-five years ago. But there are more honourable reasons for using quotations, especially in the world of politics. In mobilizing support for a project or a policy it is especially agreeable to be able to call upon the distinguished dead; their distinction adds intellectual weight and moral force to the argument, and their death makes it impossible for them to appear on television later and say that they meant something completely different.

Even more important, perhaps, than the support of the eminent is the wisdom of the ages. New ideas in politics are always suspect, but recourse to quotation can show that your ideas, far from being new and tender shoots, are rooted deep in the history of political society. Those who argue for punishment as deterrent rather than rehabilitation may find themselves out of the fashion, but a quick look at Aeschylus will enable them to demonstrate the two and a half thousand year pedigree of their belief. Those who oppose closer ties with Europe can quote Bagehot, 'Are they [the English people] not above all nations divided from the rest of the world? ... Are they not out of the current of common European causes and affairs?' from the nineteenth century, and Gibbon, 'The division of Europe into a number of independent states is productive of the most beneficial consequences to the liberty of mankind,' from the eighteenth, to show that there is nothing new in their belief that there is strength and logic in their resistance, while Europhiles can adduce the dictum of the nineteenth-century Prime Minister Lord Salisbury: 'We are part of the community of Europe and we must do our duty as such.' Just occasionally, too, quotations can be used not just for intellectual support, but for dramatic effect, as if they carried some magical power. Two Prime Ministers in living memory have felt the force of it. The first was Chamberlain in 1940, when Leo Amery quoted Cromwell's historic words to the Rump Parliament 'You have sat too long for any good you have been doing. Depart, I say, and let us have done with you. In the name of God, go!' Chamberlain went. The second was Macmillan in 1963, when a fellow Conservative, Nigel Birch, quoted just as lethally from Browning's *The Lost Leader*:

> Life's night begins; let him never come back to us!
> There would be doubt, hesitation and pain,

> Forced praise on our part—the glimmer of twilight,
> Never glad confident morning again!

Perhaps Macmillan was doomed anyway, but Birch's quotation made certain of his fall as surely as Brutus' dagger.

This dictionary, it is hoped, will be of service to those who want to support their arguments and opinions with evidence of their distinguished pedigree and ancient lineage, as well as those looking for no more than a pleasing touch of erudition or the avoidance of thought. It is not, however, simply an anthology of political wit and wisdom. It is, foremost, and above all, a work of reference. The primary qualification for an entry is not its antiquity or its profundity but its familiarity. There is a bank of political quotations which are part of the currency of political speeches and writings throughout the English-speaking world. All of them should be in these pages, and if they are not (and I am sure time and alert readers will expose some glaring omissions) then the editor is to blame.

Beyond the central core of universally recognized political quotations there is a much wider circle of entries which, while they are quoted from time to time, are not immediately recognizable to all of those to whom they are addressed. These are subject to editorial judgement, and here the editor might try to defend an omission rather than apologize for it. But in both cases the key question has been 'Should this be in a work of reference?' The two principal users for whom the book is intended are those who have encountered or partly recall a quotation and want to verify or source it, and those who are looking for a quotation on a given subject or from a given writer.

Many works of reference, however, have an appeal to browsers and grazers as well as hunters, and a dictionary of political quotations must be very close to the top of the list; it offers the delight of discovery as well as confirmation and verification. While this one is not designed as an anthology, it is bound to give the reader most of the pleasure of an anthology, and so in many cases I have tried to supply more contextual information than might be necessary in a work of pure reference. Some quotations (for instance Wellington's 'If you believe that you'll believe anything') make little sense to any but the expert reader, unless accompanied by some indication of the context. Others, while intelligible (like Margaret Thatcher's 'Now it must be business as usual'), can become much more interesting with some knowledge of the circumstances in which they were uttered. For the same reason the Dictionary is organized not by theme but by the name of the speaker or writer. I have never myself been entirely at ease with thematic organization—I always have a niggling suspicion that any thematic entry could legitimately have been included under a different heading, and often under several—whereas entries grouped under the name of the source cannot suffer under this disability, and arrangement by source is just as helpful as arrangement by theme for reference purposes. In a collection of political quotations, this form is particularly advantageous, especially for the random dipper: reading through the citations for one individual—Lloyd George, de Tocqueville, Halifax—gives a quick but vivid sense not only of what he said but also of his quality and individuality. So although this is indeed a work of reference, it is hoped that many people will also use it as an illuminating, if wildly unsystematic, compendium of opinions, ideas, and personalities that have marked our progress towards the political society we live in today.

So what makes a quotation into a political quotation? Often, of course, the answer is obvious. General truths about politics are immediate candidates: Aeschylus's 'Everyone's quick to blame the alien', Bacon's 'All rising to great place is by a winding stair', and Burke's 'To tax and to please, no more than to love and be wise, is not given to men.' Then there are the quotations specific to an event or individual which have passed into the language: Disraeli's 'I have climbed to the top of the greasy pole' ot Mary Tudor's 'When I am dead and opened, you shall find "Calais" lying in my heart', even though it is more often misquoted than quoted. Some quotations would not merit quotation but for the source; if you or I had said 'No woman in my time will be Prime Minister' we would hardly expect to find ourselves in the Dictionary. The fact that Margaret Thatcher said it makes all the difference.

There is however a disputed territory between what is obviously a political quotation and what is obviously not. There is nothing remotely political about the words 'I can't tell a lie, Pa; you know I can't tell a lie. I did cut it with my hatchet,' but because it illuminates Washington's character, and because its frequent quotation testifies to his reputation, there can be no question of leaving it out. But what about the sayings of great men when they are writing fiction and the words come from the mouths of their characters, as in Macaulay's poems or Disraeli's novels. Surely it can not be cheating to include them if exclusion would mean omitting 'A Jacobite's Epitaph'? And the 'Two Nations' speech in *Sybil* is currently at the heart of the Conservative Party's internal strife.

Another obscure territorial boundary is that which divides, or fails to divide, political quotations from those which, while having large areas that overlap politics, might more properly be classified under headings such as law, warfare, royalty, or economics. If these subjects had their own Oxford quotation dictionaries, there might have been some debate about where to place Adam Smith's observation that 'people of the same trade seldom meet together, even for merriment and diversion, but the conversation ends in a conspiracy against the public, or in some contrivance to raise prices.' Since there is however (as yet) no Oxford Dictionary of Economics Quotations, there was no argument. There is however an excellent *Oxford Book of Political Anecdotes* and, while some anecdotes are the source of quotation, anecdotes as such are not included. Obviously there were temptations. After losing office in 1964 Iain Macleod was a conspicuous absentee from the opposition front bench, which Wilson knew was a cause of much critical comment among Conservative back-benchers. One day however he did appear, to put a challenging question to the Prime Minister. Wilson rose, paused, and then said 'Do you come here often?' It produced one of the biggest laughs ever heard from a party against one of its own front-benchers. But somehow 'Do you come here often?' did not sound like a political quotation; it belongs only in that anecdote and had to be excluded.

Of course not all political quotations are either by politicians or about politics. Lewis Carroll was certainly not a politician and *Alice Through the Looking Glass* is equally certainly not a political work, but 'Jam tomorrow' and ' when I use a word it means just what I choose it to mean' are regularly quoted in political debate— as witness the quotation from Tony Benn 'Some of that jam we thought was for tomorrow we have already eaten.' The Dictionary would be failing its readers if it left them out. Politicians may no longer quote poetry as freely as they used to, but students of the politics of the recent past will find many quotations from and references to poets, and even today they may encounter Kipling's 'Paying the Dane-geld', Chesterton's 'The Secret People', and copious allusions to the Vicar of Bray. And there is of course one poet who stands out above all the others for frequency of quotation: it is not just the power and range of Shakespeare's writing that makes him so quotable in a political context, it is the fact that so many of his plays are so intensely political in their themes, characters, and conflicts. If readers feel that he is over-represented here, I can only say that I have been acutely aware of the apparently excessive space he has been given, and that the original section was considerably longer. Much weeding has been done, and the surviving entries represent the editor's judgement of those that could not be omitted without loss.

Shakespeare is not the only writer (though he is the only poet) to occupy what might seem to be a disproportionate amount of space. Four great national leaders—Churchill, Disraeli, Jefferson, and Lincoln—have been endlessly quoted by their contemporaries and successors. Certainly they had the gift of language, but it also seems as if the fame they achieved during their lifetime may have led to their words being more diligently recorded and more frequently repeated than those of their less famous contemporaries. There are however two people who figure prominently in these pages without having achieved the same world wide fame. Burke, though he was indeed a statesman, was not in their class, and Bagehot was never even a member of parliament. Both, however, consistently found a way of expressing ideas and arguments that everyone could remember and no one could improve on. Some of their ideas were original, but even those that were not have proved to be endlessly quotable. They exemplify Pope's definition:

> True wit is Nature to advantage dressed.
> What oft was thought, but ne'er so well expressed.

The editor feels no need to apologize for the amount of space they command.

There is one particular danger which confronts all quotation dictionaries: the danger of including only those quotations which have already appeared in other dictionaries. It is of course inevitable that many of the quotations will be found in other collections, but it is equally important that lexicographers should not be endlessly recycling the same material. If quotations are to refresh and invigorate political communication, they should be drawn from a living stream and not a stagnant pond. So while the starting point for this dictionary was the existing corpus of political quotations held on the files of the Oxford University Press, it was only the starting point. The principal means of bringing in new material was a team of researchers who combed the daily papers and the periodicals, and listened to radio and television programmes, to record every significant quotation they came across and submit it for consideration. Another important source has been correspondence. A living dictionary of quotations will necessarily include quotations from the living, and many of them have been kind enough not only to verify and source entries attributed to them, but also to supply other of their writings and sayings that they have found being quoted. The living have also interceded for the dead: for examples, the first draft selection, like all the quotation dictionaries I have encountered, was disturbingly short of quotations from one of Britain's most distinguished Prime Ministers, Robert Peel. It was hard to believe that he had left so few quotable remarks behind him, and a letter to the leading authority on Peel, Professor Norman Gash, produced evidence that it was not Peel but the record that was at fault. Peel's entry is now of a respectable length. Equally, one of the most astute civil servants of the nineteenth century would have remained unrepresented if Lord Dacre had not directed me to Henry Taylor's *The Statesman*.

This leads to the final aspect of the question 'What is a political quotation?', namely does it have to have been quoted, or is it sufficient for it to be quotable? Once you accept quotability as the criterion, you are on a slippery slope, at the bottom of which lie the broad acres of anthologies and commonplace books. The compilers of the first edition of the *Oxford Dictionary of Quotations* were in no doubt: 'During the whole work of selection a great effort was made to restrict the entries to actual current quotations and not to include phrases which the various editors or contributors believed to be quotable or wanted to be quoted.' Of course they were right. And yet even they said only that a great effort was made, not that it was successful in every case. I must confess to not having been quite so purist. Certainly this is essentially a dictionary of what has been quoted, but here and there I have taken one or two small steps down the slippery slope and included lines that I believed modern readers would like to quote. After all, how can one not know that they have not been quoted somewhere at some time? I took the liberty of including Laertes's advice to Ophelia about marriage to the heir to the throne:

> His greatness weighed, his will is not his own
> For he himself is subject to his birth.
> He may not, as unvalued persons do,
> Carve for himself, for on his choice depends
> The sanity and health of the whole state;
> And therefore must his choice be circumscribed
> Unto the voice and yielding of that body
> Whereof he is the head.

I had no record of its being politically quoted anywhere, but in view of the continuing current debate about the divorce and remarriage of the Prince of Wales it seemed to me that many people might like to be reminded of it. It was only after it had been passed for the press that I discovered that Stanley Baldwin had quoted that same speech in the House of Commons, in relation to the abdication of King Edward VIII. So the reader will find here a small number—and an exceedingly small percentage—of entries that I cannot swear have been previously quoted, though equally I cannot swear that they have not. They are also another way of stopping the pool of political quotations from stagnating. And another aspect of this question is, when does a political quotation stop being a political quotation? It would have been easy to decide that Bismarck's observation that the Balkan conflict was 'not worth the healthy bones of a single Pomeranian grenadier' had passed into history's out-tray; but it surfaced again in 1995 in a House of Commons debate on the role of the UN forces in Bosnia.

If I may have taken slight liberties with the quotable as opposed to the quoted, this has not been the case with verification and sourcing. My colleagues at the Press have been rigorous and scrupulous about the tracing of quotations, and many promising runners fell at this last fence. They include familiar lines like *Pas d'ennemi à gauche* and 'Whoever is in office, the Conservatives are always in power', but among the omissions are a few whose absence I particularly regret. I am sure Bacon said 'Councils to which Time hath not been called, Time will not ratify' (and I am absolutely certain I did not make it up), and I am fairly sure he said 'Great events may have small occasions, but seldom small causes', but no amount of research has been able to track either of them down. I also wish we could have found who it was who said of Gladstone that when making a speech he not only followed every bay and headland along the coastline of his argument, but also insisted on tracking every river to its source. And I believe it was the American scholar Donald Schon who said that government bureaux are memorials to dead problems, but alas I cannot prove it. Another source of regret is the quotations that appeared just too late for inclusion, in particular Shimon Peres's observations 'Television has made dictatorship impossible, but democracy unbearable.' But we were not too late for President Izetbegović's words after signing the Dayton Accord: 'And to my people I say, this may not be a just peace, but it is more just than a continuation of war.'

Perhaps the most problematic of all the quotations are the very recent ones. Ultimately, time is the judge of whether an observation can be accepted as a quotation, and whether 'Tough on crime and tough on the causes of crime' is a full member of the club or merely a short-term visitor, only time will tell. On the other hand, to set an arbitrary limit of ten or twenty years from the first citation as a qualifying period would mean excluding many quotations to which readers would want to refer. I suspect that in any future edition it will be the most topical recent entries that are the least likely to survive.

And what about speech-writers? This is surely a recent problem. It may be that politicians in the past had help from time to time, but it is hard to picture Lincoln or Disraeli or Lloyd George or Churchill asking the boys in the back room to come up with some ideas for the next speech. Today a team of speech-writers is part of the standard entourage of an international leader, and on occasions we learn, at least informally, that some famous phrase or other was coined by a hand unconnected to the tongue that uttered it. Should we seek out the names of the writers and give them due recognition? It would be an impossible task, and moreover the reader would look for the phrase under the name of the politician who delivered it. This is also true of quotations which were in circulation some time before a politician gave them national or international currency. Where we can trace the original we attribute it, but it has to be accepted that some of the quotations attributed to politicians were probably not their own coinage. Nevertheless they will always be associated with the words, just as Clark Gable, and not Margaret Mitchell or Sidney Howard, will always be associated with the line 'Frankly, my dear, I don't give a damn' (which would probably be the politician's comment on this question).

The other difficulty presented by the most recent quotations is the possibility that in their original form they reached a national or international audience without ever appearing on a printed page. Radio and television archives are not always accessible, and slow to plough through even when you know exactly what you are looking for; but when you have only an imprecise recollection or reference it can be effectively impossible to locate what would be fairly easy to find in a newspaper or press cuttings library. Of course all the memorable quotations eventually find their way into print, but not always in their original form. The chief whip's famous phrase in Michael Dobbs's *House of Cards*, 'You might very well think that. I couldn't possibly comment', is taken from the television script; it does not appear in the book. Equally, transcripts from radio and television can miss important emphases and nuances: when Neil Kinnock spoke to the Labour Party Conference about Liverpool Council, his stress on 'Labour' in the phrase, 'the grotesque chaos of a Labour council—a *Labour* council—hiring taxis to scuttle round the city handing out redundancy notices to its own workers' did not come through in the press reports as it did in the television news bulletins. And the televising of parliamentary debates has exposed the difference between the semi-incoherence of some members' speeches and the comparative lucidity and logic of the phrasing that appears subsequently in the august pages of Hansard.

Finally I must acknowledge with gratitude the large number of people whose help has been invaluable. Christopher Booker, Simon Heffer, Nigel Rees, and Peter Hennessy all read the whole of the first draft and made numerous comments and suggestions of which many were immediately incorporated. All of them are extremely busy professionals and I was astonished as well as delighted at the amount of time and care they were willing to give to the task. Indeed one of the happiest aspects of an unusually happy assignment has been the willingness of almost everyone I contacted to give up time and take trouble to make the Dictionary as full and accurate as possible. Of those who helped out on specific topics or authors I would like to offer especial thanks to the following: Lord Bauer, Tony Benn, John Biffen, John Blundell, Dr Eamonn Butler, the Bishop of Coventry, Lord Dacre, Lord Deedes, Oliver Everett, Milton Friedman, Norman Gash, Martin Gilbert, Henry Hardy, Lord Healey, Sir Bernard Ingham, Simon Jenkins, Bernard Levin, Kenneth Morgan, Nigel Nicolson, Matthew Parris, Enoch Powell, Stanley Wells, and Chris Wrigley. Above all, I want to thank the editorial team of the Quotations Dictionaries department of the Oxford University Press. Not only have they done the bulk of the work; their knowledge, expertise, and scholarly rigour have contributed immeasurably to the quality of the book.

Any credit for the final result must be shared with all of the above; the blame remains exclusively the editor's.

ANTONY JAY

Somerset, January 1996

From Rhetoric to Sound Bites

MATTHEW PARRIS

When Harold Macmillan described the then Foreign Secretary as 'forever poised between a cliché and an indiscretion' he put his finger on a universal dilemma. Every serious politician has been caught between two conflicting impulses: the desire to say something memorable, and the fear of saying something memorable. Memorability is a dangerous virtue and clarity a double-edged sword. A fine and often accidental line divides a celebrated utterance from a notorious hostage to fortune.

George W. Bush's 'Mission Accomplished' started as a celebrated phrase and ended in infamy. So did his father's 'Read my lips: no new taxes.' Margaret Thatcher's 'You turn if you want to; the lady's not for turning' looked (to many) bound at first for infamy—but ended in fame.

For politics and its consequences arrive initially and necessarily in words. Even when politics moves mountains, even when politics brings war, peace, famine, feast or the Tennessee Valley Authority, it all starts and ends in words.

Words do not oil the wheels of politics: they are the wheels of politics. How did Adolf Hitler or Benito Mussolini electrify a nation, except through words? How did Winston Churchill rally and inspire, except through words? Strip from history the phrases, slogans, and speeches that have lifted hearts or poisoned minds and you remove more than the verbal handles with which we have grappled with events: you may remove an explanation of the events themselves.

In politics words can be events. Words start wars; they forge peace treaties; they define ('to each according to his ability…') and in defining help solidify an argument or ideology; they make promises ('No, no, no') and in making them establish policy, burn bridges, corner, expose—or open up lines of retreat. Words lead us closer to an understanding of those who speak or write them—or to the illusions that bring disillusion. Phrases made memorable by fluency, irony, or circumstance serve as permanent markers in the landscape of our history.

This has not changed in five thousand years, and I am struck by just how much it has not changed. Whether chiselled into granite, penned by quill and ink, or tapped into a twenty-first-century laptop (like 'a good day to bury bad news'—a misquotation), the right phrase or felicitous utterance has remained the thing for which those ambitious to practise, to influence, or to define politics have always striven; while the wrong phrase—the inaccurate or sometimes too accurate expression—has condemned with equal finality.

In the game of politics, to find the right words is to reach first base at least, and it was ever thus. Cicero was at least a rhetorician, Caesar at least a diarist, Churchill at least a stylist, and Roosevelt at least a broadcaster. All four were more than communicators, but none would have reached 'the top of the greasy pole' (Disraeli) in the first place through their non-verbal talents alone. Elizabeth I was a spin-doctor—her own—from whose reputation it is probably now impossible to separate words, image, and reality.

Wilberforce was, at least, a persuader, Disraeli an artist, and Gladstone a Vesuvius in words. Lord Salisbury was an aphorist (if I may coin a word) of bleak and pitiless brilliance, Lloyd George a bard, and Macmillan a scriptwriter to his own music hall. Harold Wilson was a telly-publicist, Margaret Thatcher a patchy communicator with an unerring instinct for the best professional help, and John Major a forward-thinker dogged by his failure to find the right language. Tony Blair lived by words, and Gordon Brown will die for the want of them.

But among our own British statesmen from this and the last century, the happiest surprise for me in this *Oxford Dictionary of Political Quotations* is Lord Salisbury. Flicking idly through, I had at first wondered why that late-nineteenth and early-twentieth-century prime minister commanded so many pages—until I started to read. From the very first quotation (about Ireland): 'she has given us foreign invasions, domestic rebellions and in quieter times the manly sport of landlord-shooting' to the last—'Whitehall will create business for itself surely as a new railway will create traffic'—his mordant, penetrating, and deliciously reactionary prose flows like the finest vinegar.

Salisbury's remarks were aimed at—and appreciated by—the discerning only. Margaret Thatcher, by contrast, directed her phrasemaking toward millions. 'You turn if you want to; the lady's not for turning' did more than encapsulate (or caricature) a personality: it polarized an argument, etched a stereotype, hardened the edges of the way we saw her. That she didn't draft this sentence herself only demonstrates her appreciation of the importance of speech-writing: too important, as she realized, to be left to her own literary talents.

Others, too, have found the fortunate (or unfortunate) phrase that changed politics. If Harold Macmillan had not said 'You've never had it so good', if Enoch Powell had not spoken of rivers of blood, or if Henry of Navarre had not called James I 'the wisest fool in Christendom', their own and succeeding ages might never have seen or reacted to them in quite the way they did. In every case the words provided a prism through which to see individuals, subtly changing their relationship with the world.

And, often enough, changing their relationship with themselves too. In the case of those last three twentieth-century British politicians I believe these catchphrases provided a prism not only through which we saw them but through which they began to see themselves. The English playwright Christopher Fry gave 'the lady's not for turning' to the theatre, and the playwright Ronald Miller, as Margaret Thatcher's speech-writer, gave it on to his mistress—as a phrase to describe her own unswerving determination. I had worked for her in opposition and drafted statements for her myself, so I was already familiar with her style and her literary hinterland. I would be surprised if when she received Ronnie's draft she knew much (perhaps anything) about the original context of that phrase; or about the work of Christopher Fry—or even (quite possibly) who Fry was. She would have thought his plays and his linguistic playfulness unbelievably silly. His phraseology was far from her own native style, which was rather unadventurous and stilted.

But she liked what it said about her. And, more to the point, she liked the way *we* liked what it said about her. And so was continued a process I observed in her between 1975 and 1990: an unconscious evolution in which a world leader began to model herself on the caricature the world was already forming of her, playing up the bits that seemed to amuse or impress, until finally she became almost a pantomime version of the younger Mrs Thatcher I had first met. Thus can the description become father to the described, rather than the other way around: an observation that may in some measure be applied to Winston Churchill too ('simply a "Radio personality" who outlived his time,' said Evelyn Waugh in a quote that I hope may make its way into the next edition of this dictionary).

It might be thought that the gift of words is less likely to profit a politician in an age of email and instant communication, and that in the tediously managerial epoch into which this edition is published, fine words and memorable language are losing their potency in politics. Nothing could be further from the truth.

Certainly it is true that what earlier centuries called Rhetoric (with a capital R) sounds to modern ears forced and overblown. You will find less W. E. Gladstone in these pages than his reputation for eloquence (however long-winded) might suggest, and less William Pitt. But as Gladstone said himself of his public speaking—'I absorb the vapour and return it as a flood'—the phenomenon in his case lay in the sheer volume and force; his speeches were performances; you had to be there. What he less often offered were distillations of his argument short and pithy enough to be taken away, remembered, and delivered impressively by others.

A great political quotation must be quotable and intelligible in other seasons and circumstances than those in which it was first delivered. It must read memorably even when taken out of context ('*All* quotation is out of context,' Enoch Powell once snapped at an interrupter who protested that he was quoting someone out of context: another remark which I hope may find its way into future editions). This dictionary is really a collection of paragraphs and sentences with the power to speak beyond context and from beyond the political grave.

Indeed our age of information technology understands the value of such expressions so well that it has its own term for one branch of them: phrases, we say, that have 'gone viral'. Such quotations have communicated themselves easily, stuck in the memory effortlessly, and spread. When J. K. Galbraith coined the term 'conventional wisdom' in 1958 he will have had no idea what going viral entailed; but his expression has gone so viral that not one in a hundred of us who employ it routinely will be aware of the source.

Modern media-speak has another term, too, for a branch of political quotation well-represented here: the 'sound bite'. You will find explicit reference to the expression in the section devoted to Tony Blair. 'This is not a time for sound bites,' he said, at the birth of the 'Good Friday' peace agreement in Northern Ireland—continuing (without conscious self-mockery) '…I feel the hand of history upon our shoulders'. That, along with 'I'm a pretty straight sort of guy,' shot to fame in the halls of irony within days.

But though the term is new, the sound bite is as old as politics. George V probably did not intend 'bugger Bognor' as a sound bite (if he said it at all) but F. D. Roosevelt's 'new deal for the American people,' like Karl Marx's 'religion…is the opium of the people' or Mary Tudor's 'when I am dead and opened, you shall find "Calais" lying in my heart' were surely delivered with an eye to simplicity, memorability, and punch.

Sound bites, viral expressions, buzz-phrases…modern-sounding descriptions, all of them, of a characteristic of so much that makes for endurance in political quotation, ancient and modern: concision, pithiness, and (often enough) idiomatic wit. How long before a future edition of this dictionary includes a section on famous political tweets? Sneer if you like, but I can think of many former colleagues in the House of Commons whose career and reputation would have benefited—and who would have conveyed at least as much useful information in their lives—if they had been obliged to confine their utterances within sentences of no more than 140 characters.

And if the study of rhetoric has fallen out of fashion, the fashion has been replaced by another, at least as deliberate: the professional crafting of words, phrases, sentences so striking and attention-grabbing that they become marketing tools: weapons in the armoury of any twenty-first-century politician's (or political columnist's) communications strategy. This is good news for the compilers of dictionaries.

Mr Blair's 1993 'Tough on crime and tough on the causes of crime,' is a triumphant example, and you will find it here. Gordon Brown's 'No return to boom and bust' (or, as he insists, 'No return to Tory boom and bust') has recently proved itself an abject example, and looks set to enter the next edition, just as (abject or triumphant, we have yet to find out) Barack Obama's 'Yes we can' will surely do.

Far from living in an age when the skilled use of English no longer counts, we are living in an age in which finding the right phrase is so much the rage that it is thought careless to entrust it to amateurs. Whole professions now nestle under the aegis of 'communications and marketing' and politics in Europe and America has rushed headlong into the arms of their practitioners. Politicians in days gone by might have hoped that some of their choicer terms or passages would survive. Politicians (and their spin-doctors) today design their public communications entirely around that ambition.

And as any modern marketing professional will tell you, if you can't grab and hold your audience within fifty words you might as well give up; and if you haven't imparted the kernel of what you have to convey within a hundred words, then your message is lost. Such wisdom is music to the ears of lexicographers of quotation.

It follows not only that the 'keynote speech' has become the standard heavy artillery of the political campaign, but also that within the many thousands of words these hour-long sound-chews, sound-gobbles, and sound-feasts spread out before us, it is vital that at least half a dozen sound bites lurk: for it is these and these alone that will survive the real-time occasion and take on a life in the virtual world of news headlines that in modern politics can matter more than the real-time one. No speech has done its work unless one or more quotable quotes from it appear in the six-o'clock bulletins, the on-line reaction, the blogs, the following morning's front pages, and (if they stand the test of time) dictionaries like this.

Gordon Brown's entire, turgid Party Conference speech in 2008 was worth the effort for the survival beyond it of just five words: 'no time for a novice'— delivering 'a double-whammy' (the expression made famous when as Tory Party Chairman Chris Patten approved it for poster-use in 1992) to the chins of two young potential challengers: David Miliband and David Cameron. 'Double whammy' you will find here, because it lives on and helped the Tories win. 'No time for a novice' must survive at least one general election before the lexicographers begin to circle. Its chances of getting into future dictionaries depend upon the voters concurring with the sentiment. Already, this is the only quote I can remember from that party conference season.

In fact it has become almost a cliché among reporters and sketch-writers to boast how we make a point of *not* going into the conference hall to hear the set-piece speech, for fear of being too influenced by the phantom rather than the real event. The real event is the TV clips and summarized report, so we discipline ourselves not to look at the whole speech. The clips and not the speech the poor bloody party infantry thought they heard, will shape the enduring picture of the occasion. It is as though, whereas in a bygone age a political oration passed through an *in extenso* phase before shards lodged themselves in dictionaries of quotations, today's speech-writers are drafting with a view only to the shards.

We who read, compile, or contribute to collections of choice quotations thus find ourselves with the spirit of the age. Long, painstaking arguments set out in long, painstaking speeches are history. They are only the setting. Few have time to read or listen any more, and nobody's drafting for those who do. The wisdom of politics comes in bite-sized chunks, or it comes not at all.

The stakes in modern Western politics grow ever more trivial (the clash of ideology and interests being now regarded as having been concluded in favour of a liberal market economy with socially compassionate trimmings). As the issues grow ever more managerial and the squabbles more squalid, so the language (as if to compensate) grows more absurdly heroic. In an epoch cruelly short of political visions, the political language is permanently charged with what George Bush Snr called 'the vision thing'.

The boldness of political prose is becoming proportionate to the banality of political content: large words chasing small thoughts. Today's politicians mount the rostrum not so much to set out plans as to dream dreams, share visions, celebrate values, confide personal histories, champion change, and shed tears of compassion; then they return to their offices to bicker, feud, and nit-pick.

Lexicographers are therefore in for a continuing feast of fine phrases, although already I sense vision-fatigue beginning to set in. The day may come when a politician with the audacity not to hope, but to explain a modest proposal in workmanlike prose, finds himself in the *Oxford Dictionary of Political Quotations* for the sheer exoticism of using a political platform to expound a practical plan. As for the rest—the over-hyped oratory, the super-abundance of abstract nouns and the empty breast-beating that characterize so much of today's political oratory—their only hope of persistence through future editions of this dictionary must lie, as it did for Shelley's Ozymandias (whom I'm glad to see here) in the mockery of a future age. The sound bites of the modern British party conference will feel the hand not of history but of irony upon their shoulder.

Safer, then, not to be in this book at all.

How to Use the Dictionary

Finding a quotation...

...if you know the author
If you know the author of a quotation you can go straight to that entry in the dictionary: the authors are in alphabetical order. Unless the entry is very large you should be able to spot the quotation that you want.

...if you know the words but not the author
If you know some words from the quotation but not who said it, look in the Keyword Index. The most significant words from each quotation are indexed with a reference to help you find it.

...on a subject
If you want to find a quotation on a specific subject, the topic may be included in the Selective Subject Index. Signposts to these subjects are included in the alphabetical sequence of authors. If the subject is not listed, try looking for the word and related terms in the Keyword Index.

About the order...

...of authors
The authors are in alphabetical order. Author names are given in the form by which they are best known, usually a surname but where appropriate a forename, pseudonym, or nickname. Some anonymous quotations are included in special category boxes in the A-Z sequence. A full list of the special categories is given on the Contents page.

...of quotations
Within each author entry, quotations from speeches, letters, and diaries appear first, in date order. Quotations from secondary sources which can be dated are included in this chronological sequence. Literary and published works follow, in alphabetical order of title. Undated quotations, and quotations in the special category boxes, are arranged in alphabetical order of the quotation text.

Where helpful, essential background information is given before the quotation in an italicized note, while supplementary or explanatory information is given after it. Each quotation is followed by a note of its source.

Looking elsewhere in the book ...

... for quotations about an author

Following the description of the author, cross references are given to any quotations about that person elsewhere in the text, and occasionally to other quotations associated with them. Each cross reference to a quotation includes the name of its author followed by its page number and then its unique quotation number on that page.

James Callaghan 1912–2005
British Labour statesman; Prime Minister 1976–9.
On Callaghan: see **Butler 51:9, Jenkins 158:5**; see
also **Misquotations 215:5**

quotation about this author
number of quotation on page
quotation associated with the author
page on which quotation appears

... for further information

Cross references are used to direct the reader to similar or related quotations. In supplementary or background information, the names of people who have their own entries are in bold type.

Lord Acton 1834–1902
British historian

10 Power tends to corrupt and
absolute power corrupts absolutely.
often quoted as 'All power corrupts...' — supplementary information
letter to Bishop Mandell Creighton, 3 April
1887; see **Pitt 245:10** — related quotation

Gore Vidal 1925–
American novelist and critic

5 *of Ronald **Reagan**:* — background information
A triumph of the embalmer's art. — person with own entry in the dictionary
in *Observer* 26 April 1981

Index ...

... of keywords

The most significant words from each quotation appear in the Keyword Index, allowing individual quotations to be traced. Each instance of a keyword, abbreviated to its initial letter, is given with a short section of the surrounding text to help identify it. Both the headwords and the sections of text are in alphabetical order. To simplify searching, words are indexed in their standard British English form, regardless of spelling in the original.

... references

Index references are to the first four letters of the author's name, followed by the page number and the number of the quotation on the page. Thus the index entry for the word **cement**:

		index headword
cement like mixing c.	Mond 216:14	
Palestine is the c.	Araf 11:9	initial letter of headword
censorship extreme form of c.	Shaw 286:16	
fought without c.	West 330:11	
results from a c.	Bent 28:11	first four letters of author name
centralization C. and socialism	Tocq 313:4	page number
c. follows	Tocq 313:2	quotation number

leads to the quotation:

Aristophanes **11** ········· page number

········· author name

Yasser Arafat 1929–2004
Palestinian statesman, President 1996–2004. On
Arafat: see **Mandela 204:5**

········· quotation number

9 Palestine is the cement that
holds the Arab world together, or it
is the explosive that blows it apart.
in *Time* 11 November 1974

········· index headword

... of subjects

A selection of quotations on common political topics can be traced through the Selective Subject Index. Each subject heading is followed by a short extract from each of the quotations on the theme. References are given in the same form as in the Keyword Index. Thus the signpost **Slavery** in the main dictionary:

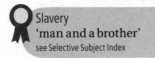

Slavery
'man and a brother'
see Selective Subject Index

leads to the Selective Subject Index entry:

Slavery

all persons held as slaves	Linc 186:2	
contrary to the laws of God	Hart 136:12	
I entered the world a slave	Brow 43:12	
man and a brother	Wedg 328:9	quotation reference
		extract from quotation

which in turn directs to quotations such as:

Josiah Wedgwood 1730–95
English potter

9 Am I not a man and a brother.
*legend on Wedgwood cameo, depicting a
kneeling Negro slave in chains*
reproduced in facsimile in E. Darwin *The
Botanic Garden* pt. 1 (1791)

Quotations

Diane Abbott 1953–
British Labour politician

1 Being an MP is the sort of job all working-class parents want for their children—clean, indoors and no heavy lifting.
   in *Independent* 18 January 1994

Lord Aberdeen 1784–1860
British statesman and scholar

2 He is terrible in the rebound.
   *of **Gladstone**'s capacity to recover from setbacks.*
   in 1859; John Morley *Life of William Ewart Gladstone* (1903)

Bella Abzug 1920–98
American Democratic politician

3 Richard Nixon impeached himself. He gave us Gerald Ford as his revenge.
   in *Rolling Stone*; Linda Botts *Loose Talk* (1980)

Accius 170–c. 86 BC
Roman poet and dramatist

4 Let them hate, so long as they fear.
   Atreus

Dean Acheson 1893–1971
American Democratic politician. On Acheson: see **Pearson 242:4**

5 I will undoubtedly have to seek what is happily known as gainful employment, which I am glad to say does not describe holding public office.
   in *Time* 22 December 1952

6 Great Britain has lost an empire and has not yet found a role.
   speech at the Military Academy, West Point, 5 December 1962

7 The first requirement of a statesman is that he be dull.
   in *Observer* 21 June 1970

8 A memorandum is written not to inform the reader but to protect the writer.
   in *Wall Street Journal* 8 September 1977

Lord Ackner 1920–2005
British judge

9 Prison is a most expensive way of making bad people worse.
   speech in the House of Lords, 23 October 1997

Lord Acton 1834–1902
British historian

10 Power tends to corrupt and absolute power corrupts absolutely.
   often quoted as 'All power corrupts…'
   letter to Bishop Mandell Creighton, 3 April 1887; see **Pitt 245:10**

11 Great men are almost always bad men, even when they exercise influence and not authority.
   letter to Bishop Mandell Creighton, 3 April 1887

12 Beware of too much explaining, lest we end by too much excusing.
   attributed by Acton to the Duc de Broglie, *Lectures in Modern History* (1906), lecture delivered Cambridge, June 1895

Abigail Adams 1744–1818
American letter writer, wife of John **Adams** and mother of John Quincy **Adams**

13 In the new code of laws which I suppose it will be necessary for you to make I desire you would remember the ladies, and be more generous and favourable to them than your ancestors. Do not put such unlimited power into the hands of the husbands. Remember

all men would be tyrants if they could.
letter to John Adams, 31 March 1776

1 These are times in which a genius would wish to live. It is not in the still calm of life, or the repose of a pacific station, that great characters are formed...Great necessities call out great virtues.
letter to John Quincy Adams, 19 January 1780

2 Patriotism in the female sex is the most disinterested of all virtues. Excluded from honours and from offices, we cannot attach ourselves to the State or Government from having held a place of eminence... Yet all history and every age exhibit instances of patriotic virtue in the female sex; which considering our situation equals the most heroic of yours.
letter to John Adams, 17 June 1782

Franklin P. Adams 1881–1960
American journalist and humorist

3 When the political columnists say 'Every thinking man' they mean themselves, and when candidates appeal to 'Every intelligent voter' they mean everybody who is going to vote for them.
Nods and Becks (1944)

4 The trouble with this country is that there are too many politicians who believe, with a conviction based on experience, that you can fool all of the people all of the time.
Nods and Becks (1944)

5 Elections are won by men and women chiefly because most people vote against somebody rather than for somebody.
Nods and Becks (1944)

Gerry Adams 1948–
Northern Irish politician; President of Sinn Féin

6 We want him to be the last British Prime Minister with jurisdiction in Ireland.
*of Tony **Blair***
in *Irish Times* 18 October 1997

Henry Brooks Adams 1838–1918
American historian

7 Politics, as a practice, whatever its professions, has always been the systematic organization of hatreds.
The Education of Henry Adams (1907)

8 A friend in power is a friend lost.
The Education of Henry Adams (1907)

9 [Charles] Sumner's mind had reached the calm of water which receives and reflects images without absorbing them; it contained nothing but itself.
*of the American politician and orator Charles **Sumner***
The Education of Henry Adams (1907)

10 The progress of evolution from President Washington to President Grant was alone evidence to upset Darwin.
The Education of Henry Adams (1907)

11 Practical politics consists in ignoring facts.
The Education of Henry Adams (1907)

John Adams 1735–1826
American statesman, 2nd President of the US; husband of Abigail **Adams** and father of John Quincy **Adams**. See also **Last words 179:15**

12 The law, in all vicissitudes of government...will preserve a steady undeviating course; it will not bend to the uncertain wishes, imaginations, and wanton tempers of men...On the one hand it is inexorable to the cries of the prisoners; on the other it is deaf, deaf as an adder to the clamours of the populace.
argument in defence of the British soldiers in the Boston Massacre Trials, 4 December 1770; see **Sidney 288:14**

13 There is danger from all men. The only maxim of a free government ought to be to trust no man living with power to endanger the public liberty.
Notes for an Oration at Braintree (Spring 1772)

14 *of the Boston Tea Party:*
There is a dignity, a majesty, a sublimity, in this last effort of the patriots that I greatly admire.

The people should never rise without doing something to be remembered—something notable and striking.
diary, 17 December 1773

1 A government of laws, and not of men.
later incorporated in the Massachusetts Constitution (1780)
in *Boston Gazette* (1774)

2 I agree with you that in politics the middle way is none at all.
letter to Horatio Gates, 23 March 1776

3 Yesterday, the greatest question was decided which ever was debated in America, and a greater perhaps never was nor will be decided among men. A resolution was passed without one dissenting colony, 'that these United Colonies are, and of right ought to be, free and independent States.'
letter to Abigail Adams, 3 July 1776

4 I am well aware of the toil and blood and treasure that it will cost us to maintain this declaration, and support and defend these states.
letter to Abigail Adams, 3 July 1776

5 I must study politics and war that my sons may have liberty to study mathematics and philosophy.
letter to Abigail Adams, 12 May 1780

6 *of the vice-presidency:*
My country has in its wisdom contrived for me the most insignificant office that ever the invention of man contrived or his imagination conceived.
letter to Abigail Adams, 19 December 1793

7 Democracy never lasts long. It soon wastes, exhausts, and murders itself. There never was a democracy that did not commit suicide.
letter to John Taylor, 15 April 1814

8 The fundamental article of my political creed is that despotism, or unlimited sovereignty, or absolute power, is the same in a majority of a popular assembly, an aristocratic council, an oligarchical junto, and a single emperor.
letter to Thomas Jefferson, 13 November 1815

9 The jaws of power are always opened to devour, and her arm is always stretched out, if possible, to destroy the freedom of thinking, speaking, and writing.
A Dissertation on the Canon and the Feudal Law (1765)

10 Liberty cannot be preserved without a general knowledge among the people, who have a right...and a desire to know; but besides this, they have a right, an indisputable, unalienable, indefeasible, divine right to that most dreaded and envied kind of knowledge, I mean of the characters and conduct of their rulers.
A Dissertation on the Canon and Feudal Law (1765)

11 The happiness of society is the end of government.
Thoughts on Government (1776)

12 Fear is the foundation of most governments.
Thoughts on Government (1776)

13 The judicial power ought to be distinct from both the legislative and executive, and independent upon both, that so it may be a check upon both, as both should be checks upon that.
Thoughts on Government (1776)

John Quincy Adams 1767–1848
American statesman, 6th President of the US; son of Abigail **Adams** and John **Adams**. See also **Last words 179:14**

14 Think of your forefathers! Think of your posterity!
Oration at Plymouth 22 December 1802

15 *Fiat justitia, pereat coelum* [Let justice be done, though heaven perish]. My toast would be, may our country be always successful, but whether successful or otherwise, always right.
letter to John Adams, 1 August 1816; see **Decatur 87:1, Mansfield 204:11, Mottoes 221:3**

16 Wherever the standard of freedom and Independence has been or

shall be unfurled, there will her heart, her benedictions and her prayers be. But she [America] goes not abroad in search of monsters to destroy.
speech to House of Representatives, 4 July 1821

1 This house will bear witness to his piety; this town [Braintree, Massachusetts], his birthplace, to his munificence; history to his patriotism; posterity to the depth and compass of his mind.
epitaph for John **Adams**, 1829

Samuel Adams 1722–1803
American revolutionary leader

2 Let us contemplate our forefathers, and posterity, and resolve to maintain the rights bequeathed to us by the former, for the sake of the latter.
speech, 1771

3 What a glorious morning this is.
on hearing gunfire at Lexington, 19 April 1775
J. K. Hosmer *Samuel Adams* (1886); see **Misquotations 216:10**

4 A nation of shopkeepers are very seldom so disinterested.
Oration in Philadelphia 1 August 1776 (the authenticity of this publication is doubtful); see **Napoleon I 224:5, Smith 293:4**

5 We cannot make events. Our business is wisely to improve them…Mankind are governed more by their feelings than by reason. Events which excite those feelings will produce wonderful effects.
J. N. Rakove *The Beginnings of National Politics* (1979)

Frank Ezra Adcock 1886–1968
British classicist and historian of Greece and Rome

6 Rome under Sulla was like a bus, with half the passengers trying to drive, and the rest trying to collect the fare.
lecture at Cambridge in the 1940s

Joseph Addison 1672–1719
English poet, dramatist, and essayist; co-founder of *The Spectator*

7 And, pleased th' Almighty's orders to perform,
Rides in the whirlwind, and directs the storm.
The Campaign (1705); see **Page 235:10**

8   What pity is it
That we can die but once to serve our country!
Cato (1713)

9 From hence, let fierce contending nations know
What dire effects from civil discord flow.
Cato (1713)

Konrad Adenauer 1876–1967
German statesman, first Chancellor of the Federal Republic of Germany

10 A thick skin is a gift from God.
in *New York Times* 30 December 1959

11 History is the sum total of the things that could have been avoided.
attributed

Aeschylus c. 525–456 BC
Greek tragedian

12 Do not taint pure laws with mere expediency
Guard well and reverence that form of government
Which will eschew alike licence and slavery.
And from your policy do not wholly banish fear
For what man living, freed from fear, will still be just?
The Eumenides

13 Let war stay abroad; it makes no difficulty in coming, for the man

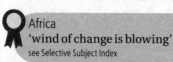
Africa
'wind of change is blowing'
see Selective Subject Index

who will have in him a strong desire for glory. I disapprove of a bird's battling in its own home.
The Eumenides

1 Everyone's quick to blame the alien.
The Suppliant Maidens

Herbert Agar 1897–1980
American poet and writer

2 The truth which makes men free is for the most part the truth which men prefer not to hear.
Time for Greatness (1942); see **Bible 33:9**

Spiro T. Agnew 1918–96
American Republican politician

3 I didn't say I wouldn't go into ghetto areas. I've been in many of them and to some extent I would say this: If you've seen one city slum you've seen them all.
in *Detroit Free Press* 19 October 1968

4 A spirit of national masochism prevails, encouraged by an effete corps of impudent snobs who characterize themselves as intellectuals.
speech in New Orleans, 19 October 1969

5 In the United States today, we have more than our share of the nattering nabobs of negativism.
speech in San Diego, 11 September 1970

Bertie Ahern 1951–
Irish Fianna Fáil statesman, Taoiseach 1997–2008

6 It is a day we should treasure. Today is about the promise of a bright future, a day when we hope a line will be drawn under the bloody past.
on the Good Friday Agreement, 10 April 1998; in *Guardian* 11 April 1998

Mahmoud Ahmadinejad 1956–
Iranian statesman; President since 2005

7 As the imam said, Israel must be wiped off the map.
speech to students in Tehran, 26 October 2005, as translated by the Iranian state news agency; see **Khomeini 170:5**

Jonathan Aitken 1942–
British Conservative politician

8 If it falls to me to start a fight to cut out the cancer of bent and twisted journalism in our country with the simple sword of truth and the trusty shield of British fair play, so be it.
statement, London, 10 April 1995

Lord Alanbrooke 1883–1963
British field marshal

9 Without him England was lost for a certainty, with him England has been on the verge of disaster time and again.
of Churchill
diary, 10 September 1944

Madeleine Albright 1937–
American diplomat

10 Hallelujah…Never again will your fates be tossed around like poker chips on a bargaining table.
accepting the admission papers for Hungary, Poland, and the Czech Republic to become members of Nato
in *Daily Telegraph* 13 March 1999

Alcuin c. 735–804
English scholar and theologian

11 And those people should not be listened to who keep saying the voice of the people is the voice of God [*Vox populi, vox Dei*], since the riotousness of the crowd is always very close to madness.
letter 164 in *Works* (1863)

Richard Aldington 1892–1962
English poet, novelist, and biographer

12 Patriotism is a lively sense of collective responsibility. Nationalism is a silly cock crowing on its own dunghill.
The Colonel's Daughter (1931)

Alexander VI 1431–1503
Spanish cleric, Pope from 1492, father of Cesare Borgia

13 The most grievous danger for any Pope lies in the fact that,

encompassed as he is by flatterers, he never hears the truth about his own person and ends by not wishing to hear it.
quoting St Bernard of Clairvaux (1090–1153) in 1497, Hubert Jedin A History of the Council of Trent (1957)

Cecil Frances Alexander 1818–95
Irish poet and hymn-writer

1 The rich man in his castle,
The poor man at his gate,
God made them, high or lowly,
And ordered their estate.
'All Things Bright and Beautiful' (1848)

Iyad Allawi 1945–
Iraqi statesman, Prime Minister 2004–5

2 If this is not civil war, then God knows what civil war is.
interview on BBC Television *Sunday AM*, 19 March 2006

Woody Allen 1935–
American film director, writer, and actor

3 I believe there is something out there watching over us. Unfortunately, it's the government.
Peter McWilliams *Ain't Nobody's Business If You Do* (1993); attributed

Joseph Alsop 1910–89
American journalist

4 Gratitude, like love, is never a dependable international emotion.
in *Observer* 30 November 1952

Julian Amery 1919–96
British Conservative politician, son of Leo **Amery**

5 *of a misinterpretation of their role made by some Members of Parliament:*
Representing Parliament in their constituencies rather than their constituents in Parliament.
attributed by Norman Tebbit in 'On the Inner Culture of the Tories'; Subroto Roy and John C. Clarke *Margaret Thatcher's Revolution* (2005)

Leo Amery 1873–1955
British Conservative politician, father of Julian **Amery**

6 *of H. H. Asquith:*
For twenty years he has held a season-ticket on the line of least resistance and has gone wherever the train of events has carried him, lucidly justifying his position at whatever point he has happened to find himself.
in *Quarterly Review* July 1914

7 Speak for England.
said to Arthur Greenwood in House of Commons, 2 September 1939; see **Boothby 39:5**

8 I will quote certain other words. I do it with great reluctance, because I am speaking of those who are old friends and colleagues of mine, but they are words which, I think, are applicable to the present situation. This is what Cromwell said to the Long Parliament when he thought it was no longer fit to conduct the affairs of the nation: 'You have sat too long here for any good you have been doing. Depart, I say, and let us have done with you. In the name of God, go.'
in the House of Commons, 7 May 1940; see **Cromwell 82:12**

Fisher Ames 1758–1808
American politician

9 A monarchy is a merchantman which sails well, but will sometimes strike on a rock, and go to the bottom; whilst a republic is a raft which would never sink, but then your feet are always in the water.
attributed to Ames, speaking in the House of Representatives, 1795, but not traced in Ames's speeches

Anacharsis
Scythian prince of the 6th century BC

10 Written laws are like spider's webs; they will catch, it is true, the weak and poor, but would be torn in pieces by the rich and powerful.
Plutarch *Parallel Lives* 'Solon'; see **Shenstone 287:14, Swift 303:10**

Kofi Annan 1938–
Ghanaian diplomat, Secretary-General of the United Nations 1997–2007

11 You can do a lot with diplomacy, but of course you can do a lot more

with diplomacy backed up by fairness and force.
of the agreement reached with Saddam Hussein over weapons inspections, February 1998
in *Mail on Sunday* 1 March 1998 'Quotes of the Week'

Anonymous

1 All the 'isms are wasms.
said to have been the comment of a Foreign Office spokesman on the signing of the Molotov–Ribbentrop Pact in August 1939
Peter Hennessy *Whitehall* (1990)

2 Always ask youself why these lying bastards are lying to you.
advice on interviewing from the industrial correspondent of the Daily Worker, *c. 1946*
Louis Heren *Growing Up on The Times* (1978)

3 The best defence against the atom bomb is not to be there when it goes off.
contributor to *British Army Journal*, in *Observer* 20 February 1949

4 But this is terrible—*they've* elected a Labour Government, and *the country* will never stand for that!
unidentified lady diner in the Savoy Hotel, 26 July 1945
Michael Sissons and Philip French (eds.) *The Age of Austerity 1945–51* (1964)

5 A community in which power, wealth and opportunity are in the hands of the many not the few, where the rights we enjoy reflect the duties we owe...in which the enterprise of the market and the rigour of competition are joined with the forces of partnership and cooperation.
new Clause Four of the Labour Party constitution, passed at a special conference 29 April 1995; see **Anonymous 10:8**

6 A Company for carrying on an undertaking of Great Advantage, but no one to know what it is.
Company Prospectus at the time of the South Sea Bubble (1711)

7 Dalton McGuinty: He's an evil reptilian kitten-eater from another planet.
Canadian Conservative press release attacking the Liberal leader (now premier) during September 2003 Ontario election campaign
in *London Free Press News* 13 September 2003

8 Every country has its own constitution; ours is absolutism moderated by assassination.
of Russia
Ernst Friedrich Herbert, Count Münster, quoting 'an intelligent Russian', in *Political Sketches of the State of Europe, 1814–1867* (1868)

9 Expletive deleted.
Submission of Recorded Presidential Conversations to the Committee on the Judiciary of the House of Representatives by President Richard M. Nixon 30 April 1974

10 Exterminate...the treacherous English, walk over General French's contemptible little army.
often attributed to Kaiser Wilhelm II, but most probably fabricated by the British; source of the nickname 'the Old Contemptibles'
Annexe to British Expeditionary Force Routine Orders of 24 September 1914; Arthur Ponsonby *Falsehood in Wartime* (1928)

11 The finest brute votes in Europe.
a 'cynical politician's' view of the parliamentary county members
Walter Bagehot *The English Constitution* (1867) 'The House of Commons'

12 For the sake of brevity we have followed the common practice of using the phrase 'Communists' throughout to include Fascists.
Radcliffe Report 'Security Procedures in the Public Service' April 1962

13 Frederick the Great lost the battle of Jena.
*attributing the Prussians' defeat at Jena by **Napoleon I** in 1806 to their rigid adherence to the strategy of **Frederick the Great** (who had died in 1786)*
Walter Bagehot *The English Constitution* (1867)

14 Happy is that city which in time of peace thinks of war.
inscription found in the armoury of Venice
Robert Burton *The Anatomy of Melancholy* (1621–51)

15 Hark the herald angels sing Mrs Simpson's pinched our king.
*contemporary children's rhyme on the abdication of **Edward VIII***
Clement Attlee letter 26 December 1938; Kenneth Harris *Attlee* (1982)

16 Have you heard? The Prime Minister has resigned and

Northcliffe has sent for the King.
*a joke (1919) suggesting that Lord **Northcliffe**, the press baron and **Lloyd George**'s implacable enemy, would succeed him as Prime Minister*
Hamilton Fyfe *Northcliffe, an Intimate Biography* (1930)

1 He talked shop like a tenth muse.
*of **Gladstone**'s Budget speech*
G. W. E. Russell *Collections and Recollections* (1898)

2 He who writes the minutes rules the roost.
Civil Service maxim

3 I cannot see the Speaker, Hal, can you?
What! Cannot see the Speaker, I see two!
satirical verse in an opposition newspaper of 1793, referring to the report that William Pitt and Henry Dundas had come into the House of Commons while drunk
William Hague *William Pitt the Younger* (2004) ch. 16

4 I like Mr Baldwin: he promises nothing and keeps his word.
unattributed comment

5 I never vote. It only encourages them.
elderly American lady quoted by comedian Jack Parr; William Safire *The New Language of Politics* (1968)

6 The iron lady.
*name given to Margaret **Thatcher**, then Leader of the Opposition, by the Soviet Defence Ministry newspaper* Red Star, *which accused her of trying to revive the cold war*
in *Sunday Times* 25 January 1976

7 It became necessary to destroy the town to save it.
comment by unidentified US Army major on Ben Tre, Vietnam
in Associated Press Report, *New York Times* 8 February 1968

8 It is a pretty pass when the headline in the *Morning Star* reads 'Back the Law Lords.'
to the Lord Chancellor on the Prevention of Terrorism legislation
comment reported by Lord Falconer, speech in House of Lords, 7 March 2005

9 The King over the Water.
Jacobite toast to the deposed and exiled James II and his heirs
current in the 18th century

10 A lass and a lakh a day.
said to be an after-dinner toast of the East India Company; a lakh was 100,000 rupees
K. Ballhatchet *Race, Sex and Class under the Raj* (1980)

11 Liberty is always unfinished business.
title of 36th Annual Report of the American Civil Liberties Union, 1 July 1955–30 June 1956

12 [Like] watching a stream of blood coming from beneath a closed door.
a contemporary expression of the feelings evoked by news of the executions after the Easter Rising, 1916
Robert Kee *Ourselves Alone* (1972)

13 Lost is our old simplicity of times,
The world abounds with laws, and teems with crimes.
On the Proceedings Against America (1775)

14 CHILD: Mamma, are Tories born wicked, or do they grow wicked afterwards?
MOTHER: They are born wicked, and grow worse.
G. W. E. Russell *Collections and Recollections* (1898)

15 Men said openly that Christ and His saints slept.
of twelfth-century England during the civil war between Stephen and Matilda
Anglo-Saxon Chronicle for 1137

16 The ministry of all the talents.
name given ironically to William Grenville's coalition of 1806, and also applied to later coalitions
G. W. Cooke *The History of Party* (1837) vol. 3

17 My name is George Nathaniel Curzon,
I am a most superior person.
My face is pink, my hair is sleek,
I dine at Blenheim once a week.
*of Lord **Curzon***
The Masque of Balliol (1870), in W. G. Hiscock *The Balliol Rhymes* (1939, the last two lines are a later addition); see **Parris 241:3**

18 Never stand when you could sit, and never miss a chance to relieve yourself.
advice given by a private secretary or equerry to **George V** or **George VI**

19 No man's life, liberty or property are safe while the legislature is

in session.
view of an unidentified New York State Surrogate Court Judge
in 1866; unattributed comment

1 Now that the Cabinet's gone to its dinner,
The Secretary stays and gets thinner and thinner,
Racking his brains to record and report
What he thinks they think they ought to have thought.
anonymous verse, undated; S. S. Wilson *The Cabinet Office* (1975)

2 One Cartwright brought a Slave from Russia, and would scourge him, for which he was questioned: and it was resolved, That England was too pure an Air for Slaves to breathe in.
'In the 11th of Elizabeth' (17 November 1568–16 November 1569); John Rushworth *Historical Collections* (1680–1722)

3 Order reigns in Warsaw.
after the brutal suppression of an uprising
the newspaper *Moniteur* reported, 16 September 1831, 'Order and calm are completely restored in the capital'; on the same day Count Sebastiani, minister of foreign affairs, declared: 'Peace reigns in Warsaw'

4 Peace, order, and good government.
British North America Act 1867 sect. 91, introduction

5 A place within the meaning of the Act.
usually taken to be a reference to the Betting Act 1853, sect. 2, which banned off-course betting on horse-races

6 The plan is called 'Shock and Awe', and its goal is 'the psychological destruction of the enemy's will to fight'.
in *New Yorker* 10 February 2003; see **Ullman and Wade 319:3**

7 Please to remember the Fifth of November,
Gunpowder Treason and Plot.
We know no reason why gunpowder treason
Should ever be forgot.
traditional rhyme on the Gunpowder Plot (1605)

8 Prudence is the other woman in

Gordon's life.
*of Gordon **Brown***
unidentified aide, quoted in BBC News online (Budget Briefing), 20 March 1998

9 Psychological flaws.
*on which, according to an unnamed source, Gordon **Brown** needed to 'get a grip'*
in *Observer* 18 January 1998; attributed to Alastair **Campbell** by Bernard **Ingham** in minutes of the Parliamentary Select Committee on Public Administration, 2 June 1998, but denied by Campbell in evidence to the Committee, 23 June 1998

10 The quality of goods includes their...fitness for all the purposes for which goods of the kind in question are commonly supplied.
Sale of Goods Act 1979; see **Reid 257:6**

11 Reorganizing the Civil Service is like drawing a knife through a bowl of marbles.
unattributed comment

12 A revolution which lacks the anchor of ideology or the compass of principle will founder on the rocks of mere personality.
an unidentified left-winger on the reported feud between New Labour's Gordon Brown and Peter Mandelson
in *The Mail on Sunday* 19 May 1996

13 *Sic transit gloria mundi.*
Thus passes the glory of the world.
said during the coronation of a new Pope, while flax is burned to represent the transitoriness of earthly glory
used at the coronation of Alexander V in Pisa, 7 July 1409, but earlier in origin

14 The silly, flat, dishwatery utterances of the man who has to be pointed out to intelligent observers as the President of the United States.
review of **Lincoln**'s Gettysburg Address, in *Chicago Times* 20 November 1863; see **Everett 108:1**

15 *Tempora mutantur, et nos mutamur in illis.*
Times change, and we change with them.
William Harrison *Description of Britain* (1577); attributed to the Emperor Lothar I (795–855) in the form '*omnia mutantur, nos et mutamur in illis* [all things change, and we change with them]'

1 There is one thing stronger than all
the armies in the world; and that is
an idea whose time has come.
in flyer for *Nation* 15 April 1943; see **Hugo 149:4**

2 There shall be a Scottish
parliament.
first clause of the Scotland Act, 1998; see
Dewar 90:5

3 *an unnamed Labour MP commenting on the
unusually pale eyes of Hugh* **Dalton***:*
They have a habit of looking
at you intently and conveying
unfathomable depths of insincerity.
*sometimes quoted as 'eyes blazing with
insincerity'*
Patricia Strauss *Bevin and Co. The Leaders of
British Labour* (1941)

4 *annotation to a ministerial brief, said to have
been read out inadvertently in the House of
Lords:*
This is a rotten argument, but
it should be good enough for
their lordships on a hot summer
afternoon.
Lord Home *The Way the Wind Blows* (1976)

5 Those on the opposite side are your
opponents; your enemies are on
your own side.
traditional advice to a new MP

6 Though I yield to no one in my
admiration for Mr Coolidge, I do
wish he did not look as if he had
been weaned on a pickle.
of President Calvin **Coolidge**
anonymous remark, in Alice Roosevelt
Longworth *Crowded Hours* (1933)

7 'Tis bad enough in man or woman
To steal a goose from off a common;
But surely he's without excuse
Who steals the common from the
goose.
'On Inclosures'; in *The Oxford Book of Light
Verse* (1938)

8 To secure for the workers by hand
or by brain the full fruits of their
industry and the most equitable
distribution thereof that may be
possible upon the basis of the
common ownership of the means
of production, distribution, and

exchange.
Clause Four of the Labour Party's Constitution
of 1918 (revised 1929); the commitment to
common ownership of services was largely
removed in 1995; see **Anonymous 7:5**

9 Under capitalism man exploits
man. And under Communism it is
just the reverse.
joke told to J. K. **Galbraith** *at a dinner given for
him during his lecture tour of Poland by the Polish
Economic Society, May 1958*
J. K. Galbraith *A Life in Our Times* (1981)

10 We hold these truths to be self-
evident, that all men are created
equal, that they are endowed
by their Creator with certain
unalienable rights, that among
these are life, liberty and the
pursuit of happiness.
The American Declaration of Independence,
4 July 1776

11 We trained hard...but it seemed
that every time we were beginning
to form up into teams we would be
reorganized. I was to learn later in
life that we tend to meet any new
situation by reorganizing; and a
wonderful method it can be for
creating the illusion of progress
while producing confusion,
inefficiency, and demoralization.
modern saying, frequently (and wrongly)
attributed to the Roman satirist Petronius
Arbiter (d. AD 65)

12 We value excellence as well as
fairness, independence as dearly as
mateship.
draft preamble to the Australian constitution,
made public 23 March 1999

13 What did the President know and
when did he know it?
question current at the time of Watergate,
associated particularly with Howard Baker,
Vice-Chairman of the Senate Watergate
Committee

14 When I left the dining room after
sitting next to Mr Gladstone I
thought he was the cleverest man
in England, but after sitting next
to Mr Disraeli I thought I was the

cleverest woman in England.
view of a young lady taken into dinner by both on successive nights, sometimes attributed to Queen
Victoria
 Princess Marie Louise *My Memories of Six Reigns* (1979)

1 When war enters a country
 It produces lies like sand.
 epigraph to Arthur Ponsonby *Falsehood in Wartime* (1928)

2 Why is there only one
 Monopolies Commission?
 British graffiti; incorporated in the Official Monster Raving Loony Party Manifesto, 1987

3 A willing foe and sea room.
 Naval toast in the time of Nelson
 W. N. T. Beckett *A Few Naval Customs, Expressions, Traditions, and Superstitions* (1931) 'Customs'

4 Winston is back.
 Board of Admiralty signal to the Fleet on Winston **Churchill***'s reappointment as First Sea Lord, 3 September 1939*
 Martin Gilbert *Winston S. Churchill* (1976) vol. 5

5 You love life and we love
 death.
 videotape statement claiming that Al Qaeda carried out the Madrid train bombings, released to the public 14 March 2004

Susan Brownell Anthony

1820–1906
American feminist and political activist

6 The men and women of the
 North are slaveholders, those of the South slaveowners. The guilt rests on the North equally with the South.
 Speech on No Union with Slaveholders 1857

7 Join the union, girls, and
 together say *Equal Pay for Equal Work*.
 in *The Revolution* 8 October 1869

8 Here, in the first
 paragraph of the Declaration [of Independence], is the assertion of the natural right of all to the ballot; for how can 'the consent of the governed' be given, if the right to vote be denied?
 speech in 1873 before her trial for voting
 Is It a Crime for a Citizen of the United States to Vote?

Yasser Arafat 1929–2004

Palestinian statesman, President 1996–2004. On Arafat: see **Mandela 204:5**

9 Palestine is the cement that
 holds the Arab world together, or it is the explosive that blows it apart.
 in *Time* 11 November 1974

John Arbuthnot 1667–1735

Scottish physician and pamphleteer

10 He [the writer] warns the heads of
 parties against believing their own lies.
 The Art of Political Lying (1712)

11 All political parties die at last of
 swallowing their own lies.
 attributed; Richard Garnett *Life of Emerson* (1887)

Hannah Arendt 1906–75

American political philosopher

12 The most radical revolutionary will
 become a conservative on the day after the revolution.
 in *New Yorker* 12 September 1970

13 Under conditions of tyranny it is far
 easier to act than to think.
 W. H. Auden *A Certain World* (1970)

Marquis d'Argenson 1694–1757

French politician and political essayist

14 *Laisser-faire.*
 No interference.
 term applied to the doctrine of minimum state intervention in economic affairs
 Mémoires et Journal Inédit du Marquis d'Argenson; see **Quesnay 253:2**

Aristophanes c. 450–c. 385 BC

Greek comic dramatist

15 How about 'Cloudcuckooland'?
 naming the capital city of the Birds
 The Birds (414 BC)

16 You have all the characteristics of a
 popular politician: a horrible voice, bad breeding and a vulgar manner.
 The Knights (424 BC)

17 Under every stone lurks a
 politician.
 Thesmophoriazusae

Aristotle 384–322 BC
Greek philosopher

1 Therefore, the good of man must be the objective of the science of politics.
 Nicomachean Ethics

2 We make war that we may live in peace.
 Nicomachean Ethics

3 Politicians also have no leisure, because they are always aiming at something beyond political life itself, power and glory, or happiness.
 Nicomachean Ethics

4 Man is by nature a political animal.
 Politics

5 He who is unable to live in society, or who has no need because he is sufficient for himself, must be either a beast or a god.
 Politics

6 For that some should rule, and others be ruled, is a thing not only necessary but expedient, for from the hour of their birth some are marked for subjection, others for rule.
 Politics

7 Poverty is the parent of revolution and crime.
 Politics

8 Where some people are very wealthy and others have nothing, the result will be either extreme democracy or absolute oligarchy, or despotism will come from either of those excesses.
 Politics

9 The most perfect political community is one in which the middle class is in control, and outnumbers both of the other classes.
 Politics

10 No tyrant need fear till men begin to feel confident in each other.
 Politics

Robert Armstrong 1927–
British civil servant; Head of the Civil Service, 1981–7

11 It contains a misleading impression, not a lie. It was being economical with the truth.
 referring to a letter during the 'Spycatcher' trial, Supreme Court, New South Wales, November 1986
 in *Daily Telegraph* 19 November 1986; see **Burke 48:18, Clark 73:5**

William Armstrong 1915–80
British civil servant, Head of the Civil Service 1968–74

12 The business of the Civil Service is the orderly management of decline.
 in 1973: Peter Hennessy *Whitehall* (1990)

Matthew Arnold 1822–88
English poet and essayist; son of Thomas **Arnold**

13 Our society distributes itself into Barbarians, Philistines, and Populace; and America is just ourselves, with the Barbarians quite left out, and the Populace nearly.
 Culture and Anarchy (1869) preface

14 The men of culture are the true apostles of equality.
 Culture and Anarchy (1869)

15 When I want to distinguish clearly the aristocratic class from the Philistines proper, or middle class, [I] name the former, in my own mind *the Barbarians*.
 Culture and Anarchy (1869)

16 That vast portion...of the working-class which, raw and half-developed, has long lain half-hidden amidst its poverty and squalor, and is now issuing from its hiding-place to assert an Englishman's heaven-born privilege of doing as he likes, and is beginning to perplex us by marching where it likes, meeting where it likes, bawling what it likes, breaking what it likes—to this vast residuum we may with great propriety give the name of Populace.
 Culture and Anarchy (1869)

Thomas Arnold 1795–1842
English historian and educator; Headmaster of Rugby School from 1828; father of Matthew **Arnold**

1 As for rioting, the old Roman way of dealing with that is always the right one; flog the rank and file, and fling the ringleaders from the Tarpeian rock.
   from an unpublished letter written before 1828

Raymond Aron 1905–83
French sociologist and political journalist

2 Political thought, in France, is retrospective or utopian.
   L'opium des intellectuels (1955)

John Ashcroft 1942–
American Republican politician, Attorney General of the US 2001–4

3 We may never know why he turned his back on our country and our values, but we cannot ignore that he did. Youth is not absolution for treachery.
   on John Walker Lindh, an American who fought for the Taliban
   in *Newsweek* 28 January 2002

Herbert Henry Asquith 1852–1928
British Liberal statesman; Prime Minister, 1908–16. On Asquith: see **Churchill 65:13, Hennessy 141:4**

4 We had better wait and see.
   phrase used repeatedly in speeches in 1910, referring to the rumour that the House of Lords was to be flooded with new Liberal peers to ensure the passage of the Finance Bill
   Roy Jenkins *Asquith* (1964)

5 We shall never sheathe the sword which we have not lightly drawn until Belgium recovers in full measure all and more than all that she has sacrificed, until France is adequately secured against the menace of aggression, until the rights of the smaller nationalities of Europe are placed upon an unassailable foundation, and until the military domination of Prussia is wholly and finally destroyed.
   speech at the Guildhall, London, 9 November 1914

6 There is no more striking illustration of the immobility of British institutions than the House of Commons.
   Fifty Years of Parliament (1926) vol. 2

7 The office of the Prime Minister is what its holder chooses and is able to make of it.
   Fifty Years of Parliament (1926) vol. 2

8 He is a Chimborazo or Everest among the sandhills of the Baldwin Cabinet.
   *of Winston **Churchill***
   Roy Jenkins *Asquith* (1964)

9 It is fitting that we should have buried the Unknown Prime Minister [Bonar Law] by the side of the Unknown Soldier.
   Robert Blake *The Unknown Prime Minister* (1955)

10 [The War Office kept three sets of figures:] one to mislead the public, another to mislead the Cabinet, and the third to mislead itself.
   Alistair Horne *Price of Glory* (1962)

11 We are bound to lose Ireland in consequence of years of cruelty, stupidity and misgovernment and I would rather lose her as a friend than as a foe.
   Margot Asquith *More Memories* (1933)

Margot Asquith 1864–1945
British political hostess; wife of Herbert **Asquith**

12 Kitchener is a great poster.
   More Memories (1933)

13 There is nothing more popular in the House of Commons than to blame yourself. 'I have killed my mother. I will never do it again,' is certain to raise a cheer.
   Off the Record (1943)

14 No amount of education will make women first-rate politicians. Can you see a woman becoming a Prime Minister? I cannot imagine a greater calamity for these islands than to be put under the guidance of a woman in 10 Downing Street.
   Off the Record (1943)

15 Lord Birkenhead is very clever but sometimes his brains go to his head.
   in *Listener* 11 June 1953 'Margot Oxford' by Lady Violet Bonham Carter

1 He can't see a belt without hitting
below it.
of Lloyd George
in *Listener* 11 June 1953 'Margot Oxford' by
Lady Violet Bonham Carter

Jacob Astley 1579–1652
English soldier and royalist

2 Gentlemen, ye may now sit and
play, for you have done all your
work, if you fall not out among
yourselves.
*to enemy officers, after being captured at Stow-
on-the-Wold, 1646*
R. Field *Stow-on-the-Wold, 1646* (1992)

Nancy Astor 1879–1964
American-born British Conservative politician

3 NANCY ASTOR: If I were your wife I
would put poison in your coffee.
WINSTON CHURCHILL: And if I were
your husband I would drink it.
Consuelo Vanderbilt *Glitter and Gold* (1952)

Kemal Atatürk 1881–1938
Turkish general and statesman, President 1923–38

4 There is no difference between
the Johnnies and the Mehmets
to us where they lie side by side
in this country of ours. You, the
mothers, who sent their sons from
faraway countries, wipe away your
tears. Your sons are now lying in
our bosom and are in peace. After
having lost their lives on this land,
they have become our sons as well.
address to a group of visiting Australians at
Anzac Cove, Gallipoli, 1934; subsequently
inscribed on the memorial there, and on the
Atatürk memorials in Canberra and Wellington

Brooks Atkinson 1894–1984
American journalist and critic

5 After each war there is a little less
democracy to save.
Once Around the Sun (1951) 7 January

6 In every age 'the good old days'
were a myth. No one ever thought
they were good at the time. For
every age had consisted of crises
that seemed intolerable to the
people who lived through them.
Once Around the Sun (1951) 8 February

7 There is a good deal of solemn
cant about the common interests
of capital and labour. As matters
stand, their only common interest is
that of cutting each other's throat.
Once Around the Sun (1951) 7 September

Clement Attlee 1883–1967
British Labour statesman; Prime Minister, 1945–51.
On Attlee: see **Churchill 71:9, Churchill 71:18,
Hennessy 141:4, Nicolson 227:4**

8 A monologue is not a decision.
*to Winston **Churchill**, who had complained that
a matter had been raised several times in Cabinet*
Francis Williams *A Prime Minister Remembers*
(1961)

9 The voice we heard was that of
Mr Churchill but the mind was that
of Lord Beaverbrook.
speech on radio, 5 June 1945

10 A period of silence on your part
would be welcome.
*in reply to a letter from the Chairman of the
Labour Party, Harold **Laski**, asking (for the second
time and at length) that Attlee should not form a
new government until the Parliamentary Labour
Party had had the chance to elect a new leader*
letter to Harold Laski, 20 August 1945

11 If the King asks you to form a
Government you say 'Yes' or 'No',
not 'I'll let you know later!'
Kenneth Harris *Attlee* (1982)

12 *at a Cabinet Meeting, when Aneurin **Bevan**
as Minister of Housing complained that he
could not get enough people for his building
programme:*
BEVAN: Where are all the people I
need for my programme?
ATTLEE: Looking for houses, Nye!
Michael Foot *Aneuran Bevan* (1973) vol. 2

13 I should be a sad subject for any
publicity expert. I have none of the
qualities which create publicity.
Harold Nicolson diary, 14 January 1949

14 *response to a memorandum from the
Ministry of Works saying, 'We have read the
Cabinet's proposals':*
The Cabinet does not propose,
it decides.
Tony Benn diary, 20 May 1974

15 I believe that conscience is a still
small voice and not a loudspeaker.
attributed, 1955

1 Few thought he was even a starter
There were many who thought
  themselves smarter
But he ended PM
CH and OM
An earl and a knight of the garter.
*describing himself in a letter to Tom Attlee,
8 April 1956*
Kenneth Harris *Attlee* (1982)

2 [Russian Communism is] the
illegitimate child of Karl Marx and
Catherine the Great.
speech at Aarhus University, 11 April 1956

3 Generally speaking the Press lives
on disaster.
attributed, 1956

4 Democracy means government by
discussion, but it is only effective if
you can stop people talking.
speech at Oxford, 14 June 1957

5 Often the 'experts' make the worst
possible Ministers in their own
fields. In this country we prefer rule
by amateurs.
speech at Oxford, 14 June 1957

6 It's a good maxim that if you have
a good dog you don't bark yourself.
I had a very good dog in Mr Ernest
Bevin.
attributed, 1960

7 *definition of the art of politics:*
Judgement which is needed to make
important decisions on imperfect
knowledge in a limited time.
attributed

W. H. Auden 1907–73
English poet

8 To save your world you asked this
  man to die:
Would this man, could he see you
  now, ask why?
'Epitaph for the Unknown Soldier' (1955)

9 He knew human folly like the back
  of his hand,
And was greatly interested in armies

and fleets;
When he laughed, respectable
  senators burst with laughter,
And when he cried the little children
  died in the streets.
'Epitaph on a Tyrant' (1940); see
Motley 220:10

10 In the nightmare of the dark
All the dogs of Europe bark,
And the living nations wait,
Each sequestered in its hate.
'In Memory of W. B. Yeats' (1940)

11 Private faces in public places
Are wiser and nicer
Than public faces in private places.
Orators (1932) dedication

12 There is no such thing as the State
And no one exists alone;
Hunger allows no choice
To the citizen or the police;
We must love one another or die.
'September 1, 1939' (1940)

13 Our researchers into Public
  Opinion are content
That he held the proper opinions for
  the time of year;
When there was peace, he was for
  peace; when there was war, he
  went.
'The Unknown Citizen' (1940)

14 This marble monument was
  erected by the state.
Was he free? Was he happy? The
  question is absurd:
Had anything been wrong, we should
  certainly have heard.
'The Unknown Citizen' (1940)

Augustus 63 BC–AD 14
first Roman emperor. On Augustus: see **Cicero 72:14**

15 Quintilius Varus, give me back my
legions.
*after the annihilation by the German leader
Arminius of three Roman legions under Quintilius
Varus*
Suetonius *Lives of the Caesars*

16 He could boast that he inherited it

Australia
'light on the hill'
see Selective Subject Index

brick and left it marble.
of the city of Rome
Suetonius *Lives of the Caesars*

Aung San Suu Kyi 1945–
Burmese political leader

1 In societies where men are truly confident of their own worth, women are not merely tolerated but valued.
videotape speech at NGO Forum on Women, China, early September 1995

2 Real freedom is freedom from fear, and unless you can live free from fear you cannot live a dignified human life.
undated interview with the BBC; transcript on BBC World Service website

Marcus Aurelius AD 121–180
Roman emperor from AD 161

3 Man, you have been a citizen in

this world city, what does it matter whether for five years or fifty?
Meditations

Jane Austen 1775–1817
English novelist

4 From politics, it was an easy step to silence.
Northanger Abbey (1818)

Ayesha fl. 1492
Moorish princess, mother of the last Sultan of Granada

5 You do well to weep as a woman over what you could not defend as a man.
reproach to her son Boabdil (Muhammad XI), who had surrendered Granada to Ferdinand and Isabella
traditional attribution; Washington Irving *The Alhambra* (1832; rev. ed. 1851) ch. 18

Isaac Babel 1894–1940
Russian short-story writer

6 Now a man talks frankly only with his wife, at night, with the blanket over his head.
remark 1937; Solomon Volkov *St Petersburg* (1996)

7 They didn't let me finish.
to his wife, on the day of his arrest by the NKVD, 16 May 1939

Francis Bacon 1561–1626
English lawyer, courtier, philosopher, and essayist. See also **Last words 178:6**

8 *Tempus, ad quae consilia non advocatur, nec rata habet.*
The counsels to which Time is not called, Time will not ratify.
De Dignitate et Augmentis Scientiarum (1623)

9 He is the fountain of honour.
An Essay of a King (1642); attribution doubtful; see **Bagehot 18:6**

10 In civil business; what first? boldness; what second and third? boldness: and yet boldness is a child of ignorance and baseness.
Essays (1625) 'Of Boldness'

11 There be [some] that can pack the cards and yet cannot play well; so there are some that are good in canvasses and factions, that are otherwise weak men.
Essays (1625) 'Of Cunning'

12 Nothing doth more hurt in a state than that cunning men pass for wise.
Essays (1625) 'Of Cunning'

13 There is surely no greater wisdom than well to time the beginnings

and endings of things.
Essays (1625) 'Of Delays'

1 The difficulties in princes' business
are many and great, but the
greatest difficulty is often in their
own mind.
Essays (1625) 'Of Empire'

2 Men in great place are thrice
servants: servants of the sovereign
or state, servants of fame, and
servants of business.
Essays (1625) 'Of Great Place'

3 The rising unto place is laborious,
and by pains men come to greater
pains; and it is sometimes base,
and by indignities men come to
dignities. The standing is slippery,
and the regress is either a downfall,
or at least an eclipse.
Essays (1625) 'Of Great Place'

4 Severity breedeth fear, but
roughness breedeth hate. Even
reproofs from authority ought to be
grave, and not taunting.
Essays (1625) 'Of Great Place'

5 All rising to great place is by a
winding stair.
Essays (1625) 'Of Great Place'

6 New nobility is but the act of power,
but ancient nobility is the act of
time.
Essays (1625) 'Of Nobility'

7 Fame is like a river, that beareth
up things light and swollen, and
drowns things weighty and solid.
Essays (1625) 'Of Praise'

8 So when any of the four pillars of
government are mainly shakened
or weakened (which are religion,
justice, counsel, and treasure) men
had need to pray for fair weather.
Essays (1625) 'Of Seditions and Troubles'

9 The surest way to prevent seditions
(if the times do bear it) is to take
away the matter of them.
Essays (1625) 'Of Seditions and Troubles'

10 Suspicions amongst thoughts are
like bats amongst birds, they ever
fly by twilight.
Essays (1625) 'Of Suspicion'

11 Neither is money the sinews of war

(as it is trivially said).
Essays (1625) 'Of the True Greatness of
Kingdoms'; see **Cicero 72:10**

12 Neither will it be, that a people
overlaid with taxes should ever
become valiant and martial.
Essays (1625) 'Of the True Greatness of
Kingdoms'

13 What is truth? said jesting Pilate;
and would not stay for an answer.
Essays (1625) 'Of Truth'

14 All colours will agree in the dark.
Essays (1625) 'Of Unity in Religion'

15 In the youth of a state arms do
flourish; in the middle age of a
state, learning; and then both of
them together for a time; in the
declining age of a state, mechanical
arts and merchandise.
Essays (1625) 'Of Vicissitude of Things'

16 For also knowledge itself is power.
Meditationes Sacrae (1597) 'Of Heresies'

17 It is well to observe the force
and virtue and consequence of
discoveries, and these are to be
seen nowhere more conspicuously
than in those three which were
unknown to the ancients, and of
which the origins, though recent,
are obscure and inglorious; namely,
printing, gunpowder, and the
magnet [Mariner's Needle]. For
these three have changed the whole
face and state of things throughout
the world.
Novum Organum (1620)

18 There be three things which make
a nation great and prosperous: a
fertile soil, busy workshops, easy
conveyance for men and goods
from place to place.
attributed; S. Platt (ed.) *Respectfully Quoted*
(1989)

Joan Baez 1941–
American singer and songwriter

19 The only thing that's been a worse
flop than the organization of non-
violence has been the organization
of violence.
Daybreak (1970) 'What Would You Do If?'

Walter Bagehot 1826–77
English economist and essayist

1 In happy states, the Conservative party must rule upon the whole a much longer time than their adversaries. In well-framed politics, innovation—great innovation that is—can only be occasional. If you are always altering your house, it is a sign either that you have a bad house, or that you have an excessively restless disposition— there is something wrong somewhere.
'The Chances for a Long Conservative Régime in England' (1874)

2 Capital must be propelled by self-interest; it cannot be enticed by benevolence.
Economic Studies (1880)

3 The mystic reverence, the religious allegiance, which are essential to a true monarchy, are imaginative sentiments that no legislature can manufacture in any people.
The English Constitution (1867) 'The Cabinet'

4 In such constitutions [as England's] there are two parts…first, those which excite and preserve the reverence of the population—the *dignified* parts…and next, the *efficient* parts—those by which it, in fact, works and rules.
The English Constitution (1867) 'The Cabinet'

5 No orator ever made an impression by appealing to men as to their plainest physical wants, except when he could allege that those wants were caused by some one's tyranny.
The English Constitution (1867) 'The Cabinet'

6 The Crown is, according to the saying, the 'fountain of honour'; but the Treasury is the spring of business.
The English Constitution (1867) 'The Cabinet'; see **Bacon 16:9**

7 A cabinet is a combining committee—a *hyphen* which joins, a *buckle* which fastens, the legislative part of the state to the executive part of the state.
The English Constitution (1867) 'The Cabinet'

8 It has been said that England invented the phrase, 'Her Majesty's Opposition'; that it was the first government which made a criticism of administration as much a part of the polity as administration itself. This critical opposition is the consequence of cabinet government.
The English Constitution (1867) 'The Cabinet'; see **Hobhouse 145:9**

9 *The Times* has made many ministries.
The English Constitution (1867) 'The Cabinet'

10 The great qualities, the imperious will, the rapid energy, the eager nature fit for a great crisis are not required—are impediments—in common times.
The English Constitution (1867) 'The Cabinet'

11 By the structure of the world we often want, at the sudden occurrence of a grave tempest, to change the helmsman—to replace the pilot of the calm by the pilot of the storm.
The English Constitution (1867) 'The Cabinet'

12 Where great questions end, little parties begin.
The English Constitution (1867) 'The Pre-Requisites of Cabinet Government'

13 *of Queen **Victoria** and the future **Edward VII**:*
It is nice to trace how the actions of a retired widow and an unemployed youth become of such importance.
The English Constitution (1867) 'The Monarchy'

14 The best reason why Monarchy is a strong government is, that it is an intelligible government. The mass of mankind understand it, and they hardly anywhere in the world understand any other.
The English Constitution (1867) 'The Monarchy'

15 The characteristic of the English Monarchy is that it retains the feelings by which the heroic kings governed their rude age, and has added the feelings by which the

constitutions of later Greece ruled in more refined ages.
The English Constitution (1867) 'The Monarchy'

1 Women—one half the human race at least—care fifty times more for a marriage than a ministry.
The English Constitution (1867) 'The Monarchy'

2 Royalty is a government in which the attention of the nation is concentrated on one person doing interesting actions. A Republic is a government in which that attention is divided between many, who are all doing uninteresting actions. Accordingly, so long as the human heart is strong and the human reason weak, Royalty will be strong because it appeals to diffused feeling, and Republics weak because they appeal to the understanding.
The English Constitution (1867) 'The Monarchy'

3 Throughout the greater part of his life George III was a kind of 'consecrated obstruction'.
The English Constitution (1867) 'The Monarchy'

4 There are arguments for not having a Court, and there are arguments for having a splendid Court; but there are no arguments for having a mean Court.
The English Constitution (1867) 'The Monarchy'

5 The Queen...must sign her own death-warrant if the two Houses unanimously send it up to her.
The English Constitution (1867) 'The Monarchy'

6 Above all things our royalty is to be reverenced, and if you begin to poke about it you cannot reverence it...Its mystery is its life. We must not let in daylight upon magic.
The English Constitution (1867) 'The Monarchy'

7 The Sovereign has, under a constitutional monarchy such as ours, three rights—the right to be consulted, the right to encourage, the right to warn.
The English Constitution (1867) 'The Monarchy'

8 The only fit material for a constitutional king is a prince who begins early to reign—who in his youth is superior to pleasure—who in his youth is willing to labour— who has by nature a genius for discretion. Such kings are among God's greatest gifts, but they are also among His rarest.
The English Constitution (1867) 'The Monarchy'

9 The order of nobility is of great use, too, not only in what it creates, but in what it prevents. It prevents the rule of wealth—the religion of gold. This is the obvious and natural idol of the Anglo-Saxon.
The English Constitution (1867) 'The House of Lords'

10 A severe though not unfriendly critic of our institutions said that 'the cure for admiring the House of Lords was to go and look at it.'
The English Constitution (1867) 'The House of Lords'

11 If you want to raise a certain cheer in the House of Commons, make a general panegyric on economy; if you want to invite a sure defeat, propose a particular saving.
The English Constitution (1867) 'The House of Lords'

12 Nations touch at their summits.
The English Constitution (1867) 'The House of Lords'

13 An ambassador is not simply an agent; he is also a spectacle.
The English Constitution (1867) 'The House of Lords'

14 The whole life of English politics is the action and reaction between the ministry and the parliament.
The English Constitution (1867) 'The House of Commons'

15 The House of Commons lives in a state of perpetual potential choice: at any moment it can choose a ruler and dismiss a ruler. And therefore party is inherent in it, is bone of its bone, and breath of its breath.
The English Constitution (1867) 'The House of Commons'

16 An Opposition, on coming into power, is often like a speculative merchant whose bills become due.

Ministers have to make good their promises, and they find a difficulty in so doing.

The English Constitution (1867) 'The House of Commons'

1 It is an inevitable defect, that bureaucrats will care more for routine than for results.

The English Constitution (1867) 'On Changes of Ministry'

2 A bureaucracy is sure to think that its duty is to augment official power, official business, or official members, rather than to leave free the energies of mankind; it overdoes the quantity of government, as well as impairs its quality.

The English Constitution (1867) 'On Changes of Ministry'

3 But would it not have been a miracle if the English people, directing their own policy, and being what they are, had directed a good policy? Are they not above all nations divided from the rest of the world, insular both in situation and in mind, both for good and for evil? Are they not out of the current of common European causes and affairs? Are they not a race contemptuous of others? Are they not a race with no special education or culture as to the modern world, and too often despising such culture? Who could expect such a people to comprehend the new and strange events of foreign places?

The English Constitution (1867) 'On Changes of Ministry'

4 It has been said, not truly, but with a possible approximation to truth, that in 1802 every hereditary monarch was insane.

The English Constitution (1867) 'Its Supposed Checks and Balances'

5 As soon as we see that England is a disguised republic we must see too that the classes for whom the disguise is necessary must be tenderly dealt with.

The English Constitution (1867) 'Its History'

6 The natural impulse of the English

people is to resist authority.

The English Constitution (1867) 'Its History'

7 A political country is like an American forest: you only have to cut down the old trees, and immediately new trees come up to replace them; the seeds were waiting in the ground, and they began to grow as soon as the withdrawal of the old ones brought in light and air.

The English Constitution: introduction to the second edition (1872)

8 No real English gentleman, in his secret soul, was ever sorry for the death of a political economist.

Estimates of some Englishmen and Scotchmen (1858)

9 Dullness in matters of government is a good sign, and not a bad one—in particular, dullness in Parliamentary government is a test of its excellence, an indication of its success.

in *Saturday Review* 16 February 1856

10 A constitutional statesman is in general a man of common opinion and uncommon abilities.

in *National Review* July 1856

11 Public opinion is a permeating influence, and it exacts obedience to itself; it requires us to think other men's thoughts, to speak other men's words, to follow other men's habits.

in *National Review* July 1856

12 He believes, with all his heart and soul and strength, that there *is* such a thing as truth; he has the soul of a martyr with the intellect of an advocate.

*of **Gladstone***

in *National Review* July 1860

13 Years of acquiescing in proposals as to which he has not been consulted, of voting for measures which he did not frame, and in the wisdom of which he often did not believe, of arguing for proposals from half of which he dissents—usually de-intellectualize a parliamentary statesman before he comes to half

his power.
in *National Review* 1861 'William Pitt'

1 There is no method by which men can be both free and equal.
in *The Economist* 5 September 1863

2 Policies must 'grow'; they cannot be suddenly made.
in *The Economist* 1874

3 The being without an opinion is so painful to human nature that most people will leap to a hasty opinion rather than undergo it.
in *The Economist* 4 December 1875

4 The characteristic danger of great nations, like the Romans or the English, which have a long history of continuous creation, is that they may at last fail from not comprehending the great institutions which they have created.
in *Fortnightly Review* 1 November 1876

Ewen Bain 1925–89
Scottish cartoonist

5 No son—they're not the same—devolution takes longer.
father to his son, who is reading a book on evolution
cartoon caption, in *Scots Independent* January 1978

Jacques Bainville 1879–1936
French historian

6 *of the Treaty of Versailles:*
Written by Bible readers *for* Bible readers.
'Les Consequences Politiques de la Paix' (1920)

Michael Bakunin 1814–76
Russian revolutionary and anarchist

7 The urge for destruction is also a creative urge!
in *Jahrbuch für Wissenschaft und Kunst* (1842)

8 We wish, in a word, equality—equality in fact as corollary, or rather, as primordial condition of liberty. From each according to his faculties, to each according to his needs; that is what we wish

sincerely and energetically.
declaration signed by forty-seven anarchists on trial after the failure of their uprising at Lyons in 1870
J. Morrison Davidson *The Old Order and the New* (1890)

James Baldwin 1924–87
American novelist and essayist

9 Freedom is not something that anybody can be given; freedom is something people take and people are as free as they want to be.
Nobody Knows My Name (1961) 'Notes for a Hypothetical Novel'

10 At the root of the American Negro problem is the necessity of the American white man to find a way of living with the Negro in order to be able to live with himself.
in *Harper's Magazine* October 1953 'Stranger in a Village'

11 It comes as a great shock around the age of 5, 6 or 7 to discover that the flag to which you have pledged allegiance, along with everybody else, has not pledged allegiance to you. It comes as a great shock to see Gary Cooper killing off the Indians and, although you are rooting for Gary Cooper, that the Indians are you.
speaking for the proposition that 'The American Dream is at the expense of the American Negro' at the Cambridge Union, England, 17 February 1965
in *New York Times Magazine* 7 March 1965

12 If they take you in the morning, they will be coming for us that night.
in *New York Review of Books* 7 January 1971 'Open Letter to my Sister, Angela Davis'

Stanley Baldwin 1867–1947
British Conservative statesman; Prime Minister, 1923–4, 1924–9, 1935–7. On Baldwin: see **Churchill 69:5**, **Churchill 69:13**, **Curzon 84:4**, **Trevelyan 315:1**; see also **Kipling 174:11**

13 They [parliament] are a lot of hard-faced men who look as if they had done very well out of the war.
J. M. Keynes *Economic Consequences of the Peace* (1919)

1 A platitude is simply a truth
repeated until people get tired of
hearing it.
speech in the House of Commons, 29 May
1924

2 There are three classes which need
sanctuary more than others—birds,
wild flowers, and Prime Ministers.
in *Observer* 24 May 1925

3 'Safety first' does not mean a smug
self-satisfaction with everything as
it is. It is a warning to all persons
who are going to cross a road in
dangerous circumstances.
in *Times* 21 May 1929

4 Had the employers of past
generations all of them dealt fairly
with their men there would have
been no unions.
speech in Birmingham, 14 January 1931

5 I think it is well also for the man
in the street to realize that there is
no power on earth that can protect
him from being bombed. Whatever
people may tell him, the bomber
will always get through. The only
defence is in offence, which means
that you have to kill more women
and children more quickly than
the enemy if you want to save
yourselves.
speech in the House of Commons,
10 November 1932

6 Since the day of the air, the old
frontiers are gone. When you think
of the defence of England you no
longer think of the chalk cliffs of
Dover; you think of the Rhine. That
is where our frontier lies.
speech in the House of Commons, 30 July 1934

7 The Yorks will do it very well.
on the future of the monarchy, on hearing of
Edward VIII's *love for Mrs Simpson*
c. 1935; Geoffrey Bocca *The Woman Who
Would Be Queen* (1954)

8 *of his reasons for excluding* **Churchill** *from
the Cabinet:*
If there is going to be a war—and no
one can say that there is not—we
must keep him fresh to be our war
Prime Minister.
letter, 17 November 1935

9 I shall be but a short time tonight.

I have seldom spoken with greater
regret, for my lips are not yet
unsealed. Were these troubles
over I would make a case, and I
guarantee that not a man would go
into the lobby against us.
speech in the House of Commons on the
Abyssinian crisis, 10 December 1935; see
Misquotations 216:1

10 Supposing I had gone to the
country and said that Germany was
rearming and that we must rearm,
does anybody think that this pacific
democracy would have rallied to
that cry at that moment? I cannot
think of anything that would have
made the loss of the election from
my point of view more certain.
speech in the House of Commons,
12 November 1936

11 *of the advice he had given to* **Edward VIII** *on
the possibility of marriage with Mrs Simpson:*
I pointed out to him that the
position of the King's wife was
different from the position of any
other citizen in the country; it
was part of the price which the
King has to pay. His wife becomes
Queen; the Queen becomes Queen
of the country; and, therefore, in
the choice of a Queen, the voice of
the people must be heard.
speech, House of Commons, 10 December
1936 (Abdication Crisis)

12 This House today is a theatre which
is being watched by the whole
world. Let us conduct ourselves
with that dignity which His Majesty
is showing in this hour of his trial.
speech, House of Commons, 10 December
1936 (Abdication Crisis)

13 Once I leave, I leave. I am not going
to speak to the man on the bridge,
and I am not going to spit on the
deck.
on resigning
statement to the Cabinet, 28 May 1937

14 LG was born a cad and never forgot
it. Winston was born a gentleman
and never remembered it.
on **Lloyd George** *and* **Churchill**
in 1937; Richard Toye *Lloyd George and
Churchill: Rivals for Greatness* (2007)

1 You will find in politics that you are much exposed to the attribution of false motive. Never complain and never explain.
   Harold Nicolson *Diary* 21 July 1943

2 Do not run up your nose dead against the Pope or the NUM!
   Lord Butler *The Art of Memory* (1982); see **Macmillan 200:2**

3 He spent his whole life in plastering together the true and the false and therefrom manufacturing the plausible.
   *of **Lloyd George***
   attributed

Arthur James Balfour 1848–1930
British Conservative statesman; Prime Minister, 1902–5. On Balfour: see **Churchill 65:13**, **Churchill 70:10**, **Lloyd George 188:11**, **Lloyd George 189:6**

4 It is unfortunate, considering that enthusiasm moves the world, that so few enthusiasts can be trusted to speak the truth.
   letter to Mrs Drew, 19 May 1891

5 The tyranny of majorities may be as bad as the tyranny of Kings.
   watching the Belfast march past of Ulster Loyalists in 1893
   in *Times* 5 April 1893

6 His Majesty's Government view with favour the establishment in Palestine of a national home for the Jewish people, and will use their best endeavours to facilitate the achievement of this object, it being clearly understood that nothing shall be done which may prejudice the civil and religious rights of existing non-Jewish communities in Palestine, or the rights and political status enjoyed by Jews in any other country.
   letter to Lord Rothschild, 2 November 1917; see **Weizmann 328:14**

7 Zionism, be it right or wrong, good or bad, is rooted in age-long traditions, in present need, in future hopes, of far profounder import than the desires and prejudices of the seven hundred thousand Arabs who now inhabit that ancient land.
   in August 1919; Max Egremont *Balfour* (1980)

8 *replying to Frank Harris, who had claimed that 'all the faults of the age come from Christianity and journalism':*
   Christianity, of course…but why journalism?
   Margot Asquith *Autobiography* (1920) vol. 1

9 *on the continuing financial dependence of **Curzon**, who had failed to become Prime Minister in succession to **Bonar Law**, on his second wife Grace Duggan:*
   He may have lost the hope of glory, but he still retains the means of Grace.
   attributed

10 Biography should be written by an acute enemy.
   in *Observer* 30 January 1927

11 I am more or less happy when being praised, not very uncomfortable when being abused, but I have moments of uneasiness when being explained.
   K. Young *A. J. Balfour* (1963)

12 I never forgive but I always forget.
   R. Blake *Conservative Party* (1970)

13 I thought he was a young man of promise, but it appears he is a young man of promises.
   describing Churchill
   Winston Churchill *My Early Life* (1930)

14 Nothing matters very much and very few things matter at all.
   Clodagh Anson *Book: discreet memoirs* (1931) ch. 13

E. Digby Baltzell 1915–96

15 There is a crisis in American leadership in the middle of the twentieth century that is partly due, I think, to the declining authority of an establishment which is now based on an increasingly castelike White-Anglo Saxon-Protestant (WASP) upper class.
   The Protestant Establishment (1964)

Honoré de Balzac 1799–1850
French novelist

16 Equality may perhaps be a right,

but no power on earth can ever turn it into a fact.
La Duchesse de Langeais (1834)

1 Despotism accomplishes great things illegally; liberty doesn't even go to the trouble of accomplishing small things legally.
La Peau de Chagrin (1831)

Lord Bancroft 1922–96
British civil servant; Head of the Civil Service 1978–81

2 Conviction politicians, certainly: conviction civil servants, no.
'Whitehall: Some Personal Reflections', lecture at the London School of Economics 1 December 1983

Joseph Banks 1743–1820
English botanist

3 Who knows but that England may revive in New South Wales when it has sunk in Europe.
letter to Governor Hunter, 30 March 1797

Imamu Amiri Baraka 1934–
American poet and dramatist

4 A man is either free or he is not. There cannot be any apprenticeship for freedom.
in *Kulchur* Spring 1962 'Tokenism'

Ernest Barker 1874–1960
British political scientist

5 Sovereignty is unlimited— unlimited and illimitable.
Principles of Social and Political Theory (1951)

Pat Barker 1943–
English novelist

6 The Somme is like the Holocaust. It revealed things about mankind that we cannot come to terms with and cannot forget. It can never become the past.
on winning the Booker Prize 1995
in *Athens News* 9 November 1995

Alben W. Barkley 1877–1956
American politician

7 If you have to eat crow, eat it

while it's hot.
attributed

Michel Barnier 1951–
French politician

8 Alliance is not allegiance.
on Europe's relations with America
in *Independent* 29 October 2004

Michael Joseph Barry 1817–89
Irish nationalist writer

9 The wild geese—the wild geese,— 'tis long since they flew, O'er the billowy ocean's bright bosom of blue.
in *Spirit of the Nation* (Dublin, 1845)

Edmund Barton 1849–1920
Australian statesman, Prime Minister 1901–3

10 A nation for a continent and a continent for a nation.
on Australian federation
quoted in Robert Garran *The Coming Commonwealth* (1897)

Bernard Baruch 1870–1965
American financier and presidential adviser

11 Let us not be deceived—we are today in the midst of a cold war.
speech to South Carolina Legislature 16 April 1947; the expression 'cold war' was suggested to him by H. B. Swope, former editor of the *New York World*

12 Vote for the man who promises least; he'll be the least disappointing.
Meyer Berger *New York* (1960)

13 You can talk about capitalism and communism and all that sort of thing, but the important thing is the struggle everybody is engaged in to get better living conditions, and they are not interested too much in government.
in *Times* 20 August 1964

14 A political leader must keep looking over his shoulder all the time to see if the boys are still there. If they aren't still there, he's no longer a political leader.
in *New York Times* 21 June 1965

Claude-Frédéric Bastiat 1801–50
French economist

1 All men's impulses, when motivated by legitimate self-interest, fall into a harmonious social pattern.
   Economic Harmonies (1964)

2 The state is the great fictitious entity by which everyone seeks to live at the expense of everyone else.
   in *Journal des débats* 25 September 1848

Lord Bauer 1915–2002
Hungarian-born British economist

3 Foreign aid is a system of taking money from poor people in rich countries and giving it to rich people in poor countries.
   attributed; not recollected by Lord Bauer but not repudiated by him.

4 *of foreign aid:*
   With every mouth God sends a pair of hands.
   saying taken from a Cambridge Economics Tripos examination question in the 1930s

Yehuda Bauer 1926–
Czech-born Israeli historian

5 I come from a people who gave the ten commandments to the world. Time has come to strengthen them by three additional ones, which we ought to adopt and commit ourselves to: thou shalt not be a perpetrator; thou shalt not be a victim; and thou shalt never, but never, be a bystander.
   speech to the German Bundestag, 1998, quoted in his own speech to the Stockholm International Forum on the Holocaust, 26 July 2000

Beverley Baxter 1891–1964
British journalist and Conservative politician

6 Beaverbrook is so pleased to be in the Government that he is like the town tart who has finally married the Mayor!
   Henry ('Chips') Channon diary, 12 June 1940

Charles Austin Beard 1874–1948 and Mary Ritter Beard 1876–1958

7 At no time, at no place, in solemn convention assembled, through no chosen agents, had the American people officially proclaimed the United States to be a democracy... When the Constitution was framed no respectable person called himself or herself a democrat.
   America in Midpassage (1939)

Lord Beaverbrook 1879–1964
Canadian-born British newspaper proprietor and Conservative politician. On Beaverbrook: see **Baxter 25:6, Lloyd George 189:15**; see also **Kipling 174:11**

8 Our cock won't fight.
   said to Winston **Churchill**, of Edward VIII, during the abdication crisis of 1936
   Frances Donaldson *Edward VIII* (1974)

9 Now who is responsible for this work of development on which so much depends? To whom must the praise be given? To the boys in the back rooms. They do not sit in the limelight. But they are the men who do the work.
   in *Listener* 27 March 1941

10 I ran the paper [the *Daily Express*] purely for propaganda and with no other purpose.
   evidence to the Royal Commission on the Press, 18 March 1948; A. J. P. Taylor *Beaverbrook* (1972)

11 [Lloyd George] did not seem to care which way he travelled providing he was in the driver's seat.
   The Decline and Fall of Lloyd George (1963)

12 Often undecided whether to desert a sinking ship for one that might not float, he would make up his mind to sit on the wharf for a day.
   *of Lord **Curzon***
   Men and Power (1956)

13 With the publication of his Private Papers in 1952, he [Earl Haig] committed suicide 25 years after his death.
   *of Earl **Haig***
   Men and Power (1956)

14 Churchill on top of the wave has in him the stuff of which tyrants are made.
   Politicians and the War (1932)

1 *of Bonar Law and Churchill:*
I have had two masters and one of them betrayed me.
A. J. P. Taylor letter, 16 December 1973

Kim Beazley Senior 1917–
Australian Labor politician, father of Kim **Beazley**

2 When I joined the Labor Party it was made up of the cream of the working-class. When I left it was made up of the dregs of the middle-class.
quoted in the Legislative Assembly of New South Wales, 29 April 1992

Kim Beazley 1948–
Australian Labor politician, Party Leader 1995–2001 and since 2005, son of Kim **Beazley** Senior

3 We have never pretended to be a small business party. The Labor Party has never pretended that.
radio interview, 7 July 2000

Henry Becque 1837–99
French dramatist and critic

4 What makes equality such a difficult business is that we only want it with our superiors.
Querelles littéraires (1890)

Brendan Behan 1923–64
Irish dramatist

5 PAT: He was an Anglo-Irishman.
MEG: In the blessed name of God what's that?
PAT: A Protestant with a horse.
The Hostage (1958)

6 When I came back to Dublin, I was courtmartialled in my absence and sentenced to death in my absence, so I said they could shoot me in my absence.
The Hostage (1958)

Lord Belhaven 1656–1708
Scottish politician

7 Good God! What, is this an entire surrender?
culmination of a speech opposing the Union with England
speech in the Scottish Parliament, 2 November 1706

George Bell 1883–1958
English clergyman, Bishop of Chichester

8 The policy is obliteration, openly acknowledged. This is not a justifiable act of war.
of the saturation bombing of Berlin
speech, House of Lords, 9 February 1944

Francis Bellamy 1856–1931
American clergyman and editor

9 I pledge allegiance to the flag of the United States of America and to the republic for which it stands, one nation under God, indivisible, with liberty and justice for all.
The Pledge of Allegiance to the Flag (1892)

Hilaire Belloc 1870–1953
British poet, essayist, historian, novelist, and Liberal politician

10 Sir! you have disappointed us!
We had intended you to be
The next Prime Minister but three:
The stocks were sold; the Press was squared;
The Middle Class was quite prepared.
But as it is!…My language fails!
Go out and govern New South Wales!
Cautionary Tales (1907) 'Lord Lundy'

11 Here richly, with ridiculous display,
The Politician's corpse was laid away.
While all of his acquaintance sneered and slanged
I wept: for I had longed to see him hanged.
'Epitaph on the Politician Himself' (1923)

12 Whatever happens we have got
The Maxim Gun, and they have not.
The Modern Traveller (1898)

13 The accursed power which stands on Privilege
(And goes with Women, and Champagne, and Bridge)
Broke—and Democracy resumed her reign:
(Which goes with Bridge, and Women and Champagne).
'On a Great Election' (1923)

14 Gentlemen, I am a Catholic…If you reject me on account of my religion, I shall thank God that He has

spared me the indignity of being your representative.
speech to voters of South Salford, 1906

Saul Bellow 1915–2005
American novelist

1 Sitting tight is power.
The Adventures of Augie March (1953)

Julien Benda 1867–1956
French philosopher and novelist

2 *La trahison des clercs.*
The treachery of the intellectuals.
title of book, 1927

Ruth Fulton Benedict 1887–1948
American anthropologist

3 The tough-minded...respect difference. Their goal is a world made safe for differences, where the United States may be American to the hilt without threatening the peace of the world, and France may be France, and Japan may be Japan on the same conditions.
The Chrysanthemum and the Sword (1946)

Peter Benenson 1921–2005
British founder of Amnesty International

4 Better to light a candle than curse the darkness.
at a Human Rights Day ceremony, 10 December 1961 (see also **Stevenson 301:9**)

David Ben-Gurion 1886–1973
Israeli statesman

5 In Israel, in order to be a realist, you must believe in miracles.
on CBS TV, 5 October 1956

Ernest Benn 1875–1954
English publisher and economist

6 Politics is the art of looking for trouble, finding it everywhere, diagnosing it wrongly and applying unsuitable remedies.
attributed, Powell Spring *What Is Truth* (1944); often later associated with the American film comedian Groucho Marx (1890–1977)

Tony Benn 1925–
British Labour politician

7 Not a reluctant peer but a persistent commoner.
at a Press Conference, 23 November 1960

8 Some of the jam we thought was for tomorrow, we've already eaten.
attributed, 1969; see **Carroll 57:15**

9 In developing our industrial strategy for the period ahead, we have the benefit of much experience. Almost everything has been tried at least once.
speech in House of Commons, 13 March 1974

10 *on seeing Harold* **Wilson**, *who had resigned as Prime Minister in March, looking 'absolutely shrunk':*
Office is something that builds up a man only if he is somebody in his own right.
diary, 12 April 1976

11 Marxism is now a world faith and must be allowed to enter into a continuous dialogue with other world faiths, including religious faiths.
Karl Marx lecture, 16 March 1982

12 *of the influence of Parliament:*
Through talk, we tamed kings, restrained tyrants, averted revolution.
Anthony Sampson *The Changing Anatomy of Britain* (1982)

13 I did not enter the Labour Party forty-seven years ago to have our manifesto written by Dr Mori, Dr Gallup and Mr Harris.
in *Guardian* 13 June 1988

14 A faith is something you die for; a doctrine is something you kill for: there is all the difference in the world.
in *Observer* 16 April 1989 'Sayings of the Week'

15 *questions habitually asked by Tony Benn on meeting somebody in power:*
What power have you got? Where did you get it from? In whose interests do you exercise it? To whom are you accountable? How

do we get rid of you?
'The Independent Mind', lecture at
Nottingham, 18 June 1993

1 I wouldn't like to go to a dentist
who, just before he drilled my teeth,
told me he was not a dentist himself
but that his father had been a very
good dentist.
on the hereditary House of Lords
in *Independent* 5 June 2006

Alan Bennett 1934–
English dramatist and actor

2 To be Prince of Wales is not a
position. It is a predicament.
The Madness of King George (1995 film); in the
1992 play *The Madness of George III* the line
was 'To be heir to the throne…'

Arnold Bennett 1867–1931
English novelist

3 Seventy minutes had passed
before Mr Lloyd George arrived at
his proper theme. He spoke for a
hundred and seventeen minutes, in
which period he was detected only
once in the use of an argument.
Things that have Interested Me (1921) 'After the
March Offensive'

4 Literature's always a good card to
play for Honours. It makes people
think that Cabinet ministers are
educated.
The Title (1918)

A. C. Benson 1862–1925
English writer

5 Land of Hope and Glory, Mother of
the Free,
How shall we extol thee who are born
of thee?
Wider still and wider shall thy
bounds be set;
God who made thee mighty, make
thee mightier yet.
'Land of Hope and Glory' written to be sung as
the Finale to Elgar's *Coronation Ode* (1902)

Jeremy Bentham 1748–1832
English philosopher

6 Right…is the child of law: from
real laws come real rights; but

from imaginary laws, from laws of
nature, fancied and invented by
poets, rhetoricians, and dealers
in moral and intellectual poisons,
come imaginary rights, a bastard
brood of monsters.
Anarchical Fallacies (1843)

7 Natural rights is simple nonsense:
natural and imprescriptible rights,
rhetorical nonsense—nonsense
upon stilts.
Anarchical Fallacies (1843)

8 It is the greatest happiness of
the greatest number that is the
measure of right and wrong.
*Bentham claims to have acquired the 'sacred
truth' either from Joseph Priestley (1733–1804) or
Cesare Beccaria (1738–94)*
A Fragment on Government (1776)

9 Every law is contrary to liberty.
Principles of the Civil Code (1843)

10 Publicity is the very soul of justice.
It is the keenest spur to exertion,
and the surest of all guards against
improbity.
Publicity in the Courts of Justice (1843)

11 As to the evil which results from
a censorship, it is impossible to
measure it, because it is impossible
to tell where it ends.
Theory of Legislation (1864) 'Principles of the
Penal Code' pt. 4, ch. 2

12 He rather hated the ruling few than
loved the suffering many.
of James Mill
H. N. Pym (ed.) *Memories of Old Friends,
being Extracts from the Journals and Letters of
Caroline Fox* (1882)

Edmund Clerihew Bentley
1875–1956
English writer

13 When their lordships asked Bacon
How many bribes he had taken
He had at least the grace
To get very red in the face.
Baseless Biography (1939) 'Bacon'

14 George the Third
Ought never to have occurred.
One can only wonder
At so grotesque a blunder.
More Biography (1929) 'George the Third'

Lloyd Bentsen 1921–2006
American Democratic politician

1 *responding to Dan Quayle's claim to have 'as much experience in the Congress as Jack **Kennedy** had when he sought the presidency':*
Senator, I served with Jack Kennedy. I knew Jack Kennedy. Jack Kennedy was a friend of mine. Senator, you're no Jack Kennedy.
in the vice-presidential debate, 5 October 1988

George Berkeley 1685–1753
Irish philosopher and Anglican bishop

2 Westward the course of empire takes its way;
The first four acts already past,
A fifth shall close the drama with the day:
Time's noblest offspring is the last.
'On the Prospect of Planting Arts and Learning in America' (1752); see John Quincy Adams *Oration at Plymouth* (1802): 'Westward the star of empire takes its way'

Irving Berlin 1888–1989
American songwriter

3 God bless America,
Land that I love,
Stand beside her and guide her
Thru the night with a light from above.
From the mountains to the prairies,
To the oceans white with foam,
God bless America,
My home sweet home.
'God Bless America' (1939)

Isaiah Berlin 1909–97
British philosopher

4 The fundamental sense of freedom is freedom from chains, from imprisonment, from enslavement by others. The rest is extension of this sense, or else metaphor.
Four Essays on Liberty (1969); introduction

5 Injustice, poverty, slavery, ignorance—these may be cured by reform or revolution. But men do not live only by fighting evils. They live by positive goals, individual and collective, a vast variety of them, seldom predictable, at times incompatible.
Four Essays on Liberty (1969)

6 Liberty is liberty, not equality or fairness or justice or human happiness or a quiet conscience.
Two Concepts of Liberty (1958)

7 It is this—the 'positive' conception of liberty: not freedom from, but freedom to—which the adherents of the 'negative' notion represent as being, at times, no better than a specious disguise for brutal tyranny.
Two Concepts of Liberty (1958)

8 Few new truths have ever won their way against the resistance of established ideas save by being overstated.
Vico and Herder (1976)

Silvio Berlusconi 1936–
Italian media entrepreneur and statesman

9 They have everything they need, they have medical care, hot food… Of course, their current lodgings are a bit temporary. But they should see it like a weekend of camping.
on the thousands of people left homeless by the L'Aquila earthquake
in *Telegraph* 8 April 2009 (online ed.)

J. D. Bernal 1901–71
Irish-born physicist

10 Men will not be content to manufacture life: they will want to improve on it.
The World, the Flesh and the Devil (1929)

Carl Bernstein 1944– and Bob Woodward 1943–

11 All the President's men.
title of book (1974) on the Watergate scandal

Pierre Berton 1920–2004
Canadian writer

12 The march of social progress is like a long and straggling parade, with the seers and prophets at its head and a smug minority bringing up the rear.
The Smug Minority (1968)

Theobald von Bethmann Hollweg 1856–1921
German statesman, Chancellor 1909–17

1 Just for a word 'neutrality'—a word which in wartime has so often been disregarded—just for a scrap of paper, Great Britain is going to make war on a kindred nation who desires nothing better than to be friends with her.
   summary of a report by E. Goschen to Edward Grey in *British Documents on Origins of the War 1898–1914* (1926) vol. 11

Mary McLeod Bethune 1875–1955
American educator

2 If we accept and acquiesce in the face of discrimination, we accept the responsibility ourselves and allow those responsible to salve their conscience by believing that they have our acceptance and concurrence.
   Rayford W. Logan (ed.) *What the Negro Wants* (1944) 'Certain Inalienable Rights'

John Betjeman 1906–84
English poet

3 Think of what our Nation stands for,
   Books from Boots' and country lanes,
   Free speech, free passes, class distinction,
   Democracy and proper drains.
   Lord, put beneath Thy special care
   One-eighty-nine Cadogan Square.
   'In Westminster Abbey' (1940)

Aneurin Bevan 1897–1960
British Labour politician

4 This island is made mainly of coal and surrounded by fish. Only an organizing genius could produce a shortage of coal and fish at the same time.
   speech at Blackpool, 24 May 1945

5 No amount of cajolery, and no attempts at ethical or social seduction, can eradicate from my heart a deep burning hatred for the Tory Party…So far as I am concerned they are lower than vermin.
   speech at Manchester, 4 July 1948

6 The language of priorities is the religion of Socialism.
   speech at Labour Party Conference in Blackpool, 8 June 1949

7 Why read the crystal when he can read the book?
   *referring to Robert **Boothby***
   debate on the Sterling Exchange Rate, House of Commons, 29 September 1949

8 [Winston Churchill] does not talk the language of the 20th century but that of the 18th. He is still fighting Blenheim all over again. His only answer to a difficult situation is send a gun-boat.
   speech at Labour Party Conference, Scarborough, 2 October 1951

9 The Tories, every election, must have a bogy man. If you haven't got a programme, a bogy man will do. In 1945 it was Harold Laski, in 1951 it is me.
   speech in the general election campaign at Stonehouse, Gloucester, 13 October 1951

10 We know what happens to people who stay in the middle of the road. They get run down.
   in *Observer* 6 December 1953

11 Damn it all, you can't have the crown of thorns *and* the thirty pieces of silver.
   on his position in the Labour Party, 1956
   Michael Foot *Aneurin Bevan* vol. 2 (1973)

12 I am not going to spend any time whatsoever in attacking the Foreign Secretary…If we complain about the tune, there is no reason to attack the monkey when the organ grinder is present.
   during a debate on the Suez crisis
   in the House of Commons, 16 May 1957

13 If you carry this resolution you will send Britain's Foreign Secretary naked into the conference chamber.
   speaking against a motion proposing unilateral nuclear disarmament by the United Kingdom
   speech at Labour Party Conference in Brighton, 3 October 1957

14 You call that statesmanship? I call it

an emotional spasm.
speaking against a motion proposing unilateral nuclear disarmament by the United Kingdom
speech at Labour Party Conference in Brighton, 3 October 1957

1 I know that the right kind of leader for the Labour Party is a desiccated calculating machine who must not in any way permit himself to be swayed by indignation. If he sees suffering, privation or injustice he must not allow it to move him, for that would be evidence of the lack of proper education or of absence of self-control. He must speak in calm and objective accents and talk about a dying child in the same way as he would about the pieces inside an internal combustion engine.
*frequently taken as referring to Hugh **Gaitskell**, although Bevan specifically denied it in an interview with Robin Day on 28 April 1959*
Michael Foot *Aneurin Bevan* vol. 2 (1973)

2 The conquest of the commanding heights of the economy.
recalling his own earlier use of the phrase (possibly originated by Lenin) at the Labour Party Conference, November 1959

3 The Prime Minister has an absolute genius for putting flamboyant labels on empty luggage.
*of Harold **Macmillan***
in the House of Commons, 3 November 1959

4 I read the newspapers avidly. It is my one form of continuous fiction.
in *Times* 29 March 1960

5 *of his handling of the consultants during the establishment of the National Health Service:*
I stuffed their mouths with gold.
Brian Abel-Smith *The Hospitals 1800–1948* (1964)

6 Listening to a speech by Chamberlain is like paying a visit to Woolworth's: everything in its place and nothing above sixpence.
Michael Foot *Aneurin Bevan* vol. 1 (1962)

Albert Jeremiah Beveridge

1862–1927
American Republican politician and member of the Senate, who in 1912 chaired the convention that organized the Progressive party and nominated Theodore **Roosevelt** for President

7 This party comes from the grass

roots. It has grown from the soil of the people's hard necessities.
address at the Bull Moose Convention in Chicago, 5 August 1912

William Henry Beveridge

1879–1963
British economist

8 Ignorance is an evil weed, which dictators may cultivate among their dupes, but which no democracy can afford among its citizens.
Full Employment in a Free Society (1944)

9 The object of government in peace and in war is not the glory of rulers or of races, but the happiness of the common man.
Social Insurance and Allied Services (1942)

10 Want is one only of five giants on the road of reconstruction...the others are Disease, Ignorance, Squalor and Idleness.
Social Insurance and Allied Services (1942)

11 The state is or can be master of money, but in a free society it is master of very little else.
Voluntary Action (1948)

Ernest Bevin 1881–1951
British Labour politician and trade unionist

12 The most conservative man in this world is the British Trade Unionist when you want to change him.
speech, 8 September 1927

13 I hope you will carry no resolution of an emergency character telling a man with a conscience like Lansbury what he ought to do... It is placing the Executive in an absolutely wrong position to be taking your conscience round from body to body to be told what you ought to do with it.
in *Labour Party Conference Report* (1935); see **Misquotations 215:11**

14 I am not one of those who decry Eton and Harrow. I was very glad of them in the Battle of Britain.
speech at Blackpool, 1945

15 There never has been a war yet which, if the facts had been put calmly before the ordinary folk,

could not have been prevented...
The common man, I think, is the
great protection against war.
in the House of Commons, 23 November 1945

1 *as Minister of Labour to his Civil Servants:*
You've just given me twenty reasons
why I can't do this; I'm sure that
clever chaps like you can go away
and produce twenty good reasons
why I can.
oral tradition; Peter Hennessy *Whitehall* (1990)

2 My [foreign] policy is to be able to
take a ticket at Victoria Station and
go anywhere I damn well please.
in *Spectator* 20 April 1951

3 I didn't ought never to have done
it. It was you, Willie, what put me
up to it.
*to Lord Strang, after officially recognizing
Communist China*
C. Parrott *Serpent and Nightingale* (1977)

4 If you open that Pandora's Box, you
never know what Trojan 'orses will
jump out.
on the Council of Europe
Roderick Barclay *Ernest Bevin and the Foreign
Office* (1975)

5 *someone had remarked that Aneurin **Bevan**
was his own worst enemy:*
Not while I'm alive 'e ain't.
*also attributed to Bevin of Herbert **Morrison***
Roderick Barclay *Ernest Bevin and the Foreign
Office* (1975)

Benazir Bhutto 1953–2007
Pakistani stateswoman; Prime Minister 1988–90 and
1993–96

6 Every dictator uses religion as a
prop to keep himself in power.
interview on *60 Minutes*, CBS-TV, 8 August 1986

7 You can't be fuelled by bitterness. It
can eat you up, but it cannot drive
you.
Daughter of Destiny (1989)

The Bible (Authorized Version)

8 Let my people go.
Exodus

9 Let them live; but let them be
hewers of wood and drawers of
water unto all the congregation.
Joshua

10 He smote them hip and thigh.
Judges

11 And she named the child I-chabod,
saying, The glory is departed from
Israel.
I Samuel

12 David therefore departed thence,
and escaped to the cave Adullam...
And every one that was in distress,
and every one that was in debt, and
every one that was discontented,
gathered themselves unto him.
I Samuel; see **Bright 42:5**

13 And Saul said, God hath delivered
him into mine hand.
I Samuel

14 He shall know that there is a
prophet in Israel.
II Kings

15 Had Zimri peace, who slew his
master?
II Kings

16 Thus shall it be done to the man
whom the king delighteth to
honour.
Esther

17 Great men are not always wise.
Job

18 Where there is no vision, the people
perish.
Proverbs

19 The race is not to the swift, nor the
battle to the strong.
Ecclesiastes

20 Woe to thee, O land, when thy king
is a child.
Ecclesiastes

21 They shall beat their swords into
plowshares, and their spears into
pruninghooks: nation shall not lift
up sword against nation, neither
shall they learn war any more.
Isaiah; see **Rendall 257:8**

22 Of the increase of his government
and peace there shall be no end.
Isaiah

23 Now, O king, establish the decree,
and sign the writing, that it be not
changed, according to the law of
the Medes and Persians, which
altereth not.
Daniel

1 They have sown the wind, and they shall reap the whirlwind.
Hosea

2 Let us now praise famous men, and our fathers that begat us.
Ecclesiasticus

3 Judge not, that ye be not judged.
St Matthew

4 I came not to send peace, but a sword.
St Matthew

5 He that is not with me is against me.
St Matthew; St Luke

6 Render therefore unto Caesar the things which are Caesar's; and unto God the things that are God's.
St Matthew

7 Ye shall hear of wars and rumours of wars: see that ye be not troubled: for all these things must come to pass but the end is not yet.
St Matthew

8 For nation shall rise against nation, and kingdom against kingdom.
St Matthew; St John

9 And ye shall know the truth, and the truth shall make you free.
St John; see **Agar 5:2**

10 Those that have turned the world upside down are come hither also.
Acts of the Apostles

11 But Paul said, I am a man which am a Jew of Tarsus, a city in Cilicia, a citizen of no mean city.
Acts of the Apostles

12 Hast thou appealed unto Caesar? unto Caesar shalt thou go.
Acts of the Apostles

13 For where no law is, there is no transgression.
Romans

Georges Bidault 1899–1983
French statesman; Prime Minister, 1946, 1949–50

14 The weak have one weapon: the errors of those who think they are strong.
in *Observer* 15 July 1962 'Sayings of the Week'

Francis Biddle 1886–1968
American lawyer and judge, Attorney-General 1941–7, senior American judge at the Nuremberg Trials

15 The Constitution has never greatly bothered any wartime President.
In Brief Authority (1962)

Ambrose Bierce 1842–c. 1914
American writer. See also **Proverbs 252:8**

16 BATTLE, *n.* A method of untying with the teeth a political knot that would not yield to the tongue.
The Cynic's Word Book (1906)

17 CONSERVATIVE, *n.* A statesman who is enamoured of existing evils, as distinguished from the Liberal, who wishes to replace them with others.
The Cynic's Word Book (1906)

18 PEACE, *n.* In international affairs, a period of cheating between two periods of fighting.
The Devil's Dictionary (1911)

John Biffen 1930–
British Conservative politician

19 *of Margaret **Thatcher** as Prime Minister:* She was a tigress surrounded by hamsters.
in *Observer* 9 December 1990

Steve Biko 1946–77
South African anti-apartheid campaigner

20 The most potent weapon in the hands of the oppressor is the mind of the oppressed.
statement as witness, 3 May 1976

Josh Billings 1818–85
American humorist

21 It is better to know nothing than to know what ain't so.
Proverb (1874)

Laurence Binyon 1869–1943
English poet

22 They shall grow not old, as we that are left grow old.
Age shall not weary them, nor the years condemn.

At the going down of the sun and in
the morning
We will remember them.
*regularly recited as part of the ritual for
Remembrance Day parades*
'For the Fallen' (1914)

Nigel Birch 1906–81
British Conservative politician. See also
Browning 44:5

1 *on hearing of the resignation of Hugh
Dalton, Chancellor of the Exchequer in the
Labour Government, 13 November 1947:*
My God! They've shot our fox!
Harold Macmillan *Tides of Fortune* (1969)

Stanley F. Birch Jr. 1945–
American judge, member of the 11th US Circuit Court
of Appeals

2 Despite sincere and altruistic
motivation, the legislative
and executive branches of our
government have acted in a manner
demonstrably at odds with our
Founding Fathers' blueprint for the
governance of a free people—our
Constitution.
opinion denying the appeal that the Federal
Court reverse the ruling in the Schiavo case,
30 March 2005 (compare **DeLay**)

Lord Birkenhead see F. E. Smith

Otto von Bismarck 1815–98
German statesman. On Bismarck: see **Taylor 306:14,
Tenniel 308:5**; see also **Misquotations 215:17**

3 The secret of politics? Make a good
treaty with Russia.
in 1863, when first in power
A. J. P. Taylor *Bismarck* (1955)

4 Politics is not an exact science.
speech to the Prussian legislature,
18 December 1863

5 Politics is the art of the possible.
*in conversation with Meyer von Waldeck,
11 August 1867; see **Galbraith 118:10***

6 Let us...put Germany in the saddle!
She will know well enough how to
ride!
*in 1867; Alan Palmer *Bismarck* (1976)*

7 We will not go to Canossa.
*during his quarrel with Pope Pius IX regarding
papal authority over German subjects, in allusion*

*to the Emperor Henry IV's submission to Pope
Gregory VII at Canossa in Modena in 1077*
speech to the Reichstag, 14 May 1872

8 Whoever speaks of Europe is
wrong, [it is] a geographical
concept.
marginal note on a letter from the Russian
Chancellor Gorchakov, November 1876; see
Metternich 211:6

9 I have always found the word
Europe on the lips of those
politicians who wanted something
from other Powers which they dared
not demand in their own names.
*to the Russian Chancellor Gorchakov, who had
urged that a rising in Bosnia in 1878 was a
European, rather than a German or Russian,
question*
A. J. P. Taylor *Bismarck* (1955)

10 I do not regard the procuring of
peace as a matter in which we
should play the role of arbiter
between different opinions...
more that of an honest broker who
really wants to press the business
forward.
before the Congress of Berlin
speech to the Reichstag, 19 February 1878

11 A lath of wood painted to look like
iron.
*of Lord **Salisbury** at the Congress of Berlin in
1878*
attributed, but vigorously denied by Sidney
Whitman in *Personal Reminiscences of Prince
Bismarck* (1902)

12 The old Jew! That is the man.
*of **Disraeli** at the Congress of Berlin*
attributed

13 Place in the hands of the King of
Prussia the strongest possible
military power, then he will be able
to carry out the policy you wish;
this policy cannot succeed through
speeches, and shooting-matches,
and songs; it can only be carried
out through blood and iron.
in the Prussian House of Deputies, 28 January
1886; in a speech on 30 September 1862,
Bismarck had used the form 'iron and blood'

14 I am bored; the great things are
done. The German *Reich* is made.
A. J. P. Taylor *Bismarck* (1955)

15 Jena came twenty years after the
death of Frederick the Great; the

crash will come twenty years after my departure if things go on like this.
*to Kaiser **Wilhelm II** at their last meeting in 1895*
A. J. P. Taylor *Bismarck* (1955)

1 If there is ever another war in Europe, it will come out of some damned silly thing in the Balkans.
reported by the shipping magnate Herr Ballen as being said by Bismarck in his later years; quoted in the House of Commons, 16 August 1945

2 Man cannot create the current of events. He can only float with it and steer.
A. J. P. Taylor *Bismarck* (1955)

3 *of possible German involvement in the Balkans:*
Not worth the healthy bones of a single Pomeranian grenadier.
George O. Kent *Bismarck and his Times* (1978); see **Harris 136:9**

4 A statesman…must wait until he hears the steps of God sounding through events; then leap up and grasp the hem of his garment.
A. J. P. Taylor *Bismarck* (1955)

5 *when asked what was the greatest political fact of modern times:*
The inherited and permanent fact that North America speaks English.
attributed; George Beer *The English-Speaking Peoples* (1917)

6 There is a providence that protects idiots, drunkards, children, and the United States of America.
attributed, perhaps apocryphal

7 When a man says he approves of something in principle, it means he hasn't the slightest intention of putting it into practice.
attributed

Johannes ('Joh') Bjelke-Petersen 1911–2005
New Zealand-born Australian National Party politician, Premier of Queensland, 1968–87

8 Don't you worry about that.
habitual response to questions
in *Times* 25 April 2005 (obituary)

9 Feeding the chooks.
term for a press conference
in *Times* 25 April 2005 (obituary)

Hugo La Fayette Black 1886–1971
American judge

10 The First Amendment has erected a wall between church and state. That wall must be kept high and impregnable. We could not approve the slightest breach.
in *Emerson v. Board of Education* 1947

11 In revealing the workings of government that led to the Vietnam War, the newspapers nobly did precisely that which the Founders hoped and trusted they would do.
concurring opinion on the publication of the Pentagon Papers, 1971

William Blackstone 1723–80
English jurist

12 The king never dies.
Commentaries on the Laws of England (1765)

13 The royal navy of England hath ever been its greatest defence and ornament; it is its ancient and natural strength; the floating bulwark of the island.
Commentaries on the Laws of England (1765)

14 That the king can do no wrong, is a necessary and fundamental principle of the English constitution.
Commentaries on the Laws of England (1765)

15 In all tyrannical governments the supreme magistracy, or the right both of making and of enforcing the laws, is vested in one and the same man, or one and the same body of men; and wherever these two powers are united together, there can be no public liberty.
Commentaries on the Laws of England (1765)

16 Herein indeed consists the excellence of the English government, that all parts of it form a mutual check upon each other.
Commentaries on the Laws of England (1765)

Tony Blair 1953–
British Labour statesman; Prime Minister 1997–2007. On Blair: see **Cameron 54:9, Newspaper headlines 225:11**

17 Labour is the party of law and order

in Britain today. Tough on crime
and tough on the causes of crime.
speech at the Labour Party Conference as
Shadow Home Secretary, 30 September 1993

1 Those who seriously believe we
cannot improve on words written
for the world of 1918 when we are
now in 1995 are not learning from
our history but living it.
on the proposed revision of Clause IV; see
Anonymous
in *Independent* 11 January 1995

2 My project will be complete when
the Labour party learns to love
Peter Mandelson.
in *Guardian* 11 February 1995

3 Ask me my three main priorities
for Government, and I tell
you: education, education and
education.
speech at the Labour Party Conference,
1 October 1996; see **Michelet 212:1**

4 We are not the masters. The people
are the masters. We are the servants
of the people...What the electorate
gives, the electorate can take away.
*addressing Labour MPs on the first day of the new
Parliament, 7 May 1997*
in *Guardian* 8 May 1997; see **Burke 49:9**

5 She was the People's Princess, and
that is how she will stay...in our
hearts and in our memories forever.
*on hearing of the death of **Diana**, Princess of
Wales, 31 August 1997*
in *Times* 1 September 1997

6 I am a pretty straight sort of guy.
*interviewed on the government's exemption of
Formula One racing from the tobacco advertising
ban*
interviewed on *On the Record* (BBC TV),
17 November 1997

7 This is not a time for soundbites.
We've left them at home. I feel
the hand of history upon our
shoulders...I'm here to try.
*arriving in Belfast for the final stage of the
Northern Irish negotiations, 8 April 1998*
in *Irish Times* 11 April 1998 'This Week They
Said'

8 In future, welfare will be a hand-up
not a hand-out.
lecture, London, 18 March 1999

9 Arrayed against us: the forces of
conservatism, the cynics, the elites,
the establishment. On our side, the
forces of modernity and justice.
speech to Labour Party Conference,
28 September 1999

10 We need two or three eye-catching
initiatives...I should be personally
associated with as much of this as
possible.
leaked memorandum, 29 April 2000; in *Times*
18 July 2000

11 This is not a battle betweeen the
United States and terrorism, but
between the free and democratic
world and terrorism. We therefore
here in Britain stand shoulder to
shoulder with our American friends
in this hour of tragedy and we, like
them, will not rest until this evil is
driven from our world.
in Downing Street, London, 11 September 2001

12 Go round smiling at everyone, and
get other people to shoot them.
on constituency party enemies
advice to David Miliband; Chris Mullin *A View
from the Foothills* (2009) 13 September 2001

13 The state of Africa is a scar on the
conscience of the world.
speech to Labour Party Conference, 2 October
2001

14 I believe we're at our best when we
are boldest.
speech to the Labour Party Conference,
30 September 2002; see **Brown 43:5**

15 This is not the time to falter.
speech in the House of Commons, 18 March
2003

16 I can only go one way. I've not got a
reverse gear.
speech, Labour Party Conference,
Bournemouth, 30 September 2003

17 I've listened, and I've learned...I,
we, the Government are going
to focus now relentlessly on the
priorities the people have set for us.
speech outside Downing Street, 6 May 2005

18 However much the right hon.
gentleman may dance around the
ring beforehand, at some point, he
will come within the reach of a big
clunking fist.
*usually taken as referring to Gordon **Brown***
to David Cameron, the House of Commons,
15 November 2006

1 BRITTON: If you had known then
that there were no WMDs, would
you still have gone on?
BLAIR: I would still have thought
it right to remove him. I mean
obviously you would have had to use
and deploy different arguments,
about the nature of the threat.
*on Saddam **Hussein***
Fern Britton Meets BBC1 TV 13 December 2009

William Blake 1757–1827
English poet

2 The strongest poison ever known
Came from Caesar's laurel crown.
'Auguries of Innocence' (1803)

3 The whore and gambler by the State
Licensed build that nation's fate
The harlot's cry from street to street
Shall weave old England's winding
sheet.
'Auguries of Innocence' (1803)

4 He who would do good to another,
must do it in minute particulars
General good is the plea of the
scoundrel, hypocrite and flatterer.
Jerusalem (1815) 'Chapter 3' (plate 55, l. 60)

5 And was Jerusalem builded here
Among these dark Satanic mills?
Milton (1804–10) preface 'And did those feet
in ancient time'

6 I will not cease from mental fight,
Nor shall my sword sleep in my hand,
Till we have built Jerusalem,
In England's green and pleasant
land.
Milton (1804–10) preface 'And did those feet
in ancient time'

Hazel Blears 1956–
British Labour politician

7 YouTube if you want to.
*of Gordon **Brown**'s YouTube videos*
in *Observer* 3 May 2009

8 Rocking the boat.
slogan on a brooch worn at her resignation
from the cabinet, 3 June 2009; in *Times* 4 June
2009

Hans Blix 1928–
Swedish diplomat

9 We have not found any

smoking guns.
of weapons inspections in Iraq
in *Newsweek* 20 January 2003

David Blunkett 1947–
British Labour politician

10 Let me say this very slowly indeed.
Watch my lips: no selection by
examination or interview under a
Labour government.
in *Daily Telegraph* (electronic edition)
5 October 1995; see **Bush 50:14**

11 We could live in a world which
is airy-fairy, libertarian, where
everybody does precisely what
they like and we believe the best of
everybody and then they destroy
us.
interview on London Weekend Television,
11 November 2001

Alfred Blunt, Bishop of Bradford 1879–1957
English clergyman

12 The benefit of the King's
Coronation depends, under God,
upon two elements: First on the
faith, prayer, and self-dedication
of the King himself, and on that it
would be improper for me to say
anything except to commend him,
and ask you to commend him,
to God's grace, which he will so
abundantly need...if he is to do his
duty faithfully. We hope that he is
aware of his need. Some of us wish
that he gave more positive signs of
his awareness.
it was this speech that broke the story of
***Edward VIII** and Mrs Simpson which the media*
had been voluntarily suppressing until then
speech to Bradford Diocesan Conference,
1 December 1936

David Boaz 1953–
American foundation executive

13 Alcohol didn't cause the high
crime rates of the '20s and '30s,
Prohibition did. Drugs don't cause
today's alarming crime rates, but
drug prohibition does.
'The Legalization of Drugs' 27 April 1988

Ivan Boesky 1937–
American financier, imprisoned in 1987 for insider dealing

1 Greed is all right...Greed is healthy. You can be greedy and still feel good about yourself.
commencement address at the University of California, Berkeley, 18 May 1986; see **Weiser and Stone 328:13**

Alan Bold 1943–
Scottish poet

2 Scotland, land of the omnipotent No.
'A Memory of Death' (1969)

Henry St John, Lord Bolingbroke 1678–1751
English politician

3 The great mistake is that of looking upon men as virtuous, or thinking that they can be made so by laws.
comment (1728) in Joseph Spence *Observations, Anecdotes, and Characters* (1820)

4 The greatest art of a politician is to render vice serviceable to the cause of virtue.
comment (1728) in Joseph Spence *Observations, Anecdotes, and Characters* (1820)

5 Nations, like men, have their infancy.
On the Study of History letter 5, in *Works* (1809) vol. 3

Simón Bolívar 1783–1830
Venezuelan patriot and statesman

6 Those who have served the cause of the revolution have ploughed the sea.
attributed

Robert Bolt 1924–95
English dramatist

7 THOMAS MORE: This country's planted thick with laws from coast to coast—Man's laws, not God's—and if you cut them down—and you're just the man to do it—d'you really think you could stand upright in the winds that would blow then?
A Man for All Seasons (1960)

Laetitia Bonaparte 1750–1836
French mother of **Napoleon I**

8 *Pourvu que ça dure!*
Let's hope it lasts!
on her son **Napoleon I** *becoming Emperor, 1804*
attributed, possibly apocryphal

Andrew Bonar Law 1858–1923
Canadian-born British Conservative statesman, Prime Minister 1922–3. On Bonar Law: see **Asquith 13:9, Beaverbrook 26:1**

9 There are things stronger than parliamentary majorities. I can imagine no length of resistance to which Ulster will not go, in which I shall not be ready to support them.
at a Unionist meeting at Blenheim in 1912
Robert Blake *The Unknown Prime Minister* (1955)

10 We cannot alone act as the policemen of the world.
letter to *Times*, 7 October 1922

11 If I am a great man, then all great men are frauds.
Lord Beaverbrook *Politicians and the War* (1932)

Dietrich Bonhoeffer 1906–45
German Lutheran theologian and martyr

12 I have come to the conclusion that I have made a mistake in coming to America. I must live through this difficult period of our national history with the Christian people of Germany. I shall have no right to participate in the reconstruction of Christian life in Germany after the war if I do not share the trials of this time with my people.
letter to Reinhold Niebuhr, July 1939

13 It is the nature, and the advantage, of strong people that they can bring out the crucial questions and form a clear opinion about them. The weak always have to decide between alternatives that are not their own.
Widerstand und Ergebung (1951)

The Book of Common Prayer
1662

1 Give peace in our time, O Lord.
Morning Prayer Versicle; see
Chamberlain 60:12

2 The Bishop of Rome hath no
jurisdiction in this Realm of
England.
Articles of Religion (1562) no. 37

Daniel J. Boorstin 1914–
American writer

3 A pseudo event…comes about
because someone has planned,
planted, or incited it. Typically, it is
not a train wreck or an earthquake,
but an interview.
The Image (1962)

John Wilkes Booth 1838–65
American actor and assassin. See also **Last
words 179:16**

4 *Sic semper tyrannis!* The South is
avenged.
*having shot President **Lincoln**, 14 April 1865
in New York Times* 15 April 1865; the second
part of the statement does not appear in
any contemporary source, and is possibly
apocryphal; see **Mottoes 221:8**

Robert Boothby 1900–86
British Conservative politician

5 *You* speak for Britain!
*to Arthur Greenwood, acting Leader of the Labour
Party, after Neville **Chamberlain** had failed to
announce an ultimatum to Germany; perhaps
taking up an appeal already voiced by Leo **Amery***
Harold Nicolson diary, 2 September 1939; see
Amery 6:7

James H. Boren 1925–
American bureaucrat

6 Guidelines for bureaucrats: (1)
When in charge, ponder. (2) When
in trouble, delegate. (3) When in
doubt, mumble.
in New York Times 8 November 1970

Jorge Luis Borges 1899–1986
Argentinian writer

7 The Falklands thing was a fight

between two bald men over a comb.
application of a proverbial phrase; in Time
14 February 1983

Cesare Borgia see Mottoes 221:1

Robert H. Bork 1927–
American judge and educationalist

8 One of the uses of history is to
free us of a falsely imagined past.
The less we know of how ideas
actually took root and grew, the
more apt we are to accept them
unquestioningly, as inevitable
features of the world in which we
move.
The Antitrust Paradox (1978)

George Borrow 1803–81
English writer

9 I am invariably of the politics of
the people at whose table I sit, or
beneath whose roof I sleep.
The Bible in Spain (1843)

10 The English have forgot that they
ever conquered the Welsh, but
some ages will elapse before the
Welsh forget that the English have
conquered them.
Wild Wales (1854)

James Boswell 1740–95
Scottish lawyer; biographer of Samuel **Johnson**

11 We [Boswell and Johnson] are
both *Tories*; both convinced of the
utility of monarchical power, and
both lovers of that reverence and
affection for a sovereign which
constitute loyalty, a principle which
I take to be absolutely extinguished
in Britain.
Journal of a Tour to the Hebrides 13 September
1773

Antoine Boulay de la Meurthe
1761–1840
French statesman

12 *on hearing of the execution of the Duc
d'Enghien, 1804:*
It is worse than a crime, it is a
blunder.
C.-A. Sainte-Beuve *Nouveaux Lundis* (1870)
vol. 12

Pierre Boulez 1925–
French conductor and composer

1 Revolutions are celebrated when
they are no longer dangerous.
in Guardian 13 January 1989

Lord Bowen 1835–94
English judge

2 The man on the Clapham omnibus.
the average man
in Law Reports (1903); attributed

Omar Bradley 1893–1981
American general

3 The way to win an atomic war is to
make certain it never starts.
speech to Boston Chamber of Commerce,
10 November 1948

4 We have grasped the mystery of the
atom and rejected the Sermon on
the Mount.
speech on Armistice Day, 1948

5 The world has achieved brilliance
without wisdom, power without
conscience. Ours is a world of
nuclear giants and ethical infants.
speech on Armistice Day, 1948

6 In war there is no second prize for
the runner-up.
in Military Review February 1950

7 This strategy would involve us in
the wrong war, at the wrong place,
at the wrong time, and with the
wrong enemy.
*on General Macarthur's wish to extend the Korean
War into China*
*in US Congressional Senate Committee on
Armed Service* (1951) vol. 2

John Bradshaw 1602–59
English judge at the trial of **Charles I**

8 Rebellion to tyrants is obedience
to God.
suppositious epitaph; Henry S. Randall
Life of Thomas Jefferson (1865) vol. 3; see
Mottoes 221:6

Edward Stuyvesant Bragg
1827–1912
American politician

9 They love him most for the enemies

he has made.
seconding the presidential nomination of Grover
Cleveland
speech, 9 July 1884

Louis D. Brandeis 1856–1941
American jurist

10 Publicity is justly commended as
a remedy for social and industrial
diseases. Sunlight is said to be the
best of disinfectants; electric light
the most efficient policeman.
Other People's Money (1914)

11 Fear of serious injury cannot alone
justify suppression of free speech
and assembly. Men feared witches
and burned women. It is the
function of speech to free men from
the bondage of irrational fears.
in Whitney v. California (1927)

12 They [the makers of the
Constitution] conferred, as against
the Government, the right to be let
alone—the most comprehensive of
rights and the right most valued by
civilized men.
in Olmstead v. United States (1928)

13 The greatest dangers to liberty lurk
in insidious encroachment by men
of zeal, well-meaning but without
understanding.
dissenting opinion *in Olmstead v. United States*
(1928)

14 Our government is the potent, the
omnipresent teacher. For good or
ill, it teaches the whole people by its
example.
*quoted by the Oklahoma bomber, Timothy
McVeigh, just prior to being sentenced to death,
14 August 1997*
dissenting opinion *in Olmstead v. United States*
(1928)

Willy Brandt 1913–92
German statesman, Chancellor of West Germany
1969–74

15 We want to risk more democracy.
speech to parliament after his election as
Chancellor, 28 October 1969

16 Where mass hunger reigns, we
cannot speak of peace.
World Armament and World Hunger (1986)

1 If I'm selling to you, I speak your language. If I'm buying *dann mussen Sie Deutsch sprechen* [then you must speak German].
   attributed by Trade Minister Richard Needham, National Languages for Exports Awards, London, 5 April 1995

William Cowper Brann 1855–98

2 No man can be a patriot on an empty stomach.
   The Iconoclast, Old Glory 4 July 1893

Joseph Brant (Thayendanegea)
1742–1807
American-born Canadian Mohawk leader

3 I bow to no man for I am considered a prince among my own people. But I will gladly shake your hand.
   on being presented to **George III**
   attributed

Bertolt Brecht 1898–1956
German dramatist

4 ANDREA: Unhappy the land that has no heroes!...
   GALILEO: No. Unhappy the land that needs heroes.
   Life of Galileo (1939)

5 One observes, they have gone too long without a war here. Where is morality to come from in such a case, I ask? Peace is nothing but slovenliness, only war creates order.
   Mother Courage (1939)

6 The finest plans are always ruined by the littleness of those who ought to carry them out, for the Emperors can actually do nothing.
   Mother Courage (1939)

7 War always finds a way.
   Mother Courage (1939)

8 Don't tell me peace has broken out, when I've just bought some new supplies.
   Mother Courage (1939)

9 Would it not be easier
   In that case for the government
   To dissolve the people
   And elect another?
   on the uprising against the Soviet occupying

forces in East Germany in 1953
'The Solution' (1953)

L. Paul Bremer 1941–
American diplomat, US Administrator for Iraq, 2003–4

10 Ladies and gentlemen, we got him.
   announcing the capture of Saddam **Hussein**, *14 December 2003*
   in *Independent* 15 December 2003

William Joseph Brennan Jr.
1906–97
American judge

11 Debate on public issues should be uninhibited, robust, and wide open, and that...may well include vehement, caustic, and sometimes unpleasantly sharp attacks on government and public officials.
   in *New York Times Co. v. Sullivan* (1964)

12 The nation's future depends upon leaders trained through wide exposure to that robust exchange of ideas which discovers truth 'out of a multitude of tongues'.
   Supreme Court decision on *Keyishian v. Board of Regents of the University of the State of New York et al.* (1967); see **Hand 135:2**

13 The genius of the Constitution rests not in any static meaning it might have had in a world that is dead and gone, but in the adaptability of its great principles to cope with current problems and needs.
   address to the Text and Teaching Symposium, Georgetown University, 12 October 1985

Aristide Briand 1862–1932
French statesman

14 The high contracting powers solemnly declare...that they condemn recourse to war and renounce it...as an instrument of their national policy towards each other...The settlement or the solution of all disputes or conflicts of whatever nature or of whatever origin they may be which may arise...shall never be sought by either side except by pacific means.
   draft, 20 June 1927, later incorporated into the Kellogg Pact, 1928

John Bright 1811–89
English Liberal politician and reformer

1 The angel of death has been abroad throughout the land; you may almost hear the beating of his wings.
on the effects of the war in the Crimea
in the House of Commons, 23 February 1855

2 *of British foreign policy:*
A gigantic system of outdoor relief for the aristocracy of Great Britain.
speech at Birmingham, 29 October 1858

3 I am for 'Peace, retrenchment, and reform', the watchword of the great Liberal party 30 years ago.
speech at Birmingham, 28 April 1859; the phrase quoted may be found in Samuel Warren's novel *Ten Thousand a Year* (1841)

4 England is the mother of Parliaments.
speech at Birmingham, 18 January 1865

5 *of Robert Lowe, leader of the dissident Whigs opposed to the Reform Bill of 1866:*
The right hon Gentleman…has retired into what may be called his political Cave of Adullam—and he has called about him every one that was in distress and every one that was discontented.
in the House of Commons, 13 March 1866; see **Bible 32:12**

6 Force is not a remedy.
speech to the Birmingham Junior Liberal Club, 16 November 1880

Vera Brittain 1893–1970
English writer

7 Politics are usually the executive expression of human immaturity.
Rebel Passion (1964)

Russell Brockbank 1913–79
British cartoonist

8 Fog in Channel—Continent isolated.
newspaper placard in cartoon, *Round the Bend with Brockbank* (1948); the phrase 'Continent isolated' was quoted as already current by John Gunther *Inside Europe* (1938)

David Broder 1929–
American columnist

9 Anybody that wants the presidency so much that he'll spend two years organizing and campaigning for it is not to be trusted with the office.
in *Washington Post* 18 July 1973

D. W. Brogan 1900–74
Scottish historian

10 Any well-established village in New England or the northern Middle West could afford a town drunkard, a town atheist, and a few Democrats.
The American Character (1944)

Henry Brooke 1703–83
Irish poet and dramatist

11 For righteous monarchs,
Justly to judge, with their own eyes should see;
To rule o'er freemen, should themselves be free.
Earl of Essex (performed 1750, published 1761)

Lord Brougham 1778–1868
Scottish lawyer and politician; Lord Chancellor. On Brougham: see **Melbourne 209:7**, **Melbourne 209:8**

12 In my mind, he was guilty of no error—he was chargeable with no exaggeration—he was betrayed by his fancy into no metaphor, who once said, that all we see about us, King, Lords, and Commons, the whole machinery of the State, all the apparatus of the system, and its varied workings, end in simply bringing twelve good men

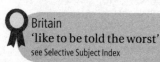

Britain
'like to be told the worst'
see Selective Subject Index

into a box.
in the House of Commons, 7 February 1828

1 Education makes a people easy to lead, but difficult to drive; easy to govern, but impossible to enslave.
attributed

Heywood Broun 1888–1939
American journalist

2 Just as every conviction begins as a whim so does every emancipator serve his apprenticeship as a crank. A fanatic is a great leader who is just entering the room.
in *New York World* 6 February 1928

3 Appeasers believe that if you keep on throwing steaks to a tiger, the tiger will turn vegetarian.
attributed

Gordon Brown 1951–
British Labour statesman, Prime Minister 2007–10. On Brown: see **Anonymous 9:8**, **Anonymous 9:9**, **Blair 36:18**, **Cable 52:8**

4 No return to Tory boom and bust.
speech, Labour Party conference, 28 September 1998; see **Clarke 73:9**, **Lawson 181:7**

5 The Labour Party—best when we are boldest, best when we are united, best when we are Labour.
speech to the Labour Party Conference, 29 September 2003; see **Blair 36:14**

6 There is nothing that you could ever say to me now that I could ever believe.
to Tony Blair, who in 2004 had allegedly gone back on a promise to resign as Prime Minister.
attributed (although denied in the House of Commons by the Prime Minister); Robert Peston *Brown's Britain* (2005)

7 There are two kinds of Chancellor. Those who fail and those who get out in time.
habitual saying recalled by Anthony Howard; in *Times* 8 February 2005

8 I learned from my mother and father that for every opportunity there was an obligation, for every demand a duty, for every chance given, a contribution to be made. And when they said

to me that for every right there was a responsibility, for them that was not just words. What they meant was quite simple and straightforward, for me my moral compass.
speech, Labour Party Conference, 26 September 2005, in *Guardian* 26 September 2005 (electronic edition)

9 Drawing on the talents of all to create British jobs for British workers.
speech, Labour Party conference, Bournemouth, 24 September 2007

10 Everyone knows I'm all in favour of apprenticeships, but let me tell you this is no time for a novice.
speech, Labour Party conference, 23 September 2008

11 We not only saved the world…Er, saved the banks.
speech, House of Commons, 10 December 2008

Henry Box Brown b. 1815
American escaped slave

12 I entered the world a slave—in the midst of a country whose most honoured writings declare that all men have a right to liberty.
Narrative of the Life of Henry Box Brown (1851)

H. Rap Brown (Jamil Abdullah Al-Amin) 1943–
American Black Power leader

13 I say violence is necessary. It is as American as cherry pie.
speech at Washington, 27 July 1967

John Brown 1800–59
American abolitionist. On Brown: see **Songs 297:1**; see also **Last words 179:12**

14 I am yet too young to understand that God is any respecter of persons.
last speech to the court at his trial on 2 November 1859

15 If it is deemed necessary that I should forfeit my life for the furtherance of the ends of justice, and mingle my blood further with the blood of my children, and

with the blood of millions in this
slave country whose rights are
disregarded by wicked, cruel, and
most unjust enactments, I submit:
so let it be done!
last speech to the court at his trial
    on 2 November 1859

Des Browne 1952–
British Labour politician

1 I have expressed a degree of regret
that can be equated with an
apology.
*on permitting British sailors to sell their stories of
their capture by Iran to the press*
    speech in the House of Commons, 16 April
    2007

William Browne 1692–1774
English physician and writer

2 The King to Oxford sent a troop of
horse,
For Tories own no argument but
force:
With equal skill to Cambridge books
he sent,
For Whigs admit no force but
argument.
    reply to Trapp's epigram, in J. Nichols *Literary
    Anecdotes* vol. 3; see **Trapp 314:8**

Frederick 'Boy' Browning
1896–1965
British soldier

3 *expressing reservations about the Arnhem
'Market Garden' operation to Field Marshal
Montgomery on 10 September 1944:*
I think we might be going a bridge
too far.
    R. E. Urquhart *Arnhem* (1958)

Robert Browning 1812–89
English poet

4 Just for a handful of silver he left us,
Just for a riband to stick in his coat.
*of **Wordsworth**'s implied abandonment of
radical principles by his acceptance of the
Laureateship*
    'The Lost Leader' (1845)

5 Life's night begins: let him never
come back to us!
There would be doubt, hesitation

and pain,
Forced praise on our part—the
glimmer of twilight,
Never glad confident morning again!
*quoted by Nigel **Birch** in the House of Commons,
17 June 1963, on Harold **Macmillan** and the
Profumo affair*
    'The Lost Leader' (1845)

Cathal Brugha 1874–1922
Irish nationalist. On Brugha: see **Collins 78:2**

6 Don't you realize that, if you sign
this thing, you will split Ireland
from top to bottom?
*to **de Valera**, December 1921, on the Treaty*
    Jim Ring *Erskine Childers* (1996)

Gro Harlem Brundtland 1939–
Norwegian stateswoman; Prime Minister 1981,
1986–89, and 1990–96

7 I do not know of any environmental
group in any country that does
not view its government as an
adversary.
    in *Time* 25 September 1989

William Jennings Bryan 1860–1925
American Democratic politician

8 The humblest citizen of all the
land, when clad in the armour of a
righteous cause, is stronger than all
the hosts of error.
    speech at the Democratic National Convention,
    Chicago, 1896

9 Destroy our farms and the grass
will grow in the streets of every city
in the country.
    speech at the Democratic National Convention,
    Chicago 1896; see **Hoover 147:5**

10 You shall not press down upon the
brow of labour this crown of thorns,
you shall not crucify mankind upon
a cross of gold.
    speech at the Democratic National Convention,
    Chicago, 1896; see **Slogans 291:9**

Zbigniew Brzezinski 1928–
American politician

11 Russia can be an empire or a
democracy, but it cannot be both.
    in *Foreign Affairs* March/April 1994 'The
    Premature Partnership'

Frank Buchman 1878–1961
American evangelist; founder of the Moral Re-
Armament movement

1 I thank heaven for a man like Adolf
Hitler, who built a front line of
defence against the anti-Christ of
Communism.
in *New York World-Telegram* 26 August 1936

Warren Buffett 1930–
American businessman

2 It's only when the tide goes out that
you learn who's been swimming
naked.
at Berkshire Hathaway annual meeting,
Omaha, 1993; *Warren Buffet Speaks* (1997)

Gerald Bullett 1893–1958
British writer

3 My Lord Archbishop, what a scold
you are!
And when your man is down how
bold you are!
Of charity how oddly scant you are!
How Lang, O Lord, how full of
Cantuar!
*on the role of Cosmo Gordon Lang, Archbishop of
Canterbury, in the abdication of Edward VIII*
in 1936

Ivor Bulmer-Thomas 1905–93
British Conservative politician

4 *of Harold **Wilson**:*
If he ever went to school without
any boots it was because he was too
big for them.
speech at the Conservative Party Conference,
in *Manchester Guardian* 13 October 1949

Prince Bernhard von Bülow
1849–1929
German statesman, Chancellor of Germany, 1900–9

5 In a word, we desire to throw no
one into the shade [in East Asia],
but we also demand our own place

in the sun.
speech in the Reichstag, 6 December 1897; see
Wilhelm II 333:4

Edward George Bulwer-Lytton
1803–73
British novelist and politician

6 Here Stanley meets,—how Stanley
scorns, the glance!
The brilliant chief, irregularly great,
Frank, haughty, rash,—the Rupert of
Debate!
*on Edward Stanley, 14th Earl of **Derby***
The New Timon (1846); see **Disraeli 92:7**

7 Beneath the rule of men entirely
great
The pen is mightier than the sword.
Richelieu (1839)

Samuel Dickinson Burchard
1812–91
American Presbyterian minister

8 We are Republicans and don't
propose to leave our party and
identify ourselves with the party
whose antecedents are rum,
Romanism, and rebellion.
speech at the Fifth Avenue Hotel, New York,
29 October 1884

Anthony Burgess 1917–93
English novelist and critic

9 The US presidency is a Tudor
monarchy plus telephones.
George Plimpton (ed.) *Writers at Work* (4th
Series, 1977)

Edmund Burke 1729–97
Irish-born Whig politician and man of letters. On
Burke: see **Gibbon 123:6, Johnson 161:14,
O'Brien 231:12, Paine 237:2, Paine 237:3**;
see also **Misquotations 215:15**

10 Those who have been once
intoxicated with power, and have
derived any kind of emolument
from it, even though for but

Bureaucracy
'When in trouble, delegate'
see Selective Subject Index

one year, can never willingly abandon it.
Letter to a Member of the National Assembly (1791)

1 Tyrants seldom want pretexts.
Letter to a Member of the National Assembly (1791)

2 You can never plan the future by the past.
Letter to a Member of the National Assembly (1791)

3 Men are qualified for civil liberty, in exact proportion to their disposition to put moral chains upon their own appetites.
Letter to a Member of the National Assembly (1791)

4 The king, and his faithful subjects, the lords and commons of this realm,—the triple cord, which no man can break.
A Letter to a Noble Lord (1796)

5 To innovate is not to reform.
A Letter to a Noble Lord (1796)

6 Bodies tied together by so unnatural a bond of union as mutual hatred are only connected to their ruin.
Letter to the Sheriffs of Bristol (1777)

7 I was persuaded that government was a practical thing made for the happiness of mankind, and not to furnish out a spectacle of uniformity to gratify the schemes of visionary politicians.
Letter to the Sheriffs of Bristol (1777)

8 Liberty too must be limited in order to be possessed.
Letter to the Sheriffs of Bristol (1777)

9 Among a people generally corrupt, liberty cannot long exist.
Letter to the Sheriffs of Bristol (1777)

10 It is a general popular error to imagine the loudest complainers for the public to be the most anxious for its welfare.
Observations on a late Publication on the Present State of the Nation (2nd ed., 1769)

11 There is, however, a limit at which forbearance ceases to be a virtue.
Observations on a late Publication on the Present State of the Nation (2nd ed., 1769)

12 It is the nature of all greatness not to be exact; and great trade will always be attended with considerable abuses.
On American Taxation (1775)

13 To tax and to please, no more than to love and to be wise, is not given to men.
On American Taxation (1775)

14 I have in general no very exalted opinion of the virtue of paper government.
On Conciliation with America (1775)

15 The concessions of the weak are the concessions of fear.
On Conciliation with America (1775)

16 When we speak of the commerce with our colonies, fiction lags after truth; invention is unfruitful, and imagination cold and barren.
On Conciliation with America (1775)

17 The use of force alone is but *temporary*. It may subdue for a moment; but it does not remove the necessity of subduing again; and a nation is not governed, which is perpetually to be conquered.
On Conciliation with America (1775)

18 Nothing less will content me, than *whole America*.
On Conciliation with America (1775)

19 I do not know the method of drawing up an indictment against an whole people.
On Conciliation with America (1775)

20 It is not, what a lawyer tells me I *may* do; but what humanity, reason, and justice, tells me I ought to do.
On Conciliation with America (1775)

21 Freedom and not servitude is the cure of anarchy; as religion, and not atheism, is the true remedy for superstition.
On Conciliation with America (1775)

22 Instead of a standing revenue, you will have therefore a perpetual quarrel.
On Conciliation with America (1775)

23 Parties must ever exist in a free country.
On Conciliation with America (1775)

24 Slavery they can have anywhere. It

is a weed that grows in every soil.
On Conciliation with America (1775)

1 Deny them this participation of freedom, and you break that sole bond, which originally made, and must still preserve the unity of the empire.
On Conciliation with America (1775)

2 It is the love of the people; it is their attachment to their government, from the sense of the deep stake they have in such a glorious institution, which gives you your army and your navy, and infuses into both that liberal obedience, without which your army would be a base rabble, and your navy nothing but rotten timber.
On Conciliation with America (1775)

3 Magnanimity in politics is not seldom the truest wisdom; and a great empire and little minds go ill together.
On Conciliation with America (1775)

4 By adverting to the dignity of this high calling, our ancestors have turned a savage wilderness into a glorious empire: and have made the most extensive, and the only honourable conquests; not by destroying, but by promoting the wealth, the number, the happiness of the human race.
On Conciliation with America (1775)

5 I flatter myself that I love a manly, moral, regulated liberty as well as any gentleman.
Reflections on the Revolution in France (1790)

6 Whenever our neighbour's house is on fire, it cannot be amiss for the engines to play a little on our own.
Reflections on the Revolution in France (1790)

7 A state without the means of some change is without the means of its conservation.
Reflections on the Revolution in France (1790)

8 Make the Revolution a parent of settlement, and not a nursery of future revolutions.
Reflections on the Revolution in France (1790)

9 People will not look forward to posterity, who never look backward to their ancestors.
Reflections on the Revolution in France (1790)

10 Those who attempt to level never equalize.
Reflections on the Revolution in France (1790)

11 Government is a contrivance of human wisdom to provide for human *wants*. Men have a right that these wants should be provided for by this wisdom.
Reflections on the Revolution in France (1790)

12 Flattery corrupts both the receiver and the giver.
Reflections on the Revolution in France (1790)

13 *of **Marie-Antoinette**:*
I thought ten thousand swords must have leapt from their scabbards to avenge even a look that threatened her with insult.
Reflections on the Revolution in France (1790)

14 The age of chivalry is gone.— That of sophisters, economists, and calculators, has succeeded; and the glory of Europe is extinguished for ever.
Reflections on the Revolution in France (1790)

15 This barbarous philosophy, which is the offspring of cold hearts and muddy understandings.
Reflections on the Revolution in France (1790)

16 In the groves of *their* academy, at the end of every vista, you see nothing but the gallows.
Reflections on the Revolution in France (1790)

17 Kings will be tyrants from policy when subjects are rebels from principle.
Reflections on the Revolution in France (1790)

18 Because half a dozen grasshoppers under a fern make the field ring with their importunate chink, whilst thousands of great cattle, reposed beneath the shadow of the British oak, chew the cud and are silent, pray do not imagine that those who make the noise are the only inhabitants of the field.
Reflections on the Revolution in France (1790)

19 Society is indeed a contract...it becomes a partnership not only between those who are living, but between those who are living, those

who are dead, and those who are to
be born.
Reflections on the Revolution in France (1790)

1 Nobility is a graceful ornament to
the civil order. It is the Corinthian
capital of polished society.
Reflections on the Revolution in France (1790)

2 By hating vices too much, they
come to love men too little.
Reflections on the Revolution in France (1790)

3 We begin our public affections in
our families. No cold relation is a
zealous citizen.
Reflections on the Revolution in France (1790)

4 Good order is the foundation of all
good things.
Reflections on the Revolution in France (1790)

5 Nothing turns out to be so
oppressive and unjust as a feeble
government.
Reflections on the Revolution in France (1790)

6 When the leaders choose to make
themselves bidders at an auction
of popularity, their talents, in the
construction of the state, will be of
no service.
Reflections on the Revolution in France (1790)

7 Ambition can creep as well as soar.
*Third Letter…on the Proposals for Peace with
the Regicide Directory* (1797)

8 And having looked to government
for bread, on the very first scarcity
they will turn and bite the hand
that fed them.
Thoughts and Details on Scarcity (1800)

9 To complain of the age we live in, to
murmur at the present possessors
of power, to lament the past,
to conceive extravagant hopes
of the future, are the common
dispositions of the greatest part of
mankind.
*Thoughts on the Cause of the Present
Discontents* (1770)

10 I am not one of those who think
that the people are never in
the wrong. They have been so,
frequently and outrageously, both
in other countries and in this.
But I do say, that in all disputes
between them and their rulers, the
presumption is at least upon a par

in favour of the people.
*Thoughts on the Cause of the Present
Discontents* (1770)

11 The power of the crown, almost
dead and rotten as Prerogative, has
grown up anew, with much more
strength, and far less odium, under
the name of Influence.
*Thoughts on the Cause of the Present
Discontents* (1770)

12 We must soften into a credulity
below the milkiness of infancy to
think all men virtuous. We must
be tainted with a malignity truly
diabolical, to believe all the world
to be equally wicked and corrupt.
*Thoughts on the Cause of the Present
Discontents* (1770)

13 When…[people] imagine that their
food is only a cover for poison, and
when they neither love nor trust
the hand that serves it, it is not
the name of the roast beef of old
England that will persuade them to
sit down to the table that is spread
for them.
*Thoughts on the Cause of the Present
Discontents* (1770)

14 When bad men combine, the good
must associate; else they will fall,
one by one, an unpitied sacrifice in
a contemptible struggle.
*Thoughts on the Cause of the Present
Discontents* (1770); see
Misquotations 215:15

15 Of this stamp is the cant of *Not
men, but measures*; a sort of
charm by which many people
get loose from every honourable
engagement.
*Thoughts on the Cause of the Present
Discontents* (1770); see **Canning 55:15**

16 Laws, like houses, lean on one
another.
A Tract on the Popery Laws (planned 1765)

17 In all forms of Government the
people is the true legislator.
A Tract on the Popery Laws (planned 1765)

18 Falsehood and delusion are allowed
in no case whatsoever: But, as in
the exercise of all the virtues, there

is an economy of truth.
Two Letters on the Proposals for Peace with the Regicide Directory (9th ed., 1796); see **Armstrong 12:11**

1 All men that are ruined are ruined on the side of their natural propensities.
Two Letters on the Proposals for Peace with the Regicide Directory (9th ed., 1796)

2 If ever there was in all the proceedings of government a rule that is fundamental, universal, invariable it is this: that you ought never to attempt a measure of authority you are not morally sure you can go through with.
in the House of Commons, 9 May 1770

3 The greater the power, the more dangerous the abuse.
speech on the Middlesex Election, 7 February 1771

4 The fire-bell at midnight disturbs your sleep, but it keeps you from being burned in your bed.
speech on the Jury Bill, 7 March 1771, in P. Langford (ed.) *Writings and Speeches of Edmund Burke* (1981) vol. 2

5 Your representative owes you, not his industry only, but his judgement; and he betrays, instead of serving you, if he sacrifices it to your opinion.
speech, 3 November 1774, in *Speeches at his Arrival at Bristol* (1774)

6 People crushed by law have no hopes but from power. If laws are their enemies, they will be enemies to laws; and those, who have much to hope and nothing to lose, will always be dangerous, more or less.
letter to Charles James Fox, 8 October 1777

7 It is the interest of the commercial world that wealth should be found everywhere.
letter to Samuel Span, 23 April 1778

8 Bad laws are the worst sort of tyranny.
Speech at Bristol, previous to the Late Election (1780)

9 The people are the masters.
in the House of Commons, 11 February 1780; see **Blair 36:4**

10 *of the younger **Pitt**'s maiden speech, February 1781:*
Not merely a chip of the old 'block', but the old block itself.
N. W. Wraxall *Historical Memoirs of My Own Time* (1904 ed.)

11 I feel an insuperable reluctance in giving my hand to destroy any established institution of government, upon a theory, however plausible it may be.
in the House of Commons on Fox's East India Bill, 1 December 1783

12 The people never give up their liberties but under some delusion.
speech at County Meeting of Buckinghamshire, 1784, attributed in E. Latham *Famous Sayings* (1904), with 'except' substituted for 'but'

13 You strike at the whole corps, if you strike at the head.
opening speech, impeachment of Warren Hastings, House of Commons 13 February 1788

14 An event has happened, upon which it is difficult to speak, and impossible to be silent.
speech, 5 May 1789; E. A. Bond (ed.) *Speeches...in the Trial of Warren Hastings* (1859) vol. 2

15 At last dying in the last dyke of prevarication.
speech, 7 May 1789; E. A. Bond (ed.) *Speeches...in the Trial of Warren Hastings* (1859) vol. 2

16 Somebody has said, that a king may make a nobleman but he cannot make a gentleman.
letter to William Smith, 29 January 1795

17 Those who carry on great public schemes must be proof against the most fatiguing delays, the most mortifying disappointments, the most shocking insults, and, worst of all, the presumptuous judgements of the ignorant upon their designs.
attributed; Benjamin Ward Richardson 'A Biographical Dissertation' ch. 4 in Edwin Chadwick *The Health of Nations* (1887)

George Burns 1896–1996
American comedian

18 Too bad all the people who know how to run the country are busy

driving taxi cabs and cutting hair.
in *Daily Mail* 30 September 1997

John Burns 1858–1943
British Liberal politician

1 The curse of the working class is the fewness of their wants, the poverty of their desires.
Brains Better Than Bets or Beer (1902)

2 I have seen the Mississippi. That is muddy water. I have seen the St Lawrence. That is crystal water. But the Thames is liquid history.
in *Daily Mail* 25 January 1943

Robert Burns 1759–96
Scottish poet

3 The rank is but the guinea's stamp,
The man's the gowd for a' that!
'For a' that and a' that' (1790)

4 A fig for those by law protected!
LIBERTY's a glorious feast!
Courts for cowards were erected,
Churches built to please the PRIEST.
'The Jolly Beggars' (1799)

5 Liberty's in every blow!
Let us do—or die!!!
'Robert Bruce's March to Bannockburn' (1799)

6 We labour soon, we labour late,
To feed the titled knave, man;
And a' the comfort we're to get,
Is that ayont the grave, man.
'The Tree of Liberty' (1838)

Burnum Burnum 1936–97
Australian political activist

7 We wish no harm to England's native people. We are here to bring you good manners, refinement and an opportunity to make a *Koompartoo*, a fresh start.
in 1988, the year of Australia's bicentenary, on planting an Aboriginal flag on the white cliffs of Dover and 'claiming' England for the Aboriginal people
on 26 January 1988; in obituary, *Independent* 20 August 1997

Aaron Burr 1756–1836
American politician

8 Law is whatever is boldly asserted

and plausibly maintained.
James Parton *The Life and Times of Aaron Burr* (1857); attributed

Barbara Bush 1925–
American wife of George **Bush**; First Lady 1989–93

9 Somewhere out in this audience may even be someone who will one day follow in my footsteps, and preside over the White House as the President's spouse. I wish him well!
at Wellesley College Commencement, 1 June 1990

10 Remember, they only name things after you when you're dead or really old.
at the naming ceremony for the George Bush Centre for Intelligence
at Wellesley College Commencement, 1 June 1990

George Bush 1924–
American Republican statesman; 41st President of the US, 1989–93; father of George W. **Bush**. On Bush: see **Richards 259:4**

11 Oh, the vision thing.
responding to the suggestion that he turn his attention from short-term campaign objectives and look to the longer term.
in *Time* 26 January 1987

12 What's wrong with being a boring kind of guy?
during the campaign for the Republican nomination; in *Daily Telegraph* 28 April 1988

13 We are a nation of communities, of tens and tens of thousands of ethnic, religious, social, business, labour union, neighbourhood, regional and other organizations, all of them varied, voluntary, and unique…a brilliant diversity spread like stars, like a thousand points of light in a broad and peaceful sky.
acceptance speech at the Republican National Convention in New Orleans, 18 August 1988

14 Read my lips: no new taxes.
accepting the Republican nomination
in *New York Times* 19 August 1988; see **Blunkett 37:10**

15 And now, we can see a new world coming into view. A world in which there is the very real prospect of a

new world order.
  speech, in *New York Times* 7 March 1991

George W. Bush 1946–
American Republican statesman; 43rd President of the US 2001–9; son of George **Bush**

1 They misunderestimated me.
  speech in Bentonville, Arkansas, November 2000

2 We will make no distinction between terrorists who committed these acts and those who harbour them.
  after the terrorist attacks of 11 September
  televised address, 12 September 2001

3 Today we feel what Franklin Roosevelt called the warm courage of national unity. This unity against terror is now extending across the world.
  address in Washington National Cathedral, 14 September 2001, at the day of mourning for those killed in the terrorist attacks of 11 September
  in *Times* 15 September 2001; see **Roosevelt 262:3**

4 This crusade, this war on terrorism is going to take a while.
  the President later retracted his use of the word 'crusade'
  at a White House press conference, 16 September 2001

5 States like these…constitute an axis of evil, arming to threaten the peace of this world.
  of Iraq, Iran, and North Korea
  State of the Union address, in *Newsweek* 11 February 2002

6 Let freedom reign!
  handwritten note as power in Iraq was officially transferred to the Interim Government
  in *Daily Telegraph* 29 June 2004; see also **Mandela 203:11**

7 Our enemies are innovative and resourceful, and so are we. They never stop thinking about new ways to harm our country and our people, and neither do we.
  at a signing ceremony for a Defense Bill, the White House, 5 August 2004

8 I earned capital in the campaign, political capital, and I

intend to spend it.
  on his re-election as President
  in *New York Times* 5 November 2004 (online edition)

David Butler 1924–
British political scientist

9 Has he got a resignation in him?
  *of James **Callaghan**, to Hugh **Dalton***
  Hugh Dalton *Political Diary* (1986) 13 July 1960

Lord Butler of Brockwell 1938–
British civil servant; Cabinet Secretary 1988–97

10 More weight was placed on the intelligence than it could bear.
  Review of Intelligence on Weapons of Mass Destruction ('Butler Report') 14 July 2004

R. A. ('Rab') Butler 1902–82
British Conservative politician. On Butler: see **Hennessy 141:6**

11 *on hearing of the appointment of Winston **Churchill** as Prime Minister in succession to Neville **Chamberlain**:*
  The good clean tradition of English politics, that of Pitt as opposed to Fox, has been sold to the greatest adventurer of modern political history.
  John Colville diary, 10 May 1940

12 REPORTER: Mr Butler, would you say that this [Anthony Eden] is the best Prime Minister we have?
  R. A. BUTLER: Yes.
  interview at London Airport, 8 January 1956; R. A. Butler *The Art of the Possible* (1971)

13 The Civil Service is a bit like a Rolls-Royce—you know it's the best machine in the world, but you're not quite sure what to do with it.
  Anthony Sampson *Anatomy of Britain* (1962)

14 I think a Prime Minister has to be a butcher and know the joints. That is perhaps where I have not been quite competent, in knowing all the ways that you can cut up a carcass.
  in *Listener* 28 June 1966

15 In politics you must always keep running with the pack. The moment that you falter and they sense that you are injured, the rest

will turn on you like wolves.
Dennis Walters *Not Always with the Pack* (1989)

Isaac Butt 1813–79
Irish nationalist politician

1 The people of this country are not idle. Let no man tell me this, when I see a peasant from Connaught going over to reap the harvest in England.
speech in defence of Thomas F. Meagher, 1848

John Byrom 1692–1763
English poet

2 God bless the King, I mean the Faith's Defender;
God bless—no harm in blessing—the Pretender;
But who Pretender is, or who is King,
God bless us all—that's quite another thing.
'To an Officer in the Army, Extempore, Intended to allay the Violence of Party-Spirit' (1773)

Lord Byron 1788–1824
English poet

3 For what were all these country patriots born?
To hunt, and vote, and raise the price of corn?
'The Age of Bronze' (1823)

4 Year after year they voted cent per cent
Blood, sweat, and tear-wrung millions—why? for rent!
'The Age of Bronze' (1823)

5 So he has cut his throat at last!— He! Who?
The man who cut his country's long ago.
on Castlereagh's suicide, 1822
'Epigram on Lord Castlereagh'

6 The Cincinnatus of the West.
*of George **Washington***
'Ode to Napoleon Bonaparte' (1814)

7 The arbiter of others' fate A suppliant for his own!
'Ode to Napoleon Bonaparte' (1814)

Vince Cable 1943–
British Liberal Democrat politician

8 The House has noticed the Prime Minister's remarkable transformation in the last few weeks from Stalin to Mr Bean, creating chaos out of order rather than order out of chaos.
*on Gordon **Brown***
speech in the House of Commons, 28 November 2007

Julius Caesar 100–44 BC
Roman general and statesman. See also **Plutarch 247:2**

9 *Gallia est omnis divisa in partes tres.*
Gaul as a whole is divided into three parts.
De Bello Gallico

10 Men are nearly always willing to believe what they wish.
De Bello Gallico

11 Caesar's wife must be above suspicion.
oral tradition, based on Plutarch *Parallel Lives* 'Julius Caesar'

12 Caesar had rather be first in a village than second at Rome.
Francis Bacon *The Advancement of Learning* (based on Plutarch *Parallel Lives* 'Julius Caesar')

13 *Iacta alea est.*
The die is cast.
at the crossing of the Rubicon
Suetonius *Lives of the Caesars* 'Divus Julius' (often quoted in Latin *'Iacta alea est'* but originally spoken in Greek)

1 *Veni, vidi, vici.*
  I came, I saw, I conquered.
    inscription displayed in Caesar's Pontic
    triumph, according to Suetonius *Lives of the
    Caesars* 'Divus Julius'; or, according to Plutarch
    Parallel Lives 'Julius Caesar', written in a letter
    by Caesar, announcing the victory of Zela
    which concluded the Pontic campaign

2 *Et tu, Brute?*
  You too, Brutus?
    traditional rendering of Suetonius *Lives of the
    Caesars* 'Divus Julius': 'Some have written that
    when Marcus Brutus rushed at him, he said in
    Greek, "You too, my child?" '

Joseph Cairns 1920–
British industrialist and politician

3 The betrayal of Ulster, the cynical
  and entirely undemocratic
  banishment of its properly elected
  Parliament and a relegation to the
  status of a fuzzy wuzzy colony is, I
  hope, a last betrayal contemplated
  by Downing Street because it is the
  last that Ulster will countenance.
    *speech on retiring as Lord Mayor of Belfast,
    31 May 1972*
    in *Daily Telegraph* 1 June 1972

John Caldwell Calhoun 1782–1850
American politician. On Calhoun: see **Jackson 153:10**

4 The very essence of a free
  government consists in considering
  offices as public trusts, bestowed for
  the good of the country, and not for
  the benefit of an individual or party.
    speech 13 February 1835

5 The surrender of life is
  nothing to sinking down into
  acknowledgement of inferiority.
    speech in the Senate, 19 February 1847

Caligula AD 12–41
Roman emperor from AD 37

6 Would that the Roman people had
  but one neck!
    Suetonius *Lives of the Caesars* 'Gaius Caligula'

James Callaghan 1912–2005
British Labour statesman; Prime Minister 1976–9.
On Callaghan: see **Butler 51:9**, **Jenkins 158:5**; see
also **Misquotations 215:5**

7 Leaking is what you do; briefing is

what *I* do.
    *when giving evidence to the Franks Committee on
    Official Secrecy in 1971*
    Franks Report (1972); oral evidence

8 We say that what Britain needs
  is a new social contract. That is
  what this document [*Labour's
  Programme for Britain*] is about.
    speech at Labour Party Annual Conference,
    2 October 1972

9 You cannot now, if you ever could,
  spend your way out of a recession.
    speech at Labour Party Conference,
    28 September 1976

10 You never reach the promised land.
   You can march towards it.
    in a television interview, 20 July 1978

11 I had known it was going to be a
   'winter of discontent'.
    television interview, 8 February 1979; see
    Newspaper headlines 225:3

12 It's the first time in recorded history
   that turkeys have been known to
   vote for an early Christmas.
    *in the debate resulting in the fall of the Labour
    government, when the pact between Labour and
    the Liberals had collapsed, and the Nationalists
    also withdrew their support in the wake of the
    failure of the devolution bills*
    in the House of Commons, 28 March 1979

13 I doubt if you accumulate much
   intellectual weight whilst you're
   in the office [of Prime Minister]…I
   think you rather spend your
   intellectual capital whilst you're in
   the office so it's important to take
   some baggage in.
    *to his Principal Private Secretary, towards the end
    of the 'Winter of Discontent', 1979*
    in conversation with Michael Cockerell, 1996;
    Peter Hennessy *The Prime Minister: the Office
    and its Holders* (2000)

14 There are times, perhaps once
   every thirty years, when there is a
   sea-change in politics. It then does
   not matter what you say or what
   you do. There is a shift in what the
   public wants and what it approves
   of. I suspect there is now such a sea-
   change—and it is for Mrs Thatcher.
    during the election campaign of 1979
    Kenneth O. Morgan *Callaghan* (1997)

15 *of the popularity of Mrs **Thatcher**:*
   The further you got from Britain,

the more admired you found she was.
in Spectator 1 December 1990

1 It's never a misfortune to become Prime Minister. It's always the greatest thing in your life. It's absolute heaven—I enjoyed every moment of it until those last few months of the 'Winter of Discontent'.
interview on *Analysis*, BBC Radio 4, 20 June 1991

2 Well, it works, doesn't it? So I think that's the answer, even if it is on the back of an envelope and doesn't have a written constitution with every comma and every semi-colon in place. Because sometimes they can make for difficulties that common sense can overcome.
Peter Hennessy and Simon Coates *The Back of the Envelope* (1991)

Italo Calvino 1923–85
Italian novelist and short-story writer

3 Revolutionaries are more formalistic than conservatives.
Il Barone Rampante (1957)

Helder Camara 1909–99
Brazilian priest

4 When I give food to the poor they call me a saint. When I ask why the poor have no food they call me a communist.
attributed, 1992

Lord Camden 1714–94
British Whig politician; Lord Chancellor, 1766–70

5 Taxation and representation are inseparable...whatever is a man's own, is absolutely his own; no man hath a right to take it from him without his consent either expressed by himself or representative; whoever attempts to do it, attempts an injury; whoever does it, commits a robbery; he throws down and destroys the distinction between

liberty and slavery.
on the taxation of Americans by the British parliament
in the House of Lords, 10 February 1766

David Cameron 1966–
British Conservative politician, Prime Minister from 2010

6 It's where you are going to, not where you have come from that matters.
in *Sunday Times* 22 May 2005

7 There is such a thing as society, it's just not the same as the state.
in *Birmingham Post* 15 September 2005, later repeated on becoming leader of the Conservative party, 6 December 2005; see **Thatcher 310:11**

8 I'm fed up with the Punch and Judy politics of Westminster.
speech on becoming leader of the Conservative party, 6 December 2005

9 I want to talk about the future. He was the future once.
of Tony Blair
at Prime Minister's Questions in House of Commons, 7 December 2005

10 We—the people in suits—often see hoodies as aggressive, the uniform of a rebel army of gangsters. But hoodies are more defensive than offensive. They're a way to stay invisible in the street.
speech to Centre for Social Justice, 10 July 2006, summed up by Vernon Coaker as 'Let's hug a hoodie'; see **Coaker 76:12**

11 The age of irresponsibility is giving way to the age of austerity.
speech, Conservative Party conference, 26 April 2009

Simon Cameron 1799–1889
American politician

12 An honest politician is one who when he's bought stays bought.
attributed

Alastair Campbell 1957–
British journalist, Press Secretary to the Prime Minister 1997–2003. See also **Anonymous 9:9**

13 The day of the bog-standard comprehensive is over.
press briefing, 12 February 2001

1 I'm sorry, we don't do God.
*when Tony **Blair** was asked about his Christian
faith in an interview for* Vanity Fair *magazine*
in *Daily Telegraph* 5 May 2003

Thomas Campbell 1777–1844
Scottish poet

2 What millions died—that Caesar
might be great!
Pleasures of Hope (1799)

Timothy Campbell 1840–1904
American politician

3 What's the Constitution between
friends?
*reported response to President **Cleveland**'s
refusing to support a bill on the grounds of its
being unconstitutional*
attributed, 1885

Henry Campbell-Bannerman
1836–1908
British Liberal statesman, Prime Minister 1905–8. On
Campbell-Bannerman: see **Cecil 59:10**

4 There is a phrase which seems in
itself somewhat self-evident, which
is often used to account for a good
deal—that 'war is war'. But when
you come to ask about it, then you
are told that the war now going on
is not war. [Laughter] When is a
war not a war? When it is carried on
by methods of barbarism in South
Africa.
speech to National Reform Union, 14 June
1901

5 Good government could never be
a substitute for government by the
people themselves.
speech at Stirling, 23 November 1905

Albert Camus 1913–60
French novelist, dramatist, and essayist

6 Politics and the fate of mankind are
formed by men without ideals and
without greatness. Those who have
greatness within them do not go in

for politics.
Notebooks, 1935–42 (1962)

7 What is a rebel? A man who says no.
The Rebel (1951)

8 All modern revolutions have ended
in a reinforcement of the State.
The Rebel (1951)

9 Every revolutionary ends as an
oppressor or a heretic.
The Rebel (1951)

Elias Canetti 1905–94
Bulgarian-born writer and novelist

10 Secrecy lies at the very core of
power.
Crowds and Power (1960)

George Canning 1770–1827
British Tory statesman; Prime Minister, 1827

11 A steady patriot of the world alone,
The friend of every country but his
own.
on the Jacobin
'New Morality' (1821)

12 And finds, with keen
discriminating sight,
Black's not so black;—nor white so
very white.
'New Morality' (1821)

13 Give me the avowed, erect and
manly foe;
Firm I can meet, perhaps return the
blow;
But of all plagues, good Heaven, thy
wrath can send,
Save me, oh, save me, from the
candid friend.
*the last two lines were quoted by **Peel** to
Disraeli in the House of Commons; Disraeli's
reply rested on the view that Peel had treated
Canning shabbily*
'New Morality' (1821)

14 Pitt is to Addington
As London is to Paddington.
'The Oracle' (1803)

15 Away with the cant of 'Measures

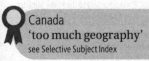

Canada
'too much geography'
see Selective Subject Index

not men'!—the idle supposition
that it is the harness and not the
horses that draw the chariot along.
If the comparison must be made,
if the distinction must be taken,
men are everything, measures
comparatively nothing.
*speech on the Army estimates, 8 December 1802
Speeches of…Canning (1828) vol. 2; the
phrase 'measures not men' may be found as
early as 1742 (in a letter from Chesterfield to
Dr Chevenix, 6 March); also in Goldsmith The
Good Natured Man (1768), 'Measures not men,
have always been my mark'; see* **Burke 48:15**

1 In matters of commerce the fault of
the Dutch
Is offering too little and asking too
much.
The French are with equal advantage
content,
So we clap on Dutch bottoms just
twenty per cent.
*dispatch, in cipher, to the English ambassador
at the Hague, 31 January 1826*

2 I called the New World into
existence, to redress the balance of
the Old.
*speech on the affairs of Portugal
in the House of Commons, 12 December 1826*

3 [The Whip's duty is] to make a
House, and keep a House, and cheer
the minister.
J. E. Ritchie Modern Statesmen (1861)

Al Capone 1899–1947
Italian-born American gangster, notorious for his
domination of organized crime in Chicago in the 1920s

4 Don't you get the idea I'm one of
these goddam radicals. Don't get
the idea I'm knocking the American
system.
*interview, 1929; Claud Cockburn In Time of
Trouble (1956)*

Benjamin Nathan Cardozo
1870–1938
American judge

5 [The Constitution] was framed
upon the theory that the peoples
of the several states must sink or
swim together, and that in the long
run prosperity and salvation are in

union and not division.
in Baldwin v. Seelig (1935)

James B. Carey 1911–73
American labour leader

6 I don't think that makes any
difference. A door-opener for the
Communist party is worse than a
member of the Communist party.
When someone walks like a duck,
swims like a duck, and quacks like a
duck, he's a duck.
of Communist affiliations during the **McCarthy**
*era
in New York Times 3 September 1948*

Richard Carleton 1943–
Australian journalist

7 How does it feel to have blood on
your hands?
to Bob **Hawke**, *new leader of the Australian
Labor Party, after the resignation of Bill* **Hayden**
as Opposition leader (see **Hayden**)
television interview, 3 February 1983

Thomas Carlyle 1795–1881
Scottish historian and political philosopher

8 A witty statesman said, you might
prove anything by figures.
Chartism (1839)

9 Surely of all 'rights of man', this
right of the ignorant man to be
guided by the wiser, to be, gently or
forcibly, held in the true course by
him, is the indisputablest.
Chartism (1839)

10 In epochs when cash payment has
become the sole nexus of man to
man.
Chartism (1839)

11 To the very last he [Napoleon] had
a kind of idea; that, namely, of *La
carrière ouverte aux talents*, The
tools to him that can handle them.
*Critical and Miscellaneous Essays (1838) 'Sir
Walter Scott'*

12 The three great elements of modern
civilization, Gunpowder, Printing,
and the Protestant Religion.
*Critical and Miscellaneous Essays (1838) 'The
State of German Literature'*

1 The seagreen Incorruptible.
   describing **Robespierre**
   History of the French Revolution (1837) vol. 2

2 France was long a despotism
   tempered by epigrams.
   History of the French Revolution (1837) vol. 3

3 Aristocracy of the Moneybag.
   History of the French Revolution (1837) vol. 3

4 A Parliament speaking through
   reporters to Buncombe and the
   twenty-seven millions mostly fools.
   Latter-Day Pamphlets (1850) 'Parliaments'; see
   Walker 323:14

5 *of political economy:*
   The Dismal Science.
   Latter-Day Pamphlets (1850) 'The Present Time'

6 *of himself:*
   Little other than a redtape talking-
   machine, and unhappy bag of
   parliamentary eloquence.
   Latter-Day Pamphlets (1850) 'The Present Time'

7 Despotism is essential in most
   enterprises.
   Past and Present (1843)

8 Councillors of state sit plotting,
   and playing their high chess-game,
   whereof the pawns are men.
   Sartor Resartus (1858)

9 *of **Disraeli**:*
   A superlative Hebrew conjuror.
   Shooting Niagara: and After? (1867)

10 Democracy, which means despair
   of finding any heroes to govern you.
   attributed

11 Vote by ballot is the dyspepsia of
   the society.
   Simon Heffer *Moral Desperado* (1995)

Stokely Carmichael 1941–98 and
Charles Vernon Hamilton 1929–
American Black Power leaders

12 Black power...is a call for black
   people in this country to unite, to
   recognize their heritage, to build a
   sense of community.
   Black Power (1967)

13 Before a group can enter the open
   society, it must first close ranks.
   Black Power (1967)

Caroline of Ansbach 1683–1737
German-born Queen of Great Britain and Ireland from
1727, wife of George II

14 My dear firstborn is the greatest
   ass, and the greatest liar, and the
   greatest *canaille*, and the greatest
   beast in the whole world, and I
   heartily wish he was out of it.
   *of her eldest son, Frederick, Prince of Wales,
   father of **George III** (he died in 1751, before he
   could succeed to the throne)*
      in *Dictionary of National Biography* (1917–)

Lewis Carroll 1832–98
English writer and logician

15 The rule is, jam to-morrow and jam
   yesterday—but never jam today.
      Through the Looking-Glass (1872); see
      Benn 27:8

16 'When *I* use a word,' Humpty
   Dumpty said in a rather scornful
   tone, 'it means just what I choose it
   to mean—neither more nor less.'
      Through the Looking-Glass (1872); see
      Shawcross 286:17

Edward Carson 1854–1935
British lawyer and politician

17 I now enter into compact with you,
   and with the help of God you and I
   joined together...will yet defeat the
   most nefarious conspiracy that has
   ever been hatched against a free
   people...We must be prepared...
   the morning Home Rule passes,
   ourselves to become responsible for
   the government of the Protestant
   Province of Ulster.
      speech at Craigavon, 23 September 1911

18 My one affection left me is my love
   for Ireland.
   after the death of his wife in 1913
      Montgomery Hyde *Carson* (1953)

19 We do not want a sentence of death
   with a stay of execution for six
   years.
   *rejecting the suggestion that the Home Rule Bill
   should allow the temporary exclusion of Ulster
   for six years*
      speech, March 1914

20 From the day I first entered
   parliament up to the present,

devotion to the union has been the guiding star of my political life.
in *Dictionary of National Biography* (1917–)

1 My only great qualification for being put at the head of the Navy is that I am very much at sea.
Ian Colvin *Life of Lord Carson* (1936) vol. 3

Jimmy Carter 1924–
American Democratic statesman, 39th President of the US, 1977–81

2 We should live our lives as though Christ were coming this afternoon.
to a Bible class at Plains, Georgia, March 1976 in *Boston Sunday Herald Advertiser* 11 April 1976

3 I'm Jimmy Carter, and I'm going to be your next president.
I'll Never Lie to You (1976); see **Gore 128:5**

4 I've looked on a lot of women with lust. I've committed adultery in my heart many times. This is something that God recognizes I will do—and I have done it—and God forgives me for it.
in *Playboy* November 1976

John Cartwright 1740–1824
English political reformer

5 One man shall have one vote.
The People's Barrier Against Undue Influence (1780) 'Principles, maxims, and primary rules of politics' no. 68

Thomas Nixon Carver 1865–1961
American economist, who had previously given the course in agricultural economics at Harvard taken over by **Galbraith** in 1934

6 The trouble with radicals is that they only read radical literature, and the trouble with conservatives is that they don't read anything.
'Carver's Law'; J. K. Galbraith *A Life in Our Times* (1981)

Roger Casement 1864–1916
Irish nationalist; executed for treason in 1916

7 Self-government is our right, a thing born in us at birth, a thing no more to be doled out to us, or withheld from us, by another

people than the right to life itself—than the right to feel the sun, or smell the flowers, or to love our kind.
statement at the conclusion of his trial, the Old Bailey, London, 29 June 1916

8 Where all your rights become only an accumulated wrong; where men must beg with bated breath for leave to subsist in their own land, to think their own thoughts, to sing their own songs, to garner the fruits of their own labours...then surely it is a braver, a saner and truer thing, to be a rebel in act and deed against such circumstances as these than tamely to accept it as the natural lot of men.
statement from prison, 29 June 1916

Barbara Castle 1910–2002
British Labour politician

9 She is so clearly the best man among them.
of Margaret **Thatcher**
diary, 11 February 1975

10 I will fight for what I believe in until I drop dead. And that's what keeps you alive.
in *Guardian* 14 January 1998

Ted Castle 1907–79
British journalist

11 In place of strife.
title of Labour Government White Paper, 17 January 1969; suggested by Castle to his wife, Barbara **Castle**, then Secretary of State for Employment

Fidel Castro 1927–
Cuban statesman, Prime Minister 1959–76 and President since 1976

12 Capitalism is using its money; we socialists throw it away.
in *Observer* 8 November 1964

Catherine the Great 1729–96
Russian monarch, Empress from 1762

13 I shall be an autocrat: that's my trade. And the good Lord will forgive me: that's his.
attributed

Wyn Catlin

1 Diplomacy is saying 'Nice doggie'
until you find a rock.
Laurence J. Peter (ed.) *Quotations for our Time*
(1977)

Cato the Elder 234–149 BC
Roman statesman, orator, and writer

2 *Delenda est Carthago.*
Carthage must be destroyed.
*words concluding every speech Cato made in the
Senate*
Pliny the Elder *Naturalis Historia*

Carrie Chapman Catt 1859–1947
American feminist

3 When a just cause reaches its flood-
tide…whatever stands in the way
must fall before its overwhelming
power.
speech at Stockholm, *Is Woman Suffrage
Progressing?* (1911)

Mr Justice Caulfield 1914–94
British judge

4 Remember Mary Archer in the
witness box. Your vision of her will
probably never disappear. Has
she elegance? Has she fragrance?
Would she have—without the strain
of this trial—a radiance?
summing up of court case between Jeffrey
Archer and the *Star*, July 1987, in *Times* 24 July
1987

Constantine Cavafy 1863–1933
Greek poet

5 What are we waiting for, gathered
in the market-place?
The barbarians are to arrive today.
'Waiting for the Barbarians' (1904)

6 And now, what will become of us
without the barbarians?
Those people were a kind of solution.
'Waiting for the Barbarians' (1904)

Edith Cavell 1865–1915
English nurse

7 Patriotism is not enough. I must
have no hatred or bitterness
towards anyone.
*on the eve of her execution by the Germans for
assisting in the escape of British soldiers from
occupied Belgium*
in *Times* 23 October 1915

Count Cavour 1810–61
Italian statesman

8 We are ready to proclaim
throughout Italy this great
principle: a free church in a free
state.
speech, 27 March 1861

Lord Edward Cecil 1867–1918
British soldier and civil servant

9 *definition of a compromise:*
An agreement between two men to
do what both agree is wrong.
letter 3 September 1911

Lord Hugh Cecil 1869–1956
British Conservative politician and educationist,
Provost of Eton

10 There is no more ungraceful figure
than that of a humanitarian with
an eye to the main chance.
*dismissal of a manoeuvre by **Campbell-
Bannerman***
in *Times* 24 June 1901

11 The socialist believes that it is
better to be rich than poor, the
Christian that it is better to be poor
than rich.
Conservatism (1912)

Robert Cecil 1563–1612
English courtier and statesman, son of William Cecil,
Lord Burghley

12 Rest content, and give heed to
one that hath sorrowed in the
bright lustre of a court, and gone
heavily even on the best-seeming
fair ground…I know it bringeth
little comfort on earth; and he is, I
reckon, no wise man that looketh
this way to Heaven.
letter to Sir John Harington; Algernon Cecil *A
Life of Robert Cecil* (1915)

**Robert Arthur James
Gascoyne-Cecil** see Lord **Salisbury**
1893–1972

**Robert Arthur Talbot
Gascoyne-Cecil** see Lord **Salisbury**
1830–1903

Paul Celan 1920–70
German poet

1 *Der Tod ist ein Meister aus
  Deutschland.*
  Death is a master from Germany.
  'Deathfugue' (written 1944)

2 There's nothing in the world for
  which a poet will give up writing,
  not even when he is a Jew and the
  language of his poems is German.
  letter to relatives, 2 August 1948

Joseph Chamberlain 1836–1914
British Liberal politician, father of Neville
Chamberlain. On Chamberlain: see **Churchill 70:9**;
see also **Slogans 291:18**

3 In politics, there is no use looking
  beyond the next fortnight.
  A. J. Balfour letter to Lord Salisbury, 24 March
  1886; see **Wilson 334:9**

4 Any universal scheme for giving
  pensions to everybody is…
  beyond the resources of the state.
  It would cost such an enormous
  sum, and would involve such an
  entire disintegration of our whole
  financial system, that it is perfectly
  impossible to contemplate it as
  practical legislation.
  speech on the Pensions Bill, House of
  Commons, 22 March 1899

5 Provided that the City of London
  remains, as it is at present, the
  clearing-house of the world, any
  other nation may be its workshop.
  speech at the Guildhall, 19 January 1904

6 Learn to think Imperially.
  *with reference to Alexander **Hamilton**'s advice to
  the newly independent United States*
  speech at the Guildhall, 19 January 1904; see
  Hamilton 135:1

7 The day of small nations has long
  passed away. The day of Empires

has come.
  speech at Birmingham, 12 May 1904

8 We are not downhearted. The only
  trouble is we cannot understand
  what is happening to our
  neighbours.
  *referring to a constituency which had remained
  unaffected by an electoral landslide*
  speech at Smethwick, 18 January 1906

Neville Chamberlain 1869–1940
British Conservative statesman; Prime Minister, 1937–
40, son of Joseph **Chamberlain**. On Chamberlain: see
Bevan 31:6, Churchill 66:11, Lloyd George 189:9

9 In spite of the hardness and
  ruthlessness I thought I saw in his
  face I got the impression that here
  was a man who could be relied
  upon when he had given his word.
  *of **Hitler***
  letter to Ida Chamberlain, 19 September 1938

10 How horrible, fantastic, incredible
  it is that we should be digging
  trenches and trying on gas-masks
  here because of a quarrel in a far
  away country between people of
  whom we know nothing.
  on Germany's annexation of the Sudetenland
  radio broadcast, 27 September 1938

11 This morning I had another talk
  with the German Chancellor, Herr
  Hitler, and here is the paper which
  bears his name upon it as well as
  mine…'We regard the agreement
  signed last night and the Anglo-
  German Naval Agreement, as
  symbolic of the desire of our two
  peoples never to go to war with one
  another again.'
  speech at Heston Airport, 30 September 1938

12 This is the second time in our
  history that there has come back
  from Germany to Downing Street
  peace with honour. I believe it is
  peace for our time.
  *speech from the window of 10 Downing Street,
  30 September 1938*
  in *Times* 1 October 1938; see **Book of
  Common Prayer 39:1, Disraeli 94:3**

1 *the British Ambassador in Berlin had handed the German government a final note stating that unless the British government had heard by eleven o'clock that Germany was prepared to withdraw her troops from Poland, a state of war would exist between the two countries:*
I have to tell you now that no such undertaking has been received, and that consequently this country is at war with Germany.
  radio broadcast, 3 September 1939

2 Whatever may be the reason— whether it was that Hitler thought he might get away with what he had got without fighting for it, or whether it was that after all the preparations were not sufficiently complete—however, one thing is certain—he missed the bus.
  speech at Central Hall, Westminster, 4 April 1940

Nicolas-Sébastien Chamfort
1741–94
French writer

3 If you would find to what extent each condition of society can corrupt a man, examine what he is when he has undergone that influence for the longest possible time, that is to say, when he is old. See what an old courtier is like, an old priest, an old judge, an old solicitor, an old surgeon.
  Maximes et Pensées (1796) ch. 2

Henry ('Chips') Channon
1897–1958
American-born British Conservative politician and diarist

4 There is nowhere in the world where sleep is so deep as in the libraries of the House of Commons.
  diary, 17 December 1937

5 I gather it has now been decided not to embrace the Russian bear, but to hold out a hand and accept its paw gingerly. No more. The worst of both worlds.
  diary, 16 May 1939

Charles I 1600–49
British monarch, King of England, Scotland, and Ireland from 1625, son of **James I** and father of **Charles II**. On Charles I: see **Marvell 206:6**; see also **Last words 179:8**

6 Never make a defence or apology before you be accused.
  letter to Lord Wentworth, 3 September 1636

7 I see all the birds are flown.
  after attempting to arrest the Five Members in the House of Commons, 4 January 1642

8 Sweet-heart, now they will cut off thy father's head. Mark, child, what I say: they will cut off my head, and perhaps make thee a king. But mark what I say: you must not be a king, so long as your brothers Charles and James do live.
  said to Prince Henry in Reliquiae Sacrae Carolinae (1650)

9 You manifestly wrong even the poorest ploughman, if you demand not his free consent.
  rejecting the jurisdiction of the High Court of Justice, 21 January 1649
    S. R. Gardiner *Constitutional Documents of the Puritan Revolution* (1906 ed.)

10 As to the King, the laws of the land will clearly instruct you for that... For the people; and truly I desire their liberty and freedom, as much as any body: but I must tell you, that their liberty and freedom consists in having the government of those laws, by which their life and their goods may be most their own; 'tis not for having share in government [sirs] that is nothing pertaining to 'em. A subject and a sovereign are clean different things...If I would have given way to an arbitrary way, for to have all laws changed according to the power of the sword, I needed not to have come here; and therefore I tell you (and I pray God it be not laid to your charge) that I am the martyr of the people.
  speech on the scaffold, 30 January 1649
    J. Rushworth *Historical Collections* vol. 2 (1701)

11 I die a Christian, according to the profession of the Church of

England, as I found it left me by my father.
J. Rushworth *Historical Collections* vol. 2 (1701)

Charles II 1630–85
British monarch, King of England, Scotland and Ireland from 1660, son of **Charles I**. On Charles II: see **Rochester 260:13, Sellar and Yeatman 276:11**

1 It is upon the navy under the good Providence of God that the safety, honour, and welfare of this realm do chiefly depend.
'Articles of War' preamble (probably a popular paraphrase); Geoffrey Callender *The Naval Side of British History* (1952)

2 This is very true: for my words are my own, and my actions are my ministers'.
*reply to Lord **Rochester**'s epitaph on him*
in *Thomas Hearne: Remarks and Collections* (1885–1921) 17 November 1706; see **Epitaphs 106:3**

3 Better than a play.
on the debates in the House of Lords on Lord Ross's Divorce Bill
A. Bryant *King Charles II* (1931)

4 I am sure no man in England will take away my life to make you King.
to his brother James, afterwards James II
William King *Political & Literary Anecdotes* (1818)

5 I am weary of travelling and am resolved to go abroad no more. But when I am dead and gone I know not what my brother will do: I am much afraid that when he comes to wear the crown he will be obliged to travel again.
on the difference between himself and his brother
attributed

6 I, who will never use arbitrary government myself, am resolved not to suffer it in others.
to the Whigs
attributed

7 Not a religion for gentlemen.
of Presbyterianism
Gilbert Burnet *History of My Own Time* (1724) vol. 1

8 He had been, he said, an unconscionable time dying; but he hoped that they would excuse it.
Lord Macaulay *History of England* (1849) vol. 1

Salmon Portland Chase 1808–73
American lawyer and politician

9 The Constitution, in all its provisions, looks to an indestructible Union composed of indestructible States.
decision in Texas v. White, 1868

Hugo Chavez 1954–
Venezuelan statesman, President 1999–

10 Fatherland, socialism or death—I swear it.
third inauguration speech, 10 January 2007, in *New York Times* (online edition) 11 January 2007

Dick Cheney 1941–
American Republican politician, Vice-President of the US 2001–9

11 Except for the occasional heart attack, I never felt better.
in June 2003; quoted on *BBC News Online* website, 6 October 2004

12 Direct threats require decisive action.
in *Chicago Sun-Times* 25 January 2004

Lord Chesterfield 1694–1773
English writer and politician. On Chesterfield: see **Johnson 160:16, Walpole 324:8**

13 Politicians neither love nor hate. Interest, not sentiment, directs them.
Letters, 1748

14 I...could not help reflecting in my way upon the singular ill-luck of this my dear country, which, as long as ever I remember it, and as far back as I have read, has always been governed by the only two or three people, out of two or three millions, totally incapable of governing, and unfit to be trusted.
in *The World* 7 October 1756

G. K. Chesterton 1874–1936
English essayist, novelist, and poet

15 'My country, right or wrong' is a thing no patriot would ever think of saying except in a desperate case. It is like saying, 'My mother, drunk

or sober.'
The Defendant (1901)

1 Tradition means giving votes to the most obscure of all classes, our ancestors. It is the democracy of the dead.
Orthodoxy (1908)

2 Democrats object to men being disqualified by the accident of birth; tradition objects to their being disqualified by the accident of death. Tradition refuses to submit to the small and arrogant oligarchy of those who merely happen to be walking around.
Orthodoxy (1908)

3 All conservatism is based upon the idea that if you leave things alone you leave them as they are. But you do not. If you leave a thing alone you leave it to a torrent of change.
Orthodoxy (1908)

4 Talk about the pews and steeples And the Cash that goes therewith! But the souls of Christian peoples...
Chuck it, Smith!
*satirizing F. E. **Smith**'s response to the Welsh Disestablishment Bill*
'Antichrist' (1912)

5 They died to save their country and they only saved the world.
'English Graves' (1922)

6 Smile at us, pay us, pass us; but do not quite forget.
For we are the people of England, that never have spoken yet.
'The Secret People' (1915)

7 They have given us into the hand of new unhappy lords,
Lords without anger and honour, who dare not carry their swords.
They fight us by shuffling papers; they have bright dead alien eyes;
And they look at our labour and laughter as a tired man looks at flies.
And the load of their loveless pity is worse than the ancient wrongs,
Their doors are shut in the evening; And they know no songs.
'The Secret People' (1915)

8 Lancashire merchants whenever

they like
Can water the beer of a man in Klondike
Or poison the meat of a man in Bombay;
And that is the meaning of Empire Day.
'Songs of Education: II Geography' (1922)

9 Democracy means government by the uneducated, while aristocracy means government by the badly educated.
in *New York Times* 1 February 1931

Joseph Benedict 'Ben' Chifley
1885–1951
Australian Labor statesman; Prime Minister 1945–9

10 We have a great objective—the light on the hill—which we aim to reach by working for the betterment of mankind not only here but anywhere we may give a helping hand.
speech to the Annual Conference of the New South Wales branch of the Australian Labor Party, 12 June 1949

Lydia Maria Child 1802–80
American abolitionist and suffragist

11 We first crush people to the earth, and then claim the right of trampling on them forever, because they are prostrate.
An Appeal on Behalf of That Class of Americans Called Africans (1833)

12 Woman stock is rising in the market. I shall not live to see women vote, but I'll come and rap at the ballot box.
letter to Sarah Shaw, 3 August 1856

Erskine Childers see Last words 178:3

Jacques Chirac 1932–
French statesman, Prime Minister 1974–6 and 1986–8, President 1995–2007

13 You have been very rude, and I have never been spoken to like this before.
*to Tony **Blair** at the EU enlargement summit in Brussels*
in *Guardian* online 29 October 2002

1 It is not well-brought-up behaviour.
They missed a good opportunity to
keep quiet.
*criticizing the support from Central and Eastern
European states for the Anglo-American stance
on Iraq*
in *Times* 19 February 2003

Shirley Chisholm 1924–2005
American Democratic politician and social activist

2 Of my two 'handicaps', being
female put many more obstacles in
my path than being black.
Unbought and Unbossed (1970) introduction

Rufus Choate 1799–1859
American lawyer and politician

3 We join ourselves to no party that
does not carry the flag and keep
step to the music of the Union.
letter to the Whig Convention, Worcester,
Massachusetts, 1 October 1855

4 Its constitution the glittering
and sounding generalities of
natural right which make up the
Declaration of Independence.
letter to the Maine Whig State Central
Committee, 9 August 1856

Duc de Choiseul 1719–85
French politician

5 A minister who moves about in
society is in a position to read the
signs of the times even in a festive
gathering, but one who remains
shut up in his office learns nothing.
Jack F. Bernard *Talleyrand* (1973)

Jean Chrétien 1934–
Canadian Liberal statesman; Prime Minister
1993–2003

6 Leadership means making people
feel good.
in *Toronto Star* 7 June 1984

7 The art of politics is learning to
walk with your back to the wall,
your elbows high, and a smile
on your face. It's a survival game
played under the glare of lights.
Straight from the Heart (1985)

8 *asked about the kind of proof he needed to
be convinced that Iraq had weapons of mass
destruction:*
What kind of a proof?…A proof is a
proof. And when you have a good
proof, it's because it's proven.
interview on CBC News, 6 September 2002

9 He's not a moron at all, he's a friend.
*after reports of an off-the-record comment on
George W.* **Bush** *by a Canadian political aide,
Françoise* **Ducros**
attributed; reported in *CTVnews* (online
edition) 21 November 2002

Christina of Denmark 1522–90
Danish princess

10 If I had two heads, I would happily
place one at the disposal of the King
of England.
on the possibility of marrying Henry VIII
attributed in varying forms since the 19th
century

David Christy 1802–c. 68

11 Cotton is King; or, the economical
relations of slavery.
title of book, 1855; see **Hugo 149:5**

Clementine Churchill 1885–1977
British wife of Winston **Churchill**

12 Winston…has the supreme
quality which I venture to say
very few of your present or future
Cabinet possess, the power, the
imagination, the deadliness to fight
Germany.
letter to **Asquith** *on Winston* **Churchill**'s
dismissal from the Admiralty, May 1915
Martin Gilbert *In Search of Churchill* (1994)

Lord Randolph Churchill 1849–94
British Conservative politician. On Churchill: see
Gladstone 125:8

13 To tell the truth I don't know
myself what Tory Democracy
is. But I believe it is principally
opportunism.
*having urged Wilfrid Scawen Blunt in 1885 to
stand for Parliament as a Tory Democrat*
Elizabeth Longford *A Pilgrimage of Passion*
(1979)

1 For the purposes of recreation
he [Gladstone] has selected the
felling of trees, and we may usefully
remark that his amusements,
like his politics, are essentially
destructive...The forest laments
in order that Mr Gladstone may
perspire.
    speech on Financial Reform, delivered in
    Blackpool, 24 January 1884

2 I decided some time ago that if the
G.O.M. [Gladstone] went for Home
Rule, the Orange card would be the
one to play. Please God it may turn
out the ace of trumps and not the
two.
    often quoted as 'Play the Orange card'; see
    Shapiro
        letter to Lord Justice FitzGibbon, 16 February
        1886

3 Ulster will fight; Ulster will be right.
    public letter, 7 May 1886

4 An old man in a hurry.
    *of **Gladstone***
        in an address to the electors of South
        Paddington, 19 June 1886; see also
        Salisbury 270:10

5 All great men make mistakes.
Napoleon forgot Blücher, I forgot
Goschen.
    *when Lord Randolph suddenly resigned the
    position of Chancellor of the Exchequer in 1886,
    Goschen had been appointed in his place*
        in *Leaves from the Notebooks of Lady Dorothy
        Nevill* (1907)

6 I never could make out what those
damned dots meant.
    of decimal points
        Winston Churchill *Lord Randolph Churchill*
        (1906) vol. 2

7 I have tried all forms of excitement,
from tip-cat to tiger-shooting;
all degrees of gambling, from
beggar-my-neighbour to Monte
Carlo; but have found no gambling
like politics, and no excitement
like a big division in the House of
Commons.
    Robert Rhodes James *An Introduction to the
    House of Commons* (1961)

Winston Churchill 1874–1965
British Conservative statesman; Prime Minister,
1940–5, 1951–5. On Churchill: see **Alanbrooke 5:9**,
Asquith 13:8, **Baldwin 22:8**, **Baldwin 22:14**,
Balfour 23:13, **Bevan 30:8**, **Butler 51:11**,
Laski 180:6, **Lloyd George 189:11**, **Lloyd
George 189:19**, **Nicolson 227:4**, **Webb 327:3**;
see also **Spears 298:4**

8 A labour contract into which men
enter voluntarily for a limited and
for a brief period, under which they
are paid wages which they consider
adequate...may not be a healthy
or proper contract, but it cannot
in the opinion of His Majesty's
Government be classified as
slavery in the extreme acceptance
of the word without some risk of
terminological inexactitude.
    in the House of Commons, 22 February 1906

9 He is one of those orators of whom
it was well said, 'Before they get
up, they do not know what they
are going to say; when they are
speaking, they do not know what
they are saying; and when they
have sat down, they do not know
what they have said.'
    of Lord Charles Beresford
        in the House of Commons, 20 December 1912

10 Business carried on as usual during
alterations on the map of Europe.
    on the self-adopted 'motto' of the British people
        speech at Guildhall, 9 November 1914

11 I have derived continued benefit
from criticism at all periods of my
life and I do not remember any time
when I was ever short of it.
    speech in House of Commons, 27 November
    1914

12 A drizzle of Empires...falling
through the air.
    *of the Austro-Hungarian and Ottoman empires
    in 1918*
        Martin Gilbert *In Search of Churchill* (1994)

13 *comparing H. H. **Asquith** with Arthur
Balfour:*
The difference between him and
Arthur is that Arthur is wicked
and moral, Asquith is good and
immoral.
    E. T. Raymond *Mr Balfour* (1920)

1 The whole map of Europe has been changed…but as the deluge subsides and the waters fall short we see the dreary steeples of Fermanagh and Tyrone emerging once again.
in the House of Commons, 16 February 1922

2 Anyone can rat, but it takes a certain amount of ingenuity to re-rat.
on rejoining the Conservatives twenty years after leaving them for the Liberals, 1924
Kay Halle Irrepressible Churchill (1966)

3 of a meeting in 1926 with **Lloyd George**, by then out of office:
Within five minutes the old relationship between us was completely re-established. The relationship between Master and Servant. And I was the Servant.
Lord Boothby Recollections of a Rebel (1978)

4 I decline utterly to be impartial as between the fire brigade and the fire.
replying to complaints of his bias in editing the British Gazette during the General Strike
in the House of Commons, 7 July 1926

5 Cultured people are merely the glittering scum which floats upon the deep river of production.
on hearing his son Randolph criticize the lack of culture of the Calgary oil magnates, probably 1929
Martin Gilbert In Search of Churchill (1994)

6 We are with Europe, but not of it. We are linked but not comprised. We are interested and associated, but not absorbed.
in Saturday Evening Post 15 February 1930

7 I remember, when I was a child, being taken to the celebrated Barnum's circus, which contained an exhibition of freaks and monstrosities, but the exhibit on the programme which I most desired to see was the one described as 'The Boneless Wonder'. My parents judged that that spectacle would be too revolting and demoralizing for my youthful eyes, and I have waited 50 years to see the boneless wonder sitting on the Treasury Bench.
of Ramsay **MacDonald**
speech in the House of Commons, 28 January 1931

8 There is not much collective security in a flock of sheep on the way to the butcher.
speech at the New Commonwealth Society luncheon, Dorchester Hotel, 25 November 1936

9 [The Government] go on in strange paradox, decided only to be undecided, resolved to be irresolute, adamant for drift, solid for fluidity, all-powerful to be impotent.
in the House of Commons, 12 November 1936

10 Dictators ride to and fro upon tigers which they dare not dismount. And the tigers are getting hungry.
letter, 11 November 1937

11 The utmost he [Neville Chamberlain] has been able to gain for Czechoslovakia and in the matters which were in dispute has been that the German dictator, instead of snatching his victuals from the table, has been content to have them served to him course by course.
in the House of Commons, 5 October 1938

12 I cannot forecast to you the action of Russia. It is a riddle wrapped in a mystery inside an enigma.
radio broadcast, 1 October 1939

13 on being asked where to set the podium from which Neville **Chamberlain** was to give an address to local Conservatives:
It doesn't matter where you put it as long as he has the sun in his eyes and the wind in his teeth.
Martin Gilbert In Search of Churchill (1994)

14 An appeaser is one who feeds a crocodile hoping it will eat him last.
in the House of Commons, January 1940

15 as Prime Minister:
[I was] conscious of a profound sense of relief. I felt as if I was walking with destiny, and that all my past life had been but a preparation for this hour and this trial.
on 10 May 1940

1 I have nothing to offer but blood, toil, tears and sweat.
speech in the House of Commons, 13 May 1940

2 What is our policy?...to wage war against a monstrous tyranny, never surpassed in the dark, lamentable catalogue of human crime.
speech in the House of Commons, 13 May 1940

3 We shall not flag or fail. We shall go on to the end. We shall fight in France, we shall fight on the seas and oceans, we shall fight with growing confidence and growing strength in the air, we shall defend our island, whatever the cost may be. We shall fight on the beaches, we shall fight on the landing grounds, we shall fight in the fields and in the streets, we shall fight in the hills; we shall never surrender.
speech in the House of Commons, 4 June 1940

4 Let us therefore brace ourselves to our duty, and so bear ourselves that, if the British Empire and its Commonwealth lasts for a thousand years, men will still say, 'This was their finest hour.'
speech in the House of Commons, 18 June 1940

5 Never in the field of human conflict was so much owed by so many to so few.
on the skill and courage of British airmen
speech in the House of Commons, 20 August 1940

6 Death and sorrow will be the companions of our journey; hardship our garment; constancy and valour our only shield. We must be united, we must be undaunted, we must be inflexible.
speech in the House of Commons, 8 October 1940

7 *comment allegedly made on a long-winded report submitted by Anthony **Eden** on his tour of the Near East:*
As far as I can see you have used every cliché except 'God is Love' and 'Please adjust your dress before leaving.'
in *Life* December 1940

8 What I want is for you to keep the flies off the meat. It becomes bad if they are allowed to settle even for a moment. I am the meat and you must show me the warning light when troubles arise in the Parliamentary and political scene.
to his newly appointed Parliamentary Private Secretary, 1941; Andrew Roberts *Eminent Churchillians* (1994)

9 I owe my advancement entirely to the House of Commons, whose servant I am. In my country, as in yours, public men are proud to be the servants of the state and would be ashamed to be its masters.
speech to US Congress, 26 December 1941

10 It becomes still more difficult to reconcile Japanese action with prudence or even with sanity. What kind of a people do they think we are?
speech to US Congress, 26 December 1941

11 The British nation is unique in this respect. They are the only people who like to be told how bad things are, who like to be told the worst.
speech in the House of Commons, 10 June 1941

12 The people of London with one voice would say to Hitler: 'You have committed every crime under the sun...We will have no truce or parley with you, or the grisly gang who work your wicked will. You do your worst—and we will do our best.'
speech at County Hall, London, 14 July 1941

13 Here is the answer which I will give to President Roosevelt...Give us the tools and we will finish the job.
radio broadcast, 9 February 1941

14 When I warned them [the French Government] that Britain would fight on alone whatever they did, their generals told their Prime Minister and his divided Cabinet, 'In three weeks England will have her neck wrung like a chicken.' Some chicken! Some neck!
speech to Canadian Parliament, 30 December 1941

15 A medal glitters, but it also casts

a shadow.
a reference to the envy caused by the award of honours
in 1941; Kenneth Rose *King George V* (1983)

1 I have not become the King's First Minister in order to preside over the liquidation of the British Empire.
speech in London, 10 November 1942

2 Now this is not the end. It is not even the beginning of the end. But it is, perhaps, the end of the beginning.
on British success in the North African campaign
speech at the Mansion House, London, 10 November 1942

3 We make this wide encircling movement in the Mediterranean, having for its primary object the recovery of the command of that vital sea, but also having for its object the exposure of the under-belly of the Axis, especially Italy, to heavy attack.
speech in the House of Commons, 11 November 1942; see **Misquotations 216:3**

4 National compulsory insurance for all classes for all purposes from the cradle to the grave.
radio broadcast, 21 March 1943

5 There is no finer investment for any community than putting milk into babies.
radio broadcast, 21 March 1943

6 The empires of the future are the empires of the mind.
speech at Harvard, 6 September 1943

7 This is something you ought to know: each time we have to choose between Europe and the open sea, we shall always choose the open sea.
to de Gaulle, 4 June 1944; Charles de Gaulle *War Memoirs: Unity 1942–1944* (1959)

8 *on rebuilding the Houses of Parliament:*
We shape our dwellings, and afterwards our dwellings shape us.
speech in the House of Commons, 28 October 1944

9 In wartime...truth is so precious that she should always be attended by a bodyguard of lies.
The Second World War vol. 5 (1951)

10 I do not see any other way of realizing our hopes about World Organization in five or six days. Even the Almighty took seven.
*to Franklin **Roosevelt** on the likely duration of the Yalta conference with **Stalin** in 1945*
The Second World War vol. 6 (1954)

11 There is only one thing worse than fighting with allies, and that is fighting without them!
attributed; Lord Alanbrooke's diary, 1 April 1945

12 He devised the extraordinary measure of assistance called Lend-Lease, which will stand forth as the most unselfish and unsordid financial act of any country in all history.
*of President **Roosevelt***
speech in the House of Commons, 17 April 1945

13 *after the General Election of 1945:*
Why should I accept the Order of the Garter from His Majesty when the people have just given me the order of the boot?
D. Bardens *Churchill in Parliament* (1967)

14 *of Aneurin **Bevan**:*
Unless the right hon. gentleman changes his policy and methods and moves without the slightest delay, he will be as great a curse to this country in time of peace, as he was a squalid nuisance in time of war.
speech in the House of Commons, 6 December 1945

15 The Prime Minister has nothing to hide from the President of the United States
*on stepping from his bath in the presence of a startled President **Roosevelt***
as recalled by Roosevelt's son in *Churchill* (BBC television series presented by Martin Gilbert, 1992) pt. 3

16 Neither the sure prevention of war, nor the continuous rise of world organisation will be gained without what I have called the fraternal association of the English-speaking peoples. This means a special relationship between the British Commonwealth and Empire and

the United States
speech at Westminster College, Fulton,
Missouri, 5 March 1946; Churchill had earlier
referred to a 'special relationship' in the House
of Commons, 7 November 1945

1 From Stettin in the Baltic to Trieste
in the Adriatic an iron curtain has
descended across the Continent.
*the expression 'iron curtain' previously had been
applied by others to the Soviet Union or her
sphere of influence, e.g. Ethel Snowden* Through
Bolshevik Russia *(1920), Dr Goebbels* Das Reich,
*25 February 1945, and by Churchill himself in a
cable to President Truman, 4 June 1945*
speech at Westminster College, Fulton,
Missouri, 5 March 1946

2 The first step in the re-creation
of the European family must be
a partnership between France
and Germany. In this way only
can France recover the moral
leadership of Europe. There can
be no revival of Europe without
a spiritually great France and a
spiritually great Germany.
speech in Zurich, 19 September 1946

3 Time may be short...The fighting
has stopped; but the dangers have
not stopped. If we are to form the
United States of Europe or whatever
name or form it may take, we must
begin now.
speaking of the threat posed by the atom bomb
speech in Zurich, 19 September 1946

4 *after the Nuremberg war trials:*
From now on I shall have to take
care not to lose wars.
attributed

5 I wish Stanley Baldwin no ill, but it
would have been much better if he
had never lived.
*on being asked to send **Baldwin** an 80th
birthday tribute*
Martin Gilbert *In Search of Churchill* (1994)

6 It would be a great reform in
politics if wisdom could be made
to spread as easily and as rapidly
as folly.
speech at the Guildhall, London, 10 September
1947

7 Democracy is the worst form of
Government except all those other
forms that have been tried from

time to time.
speech in the House of Commons,
11 November 1947

8 When I am abroad I always make it
a rule never to criticize or attack the
Government of my country. I make
up for lost time when I am at home.
speech in the House of Commons, 18 April
1947

9 For my part, I consider that it
will be found much better by all
Parties to leave the past to history,
especially as I propose to write that
history myself.
speech in the House of Commons, 23 January
1948

10 This is the sort of English up with
which I will not put.
*after an official had gone through one of his
papers moving prepositions away from the ends
of sentences*
Ernest Gowers *Plain Words* (1948) 'Troubles
with Prepositions'

11 *on why Clement Attlee was unlikely to go to
America to deal with the financial crisis:*
When the mouse is away the cats
might play.
Cynthia Gladwyn diary, 17 August 1949

12 Naval tradition? Monstrous.
Nothing but rum, sodomy, prayers,
and the lash.
*often quoted as, 'rum, sodomy, and the lash', as
in Peter Gretton* Former Naval Person *(1968)*
Harold Nicolson diary, 17 August 1950

13 The candle in that great turnip has
gone out.
*in reply to the comment 'One never hears of
Baldwin nowadays — he might as well be dead'*
Harold Nicolson diary, 17 August 1950

14 The object of Parliament is to
substitute argument for fisticuffs.
speech in the House of Commons, 6 June 1951

15 When the English history of the
first quarter of the twentieth
century is written, it will be seen
that the greater part of our fortunes
in peace and in war were shaped by
this one man.
*of **Lloyd George***
in *Evening Standard* 4 October 1951

16 It is an error to believe that the
world began when any particular
party or statesman got into office.

It has all been going on quite a long time.
speech at the Guildhall, London, 9 November 1951

1 She comes to the throne at a time when a tormented mankind stands uncertainly poised between world catastrophe and a golden age.
on the accession of **Elizabeth II**
in the House of Commons, 11 February 1952

2 A modest man who has much to be modest about.
of Clement **Attlee**
in *Chicago Sunday Tribune Magazine of Books* 27 June 1954

3 I am prepared to meet my Maker. Whether my Maker is prepared for the great ordeal of meeting me is another matter.
at a news conference in Washington in 1954

4 To jaw-jaw is always better than to war-war.
speech at the White House, 26 June 1954

5 It was the nation and the race dwelling all round the globe that had the lion's heart. I had the luck to be called upon to give the roar.
speech at Westminster Hall, 30 November 1954

6 Foster Dulles is the only case I know of a bull who carries his china shop with him.
c. 1956, Leonard Mosley *Dulles* (1978)

7 I still have the ideas, Walter, but I can't find the words to clothe them.
to Walter Monckton
Tony Benn diary, 15 December 1956

8 *of Lord* **Montgomery**:
In defeat unbeatable: in victory unbearable.
Edward Marsh *Ambrosia and Small Beer* (1964)

9 'Joe' was the one who made the weather.
of Joseph **Chamberlain**
Great Contemporaries (1937)

10 *of* **Balfour**'s *moving from* **Asquith**'s *Cabinet to that of* **Lloyd George**:
Like a powerful graceful cat walking delicately and unsoiled across a rather muddy street.
Great Contemporaries (1937)

11 *of the career of Lord* **Curzon**:
The morning had been golden; the noontide was bronze; and the evening lead. But all were solid, and each was polished till it shone after its fashion.
Great Contemporaries (1937)

12 No part of the education of a politician is more indispensable than the fighting of elections.
Great Contemporaries (1937)

13 *when taking the entrance examination for Harrow, Churchill's answer paper consisted of his own name and a bracketed figure 1 for the first question:*
It was from these slender indications of scholarship that Mr Welldon drew the conclusion that I was worthy to pass into Harrow. It is very much to his credit.
My Early Life (1930)

14 Headmasters have powers at their disposal with which Prime Ministers have never yet been invested.
My Early Life (1930)

15 I am biased in favour of boys learning English. I would make them all learn English: and then I would let the clever ones learn Latin as an honour, and Greek as a treat.
My Early Life (1930)

16 Mr Gladstone read Homer for fun, which I thought served him right.
My Early Life (1930)

17 It may be that vengeance is sweet, and that the gods forbade vengeance to men because they reserved for themselves so delicious and intoxicating a drink. But no one should drain the cup to the bottom. The dregs are often filthy-tasting.
The River War (1899)

18 The influence of the religion [Islam] paralyses the social development of those who follow it. No stronger retrograde force exists in the world.
The River War (1899)

19 In war: resolution. In defeat: defiance. In victory: magnanimity.

In peace: goodwill.
The Second World War vol. 1 (1948) epigraph, which according to Edward Marsh in *A Number of People* (1939), occurred to Churchill shortly after the conclusion of the First World War

1 The loyalties which centre upon number one are enormous. If he trips he must be sustained. If he makes mistakes they must be covered. If he sleeps he must not be wantonly disturbed. If he is no good he must be pole-axed. But this last extreme process cannot be carried out every day; and certainly not in the days just after he has been chosen.
The Second World War vol. 2 (1949)

2 It may almost be said, 'Before Alamein we never had a victory. After Alamein we never had a defeat.'
The Second World War (1951) vol. 4

3 I did not suffer from any desire to be relieved of my responsibilities. All I wanted was compliance with my wishes after reasonable discussion.
The Second World War (1951) vol. 4

4 *of the General Election of 1922:*
In the twinkling of an eye I found myself without an office, without a seat, without a party, and without an appendix.
Thoughts and Adventures (1932)

5 *of the qualifications desirable in a prospective politician:*
The ability to foretell what is going to happen tomorrow, next week, next month, and next year. And to have the ability afterwards to explain why it didn't happen.
B. Adler *Churchill Wit* (1965)

6 As to freedom of the press, why should any man be allowed to buy a printing press and disseminate pernicious opinions calculated to embarrass the government?
Piers Brendon *Winston Churchill* (1984)

7 *of his recurring depression:*
Black dog is back again.
attributed

8 An empty taxi arrived at 10 Downing Street, and when the door was opened Attlee got out.
attributed to Churchill, but strongly repudiated by him
Kenneth Harris *Attlee* (1982)

9 Feed a bee on royal jelly, and it becomes a queen.
on Attlee's showing unexpected authority as Prime Minister
attributed

10 The geese who laid the golden eggs but never cackled.
on the Enigma code-breakers at Bletchley Park, who never spoke of their work
attributed; Ronald Lewin *Ultra Goes to War* (1978)

11 *of Stanley **Baldwin**:*
He occasionally stumbled over the truth, but hastily picked himself up and hurried on as if nothing had happened.
attributed

12 I am fond of pigs. Dogs look up to us. Cats look down on us. Pigs treat us as equals.
Martin Gilbert *Never Despair* (1988); attributed

13 If you have ten thousand regulations you destroy all respect for the law.
attributed

14 I have taken more out of alcohol than alcohol has taken out of me.
Quentin Reynolds *By Quentin Reynolds* (1964)

15 I know of no case where a man added to his dignity by standing on it.
attributed

16 In the course of my life I have often had to eat my words, and I must confess that I have always found it a wholesome diet.
W. Manchester *The Caged Lion* (1988)

17 Most wars in history have been avoided simply by postponing them.
J. K. Galbraith *A Life in Our Times* (1981)

18 A sheep in sheep's clothing.
*of Clement **Attlee***
Lord Home *The Way the Wind Blows* (1976)

19 Take away that pudding—it has no theme.
Lord Home *The Way the Wind Blows* (1976)

1 There but for the grace of God, goes God.
of Stafford Cripps
P. Brendon *Churchill* (1984)

2 The United States always does the right thing, after exploring every other possible course of action.
attributed; H. Rawson and M. Miner *Oxford Dictionary of American Quotations* (2006)

3 *of Alfred Bossom:*
Who is this man whose name is neither one thing nor the other?
attributed

4 BESSIE BRADDOCK: Winston, you're drunk.
CHURCHILL: Bessie, you're ugly. But tomorrow I shall be sober.
an exchange with the Labour MP Bessie Braddock; J. L. Lane (ed.) *Sayings of Churchill* (1992)

Count Galeazzo Ciano 1903–44
Italian fascist politician; son-in-law of **Mussolini**

5 Victory has a hundred fathers, but defeat is an orphan.
diary, 9 September 1942 (literally 'no-one wants to recognize defeat as his own')

Cicero 106–43 BC
Roman orator and statesman. On Cicero:
see **Plutarch 247:3**, **Stevenson 301:8**; see also **Misquotations 215:3**

6 For he delivers his opinions as though he were living in Plato's Republic rather than among the dregs of Romulus.
of M. Porcius Cato, the Younger
Ad Atticum

7 *Salus populi suprema est lex.*
The good of the people is the chief law.
De Legibus; see **Selden 276:7**

8 Let war yield to peace, laurels to paeans.
De Officiis

9 In men of the highest character and noblest genius there is to be found

an insatiable desire for honour, command, power, and glory.
De Officiis

10 The sinews of war, unlimited money.
Fifth Philippic; see **Bacon 17:11**

11 *O tempora, O mores!*
Oh, the times! Oh, the manners!
In Catilinam

12 *Civis Romanus sum.*
I am a Roman citizen.
In Verrem

13 Laws are silent in time of war.
Pro Milone

14 The young man should be praised, decorated, and got rid of.
*of Octavian, the future Emperor **Augustus***
referred to in a letter from Decimus Brutus to Cicero; *Epistulae ad Familiares*

Edward Hyde, Lord Clarendon
1609–74
English statesman and historian

15 Without question, when he first drew the sword, he threw away the scabbard.
of the parliamentarian John Hampden (1594–1643)
The History of the Rebellion (1703) vol. 3

16 He had a head to contrive, a tongue to persuade, and a hand to execute any mischief.
of the parliamentarian John Hampden (1594–1643)
The History of the Rebellion (1703) vol. 3

17 He...would, with a shrill and sad accent, ingeminate the word *Peace, Peace.*
*of **Falkland***
The History of the Rebellion (1703) vol. 3

18 So enamoured on peace that he would have been glad the King should have bought it at any price.
*of **Falkland***
The History of the Rebellion (1703) vol. 3

19 He will be looked upon by posterity

Civil Service
'Yes, Minister! No, Minister'
see Selective Subject Index

as a brave bad man.
of Cromwell
The History of the Rebellion (1703) vol. 6

Alan Clark 1928–99
British Conservative politician

1 In the end we are all sacked and it's always awful. It is as inevitable as death following life. If you are elevated there comes a day when you are demoted. Even Prime Ministers.
diary, 21 June 1983

2 Give a civil servant a good case and he'll wreck it with clichés, bad punctuation, double negatives and convoluted apology.
diary, 22 July 1983

3 Like most Chief Whips he knew who the shits were.
of Michael Jopling
diary, 17 June 1987

4 There are no true friends in politics. We are all sharks circling, and waiting, for traces of blood to appear in the water.
diary, 30 November 1990

5 Our old friend economical...with the *actualité*.
under cross-examination at the Old Bailey during the Matrix Churchill case
in *Independent* 10 November 1992; see **Armstrong 12:11**

6 If I can comport myself with the dignity and competence of Ms Mo Mowlam, I shall be very satisfied.
after surgery for a brain tumour
in *Sunday Times* 6 June 1999 'Talking Heads'

Helen Clark 1950–
New Zealand stateswoman

7 I sometimes wonder whether I'm a victim of my own success as a popular and competent Prime Minister.
accusing the Green Party of colluding in a smear campaign against her
in *New Zealand Herald* 2 September 2003

Kenneth Clarke 1940–
British Conservative politician

8 Tell your kids to get their scooters off my lawn.
*allegedly said to the Party Chairman, Brian Mawhinney; see **Wilson***
in *Guardian* 7 December 1996

9 One of the guidelines which I have laid down throughout my chancellorship is no return to boom and bust.
speech, House of Commons, 30 October 1996; see **Brown 43:4, Lawson 181:7**

Karl von Clausewitz 1780–1831
Prussian soldier and military theorist

10 The first, the supreme, the most far-reaching act of judgement that the statesman and commander have to make is to establish...the kind of war on which they are embarking.
On War (1832–4) bk 1, ch. 27

11 The general unreliability of all information presents a special problem in war: all action takes place, so to speak, in a kind of twilight, which, like fog or moonlight, often tends to make things seem grotesque and larger than they really are.
often alluded to by the phrase 'fog of war'
On War (1832–4) bk 2, ch. 2

12 The closer these practical probabilities drive war toward the absolute, the more the belligerent states are involved and drawn into its vortex, the clearer appear the connections between its separate actions, and the more imperative the need not to take the first step without considering the last.
On War (1832–4) bk. 8, ch. 3

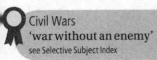

Civil Wars
'war without an enemy'
see Selective Subject Index

1 War is nothing but a continuation of politics with the admixture of other means.
   commonly rendered 'War is the continuation of politics by other means'
   On War (1832–4) bk. 8, ch. 6

Henry Clay 1777–1852
American politician. On Clay: see **Glasscock 126:3**, **Jackson 153:10**

2 I am for resistance by the *sword*. No man in the nation desires peace more than I. But I prefer the troubled ocean of war...to the tranquil, putrescent pool of ignominious peace.
   speech in the US Senate on the Macon Bill, 22 February 1810

3 If you wish to avoid foreign collision, you had better abandon the ocean.
   in the House of Representatives, 22 January 1812

4 The gentleman [Josiah Quincy] can not have forgotten his own sentiment, uttered even on the floor of this House, 'peaceably if we can, forcibly if we must'.
   speech in Congress, 8 January 1813

5 [Andrew Jackson] is ignorant, passionate, hypocritical, corrupt, and easily swayed by the basest men who surround him.
   letter to Francis T. Brooke, 2 August 1833

6 The arts of power and its minions are the same in all countries and in all ages. It marks a victim; denounces it; and excites the public odium and the public hatred, to conceal its own abuses and encroachments.
   speech in the Senate, 14 March 1834

7 Sir, politics make strange bed-fellows!
   speech in the Senate, 24 February 1835; see **Warner 325:13**

8 I had rather be right than be

President.
   to Senator Preston of South Carolina, 1839

9 It has been my invariable rule to do all for the Union. If any man wants the key of my heart, let him take the key of the Union, and that is the key to my heart.
   speech in Norfolk, 22 April 1844

10 I have heard something said about allegiance to the South. I know no South, no North, no East, no West, to which I owe any allegiance...The Union, sir, is my country.
   speech in the US Senate, 1848

Eldridge Cleaver 1935–98
American political activist

11 What we're saying today is that you're either part of the solution or you're part of the problem.
   speech in San Francisco, 1968; R. Scheer *Eldridge Cleaver, Post Prison Writings and Speeches* (1969)

John Cleese 1939– and Connie Booth 1944–

12 They're Germans. Don't mention the war.
   Fawlty Towers 'The Germans' (BBC TV programme, 1975)

Nick Clegg 1967–
British Liberal Democrat politician, Deputy Prime Minister from 2010

13 We are talking about the biggest foreign policy mistake since Suez.
   on the Iraq war
   in *Observer* 14 June 2009

Georges Clemenceau 1841–1929
French statesman; Prime Minister of France, 1906–9, 1917–20. On Clemenceau: see **Keynes 169:1**, **Lloyd George 189:4**; see also **Proverbs 252:1**

14 My home policy: I wage war; my foreign policy: I wage war. All the

Class
'know our proper stations'
see Selective Subject Index

time I wage war.
speech to French Chamber of Deputies,
8 March 1918

1 *to André Tardieu, on being asked why he
always gave in to Lloyd George at the Paris
Peace Conference, 1918*
What do you expect when I'm
between two men of whom
one [Lloyd George] thinks he is
Napoleon and the other [Woodrow
Wilson] thinks he is Jesus Christ?
Harold Nicolson letter, 20 May 1919

2 It is easier to make war than to
make peace.
speech at Verdun, 20 July 1919

3 God Almighty was satisfied with
Ten Commandments. Mr Wilson
requires Fourteen Points.
during the Peace Conference negotiations in
1919; Leon Harris *The Fine Art of Political Wit*
(1965)

4 *on seeing a pretty girl on his eightieth
birthday:*
Oh, to be seventy again!
James Agate diary, 19 April 1938; has also
been attributed to Oliver Wendell **Holmes** Jr.

5 War is too serious a matter to
entrust to military men.
attributed to Clemenceau, but also to Briand
and Talleyrand; see also **de Gaulle 87:16**

Grover Cleveland 1837–1908
American Democratic statesman; 22nd and 24th
President of the US 1885–9 and 1893–7. On
Cleveland: see **Bragg 40:9**

6 Your every voter, as surely as your
chief magistrate, exercises a public
trust.
*'public office is a public trust' was used as the
motto of the Cleveland administration*
inaugural address, 4 March 1885

7 I have considered the pension list of
the republic a roll of honour.
veto of Dependent Pension Bill, 5 July 1888

8 The lessons of paternalism ought
to be unlearned and the better
lesson taught that, while the people
should patriotically and cheerfully
support their government, its
functions do not include the
support of the people.
inaugural address, 4 March 1893

Harlan Cleveland 1918–2008
American government official

9 The revolution of rising
expectations.
phrase coined, 1950; see Arthur Schlesinger *A
Thousand Days* (1965)

Hillary Rodham Clinton 1947–
American lawyer and Democratic politician, wife of Bill
Clinton, First Lady of the US 1993–2001

10 I am not standing by my man,
like Tammy Wynette. I am sitting
here because I love him, I respect
him, and I honour what he's been
through and what we've been
through together.
interview on *60 Minutes*, CBS-TV, 27 January
1992

11 I could have stayed home and
baked cookies and had teas. But
what I decided was to fulfil my
profession, which I entered before
my husband was in public life.
comment on questions raised by rival
Democratic contender Edmund G. Brown Jr.; in
Albany Times-Union 17 March 1992

12 The great story here…is this vast
right-wing conspiracy that has been
conspiring against my husband
since the day he announced for
president.
interview on *Today* (NBC television),
27 January 1998

13 A hard dog to keep on the porch.
on her husband
in *Guardian* 2 August 1999

14 If I misspoke that was just a
misstatement.
*after wrongly claiming during her presidential
campaign that she had been under sniper fire
in Bosnia*
meeting with editorial board of the
Philadelphia Daily News, 24 March 2008

15 Although we weren't able to shatter
that highest, hardest glass ceiling
this time, thanks to you, it has
about 18 million cracks in it.
speech to her supporters, conceding the
Democratic party presidential nomination to
Barack Obama, 7 June 2008

16 My husband is not the Secretary of
State, I am. So you ask my opinion.
I will tell my opinion. I'm not going

to be channelling my husband.
when asked what her husband thought about an issue
    interview in Kinshasa, 10 August 2009

William Jefferson ('Bill') Clinton 1946–
American Democratic statesman; 42nd President of the US 1993–2001; husband of Hillary Rodham **Clinton**. On Clinton: see **Jackson 154:2**

1 I experimented with marijuana a time or two. And I didn't like it, and I didn't inhale.
    in *Washington Post* 30 March 1992

2 The comeback kid!
description of himself after coming second in the New Hampshire primary in the 1992 presidential election (since 1952, no presidential candidate had won the election without first winning in New Hampshire)
    Michael Barone and Grant Ujifusa *The Almanac of American Politics 1994*

3 The urgent question of our time is whether we can make change our friend and not our enemy.
    inaugural address, 1993

4 There is nothing wrong with America that cannot be fixed by what is right with America.
    inaugural address, 1993

5 I did not have sexual relations with that woman.
    in a television interview, *Daily Telegraph* (electronic edition) 27 January 1998

6 I did have a relationship with Ms Lewinsky that was not appropriate. In fact, it was wrong.
broadcast to the American people, 18 August 1998
    in *Times* 19 August 1998

7 It depends on what the meaning of 'is' is.
videotaped evidence to the grand jury; tapes broadcast 21 September 1998
    in *Guardian* 22 September 1998

8 The American people have spoken—but it's going to take a little while to determine exactly what they said.
on the US presidential election of 2000
    in *Mail on Sunday* 12 November 2000; compare **Salisbury**

9 I tried to walk a fine line between

acting lawfully and testifying falsely but I now recognize that I did not fully accomplish that goal.
    in *Daily Telegraph* 20 January 2001

Lord Clive 1725–74
British general; Governor of Bengal

10 By God, Mr Chairman, at this moment I stand astonished at my own moderation!
reply during Parliamentary cross-examination, 1773
    G. R. Gleig *The Life of Robert, First Lord Clive* (1848)

11 *while attempting to take his own life, his pistol twice failed to fire:*
I feel that I am reserved for some end or other.
    G. R. Gleig *The Life of Robert, First Lord Clive* (1848)

Vernon Coaker 1953–
British Labour politician

12 Cameron's empty idea seems to be 'let's hug a hoodie', whatever they have done.
commenting on the text of a forthcoming speech by David Cameron: see **Cameron 54:10**;
    in *Observer* 9 July 2006

Thomas W. Cobb 1784–1830
American politician

13 If you persist, the Union will be dissolved. You have kindled a fire which all the waters of the ocean cannot put out, which seas of blood can only extinguish.
to James Tallmadge, on his amendment to the bill to admit Missouri to the Union as a slave state in 1820
    Robert V. Remini *Henry Clay* (1991)

William Cobbett 1762–1835
English political reformer and radical journalist

14 Nouns of number, or multitude, such as Mob, Parliament, Rabble, House of Commons, Regiment, Court of King's Bench, Den of Thieves, and the like.
    English Grammar (1817) letter 17 'Syntax as Relating to Pronouns'

15 From a very early age, I had

imbibed the opinion, that it was every man's duty to do all that lay in his power to leave his country as good as he had found it.
Political Register 22 December 1832

1 But what is to be the fate of the great wen of all? The monster, called...'the metropolis of the empire'?
of London
Rural Rides: The Kentish Journal 5 January 1822

Claud Cockburn 1904–81
British writer and journalist

2 I am prepared to believe that a lot of the people I had cast as principal figures were really mere cat's-paws. But then a cat's-paw is a cat's-paw and must expect to be treated as part of the cat.
of his writing about the 'Cliveden Set'
Crossing the Line (1958)

3 Believe nothing until it has been officially denied.
advice frequently given to the young Claud Cockburn
In Time of Trouble (1956)

George M. Cohan 1878–1942
American songwriter, dramatist, and producer

4 Over there, over there,
Send the word, send the word over there
That the Yanks are coming, the Yanks are coming,
The drums rum-tumming everywhere.
So prepare, say a prayer,
Send the word, send the word to beware.
We'll be over, we're coming over
And we won't come back till it's over, over there.
'Over There' (1917 song)

Edward Coke 1552–1634
English jurist

5 Magna Charta is such a fellow, that he will have no sovereign.
on the Lords' Amendment to the Petition of Right, 17 May 1628; J. Rushworth Historical Collections *(1659) vol. 1*

Jean-Baptiste Colbert 1619–83
French statesman; chief minister to Louis XIV 1665–83

6 The art of taxation consists in so plucking the goose as to obtain the largest possible amount of feathers with the smallest possible amount of hissing.
attributed

Richard Law, Lord Coleraine
1901–80
British writer, son of Andrew **Bonar Law**

7 When all is said, the floating vote lives up to its name. It floats with the tide; and whoever would influence it must first influence the tide.
For Conservatives Only (1970)

Samuel Taylor Coleridge
1772–1834
English poet, critic, and philosopher

8 State policy, a cyclops with one eye, and that in the back of the head!
On the Constitution of the Church and State (1839)

9 In politics, what begins in fear usually ends in folly.
Table Talk (1835) 5 October 1830

Michael Collins 1890–1922
Irish revolutionary

10 That volley which we have just heard is the only speech which it is proper to make over the grave of a dead Fenian.
at the funeral of Thomas Ashe, who had died in prison while on hunger strike
at Glasnevin cemetery, 30th September 1917

11 Think—what I have got for Ireland? Something which she has wanted these past seven hundred years. Will anyone be satisfied at the bargain? Will anyone? I tell you this—early this morning I signed my death warrant. I thought at the time how odd, how ridiculous—a bullet may just as well have done the job five years ago.
on signing the treaty establishing the Irish Free State; he was shot from ambush in the following year
letter, 6 December 1921

1 *on arriving at Dublin Castle for the handover*
   by British forces on 16 January 1922, and
   being told that he was seven minutes late:
   We've been waiting 700 years, you
   can have the seven minutes.
     Tim Pat Coogan *Michael Collins* (1990);
     attributed

2 Because of his sincerity, I would
   forgive him anything.
     after the death of Cathal **Brugha**, *July 1922*
     Robert Kee *Ourselves Alone* (1976)

3 My own fellow-countrymen won't
   kill me.
     before leaving for Cork where he was ambushed
     and killed, 20 August 1922
     James Mackay *Michael Collins* (1996)

John Robert Colombo 1936–
Canadian writer

4 Canada could have enjoyed:
   English government,
   French culture,
   and American know-how.
   Instead it ended up with:
   English know-how,
   French government,
   and American culture.
     'O Canada' (1965)

Henry Steele Commager 1902–98
American historian

5 It was observed half a century
   ago that what is a stone wall to a
   layman, to a corporate lawyer is a
   triumphant arch. Much the same
   might be said of civil rights and
   freedoms. To the layman the Bill
   of Rights seems to be a stone wall
   against the misuse of power. But
   in the hands of a congressional
   committee, or often enough of a
   judge, it turns out to be so full of
   exceptions and qualifications that
   it might be a whole series of arches.
     'The Right to Dissent' in *Current History*
     October 1955; see **Dunne 100:3**

Barber B. Conable Jr. 1922–
American Republican politician and banker

6 I guess we have found the smoking
   pistol, haven't we?
     on hearing a tape of President **Nixon**'s *discussion*
     with H. R. **Haldeman**, *on 23 June 1972, as to*
     how the FBI's investigation of the Watergate
     burglary could be limited
     Nigel Rees *Brewer's Quotations* (1994)

Gerry Conlon 1954–
Northern Irish member of the Guildford Four, the first
to be released from prison

7 The life sentence goes on. It's like
   a runaway train that you can't just
   get off.
     of life after his conviction was quashed by the
     Court of Appeal
     in *Irish Post* 13 September 1997

James M. Connell see Songs 297:5

Sean Connery 1930–
Scottish actor

8 We have waited nearly 300 years.
   My hope is that it will evolve
   with dignity and integrity and it
   will truly reflect the new voice of
   Scotland. My position on Scotland
   has never changed in 30-odd years.
   Scotland should be nothing less
   than an equal of other nations of
   the world.
     in *Daily Telegraph* 27 April 1999

Billy Connolly 1942–
Scottish comedian

9 I don't want a Stormont. I don't
   want a wee pretendy government in
   Edinburgh.
     on the prospective Scottish Parliament; often
     quoted as 'a wee pretendy Parliament'
     interview on *Breakfast with Frost* (BBC TV),
     9 February 1997

Communism
'Workers of the world, unite'
see Selective Subject Index

Cyril Connolly 1903–74
English writer

1 In the eighteenth century he would have become Prime Minister before he was thirty; as it was he appeared honourably ineligible for the struggle of life.
on **Home**
Enemies of Promise (1938)

James Connolly 1868–1916
Irish labour leader and nationalist; executed after the Easter Rising, 1916

2 Apostles of freedom are ever idolised when dead, but crucified when alive.
in *Workers' Republic* August 1898

3 The worker is the slave of capitalist society, the female worker is the slave of that slave.
The Re-conquest of Ireland (1915)

4 The time for Ireland's battle is NOW, the place for Ireland's battle is HERE.
in *The Workers' Republic* 22 January 1916

5 I can always guarantee that the Irish Citizen Army will fight, but I cannot guarantee that it will be on time.
Diana Norman *Terrible Beauty* (1987)

Joseph Conrad 1857–1924
Polish-born English novelist

6 The terrorist and the policeman both come from the same basket.
The Secret Agent (1907)

7 The scrupulous and the just, the noble, humane, and devoted natures; the unselfish and the intelligent may begin a movement—but it passes away from them. They are not the leaders of a revolution. They are its victims.
Under Western Eyes (1911)

Constitution of the United States 1787
the first ten amendments are known as the Bill of Rights

8 We the people of the United States, in order to form a more perfect Union, establish justice, insure domestic tranquillity, provide for the common defense, promote the general welfare, and secure the blessings of liberty to ourselves and our posterity do ordain and establish this Constitution for the United States of America.
preamble (see also **Rice 258:8**)

9 Representatives and direct taxes shall be apportioned among the several States which may be included within this Union, according to their respective numbers, which shall be determined by adding to the whole number of free persons, including those bound to service for a term of years, and excluding Indians not taxed, three fifths of all other persons.
article 1, sect. 2 (see also **Rice 258:8**)

10 He shall from time to time give to the Congress information of the state of the Union, and recommend to their consideration such measures as he shall judge necessary and expedient.
origin of the 'State of the Union' address
article 2, sect. 3 'President shall communicate to Congress'

11 Congress shall make no law respecting an establishment of religion, or prohibiting the free exercise thereof; or abridging the freedom of speech, or of the press; or the right of the people peaceably to assemble, and to petition the government for a redress of grievances.
First Amendment (1791)

12 A well-regulated militia, being necessary to the security of a free State, the right of the people to keep and bear arms, shall not be infringed.
Second Amendment (1791)

13 Nor shall any person subject for the same offense to be twice put in jeopardy of life or limb; nor shall be compelled in any criminal case to

be a witness against himself, nor be deprived of life, liberty, or property, without due process of law.
Fifth Amendment (1791)

1 Excessive bail shall not be required, nor excessive fines imposed, nor cruel and unusual punishment inflicted.
Eighth Amendment (1791)

A. J. Cook 1885–1931
English labour leader; Secretary of the Miners' Federation of Great Britain, 1924–31

2 Not a penny off the pay, not a second on the day.
often quoted with 'minute' substituted for 'second'
speech at York, 3 April 1926

Peter Cook 1937–95
British satirist and performer

3 We need a futile gesture at this stage. It will raise the whole tone of the war.
Beyond the Fringe (1961)

Robin Cook 1946–2005
British Labour politician

4 Our foreign policy must have an ethical dimension and must support the demands of other people for the democratic rights on which we insist for ourselves.
mission statement as the new Foreign Secretary, 12 May 1997, in *Times* 13 May 1997

5 Why is it now so urgent that we should take military action to disarm a military capacity that has been there for 20 years, and which we helped to create?
resigning from the government over Iraq
speech in the House of Commons, 17 March 2003

6 They found more dangerous chemicals in Coca-Cola's Dasani mineral water than they did in the whole of Iraq.
speaking at the Edinburgh Book Festival, in *Observer* 29 August 2004

Calvin Coolidge 1872–1933
American Republican statesman; 30th President of the US 1923–9. On Coolidge: see **Anonymous 10:6**, **Mencken 211:2**, **Parker 239:12**

7 There is no right to strike against the public safety by anybody, anywhere, any time.
telegram to Samuel Gompers, 14 September 1919

8 Civilization and profits go hand in hand.
speech in New York, 27 November 1920

9 The chief business of the American people is business.
speech in Washington, 17 January 1925

10 That man has offered me unsolicited advice for six years, all of it bad.
in 1928, when asked to support the Presidential nomination of his eventual successor Herbert **Hoover**
Donald R. McCoy *Calvin Coolidge: the Quiet President* (1967)

11 The political mind is the product of men in public life who have been twice spoiled. They have been spoiled with praise and they have been spoiled with abuse. With them nothing is natural, everything is artificial.
The Autobiography of Calvin Coolidge (1929)

12 They hired the money, didn't they?
on the subject of war debts incurred by England and others
John H. McKee *Coolidge: Wit and Wisdom* (1933)

13 *account (probably apocryphal) supposedly given by Coolidge to his wife of what a preacher had said about sin:*
He was against it.
John H. McKee *Coolidge: Wit and Wisdom* (1933)

14 Nothing is easier than spending the public money. It does not appear to belong to anybody. The temptation is overwhelming to bestow it on somebody.
attributed

15 When more and more people are thrown out of work, unemployment results.
attributed; Stanley Walker *City Editor* (1934)

Francis M. Cornford 1874–1943
English academic

1 Every public action, which is not
customary, either is wrong, or, if it
is right, is a dangerous precedent. It
follows that nothing should ever be
done for the first time.
Microcosmographia Academica (1908)

2 *of propaganda:*
That branch of the art of lying
which consists in very nearly
deceiving your friends without
quite deceiving your enemies.
Microcosmographia Academica (1922 ed.)

Coronation Service

3 We present you with this Book, the
most valuable thing that this world
affords. Here is wisdom; this is
the royal Law; these are the lively
Oracles of God.
'The Presenting of the Holy Bible'; L. G.
Wickham Legge *English Coronation Records*
(1901)

Thomas Coventry 1578–1640
English judge

4 The dominion of the sea, as it is an
ancient and undoubted right of the
crown of England, so it is the best
security of the land...The wooden
walls are the best walls of this
kingdom.
speech to the Judges, 17 June 1635

Crazy Horse (Ta-Sunko-Witko)
c. 1849–77
American Sioux chief

5 One does not sell the earth upon
which the people walk.
Dee Brown *Bury My Heart at Wounded Knee*
(1970) ch. 12

Michel Guillaume Jean de Crèvecoeur 1735–1813
French-born immigrant to America

6 What then is the American, this
new man? He is either a European,
or the descendant of a European,
hence that strange mixture of
blood, which you will find in no
other country...Here individuals
of all nations are melted into a new
race of men, whose labours and
posterity will one day cause great
changes in the world.
Letters from an American Farmer (1782)

Ivor Crewe 1945–
British political scientist

7 The British public has always
displayed a healthy cynicism of
MPs. They have taken it for granted
that MPs are self-serving impostors
and hypocrites who put party
before country and self before
party.
addressing the Nolan inquiry into standards in
public life, in *Guardian* 18 January 1995

Ranulphe Crewe 1558–1646
English judge

8 And yet time hath his revolution;
there must be a period and an end
to all temporal things, *finis rerum*,
an end of names and dignities
and whatsoever is terrene; and
why not of De Vere? Where is
Bohun, where's Mowbray, where's
Mortimer? Nay, which is more and
most of all, where is Plantagenet?
They are entombed in the urns and
sepulchres of mortality. And yet let
the name and dignity of De Vere
stand so long as it pleaseth God.
speech in Oxford Peerage Case, 22 March
1626; in *Dictionary of National Biography*
(1917–) vol. 5

Corruption
'All those men have their price'
see Selective Subject Index

George Washington Crile
1864–1943
American surgeon and physiologist

1 France…a nation of forty millions
with a deep-rooted grievance and
an iron curtain at its frontier.
A Mechanistic View of War and Peace (1915)

Julian Critchley 1930–2000
British Conservative politician and journalist

2 The only safe pleasure for a
parliamentarian is a bag of boiled
sweets.
in *Listener* 10 June 1982

3 She cannot see an institution
without hitting it with her handbag.
of Margaret **Thatcher**
in *Times* 21 June 1982

4 Disloyalty is the secret weapon of
the Tory Party.
in *Observer* 11 November 1990; see
Kilmuir 171:2

Oliver Cromwell 1599–1658
English soldier and statesman; Lord Protector from
1653. See also **Last words 179:3**,
Misquotations 216:6

5 *on being asked by Lord* **Falkland** *what he
would have done if the Grand Remonstrance
of 1641 against the King had not passed:*
I would have sold all I had the next
morning, and never have seen
England more.
Clarendon *History of the Rebellion* (1826)

6 A few honest men are better than
numbers.
letter to William Spring, September 1643

7 I would rather have a plain russet-
coated captain that knows what
he fights for, and loves what he
knows, than that which you call 'a
gentleman' and is nothing else.
letter to William Spring, September 1643

8 Cruel necessity.
on the execution of **Charles I**
Joseph Spence *Anecdotes* (1820)

9 For that which you mention
concerning liberty of conscience,
I meddle not with any man's

conscience.
letter to the Governor of Ross in Ireland,
19 October 1649; W. C. Abbott *Writings and
Speeches of Oliver Cromwell* (1939) vol. 3

10 I beseech you, in the bowels of
Christ, think it possible you may be
mistaken.
letter to the General Assembly of the Kirk of
Scotland, 3 August 1650

11 The dimensions of this mercy are
above my thoughts. It is, for aught I
know, a crowning mercy.
letter to William **Lenthall**, Speaker of the
Parliament of England, 4 September 1651

12 You have sat too long here for any
good you have been doing. Depart,
I say, and let us have done with you.
In the name of God, go!
*addressing the Rump Parliament, 20 April
1653 (oral tradition; quoted by Leo* **Amery** *to
Neville* **Chamberlain** *in the House of Commons,
7 May 1940)*
Bulstrode Whitelock *Memorials of the English
Affairs* (1732 ed.)

13 Take away that fool's bauble, the
mace.
at the dismissal of the Rump Parliament,
20 April 1653; Bulstrode Whitelock *Memorials
of the English Affairs* (1732 ed.); see
Misquotations 216:5

14 It's a maxim not to be despised,
'Though peace be made, yet it's
interest that keeps peace.'
speech to Parliament, 4 September 1654

15 Necessity hath no law. Feigned
necessities, imaginary
necessities…are the greatest
cozenage that men can put upon
the Providence of God, and make
pretences to break known rules by.
speech to Parliament, 12 September 1654

16 Your poor army, those poor
contemptible men, came up hither.
speech to Parliament, 21 April 1657

17 You have accounted yourselves
happy on being environed with
a great ditch from all the world
besides.
speech to Parliament, 25 January 1658

18 Hell or Connaught.
*summary of the choice offered to the Catholic
population of Ireland, transported to the western
counties to make room for settlers*
traditionally attributed

1 None climbs so high as he who knows not whither he is going.
   attributed

2 There is no one I am more at a loss how to manage than that Marcus Tullius Cicero, the little man with three names.
   of Anthony Ashley Cooper, Lord **Shaftesbury**
   B. Martyn and Dr Kippis *The Life of the First Earl of Shaftesbury* (1836)

Walter Cronkite 1916–2009
American broadcaster and journalist

3 It seems now more certain than ever that the bloody experience of Vietnam is to end in a stalemate.
   after visiting Vietnam; see **Johnson**
   CBS special television report, 27 February 1968; quoted in D. Halberstam *The Powers That Be* (1979)

Anthony Crosland 1918–77
British Labour politician

4 Total abstinence and a good filing system are not now the right signposts to the socialist Utopia; or at least, if they are, some of us will fall by the wayside.
   The Future of Socialism (1956)

5 Harold knows best. Harold is a bastard, but he is a genius. He's like Odysseus. Odysseus was a bastard, but he managed to steer the ship between Scylla and Charybdis.
   on Harold **Wilson**
   Susan Crosland *Tony Crosland* (1982)

6 If it's the last thing I do, I'm going to destroy every fucking grammar school in England. And Wales, and Northern Ireland.
   in 1965, while Secretary of State for Education and Science; Susan Crosland *Tony Crosland* (1982)

7 The party's over.
   cutting back central government's support for rates, as Minister of the Environment in the 1970s
   Anthony Sampson *The Changing Anatomy of Britain* (1982)

Richard Crossman 1907–74
British Labour politician. On Crossman: see **Dalton 84:9**

8 The Civil Service is profoundly

deferential — 'Yes, Minister! No, Minister! If you wish it, Minister!'
   Diaries of a Cabinet Minister vol. 1 (1975) 22 October 1964

9 [To strip away] the thick masses of foliage which we call the myth of democracy.
   introduction to *Diaries of a Cabinet Minister* vol. 1 (1975)

10 As Harold Laski used to remind us, in British politics while there is death there is hope.
   on the effect of the death of Hugh **Gaitskell** *on his own career*
   introduction to *Diaries of a Cabinet Minister* vol.1 (1975)

e. e. cummings 1894–1962
American poet

11 a politician is an arse upon which everyone has sat except a man.
   1 x 1 (1944) no. 10

Mario Cuomo 1932–
American Democratic politician

12 You campaign in poetry. You govern in prose.
   in *New Republic*, Washington, DC, 8 April 1985

John Philpot Curran 1750–1817
Irish judge

13 The condition upon which God hath given liberty to man is eternal vigilance; which condition if he break, servitude is at once the consequence of his crime, and the punishment of his guilt.
   speech on the right of election of the Lord Mayor of Dublin, 10 July 1790; see **Demosthenes 88:12**

14 *of Robert* **Peel**'s smile:
   Like the silver plate on a coffin.
   quoted by Daniel **O'Connell** in the House of Commons, 26 February 1835

Edwina Currie 1946–
British Conservative politician

15 I wasn't even in the index.
   on the omission of their affair from John **Major**'s *autobiography*
   in *Times* 28 September 2002

John Curtin 1885–1945
Australian Labor statesman; Prime Minister 1941–5

1 Australia looks to America, free of any pangs as to our traditional links or kinship with the United Kingdom.
of the threat from Japan, and British reluctance to recall Australian troops from the Middle East
in *Herald* (Melbourne) 27 December 1941

Lord Curzon 1859–1925
British Conservative politician; Viceroy of India 1898–1905. On Curzon: **Anonymous 8:17, Balfour 23:9, Beaverbrook 25:12, Churchill 70:11, Nehru 224:17**

2 Other countries have but one capital—Paris, Berlin, Madrid. Great Britain has a series of capitals all over the world, from Ottawa to Shanghai.
notebook, 1887; Kenneth Rose *Superior Person* (1969)

3 When a group of Cabinet Ministers begins to meet separately and to discuss independent action, the death-tick is audible in the rafters.
*in November 1922, shortly before the fall of **Lloyd George**'s Coalition Government*
David Gilmour *Curzon* (1994)

4 Not even a public figure. A man of no experience. And of the utmost insignificance.
*of Stanley **Baldwin**, appointed Prime Minister in 1923 in succession to **Bonar Law***
Harold Nicolson *Curzon: the Last Phase* (1934)

5 I never knew that the lower classes had such white skins.
supposedly said when watching troops bathing during the First World War
Kenneth Rose *Superior Person* (1969)

Astolphe Louis Léonard, Marquis de Custine 1790–1857
French writer and traveller

6 This empire, vast as it is, is only a prison to which the emperor holds the key.
of Russia
La Russie en 1839; at Peterhof, 23 July 1839

7 Whoever has really seen Russia will find himself content to live anywhere else. It is always good to know that a society exists where no happiness is possible because, by a law of nature, man cannot be happy unless he is free.
La Russie en 1839; at Peterhof, 23 July 1839; conclusion

Richard J. Daley 1902–76
American Democratic politician and Mayor of Chicago

8 The policeman isn't there to create disorder; the policeman is there to preserve disorder.
to the press, on the riots during the Democratic Convention in 1968
Milton N. Rakove *Don't Make No Waves: Don't Back No Losers* (1975)

Hugh Dalton 1887–1962
British Labour politician. On Dalton: see **Anonymous 10:3, Birch 34:1**

9 I view this able and energetic

man with some detachment. He is loyal to his own career but only incidentally to anything or anyone else.
*of Richard **Crossman***
diary, 17 September 1941

Tam Dalyell 1932–
Scottish-born Labour politician

10 Under the new Bill, shall I still be able to vote on many matters in relation to West Bromwich but not West Lothian, as I was under the last Bill, and will my right hon.

Friend [James Callaghan, MP for Cardiff] be able to vote on many matters in relation to Carlisle but not Cardiff?
formulation of the 'West Lothian question', identifying the constitutional anomaly that would arise if devolved assemblies were established for Scotland and for Wales but not for England
in the House of Commons, 3 November 1977

1 The West-Lothian-West-Bromwich problem pinpoints a basic design fault in the steering of the devolutionary coach which will cause it to crash into the side of the road.
in the House of Commons, 14 November 1977

2 I make no apology for returning yet again to the subject of the sinking of the *Belgrano*.
on the question of whether the Argentine cruiser Belgrano had been a legitimate target in the Falklands War
in the House of Commons, 13 May 1983

George Dangerfield 1904–86
British historian

3 To reform the House of Lords [in 1910] meant to set down in writing a Constitution which for centuries had remained happily unwritten, to conjure a great ghost into the narrow and corruptible flesh of a code.
The Strange Death of Liberal England (1936)

Samuel Daniel 1563–1619
English poet and dramatist

4 Princes in this case
Do hate the traitor, though they love the treason.
The Tragedy of Cleopatra (1594)

Georges Jacques Danton 1759–94
French revolutionary

5 *De l'audace, et encore de l'audace, et toujours de l'audace!*
Boldness, and again boldness, and always boldness!
speech to the Legislative Committee of General Defence, 2 September 1792

6 Thou wilt show my head to the

people: it is worth showing.
to his executioner, 5 April 1794
Thomas Carlyle *History of the French Revolution* (1837) vol. 3

Bill Darnell
Canadian environmentalist

7 Make it a *green* peace.
at a meeting of the Don't Make a Wave Committee, which preceded the formation of Greenpeace
in Vancouver, 1970; Robert Hunter *The Greenpeace Chronicle* (1979); see
Hunter 150:4

Clarence Darrow 1857–1938
American lawyer

8 When I was a boy I was told that anybody could become President. I'm beginning to believe it.
Irving Stone *Clarence Darrow for the Defence* (1941)

Harry Daugherty 1860–1941
American Republican supporter

9 Some twelve or fifteen men, worn out and bleary-eyed for lack of sleep, will sit down about two o'clock in the morning around a table in a smoke-filled room in some hotel and decide the nomination.
the way in which the Republican Party's presidential candidate for 1920 would be selected if (as in fact happened) no clear nomination emerged from the convention; see
Simpson
attributed (although subsequently denied by Daugherty); William Safire *The New Language of Politics* (1968)

Charles D'Avenant 1656–1714
English dramatist and political economist

10 Custom, that unwritten law,
By which the people keep even kings in awe.
Circe (1677)

Robertson Davies 1913–95
Canadian novelist

11 I see Canada as a country torn between a very northern, rather extraordinary, mystical spirit which it fears and its desire to

present itself to the world as a
Scotch banker.
The Enthusiasms of Robertson Davies (1990)

Ron Davies 1946–
British Labour politician

1 It was a moment of madness for
which I have subsequently paid a
very, very heavy price.
*of the episode on Clapham Common leading to
his resignation as Welsh Secretary*
interview with BBC Wales and HTV, 30 October
1998

Jefferson Davis 1808–89
American statesman; President of the Confederate
states 1861–5. On Davis: see **Yancey 339:2**

2 If the Confederacy fails, there
should be written on its tombstone:
Died of a Theory.
in 1865; Geoffrey C. Ward *The Civil War* (1991)

Thomas Davis 1814–45
Irish poet and nationalist

3 But the land of their heart's hope
they never saw more,
For in far, foreign fields, from
Dunkirk to Belgrade
Lie the soldiers and chiefs of the Irish
Brigade.
'The Battle-Eve of the Brigade' (1845)

4 Viva la the New Brigade!
Viva la the Old One, too!
Viva la, the Rose shall fade,
And the shamrock shine for ever new.
'Clare's Dragoons' (1845)

5 And then I prayed I yet might see
Our fetters rent in twain,
And Ireland, long a province, be
A Nation once again.
'A Nation Once Again' (1846)

6 But—hark!—some voice like
thunder spake:
The West's awake! the West's awake!
'The West's Asleep' (1845); see
Robinson 260:11

Michael Davitt 1846–1905
Irish nationalist

7 An Englishman of the strongest

type moulded for an Irish purpose.
of Charles Stewart **Parnell**
The Fall of Feudalism in Ireland (1906)

Lord Dawson of Penn 1864–1945
British physician to King **George V**

8 The King's life is moving peacefully
towards its close.
*bulletin, drafted on a menu card at Buckingham
Palace on the eve of the king's death, 20 January
1936*
Kenneth Rose *King George V* (1983)

Stockwell Burt Day 1950–
Canadian Progressive Conservative politician

9 God's law is clear. Standards
of education are not set by
government, but by God, the Bible,
the home and the school.
Alberta Report, 1984

John Dean 1938–
American lawyer and White House counsel during the
Watergate affair

10 We have a cancer within, close to
the Presidency, that is growing.
from the [Nixon] Presidential Transcripts,
21 March 1973

Régis Debray 1940–
French Marxist theorist

11 International life is right-wing, like
nature. The social contract is left-
wing, like humanity.
Charles de Gaulle (1994)

Eugene Victor Debs 1855–1926
American socialist

12 When great changes occur in
history, when great principles are
involved, as a rule the majority are
wrong. The minority are right.
*speech at his trial for sedition in Cleveland, Ohio,
11 September 1918*
Speeches (1928)

13 While there is a lower class, I am in
it; while there is a criminal element,
I am of it; while there is a soul in
prison, I am not free.
*speech at his trial for sedition in Cleveland, Ohio,
11 September 1918*
in *Liberator* November 1918

Stephen Decatur 1779–1820
American naval officer

1 Our country! In her intercourse with foreign nations, may she always be in the right; but our country, right or wrong.
Decatur's toast at Norfolk, Virginia, April 1816
A. S. Mackenzie *Life of Stephen Decatur* (1846); see **Adams 3:15**

Declaration of Arbroath

2 So long as there shall but one hundred of us remain alive, we will never subject ourselves to the dominion of the English. For it is not glory, it is not riches, neither is it honour, but it is freedom alone that we fight and contend for, which no honest man will lose but with his life.
letter sent by the Scottish Parliament, 6 April 1320, to the Pope, asserting the independence of Scotland.

Daniel Defoe 1660–1731
English novelist and journalist

3 Nature has left this tincture in the blood,
That all men would be tyrants if they could.
The History of the Kentish Petition (1712–13)

4 Fools out of favour grudge at knaves in place.
The True-Born Englishman (1701) introduction

5 From this amphibious ill-born mob began
That vain, ill-natured thing, an Englishman.
The True-Born Englishman (1701)

6 Your Roman-Saxon-Danish-Norman English.
The True-Born Englishman (1701)

7 His lazy, long, lascivious reign.
of **Charles II**
The True-Born Englishman (1701)

8 Great families of yesterday we show,
And lords whose parents were the Lord knows who.
The True-Born Englishman (1701)

9 And of all plagues with which

mankind are curst,
Ecclesiastic tyranny's the worst.
The True-Born Englishman (1701)

10 When kings the sword of justice first lay down,
They are no kings, though they possess the crown.
Titles are shadows, crowns are empty things,
The good of subjects is the end of kings.
The True-Born Englishman (1701)

Charles de Gaulle 1890–1970
French soldier and statesman; President of France, 1959–69. On de Gaulle: see **Spears 298:4**

11 France has lost a battle. But France has not lost the war!
proclamation, 18 June 1940

12 Faced by the bewilderment of my countrymen, by the disintegration of a government in thrall to the enemy, by the fact that the institutions of my country are incapable, at the moment, of functioning, I General de Gaulle, a French soldier and military leader, realize that I now speak for France.
speech in London, 19 June 1940

13 Since they whose duty it was to wield the sword of France have let it fall shattered to the ground, I have taken up the broken blade.
speech, 13 July 1940

14 Men can have friends. Statesmen cannot.
interview, spring 1959, David Schoenbrun *The Three Lives of Charles de Gaulle* (1966)

15 Yes, it is Europe, from the Atlantic to the Urals, it is Europe, it is the whole of Europe, that will decide the fate of the world.
speech to the people of Strasbourg, 23 November 1959

16 Politics are too serious a matter to be left to the politicians.
*replying to Clement **Attlee**'s remark that 'De Gaulle is a very good soldier and a very bad politician'*
Clement Attlee *A Prime Minister Remembers* (1961)

17 How can you govern a country

which has 246 varieties of cheese?
Ernest Mignon *Les Mots du Général* (1962)

1 Since a politician never believes
what he says, he is quite surprised
to be taken at his word.
Ernest Mignon *Les Mots du Général* (1962)

2 *Europe des patries.*
A Europe of nations.
1962; widely associated with de Gaulle and
taken as encapsulating his views, although
perhaps not coined by him; J. Lacouture *De
Gaulle: the Ruler* (1991)

3 Treaties, you see, are like girls and
roses: they last while they last.
speech at Elysée Palace, 2 July 1963

4 *Vive Le Québec Libre.*
Long Live Free Quebec.
*quoting the slogan of the separatist movement for
an independent Quebec*
speech in Montreal, 24 July 1967

5 I respect only those who resist me,
but I cannot tolerate them.
in *New York Times Magazine* 12 May 1968

6 Authority doesn't work without
prestige, or prestige without
distance.
Le Fil de l'épée (1932) 'Du caractère'

7 The sword is the axis of the world
and its power is absolute.
Vers l'armée de métier (1934) 'Comment?'
Commandement 3

8 *on the death of his daughter, who had been
born with Down's Syndrome:*
And now she is like everyone else.
in 1948; Jean Lacouture *De Gaulle* (1965)

9 The EEC is a horse and carriage:
Germany is the horse and France is
the coachman.
attributed; Bernard Connolly *The Rotten Heart
of Europe* (1995)

Tom DeLay 1947–
American Republican politician; Senate Majority
Leader 2002–5

10 An arrogant, out-of-control,
unaccountable judiciary that
thumbed their nose at Congress
and the president.
*statement issued after the death of the brain-
damaged Terri Schiavo, whose feeding tube was
removed by court order; an extraordinary session
of Congress had passed a bill forcing the Federal
Court to review the decision, but appeals for*

replacement of the tube were not upheld
in *The Age* (online edition) 2 April 2005

Vine Victor Deloria Jr. 1933–
American Standing Rock Sioux

11 This country was a lot better off
when the Indians were running it.
in *New York Times Magazine* 3 March 1970

Demosthenes c. 384–c. 322 BC
Greek orator and Athenian statesman

12 There is one safeguard known
generally to the wise, which is an
advantage and security to all, but
especially to democracies against
despots—suspicion.
Second Philippic; see **Curran 83:13**

13 Excessive dealings with tyrants
are not good for the security of free
states.
Second Philippic

14 When asked what was first
in oratory, [he] replied to his
questioner, 'action,' what second,
'action,' and again third, 'action'.
Cicero *Brutus* ch. 37, sect. 142

Jack Dempsey 1895–1983
American boxer

15 Honey, I just forgot to duck.
*to his wife, on losing the World Heavyweight title,
23 September 1926; after a failed attempt on his
life in 1981, Ronald **Reagan** quipped to his wife
'Honey, I forgot to duck'*
J. and B. P. Dempsey *Dempsey* (1977)

Deng Xiaoping 1904–97
Chinese Communist statesman; from 1977 paramount
leader of China

16 The colour of the cat doesn't matter
as long as it catches the mice.
proverbial expression; in *Financial Times*
18 December 1986

Lord Denning 1899–1999
British judge

17 The Treaty [of Rome] is like an
incoming tide. It flows into the
estuaries and up the rivers. It
cannot be held back.
in 1975; Anthony Sampson *The Essential
Anatomy of Britain* (1992)

1 To every subject of this land,
   however powerful, I would use
   Thomas Fuller's words over three
   hundred years ago, 'Be ye never so
   high, the law is above you.'
     in a High Court ruling against the Attorney-
     General, January 1977; see **Fuller 117:1**

2 The keystone of the rule of
   law in England has been the
   independence of judges. It is the
   only respect in which we make any
   real separation of powers.
     The Family Story (1981)

3 We shouldn't have all these
   campaigns to get the Birmingham
   Six released if they'd been hanged.
   They'd have been forgotten and
   the whole community would be
   satisfied.
     in *Spectator* 18 August 1990

4 Properly exercised the new powers
   of the executive lead to the welfare
   state; but abused they lead to the
   totalitarian state.
     Anthony Sampson *The Changing Anatomy of
     Britain* (1982)

Edward Stanley, 14th Earl of Derby 1799–1869
British Conservative statesman; Prime Minister,
1852, 1858–9, 1866–8. On Derby: see **Bulwer-
Lytton 45:6**, **Disraeli 92:7**

5 The duty of an Opposition [is] very
   simple...to oppose everything, and
   propose nothing.
     quoting 'Mr Tierney, a great Whig authority', in
     the House of Commons, 4 June 1841

6 Definition of an independent
   Member of Parliament, viz. one that
   could not be depended upon.
     memorandum by Prince Albert, 1 February
     1855, in *The Letters of Queen Victoria*
     vol. 3 (1907)

7 Meddle and muddle.
     summarizing Lord John **Russell**'s foreign policy
     speech on the Address, in the House of Lords
     4 February 1864

Camille Desmoulins 1760–94
French revolutionary

8 My age is that of the *bon Sansculotte*

Jésus; an age fatal to Revolutionists.
  reply given at his trial
  Thomas Carlyle *History of the French Revolution*
  (1837)

Eamonn de Valera 1882–1975
American-born Irish statesman; Taoiseach 1937–48,
1951–4, and 1957–9, and President of the Republic
of Ireland 1959–73. On de Valera: see **Lloyd
George 189:20**

9 I am against this Treaty, not
   because I am a man of war, but
   because I am a man of peace.
     in 1921

10 Whenever I wanted to know what
   the Irish people wanted, I had only
   to examine my own heart and it
   told me straight off what the Irish
   people wanted.
     speech in Dáil Éireann, 6 January 1922

11 Further sacrifice of life would now
   be in vain...Military victory must
   be allowed to rest for the moment
   with those who have destroyed the
   Republic.
     message to the Republican armed forces,
     24 May 1923

12 I signed it the same way as I signed
   an autograph for a newspaper.
     on taking the oath of allegiance to the King
     before entering Dáil Éireann
     in 1932, attributed

13 If I were told tomorrow, 'You can
   have a united Ireland if you give up
   the idea of restoring the national
   language to be the spoken language
   of the majority of the people,' I
   would for myself say no.
     speech in the Dáil, 1939

14 That Ireland which we dreamed of
   would be the home of a people who
   valued material wealth only as a
   basis of right living, of a people who
   were satisfied with frugal comfort
   and devoted their leisure to the
   things of the spirit; a land whose
   countryside would be bright with
   cosy homesteads, whose fields
   and villages would be joyous with
   sounds of industry, the romping
   of sturdy children, the contests
   of athletic youths, the laughter of
   comely maidens; whose firesides

would be the forums of the wisdom of serene old age.
St Patrick's Day broadcast, 17 March 1943

1 Mr Churchill is proud of Britain's stand alone, after France had fallen, and before America had entered the war. Could he not find in his heart the generosity to acknowledge that there is a small nation that stood alone, not for one year or two, but for several hundred years, against aggression; that endured spoliation, famines, massacres in endless succession; that was clubbed many times into insensibility but each time, on returning consciousness, took up the fight anew; a small nation that could never be got to accept defeat and has never surrendered her soul?
radio broadcast, 16 May 1945

2 I sometimes admit that when I think of television and radio and their immense power, I feel somewhat afraid.
at the inauguration of Telefís Éireann in 1961

3 Whoever misunderstood Madame, the poor did not.
of Constance **Markievicz**
Diana Norman *Terrible Beauty* (1987)

4 Women are at once the boldest and most unmanageable revolutionaries.
in conversation, 1975

Donald Dewar 1937–2000
Scottish Labour politician; First Minister for Scotland from 1999

5 'There shall be a Scottish parliament.' Through long years, those words were first a hope, then a belief, then a promise. Now they are a reality.
at the official opening of the Scottish Parliament speech, 1 July 1999; see **Anonymous 10:2**

6 This is about more than our politics and our laws. This is about who we are, how we carry ourselves.
at the official opening of the Scottish Parliament speech, 1 July 1999

Thomas E. Dewey 1902–71
American Republican politician and presidential candidate. On Dewey: see **Newspaper headlines 225:4**

7 That's why it's time for a change!
phrase used extensively in campaigns of 1944, 1948, and 1952
campaign speech in San Francisco, 21 September 1944

Diana, Princess of Wales 1961–97
British princess, former wife of Charles, Prince of Wales

8 I'd like to be a queen in people's hearts but I don't see myself being Queen of this country.
interview on *Panorama*, BBC1 TV, 20 November 1995

9 I'm not a political figure…I'm a humanitarian figure. I always have been and I always will be.
on taking part in the campaign against landmines in *Daily Telegraph* 17 January 1997

10 The press is ferocious. It forgives nothing, it only hunts for mistakes…In my position anyone sane would have left a long time ago.
contrasting British and foreign press in *Le Monde* 27 August 1997

Porfirio Diaz 1830–1915
Mexican revolutionary and statesman; President of Mexico, 1877–80, 1884–1911

11 Poor Mexico, so far from God and so close to the United States.
attributed

A. V. Dicey 1835–1922
British jurist

12 The beneficial effect of state intervention, especially in the form of legislation, is direct, immediate, and, so to speak, visible, while its evil effects are gradual and indirect, and lie out of sight… Hence the majority of mankind must almost of necessity look with undue favour upon government intervention.
Lectures on the Relation between Law and Public Opinion (1914)

Charles Dickens 1812–70
English novelist

1 O let us love our occupations,
Bless the squire and his relations,
Live upon our daily rations,
And always know our proper stations.
The Chimes (1844) 'The Second Quarter'

2 Annual income twenty pounds,
annual expenditure nineteen
nineteen six, result happiness.
Annual income twenty pounds,
annual expenditure twenty pounds
ought and six, result misery.
David Copperfield (1850)

3 'It's always best on these occasions
to do what the mob do.' 'But
suppose there are two mobs?'
suggested Mr Snodgrass. 'Shout
with the largest,' replied Mr
Pickwick.
Pickwick Papers (1837)

4 It was the best of times, it was
the worst of times, it was the
age of wisdom, it was the age
of foolishness, it was the epoch
of belief, it was the epoch of
incredulity, it was the season
of Light, it was the season of
Darkness, it was the spring of hope,
it was the winter of despair.
of the French Revolution
A Tale of Two Cities (1859)

5 'It is possible—that it may not
come, during our lives…We shall
not see the triumph.' 'We shall have
helped it,' returned madame.
A Tale of Two Cities (1859)

6 Detestation of the high is the
involuntary homage of the low.
A Tale of Two Cities (1859)

7 My faith in the people governing
is, on the whole, infinitesimal; my
faith in The People governed is, on
the whole, illimitable.
speech at Birmingham and Midland Institute,
27 September 1869

John Dickinson 1732–1808
American politician

8 We have counted the cost of this
contest, and find nothing so
dreadful as voluntary slavery…Our
cause is just, our union is perfect.
declaration of reasons for taking up arms against
England, presented to Congress, 8 July 1775
C. J. Stillé *The Life and Times of John Dickinson*
(1891)

9 Then join hand in hand, brave
Americans all,—
By uniting we stand, by dividing we
fall.
'The Liberty Song' (1768)

Denis Diderot 1713–84
French philosopher and man of letters

10 And [with] the guts of the last priest
Let's shake the neck of the last king.
Dithrambe sur fete de rois; see **Meslier 211:5**

Joan Didion 1934–
American writer

11 When we start deceiving ourselves
into thinking not that we want
something or need something, not
that it is a pragmatic necessity for
us to have it, but that it is a *moral
imperative* that we have it, then
is when we join the fashionable
madmen, and then is when the thin
whine of hysteria is heard in the
land, and then is when we are in
bad trouble.
Slouching towards Bethlehem (1968) 'On
Morality'

John G. Diefenbaker 1895–1979
Canadian Progressive Conservative statesman; Prime
Minister 1957–63

12 There can be no dedication
to Canada's future without a
knowledge of its past.
in *Toronto Star* 9 October 1964

John Dillon 1851–1927
Irish nationalist politician

13 I say I am proud of their courage
and if you were not so dense and
stupid, as some of you English
people are, you could have had
these men fighting for you…It is not
murderers who are being executed;
it is insurgents who have fought a
clean fight, however misguided,

and it would have been a damned good thing for you if your soldiers were able to put up as good a fight as did those men in Dublin.
of those executed after the Easter Rising
speech in the British House of Commons, 11 May 1916

Everett Dirksen 1896–1969
American Republican politician

1 A billion here and a billion there, and pretty soon you're talking real money.
on federal spending
attributed, perhaps apocryphal; in *United States Senate Historical Minute Essays* (online edition, July 2006)

Benjamin Disraeli 1804–81
British Tory statesman and novelist; Prime Minister, 1868, 1874–80. On Disraeli: see **Anonymous 10:14**, **Bismarck 34:12**, **Carlyle 57:9**, **Palmerston 238:13**; see also **Last words 179:4**

2 Between ourselves I could floor them all. This *entre nous*. I was never more confident of anything than that I could carry everything before me in that House. The time will come.
four years before he entered Parliament
letter, 7 February 1833

3 In the 'Town' yesterday, I am told 'some one asked Disraeli, in offering himself for Marylebone, on what he intended *to stand*. "On my head," was the reply.'
letter, 8 April 1833

4 Though I sit down now, the time will come when you will hear me.
maiden speech in the House of Commons, 7 December 1837

5 The Continent will [not] suffer England to be the workshop of the world.
in the House of Commons, 15 March 1838

6 Thus you have a starving population, an absentee aristocracy, and an alien Church, and in addition the weakest executive in the world. That is the Irish Question.
in the House of Commons, 16 February 1844

7 The noble Lord is the Prince Rupert of Parliamentary discussion.
of Lord Stanley, later the 14th Earl of **Derby**
in the House of Commons, 24 April 1844; see **Bulwer-Lytton 45:6**

8 The right hon. Gentleman caught the Whigs bathing, and walked away with their clothes.
on Robert **Peel***'s abandoning protection in favour of free trade, traditionally the policy of the Whig Opposition*
in the House of Commons, 28 February 1845

9 Protection is not a principle, but an expedient.
in the House of Commons, 17 March 1845

10 A Conservative Government is an organized hypocrisy.
in the House of Commons, 17 March 1845; (Bagehot, quoting Disraeli in *The English Constitution* (1867) 'The House of Lords', elaborated on the theme with the words 'so much did the ideas of its "head" differ from the sensations of its "tail"')

11 He traces the steam-engine always back to the tea-kettle.
of Robert **Peel**
in the House of Commons, 11 April 1845

12 Justice is truth in action.
in the House of Commons, 11 February 1851

13 I read this morning an awful, though monotonous, manifesto in the great organ of public opinion, which always makes me tremble: Olympian bolts; and yet I could not help fancying amid their rumbling terrors I heard the plaintive treble of the Treasury Bench.
in the House of Commons, 13 February 1851

14 These wretched colonies will all be independent, too, in a few years, and are a millstone round our necks.
letter to Lord Malmesbury, 13 August 1852

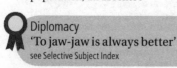
Diplomacy
'To jaw-jaw is always better'
see Selective Subject Index

1 England does not love coalitions.
   in the House of Commons, 16 December 1852

2 Finality is not the language of politics.
   in the House of Commons, 28 February 1859

3 It is, I say, in the noble Lord's power to come to some really cordial understanding...between this country and France...and to put an end to these bloated armaments which only involve states in financial embarrassment.
   in the House of Commons, 8 May 1862

4 Colonies do not cease to be colonies because they are independent.
   in the House of Commons, 5 February 1863

5 You are not going, I hope, to leave the destinies of the British Empire to prigs and pedants.
   in the House of Commons, 5 February 1863

6 Party is organized opinion.
   speech at Oxford, 25 November 1864

7 I hold that the characteristic of the present age is craving credulity.
   speech at Oxford, 25 November 1864

8 Is man an ape or an angel? Now I am on the side of the angels.
   speech at Oxford, 25 November 1864

9 Assassination has never changed the history of the world.
   in the House of Commons, 1 May 1865

10 I had to prepare the mind of the country, and...to educate our party.
   speech at Edinburgh, 29 October 1867

11 Change is inevitable in a progressive country. Change is constant; and the great question is, not whether you still resist change which is inevitable, but whether that change shall be carried out in deference to the manners, the customs, the laws and the traditions of a people, or...in deference to abstract principles and arbitrary and general doctrines.
   speech at Edinburgh, 29 October 1867

12 There can be no economy where there is no efficiency.
   address to his Constituents, 1 October 1868

13 *to Queen Victoria after the publication of* Leaves from the Journal of our Life in the Highlands *in 1868:*
   We authors, Ma'am.
   Elizabeth Longford *Victoria R.I.* (1964)

14 We have legalized confiscation, consecrated sacrilege, and condoned high treason.
   on **Gladstone**'s *Irish policy*
   in the House of Commons, 27 February 1871

15 I look upon Parliamentary Government as the noblest government in the world.
   speech at Manchester, 3 April 1872

16 I believe that without party Parliamentary government is impossible.
   speech at Manchester, 3 April 1872

17 You behold a range of exhausted volcanoes.
   of the Liberal Government
   speech at Manchester, 3 April 1872

18 Increased means and increased leisure are the two civilizers of man.
   speech at Manchester, 3 April 1872

19 The very phrase 'foreign affairs' makes an Englishman convinced that I am about to treat of subjects with which he has no concern.
   speech at Manchester, 3 April 1872

20 A University should be a place of light, of liberty, and of learning.
   in the House of Commons, 11 March 1873

21 An author who speaks about his own books is almost as bad as a mother who talks about her own children.
   at a banquet given in Glasgow on his installation as Lord Rector, 19 November 1873; in *Times* 20 November 1873

22 Upon the education of the people of this country the fate of this country depends.
   in the House of Commons, 15 June 1874

23 He is a great master of gibes and flouts and jeers.
   of Lord **Salisbury**
   in the House of Commons, 5 August 1874

24 Mr Gladstone not only appeared but rushed into the debate... The new Members trembled and

fluttered like small birds when a hawk is in the air.
letter to Queen Victoria, March 1875, after an election in which **Gladstone**'s *party had lost office*

1 Coffee house babble.
on the Bulgarian Atrocities, 1876
R. W. Seton-Watson *Britain in Europe 1789–1914* (1955)

2 Cosmopolitan critics, men who are the friends of every country save their own.
speech at Guildhall, 9 November 1877

3 Lord Salisbury and myself have brought you back peace—but a peace I hope with honour.
on returning from the Congress of Berlin
speech, 16 July 1878, in *Times* 17 July 1878;
see **Chamberlain 60:12**, **Russell 267:14**

4 A series of congratulatory regrets.
of Lord Harrington's Resolution on the Berlin Treaty
at a banquet, Knightsbridge, 27 July 1878

5 A sophistical rhetorician, inebriated with the exuberance of his own verbosity.
of **Gladstone**
in *Times* 29 July 1878

6 I admit that there is gossip…But the government of the world is carried on by sovereigns and statesmen, and not by anonymous paragraph writers…or by the hare-brained chatter of irresponsible frivolity.
speech at Guildhall, London, 9 November 1878

7 One of the greatest of Romans, when asked what were his politics, replied, *Imperium et Libertas*. That would not make a bad programme for a British Ministry.
speech at Mansion House, London, 10 November 1879, quoting a paraphrase of Tacitus by Winston Churchill (1620–88) Divi Britannici (1675): 'Here the two great interests Imperium & Libertas, res olim insociabiles (saith Tacitus), began to incounter each other';
see **Tacitus 304:3**

8 Take away that emblem of mortality.
on being offered an air cushion to sit on, 1881
Robert Blake *Disraeli* (1966)

9 I will not go down to posterity

talking bad grammar.
while correcting proofs of his last Parliamentary speech, 31 March 1881
Robert Blake *Disraeli* (1966)

10 The House of Commons is absolute. It is the State. 'L'État c'est moi.'
Coningsby (1844); see **Louis XIV 190:14**

11 A government of statesmen or of clerks? Of Humbug or Humdrum?
Coningsby (1844)

12 We owe the English peerage to three sources: the spoliation of the Church; the open and flagrant sale of honours by the elder Stuarts; and the borough-mongering of our own time.
Coningsby (1844)

13 Conservatism discards Prescription, shrinks from Principle, disavows Progress; having rejected all respect for antiquity, it offers no redress for the present, and makes no preparation for the future.
Coningsby (1844)

14 'A sound Conservative government,' said Taper, musingly. 'I understand: Tory men and Whig measures.'
Coningsby (1844)

15 Youth is a blunder; Manhood a struggle; Old Age a regret.
Coningsby (1844)

16 It seems to me a barren thing this Conservatism—an unhappy cross-breed, the mule of politics that engenders nothing.
Coningsby (1844); see **Donnelly 97:3**, **Power 249:9**

17 No Government can be long secure without a formidable Opposition.
Coningsby (1844)

18 Read no history: nothing but biography, for that is life without theory.
Contarini Fleming (1832)

19 The practice of politics in the East may be defined by one word—dissimulation.
Contarini Fleming (1832)

20 The transient and embarrassed phantom of Lord Goderich.
of Lord Goderich as Prime Minister
Endymion (1880)

1 An insular country, subject to fogs,
and with a powerful middle class,
requires grave statesmen.
of England
Endymion (1880)

2 As for our majority…one is enough.
Endymion (1880)

3 The greatest opportunity that can
be offered to an Englishman—a
seat in the House of Commons.
Endymion (1880)

4 The sweet simplicity of the three
per cents.
Endymion (1880); see **Stowell 302:9**

5 I believe they went out, like all good
things, with the Stuarts.
Endymion (1880)

6 What we anticipate seldom occurs;
what we least expected generally
happens.
Henrietta Temple (1837)

7 An aristocracy is rather apt to
exaggerate the qualities and
magnify the importance of a
plebeian leader.
Lord George Bentinck (1852)

8 *of Robert* **Peel**:
Wanting imagination he lacked
prescience…His judgement was
faultless provided he had not to
deal with the future.
Lord George Bentinck (1852)

9 'Two nations; between whom
there is no intercourse and no
sympathy; who are as ignorant of
each other's habits, thoughts, and
feelings, as if they were dwellers in
different zones, or inhabitants of
different planets; who are formed
by a different breeding, are fed by
a different food, are ordered by
different manners, and are not
governed by the same laws.'
'You speak of—' said Egremont,
hesitatingly, 'THE RICH AND THE
POOR.'
Sybil (1845)

10 Pretending that people can
be better off than they are is
radicalism and nothing else.
Sybil (1845)

11 'Frank and explicit'—that is the

right line to take when you wish
to conceal your own mind and to
confuse the minds of others.
Sybil (1845)

12 The Youth of a Nation are the
trustees of Posterity.
Sybil (1845)

13 That fatal drollery called a
representative government.
Tancred (1847)

14 A majority is always the best
repartee.
Tancred (1847)

15 Progress to what and from
where…The European talks of
progress because by an ingenious
application of some scientific
acquirements he has established
a society which has mistaken
comfort for civilization.
Tancred (1847)

16 London is a modern Babylon.
Tancred (1847)

17 We should never lose an occasion.
Opportunity is more powerful even
than conquerors and prophets.
Tancred (1847)

18 The grovelling tyranny of self-
government.
Tancred (1847)

19 There is no act of treachery or
meanness of which a political party
is not capable; for in politics there
is no honour.
Vivian Grey (1826)

20 Experience is the child of thought
and thought is the child of action.
We cannot learn men from books.
Vivian Grey (1826)

21 I repeat…that all power is a trust—
that we are accountable for its
exercise—that, from the people,
and for the people, all springs, and
all must exist.
Vivian Grey (1826)

22 Damn your principles! Stick to your
party.
attributed to Disraeli and believed to have been
said to Edward **Bulwer-Lytton**; E. Latham
Famous Sayings and their Authors (1904)

23 Everyone likes flattery; and when
you come to Royalty you should lay

it on with a trowel.
*to Matthew **Arnold**, in G. W. E. Russell*
Collections and Recollections (1898) ch. 23

1 I have climbed to the top of the
greasy pole.
on becoming Prime Minister
W. Monypenny and G. Buckle *Life of Benjamin
Disraeli* vol. 4 (1916)

2 I am dead; dead, but in the Elysian
fields.
to a peer, on his elevation to the House of Lords
W. Monypenny and G. Buckle *Life of Benjamin
Disraeli* vol. 5 (1920)

3 I never deny; I never contradict; I
sometimes forget.
*said to Lord Esher of his relations with Queen
Victoria*
Elizabeth Longford *Victoria R. I* (1964)

4 Never complain and never explain.
J. Morley *Life of William Ewart Gladstone*
(1903) vol. 1; see **Fisher 110:6**

5 The palace is not safe when the
cottage is not happy.
Robert Blake *Disraeli* (1966)

6 Palmerston is now seventy. If he
could prove evidence of his potency
in his electoral address he'd sweep
the country.
*to the suggestion that capital could be made from
one of Palmerston's affairs*
Hesketh Pearson *Dizzy* (1951); attributed,
probably apocryphal

7 Posterity will do justice to that
unprincipled maniac Gladstone—
extraordinary mixture of envy,
vindictiveness, hypocrisy and
superstition; and with one
commanding characteristic—
whether Prime Minister or Leader
of the Opposition, whether
preaching, praying, speechifying or
scribbling—never a gentleman.
W. Monypenny and G. Buckle *Life of Benjamin
Disraeli* vol. 6 (1920)

8 Pray remember, Mr Dean, no
dogma, no Dean.
W. Monypenny and G. Buckle *Life of Benjamin
Disraeli* vol. 4 (1916)

9 Protection is not only dead, but
damned.
W. Monypenny and G. Buckle *Life of Benjamin
Disraeli* vol. 3 (1914)

10 The school of Manchester.
*of the free trade politics of Cobden and **Bright***
Robert Blake *Disraeli* (1966)

11 There are three kinds of lies: lies,
damned lies and statistics.
attributed to Disraeli in Mark Twain
Autobiography (1924) vol. 1; anonymous
versions of this occur earlier, e.g. in *Economic
Journal* June 1892

12 We came here for fame.
*to John **Bright**, in the House of Commons*
Robert Blake *Disraeli* (1966)

13 When Gentlemen cease to be
returned to Parliament this Empire
will perish.
W. Fraser *Disraeli and His Day* (1891)

14 When I want to read a novel, I write
one.
W. Monypenny and G. Buckle *Life of Benjamin
Disraeli* vol. 6 (1920)

15 You will find as you grow older that
courage is the rarest of all qualities
to be found in public life.
*to Lady Gwendolen Cecil, telling her that her
father Lord **Salisbury** was the only man of real
courage with whom Disraeli had worked*
Lady Gwendolen Cecil *Life of Robert Marquis of
Salisbury* (1931)

Milovan Djilas 1911–95
Yugoslav political writer and former member of the
Yugoslav Communist Party (from which he resigned in
April 1954)

16 The Party line is that there is no
Party line.
*comment on reforms of the Yugoslavian
Communist Party, November 1952*
Fitzroy Maclean *Disputed Barricade* (1957)

Michael Dobbs 1948–
British writer

17 You might very well think that. I
couldn't possibly comment.
the Chief Whip's habitual response to questioning
House of Cards *(as dramatized for television,
1990)*

Frank Dobson 1940–
British Labour politician

18 The ego has landed.
*of Ken **Livingstone's** independent candidacy for
Mayor of London*
in *Times* 7 March 2000

Bubb Dodington 1691–1762
English politician

1 Love thy country, wish it well,
Not with too intense a care,
'Tis enough, that when it fell,
Thou its ruin didst not share.
'Ode' (written 1761) in Joseph Spence
Anecdotes (1820)

Robert Dole 1923–
American Republican politician

2 *announcing his decision to relinquish his
Senate seat and step down as majority
leader:*
I will seek the presidency with
nothing to fall back on but the
judgement of the people and with
nowhere to go but the White House
or home.
on Capitol Hill, 15 May 1996

Ignatius Donnelly 1831–1901
American politician

3 The Democratic Party is like a
mule—without pride of ancestry or
hope of posterity.
attributed; see **Disraeli 94:16, Power 249:9**

John Dos Passos 1896–1970
American novelist

4 America our nation has been
beaten by strangers who have
bought the laws and fenced off the
meadows and cut down the woods
for pulp and turned our pleasant
cities into slums and sweated
the wealth out of our people and
when they want to they hire the
executioner to throw the switch.
The Big Money (1936)

James Douglas, Earl of Mar
c. 1358–88
Scottish soldier

5 God be praised, not many of my
ancestors have died in their beds.
dying at the battle of Otterburn, 1388; Jean
Froissart *Chronicles*

William O. Douglas 1898–1980
American judge, Justice of the Supreme Court

6 The Fifth Amendment is an old
friend and a good friend. It is one
of the great landmarks in man's
struggle to be free of tyranny, to be
decent and civilized.
An Almanac of Liberty (1954)

7 The search…for ways and means to
make the machine—and the vast
bureaucracy of the corporation
state and of government that runs
that machine—the servant of
man. That is the revolution that is
coming.
in 1970; Anthony Sampson *The Company Man*
(1995)

Alec Douglas-Home see Lord **Home**

Frederick Douglass *c.* 1818–95
American former slave and civil rights campaigner

8 Every tone [of the songs of the
slaves] was a testimony against
slavery, and a prayer to God for
deliverance from chains.
Narrative of the Life of Frederick Douglass
(1845) ch. 2

9 What, to the American slave, is
your Fourth of July? I answer: A day
that reveals to him, more than all
other days in the year, the gross
injustice and cruelty to which he is
the constant victim. To him your
celebration is a sham.
speech at Rochester, New York, 4 July 1852

10 In all the relations of life and death,
we are met by the colour line.
speech at the Convention of Coloured Men,
Louisville, Kentucky, 24 September 1883

11 No man can put a chain about the
ankle of his fellow man without at
last finding the other end fastened
about his own neck.
speech at Civil Rights Mass Meeting,
Washington, DC, 22 October 1883

Margaret Drabble 1939–
English novelist

12 England's not a bad country…It's
just a mean, cold, ugly, divided,
tired, clapped-out, post-imperial,

post-industrial slag-heap covered in polystyrene hamburger cartons.
A Natural Curiosity (1989)

Francis Drake c. 1540–96
English sailor and explorer

1 The singeing of the King of Spain's Beard.
on the expedition to Cadiz, 1587
Francis Bacon *Considerations touching a War with Spain* (1629)

2 There is plenty of time to win this game, and to thrash the Spaniards too.
attributed, in *Dictionary of National Biography* (1917–) vol. 5

Joseph Rodman Drake 1795–1820
American poet

3 Forever float that standard sheet! Where breathes the foe but falls before us,
With Freedom's soil beneath our feet, And Freedom's banner streaming o'er us?
'The American Flag' in *New York Evening Post*, 29 May 1819 (also attributed to Fitz-Greene Halleck)

William Driver 1803–86
American sailor

4 I name thee Old Glory.
as the flag was hoisted to the masthead of his ship (Driver was captain of the Charles Doggett, *the ship on which the Bounty mutineers were returned from Tahiti to Pitcairn, and was presented with a large American flag by a band of women in recognition of this)*
attributed

Maurice Druon 1918–2009
French novelist

5 The people who come knocking on the door of this ministry with a begging bowl in one hand and a Molotov cocktail in the other will have to make a choice.
as Minister of Culture, of France's generally left-wing subsidised theatre
in 1973; in *Times* 17 April 2009

John Dryden 1631–1700
English poet, critic, and dramatist

6 Plots, true or false, are necessary things,
To raise up commonwealths and ruin kings.
Absalom and Achitophel (1681)

7 Of these the false Achitophel was first,
A name to all succeeding ages curst.
For close designs and crooked counsels fit,
Sagacious, bold, and turbulent of wit,
Restless, unfixed in principles and place,
In power unpleased, impatient of disgrace.
in Dryden's political satire relating to the Protestant succession 'Achitophel' represented **Shaftesbury**, *and 'Absalom' the Duke of* **Monmouth**
Absalom and Achitophel (1681)

8 A daring pilot in extremity;
Pleased with the danger, when the waves went high
He sought the storms; but for a calm unfit,
Would steer too nigh the sands to boast his wit.
Absalom and Achitophel (1681)

9 In friendship false, implacable in hate:
Resolved to ruin or to rule the state.
Absalom and Achitophel (1681)

10 The people's prayer, the glad diviner's theme,
The young men's vision and the old men's dream!
Absalom and Achitophel (1681)

11 All empire is no more than power in trust.
Absalom and Achitophel (1681)

12 Better one suffer, than a nation grieve.
Absalom and Achitophel (1681)

13 For who can be secure of private right,
If sovereign sway may be dissolved by might?
Nor is the people's judgement always true:
The most may err as grossly as

the few.
Absalom and Achitophel (1681)

1 Never was patriot yet, but was a
fool.
Absalom and Achitophel (1681)

2 Reason to rule, but mercy to
forgive:
The first is law, the last prerogative.
The Hind and the Panther (1687)

3 Either be wholly slaves or wholly
free.
The Hind and the Panther (1687)

4 T'abhor the makers, and their laws
approve,
Is to hate traitors and the treason
love.
The Hind and the Panther (1687)

5 War is the trade of kings.
King Arthur (1691)

6 But treason is not owned when 'tis
descried;
Successful crimes alone are justified.
The Medal (1682)

7 But 'tis the talent of our English
nation,
Still to be plotting some new
reformation.
'The Prologue at Oxford, 1680' (prologue to
Nathaniel Lee *Sophonisba*, 2nd ed., 1681)

8 Freedom which in no other land
will thrive,
Freedom an English subject's sole
prerogative.
Threnodia Augustalis (1685)

9 If by the people you understand
the multitude, the *hoi polloi*, 'tis no
matter what they think; they are
sometimes in the right, sometimes
in the wrong: their judgement is a
mere lottery.
An Essay of Dramatic Poesy (1668)

Alexander Dubček 1921–92
Czechoslovak statesman; First Secretary of the
Czechoslovak Communist Party, 1968–9

10 In the service of the people
we followed such a policy that
socialism would not lose its human
face.
in *Rudé Právo* 19 July 1968

Joachim Du Bellay 1522–60
French poet

11 France, mother of arts, of warfare,
and of laws.
Les Regrets (1558) Sonnet no. 9

W. E. B. Du Bois 1868–1963
American social reformer and political activist

12 The cost of liberty is less than the
price of repression.
John Brown (1909)

13 The problem of the twentieth
century is the problem of the colour
line—the relation of the darker to
the lighter races of men in Asia and
Africa, in America and the islands
of the sea.
The Souls of Black Folk (1905)

Françoise Ducros
Canadian political aide

14 What a moron.
off-the-record comment on George W. **Bush***;
she subsequently resigned as Jean* **Chrétien***'s
director of communications*
attributed; reported in *CTV news* (online
edition) 21 November 2002

John Foster Dulles 1888–1959
American international lawyer and Republican
politician. On Dulles: see **Churchill 70:6**

15 If…the European Defence
Community should not become
effective; if France and Germany
remain apart…That would compel
an agonizing reappraisal of basic
United States policy.
speech to NATO Council in Paris, 14 December
1953

16 The ability to get to the verge
without getting into the war is
the necessary art. If you cannot
master it, you inevitably get into
war. If you try to run away from it,
if you are scared to go to the brink,
you are lost. We've had to look it
square in the face—on the question
of enlarging the Korean war, on
the question of getting into the
Indochina war, on the question of

Formosa. We walked to the brink and we looked it in the face.
this policy became known as 'brinkmanship' in *Life* 16 January 1956; see **Stevenson 301:5**

Alan Duncan 1957–
British Conservative politician

1 Basically, it's being nationalised, you have to live on rations and are treated like shit.
on why no-one would wish to become an MP following the expenses scandal
interview secretly recorded by campaigner Heydon Prowse; in *Independent* (online edition) 12 August 2009

Henry Dundas 1742–1811
Scottish-born politician

2 When it is said that no alternative is left to the New Englanders but to starve or rebel, this is not the fact, for there is another way, to submit.
the word 'starvation' was said to have been coined in relation to this speech, and Dundas became known as 'Starvation Dundas'
in the House of Commons, 1775

Finlay Peter Dunne 1867–1936
American humorous writer

3 A law, Hinnissey, that might look like a wall to you or me wud look like a triumphal arch to th'expeeryenced eye iv a lawyer.
'Mr Dooley on the Power of the Press'
in *American Magazine* no. 62 1906; see **Commager 78:5**

John Dunning, Lord Ashburton
1731–83
English lawyer and politician

4 The influence of the Crown has increased, is increasing, and ought to be diminished.
resolution passed in the House of Commons, 6 April 1780

Ray Durem 1915–63
American poet

5 Some of my best friends are white boys.
when I meet 'em
I treat 'em
just the same as if they was people.
'Broadminded' (written 1951)

John George Lambton, Lord Durham 1792–1840
English Whig politician

6 £40,000 a year a moderate income— such a one as a man *might jog on with*.
Thomas Creevey, letter to Elizabeth Ord, 13 September 1821

7 I expected to find a contest between a government and a people: I found two nations warring in the bosom of a single state.
Report of the Affairs of British North America (1839)

James Dyson 1947–
English inventor and businessman

8 Making money from money should be replaced with making money from making.
in *Observer* 8 February 2009

Stephen T. Early 1889–1951

1 Don't Worry Me—I am an 8 Ulcer Man on 4 Ulcer Pay.
card received by Harry Truman; William Hillman *Mr President: the First Publication from the Personal Diaries, Private Letters, Papers and Revealing Interviews of Harry S. Truman* (1952)

Abba Eban 1915–
Israeli diplomat

2 History teaches us that men and nations behave wisely once they have exhausted all other alternatives.
speech in London, 16 December 1970

3 *of the British Foreign Office:*
A hotbed of cold feet.
in conversation with Antony Jay

Anthony Eden 1897–1977
British Conservative statesman, Prime Minister 1955–7. On Eden: see **Butler 51:12**, **Muggeridge 221:17**, **Newspaper headlines 225:16**

4 Everyone is always in favour of general economy and particular expenditure.
in *Observer* 17 June 1956

5 We are in an armed conflict; that is the phrase I have used. There has been no declaration of war.
on the Suez crisis
in the House of Commons, 1 November 1956

6 Long experience has taught me that to be criticized is not always to be wrong.
during the Suez crisis
speech at Lord Mayor's Guildhall banquet; in *Daily Herald* 10 November 1956

Clarissa Eden 1920–
British wife of Anthony **Eden**

7 For the past few weeks I have really felt as if the Suez Canal was flowing through my drawing room.
speech at Gateshead, 20 November 1956

John Maxwell Edmonds 1875–1958
English classicist

8 When you go home, tell them of us and say,
'For your tomorrows these gave their today.'
Inscriptions Suggested for War Memorials (1919); see **Epitaphs 106:12**

Edward VII 1841–1910
British monarch, King of the United Kingdom from 1901

9 The last King of England.
introducing his son, the future George V, to Lord Haldane, expressing his pessimism for the survival of the British monarchy
Andrew Roberts *Eminent Churchillians* (1994)

Edward VIII 1894–1972
King of the United Kingdom, 1936; afterwards Duke of Windsor. On Edward VIII: see **George V 121:8**, **Mary 207:11**, **Thomas 311:11**

10 These works brought all these people here. Something should be done to get them at work again.
speaking at the derelict Dowlais Iron and Steel Works, 18 November 1936
in *Western Mail* 19 November 1936; see **Misquotations 216:4**

11 At long last I am able to say a few words of my own...you must believe me when I tell you that I have found it impossible to carry the heavy burden of responsibility and to discharge my duties as King as I would wish to do without the help and support of the woman I love.
radio broadcast following his abdication, 11 December 1936
in *Times* 12 December 1936

John Edwards 1953–
American Democratic politician, vice-presidential
candidate in 2004

1 The president of the United States
actually has to be able to walk and
chew gum at the same time.
*in January 2004; quoted on BBC News Online
website, 6 October 2004 (see* **Johnson 160:6**)

2 We have been 'The Little Engine
that Could'. I am proud of what
we've done.
*to his supporters, acknowledging defeat in
the contest for the Democratic presidential
nomination*
*in Chicago Tribune 3 March 2004 (online
edition)*

John Ehrlichman 1925–99
American Presidential assistant to Richard **Nixon**

3 I think we ought to let him hang
there. Let him twist slowly, slowly
in the wind.
*speaking of Patrick Gray (regarding his
nomination as director of the FBI) in a telephone
conversation with John Dean*
in Washington Post 27 July 1973

Albert Einstein 1879–1955
German-born theoretical physicist; originator of the
theory of relativity

4 The prestige of government
has undoubtedly been lowered
considerably by the Prohibition
laws. For nothing is more
destructive of respect for the
government and the law of the land
than passing laws which cannot be
enforced.
*after visiting America in 1921; The World As I
See It (1935)*

5 Nationalism is an infantile
sickness. It is the measles of the
human race.
*Helen Dukas and Banesh Hoffman Albert
Einstein, the Human Side (1979)*

6 One must divide one's time
between politics and equations.
But our equations are much more
important to me.
*C. P. Snow 'Einstein' in M. Goldsmith et al.
(eds.) Einstein (1980)*

Dwight D. Eisenhower 1890–1969
American Republican statesman; 34th President of the
US. On Eisenhower: see **Truman 317:7**

7 Soldiers, sailors and airmen of the
Allied Expeditionary Force: You
are about to embark upon the great
crusade, toward which we have
striven these many months. The
eyes of the world are upon you. The
hope and prayers of liberty-loving
people everywhere march with you.
*order to troops preparing to invade Normandy,
6 June 1944*

8 People of Western Europe: A
landing was made this morning
on the coast of France by troops
of the Allied Expeditionary
Force. This landing is part of the
concerted United Nations plan for
the liberation of Europe, made in
conjunction with our great Russian
allies...I call upon all who love
freedom to stand with us now.
Together we shall achieve victory.
broadcast on D-Day, 6 June 1944

9 Every gun that is made, every
warship launched, every rocket
fired signifies, in the final sense, a
theft from those who hunger and
are not fed, those who are cold and
are not clothed. This world in arms
is not spending money alone. It is
spending the sweat of its labourers,
the genius of its scientists, the
hopes of its children.
speech in Washington, 16 April 1953

10 I just will not—I *refuse*—to get into
the gutter with that guy.
explaining why he did not try to restrain Senator
McCarthy
*in 1953; in American National Biography
(online edition) 'Joseph McCarthy'*

11 You have broader considerations
that might follow what you might
call the 'falling domino' principle.
You have a row of dominoes set up.
You knock over the first one, and
what will happen to the last one
is that it will go over very quickly.
So you have the beginning of a
disintegration that would have the

most profound influences.
speech at press conference, 7 April 1954

1 What counts is not necessarily the size of the dog in the fight — it's the size of the fight in the dog.
remark, Republican National Committee Breakfast, 31 January 1958

2 Governments are far more stupid than their people.
attributed, 1958

3 I think that people want peace so much that one of these days governments had better get out of the way and let them have it.
broadcast discussion, 31 August 1959

4 In the councils of government, we must guard against the acquisition of unwarranted influence, whether sought or unsought, by the military-industrial complex. The potential for the disastrous rise of misplaced power exists and will persist.
farewell broadcast, 17 January 1961
in *New York Times* 18 January 1961

5 No *easy* problems ever come to the president of the United States. If they are easy to solve, someone else has solved them.
quoted by John F. Kennedy, in *Parade* 8 April 1962

George Eliot 1819–80
English novelist

6 An election is coming. Universal peace is declared, and the foxes have a sincere interest in prolonging the lives of the poultry.
Felix Holt (1866)

T. S. Eliot 1888–1965
American-born British poet, critic, and dramatist

7 This is the way the world ends
Not with a bang but a whimper.
'The Hollow Men' (1925)

Queen Elisabeth of Belgium
1876–1965
German-born consort of King Albert of the Belgians

8 Between them [Germany] and me there is now a bloody curtain which

has descended forever.
on Germany's invasion of Belgium in 1914
attributed

Elizabeth I 1533–1603
English monarch, Queen of England and Ireland from 1558. See also **Last words 178:1, Mottoes 221:7**

9 This judgement I have of you that you will not be corrupted by any manner of gift and that you will be faithful to the state; and that without respect of my private will you will give me that counsel which you think best.
to William Cecil, appointing him her Secretary of State in 1558
Conyers Read *Mr Secretary Cecil and Queen Elizabeth* (1955)

10 I have already joined myself in marriage to a husband, namely, the kingdom of England.
in reply to her first Parliament pleading with her to consider marriage for the safety of the country in February 1559

11 The queen of Scots is this day leichter of a fair son, and I am but a barren stock.
to her ladies, June 1566, in Sir James Melville Memoirs of His Own Life (1827 ed.)

12 I am your anointed Queen. I will never be by violence constrained to do anything. I thank God that I am endued with such qualities that if I were turned out of the Realm in my petticoat, I were able to live in any place in Christome.
speech to Members of Parliament, 5 November 1566

13 I know what it is to be a subject, what to be a Sovereign, what to have good neighbours, and sometimes meet evil-willers.
speech to a Parliamentary deputation at Richmond, 12 November 1586; J. E. Neale *Elizabeth I and her Parliaments 1584–1601* (1957), from a report 'which the Queen herself heavily amended in her own hand'; see **Misquotations 215:14**

14 I will make you shorter by the head.
*to the leaders of her Council, who were opposing her course towards **Mary** Queen of Scots*
F. Chamberlin *Sayings of Queen Elizabeth* (1923)

15 I know I have the body of a weak

and feeble woman, but I have the heart and stomach of a king, and of a king of England too; and think foul scorn that Parma or Spain, or any prince of Europe, should dare to invade the borders of my realm.
speech to the troops at Tilbury on the approach of the Armada, 1588
Lord Somers *A Third Collection of Scarce and Valuable Tracts* (1751)

1 The daughter of debate, that eke discord doth sow.
*on **Mary** Queen of Scots*
George Puttenham (ed.) *The Art of English Poesie* (1589)

2 I will have here but one Mistress, and no Master.
reproving the presumption of the Earl of Leicester
Robert Naunton *Fragmenta Regalia* (1641)

3 My lord, we make use of you, not for your bad legs, but for your good head.
to William Cecil, who suffered from gout
F. Chamberlin *Sayings of Queen Elizabeth* (1923)

4 I do entreat heaven daily for your longer life, else will my people and myself stand in need of cordials too. My comfort hath been in my people's happiness and their happiness in thy discretion.
to William Cecil on his death-bed
F. Chamberlin *Sayings of Queen Elizabeth* (1923)

5 Though God hath raised me high, yet this I count the glory of my crown: that I have reigned with your loves.
the Golden Speech, 1601
in *The Journals of All the Parliaments...* Collected by Sir Simonds D'Ewes (1682)

6 God may pardon you, but I never can.
*to the dying Countess of Nottingham, February 1603, for her part in the death of the Earl of **Essex**; the story is almost certainly apocryphal*
David Hume *The History of England under the House of Tudor* (1759) vol. 2

7 Must! Is *must* a word to be addressed to princes? Little man, little man! thy father, if he had been alive, durst not have used that word.
*to Robert **Cecil**, on his saying in her last illness*

that she must go to bed
J. R. Green *A Short History of the English People* (1874); *Dodd's Church History of England* vol. 3 (ed. M. A. Tierney, 1840) adds, 'but thou knowest I must die, and that maketh thee so presumptuous'

8 If thy heart fails thee, climb not at all.
*lines after Walter **Ralegh**, written on a window-pane*
Thomas Fuller *Worthies of England* vol. 1; see **Ralegh 254:5**

9 I think that, at the worst, God has not yet ordained that England shall perish.
F. Chamberlin *Sayings of Queen Elizabeth* (1923)

10 I would not open windows into men's souls.
oral tradition, in J. B. Black Reign of Elizabeth 1558–1603 (1936) (the words very possibly originating in a letter drafted by Bacon)

11 Like strawberry wives, that laid two or three great strawberries at the mouth of their pot, and all the rest were little ones.
describing the tactics of the Commission of Sales, in their dealings with her
Francis Bacon *Apophthegms New and Old* (1625)

12 Madam I may not call you; mistress I am ashamed to call you; and so I know not what to call you; but howsoever, I thank you.
to the wife of the Archbishop of Canterbury, the Queen disapproving of marriage among the clergy
John Harington *A Brief View of the State of the Church of England* (1653)

13 *welcoming Edward de Vere, Earl of Oxford, on his return from seven years self-imposed exile, occasioned by the acute embarrassment to himself of breaking wind in the presence of the Queen:*
My Lord, I had forgot the fart.
John Aubrey *Brief Lives* 'Edward de Vere'

14 *on being asked her opinion of Christ's presence in the Sacrament:*
'Twas God the word that spake it, He took the bread and brake it; And what the word did make it; That I believe, and take it.
S. Clarke *The Marrow of Ecclesiastical History* (1675) 'The Life of Queen Elizabeth'

Elizabeth II 1926–
British monarch, Queen of the United Kingdom from 1952; daughter of **George VI** and Queen **Elizabeth** the Queen Mother. On Elizabeth: see **Churchill 70:1**

1 I declare before you all that my whole life, whether it be long or short, shall be devoted to your service and the service of our great Imperial family to which we all belong.
   broadcast speech, as Princess Elizabeth, to the Commonwealth from Cape Town, 21 April 1947 in *Times* 22 April 1947

2 *speech at Guildhall, London, on her 25th wedding anniversary:*
   I think everybody really will concede that on this, of all days, I should begin my speech with the words 'My husband and I'.
   in *Times* 21 November 1972

3 In the words of one of my more sympathetic correspondents, it has turned out to be an 'annus horribilis'.
   speech at Guildhall, London, 24 November 1992

4 I for one believe that there are lessons to be drawn from her life and from the extraordinary and moving reaction to her death.
   broadcast from Buckingham Palace on the evening before the funeral of **Diana**, Princess of Wales, 5 September 1997 in *Times* 6 September 1997

5 *Vive la différence, mais vive l'entente cordiale.*
   Long live the difference, but long live the Entente Cordiale.
   speech, Paris, 5 April 2004 in *Times* 6 April 2004

Queen Elizabeth, the Queen Mother 1900–2002
British Queen Consort of **George VI**, mother of **Elizabeth II**

6 I'm glad we've been bombed. It makes me feel I can look the East End in the face.
   to a London policeman, 13 September 1940
   John Wheeler-Bennett *King George VI* (1958)

7 *on the suggestion that the royal family be evacuated during the Blitz:*
   The Princesses would never leave without me and I couldn't leave without the King, and the King will never leave.
   Penelope Mortimer *Queen Elizabeth* (1986)

Ebenezer Elliott 1781–1849
English poet known as the 'Corn Law Rhymer'

8 What is a communist? One who hath yearnings
   For equal division of unequal earnings.
   'Epigram' (1850)

Thomas Edward Ellis 1859–99
British Liberal politician and Welsh nationalist

9 Over and above all, we shall work for a Legislature, elected by the manhood and womanhood of Wales.
   speech at Bala, 1890

Rahm Emanuel 1959–
American Democratic politician

10 You never want a serious crisis to go to waste.
   often quoted as 'Never waste a good crisis'
   to business leaders, 18 November 2008, in *Globe and Mail* (Canada) 20 November 2008

Ralph Waldo Emerson 1803–82
American philosopher and poet

11 The two parties which divide the state, the party of Conservatism and that of Innovation, are very old, and have disputed the possession of the world ever since it was made.
   'The Conservative' (lecture, 1841)

12 The louder he talked of his honour, the faster we counted our spoons.
   The Conduct of Life (1860) 'Worship'

England
'This royal throne of kings'
see Selective Subject Index

Epitaphs

1 Free at last, free at last
  Thank God almighty
  We are free at last.
  *epitaph of Martin Luther **King** (1929–68),*
  Atlanta, Georgia
  anonymous spiritual; see **King 171:9**

2 Go, tell the Spartans, thou who
    passest by,
  That here obedient to their laws
    we lie.
  epitaph for the 300 Spartans killed at
  Thermopylae, 480 BC
  attributed to the Greek poet **Simonides**
  (*c.* 556–468 BC); Herodotus *Histories* bk. 7,
  ch. 228

3 Here lies a great and mighty king
  Whose promise none relies on;
  He never said a foolish thing,
  Nor ever did a wise one.
  *of **Charles II** (1630–85); an alternative first line*
  reads: 'Here lies our sovereign lord the King'
  John Wilmot, Earl of **Rochester** 'The King's
  Epitaph'; in C. E. Doble et al. *Thomas Hearne:*
  Remarks and Collections (1885–1921)
  17 November 1706; see **Charles II 62:2**

4 Here lies a valiant warrior
  Who never drew a sword;
  Here lies a noble courtier
  Who never kept his word;
  Here lies the Earl of Leicester
  Who governed the estates
  Whom the earth could never living
    love,
  And the just heaven now hates.
  of Robert Dudley, Earl of Leicester (1532–88)
  attributed to Ben **Jonson** in Silvester
  Tissington *A Collection of Epitaphs and*
  Monumental Inscriptions (1857)

5 Here lies Fred,
  Who was alive and is dead:
  Had it been his father,
  I had much rather;
  Had it been his brother,
  Still better than another;
  Had it been his sister,
  No one would have missed her;
  Had it been the whole generation,
  Still better for the nation:
  But since 'tis only Fred,

Who was alive and is dead,—
There's no more to be said.
of Frederick Louis, Prince of Wales (1707–1751),
son of George II and Caroline of Ansbach
in Horace Walpole *Memoirs of George II* (1847)
vol. 1

6 Here lies he who neither feared nor
  flattered any flesh.
  *of John **Knox**, said as he was buried,*
  26 November 1572
  Earl of Morton (1516–81); George R. Preedy
  The Life of John Knox (1940)

7 I will return. And I will be millions.
  inscription on the tomb of Eva **Perón**, Buenos
  Aires

8 O Death, where is thy sting?
  To take the Queen and leave the
    King?
  on the death of Caroline of Ansbach, consort of
  George II, in 1737 (anonymous verse found at
  the Royal Exchange)
  in *Manuscripts of the earl of Egmont: diary of*
  Viscount Percival, afterwards first earl of Egmont
  (1920–3) vol. 2

9 Rest in peace. The mistake shall not
  be repeated.
  inscription on the cenotaph at Hiroshima, Japan

10 A soldier of the Great War known
   unto God.
   standard epitaph for the unidentified dead of
   World War One
   adopted by the War Graves Commission

11 Their name liveth for evermore.
   standard inscription on the Stone of Sacrifice
   in each military cemetery of World War One,
   *proposed by Rudyard **Kipling** as a member of*
   the War Graves Commission
   Charles Carrington *Rudyard Kipling* (rev. ed.
   1978)

12 When you go home, tell them of us
   and say,
   'For your tomorrow we gave our
   today.'
   Kohima memorial to the Burma campaign of
   the Second World War, from a poem by John
   Maxwell Edmonds; in recent years used at
   Remembrance Day parades in the UK; see
   Edmonds 101:8

1 Here once the embattled farmers
   stood,
   And fired the shot heard round the
   world.
   'Concord Hymn' (1837)

2 When you strike at a king, you must
   kill him.
   attributed to Emerson by Oliver Wendell
   Holmes Jr.; Max Lerner *The Mind and Faith of
   Justice Holmes* (1943)

Robert Emmet 1778–1803
Irish nationalist

3 Let no man write my epitaph…
   When my country takes her place
   among the nations of the earth,
   then, and *not till then*, let my
   epitaph be written.
   speech from the dock when condemned to
   death, 19 September 1803

Friedrich Engels 1820–95
German socialist; founder, with Karl **Marx**, of modern
Communism. See also **Marx and Engels**

4 The State is not 'abolished', *it
   withers away.*
   Anti-Dühring (1878)

5 Naturally, the workers are perfectly
   free; the manufacturer does not
   force them to take his materials and
   his cards, but he says to them…'If
   you don't like to be frizzled in my
   frying-pan, you can take a walk into
   the fire'.
   *The Condition of the Working Class in England
   in 1844* (1892)

Ennius 239–169 BC
Roman writer

6 *Moribus antiquis res stat Romana
   virisque.*
   The Roman state survives by its
   ancient customs and its manhood.
   Annals

7 *Unus homo nobis cunctando*

restituit rem.
One man by delaying put the state
to rights for us.
*referring to the Roman general Fabius Cunctator
('The Delayer')
Annals*

Erasmus c. 1469–1536
Dutch Christian humanist

8 In the country of the blind the one-
   eyed man is king.
   Adages

Ludwig Erhard 1897–1977
German statesman, Chancellor of West Germany
(1963–6)

9 Without Britain Europe would
   remain only a torso.
   remark on W. German television, 27 May 1962;
   in *Times* 28 May 1962

Dudley Erwin 1917–84
Australian politician

10 *claiming that the 'political manoeuvre'
   which had cost him his job in the reshuffled
   Government was actually the Prime Minister's
   secretary:*
   It wiggles, it's shapely and its name
   is Ainsley Gotto.
   in *Times* 14 November 1969

Robert Devereux, Lord Essex
1566–1601
English soldier and courtier, executed for treason

11 Reasons are not like garments, the
   worse for wearing.
   letter to Lord Willoughby, 4 January 1599

William Maxwell Evarts 1818–83
American politician and lawyer

12 The pious ones of Plymouth, who,
   reaching the Rock, first fell upon
   their own knees and then upon the
   aborigines.
   in *Louisville Courier-Journal* 4 July 1913; a pun
   which has been variously attributed

Equality
'some animals are more equal than others'
see Selective Subject Index

Edward Everett 1794–1865
American orator and politician

1 I should be glad if I could flatter myself that I came as near the central idea of the occasion in two hours as you did in two minutes.
*to Abraham **Lincoln** on the Gettysburg address, which had been publicly criticized while Everett's two hour speech had received adulatory attention in the press*
  letter to Lincoln, 20 November 1863; see **Anonymous 9:14**

William Norman Ewer 1885–1976
British writer

2 I gave my life for freedom — This I know:
For those who bade me fight had told me so.
'Five Souls' (1917)

Winifred Ewing 1929–
Scottish Nationalist politician

3 As I took my seat it was said by political pundits that 'a chill ran along the Labour back benches looking for a spine to run up.'
of her arrival at Westminster after winning the Hamilton by-election in 1967; use of a general political expression
  in 1988, attributed; Angela Cran and James Robertson *Dictionary of Scottish Quotations* (1996)

4 The Scottish Parliament which adjourned on 25 March in the year 1707 is hereby reconvened.
opening speech, as oldest member of the new Parliament
  in *Scottish Parliament* 12 May 1999

5 I am an expert in being a minority. I was alone in the House of Commons for three years and alone in the European Parliament for nineteen years, but we are all minorities now.
opening speech, as oldest member of the new Parliament
  in *Scottish Parliament* 12 May 1999

 Europe
'continent of energetic mongrels'
see Selective Subject Index

Quintus Fabius Maximus
c. 275–203 BC
Roman politician and general

6 To be turned from one's course by men's opinions, by blame, and by misrepresentation shows a man unfit to hold an office.
  Plutarch *Parallel Lives* 'Fabius Maximus'

Émile Faguet 1847–1916
French writer and critic

7 *commenting on **Rousseau**'s 'Man was born free, and everywhere he is in chains':*
It would be equally correct to say that sheep are born carnivorous, and everywhere they nibble grass.
  paraphrasing Joseph de Maistre; *Politiques et Moralistes du Dix-Neuvième Siècle* (1899)

Thomas Fairfax 1621–71
English Parliamentary general

8 Human probabilities are not sufficient grounds to make war upon a neighbour nation.
to the proposal in 1650 that the expected attack

by the Scots should be anticipated by the invasion of Scotland
  in Dictionary of National Biography

Lucius Cary, Lord Falkland
1610–43
English royalist politician. On Falkland: see
Clarendon 72:18

1 When it is not necessary to change, it is necessary not to change.
  Discourses of Infallibility (1660) 'A Speech concerning Episcopacy' delivered in 1641

Frantz Fanon 1925–61
French West Indian psychoanalyst and writer

2 The shape of Africa resembles a revolver, and the Congo is the trigger.
  attributed

Michael Faraday 1791–1867
English physicist and chemist

3 *to **Gladstone**, when asked about the usefulness of electricity:*
  Why sir, there is every possibility that you will soon be able to tax it!
  W. E. H. Lecky *Democracy and Liberty* (1899 ed.)

Wallace Fard c. 1891–1934
American religious leader, founder of the Nation of Islam

4 The blue-eyed devil white man.
  Malcolm X with Alex Haley *The Autobiography of Malcolm X* (1965); see **Malcolm X 202:14**

James A. Farley 1888–1976
American Democratic politician

5 As Maine goes, so goes Vermont.
  *after predicting correctly that Franklin **Roosevelt** would carry all but two states in the election of 1936*
    statement to the press, 4 November 1936; see **Proverbs 251:3**

Farouk 1920–65
Egyptian monarch, King 1936–52

6 The whole world is in revolt. Soon there will be only five Kings left— the King of England, the King of Spades, the King of Clubs, the King of Hearts and the King of Diamonds.
  Lord Boyd-Orr *As I Recall* (1966), addressed to the author at a conference in Cairo, 1948

Guy Fawkes 1570–1606
English conspirator in the Gunpowder Plot, 1605

7 A desperate disease requires a dangerous remedy.
  on 6 November 1605, in *Dictionary of National Biography* (1917–) vol. 6

Dianne Feinstein 1933–
American Democratic politician

8 Toughness doesn't have to come in a pinstripe suit.
  in *Time* 4 June 1984

Ferdinand I see Mottoes 221:3

Paul Feyerabend 1924–94
Austrian philosopher

9 The time is overdue for adding the separation of state and science to the by now customary separation of state and church. Science is only *one* of the many instruments man has invented to cope with his surroundings. It is not the only one, it is not infallible, and it has become too powerful, too pushy, and too dangerous to be left on its own.
  Against Method (1975)

Elizabeth Filkin 1940–
British academic and administrator, Parliamentary Commissioner for Standards, 1999–2001

10 I don't think you can investigate anything too rigorously, because

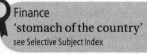

Finance
'stomach of the country'
see Selective Subject Index

you're not being fair to people
unless you do that.
interview, in *Guardian* 16 February 2002

L'Abbé Edgeworth de Firmont
1745–1807
Irish-born priest, confessor to **Louis XVI**

1 Son of Saint Louis, ascend to
heaven.
*to Louis XVI as he mounted the steps of the
guillotine, 1793*
attributed

H. A. L. Fisher 1856–1940
English historian

2 Men wiser and more learned
than I have discerned in history a
plot, a rhythm, a predetermined
pattern. These harmonies are
concealed from me. I can see only
one emergency following upon
another as wave follows upon wave,
only one great fact with respect
to which, since it is unique, there
can be no generalizations, only
one safe rule for the historian:
that he should recognize in the
development of human destinies
the play of the contingent and the
unforeseen.
A History of Europe (1935)

3 Purity of race does not exist.
Europe is a continent of energetic
mongrels.
A History of Europe (1935)

4 Nothing commends a radical
change to an Englishman more
than the belief that it is really
conservative.
A History of Europe (1935)

John Arbuthnot Fisher 1841–1920
British admiral

5 Sack the lot!
*on overmanning and overspending within
government departments*
letter to *Times*, 2 September 1919

6 Never contradict
Never explain
Never apologize.
letter to *Times*, 5 September 1919; see
Disraeli 96:4

John Fiske 1842–1901

7 The United States—bounded on
the north by the Aurora Borealis,
on the south by the precession of
the equinoxes, on the east by the
primeval chaos, and on the west by
the Day of Judgement.
Bounding the United States

Gerry Fitt 1926–2005
Northern Irish politician

8 People [in Northern Ireland]
don't march as an alternative to
jogging. They do it to assert their
supremacy. It is pure tribalism,
the cause of troubles all over the
world.
in *Times* 5 August 1994

F. Scott Fitzgerald 1896–1940
American novelist

9 See that little stream—we could
walk to it in two minutes. It took
the British a month to walk it—a
whole empire walking very slowly,
dying in front and pushing forward
behind. And another empire
walked very slowly backward a few
inches a day, leaving the dead like a
million bloody rugs.
Tender is the Night (1934)

Ari Fleischer 1960–
American government spokesman, White House Press
Secretary 2001–3

10 The problem with guns that
are hidden is you can't see their
smoke.
on BBC News Online, 10 January 2003; see
Blix 37:9

Robert, Marquis de Flers
1872–1927 and **Arman de Caillavet**
1869–1915

11 Democracy is the name we give the
people whenever we need them.
L'habit vert, in *La petite illustration série théâtre*
31 May 1913

Andrew Fletcher of Saltoun
1655–1716
Scottish patriot and anti-Unionist. See also **Last words 179:1**

1 I knew a very wise man so much of Sir Chr—'s sentiment, that he believed if a man were permitted to make all the ballads, he need not care who should make the laws of a nation.
   'An Account of a Conversation concerning a Right Regulation of Government for the Good of Mankind. In a Letter to the Marquis of Montrose' (1704)

2 The Scots deserve no pity, if they voluntarily surrender their united and separate interests to the mercy of an united Parliament, where the English have so vast a majority... their 45 Scots members may dance round to all eternity, in this trap of their own making.
   State of the Controversy betwixt United and Separate Parliaments (1706)

Caroline Flint 1961–
British Labour politician

3 Several of the women attending Cabinet —myself included—have been treated by you as little more than female window dressing.
   resignation letter to Gordon Brown, 5 June 2009, in *Times* 6 June 2009

Dario Fo 1926–
Italian dramatist

4 *Non si paga, non si paga.*
   We won't pay, we won't pay.
   title of play (1975; translated by Lino Pertile in 1978 as 'We Can't Pay? We Won't Pay!' and performed in London in 1981 as *'Can't Pay? Won't Pay!'*); see **Slogans 290:11**

Ferdinand Foch 1851–1929
French Marshal

5 My centre is giving way, my right is retreating, situation excellent, I am attacking.
   message sent during the first Battle of the Marne, September 1914; R. Recouly *Foch* (1919)

6 This is not a peace treaty, it is an armistice for twenty years.
   at the signing of the Treaty of Versailles, 1919; Paul Reynaud *Mémoires* (1963) vol. 2

Michael Foot 1913–2010
British Labour politician

7 Think of it! A second Chamber selected by the Whips. A seraglio of eunuchs.
   in the House of Commons, 3 February 1969

8 It is not necessary that every time he rises he should give his famous imitation of a semi-house-trained polecat.
   *of Norman **Tebbit***
   in the House of Commons, 2 March 1978

9 *of David **Steel**, Leader of the Liberal Party:*
   He's passed from rising hope to elder statesman without any intervening period whatsoever.
   in the House of Commons, 28 March 1979

10 A speech from Ernest Bevin on a major occasion had all the horrific fascination of a public execution. If the mind was left immune, eyes and ears and emotions were riveted.
   Aneurin Bevan (1962) vol. 1

Gerald Ford 1909–2006
American Republican statesman; 38th President of the US, 1974–7. On Ford: see **Abzug 1:3**, **Johnson 160:6**, **Morton 220:7**

11 If the Government is big enough to give you everything you want, it is big enough to take away everything you have.
   John F. Parker *If Elected* (1960); a similar remark has been attributed to Barry **Goldwater**

12 I am a Ford, not a Lincoln.
   on taking the vice-presidential oath, 6 December 1973, in *Washington Post* 7 December 1973

13 Our long national nightmare is over. Our Constitution works; our great Republic is a Government of laws and not of men.
   *on being sworn in as President in succession to Richard **Nixon***
   speech on 9 August 1974; see **Adams 3:1**

14 I believe that truth is the glue

that holds Government together, not only our Government, but civilization itself.
speech on being sworn in as President, 9 August 1974

Henry Ford 1863–1947
American car manufacturer and businessman

1 History is more or less bunk.
interview with Charles N. Wheeler in *Chicago Tribune* 25 May 1916

Howell Forgy 1908–83
American naval chaplain

2 Praise the Lord and pass the ammunition.
at Pearl Harbor, 7 December 1941, as Forgy moved along a line of sailors passing ammunition by hand to the deck (later the title of a song by Frank Loesser, 1942)
in *New York Times* 1 November 1942

E. M. Forster 1879–1970
English novelist

3 If I had to choose between betraying my country and betraying my friend, I hope I should have the guts to betray my country.
Two Cheers for Democracy (1951) 'What I Believe'

4 So Two cheers for Democracy: one because it admits variety and two because it permits criticism. Two cheers are quite enough: there is no occasion to give three. Only Love the Beloved Republic deserves that.
Two Cheers for Democracy (1951) 'What I Believe' ('Love, the beloved republic' borrowed from Swinburne's poem 'Hertha')

Harry Emerson Fosdick 1878–1969
American Baptist minister

5 I renounce war for its consequences, for the lies it lives on and propagates, for the undying hatred it arouses, for the dictatorships it puts in the place of democracy, for the starvation that stalks after it.
Armistice Day Sermon in New York, 1933, in *The Secret of Victorious Living* (1934)

6 War's tragedy is that it uses man's best to do man's worst.
On Being Fit to Live With (1946)

Charles Foster 1828–1904
American politician

7 Isn't this a billion dollar country?
at the 51st Congress, responding to a Democratic gibe about a 'million dollar Congress'
also attributed to Thomas B. Reed, who reported the exchange in *North American Review* March 1892, vol. 154

George Foster 1847–1931
Canadian politician

8 In these somewhat troublesome days when the great Mother Empire stands splendidly isolated in Europe.
in *Official Report of the Debates of the House of Commons of the Dominion of Canada* (1896) vol. 41, for 16 January 1896; on 22 January 1896; see **Newspaper headlines 226:1**

Allan Fotheringham 1932–
Canadian journalist

9 In the Maritimes, politics is a disease, in Quebec a religion, in Ontario a business, on the Prairies a protest and in British Columbia entertainment.
in 1975; *Last Page First* (1999)

10 Canada is ten independent personalities, united only by a common suspicion of Ottawa.
in *Maclean's* 11 February 1985

Charles Fourier 1772–1837
French social theorist

11 The extension of women's rights is the basic principle of all social progress.
Théorie des Quatre Mouvements (1808) vol. 2

Foreign Policy
'through blood and iron'
see Selective Subject Index

Norman Fowler 1938–
British Conservative politician

1 I have a young family and for the next few years I should like to devote more time to them.
often quoted as 'spend more time with my family'
resignation letter to the Prime Minister, in *Guardian* 4 January 1990; see **Thatcher 310:15**

Caroline Fox d. 1774
English wife of Henry Fox, Lord **Holland**, and mother of Charles James **Fox**

2 That little boy will be a thorn in Charles's side as long as he lives.
*seeing in the young William **Pitt** a prospective rival for her son Charles James **Fox***
attributed

Charles James Fox 1749–1806
English Whig politician. On Fox: see **Gibbon 123:7**, **Holland 146:1**, **Johnson 161:15**, **Shaw-Lefevre 286:18**; see also **Last words 178:9**

3 The brightest jewel that now remained in his Majesty's crown.
on India
speech in the House of Commons, 1782; William Cobbett *The Parliamentary History of England* (1814)

4 He [Pitt the Younger] was uniformly of an opinion which, though not a popular one, he was ready to aver, that the right of governing was not property but a trust.
*on **Pitt**'s scheme of Parliamentary Reform, 1785*
J. L. Hammond *Charles James Fox* (1903)

5 How much the greatest event it is that ever happened in the world! and how much the best!
on the fall of the Bastille
letter to Richard Fitzpatrick, 30 July 1789

6 Humanity…does not consist in a squeamish ear. It belongs to the mind as well as the nerves, and leads a man to take measures for the prevention of cruelty which the hypocritical cant of humanity

contents itself in deploring.
speech in a House of Commons debate on the slave trade, 18 April 1791

7 If you silence demonstrance and stifle complaint, you then leave no other alternative but force and violence.
speech in the House of Commons, 10 November 1795

8 One feels as if there was something missing in the world—a chasm, a blank that cannot be supplied.
on the death of his rival, William Pitt
Lady Bessborough, letter 23 January 1806, in Countess Granville *Lord Granville Leveson Gower: Private Correspondence 1781–1821* (1916) vol. 2

9 *in the last year of his life Fox's friends suggested that he should accept a peerage:* I will not close my politics in that foolish way.
in *Dictionary of National Biography* (1917–)

Henry Fox see Lord Holland

Anatole France 1844–1924
French novelist and man of letters

10 In every well-governed state, wealth is a sacred thing; in democracies it is the only sacred thing.
L'Île des pingouins (1908)

11 They [the poor] have to labour in the face of the majestic equality of the law, which forbids the rich as well as the poor to sleep under bridges, to beg in the streets, and to steal bread.
Le Lys rouge (1894)

Francis I 1494–1547
French monarch, King from 1515

12 Of all I had, only honour and life

France
'despotism tempered by epigrams'
see Selective Subject Index

have been spared.
letter to his mother following his defeat at Pavia, 1525, usually quoted as 'All is lost, save honour' in *Collection des Documents Inédits sur l'Histoire de France* (1847) vol. 1; see **Misquotations 215:1**

St Francis of Assisi 1181–1226
Italian monk, founder of the Franciscan Order

1 Where there is doubt, let me bring faith;
Where there is despair, let me bring hope.
*paraphrased by Margaret **Thatcher**, Downing Street, 4 May 1979*
'Prayer of St Francis' (attributed)

Anne Frank 1929–45
German-born Jewish diarist

2 I want to go on living even after death!
diary, 4 April 1944

Felix Frankfurter 1882–1965
American judge

3 It is a fair summary of history to say that the safeguards of liberty have been forged in controversies involving not very nice people.
dissenting opinion in *United States v. Rabinowitz* (1950)

Benjamin Franklin 1706–90
American politician, inventor, and scientist. On Franklin: see **Turgot 318:6**; see also **Otis 235:3**

4 Idleness and pride tax with a heavier hand than kings and parliaments. If we can get rid of the former, we may easily bear the latter.
on the Stamp Act
letter 11 July 1765

5 We must indeed all hang together, or, most assuredly, we shall all hang separately.
at the signing of the Declaration of Independence, 4 July 1776 (possibly not original)
P. M. Zall *Ben Franklin* (1980)

6 There never was a good war, or a bad peace.
letter to Josiah Quincy, 11 September 1783

7 I wish the bald eagle had not been

chosen as the representative of our country; he is a bird of bad moral character...like those among men who live by sharping and robbing, he is generally poor, and often very lousy.
The turkey...is a much more respectable bird, and withal a true original native of America.
letter to Sarah Bache, 26 January 1784

8 *on being asked, 'have we got a republic or a monarchy?':*
A republic, if you can keep it.
in conversation, 18 September 1787

9 In this world nothing can be said to be certain, except death and taxes.
letter to Jean Baptiste Le Roy, 13 November 1789; see Daniel Defoe *History of the Devil* (1726) 'Things as certain as death and taxes, can be more firmly believed'

10 George Washington, Commander of the American Armies, who, like Joshua of old, commanded the sun and the moon to stand still, and they obeyed him.
*toast given at a dinner at Versailles, when the British minister had proposed a toast to **George III**, likening him to the sun, and the French minister had likened **Louis XVI** to the moon* attributed

11 They that can give up essential liberty to obtain a little temporary safety deserve neither liberty nor safety.
Historical Review of Pennsylvania (1759)

12 No nation was ever ruined by trade.
Thoughts on Commercial Subjects

Lord Franks 1905–92
British philosopher and administrator

13 The Pentagon, that immense monument to modern man's subservience to the desk.
in *Observer* 30 November 1952

14 A secret in the Oxford sense: you may tell it to only one person at a time.
in *Sunday Telegraph* 30 January 1977

Tommy Franks 1945–
American general

15 This will be a campaign unlike

any other in history. A campaign characterized by shock, by surprise, by flexibility, by the employment of precise munitions on a scale never before seen, and by the application of overwhelming force.
encapsulated in the phrase 'shock and awe', originally deriving from a Pentagon briefing document by Harlan Ullman and James P. Wade; see **Ullman and Wade**
briefing in Qatar, 22 March 2003

Malcolm Fraser 1930–
Australian Liberal statesman; Prime Minister 1975–83. On Fraser: see **Keating 165:7**

1 He [the Prime Minister] has a dangerous reluctance to consult Cabinet, and an obstinate determination to get his own way.
of John Grey Gorton (1911–2002), when resigning from his administration
speech in the Australian Parliament, March 1971

2 Life is not meant to be easy.
5th Alfred Deakin Lecture, 20 July 1971; see **Shaw 285:11**

Michael Frayn 1933–
British writer

3 To be absolutely honest, what I feel really bad about is that I don't feel worse. That's the ineffectual liberal's problem in a nutshell.
in *Observer* 8 August 1965

Frederick the Great 1712–86
Prussian monarch, King from 1740. See also **Napoleon I 224:2**

4 All religions must be tolerated and the sole concern of officials is to ensure that one denomination does not interfere with another, for here everyone can seek salvation in the manner that seems best to him.
scribbled in the margin of an official reply to an enquiry from the General Directory on the civic rights of Roman Catholics, June 1740; T. C. W. Blanning *Culture of Power* (2002) ch. 6

5 Rascals, would you live for ever?
to hesitant Guards at Kolin, 18 June 1757
attributed

6 Drive out prejudices through the door, and they will return through

the window.
letter to Voltaire, 19 March 1771

7 My people and I have come to an agreement which satisfies us both. They are to say what they please, and I am to do what I please.
his interpretation of benevolent despotism
attributed

Cathy Freeman 1973–
Australian athlete

8 I was so angry because they were denying they had done anything wrong, denying that a whole generation was stolen.
of official response to concerns about the 'stolen generation' of Aboriginal children forcibly removed from their families
interview in *Daily Telegraph* 16 July 2000

E. A. Freeman 1823–92
English historian

9 History is past politics, and politics is present history.
Methods of Historical Study (1886)

John Freeth c. 1731–1808
English poet

10 The loss of America what can repay? New colonies seek for at Botany Bay.
'Botany Bay' in *New London Magazine* (1786)

Milton Friedman 1912–2006
American economist and exponent of monetarism; policy adviser to President **Reagan** 1981–9. See also **Proverbs 252:6**

11 There is an invisible hand in politics that operates in the opposite direction to the invisible hand in the market. In politics, individuals who seek to promote only the public good are led by an invisible hand to promote special interests that it was no part of their intention to promote.
Bright Promises, Dismal Performance: An Economist's Protest (1983); see **Smith 293:1**

12 Few trends could so thoroughly undermine the very foundations of our free society as the acceptance by corporate officials of a social responsibility other than to

make as much money for their
stockholders as possible.
Capitalism and Freedom (1962)

1 A society that puts equality—in
the sense of equality of outcome—
ahead of freedom will end up with
neither equality nor freedom.
Free to Choose (1980)

2 A society that puts freedom first
will, as a happy by-product, end
up with both greater freedom and
greater equality.
Free to Choose (1980)

3 The high rate of unemployment
among teenagers, and especially
black teenagers, is both a scandal
and a serious source of social
unrest. Yet it is largely a result of
minimum wage laws…We regard
the minimum wage law as one of
the most, if not the most, antiblack
laws on the statute books.
Free to Choose (1980)

4 *Inflation is always and everywhere a
monetary phenomenon* in the sense
that it is and can be produced only
by a more rapid increase in the
quantity of money than in output.
The Counter-Revolution in Monetary Theory
(1970)

5 There's only one place where
inflation is made: that's in
Washington.
in 1977; attributed

6 Thank heavens we do not get all of
the government that we are made
to pay for.
attributed; quoted by Lord Harris in the House
of Lords, 24 November 1994

Max Frisch 1911–91
Swiss novelist and dramatist

7 Strictly speaking, every citizen
above a certain level of income is
guilty of some offence.
The Fire Raisers (1953) sc. 3, translated by
Michael Bullock

Robert Frost 1874–1963
American poet

8 I never dared be radical when
young

For fear it would make me
conservative when old.
'Desert Places' (1936)

9 My apple trees will never get across
And eat the cones under his pines, I
tell him.
He only says, 'Good fences make
good neighbours.'
'Mending Wall' (1914)

Francis Fukuyama 1952–
American historian

10 What we may be witnessing is not
just the end of the Cold War but
the end of history as such: that is,
the end point of man's ideological
evolution and the universalism of
Western liberal democracy.
in *Independent* 20 September 1989

J. William Fulbright 1905–95
American Democratic politician

11 The Soviet Union has indeed
been our greatest menace, not so
much because of what it has done,
but because of the excuses it has
provided us for our failures.
in *Observer* 21 December 1958 'Sayings of
the Year'

12 A policy that can be accurately,
though perhaps not prudently,
defined as one of 'peaceful
coexistence'.
speech in the US Senate, 27 March 1964

13 We must dare to think
'unthinkable' thoughts. We must
learn to explore all the options and
possibilities that confront us in
a complex and rapidly changing
world. We must learn to welcome
and not to fear the voices of dissent.
We must dare to think about
'unthinkable things' because
when things become unthinkable,
thinking stops and action becomes
mindless.
speech in the US Senate, 27 March 1964

14 The arrogance of power.
title of book, 1966

15 There is a kind of voodoo about
American foreign policy. Certain
drums have to be beaten regularly

to ward off evil spirits.
The Arrogance of Power (1966)

Thomas Fuller 1654–1734
English writer and physician

1 Be you never so high, the law is above you.
Gnomologia (1732) no. 943; see **Denning 89:1**

Alfred Funke 1869–1941
German writer

2 *Gott strafe England!*
God punish England!
Sword and Myrtle (1914)

David Maxwell Fyfe see Lord **Kilmuir**

Hugh Gaitskell 1906–63
British Labour politician. On Gaitskell: see **Bevan 31:1**, **Crossman 83:10**

3 The subtle terrorism of words.
in a warning given to his Party, 1957
Harry Hopkins *The New Look* (1963); attributed

4 There are some of us...who will fight and fight and fight again to save the Party we love.
opposing the vote in favour of unilateral disarmament
speech at Labour Party Conference, 5 October 1960

5 It means the end of a thousand years of history.
on a European federation
speech at Labour Party Conference, 3 October 1962

John Kenneth Galbraith
1908–2006
Canadian-born American economist, US Ambassador to India 1961–3

6 The affluent society.
title of book (1958)

7 The conventional wisdom.
ironic term for 'the beliefs that are at any time assiduously, solemnly and mindlessly traded between the conventionally wise'
The Affluent Society (1958)

8 It is a far, far better thing to have a firm anchor in nonsense than to put out on the troubled seas of thought.
The Affluent Society (1958)

9 In a community where public services have failed to keep abreast of private consumption things are very different. Here, in an atmosphere of private opulence and public squalor, the private goods have full sway.
The Affluent Society (1958)

10 The greater the wealth, the thicker will be the dirt.
The Affluent Society (1958)

11 It is not necessary to advertise food to hungry people, fuel to cold people, or houses to the homeless.
American Capitalism (1952)

12 Trickle-down theory—the less than elegant metaphor that if one feeds the horse enough oats, some will pass through to the road for the sparrows.
The Culture of Contentment (1992)

13 You cannot know the intentions of a government that doesn't know them itself.
'Galbraith's First Law of Intelligence', formulated in early 1960s
A Life in Our Times (1981)

14 The reduction of politics to a spectator sport...has been one of the more malign accomplishments of television. Television newsmen are breathless on how the game is being played, largely silent on what the game is all about.
A Life in Our Times (1981)

1 The experience of being disastrously wrong is salutary; no economist should be denied it, and not many are.
A Life in Our Times (1981)

2 In public administration good sense would seem to require the public expectation be kept at the lowest possible level in order to minimize eventual disappointment.
A Life in Our Times (1981)

3 After a lifetime in public office, self-censorship becomes not only automatic but a part of one's personality.
A Life in Our Times (1981)

4 Nothing is so firmly established in Puritan and Presbyterian belief as that people cannot be suffering very much if they are out in healthy fresh air—and also safely out of sight.
of the public view of rural as opposed to urban poverty
A Life in Our Times (1981)

5 Of all the races on earth, the Indians have the most nearly inexhaustible appetite for oratory.
A Life in Our Times (1981)

6 One of the recurrent and dangerous influences on our foreign policy—fear of the political consequences of doing the sensible thing, which in many cases is nothing much at all.
A Life in Our Times (1981)

7 Migration…is the oldest action against poverty. It selects those who most want help. It is good for the country to which they go; it helps break the equilibrium of poverty in the country from which they came.
The Nature of Mass Poverty (1979)

8 *of the defeat of Germany in World War Two:*
That they were defeated is conclusive testimony to the inherent inefficiencies of dictatorship, the inherent efficiencies of freedom.
in *Fortune* December 1945

9 [Intellectual torpor is] the disease of opposition parties, for initiative and imagination ordinarily lie with responsibility for action.
letter to Adlai Stevenson, September 1953

10 Politics is not the art of the possible. It consists in choosing between the disastrous and the unpalatable.
letter to President **Kennedy**, 2 March 1962; see **Bismarck 34:5**

11 The modern conservative is… engaged…in one of man's oldest, best financed, most applauded, and, on the whole, least successful exercises in moral philosophy. That is the search for a superior moral justification for selfishness.
in *Harper's Magazine* March 1964

12 There are times in politics when you must be on the right side and lose.
attributed, 1968

13 Galbraith's law states that anyone who says he won't resign four times, will.
attributed, 1973

George Galloway 1954–
Scottish politician, expelled from the Labour Party in 2003 and now a member of Respect

14 Sir, I salute your courage, your strength, your indefatigability
*to Saddam **Hussein***
in Baghdad, 1994; quoted in *The Scotsman* 20 October 2003 (online edition)

15 I met Saddam Hussein exactly the same number of times as Donald Rumsfeld met him. The difference is that Donald Rumsfeld met him to sell him guns.
appearing before the US Senate Permanent Subcommittee on Investigations, 17 May 2005
in *Times Online* 23 May 2005 (online edition)

Indira Gandhi 1917–84
Indian stateswoman; Prime Minister 1966–77 and 1980–4

16 Politics is the art of acquiring, holding, and wielding power.
attributed, 1975

17 We do not tilt on either side…we

walk upright.
when asked by a reporter why India 'always tilted towards the Soviet Union'
in Washington, 1982; Inder Malhotra *Indira Gandhi* (1989)

1 I have lived a long life and I am proud that I spent the whole of my life in the service of my people. I am only proud of this and of nothing else. I shall continue to serve until my last breath and when I die, I can say, that every drop of my blood will invigorate India and strengthen it.
speech, Bhubaneshwar, 30 October 1984 (the night before she was assassinated); *Selected Speeches* (1986) vol. 5

Mahatma Gandhi 1869–1948
Indian statesman. On Gandhi: see **Naidu 223:1, Nehru 224:11**

2 What difference does it make to the dead, the orphans and the homeless, whether the mad destruction is wrought under the name of totalitarianism or the holy name of liberty or democracy?
Non-Violence in Peace and War (1942) vol. 1

3 The moment the slave resolves that he will no longer be a slave, his fetters fall. He frees himself and shows the way to others. Freedom and slavery are mental states.
Non-Violence in Peace and War (1949) vol. 2

4 Non-violence is the first article of my faith. It is also the last article of my creed.
speech at Shahi Bag, 18 March 1922, on a charge of sedition; in *Young India* 23 March 1922

5 *on being asked what he thought of modern civilization:*
That would be a good idea.
while visiting England in 1930
E. F. Schumacher *Good Work* (1979)

6 Capital as such is not evil, it is its wrong use that is evil. Capital in some form or other will always be needed.
in *Harijan* 28 July 1940

7 Please go on. It is my day of silence.
note passed to the British Cabinet Mission at a meeting in 1942; Peter Hennessy *Never Again* (1992)

8 We must be the change we wish to see in the world.
not traced in Gandhi's writings, but said to be a favourite saying; attributed (1989) in *Yale Book of Quotations*

Gabriel García Márquez 1928–
Colombian novelist

9 To the Europeans, South America is a man with a moustache, a guitar and a gun.
No One Writes to the Colonel (1961)

James A. Garfield 1831–81
American Republican statesman; 20th President of the US 1881

10 Fellow-citizens: God reigns, and the Government at Washington lives!
speech on the assassination of President **Lincoln**, 1865; in *Death of President Garfield* (1881)

11 I am not willing that this discussion should close without any mention of the value of a true teacher. Give me a log hut, with only a simple bench, Mark Hopkins [president of Williams College] on one end and I on the other, and you may have all the buildings, apparatus and libraries without him.
address to Williams College Alumni, New York, 28 December 1871

Giuseppe Garibaldi 1807–82
Italian patriot and military leader

12 Men, I'm getting out of Rome. Anyone who wants to carry on the war against the outsiders, come with me. I can offer you neither honours nor wages; I offer you hunger, thirst, forced marches, battles and death. Anyone who loves his country, follow me.
Giuseppe Guerzoni *Garibaldi* (1882) vol. 1 (not a verbatim record)

John Nance Garner 1868–1967
American Democratic politician; vice-president 1933–41

13 The vice-presidency isn't worth a pitcher of warm piss.
O. C. Fisher *Cactus Jack* (1978)

William Lloyd Garrison 1805–79
American anti-slavery campaigner

1 I am in earnest—I will not
equivocate—I will not excuse—I
will not retreat a single inch—and I
will be heard!
in *The Liberator* 1 January 1831 'Salutatory
Address'

2 The compact which exists
between the North and the South
is 'a covenant with death and an
agreement with hell'.
resolution adopted by the Massachusetts Anti-
Slavery Society, 27 January 1843

James Louis Garvin 1868–1947
British journalist and editor of the *Observer*

3 He spoke for an hour and put the
house in his pocket.
of F. E. **Smith**'s maiden speech in the House of
Commons, 12 May 1906
attributed

Eric Geddes 1875–1937
British politician and administrator

4 The Germans, if this Government
is returned, are going to pay
every penny; they are going to be
squeezed as a lemon is squeezed—
until the pips squeak.
speech at Cambridge, 10 December 1918

Martha Gellhorn 1908–98
American journalist

5 *of the defeat of the Spanish Republic:*
I daresay we all became more
competent press tourists because
of it, since we never again cared so
much. You can only love one war;
afterward, I suppose, you do your
duty.
The Honeyed Peace (1953)

Jean Genet 1910–86
French novelist, poet, and dramatist

6 What we need is hatred. From it our
ideas are born.
The Blacks (1959); epigraph

7 Are you there…Africa of the
millions of royal slaves, deported
Africa, drifting continent, are

you there? Slowly you vanish,
you withdraw into the past, into
the tales of castaways, colonial
museums, the works of scholars.
The Blacks (1959)

Genghis Khan (Temujin) 1162–1227
Mongol ruler, who took the name Genghis Khan ('ruler
of all') in 1206

8 Happiness lies in conquering
one's enemies, in driving them
in front of oneself, in taking
their property, in savouring their
despair, in outraging their wives
and daughters.
Witold Rodzinski *The Walled Kingdom: A
History of China* (1979)

George III 1738–1820
British monarch, King of Great Britain and Ireland from
1760. On George III: see **Walpole 324:13**

9 Born and educated in this country,
I glory in the name of Briton.
The King's Speech on Opening the Session
18 November 1760

10 When he has wearied me for two
hours he looks at his watch, to see
if he may not tire me for an hour
more.
of George **Grenville**
in 1765; Horace Walpole *The Reign of
George III* (1845)

11 *of America:*
Knavery seems to be so much the
striking feature of its inhabitants
that it may not in the end be an
evil that they become aliens to this
kingdom.
draft of letter to Lord Shelburne, 10 November
1782

George IV 1762–1830
British monarch, King of Great Britain and Ireland
from 1820

12 PRINCE OF WALES: True blue and Mrs
Crewe.
MRS CREWE: Buff and blue and all of
you.
*toast proposed by George IV when Prince of
Wales to Mrs Crewe, in honour of her support
for the Whigs and Charles James Fox in the
Westminster election of 1784 (buff and blue*

were the Whig colours)
at a dinner at Carlton House, May 1784;
Amanda Foreman *Georgiana Duchess of Devonshire* (1998)

George V 1865–1936

British monarch, King of Great Britain and Ireland from 1910. On George V: see **Nicolson 227:6**; see also **Last words 178:8**

1 I venture to allude to the impression which seemed generally to prevail among their brethren across the seas, that the Old Country must wake up if she intends to maintain her old position of pre-eminence in her Colonial trade against foreign competitors.
speech at Guildhall, 5 December 1901 (the speech was reprinted in 1911 with the title 'Wake up, England')

2 I pray that my coming to Ireland today may prove to be the first step towards an end of strife among her people, whatever their race or creed. In that hope I appeal to all Irishmen to pause, to stretch out the hand of forbearance and conciliation, to forgive and forget, and to join with me in making for the land they love a new era of peace, contentment and goodwill.
speech to the new Ulster Parliament at Stormont, 22 June 1921; Kenneth Rose *King George V* (1983)

3 I have many times asked myself whether there can be more potent advocates of peace upon earth through the years to come than this massed multitude of silent witnesses to the desolation of war.
message read at Terlincthun Cemetery, Boulogne, 13 May 1922; in *Times* 15 May 1922

4 You have kept up the dignity of the office without using it to give you dignity.
to the outgoing Prime Minister, Ramsay MacDonald
Ramsay MacDonald diary, 7 June 1934

5 The complex forms and balanced spirit of our constitution were not the discovery of a single era, still less of a single party or of a single person. They are the slow accretion of centuries, the outcome of patience, tradition and experience.
the words of G. M. Trevelyan in the King's Silver Jubilee address to Parliament, 1935
David Cannadine *G. M. Trevelyan: a Life in History* (1992)

6 I will not have another war. *I will not*. The last one was none of my doing and if there is another one and we are threatened with being brought into it, I will go to Trafalgar Square and wave a red flag myself sooner than allow this country to be brought in.
in 1935, in Andrew Roberts *Eminent Churchillians* (1994)

7 *in conversation with Anthony **Eden**, 23 December 1935, following Samuel Hoare's resignation as Foreign Secretary:*
I said to your predecessor: 'You know what they're all saying, no more coals to Newcastle, no more Hoares to Paris.' The fellow didn't even laugh.
Earl of Avon *Facing the Dictators* (1962)

8 After I am dead, the boy will ruin himself in twelve months.
*on his son, the future **Edward VIII***
Keith Middlemas and John Barnes *Baldwin* (1969)

9 *on H. G. Wells's comment on 'an alien and uninspiring court':*
I may be uninspiring, but I'll be damned if I'm an alien!
Sarah Bradford *George VI* (1989); attributed

10 My father was frightened of his mother; I was frightened of my father, and I am damned well going to see to it that my children are frightened of me.
attributed in Randolph S. Churchill *Lord Derby* (1959), but almost certainly apocryphal; see Kenneth Rose *George V* (1983)

George VI 1895–1952

British monarch, King of Great Britain and Northern Ireland from 1936. See also **Haskins 136:13**

11 Personally I feel happier now that we have no allies to be polite to and to pamper.
to Queen Mary, 27 June 1940
John Wheeler-Bennett *King George VI* (1958)

1 ATTLEE: I've won the election.
GEORGE VI: I know. I heard it on the Six
O'Clock News.
*first exchange between the King and his newly
elected Labour Prime Minister, 26 July 1945;
perhaps apocryphal*
Peter Hennessy *Never Again* (1992)

2 TRUMAN: You've had a revolution.
GEORGE VI: Oh no! we don't have those
here.
*during President **Truman**'s visit to Britain just
after Labour's election victory.*
Hugh Dalton *Political Diary* (1986) 28 July 1945

Geronimo c. 1829–1909
American Apache chief

3 Once I moved about like the wind.
Now I surrender to you and that is
all.
surrendering to General Crook, 25 March
1886; Dee Brown *Bury My Heart at Wounded
Knee* (1970) ch. 17

Edward Gibbon 1737–94
English historian

4 The division of Europe into a
number of independent states
connected, however, with each
other, by the general resemblance
of religion, language, and manners,
is productive of the most beneficial
consequences to the liberty of
mankind.
The Decline and Fall of the Roman Empire
(1776–88)

5 In elective monarchies, the vacancy
of the throne is a moment big with
danger and mischief.
The Decline and Fall of the Roman Empire
(1776–88)

6 The various modes of worship,
which prevailed in the Roman
world, were all considered by the
people as equally true; by the
philosopher, as equally false; and
by the magistrate, as equally useful.
And thus toleration produced not
only mutual indulgence, but even
religious concord.
The Decline and Fall of the Roman Empire
(1776–88)

7 The principles of a free constitution
are irrecoverably lost, when the
legislative power is nominated by
the executive.
The Decline and Fall of the Roman Empire
(1776–88)

8 The ascent to greatness, however
steep and dangerous, may
entertain an active spirit with the
consciousness and exercise of its
own powers; but the possession of
a throne could never yet afford a
lasting satisfaction to an ambitious
mind.
The Decline and Fall of the Roman Empire
(1776–88)

9 History…is, indeed, little more than
the register of the crimes, follies,
and misfortunes of mankind.
The Decline and Fall of the Roman Empire
(1776–88); see **Voltaire 323:3**

10 In every age and country, the wiser,
or at least the stronger, of the two
sexes, has usurped the powers of
the state, and confined the other to
the cares and pleasures of domestic
life.
The Decline and Fall of the Roman Empire
(1776–88)

11 According to the reasoning of
tyrants, those who have been
esteemed worthy of the throne
deserve death, and those who
deliberate have already rebelled.
The Decline and Fall of the Roman Empire
(1776–88)

12 All taxes must, at last, fall upon
agriculture.
quoting Artaxerxes, in *The Decline and Fall of
the Roman Empire* (1776–88) ch. 8

13 Whenever the offence inspires less
horror than the punishment, the
rigour of penal law is obliged to
give way to the common feelings of
mankind.
The Decline and Fall of the Roman Empire
(1776–88) ch. 14

14 Corruption, the most infallible
symptom of constitutional liberty.
The Decline and Fall of the Roman Empire
(1776–88)

15 In every deed of mischief he had a
heart to resolve, a head to contrive,

and a hand to execute.
of Comnenus
  The Decline and Fall of the Roman Empire
  (1776–88)

1 Our sympathy is cold to the relation of distant misery.
  The Decline and Fall of the Roman Empire
  (1776–88)

2 There is nothing perhaps more adverse to nature and reason than to hold in obedience remote countries and foreign nations in opposition to their inclination and interest.
  The Decline and Fall of the Roman Empire
  (1776–88)

3 Persuasion is the resource of the feeble; and the feeble can seldom persuade.
  The Decline and Fall of the Roman Empire
  (1776–88)

4 All that is human must retrograde if it does not advance.
  The Decline and Fall of the Roman Empire
  (1776–88)

5 The satirist may laugh, the philosopher may preach, but Reason herself will respect the prejudices and habits which have been consecrated by the experience of mankind.
  Memoirs of My Life (1796)

6 I admire his eloquence, I approve his politics, I adore his chivalry, and I can even forgive his superstition.
  of Edmund **Burke**
  letter to Lord Sheffield, 5 February 1791

7 Let him do what he will I must love the dog.
  of Charles James **Fox**
  letter to Lord Sheffield, 6 January 1793

Kahlil Gibran 1883–1931
Lebanese-born American writer and painter

8 Are you a politician who says to himself: 'I will use my country for my own benefit'?…Or are you a devoted patriot, who whispers in the ear of his inner self: 'I love to serve my country as a faithful servant.'
  The New Frontier (1931); see **Kennedy 167:4**

W. S. Gilbert 1836–1911
English writer of comic and satirical verse

9 All shall equal be.
  The Earl, the Marquis, and the Dook,
  The Groom, the Butler, and the Cook,
  The Aristocrat who banks with
    Coutts,
  The Aristocrat who cleans the boots.
  The Gondoliers (1889)

10 When every one is somebodee,
  Then no one's anybody.
  The Gondoliers (1889) act 2

11 I always voted at my party's call,
  And I never thought of thinking for
    myself at all.
  HMS Pinafore (1878)

12 I often think it's comical
  How Nature always does contrive
  That every boy and every gal,
  That's born into the world alive,
  Is either a little Liberal,
  Or else a little Conservative!
  Iolanthe (1882)

13 The House of Peers, throughout
    the war,
  Did nothing in particular,
  And did it very well.
  Iolanthe (1882)

14 When in that House MPs divide,
  If they've a brain and cerebellum too,
  They have to leave that brain outside,
  And vote just as their leaders tell
    'em to.
  Iolanthe (1882)

15 The prospect of a lot
  Of dull MPs in close proximity,
  All thinking for themselves is what
  No man can face with equanimity.
  Iolanthe (1882)

16 The idiot who praises, with
    enthusiastic tone,
  All centuries but this, and every
    country but his own.
  The Mikado (1885)

17 No Englishman unmoved that
    statement hears,
  Because, with all our faults, we love
    our House of Peers.
  The Pirates of Penzance (1879)

Andrew Gilligan 1968–
British journalist

1 I have spoken to a British
official who was involved in the
preparation of the dossier, and he
told me that until the week before
it was published, the draft dossier
produced by the intelligence
services added little to what was
already publicly known. He said:
[Voiceover]: 'It was transformed in
the week before it was published, to
make it sexier'.
BBC Radio 4 *Today* programme, 29 May 2003;
in *Guardian* 27 June 2003

Newton Gingrich 1943–
American Republican politician; Speaker of the House
of Representatives 1995–9

2 No society can survive, no
civilization can survive, with
12-year-olds having babies, with
15-year-olds killing each other,
with 17-year-olds dying of Aids,
with 18-year-olds getting diplomas
they can't read.
*in December 1994, after the Republican electoral
victory*
in *Times* 9 February 1995

George Gipp 1895–1920
American footballer

3 Win just one for the Gipper.
catch-phrase later associated with Ronald
Reagan, who uttered the immortal words in
the 1940 film *Knute Rockne, All American*

Rudy Giuliani 1944–
American Republican politician, Mayor of New York
1993–2001

4 Freedom is about the willingness of
every single human being to cede
to lawful authority a great deal of
discretion about what you do, and
how you do it.
attributed, in *Independent* 10 July 1999

5 The number of casualties will be
more than any of us can bear.
*in the aftermath of the terrorist attacks which
destroyed the World Trade Center in New York,
and damaged the Pentagon, 11 September 2001*
in *Times* 12 September 2001

Catherine Gladstone 1812–1900
British wife of William Ewart **Gladstone**

6 *to her husband:*
Oh, William dear, if you weren't
such a great man you would be a
terrible bore.
Roy Jenkins *Gladstone* (1995)

William Ewart Gladstone 1809–98
British Liberal statesman; Prime Minister, 1868–74,
1880–5, 1886, 1892–4. On Gladstone: see
**Aberdeen 1:2, Anonymous 10:14, Bagehot 20:12,
Churchill 65:1, Churchill 65:2, Churchill 70:16,
Disraeli 93:24, Disraeli 94:5, Hennessy 141:4,
Labouchere 176:7, Macaulay 194:4,
Salisbury 272:13, Victoria 321:10, Victoria 322:3**

7 Ireland, Ireland! that cloud in the
west, that coming storm.
letter to his wife, 12 October 1845

8 This is the negation of God erected
into a system of Government.
*A Letter to the Earl of Aberdeen on the State
Prosecutions of the Neapolitan Government*
(1851)

9 Your business is not to govern the
country but it is, if you think fit, to
call to account those who do govern
it.
speech to the House of Commons, 29 January
1855

10 Finance is, as it were, the stomach
of the country, from which all the
other organs take their tone.
article on finance, 1858, in H. C. G. Matthew
Gladstone 1809–1874 (1986)

11 I am come among you 'unmuzzled'.
after his parliamentary defeat at Oxford University
speech in Manchester, 18 July 1865

12 You cannot fight against the future.
Time is on our side.
on the Reform Bill
speech, House of Commons, 27 April 1866

13 Justice delayed is justice denied.
speech on the state of Ireland, House of
Commons, 16 March 1868; see **Magna
Carta 201:12**

14 My mission is to pacify Ireland.
*on receiving the news that he was to form his first
cabinet, 1 December 1868*
H. C. G. Matthew *Gladstone 1809–1874* (1986)

15 Swimming for his life, a man
does not see much of the country

through which the river winds.
diary, 31 December 1868

1 We have been borne down in a
torrent of gin and beer.
letter to his brother, 6 February 1874

2 Human justice is ever lagging after
wrong, as the prayers in Homer
came limping after sin.
in *Contemporary Review* December 1876

3 The love of freedom itself is hardly
stronger in England than the love of
aristocracy.
in *Nineteenth Century* 1877

4 Let the Turks now carry away
their abuses in the only possible
manner, namely by carrying off
themselves...one and all, bag and
baggage, shall I hope clear out from
the province they have desolated
and profaned.
Bulgarian Horrors and the Question of the East
(1876)

5 [The British Constitution]
presumes more boldly than any
other the good sense and the good
faith of those who work it.
Gleanings of Past Years (1879) vol. 1

6 [An] Established Clergy will always
be a Tory Corps d'Armée.
letter to Bishop Goodwin, 8 September 1881

7 To the actual, as distinct from the
reported, strength of the Empire,
India adds nothing. She immensely
adds to the responsibility of
Government.
H. C. G. Matthew *Gladstone 1875–1898* (1995)

8 There never was a Churchill
from John of Marlborough down
that had either morals or principles.
in conversation in 1882, recorded by Captain
R. V. Briscoe; R. F. Foster *Lord Randolph
Churchill* (1981)

9 I would tell them of my own
intention to keep my counsel...and
I will venture to recommend them,
as an old Parliamentary hand, to do
the same.
in the House of Commons, 21 January 1886

10 This, if I understand it, is one of
those golden moments of our
history, one of those opportunities
which may come and may go, but

which rarely returns.
on the Second Reading of the Home Rule Bill
in the House of Commons, 7 June 1886

11 I will venture to say, that upon
the one great class of subjects, the
largest and the most weighty of
them all, where the leading and
determining considerations that
ought to lead to a conclusion are
truth, justice, and humanity—upon
these, gentlemen, all the world
over, I will back the masses against
the classes.
speech in Liverpool, 28 June 1886

12 One prayer absorbs all others:
Ireland, Ireland, Ireland.
diary, 10 April 1887

13 Welsh nationality is as great a
reality as English nationality.
speech at Swansea, 4 June 1887

14 The blubbering Cabinet.
*of the colleagues who wept at his final Cabinet
meeting*
diary, 1 March 1894; note

15 What that Sicilian mule was to me, I
have been to the Queen.
*of a mule on which Gladstone rode, which he
'could neither love nor like', although it had
rendered him 'much valuable service'*
memorandum, 20 March 1894

16 Former Prime Ministers are like
great rafts floating untethered in a
harbour.
Roy Jenkins *Gladstone* (1995)

17 I absorb the vapour and return it as
a flood.
on public speaking
Lord Riddell *Some Things That Matter*
(1927 ed.)

18 I am sorry to say that I have a long
speech fermenting in me, and I feel
as a loaf might in the oven.
Roy Jenkins *Gladstone* (1995)

19 It is not a Life at all. It is a Reticence,
in three volumes.
on J. W. Cross's Life of George Eliot
E. F. Benson *As We Were* (1930)

20 Liberalism is trust of the
people, tempered by prudence;
conservatism is distrust of the
people, tempered by fear.
attributed; S. A. Bent *Familiar Short Sayings of
Great Men* (1887)

1 [Money should] fructify in the pockets of the people.
　H. G. C. Matthew *Gladstone 1809–1874* (1986)

2 There is scarcely a single moral action of a single man of which other men can have such a knowledge, in its ultimate grounds, its surrounding incidents, and the real determining cause of its merits, as to warrant their pronouncing a conclusive judgement upon it.
　H. C. G. Matthew *Gladstone 1875–1898* (1995)

Thomas Glascock
American politician

3 *when General Thomas Glascock of Georgia took his seat in the US Senate, a mutual friend expressed the wish to introduce him to Henry **Clay** of Virginia:*
　No, sir! I am his adversary, and choose not to subject myself to his fascination.
　Robert V. Remini *Henry Clay* (1991)

Joseph Goebbels 1897–1945
German Nazi leader

4 We can manage without butter but not, for example, without guns. If we are attacked we can only defend ourselves with guns not with butter.
　speech in Berlin, 17 January 1936; see **Goering 126:6**

5 Making noise is an effective means of opposition.
　Ernest K. Bramsted *Goebbels and National Socialist Propaganda 1925–45* (1965)

Hermann Goering 1893–1946
German Nazi leader

6 We have no butter...but I ask you—would you rather have butter or guns?...preparedness makes us powerful. Butter merely makes us fat.
　speech at Hamburg, 1936; W. Frischauer *Goering* (1951); see **Goebbels 126:4**

7 I herewith commission you to carry out all preparations with regard to...a *total solution* of the Jewish question in those territories of Europe which are under German influence.
　instructions to Heydrich, 31 July 1941
　　W. L. Shirer *The Rise and Fall of the Third Reich* (1962)

8 The people can always be brought to the bidding of the leaders. That is easy. All you have to do is tell them they are being attacked and denounce the pacifists for lack of patriotism and exposing the country to danger. It works the same in any country.
　in conversation in his cell in Nuremburg, 18 April 1946; Gustave Gilbert *Nuremburg Diary* (1947)

Nikolai Gogol 1809–52
Russian writer

9 [Are not] you too, Russia, speeding along like a spirited *troika* that nothing can overtake?...Everything on earth is flying past, and looking askance, other nations and states draw aside and make way.
　Dead Souls (1842)

Isaac Goldberg 1887–1938

10 Diplomacy is to do and say The nastiest thing in the nicest way.
　The Reflex October 1927

Ludwig Max Goldberger 1848–1913

11 America, the land of unlimited possibilities.
　Land of Unlimited Possibilities: Observations on Economic Life in the United States of America (1903)

William Golding 1911–93
English novelist

12 Anyone who moved through those years without understanding that man produces evil as a bee produces honey, must have been blind or wrong in the head.
　of the Second World War
　　The Hot Gates (1965) 'Fable'

Emma Goldman 1869–1940
American anarchist

13 Anarchism, then, really, stands for

the liberation of the human mind
from the dominion of religion;
the liberation of the human body
from the dominion of property;
liberation from the shackles and
restraint of government.
Anarchism and Other Essays (1910)

1 The political arena leaves one no
alternative, one must either be a
dunce or a rogue.
Anarchism and Other Essays (1910)

Oliver Goldsmith 1728–74
Irish writer, poet, and dramatist

2 Ill fares the land, to hast'ning ills
a prey,
Where wealth accumulates, and men
decay;
Princes and lords may flourish, or
may fade;
A breath can make them, as a breath
has made;
But a bold peasantry, their country's
pride,
When once destroyed, can never be
supplied.
The Deserted Village (1770)

3 How wide the limits stand
Between a splendid and a happy land.
The Deserted Village (1770)

4 Such is the patriot's boast, where'er
we roam,
His first, best country ever is, at
home.
The Traveller (1764)

5 Laws grind the poor, and rich men
rule the law.
The Traveller (1764)

6 How small, of all that human hearts
endure,
That part which laws or kings can
cause or cure!
The Traveller (1764); see **Johnson 160:14**

Barry Goldwater 1909–98
American Republican politician

7 I would remind you that extremism
in the defence of liberty is no vice!
And let me remind you also that
moderation in the pursuit of justice

is no virtue!
speech accepting the presidential nomination,
16 July 1964, in *New York Times* 17 July 1964

Maud Gonne 1867–1953
Irish nationalist and actress

8 The Famine Queen.
of Queen Victoria
in *L'Irlande Libre* 1900

Alberto Gonzales 1955–
American lawyer, White House Counsel 2001–5 and
Attorney General 2005–7

9 The nature of the new war
[against terrorism] places a high
premium on other factors, such
as the ability to quickly obtain
information from captured
terrorists and their sponsors in
order to avoid further atrocities or
war crimes…In my judgment, this
new paradigm renders obsolete
Geneva's strict limitations on
questioning of enemy prisoners
and renders quaint some of its
provisions requiring that captured
enemy be afforded such things
as commissary privileges, scrip
(i.e. advances of monthly pay),
athletic uniforms and scientific
instruments.
memorandum, 25 January 2002

Charles Goodhart 1936–
English economist

10 Any observed statistical regularity
will tend to collapse once pressure is
placed upon it for control purposes.
*known as Goodhart's Law, and often quoted as
'When a measure becomes a target it ceases to be
a good measure'*
*Monetary Theory and Practice: the UK
Experience* (1984)

Amy Goodman 1957–
American journalist

11 Go to where the silence is and say
something.
*accepting an award from Columbia University for
her coverage of the 1991 massacre in East Timor
by Indonesian troops*
in *Columbia Journalism Review* March/April
1994

Richard Goodwin 1931–
American writer

1 People come to Washington believing it's the centre of power. I know I did. It was only much later that I learned that Washington is a steering wheel that's not connected to the engine.
   Peter McWilliams *Ain't Nobody's Business If You Do* (1993)

Mikhail Sergeevich Gorbachev 1931–
Soviet statesman; General Secretary of the Communist Party of the USSR 1985–91 and President 1988–91. On Gorbachev: see **Gromyko 131:4**, **Thatcher 310:6**, **Zhvanetsky 340:10**

2 The guilt of Stalin and his immediate entourage before the Party and the people for the mass repressions and lawlessness they committed is enormous and unforgivable.
   speech on the seventieth anniversary of the Russian Revolution, 2 November 1987

3 The idea of restructuring [*perestroika*]…combines continuity and innovation, the historical experience of Bolshevism and the contemporaneity of socialism.
   speech on the seventieth anniversary of the Russian Revolution, 2 November 1987

4 After leaving the Kremlin…my conscience was clear. The promise I gave to the people when I started the process of perestroika was kept: I gave them freedom.
   Memoirs (1995)

Albert Gore Jnr. 1948–
American Democratic politician, Vice-President 1993–2001; presidential candidate 2000

5 I am Al Gore, and I used to be the next president of the United States of America.
   addressing Bocconi University in Milan, in *Newsweek* 19 March 2001; see **Carter 58:3**

Maxim Gorky 1868–1936
Russian writer and revolutionary

6 The proletarian state must bring up thousands of excellent 'mechanics of culture', 'engineers of the soul'.
   speech at the Writers' Congress 1934; see **Kennedy 167:14**, **Stalin 299:4**

George Joachim, Lord Goschen 1831–1907
British Liberal Unionist politician. On Goschen: see **Churchill 65:5**

7 I have the courage of my opinions, but I have not the temerity to give a political blank cheque to Lord Salisbury.
   in the House of Commons, 19 February 1884

Ernest Gowers 1880–1966
British public servant

8 It is not easy nowadays to remember anything so contrary to all appearances as that officials are the servants of the public; and the official must try not to foster the illusion that it is the other way round.
   Plain Words (1948)

D. M. Graham 1911–99
British broadcaster

9 That this House will in no circumstances fight for its King and Country.
   motion for a debate at the Oxford Union, 9 February 1933 (passed by 275 votes to 153)
   motion worded by Graham when Librarian of the Oxford Union

James Graham see Marquess of Montrose

Phil Gramm 1942–
American Republican politician

10 Balancing the budget is like going to heaven. Everybody wants to do

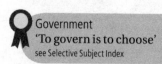

Government
'To govern is to choose'
see Selective Subject Index

it, but nobody wants to do what you have to do to get there.
in a television interview, 16 September 1990

Antonio Gramsci 1891–1937
Italian political theorist and activist

1 Our motto is still alive and to the point: Pessimism of the intellect, optimism of the will.
the motto of the periodical L'Ordine Nuovo *was borrowed from the French writer Romain Rolland (1866–1944)*
in *L'Ordine Nuovo* 4 March 1921

Bernie Grant 1944–2000
British Labour politician

2 The police were to blame for what happened on Sunday night and what they got was a bloody good hiding.
after the Broadwater Farm riots in which a policeman was killed
as leader of Haringey Council outside Tottenham Town Hall, 8 October 1985

Ulysses S. Grant 1822–85
American Unionist general and statesman; 18th President of the US 1869–77. On Grant: see **Sherman 288:3**

3 I purpose to fight it out on this line, if it takes all summer.
dispatch to Washington, from headquarters in the field, 11 May 1864
P. C. Headley *The Life and Campaigns of General U. S. Grant* (1869)

4 The war is over—the rebels are our countrymen again.
*preventing his men from cheering after **Lee**'s surrender at Appomattox*
on 9 April 1865

5 Let us have peace.
letter to General Joseph R. Hawkey, 29 May 1868, accepting the presidential nomination
P. C. Headley *The Life and Campaigns of General U. S. Grant* (1869)

6 I know no method to secure the repeal of bad or obnoxious laws so effective as their stringent execution.
inaugural address, 4 March 1869

7 Leave the matter of religion to the family altar, the church, and the private school, supported entirely by private contributions. Keep the church and state forever separate.
speech at Des Moines, Iowa, 1875

8 Labour disgraces no man; unfortunately you occasionally find men disgrace labour.
speech at Midland International Arbitration Union, Birmingham, England, 1877

Günter Grass 1927–
German novelist, poet, and dramatist

9 The citizen's first duty is unrest.
The Citizen's First Duty address delivered 1967; in *Speak Out!* (1968)

Henry Grattan 1746–1820
Irish nationalist leader

10 The thing he proposes to buy is what cannot be sold—liberty.
speech in the Irish Parliament against the proposed union, 16 January 1800, in *Dictionary of National Biography*

Frank Graves
Canadian pollster

11 It is like sleeping with an elephant who is an insomniac.
on relations between Canada and the US; see **Trudeau**
in *Guardian* 1 November 2004

John Chipman Gray 1839–1915
American lawyer

12 Dirt is only matter out of place; and what is a blot on the escutcheon of the Common Law may be a jewel in the crown of the Social Republic.
Restraints on the Alienation of Property (2nd ed., 1895) preface

Patrick, Lord Gray d. 1612

13 A dead woman bites not.
*oral tradition, Gray being said to have pressed hard for the execution of **Mary** Queen of Scots in 1587, with the words 'Mortua non mordet [Being dead, she will bite no more]'*
A. Darcy's 1625 translation of William Camden's *Annals of the Reign of Queen Elizabeth* (1615) vol. 1

Thomas Gray 1716–71
English poet

1 The boast of heraldry, the pomp of
pow'r,
And all that beauty, all that wealth
e'er gave,
Awaits alike th' inevitable hour,
The paths of glory lead but to the
grave.
Elegy Written in a Country Churchyard (1751)

2 Some village-Hampden, that with
dauntless breast
The little tyrant of his fields
withstood;
Some mute inglorious Milton here
may rest,
Some Cromwell guiltless of his
country's blood.
Elegy Written in a Country Churchyard (1751)

3 Forbad to wade through slaughter
to a throne,
And shut the gates of mercy on
mankind.
Elegy Written in a Country Churchyard (1751)

Horace Greeley 1811–72
American founder and editor of the *New York Tribune*

4 The illusion that times that were
are better than those that are, has
probably pervaded all ages.
The American Conflict (1864–6)

5 I never said all Democrats were
saloon keepers. What I said was
that all saloon keepers were
Democrats.
attributed

Alan Greenspan 1926–
American economist

6 How do we know when irrational
exuberance has unduly escalated
asset values?
speech in Washington, 5 December 1996

7 An infectious greed seemed to grip
much of our business community.
of the late 1990s
in *New York Times* 17 July 2002 (online edition)

8 The free lunch has still to be
invented.
in *Independent* 7 May 2004

Pope Gregory VII see Last words **178:11**

George Grenville 1712–70
British Whig statesman; Prime Minister 1763–5. On
Grenville: see **George III 120:10**, **Walpole 324:12**

9 A wise government knows how
to enforce with temper, or to
conciliate with dignity.
speaking against the expulsion of John Wilkes
in the House of Commons, 3 February 1769

Lord Grey of Fallodon 1862–1933
British Liberal politician

10 The lamps are going out all over
Europe; we shall not see them lit
again in our lifetime.
on the eve of the First World War
25 Years (1925) vol. 2

Arthur Griffith 1871–1922
Irish statesman

11 What I have signed I will stand by,
in the belief that the end of the
conflict of centuries is at hand.
statement to Dáil Éireann before the debate on
the Treaty, December 1921

12 We have brought back the flag; we
have brought back the evacuation
of Ireland after 700 years by British
troops and the formation of an Irish
army. We have brought back to
Ireland her full rights.
when moving acceptance of the Treaty in the
Dáil, December 1921

Roy Griffiths 1926–94
British businessman

13 If Florence Nightingale were
carrying her lamp through
the corridors of the NHS today
she would almost certainly be
searching for the people in charge.
in *Report of the NHS Management Inquiry*,
DHSS, 1983

John Grigg 1924–2001
British writer and journalist, who as Lord Altrincham
disclaimed his hereditary title in 1963

14 The personality conveyed by the
utterances which are put into
her mouth is that of a priggish

schoolgirl, captain of the hockey team, a prefect, and a recent candidate for confirmation. It is not thus that she will be able to come into her own as an independent and distinctive character.
of Queen *Elizabeth II*
  in *National and English Review* August 1957

1 Lloyd George would have a better rating in British mythology if he had shared the fate of Abraham Lincoln.
  attributed, 1963

2 Politicians are exiles from the normal, private world.
  attributed, 1964

Joseph ('Jo') Grimond 1913–93
British Liberal politician, Leader of the Liberal Party 1956–67

3 In bygone days, commanders were taught that when in doubt, they should march their troops towards the sound of gunfire. I intend to march my troops towards the sound of gunfire.
  speech to the Liberal Party Assembly, 14 September 1963

Andrei Gromyko 1909–89
Soviet statesman; President of the USSR 1985–8

4 Comrades, this man has a nice smile, but he's got iron teeth.
of *Mikhail Gorbachev*
  speech to Soviet Communist Party Central Committee, 11 March 1985

Philip Guedalla 1889–1944
British historian and biographer

5 *of the Admiralty committee to examine inventions:*
There they sit, like inverted Micawbers, waiting for something to turn down.
  in a speech at the Oxford Union, 1912; a similar comment has also been attributed to Winston Churchill of Treasury staff (Anthony Sampson *The Anatomy of Britain Today*)

6 Don't shoot till you see the stripes on their ties.
  attributed

Ernesto ('Che') Guevara 1928–67
Argentinian revolutionary and guerrilla leader

7 The Revolution is made by man, but man must forge his revolutionary spirit from day to day.
  Socialism and Man in Cuba (1968)

Nell Gwyn 1650–87
English actress and courtesan

8 Pray, good people, be civil. I am the Protestant whore.
  at Oxford, during the Popish Terror, 1681; B. Bevan *Nell Gwyn* (1969)

William Hague 1961–
British Conservative politician; Leader of the Conservative Party 1997–2001

9 Feather-bedding, pocket-lining, money-grabbing cronies.
  during the debate on lobbyists' influence and 'cronyism'
  in the House of Commons, 8 July 1998

10 Let me take you on a journey to a foreign land—to Britain after a second term of Tony Blair.
  speech to Conservative Party spring conference, Harrogate, 4 March 2001

Earl Haig 1861–1928
British general, Commander in France, 1915–18

11 A very weak-minded fellow I am afraid, and, like the feather pillow, bears the marks of the last person

who has sat on him!
describing the 17th Earl of Derby
  letter to Lady Haig, 14 January 1918; R. Blake
  Private Papers of Douglas Haig (1952)

1 Every position must be held to
the last man: there must be no
retirement. With our backs to the
wall, and believing in the justice of
our cause, each one of us must fight
on to the end.
  order to British troops, 12 April 1918; A. Duff
  Cooper *Haig* (1936) vol. 2

Lord Hailsham 1907–2001
British Conservative politician

2 A great party is not to be brought
down because of a squalid affair
between a woman of easy virtue
and a proved liar.
on the Profumo affair
  in a television interview, 13 June 1963; in
  Times 14 June 1963

3 I believe there is a golden thread
which alone gives meaning to the
political history of the West, from
Marathon to Alamein, from Solon
to Winston Churchill and after.
This I chose to call the doctrine of
liberty under the law.
  in 1975; Anthony Sampson *The Changing
  Anatomy of Britain* (1982)

4 The elective dictatorship.
of the British Constitution
  title of the Dimbleby Lecture, 19 October 1976

5 In a confrontation with the politics
of power, the soft centre has always
melted away.
  in October 1981; Anthony Sampson *The
  Changing Anatomy of Britain* (1982)

6 *of Denis Healey:*
A piratical old bruiser with a first-
class mind and very bad manners.
  interview in *Times* 2 June 1987

7 The English and, more latterly, the
British, have the habit of acquiring
their institutions by chance or
inadvertence, and shedding them
in a fit of absent-mindedness.
  'The Granada Guildhall Lecture 1987'
  10 November 1987; see **Seeley 276:4**

8 Conservatives do not believe
that the political struggle is the
most important thing in life…

The simplest of them prefer fox-
hunting—the wisest religion.
  The Case for Conservatism (1947)

9 I've known every Prime Minister
to a greater or lesser extent since
Balfour, and most of them have
died unhappy.
  attributed, 1997

Richard Burdon Haldane
1856–1928
British politician, lawyer, and philosopher

10 We have come to the
conclusion… that in the sphere
of civil government the duty of
investigation and thought, as
preliminary to action, might with
great advantage be more definitely
added.
  Peter Hennessy *Whitehall* (1990)

H. R. Haldeman 1929–93
American Presidential assistant to Richard **Nixon**

11 Once the toothpaste is out of the
tube, it is awfully hard to get it
back in.
*on the Watergate affair, to John Dean, 8 April
1973*
  in *Hearings Before the Select Committee on
  Presidential Campaign Activities of US Senate:
  Watergate and Related Activities* (1973) vol. 4

Edward Everett Hale 1822–1909
American Unitarian clergyman; Senate chaplain for
1903

12 'Do you pray for the senators,
Dr Hale?' 'No, I look at the senators
and I pray for the country.'
  Van Wyck Brooks *New England Indian Summer*
  (1940)

Matthew Hale 1609–76
English judge

13 Christianity is part of the laws of
England.
  William Blackstone's summary of Hale's words
  (Taylor's case, 1676) in *Commentaries* (1769)
  vol. 4; the origin of the expression has been
  traced to Sir John Prisot (d. 1460)

Nathan Hale 1755–76
American revolutionary. See also **Last words 178:12**

1 Every kind of service necessary
to the public good becomes
honourable by being necessary.
his defence of espionage
letter to William Hull, 10 September 1776

Lord Halifax 1633–95
English politician and essayist

2 This innocent word *Trimmer*
signifieth no more than this, that
if men are together in a boat, and
one part of the company would
weigh it down on one side, another
would make it lean as much to the
contrary.
Character of a Trimmer (1685, printed 1688)

3 Men in business are in as much
danger from those that work under
them, as from those that work
against them.
*Political, Moral, and Miscellaneous Thoughts
and Reflections* (1750) 'Instruments of State
Ministers'

4 The best way to suppose what may
come, is to remember what is past.
*Political, Moral, and Miscellaneous Thoughts
and Reflections* (1750) 'Miscellaneous:
Experience'

5 A known liar should be outlawed in
a well-ordered government.
*Political, Moral, and Miscellaneous Thoughts
and Reflections* (1750) 'Miscellaneous: Lying'

6 After a revolution, you see the same
men in the drawing-room, and
within a week the same flatterers.
*Political, Moral, and Miscellaneous Thoughts
and Reflections* (1750) 'Of Courts'

7 Most men make little other use of
their speech than to give evidence
against their own understanding.
*Political, Moral, and Miscellaneous Thoughts
and Reflections* (1750) 'Of Folly and Fools'

8 There is...no fundamental, but
that *every supreme power must be
arbitrary.*
*Political, Moral, and Miscellaneous Thoughts
and Reflections* (1750) 'Of Fundamentals'

9 The people are never so perfectly
backed, but that they will
kick and fling if not stroked at

seasonable times.
*Political, Moral, and Miscellaneous Thoughts
and Reflections* (1750) 'Of Fundamentals'

10 In corrupted governments the place
is given for the sake of the man; in
good ones the man is chosen for the
sake of the place.
*Political, Moral, and Miscellaneous Thoughts
and Reflections* (1750) 'Of Fundamentals'

11 It is in a disorderly government as
in a river, the lightest things swim
at the top.
*Political, Moral, and Miscellaneous Thoughts
and Reflections* (1750) 'Of Government'

12 The best definition of the best
government is, that it has no
inconveniences but such as are
supportable; but inconveniences
there must be.
*Political, Moral, and Miscellaneous Thoughts
and Reflections* (1750) 'Of Government'

13 If the laws could speak for
themselves, they would complain
of the lawyers in the first place.
*Political, Moral, and Miscellaneous Thoughts
and Reflections* (1750) 'Of Laws'

14 Malice is of a low stature, but it hath
very long arms.
*Political, Moral, and Miscellaneous Thoughts
and Reflections* (1750) 'Of Malice and Envy'

15 The best party is but a kind of
conspiracy against the rest of the
nation.
*Political, Moral, and Miscellaneous Thoughts
and Reflections* (1750) 'Of Parties'

16 When the people contend for their
liberty, they seldom get anything by
their victory but new masters.
*Political, Moral, and Miscellaneous Thoughts
and Reflections* (1750) 'Of Prerogative, Power
and Liberty'

17 Power is so apt to be insolent and
Liberty to be saucy, that they are
very seldom upon good terms.
*Political, Moral, and Miscellaneous Thoughts
and Reflections* (1750) 'Of Prerogative, Power
and Liberty'

18 If none were to have liberty but
those who understand what it is,
there would not be many freed men

in the world.
*Political, Moral, and Miscellaneous Thoughts
and Reflections* (1750) 'Of Prerogative, Power
and Liberty'

1 Men are not hanged for stealing
horses, but that horses may not be
stolen.
*Political, Moral, and Miscellaneous Thoughts
and Reflections* (1750) 'Of Punishment'

2 Wherever a knave is not punished,
an honest man is laughed at.
*Political, Moral, and Miscellaneous Thoughts
and Reflections* (1750) 'Of Punishment'

3 State business is a cruel trade; good
nature is a bungler in it.
*Political, Moral, and Miscellaneous Thoughts
and Reflections* (1750) 'Wicked Ministers'

4 To the question, What shall we do
to be saved in this World? there is
no other answer but this, Look to
your Moat.
A Rough Draft of a New Model at Sea (1694)

5 Lord Rochester was made Lord
president: which being a post
superior in rank, but much inferior
both in advantage and credit to that
he held formerly, drew a jest from
Lord Halifax...he had heard of many
kicked down stairs, but never of any
that was kicked up stairs before.
Gilbert Burnet *History of My Own Time* (written
1683–6) vol. 1 (1724)

Lord Halifax 1881–1959
British Conservative politician and Foreign Secretary

6 *on being asked immediately after the Munich
crisis if he were not worn out by the late
nights:*
No, not exactly. But it spoils one's
eye for the high birds.
attributed

Margaret Halsey 1910–97
American writer

7 The English never smash in a face.
They merely refrain from asking it
to dinner.
With Malice Toward Some (1938)

W. F. ('Bull') Halsey 1882–1959
American admiral

8 The Third Fleet's sunken and

damaged ships have been salvaged
and are retiring at high speed
toward the enemy.
*on hearing claims that the Japanese had virtually
annihilated the US fleet*
report, 14 October 1944; E. B. Potter *Bull
Halsey* (1985)

Alexander Hamilton c. 1755–1804
American politician. On Hamilton: see **Webster 328:2**

9 A national debt, if it is not excessive,
will be to us a national blessing.
letter to Robert Morris, 30 April 1781

10 I believe the British government
forms the best model the world ever
produced...This government has
for its object public strength and
individual security.
in *Debates of the Federal Convention* 18 June
1787

11 We are now forming a republican
government. Real liberty is neither
found in despotism or the extremes
of democracy, but in moderate
government.
in *Debates of the Federal Convention* 26 June
1787

12 Let Americans disdain to be the
instruments of European greatness.
Let the thirteen States, bound
together in a strict and indissoluble
Union, concur in erecting one great
American system, superior to the
control of all transatlantic force or
influence, and able to dictate the
terms of the connection between
the old and the new world!
in *The Federalist* (1787–8) no. 11

13 Why has government been
instituted at all? Because the
passions of men will not conform to
the dictates of reason and justice,
without constraint.
in *The Federalist* (1787–8) no. 15

14 To admit foreigners
indiscriminately to the rights of
citizens...would be nothing less
than to admit the Grecian horse
into the citadel of our liberty and
sovereignty.
Works (1886) vol.7

1 Learn to think continentally.
advice to the newly independent United States
attributed; see **Chamberlain 60:6**

Learned Hand 1872–1961
American judge

2 Right conclusions are more likely to be gathered out of a multitude of tongues, than through any kind of authoritative selection. To many this is, and will always be, folly; but we have staked upon it our all.
in *United States v. Associated Press* 1943; see **Brennan 41:12**

Mark Hanna 1837–1904
American Republican politician and businessman

3 *of Theodore **Roosevelt**'s acceding to the Presidency on the assassination of William McKinley*
Now look, that damned cowboy is President of the United States.
in September 1901

Daniel Hannan 1971–
British Conservative politician

4 You cannot spend your way out of a recession or borrow your way out of debt.
speech to European Parliament, Strasbourg, 24 March 2009

Brian Hanrahan 1949–
British journalist

5 I counted them all out and I counted them all back.
on the number of British aeroplanes joining the raid on Port Stanley
BBC broadcast report, 1 May 1982

William Harcourt 1827–1904
British Liberal politician

6 We are all socialists now.
*during the passage of Lord **Goschen**'s 1888 budget, noted for the reduction of the national debt*
G. B. Shaw (ed.) *Fabian Essays in Socialism* (1889)

7 The value of the political heads of departments is to tell the permanent officials what the public will not stand.
A. G. Gardiner *The Life of Sir William Harcourt* (1923) vol. 2

Keir Hardie 1856–1915
Scottish Labour politician

8 From his childhood onward this boy [the future Edward VIII] will be surrounded by sycophants and flatterers by the score—[*Cries of* 'Oh, oh!']—and will be taught to believe himself as of a superior creation. [*Cries of* 'Oh, oh!'] A line will be drawn between him and the people whom he is to be called upon some day to reign over. In due course, following the precedent which has already been set, he will be sent on a tour round the world, and probably rumours of a morganatic alliance will follow—[*Loud cries of* 'Oh, oh!' *and* 'Order!']—and the end of it all will be that the country will be called upon to pay the bill. [*Cries of* Divide!]
in the House of Commons, 28 June 1894

9 Woman, even more than the working class, is the great unknown quantity of the race.
speech at Bradford, 11 April 1914

Warren G. Harding 1865–1923
American Republican statesman; 29th President of the US, 1921–3. On Harding: see **Longworth 190:13**

10 In the great fulfillment we must have a citizenship less concerned about what the government can do for it and more anxious about what it can do for the nation.
speech at the Republican National Convention, 7 June 1916; see **Kennedy 167:4**

11 America's present need is not heroics, but healing; not nostrums but normalcy; not revolution, but restoration.
speech at Boston, 14 May 1920

12 I must utter my belief in the divine inspiration of the founding fathers.
inaugural address, 4 March 1921

Thomas Hardy 1840–1928
English novelist and poet

1 War makes rattling good history;
  but Peace is poor reading.
  The Dynasts (1904) pt. 1, act 2, sc. 5

2 'Peace upon earth!' was said. We
  sing it,
  And pay a million priests to bring it.
  After two thousand years of mass
  We've got as far as poison-gas.
  'Christmas: 1924' (1928)

3 The offhand decision of some
  commonplace mind high in office
  at a critical moment influences
  the course of events for a hundred
  years.
  Florence Hardy *The Early Life of Thomas Hardy
  1840–91* (1928)

John Harington 1561–1612
English writer and courtier

4 Treason doth never prosper, what's
  the reason?
  For if it prosper, none dare call it
  treason.
  Epigrams (1618)

Lord Harlech 1918–85
British diplomat, Ambassador to Washington, 1961–5

5 Britain will be honoured by
  historians more for the way she
  disposed of an empire than for the
  way in which she acquired it.
  in *New York Times* 28 October 1962

Harold II c. 1019–66
English monarch, King 1066

6 He will give him seven feet of
  English ground, or as much more as
  he may be taller than other men.
  *his offer to Harald Hardrada of Norway, invading
  England, before the battle of Stamford Bridge*
  Snorri Sturluson *King Harald's Saga* (1260)

Stephen Harper 1959–
Canadian Conservative statesman, Prime Minister
from 2006

7 I've never really noticed complexity

to be Belinda's strong point.
  *responding to Belinda **Stronach**'s comment
  that he was not sensitive to the complex nature
  of Canada*
  in *CTV.ca* 18 May 2005 (online)

8 I'm basically a cautious person…I
  believe that it is better to light one
  candle than promise a million light
  bulbs.
  *announcing his party's full platform on 13 January
  2006*
  in *New York Times* 24 January 2006

Arthur Harris 1892–1984
British Air Force Marshal

9 I would not regard the whole of
  the remaining cities of Germany
  as worth the bones of one British
  Grenadier.
  *supporting the continued strategic bombing of
  German cities*
  letter to Norman Bottomley, deputy Chief of Air
  Staff, 29 March 1945; see **Bismarck 35:3**

William Henry Harrison 1773–1841
American Whig statesman and soldier, noted for his
victory at the battle of Tippecanoe in 1811, and 9th
President of the US, 1841, who died of pneumonia
one month after his inauguration. On Harrison: see
Slogans 291:19, Songs 296:12

10 We admit of no government by
  divine right…the only legitimate
  right to govern is an express grant
  of power from the governed.
  inaugural address, 4 March 1841

11 A decent and manly examination
  of the acts of government should be
  not only tolerated, but encouraged.
  inaugural address, 4 March 1841

David Hartley 1731–1813
English Whig politician

12 That the slave trade is contrary to
  the laws of God and to the rights of
  men.
  *proposing its abolition in the House of Commons
  in 1776*
  Charles Stuart *A Memoir of Granville Sharp*
  (1836)

Minnie Louise Haskins 1875–1957
English teacher and writer

13 And I said to the man who stood

at the gate of the year: 'Give me a light that I may tread safely into the unknown.'
And he replied:
'Go out into the darkness and put your hand into the Hand of God. That shall be to you better than light and safer than a known way.'
quoted by King George VI in his Christmas broadcast, 25 December 1939
Desert (1908) 'God Knows'

Roy Hattersley 1932–
British Labour politician

1 Politicians are entitled to change their minds. But when they adjust their principles some explanation is necessary.
in Observer 21 March 1999

Charles Haughey 1925–2006
Irish Fianna Fáil statesman; Taoiseach 1979–81, 1982, and 1987–92. On Haughey: see **O'Brien 231:13**

2 Every TD, from the youngest or newest in the House, dreams of being Taoiseach.
in Irish Times 23 May 1970 'This Week They Said'

3 It was a bizarre happening, an unprecedented situation, a grotesque situation, an almost unbelievable mischance.
on the series of events leading to the resignation of the Attorney General; the acronym GUBU was subsequently coined by Conor Cruise O'Brien to describe Haughey's style of government
at a press conference in 1982; T. Ryle Dwyer Charlie: the Political Biography of Charles Haughey (1987) ch. 12

Václav Havel 1936–
Czech dramatist and statesman; President of Czechoslovakia 1989–92 and of the Czech Republic 1993–2003

4 A spectre is haunting eastern Europe: the spectre of what in the West is called 'dissent'.
The Power of the Powerless (1978)

5 I see a renewed focus of politics on real people as something far more profound than merely returning to the everyday mechanisms of western (or if you like bourgeois)

democracy.
Václav Havel et al. The Power of the Powerless (1985)

6 To respond to evil by committing another evil does not eliminate evil but allows it to go on forever.
letter 5 November 1989

Bob Hawke 1929–
Australian Labor statesman, Prime Minister 1983–91

7 No longer content to be just the lucky country, Australia must now become the clever country.
*speech, 1990; attributed; see **Horne 147:10***

R. S. Hawker 1803–75
English clergyman and poet

8 And have they fixed the where and when?
And shall Trelawny die?
Here's twenty thousand Cornish men
Will know the reason why!
the last three lines are taken from a traditional rhyme dating from the imprisonment by James II, in 1688, of the seven Bishops, including Trelawny, Bishop of Bristol
'The Song of the Western Men'

Ian Hay 1876–1952
Scottish novelist and dramatist

9 War is hell, and all that, but it has a good deal to recommend it. It wipes out all the small nuisances of peace-time.
The First Hundred Thousand (1915)

John Milton Hay 1838–1905
American politician

10 It has been a splendid little war, begun with the highest motives, carried on with magnificent intelligence and spirit, favoured by that fortune which loves the brave.
on the Spanish-American War of 1898
letter to Theodore Roosevelt, 27 July 1898

11 The open door.
on the completion of the trade policy he had negotiated with China
letter to the Cabinet, 2 January 1900

Bill Hayden 1933–
Australian Labor politician

1 *Hayden had resigned as Opposition leader in 1983 as Malcolm Fraser was in the process of calling the election, but remained convinced that he would have won:*
I am not convinced the Labor Party could not win under my leadership. I believe a drover's dog could lead the Labor Party to victory the way the country is.
John Stubbs *Hayden* (1989)

Friedrich August von Hayek
1899–1992
Austrian-born economist. On Hayek: see **Oakeshott 230:7**

2 I am certain that nothing has done so much to destroy the juridical safeguards of individual freedom as the striving after this miracle of social justice.
Economic Freedom and Representative Government (1973)

3 The system of private property is the most important guarantee of freedom, not only for those who own property, but scarcely less for those who do not.
The Road to Serfdom (1944)

4 Probably nothing has done so much harm to the liberal cause as the wooden insistence of some liberals on certain rough rules of thumb, above all the principle of *laissez-faire*.
The Road to Serfdom (1944)

5 We need good principles rather than good people. We need fixed rules, not fixers.
Studies in Philosophy, Politics and Economics (1967)

6 One cannot help a country to maintain its standard of life by assisting people to consume more than they produce.
in *Daily Telegraph* 26 August 1976

Alfred Hayes 1911–85
American songwriter

7 I dreamed I saw Joe Hill last night

Alive as you and me.
Says I, 'But Joe, you're ten years dead.'
'I never died,' says he.
'I Dreamed I Saw Joe Hill Last Night' (1936 song)

William Hazlitt 1778–1830
English essayist

8 Talk of mobs! Is there any body of people that has this character in a more consummate degree than the House of Commons? Is there any set of men that determines more by acclamation, and less by deliberation and individual conviction?
'On the Difference between Writing and Speaking'; in *London Magazine* July 1820

9 The greatest test of courage I can conceive is to speak the truth in the House of Commons.
'On the Difference between Writing and Speaking'; in *London Magazine* July 1820

Cuthbert Morley Headlam
1876–1964
British Conservative politician

10 This Parliament is enough to discourage anyone from entering political life—a vast untutored majority with a helpless minority and an extremely uninteresting Government.
diary, 27 March 1933

11 Better to break your party on a matter of principle than to let it fall to pieces because you cannot yourself make up your mind what you want to do.
diary, 2 April 1934

Denis Healey 1917–
British Labour politician, husband of Edna **Healey**. See also **Phillips 244:13**

12 There are going to be howls of anguish from the 80,000 people who are rich enough to pay over 75% [tax] on the last slice of their income.
speech at the Labour Party Conference, 1 October 1973

13 Like long-term weather forecasts

they are better than nothing...But their origin lies in the extrapolation from a partially known past, through an unknown present, to an unknowable future.
on economic forecasts
in the House of Commons, 12 November 1974

1 It's no good ceasing to become the world's policeman in order to become the world's parson instead.
at a meeting of the Cabinet at Chequers, 17 November 1974; Peter Hennessy *Whitehall* (1990)

2 *of being criticized by Geoffrey* **Howe** *in the House of Commons:*
Like being savaged by a dead sheep.
in the House of Commons, 14 June 1978

3 *of Margaret* **Thatcher:**
And who is the Mephistopheles behind this shabby Faust [the Foreign Secretary, Geoffrey Howe]?...To quote her own backbenchers, the Great She-elephant, She-Who-Must-Be-Obeyed, the Catherine the Great of Finchley, the Prime Minister herself.
in the House of Commons, 27 February 1984

4 Mrs Thatcher tells us she has given the French president a piece of her mind...not a gift I would receive with alacrity.
in *Today* 5 September 1989

5 The Fabians...found socialism wandering aimlessly in Cloud-cuckoo-land and set it working on the gas and water problems of the nearest town or village.
of the parochialism of the Fabians
New Fabian Essays (1952)

6 La Passionaria of middle-class privilege.
of Margaret **Thatcher**
Kenneth Minogue and Michael Biddiss *Thatcherism* (1987)

7 Healey's first law of politics: when you're in a hole, stop digging.
attributed

Edna Healey 1918–
British writer, wife of Denis **Healey**

8 She has no hinterland; in particular

she has no sense of history.
of Margaret **Thatcher**
Denis Healey *The Time of My Life* (1989)

Timothy Michael Healy 1855–1931
Irish nationalist politician

9 REDMOND: Gladstone is now master of the Party!
HEALY: Who is to be mistress of the Party?
at the meeting of the Irish Parliamentary Party on 6 December 1890, when the Party split over **Parnell**'s *involvement in the O'Shea divorce; Healy's reference to Katherine O'Shea was particularly damaging to Parnell*
Robert Kee *The Laurel and the Ivy* (1993)

10 I am for doing business and making peace.
letter to Beaverbrook, 1920; Frank Callanan *T. M. Healy* (1996)

11 The Sinns won in three years what we did not win in forty. You cannot make revolutions with rosewater, or omelettes without breaking eggs.
letter to his brother; Frank Callanan *T. M. Healy* (1996); see **Proverbs 252:4**

12 There is the noble Marquis. Like a pike at the bottom of a pool.
of Lord Hartington, apparently asleep on the Opposition bench
Herbert Gladstone *After Thirty Years* (1928)

Seamus Heaney 1939–
Irish poet

13 Don't be surprised
If I demur, for, be advised
My passport's green.
No glass of ours was ever raised
To toast *The Queen*.
rebuking the editors of The Penguin Book of Contemporary British Poetry *for including him among its authors*
Open Letter (1983)

14 Who would connive
in civilised outrage
yet understand the exact
and tribal, intimate revenge.
'Punishment' (1975)

15 My heart besieged by anger, my mind a gap of danger,
I walked among their old haunts, the home ground where they bled;
And in the dirt lay justice like an

acorn in the winter
Till its oak would sprout in Derry
where the thirteen men lay dead.
of Bloody Sunday, Londonderry, 30 January 1972
'The Road to Derry'

1 The famous
Northern reticence, the tight gag of
place
And times: yes, yes. Of the 'wee six'
I sing
Where to be saved you only must save
face
And whatever you say, you say
nothing.
'Whatever You Say Say Nothing' (1975)

William Randolph Hearst
1863–1951
American newspaper publisher and tycoon

2 You furnish the pictures and I'll
furnish the war.
*message to the artist Frederic Remington in
Havana, Cuba, during the Spanish-American War
of 1898*
attributed

3 The day when this nation ceases to
shape its foreign policy primarily
for the safety and welfare of the
American people will be the day on
which its national doom is sealed—
and its international doom too.
in *San Francisco Examiner* 7 May 1924

4 News is something which
somebody wants suppressed—all
the rest is advertising.
attributed; Ian Gilmour *The Body Politic* (1969)

Edward Heath 1916–2005
British Conservative statesman; Prime Minister,
1970–4. On Heath: see **Hennessy 141:4**,
Jenkins 158:3, Thatcher 309:3

5 Music means everything to me
when I'm here alone. And it's the
best way of getting that bloody man
Wilson out of my hair.
*after playing Chopin and Liszt for a visiting
journalist, late 1960s*
James Margach *The Abuse of Power* (1978)

6 This would, at a stroke, reduce the
rise in prices, increase productivity

and reduce unemployment.
*press release, never actually spoken by Heath,
on proposed tax cuts and a freeze on prices in
nationalized industries*
from Conservative Central Office, 16 June 1970

7 The unpleasant and unacceptable
face of capitalism.
on the Lonrho affair
in the House of Commons, 15 May 1973

8 If politicians lived on praise and
thanks they'd be forced into some
other line of business.
attributed, 1973

9 Rejoice, rejoice, rejoice.
*telephone call to his office on hearing of Margaret
Thatcher's fall from power in 1990*
attributed; in *Daily Telegraph* 24 September
1998 (online edition)

G. W. F. Hegel 1770–1831
German idealist philosopher

10 Gangrenous limbs cannot be cured
with lavender water.
The German Constitution (1798–1802)

11 What experience and history
teach is this—that nations and
governments have never learned
anything from history, or acted
upon any lessons they might have
drawn from it.
*Lectures on the Philosophy of World History:
Introduction* (1830); see **Marx 206:12**

Heinrich Heine 1797–1856
German poet

12 Wherever books will be burned,
men also, in the end, are burned.
Almansor (1823)

Lillian Hellman 1905–84
American dramatist

13 I cannot and will not cut my
conscience to fit this year's
fashions.
letter to John S. Wood, 19 May 1952

Leona Helmsley c. 1920–2007
American hotelier

14 Only the little people pay taxes.
reported at her trial for tax evasion
to her housekeeper; in *New York Times* 12 July
1983

Arthur Henderson 1863–1935
British Labour politician

1 *to critics in his own party, when as adviser on labour matters he was made minister without portfolio in* **Lloyd George**'s *War Cabinet (December 1916):*
I am not here either to please myself or you; I am here to see the war through.
in *Dictionary of National Biography* (1917–)

2 The first forty-eight hours decide whether a Minister is going to run his office or whether his office is going to run him.
Susan Crosland *Tony Crosland* (1982)

Leon Henderson 1895–1956
American economist; appointed by Franklin **Roosevelt** to the National Defense Advisory Commission in 1940

3 Having a little inflation is like being a little pregnant.
J. K. Galbraith *A Life in Our Times* (1981)

Peter Hennessy 1947–
English historian

4 The model of a modern Prime Minister would be a kind of grotesque composite freak—someone with the dedication to duty of a Peel, the physical energy of a Gladstone, the detachment of a Salisbury, the brains of an Asquith, the balls of a Lloyd George, the word-power of a Churchill, the administrative gifts of an Attlee, the style of a Macmillan, the managerialism of a Heath, and the sleep requirements of a Thatcher. Human beings do not come like that.
The Hidden Wiring (1995); see **Pearson 242:3**

5 MI5 is a job creation scheme for muscular underachievers from the ancient universities.
in *Times* 1981, profile of Roger Hollis

6 *of Rab* **Butler** *in his last years:*
He seemed like a benign and decent beached whale washed up on the harder shores of modern Conservatism.
in *Independent* 8 May 1987

Henri IV (of Navarre) 1553–1610
French monarch, King from 1589

7 I want there to be no peasant in my kingdom so poor that he is unable to have a chicken in his pot every Sunday.
In Hardouin de Péréfixe *Histoire de Henry le Grand* (1681); see **Hoover 147:3**

8 Hang yourself, brave Crillon; we fought at Arques and you were not there.
traditional form given by Voltaire to a letter from Henri to Crillon, 20 September 1597; Henri's actual words were: 'My good man, Crillon, hang yourself for not having been at my side last Monday at the greatest event that's ever been seen and perhaps ever will be seen'

9 Paris is well worth a mass.
when told that, though a Protestant, he must hear mass at Notre-Dame Cathedral to be consecrated king
attributed to Henri IV; alternatively to his minister Sully, in conversation with Henri

10 The wisest fool in Christendom.
of **James I** *of England*
attributed both to Henri IV and **Sully**

Henry II 1133–89
English monarch, King from 1154

11 Will no one rid me of this turbulent priest?
of Thomas Becket, Archbishop of Canterbury, murdered in Canterbury Cathedral, December 1170
oral tradition, conflating a number of variant forms, including G. Lyttelton *History of the Life of King Henry the Second* (1769): 'so many cowardly and ungrateful men in his court, none of whom would revenge him of the injuries he sustained from one turbulent priest'

Henry VIII 1491–1547
English monarch, King from 1509

12 This man hath the right sow by the ear.
of Thomas Cranmer, June 1529
in *Acts and Monuments of John Foxe* ['Foxe's Book of Martyrs'] (1570)

13 The King found her [Anne of Cleves] so different from her picture... that...he swore they had brought

him a Flanders mare.
Tobias Smollett *A Complete History of England* (3rd ed., 1759)

Patrick Henry 1736–99
American statesman

1 Caesar had his Brutus—Charles the First, his Cromwell—and George the Third—('Treason,' cried the Speaker)...*may profit by their example.* If *this* be treason, make the most of it.
speech in the Virginia assembly, May 1765

2 I am not a Virginian, but an American.
in [John Adams's] Notes of Debates in the Continental Congress, Philadelphia, 6 September 1774

3 I know not what course others may take; but as for me, give me liberty, or give me death!
speech in Virginia Convention, 23 March 1775

4 We are not weak if we make a proper use of those means which the God of Nature has placed in our power...The battle, sir, is not to the strong alone; it is to the vigilant, the active, the brave.
speech in Virginia Convention, Richmond, 23 March 1775

5 Guard with jealous attention the public liberty. Suspect everyone who approaches that jewel. Unfortunately, nothing will preserve it but downright force. Whenever you give up that force, you are inevitably ruined.
attributed

A. P. Herbert 1890–1971
English writer and humorist

6 This high official, all allow,
Is grossly overpaid;
There wasn't any Board, and now There isn't any Trade.
'The President of the Board of Trade' (1922)

7 People must not do things for fun. We are not here for fun. There is no reference to fun in any Act of Parliament.
Uncommon Law (1935) 'Is it a Free Country?'

8 The Common Law of England has been laboriously built about a mythical figure—the figure of 'The Reasonable Man'.
Uncommon Law (1935) 'The Reasonable Man'

Frank Herbert 1920–86
American writer of science fiction

9 If you think of yourselves as helpless and ineffectual, it is certain that you will create a despotic government to be your master. The wise despot, therefore, maintains among his subjects a popular sense that they are helpless and ineffectual.
The Dosadi Experiment (1978)

Herodotus c. 485–c. 425 BC
Greek historian

10 In peace, children bury their parents; war violates the order of nature and causes parents to bury their children.
Histories

11 The most hateful torment for men is to have knowledge of everything but power over nothing.
Histories

Lord Hervey 1696–1743
English politician and writer

12 Whoever would lie usefully should lie seldom.
Memoirs of the Reign of George II (ed. J. W. Croker, 1848) vol. 1

13 I am fit for nothing but to carry candles and set chairs all my life.
letter to Sir Robert Walpole, 1737

Alexander Ivanovich Herzen 1812–70
Russian writer and revolutionary

14 Communism is a Russian autocracy turned upside down.
The Development of Revolutionary Ideas in Russia (1851)

15 Russia's future will be a great danger for Europe and a great misfortune for Russia if there is no emancipation of the individual. One more century of present

despotism will destroy all the good qualities of the Russian people.
The Development of Revolutionary Ideas in Russia (1851)

Michael Heseltine 1933–
British Conservative politician

1 I knew that, 'He who wields the knife never wears the crown.'
in *New Society* 14 February 1986

2 The market has no morality.
on *Panorama* BBC1 27 June 1988

3 Polluted rivers, filthy streets, bodies bedded down in doorways are no advertisement for a prosperous or caring society.
speech at Conservative Party Conference 10 October 1989

4 The Tory recognizes the contrast between laissez-faire and noblesse oblige.
in *Observer* 18 March 1990 'Sayings of the Week'

5 The fundamental question is is the Conservative Party leadable?
in the aftermath of disastrous electoral defeat
in *Daily Telegraph* 9 June 2001 (electronic edition)

Gordon Hewart 1870–1943
British lawyer and politician

6 A long line of cases shows that it is not merely of some importance, but is of fundamental importance that justice should not only be done, but should manifestly and undoubtedly be seen to be done.
in *Rex v Sussex Justices* 9 November 1923

John Hewitt 1907–87
Northern Irish poet

7 Kelt, Briton, Roman, Saxon, Dane, and Scot,
time and this island tied a crazy knot.
'Ulsterman' (*Collected Poems*, 1991)

8 I'm an Ulsterman, of planter stock. I was born in the island of Ireland, so secondarily I'm an Irishman. I was born in the British archipelago and English is my native tongue, so I am British. The British archipelago consists of offshore islands to the continent of Europe, so I'm European. This is my hierarchy of values and so far as I am concerned, anyone who omits one step in that sequence of values is falsifying the situation.
in *Irish Times* 4 July 1974

Reinhard Heydrich 1904–42
German Nazi leader

9 Now the rough work has been done we begin the period of finer work. We need to work in harmony with the civil administration. We count on you gentlemen as far as the final solution is concerned.
on the planned mass murder of eleven million European Jews
speech in Wannsee, 20 January 1942; see **Goering 126:7**

J. R. Hicks 1904–89
British economist

10 The best of all monopoly profits is a quiet life.
Econometrica (1935) 'The Theory of Monopoly'

Jim Hightower 1943–
American writer and broadcaster

11 There's nothing in the middle of the road but yellow stripes and dead armadillos.
attributed, 1984

Charles Hill 1904–89
British Conservative politician, doctor, and broadcaster

12 It does not do to appear clever. Advancement in this man's party is due entirely to alcoholic stupidity.
*advice given in 1959 to the newly elected MP, Julian **Critchley**, seen reading in the Smoking Room of the House of Commons*
Julian Critchley *A Bag of Boiled Sweets* (1994)

Joe Hill 1879–1915
Swedish-born American labour leader and songwriter. See also **Last words 178:15**

13 You will eat, bye and bye,
In that glorious land above the sky;
Work and pray, live on hay,

You'll get pie in the sky when you die.
'Preacher and the Slave' in *Songs of the Workers* (Industrial Workers of the World, 1911)

Paul von Hindenburg 1847–1934
German Field Marshal and statesman, President of the Weimar Republic 1925–34

1 That man for a Chancellor? I'll make him a postmaster and he can lick the stamps with my head on them.
of **Hitler**
to Meissner, 13 August 1932; J. W. Wheeler-Bennett *Hindenburg: the Wooden Titan* (1936)

Emperor Hirohito 1901–89
Japanese monarch, Emperor from 1926

2 The war situation has developed not necessarily to Japan's advantage.
announcing Japan's surrender, in a broadcast to his people after atom bombs had destroyed Hiroshima and Nagasaki
on 15 August 1945

3 Certainly things happened during the Second World War for which I feel personally sorry.
attributed, 1971

Adolf Hitler 1889–1945
German dictator. On Hitler: see **Chamberlain 60:9**

4 The broad mass of a nation...will more easily fall victim to a big lie than to a small one.
Mein Kampf (1925) vol. 1

5 The night of the long knives.
applied to the massacre of Ernst Roehm and his associates by Hitler on 29–30 June 1934, though taken from an early Nazi marching song; the phrase was subsequently associated with Harold **Macmillan**'s *Cabinet dismissals of 13 July 1962*
speech in the Reichstag, 13 July 1934

6 I go the way that Providence dictates with the assurance of a sleepwalker.
speech in Munich, 15 March 1936

7 It is the last territorial claim which I have to make in Europe, but it is the claim from which I will not recede and which, God-willing, I will

make good.
on the Sudetenland
speech at Berlin Sportpalast, 26 September 1938

8 With regard to the problem of the Sudeten Germans, my patience is now at an end!
speech at Berlin Sportpalast, 26 September 1938

9 Anyone who does not wish to be the hammer in history will be the anvil.
unpublished sequel to *Mein Kampf*, written 1928; Gerhard L. Weinberg (ed.) *Hitler's Second Book* (2003)

10 *to Mussolini, having spent nine hours intermittently in Franco's company:*
Rather than go through that again, I would prefer to have three or four teeth taken out.
Paul Preston *Franco* (1993)

Thomas Hobbes 1588–1679
English philosopher

11 By art is created that great Leviathan, called a commonwealth or state, (in Latin *civitas*) which is but an artificial man...and in which, the sovereignty is an artificial soul.
Leviathan (1651); introduction

12 I put for a general inclination of all mankind, a perpetual and restless desire of power after power, that ceaseth only in death.
Leviathan (1651)

13 They that approve a private opinion, call it opinion; but they that mislike it, heresy: and yet heresy signifies no more than private opinion.
Leviathan (1651)

14 During the time men live without a common power to keep them all in awe, they are in that condition which is called war; and such a war as is of every man against every man.
Leviathan (1651)

15 For as the nature of foul weather, lieth not in a shower or two of rain; but in an inclination thereto of many days together: so the

nature of war consisteth not in actual fighting, but in the known disposition thereto during all the time there is no assurance to the contrary.
  Leviathan (1651)

1 No arts; no letters; no society; and which is worst of all, continual fear and danger of violent death; and the life of man, solitary, poor, nasty, brutish, and short.
  Leviathan (1651)

2 Force, and fraud, are in war the two cardinal virtues.
  Leviathan (1651)

3 Covenants, without the sword, are but words, and of no strength to secure a man at all.
  Leviathan (1651)

4 Liberties...depend on the silence of the law.
  Leviathan (1651)

5 The obligation of subjects to the sovereign, is understood to last as long, and no longer, than the power lasteth, by which he is able to protect them.
  Leviathan (1651)

6 I put down for one of the most effectual seeds of the death of any state, that the conquerors require not only a submission of men's actions to them for the future, but also an approbation of all their actions past.
  Leviathan (1651)

7 They that are discontented under *monarchy*, call it *tyranny*; and they that are displeased with *aristocracy*, call it *oligarchy*: so also, they which find themselves grieved under a *democracy*, call it *anarchy*, which signifies the want of government; and yet I think no man believes, that want of government, is any new kind of government.
  Leviathan (1651)

8 The papacy is not other than the ghost of the deceased Roman Empire, sitting crowned upon the grave thereof.
  Leviathan (1651)

John Cam Hobhouse 1786–1869
English politician

9 It is said to be very hard on his majesty's ministers to raise objections to this proposition. For my own part, I think it is more hard on his majesty's opposition (a laugh) to compel them to take this course.
  speech, House of Commons, 10 April 1826; see **Bagehot 18:8**

August Heinrich Hoffman
1798–1874
German poet

10 *Deutschland über alles.*
  Germany above all.
  Title of poem (1841)

Lancelot Hogben 1895–1975
English scientist

11 This is not the age of pamphleteers. It is the age of the engineers. The spark-gap is mightier than the pen. Democracy will not be salvaged by men who talk fluently, debate forcefully and quote aptly.
  Science for the Citizen (1938) epilogue; see **Bulwer-Lytton 45:7**

Sarah Hogg 1946–
British political advisor, former head of John Major's policy unit

12 Ministers say one of two things in Cabinet. Some say, 'Look, Daddy, no hands.' Others say, 'Look, Daddy, me too.'
  unidentified senior official to Sarah Hogg on her arrival to take over the Prime Minister's policy unit in *Sunday Times* 9 April 1995

Simon Hoggart 1946–
British journalist

13 Peter Mandelson is someone who can skulk in broad daylight.
  in *Guardian* 10 July 1998

Patrick Holden 1937–
British businessman: director of the Soil Association

14 Tony Blair and his ministers are operating on a 'pollute now, pay

later' policy. Farm-scale trial plots are rather like letting a rat with bubonic plague out into the environment and then seeing what happens.
on GM foods
in *Independent* 18 June 1999

Henry Fox, Lord Holland 1705–74
English Whig politician. On Holland: see **Walpole 325:12**

1 Let nothing be done to break his spirit. The world will do that business fast enough.
of his son Charles James Fox as a child
attributed

2 If Mr Selwyn calls again, shew him up: if I am alive I shall be delighted to see him; and if I am dead he would like to see me.
during his last illness
J. H. Jesse *George Selwyn and his Contemporaries* (1844) vol. 3

Oliver Wendell Holmes Jr.
1841–1935
American lawyer

3 The most stringent protection of free speech would not protect a man falsely shouting fire in a theatre and causing a panic.
sometimes quoted as, 'shouting fire in a crowded theatre'
in *Schenck v. United States* (1919)

4 Men must turn square corners when they deal with the Government.
in *Rock Island, Arkansas & Louisiana Ry. v. United States* (1920)

5 I pay my tax bills more readily than any others—for whether the money is well or ill spent I get civilized society for it.
letter to Harold Laski, 12 May 1930

6 A second-class intellect. But a first-class temperament!
of Franklin Roosevelt
on 8 March 1933

7 The mind of a bigot is like the pupil of the eye; the more light you pour upon it, the more it will contract.
attributed

Alec Douglas-Home, Lord Home 1903–95
British Conservative statesman; Prime Minister, 1963–4. On Home: see **Connolly 79:1**

8 Oh, they must find someone else, once they get away from this Blackpool hot-house. Even if they can't agree on Rab or Quintin there must be someone else. But please, please, not me!
to James Margach during the Conservative Party Conference, October 1963; James Margach *The Abuse of Power* (1978)

9 When I have to read economic documents I have to have a box of matches and start moving them into position to simplify and illustrate the points to myself.
in *Observer* 16 September 1962

10 As far as the fourteenth earl is concerned, I suppose Mr Wilson, when you come to think of it, is the fourteenth Mr Wilson.
replying to Harold Wilson's remark (on Home's becoming leader of the Conservative party) that 'the whole [democratic] process has ground to a halt with a fourteenth Earl'
in *Daily Telegraph* 22 October 1963

11 There are two problems in my life. The political ones are insoluble and the economic ones are incomprehensible.
attributed, 1964

Richard Hooker c. 1554–1600
English theologian

12 He that goeth about to persuade a multitude, that they are not so well governed as they ought to be, shall never want attentive and favourable hearers.
Of the Laws of Ecclesiastical Polity (1593)

13 Alteration though it be from worse to better hath in it inconveniences, and those weighty.
Of the Laws of Ecclesiastical Polity (1593)

Geoffrey Hoon 1953–
British Labour politician, Secretary of State for Defence 1999–2005

14 I accept responsibility for everything that goes on in the

MoD. But that does not mean I'm to blame for everything.
in *Sunday Times* 15 February 2004

Herbert Hoover 1874–1964
American Republican statesman, 31st President of the US, 1929–33

1 Our country has deliberately undertaken a great social and economic experiment, noble in motive and far-reaching in purpose.
on the Eighteenth Amendment enacting Prohibition, often referred to as 'the noble experiment'
letter to Senator W. H. Borah, 23 February 1928

2 The American system of rugged individualism.
speech in New York City, 22 October 1928

3 The slogan of progress is changing from the full dinner pail to the full garage.
sometimes paraphrased as, 'a car in every garage and a chicken in every pot'
speech in New York, 22 October 1928; see **Henri IV 141:7**

4 Words without actions are the assassins of idealism.
attributed, in *Capital Times* (Madison, Wisconsin) 15 April 1930

5 The grass will grow in the streets of a hundred cities, a thousand towns.
on proposals 'to reduce the protective tariff to a competitive tariff for revenue'
speech, 31 October 1932; see **Bryan 44:9**

6 Older men declare war. But it is youth who must fight and die.
speech at the Republican National Convention, Chicago, 27 June 1944

Bob Hope 1903–2003
American comedian

7 I must say the Senator's victory in Wisconsin was a triumph for democracy. It proves that a millionaire has just as good a chance as anybody else.
*of John F. **Kennedy**'s electoral victory in 1960; William Robert Faith *Bob Hope* (1983)*

Harry Lloyd Hopkins 1890–1946
American government official and presidential adviser

8 Give a man a dole and you save his

body and destroy his spirit. Give him a job and pay him an assured wage and you save both body and spirit.
in 1934

Horace 65–8 BC
Roman poet

9 O citizens, first acquire wealth; you can practise virtue afterwards.
Epistles; see **Pope 248:1**

Donald Richmond Horne
1921–2005
Australian journalist and writer

10 Australia is a lucky country run mainly by second-rate people who share its luck.
The Lucky Country: Australia in the Sixties (1964)

Samuel Horsley 1733–1806
English bishop

11 In this country...the individual subject...'has nothing to do with the laws but to obey them.'
defending a maxim he had used earlier in committee, in the House of Lords, 13 November 1795

John Hoskyns 1927–
British businessman; head of the Prime Minister's Policy Unit 1979–82

12 The House of Commons is the greatest closed shop of all...For the purposes of government, a country of 55 million people is forced to depend on a talent pool which could not sustain a single multinational company.
'Conservatism is Not Enough' (Institute of Directors Annual Lecture) 25 September 1983

13 The Tory party never panics, except in a crisis.
in *Sunday Times* 19 February 1989

A. E. Housman 1859–1936
English poet

14 These, in the day when heaven was falling,
The hour when earth's foundations fled,

Followed their mercenary calling
And took their wages and are dead.
Their shoulders held the sky
  suspended;
They stood, and earth's foundations
  stay;
What God abandoned, these
  defended,
And saved the sum of things for pay.
    Last Poems (1922) no. 37 'Epitaph on an Army
    of Mercenaries'

Samuel Houston 1793–1863
American politician and military leader

1 The North is determined to
preserve this Union. They are
not a fiery, impulsive people as
you are, for they live in colder
climates. But when they begin to
move in a given direction…they
move with the steady momentum
and perseverance of a mighty
avalanche.
    *in 1861, warning the people of Texas against
    secession*
    Geoffrey C. Ward *The Civil War* (1991)

John Howard 1939–
Australian Liberal statesman; Prime Minister
1996–2007

2 That's Lazarus with a triple bypass.
    *asked if he thought he could regain leadership
    of his party*
    at a press conference, 9 May 1989; David
    Barnett *John Howard: Prime Minister* (1997)

3 I want people to reflect on the loss
of life. I want them to reflect on
what it means in terms of the loss
of innocence…in relation to this
country's dealings with different
parts of the world.
    on the Bali bombing, 12 October 2002
    interview on Australian television (Channel Ten
    News), 14 October 2002

4 I have said since September 11 last
year that you can't rule out the
possibility of a terror attack of this
sort in Australia. Because of the
nature of our society, I believe it is
less likely than in many other parts
of the world. But I cannot guarantee
that it won't happen. I can't.
    in *The Age* (electronic edition) 19 October 2002

Michael Howard 1941–
British Conservative politician, Party Leader 2003–5.
On Howard: see **Widdecombe 332:9**

5 I am happy to debate the past with
the Prime Minister any day he likes.
I have a big dossier on his past, and
I did not even have to sex it up.
    at Prime Minister's Questions in the House of
    Commons, 12 November 2003

Geoffrey Howe 1926–
British Conservative politician. On Howe: see
Healey 139:2

6 It is rather like sending your
opening batsmen to the crease only
for them to find, the moment the
first balls are bowled, that their
bats have been broken before the
game by the team captain.
    *resignation speech which precipitated the fall of
    Margaret **Thatcher***
    in the House of Commons, 13 November 1990

7 The time has come for others to
consider their own response to
the tragic conflict of loyalties with
which I have myself wrestled for
perhaps too long.
    resignation speech, House of Commons,
    13 November 1990

Julia Ward Howe 1819–1910
American Unitarian lay preacher

8 Mine eyes have seen the glory of the
  coming of the Lord:
He is trampling out the vintage where
  the grapes of wrath are stored;
He hath loosed the fateful lightning
  of his terrible swift sword:
His truth is marching on.
    'Battle Hymn of the Republic' (1862)

9 As He died to make men holy, let us
  die to make men free.
    'Battle Hymn of the Republic' (1862)

Louis McHenry Howe 1871–1936
American Democratic politician

10 You can't adopt politics as a
profession, and remain honest.
    speech, 17 January 1933

Langston Hughes 1902–67
American writer and poet

1 I, too, sing America.
  I am the darker brother.
  They send me to eat in the kitchen
  When company comes.
    'I, Too' (1925)

2 'It's powerful,' he said.
  'What?'
  'That one drop of Negro blood—
    because just *one* drop of black blood
    makes a man coloured. *One* drop—
    you are a Negro!'
    Simple Takes a Wife (1953)

Robert Hughes 1938–
Australian writer

3 What the convict system
  bequeathed to later Australian
  generations was not the sturdy,
  skeptical independence...but an
  intense concern with social and
  political respectability. The idea
  of the 'convict stain', a moral blot
  soaked into our fabric, dominated
  all argument about Australian
  selfhood by the 1840s.
    The Fatal Shore (1987) introduction

Victor Hugo 1802–85
French poet, novelist, and dramatist

4 A stand can be made against
  invasion by an army; no stand can
  be made against invasion by an
  idea.
    Histoire d'un Crime (written 1851–2, published
    1877); see **Anonymous 10:1**

5 Take away *time is money*, and what
  is left of England? take away *cotton
  is king*, and what is left of America?
    Les Misérables (1862); see **Christy 64:11**

David Hume 1711–76
Scottish philosopher

6 Money...is none of the wheels of
  trade: it is the oil which renders the

motion of the wheels more smooth
and easy.
  Essays: Moral and Political (1741–2) 'Of Money'

7 That policy is violent, which
  aggrandizes the public by the
  poverty of individuals.
    Essays: Moral and Political (1741–2) 'Of Money'

8 Should it be said, that, by living
  under the dominion of a prince,
  which one might leave, every
  individual has given a tacit assent
  to his authority...We may as well
  assert, that a man by remaining
  in a vessel, freely consents to the
  dominion of the master; though he
  was carried on board while asleep,
  and must leap into the ocean, and
  perish, the moment he leaves her.
    'Of the Original Contract' (1748)

9 In all ages of the world, priests have
  been enemies of liberty.
    'Of the Parties of Great Britain' (1741–2)

10 It is a just political maxim, that
   every man must be supposed a
   knave.
    Political Discourses (1751)

John Hume 1937–
Northern Irish politician

11 There's a very thin line between
   dying for Ireland and killing for
   Ireland.
    in 1994, attributed

Hubert Humphrey 1911–78
American Democratic politician

12 There are not enough jails, not
   enough policemen, not enough
   courts to enforce a law not
   supported by the people.
    speech at Williamsburg, 1 May 1965

13 The right to be heard does not
   automatically include the right to
   be taken seriously.
    speech to National Student Association at
    Madison, 23 August 1965

Human Rights
'born free and equal'
see Selective Subject Index

1 Here we are the way politics ought
to be in America, the politics of
happiness, the politics of purpose
and the politics of joy.
   speech in Washington, 27 April 1968

2 Compassion is not weakness, and
concern for the unfortunate is not
socialism.
   attributed

G. W. Hunt see **Songs 297:8**

Lord Hunt of Tanworth 1919–
British civil servant; Secretary of the Cabinet 1973–9

3 *of British Cabinet government, described as*
'a shambles':
   It has got to be, so far as possible,
a democratic and accountable
shambles.
   at a seminar at the Institute of Historical
   Research, 20 October 1993

Robert Hunter 1941–2005
Canadian writer

4 The word *Greenpeace* had a ring
to it—it conjured images of Eden;
it said ecology and antiwar in two
syllables; it fit easily into even a
one-column headline.
   Warriors of the Rainbow (1979); see
   Darnell 85:7

Douglas Hurd 1930–
British Conservative politician; Foreign Secretary
1989–95

5 Lord Rothschild roamed like a
condottiere through Whitehall,
laying an ambush here, there
breaching some crumbling fortress
which had outlived its usefulness…
He respected persons occasionally
but rarely policies.
   *of Lord **Rothschild** as first Director of the Central*
   Policy Review Staff
   An End to Promises (1979)

6 If President Clinton decides
to accelerate the run-down
in US forces in Europe—and
by implication the priority
Washington attaches to Nato—that

wedge will be removed. With it will
go one of the principal props which
have allowed Britain to punch
above its weight in the world.
   speech at Chatham House; in *Financial Times*
   4 February 1993

7 People in the forefront of
environmental causes are
destroying experimental crops.
That's not logical. That's Luddite.
   in *Sunday Times* 19 September 1999

8 Inertia can develop its own
momentum.
   in *Mail on Sunday* 27 May 2001

Saddam Hussein 1937–2006
Iraqi statesman; President 1979–2003

9 The mother of battles.
   popular interpretation of his description of the
   approaching Gulf War, given in a speech in
   Baghdad, 6 January 1991
      in *Times* 7 January 1991 it was reported that
      Saddam had no intention of relinquishing
      Kuwait and was ready for the 'mother of all
      wars'

10 Baghdad is determined to force
the Mongols of our age to commit
suicide at its gates.
   in *Independent* 18 January 2003

11 I am Saddam Hussein, the
president of Iraq.
   response when asked who he was at the
   beginning of his trial; the judge ordered the clerk
   to 'put down "former" in brackets'
      in *Guardian* 2 July 2004

Lord Hutton 1931–
British judge, Lord Chief Justice for Northern Ireland

12 I make it clear that it will be for me
to decide as I think right within
my terms of reference the matters
which will be the subject of my
investigation.
   statement on the terms of the inquiry into the
   death of Dr David Kelly, 21 July 2003

13 The term 'sexed-up' is a slang
expression, the meaning of which
lacks clarity in the context of the
discussion of the dossier.
   statement, 28 January 2004

Aldous Huxley 1894–1963
English novelist

1 So long as men worship the Caesars
and Napoleons, Caesars and
Napoleons will duly arise and make
them miserable.
Ends and Means (1937)

2 The propagandist's purpose is to
make one set of people forget that
certain other sets of people are
human.
The Olive Tree (1937)

3 Idealism is the noble toga that
political gentlemen drape over
their will to power.
in *New York Herald Tribune* 25 November 1963

T. H. Huxley 1825–95
English biologist

4 Why, put him in the middle of a
moor, with nothing in the world but
his shirt, and you could not prevent
him being anything he liked.
*of **Gladstone***
Roy Jenkins *Gladstone* (1995)

Douglas Hyde 1860–1949
Irish nationalist

5 The devouring demon of
Anglicization in Ireland…with
its foul jaws has devoured, one
after another, everything that was
hereditary, national, instructive,
ancient, intellectual and noble
in our race, our language, our
music, our songs, our industries,
our dances, and our pastimes—I
know, I say, that you will plant your
feet firmly, and say with us, 'Back,
Demon, back!'
speaking on behalf of the Gaelic League in
America, 1904

Joe Hyman 1921–99
English businessman

6 There are three kinds of banks, and
in descending order of integrity
they are High Street banks,
mountebanks, and merchant
banks.
in conversation with Antony Jay

Dolores Ibarruri 1895–1989
Spanish Communist leader

7 *No pasarán.*
They shall not pass.
radio broadcast, Madrid, 19 July 1936; see
Proverbs 251:15

8 It is better to die on your feet than
to live on your knees.
speech in Paris, 3 September 1936;
also attributed to Emiliano Zapata; see
Roosevelt 262:13

Henrik Ibsen 1828–1906
Norwegian dramatist

9 The majority never has right on

its side. Never I say! That is one of
the social lies that a free, thinking
man is bound to rebel against.
Who makes up the majority in
any given country? Is it the wise
men or the fools? I think we must
agree that the fools are in a terrible
overwhelming majority, all the
wide world over. But, damn it, it can
surely never be right that the stupid
should rule over the clever!
An Enemy of the People (1882)

10 You should never have your best
trousers on when you go out to fight
for freedom and truth.
An Enemy of the People (1882)

Harold L. Ickes 1874–1952
American lawyer and administrator

1 The trouble with Senator Long…
is that he's suffering from halitosis
of the intellect. That's presuming
Emperor Long has an intellect.
of Huey **Long**
speech, 1935; G. Wolfskill and J. A. Hudson *All
But the People: Franklin D. Roosevelt and his
Critics, 1933–39* (1969)

2 Dewey threw his diaper into the
ring.
on the Republican candidate for the presidency
in *New York Times* 12 December 1939

3 I am against government by crony.
on resigning as secretary of the interior,
February 1946

Ivan Illich 1926–2002
American sociologist

4 In a consumer society there are
inevitably two kinds of slaves: the
prisoners of addiction and the
prisoners of envy.
Tools for Conviviality (1973)

William Ralph Inge 1860–1954
English writer; Dean of St. Paul's, 1911–34

5 A nation is a society united by a
delusion about its ancestry and by a
common hatred of its neighbours.
The End of an Age (1948)

6 The enemies of Freedom do not
argue; they shout and they shoot.
End of an Age (1948)

7 The effect of boredom on a large
scale in history is underestimated.
It is a main cause of revolutions,
and would soon bring to an end all
the static Utopias and the farmyard
civilization of the Fabians.
End of an Age (1948)

8 It takes in reality only one to make
a quarrel. It is useless for the sheep
to pass resolutions in favour of
vegetarianism, while the wolf

remains of a different opinion.
Outspoken Essays: First Series (1919)

9 The nations which have put
mankind and posterity most
in their debt have been small
states—Israel, Athens, Florence,
Elizabethan England.
Outspoken Essays: Second Series (1922) 'State,
visible and invisible'

10 A man may build himself a throne
of bayonets, but he cannot sit on it.
a similar image was used by Boris **Yeltsin** *at the
time of the failed military coup in Russia, August
1991*
Philosophy of Plotinus (1923) vol. 2

Bernard Ingham 1932–
British journalist and public relations specialist;
press secretary to Margaret **Thatcher** 1979–90. On
Ingham: see **Morgan 219:5**

11 Blood sport is brought to its ultimate
refinement in the gossip columns.
speech, 5 February 1986

12 The media…is like an oil painting.
Close up, it looks like nothing on
earth. Stand back and you get the
drift.
speech to the Parliamentary Press Gallery,
February 1990

13 *at a meeting of the Parliamentary Lobby,
noticing that he had a spot of blood on his
shirt:*
My God, I've been stabbed in the
front.
recalled in a letter to Antony Jay, January 1995

Eugène Ionesco 1912–94
French dramatist

14 A civil servant doesn't make jokes.
The Killer (1958)

Hastings Lionel ('Pug') Ismay
1887–1965
British general and Secretary to the Committee of
Imperial Defence; first Secretary-General of NATO

15 NATO exists for three reasons—

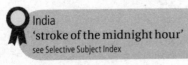
India
'stroke of the midnight hour'
see Selective Subject Index

to keep the Russians out, the Americans in and the Germans down.
to a group of British Conservative backbenchers in 1949; Peter Hennessy *Never Again* (1992); oral tradition

Molly Ivins 1944–2007 and **Lou Dubose**

1 Young political reporters are always told there are three ways to judge a politician. The first is to look at the record. The second is to look at the record. And third, look at the record.
Molly Ivins and Lou Dubose *Shrub* (2000)

2 If you think his daddy had trouble with 'the vision thing', wait till you meet this one.
*of presidential candidate George W. **Bush**; see **Bush***
Molly Ivins and Lou Dubose *Shrub* (2000)

Alija Izetbegović 1925–2003
Bosnian statesman; President of Bosnia and Herzegovina 1990–2003

3 And to my people I say, this may not be a just peace, but it is more just than a continuation of war.
after signing the Dayton accord with representatives of Serbia and Croatia
in Dayton, Ohio, 21 November 1995

Ireland
'come dance with me in Ireland'
see Selective Subject Index

Andrew Jackson 1767–1845
American Democratic statesman; 7th President of the US, 1829–37. On Jackson: see **Clay 74:5**

4 The individual who refuses to defend his rights when called by his Government, deserves to be a slave, and must be punished as an enemy of his country and friend to her foe.
proclamation to the people of Louisiana from Mobile, 21 September 1814

5 The brave man inattentive to his duty, is worth little more to his country, than the coward who deserts her in the hour of danger.
to troops who had abandoned their lines during the battle of New Orleans, 8 January 1815
attributed

6 Our Federal Union: it must be preserved.
toast given on the Jefferson Birthday Celebration, 13 April 1830; Thomas Hart Benton *Thirty Years' View* (1856) vol. 1

7 There are no necessary evils in government. Its evils exist only in its abuses.
veto of the Bank Bill, 10 July 1832

8 You are uneasy; you never sailed with *me* before, I see.
James Parton *Life of Jackson* (1860) vol. 3

9 One man with courage makes a majority.
attributed

10 *shortly before his death, Jackson was asked if he had left anything undone:*
I didn't shoot Henry Clay, and I didn't hang John C. Calhoun.
Robert V. Remini *Henry Clay* (1991); attributed

Jesse Jackson 1941–
American Democratic politician and clergyman

11 My right and my privilege to stand here before you has been won— won in my lifetime—by the blood

and the sweat of the innocent.
speech at Democratic National Convention, Atlanta, 19 July 1988

1 When I look out at this convention, I see the face of America, red, yellow, brown, black, and white. We are all precious in God's sight—the real rainbow coalition.
speech at Democratic National Convention, Atlanta, 19 July 1988

2 You can't keep on running from labour, running from blacks, running from cities and expect to inspire them to vote.
on President Clinton, after the results of the 1994 election
in Guardian 28 November 1994

3 She sat down in order that we all might stand up—and the walls of segregation came down.
of the civil rights activist Rosa Parks
in BBC News (online edition) 25 October 2005

Robert H. Jackson 1892–1954
American lawyer and judge

4 That four great nations, flushed with victory and stung with injury, stay the hands of vengeance and voluntarily submit their captive enemies to the judgement of the law, is one of the most significant tributes that Power has ever paid to Reason.
opening statement for the prosecution at Nuremberg
before the International Military Tribunal in Nuremberg, 21 November 1945

James I 1566–1625
British monarch, King of Scotland from 1567 and of England from 1603. On James: see **Henri IV 141:10**

5 No bishop, no King.
to a deputation of Presbyterians from the Church of Scotland, seeking religious tolerance in England
W. Barlow Sum and Substance of the Conference (1604)

6 The state of monarchy is the supremest thing upon earth; for kings are not only God's lieutenants upon earth, and sit upon God's throne, but even by God himself they are called gods.
speech to Parliament, 21 March 1610

7 The king is truly *parens patriae*, the polite father of his people.
speech to Parliament, 21 March 1610

8 That which concerns the mystery of the king's power is not lawful to be disputed; for that is to wade into the weakness of Princes and to take away the mystical reverence, that belongs unto them that sit in the throne of God.
'A Speech in the Star Chamber' [speech to the judges] 20 June 1616

9 I will govern according to the common weal, but not according to the common will.
in December, 1621; J. R. Green History of the English People vol. 3 (1879)

James V 1512–42
Scottish monarch, King from 1513

10 *of the crown of Scotland (which had come to the Stuarts through the female line), on learning of the birth of his daughter Mary Queen of Scots, December 1542:*
It came with a lass, and it will pass with a lass.
Robert Lindsay of Pitscottie (1500–65) History of Scotland (1728)

Antony Jay see **Lynn and Jay**

Douglas Jay 1907–96
British Labour politician. See also **Slogans 290:13**

11 In the case of nutrition and health, just as in the case of education, the gentleman in Whitehall really does know better what is good for people than the people know themselves.
The Socialist Case (1939)

12 He never used one syllable where none would do.
of Attlee
Peter Hennessy Muddling Through (1996)

Thomas Jefferson 1743–1826
American Democratic Republican statesman; 3rd President of the US, 1801–9. On Jefferson: see **Kennedy 167:9, Last words 179:15**; see also **Last words 179:13, Mottoes 221:6, Proverbs 251:16**

13 We hold these truths to be sacred and undeniable; that all men are created equal and independent,

that from that equal creation they derive rights inherent and inalienable, among which are the preservation of life, and liberty, and the pursuit of happiness.
'Rough Draft' of the American Declaration of Independence; J. P. Boyd et al. *Papers of Thomas Jefferson* vol. 1 (1950)

1 Our liberty depends on freedom of the press, and that cannot be limited without being lost.
letter to James Currie, 28 January 1786, in *Papers of Thomas Jefferson* (1954) vol. 9

2 Were it left to me to decide whether we should have a government without newspapers or newspapers without a government, I should not hesitate for a moment to prefer the latter.
letter to Colonel Edward Carrington, 16 January 1787

3 Experience declares that man is the only animal which devours its own kind, for I can apply no milder term to the governments of Europe, and to the general prey of the rich on the poor.
letter to Colonel Edward Carrington, 16 January 1787

4 A little rebellion now and then is a good thing.
letter to James Madison, 30 January 1787

5 The tree of liberty must be refreshed from time to time with the blood of patriots and tyrants. It is its natural manure.
letter to W. S. Smith, 13 November 1787

6 The natural progress of things is for liberty to yield and governments to gain ground.
letter to Colonel Edward Carrington, 27 May 1788

7 If I could not go to Heaven but with a party, I would not go there at all.
letter to Francis Hopkinson, 13 March 1789

8 The republican is the only form of government which is not eternally at open or secret war with the rights of mankind.
letter to William Hunter, 11 March 1790

9 No government ought to be without censors: and where the press is free,

no one ever will.
letter to George Washington, 9 September 1792

10 The second office of government is honourable and easy, the first is but a splendid misery.
letter to Elbridge Gerry, 13 May 1797

11 Offices are acceptable here as elsewhere, and whenever a man has cast a longing eye on them [official positions], a rottenness begins in his conduct.
letter to Tench Coxe, 21 May 1799

12 What an augmentation of the field for jobbing, speculating, plundering, office-building and office-hunting would be produced by an assumption of all the state powers into the hands of the general government.
letter, 13 August 1800

13 If the principle were to prevail, of a common law [i.e. a single government] being in force in the U.S.…it would become the most corrupt government on the earth.
letter to Gideon Granger, 13 August 1800

14 A wise and frugal government, which shall restrain men from injuring one another, which shall leave them otherwise free to regulate their own pursuits of industry and improvement, and shall not take from the mouth of labour the bread it has earned. This is the sum of good government, and this is necessary to close the circle of our felicities.
first inaugural address, 4 March 1801

15 All, too, will bear in mind this sacred principle, that though the will of the majority is in all cases to prevail, that will to be rightful must be reasonable; that the minority possess their equal rights, which equal law must protect, and to violate would be oppression.
first inaugural address, 4 March 1801

16 Would the honest patriot, in the full tide of successful experiment, abandon a government which has so far kept us free and firm?
first inaugural address, 4 March 1801

1 Peace, commerce, and honest friendship with all nations— entangling alliances with none.
first inaugural address, 4 March 1801

2 Freedom of religion; freedom of the press, and freedom of person under the protection of *habeas corpus*, and trial by juries impartially selected. These principles form the bright constellation which has gone before us, and guided our steps through an age of revolution and reformation.
first inaugural address, 4 March 1801

3 I have learned to expect that it will rarely fall to the lot of imperfect man to retire from this station with the reputation and the favour which bring him into it.
first inaugural address, 4 March 1801

4 If a due participation of office is a matter of right, how are vacancies to be obtained? Those by death are few; by resignation none.
letter to E. Shipman and others, 12 July 1801; see **Misquotations 215:8**

5 If we can prevent the government from wasting the labours of the people, under the pretence of taking care of them, they must become happy.
letter to Thomas Cooper, 29 November 1802

6 Nothing can now be believed which is seen in a newspaper. Truth itself becomes suspicious by being put into that polluted vehicle.
letter to John Norvell, 14 June 1807, in *The Portable Thomas Jefferson* (1977)

7 When a man assumes a public trust, he should consider himself as public property.
to Baron von Humboldt, 1807
B. L. Rayner *Life of Jefferson* (1834)

8 The care of human life and happiness, and not their destruction, is the first and only legitimate object of good government.
to the Republican Citizens of Washington County, Maryland, 31 March 1809

9 Politics, like religion, hold up the torches of martyrdom to the reformers of error.
letter to James Ogilvie, 4 August 1811

10 I agree with you that there is a natural aristocracy among men. The grounds of this are virtue and talents.
letter to John Adams, 28 October 1813

11 Merchants have no country. The mere spot they stand on does not constitute so strong an attachment as that from which they draw their gains.
letter to Horatio G. Spafford, 17 March 1814

12 If a nation expects to be ignorant and free, in a state of civilization, it expects what never was and never will be.
letter to Colonel Charles Yancey, 6 January 1816

13 If it is believed that these elementary schools will be better managed by the Governor and Council, the commissioners of the literary fund, or any other general authority of the government, than by the parents in each ward, it is a belief against all experience...What has destroyed liberty and the rights of man in every government which has ever existed under the sun? The generalizing and concentrating all cares and powers into one body.
letter to Joseph C. Cabell, 2 February 1816

14 Nothing gives one person so great advantage over another, as to remain always cool and unruffled under all circumstances.
letter to Francis Wayles Eppes, 21 May 1816, in Jerry Holmes (ed.) *Thomas Jefferson: A Chronology of His Thoughts* (2002)

15 Banking establishments are more dangerous than standing armies.
letter to John Taylor, 28 May 1816, in T. Jefferson Randolph (ed.) *Memoirs, Correspondence & Private Papers of T. Jefferson* (1829) vol. 3

16 But this momentous question [the Missouri Compromise], like a firebell in the night awakened and filled me with terror. I considered it the knell of the Union.
letter to John Holmes, 22 April 1820

17 We have the wolf by the ears; and

we can neither hold him, nor safely let him go. Justice is in one scale, and self-preservation in the other.
on slavery
letter to John Holmes, 22 April 1820

1 I know no safe depository of the ultimate powers of the society but the people themselves; and if we think them not enlightened enough to exercise their control with a wholesome discretion, the remedy is not to take it from them, but to inform their discretion by education.
letter to William Charles Jarvis, 28 September 1820

2 That one hundred and fifty lawyers should do business together ought not to be expected.
on the United States Congress
Autobiography 6 January 1821

3 To attain all this [universal republicanism], however, rivers of blood must yet flow, and years of desolation pass over; yet the object is worth rivers of blood, and years of desolation.
letter to John Adams, 4 September 1823

4 The generation which commences a revolution can rarely complete it.
letter to John Adams, 4 September 1823, in P. L. Ford *Writings of Thomas Jefferson* (1899) vol. 10

5 Were we directed from Washington when to sow, and when to reap, we should soon want bread.
Autobiography

6 Ignorance is preferable to error; and he is less remote from the truth who believes nothing, than he who believes what is wrong.
Notes on the State of Virginia (1781–5)

7 Millions of innocent men, women, and children, since the introduction of Christianity, have been burnt, tortured, fined, imprisoned; yet we have not advanced one inch towards uniformity [of opinion]. What has been the effect of coercion? To make one half the world fools, and the other half hypocrites.
Notes on the State of Virginia (1781–5)

8 Indeed I tremble for my country when I reflect that God is just.
Notes on the State of Virginia (1781–5)

9 To the press alone, chequered as it is with abuses, the world is indebted for all the triumphs which have been gained by reason and humanity over error and oppression.
Virginia and Kentucky Resolutions (1799)

10 No duty the Executive had to perform was so trying as to put the right man in the right place.
J. B. MacMaster *History of the People of the United States* (1883–1913) vol. 2

11 The legitimate powers of government extend to such acts only as are injurious to others. But it does me no injury for my neighbour to say there are twenty gods, or no God. It neither picks my pocket nor breaks my leg.
attributed

12 The policy of the American government is to leave their citizens free, neither restraining nor aiding them in their pursuits.
attributed

Patrick Jenkin 1926–
British Conservative politician

13 People can clean their teeth in the dark, use the top of the stove instead of the oven, all sorts of savings, but they must use less electricity.
as Minister for Energy, asking the public to save electricity as a miners' strike reduced supplies; often summarized as, 'clean your teeth in the dark'
radio broadcast, 15 January 1974

Roy Jenkins 1920–2003
British politician; co-founder of the Social Democratic Party, 1981

14 The politics of the left and centre of this country are frozen in an out-of-date mould which is bad for the political and economic health of Britain and increasingly inhibiting for those who live within the

mould. Can it be broken?
speech to Parliamentary Press Gallery, 9 June 1980

1 *of Margaret **Thatcher**:*
A First Minister whose self-righteous stubbornness has not been equalled, save briefly by Neville Chamberlain, since Lord North.
in Observer 11 March 1990

2 The record does not provide much sustenance for the view that limpet-like Prime Ministers can be easily disposed of by their parties.
in Guardian 14 April 1990

3 *of Edward **Heath**:*
A great lighthouse which stands there, flashing out beams of light, indifferent to the waves which beat against him.
in Independent 22 September 1990

4 Nearly all Prime Ministers are dissatisfied with their successors, perhaps even more so if they come from their own party.
Gladstone (1995)

5 There is nobody in politics I can remember and no case I can think of in history where a man combined such a powerful political personality with so little intelligence.
*of James **Callaghan***
Richard Crossman diary, 5 September 1969

John Jervis, Earl St Vincent
1735–1823
British admiral

6 I do not say the French cannot come. I only say they cannot come by water!
on the possibility of invasion in 1804
Arthur Bryant Years of Victory 1802–1812 (1944)

W. Stanley Jevons 1835–82
English economist

7 All classes of society are trades unionists at heart, and differ chiefly in the boldness, ability, and secrecy with which they pursue their respective interests.
The State in Relation to Labour (1882)

Muhammad Ali Jinnah 1876–1948
Indian statesman and founder of Pakistan

8 You are free; you are free to go to your temples, you are free to go to your mosques or to any other place of worship in this State of Pakistan. You may belong to any religion or caste or creed—that has nothing to do with the fundamental principle that we are all citizens and equal citizens of one state.
Presidential Address to the Constituent Assembly, 11 August 1947

John XXIII 1881–1963
Italian cleric, Pope from 1958

9 If civil authorities legislate for or allow anything that is contrary to that order and therefore contrary to the will of God, neither the laws made or the authorizations granted can be binding on the consciences of the citizens, since God has more right to be obeyed than man.
Pacem in Terris (1963)

10 The social progress, order, security and peace of each country are necessarily connected with the social progress, order, security and peace of all other countries.
Pacem in Terris (1963)

11 [In the universal *Declaration of Human Rights* (December, 1948)] in most solemn form, the dignity of a person is acknowledged to all human beings; and as a consequence there is proclaimed, as a fundamental right, the right of free movement in search for truth and in the attainment of moral good and of justice, and also the right to a dignified life.
Pacem in Terris (1963)

Elton John 1947– and Bernie Taupin 1950–

12 Goodbye England's rose;
May you ever grow in our hearts.
*rewritten for and sung at the funeral of **Diana**, Princess of Wales, 7 September 1997*
'Candle in the Wind' (song, revised version, 1997)

John Paul II 1920–2005
Polish cleric, Pope 1978–2005

1 It would be simplistic to say that Divine Providence caused the fall of communism. It fell by itself as a consequence of its own mistakes and abuses. It fell by itself because of its own inherent weaknesses.
when asked by the Italian writer Vittorio Missori if the fall of the USSR could be ascribed to God
Carl Bernstein and Marco Politi *His Holiness: John Paul II and the Hidden History of our Time* (1996)

Boris Johnson 1964–
British Conservative politician

2 It is complete balderdash. It is an inverted pyramid of piffle.
denying accusations of his having an affair with Petronella Wyatt
in *Mail on Sunday* 7 November 2004

3 All politicians in the end are like crazed wasps in a jam jar, each individually convinced that they are going to make it.
on *Desert Island Discs* BBC Radio 4, 30 October 2005

Lyndon Baines Johnson 1908–73
American Democratic statesman; 36th President of the US 1963–9. On Johnson: see **White 331:5**

4 *to a reporter who had queried his embracing Richard **Nixon** on the vice-president's return from a controversial tour of South America in 1958:*
Son, in politics you've got to learn that overnight chicken shit can turn to chicken salad.
Fawn Brodie *Richard Nixon* (1983)

5 I am a free man, an American, a United States Senator, and a Democrat, in that order.
in *Texas Quarterly* Winter 1958

6 I'll tell you what's at the bottom of it. If you can convince the lowest white man that he's better than the best coloured man, he won't notice you're picking his pocket. Hell, give him someone to look down on and he'll empty his pockets for you.
during the 1960 Presidential campaign, to Bill Moyers
Robert Dallek *Lone Star Rising* (1991)

7 All I have I would have given gladly not to be standing here today.
*following the assassination of John F. **Kennedy***
first speech to Congress as President, 27 November 1963

8 We have talked long enough in this country about equal rights. We have talked for a hundred years or more. It is time now to write the next chapter, and to write it in the books of law.
speech to Congress, 27 November 1963

9 This administration, here and now declares unconditional war on poverty in America.
State of the Union address to Congress, 8 January 1964

10 For the first time in our history, it is possible to conquer poverty.
speech to Congress, 16 March 1964

11 In your time we have the opportunity to move not only toward the rich society and the powerful society, but upward to the Great Society.
speech at University of Michigan, 22 May 1964

12 We Americans know, although others appear to forget, the risks of spreading conflict. We still seek no wider war.
speech on radio and television, 4 August 1964

13 We are not about to send American boys 9 or 10,000 miles away from home to do what Asian boys ought to be doing for themselves.
speech at Akron University, 21 October 1964

14 Extremism in the pursuit of the Presidency is an unpardonable vice. Moderation in the affairs of the nation is the highest virtue.
speech in New York, 31 October 1964; see **Goldwater 127:7**

15 A President's hardest task is not to *do* what is right, but to *know* what is right.
State of the Union address to Congress, 4 January 1965

16 It is not enough to open the gates of opportunity. All of our citizens must have the ability to walk

through those gates.
  speech at Harvard in 1965; Paul L. Fisher and
  Ralph L. Lavenstein (eds.) *Race and the News
  Media* (1967)

1 If I've lost Walter Cronkite I've lost
Mr Average Citizen.
  *in 1968, after hearing Walter Cronkite's comment
  on the position in Vietnam (now often quoted as
  '...I've lost the country'); see **Cronkite***
  to his press secretary George Christian;
  reported in D. Halberstam *The Powers That
  Be* (1979)

2 Better to have him inside the tent
pissing out, than outside pissing in.
  of J. Edgar Hoover
  David Halberstam *The Best and the Brightest*
  (1972)

3 Come now, let us reason together.
  habitual saying

4 Did you ever think that making a
speech on economics is a lot like
pissing down your leg? It seems hot
to you, but it never does to anyone
else.
  to J. K. Galbraith; J. K. Galbraith *A Life in Our
  Times* (1981)

5 I don't want loyalty. I want *loyalty*.
I want him to kiss my ass in Macy's
window at high noon and tell me it
smells like roses. I want his pecker
in my pocket.
  discussing a prospective assistant
  David Halberstam *The Best and the Brightest*
  (1972)

6 So dumb he can't fart and chew
gum at the same time.
  *of Gerald **Ford***
  Richard Reeves *A Ford, not a Lincoln* (1975)

Philander Chase Johnson
1866–1939
American journalist

7 Politics is the art of turning
influence into affluence.
  Senator Sorghum's Primer of Politics (1906)

Samuel Johnson 1709–84
English poet, critic, and lexicographer

8 Liberty is, to the lowest rank of
every nation, little more than the
choice of working or starving.
  'The Bravery of the English Common Soldier' in
  The British Magazine January 1760

9 If the changes we fear be thus
irresistible, what remains but to
acquiesce with silence, as in the
other insurmountable distresses
of humanity? It remains that we
retard what we cannot repel, that
we palliate what we cannot cure.
  A Dictionary of the English Language (1755)
  preface

10 *Pension*. Pay given to a state
hireling for treason to his country.
  A Dictionary of the English Language (1755)

11 Among the calamities of war
may be jointly numbered the
diminution of the love of truth,
by the falsehoods which interest
dictates and credulity encourages.
  The Idler 11 November 1758; see
  Proverbs 252:11

12 Faction seldom leaves a man
honest, however it might find him.
  Lives of the English Poets (1779–81)

13 How is it that we hear the loudest
yelps for liberty among the drivers
of negroes?
  Taxation No Tyranny (1775)

14 How small of all that human hearts
endure,
That part which laws or kings can
cause or cure.
  lines added to Oliver Goldsmith's *The Traveller*
  (1764); see **Goldsmith 127:6**

15 I do not much like to see a Whig in
any dress; but I hate to see a Whig
in a parson's gown.
  James Boswell *Journal of a Tour to the Hebrides*
  (1785) 24 September 1773

16 This man [Lord Chesterfield] I
thought had been a Lord among
wits; but, I find, he is only a wit
among Lords.
  James Boswell *Life of Samuel Johnson* (1791)
  1754

17 Your levellers wish to level *down* as
far as themselves; but they cannot
bear levelling *up* to themselves.
  James Boswell *Life of Samuel Johnson* (1791)
  21 July 1763

18 BOSWELL: So, Sir, you laugh
at schemes of political
improvement.
  JOHNSON: Why, Sir, most schemes
  of political improvement are very

laughable things.
James Boswell *Life of Samuel Johnson* (1791)
26 October 1769

1 So many objections may be made
to everything, that nothing can
overcome them but the necessity of
doing something.
James Boswell *Life of Samuel Johnson* (1791)
1770

2 A decent provision for the poor, is
the true test of civilization.
James Boswell *Life of Samuel Johnson* (1791)
1770

3 I would not give half a guinea to
live under one form of government
rather than another. It is of no
moment to the happiness of an
individual.
James Boswell *Life of Samuel Johnson* (1791)
31 March 1772

4 Sir, I perceive you are a vile Whig.
to Sir Adam Fergusson; James Boswell *Life of
Samuel Johnson* (1791) 31 March 1772

5 There are few ways in which a man
can be more innocently employed
than in getting money.
James Boswell *Life of Samuel Johnson* (1791)
27 March 1775

6 George the First knew nothing,
and desired to know nothing; did
nothing, and desired to do nothing;
and the only good thing that is
told of him is, that he wished to
restore the crown to its hereditary
successor.
James Boswell *Life of Samuel Johnson* (1791)
6 April 1775

7 Patriotism is the last refuge of a
scoundrel.
James Boswell *Life of Samuel Johnson* (1791)
7 April 1775

8 Politics are now nothing more than
means of rising in the world.
James Boswell *Life of Samuel Johnson* (1791)
18 April 1775

9 Every man who attacks my belief,
diminishes in some degree my
confidence in it, and therefore
makes me uneasy; and I am angry
with him who makes me uneasy.
James Boswell *Life of Samuel Johnson* (1791)
3 April 1776

10 It is better that some should be

unhappy than that none should be
happy, which would be the case in a
general state of equality.
James Boswell *Life of Samuel Johnson* (1791)
7 April 1776

11 Though we cannot out-vote them
we will out-argue them.
James Boswell *Life of Samuel Johnson* (1791)
3 April 1778

12 I have always said, the first Whig
was the Devil.
James Boswell *Life of Samuel Johnson* (1791)
28 April 1778

13 A wise Tory and a wise Whig, I
believe, will agree. Their principles
are the same, though their modes
of thinking are different.
James Boswell *Life of Samuel Johnson* (1791)
May 1781; written statement given to Boswell

14 If a man were to go by chance at
the same time with Burke under a
shed, to shun a shower, he would
say—'this is an extraordinary man.'
on Edmund **Burke**
James Boswell *Life of Samuel Johnson* (1791)
15 May 1784

15 Fox divided the kingdom with
Caesar; so that it was a doubt
whether the nation should be ruled
by the sceptre of George III or the
tongue of Fox.
on the Parliamentary defeat of Charles James **Fox**,
and the subsequent dissolution, in 1784
in *Dictionary of National Biography* (1917–)

16 Mankind are happier in a state
of inequality and subordination.
Were they to be in this pretty
state of equality, they would soon
degenerate into brutes.
attributed

Tom Johnston 1881–1965
Scottish Labour politician

17 I have become...uneasy lest
we should get political power
without our first having, or at
least simultaneously having, an
adequate economy to administer.
What purport would there be in
our getting a Scots parliament in
Edinburgh if it has to administer an
emigration system, a glorified Poor

Law, and a graveyard!
Memories (1952)

1 They have barred us by barbed wire
fences from the bens and glens:
the peasant has been ruthlessly
swept aside to make room for the
pheasant, and the mountain hare
now brings forth her young on the
hearthstone of the Gael!
Our Scots Noble Families (1909)

Hanns Johst 1890–1978
German dramatist

2 Whenever I hear the word
culture...I release the safety-catch
of my Browning!
*often quoted as: 'Whenever I hear the word
culture, I reach for my pistol!', and attributed to
Hermann **Goering***
Schlageter (1933)

Ieuan Wyn Jones 1949–
Welsh nationalist politician, president of Plaid Cymru

3 The priority for us now is for
Wales to gain the same powers as
Scotland.
*speech to the Plaid Cymru Party Conference
in Guardian 23 September 2000*

John Paul Jones 1747–92
American admiral

4 I have not yet begun to fight.
*as his ship was sinking, 23 September 1779,
having been asked whether he had lowered his
flag*
Mrs Reginald De Koven *Life and Letters of John
Paul Jones* (1914) vol. 1

Mary Harris 'Mother' Jones
c. 1837–1930
Irish-born American labour activist

5 Pray for the dead and fight like hell
for the living!
The Autobiography of Mother Jones (1925)

William Jones 1746–94
English jurist

6 My opinion is, that power should
always be distrusted, in whatever
hands it is placed.
letter to Lord Althorpe, 5 October 1782

Ben Jonson c. 1573–1637
English dramatist and poet. See also **Epitaphs 106:4**

7 PEOPLE: The Voice of Cato is the
voice of Rome.
CATO: The voice of Rome is the
consent of heaven!
Catiline his Conspiracy (1611)

Janis Joplin 1943–70
American singer

8 Fourteen heart attacks and he had
to die in my week. In MY week.
*when ex-President **Eisenhower**'s death
prevented her photograph appearing on the cover
of Newsweek
in New Musical Express 12 April 1969*

Barbara Jordan 1936–96
American Democratic politician

9 The Bill of Rights was not ordained
by nature or God. It's very human,
very fragile.
in New York Times Magazine 21 October 1990

Michael Jordan 1963–
American basketball player

10 Republicans buy sneakers, too.
*when Jordan, sponsored by the shoe
manufacturer Nike, was asked to endorse the
campaign to unseat the Republican senator Jesse
Helms in 1990*
David Halberstam *Playing for Keeps: Michael
Jordan and the World He Made* (1999)

Thomas Jordan c. 1612–85
English poet and dramatist

11 They plucked communion tables
down
And broke our painted glasses;
They threw our altars to the ground
And tumbled down the crosses.
They set up Cromwell and his heir—
The Lord and Lady Claypole—
Because they hated Common Prayer,
The organ and the maypole.
'How the War began' (1664)

Chief Joseph (Hinmaton-Yalaktit) c. 1840–1904
American Nez Percé chief

12 From where the sun now stands I

will fight no more forever.
speech at the end of the Nez Percé war in
1877; Dee Brown *Bury My Heart at Wounded
Knee* (1970) ch. 13

1 Good words do not last long unless
they amount to something. Words
do not pay for my dead people.
on a visit to Washington in 1879; Chester
Anders Fee *Chief Joseph* (1936)

Keith Joseph 1918–94
British Conservative politician

2 Problems reproduce themselves
from generation to generation…I
refer to this as a 'cycle of
deprivation'.
speech in London to the Pre-School Playgroups
Association, 29 June 1972

3 The balance of our population, our
human stock, is threatened…a high
and rising proportion of children
are being born to mothers least
fitted to bring children into the
world and bring them up.
speech in Birmingham, 19 October 1974

4 If we are to be prosperous we
need more millionaires and more
bankrupts.
maiden speech in the House of Lords,
19 February 1988

5 There are no illegitimate children,
only illegitimate parents.
in Kiss Hollywood Good-Bye *(1978), Anita Loos
attributes an earlier coinage of this statement to
the American philanthropist Edna Gladney*
speech to National Children's Home,
6 November 1991

Lionel Jospin 1937–
French statesman, Prime Minister of France
1997–2002

6 Yes to the market economy, No to
the market society.
in *Independent* 16 September 1998

Joseph Joubert 1754–1824
French essayist and moralist

7 One of the surest ways of killing
a tree is to lay bare its roots. It is
the same with institutions. We
must not be too ready to disinter
the origins of those we wish to
preserve. All beginnings are small.
Pensées (1842)

8 It's better to debate a question
without settling it than to settle a
question without debating it.
attributed

Tessa Jowell 1947–
British Labour politician

9 In the last Parliament, the House
of Commons had more MPs called
John than all the women MPs put
together.
in *Independent on Sunday* 14 March
1999 'Quotes'

James Joyce 1882–1941
Irish novelist

10 Poor Parnell! he cried loudly. My
dead king!
A Portrait of the Artist as a Young Man (1916)
ch. 1

William Joyce ('Lord Haw-Haw') 1906–46
American-born Fascist supporter and wartime
broadcaster from Nazi Germany; executed for treason
in 1946

11 Germany calling! Germany calling!
habitual introduction to propaganda broadcast
broadcasts from Germany to Britain during the
Second World War

Juan Carlos I 1938–
Spanish monarch, King from 1975

12 The Crown, the symbol of the
permanence and unity of Spain,
cannot tolerate any actions by
people attempting to disrupt by

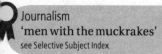

Journalism
'men with the muckrakes'
see Selective Subject Index

force the democratic process.
on the occasion of the attempted coup in 1981
television broadcast at 1.15 a.m., 24 February
1981

1 I will neither abdicate the Crown
nor leave Spain. Whoever rebels
will provoke a new civil war and
will be responsible.
on the occasion of the attempted coup
television broadcast, 24 February 1981

'Junius'
English 18th-century pseudonymous writer

2 The right of election is the very
essence of the constitution.
in *Public Advertiser* 24 April 1769, letter 11

3 Is this the wisdom of a great
minister? or is it the ominous
vibration of a pendulum?
in *Public Advertiser* 30 May 1769, letter 12

4 There is a holy mistaken zeal in
politics as well as in religion. By
persuading others, we convince
ourselves.
in *Public Advertiser* 19 December 1769,
letter 35

5 However distinguished by rank or
property, in the rights of freedom
we are all equal.
in *Public Advertiser* 19 March 1770, letter 37

6 The injustice done to an individual
is sometimes of service to the
public.
in *Public Advertiser* 14 November 1770,
letter 41

7 As for Mr Wedderburne, there is
something about him, which even
treachery cannot trust.
in *Public Advertiser* 22 June 1771, letter 49

8 The liberty of the press is
the *Palladium* of all the civil,
political, and religious rights of an
Englishman.
The Letters of Junius (1772 ed.) 'Dedication to
the English Nation'

John Junor 1919–97
British journalist

9 I do not know the answer to this
question, but I think we should be
told.
used in *Sunday Express* and elsewhere

10 Such a graceful exit. And then
he had to go and do this on the
doorstep.
*on Harold **Wilson**'s 'Lavender List', the
honours list he drew up on resigning the British
premiership in 1976*
in *Observer* 23 January 1990

Juvenal *c. AD 60–c. 130*
Roman satirist

11 *Quis tulerit Gracchos de seditione
querentes?*
Who would put up with the Gracchi
complaining about subversion?
*referring to the Roman tribune Tiberius
Sempronius Gracchus (163–133 BC) and his brother
Gaius Sempronius Gracchus (153–121 BC), who
were responsible for radical social and economic
legislation, passed against the wishes of the
senatorial class*
Satires

12 *Sed quis custodiet ipsos
Custodes?*
But who is to guard the guards
themselves?
Satires

13 ...*Verbosa et grandis epistula venit
A Capreis.*
A huge wordy letter came from
Capri.
*on the Emperor Tiberius's letter to the Senate,
which caused the downfall of Sejanus in AD 31*
Satires

14 ...*Duas tantum res anxius optat,
Panem et circenses.*
Only two things does he [the
modern citizen] anxiously wish
for—bread and circuses.
Satires

Franz Kafka 1883–1924
Czech novelist

1 It's often better to be in chains than to be free.
The Trial (1925)

Immanuel Kant 1724–1804
German philosopher

2 There is, therefore, only one categorical imperative. It is: Act only according to that maxim which you can at the same time will that it should become a universal law.
Fundamental Principles of the Metaphysics of Ethics (1785)

3 Out of the crooked timber of humanity no straight thing was ever made.
Idee zu einer allgemeinen Geschichte in weltbürgerliche Absicht (1784)

Gerald Kaufman 1930–
British Labour politician

4 The longest suicide note in history.
on the Labour Party's New Hope for Britain *(1983)*
Denis Healey *The Time of My Life* (1989)

5 We would prefer to see the House [the Royal Opera House] run by a philistine with the requisite financial acumen than by the succession of opera and ballet lovers who have brought a great and valuable institution to its knees.
report of the Commons' Culture, Media and Sport Select Committee on Covent Garden, 3 December 1997

6 Cabinet minutes are studied in Government Departments with the reverence generally reserved for sacred texts, and can be triumphantly produced conclusively to settle any arguments.
How to be a Minister (1980)

Paul Keating 1944–
Australian Labor statesman; Prime Minister 1991–6

7 You look like an Easter Island statue with an arse full of razor blades.
in the Australian Parliament to the then Prime Minister, Malcolm **Fraser**
Michael Gordon *A Question of Leadership* (1993)

8 This is a recession that Australia had to have.
speaking as Federal Treasurer, 29 November 1990

9 Even as it [Great Britain] walked out on you and joined the Common Market, you were still looking for your MBEs and your knighthoods, and all the rest of the regalia that comes with it. You would take Australia right back down the time tunnel to the cultural cringe where you have always come from.
addressing Australian Conservative supporters of Great Britain in the Australian Parliament
speech, 27 February 1992, in *House of Representatives Weekly Hansard* [Australia] (1992) no. 1

10 These are the same old fogies who doffed their lids and tugged the forelock to the British establishment.
of Australian Conservative supporters of Great Britain
speech, 27 February 1992, in *House of Representatives Weekly Hansard* [Australia] (1992) no. 1

11 I'm a bastard. But I'm a bastard who gets the mail through. And they appreciate that.
in 1994, to a senior colleague, in *Sunday Telegraph* 20 November 1994

1 Leadership is not about being nice. It's about being right and being strong.
   in *Time* 9 January 1995

Garrison Keillor 1942–
American humorous writer and broadcaster

2 Ronald Reagan, the President who never told bad news to the American people.
   We Are Still Married (1989), introduction

3 My ancestors were Puritans from England. They arrived here in 1648 in the hope of finding greater restrictions than were permissible under English law at that time.
   attributed, 1993

Tom Kelly
British government press officer

4 This is now a game of chicken with the Beeb.
   on the argument between Downing Street and the BBC about the content of Andrew Gilligan's Today *report; see* **Gilligan**
   email of 10 July 2003; in *Guardian* 19 August 2003 (online edition)

George F. Kennan 1904–2005
American diplomat and historian

5 Government…is simply not the channel through which men's noblest impulses are to be realized. Its task, on the contrary, is largely to see to it that the ignoble ones are kept under restraint and not permitted to go too far.
   Around the Cragged Hill (1993)

6 A war regarded as inevitable or even probable, and therefore much prepared for, has a very good chance of being eventually fought.
   The Cloud of Danger (1977)

Charles Kennedy 1959–
British Liberal Democrat politician, Party Leader 1999–2006

7 War is not the word; nor is crusade. Resolve is.
   of the appropriate response to terrorism; see **Bush**
   speech to the Liberal Democrat Party Conference, 24 December 2001

8 The era of three-party politics right across the UK is now with us.
   speech, 6 May 2005

Florynce Kennedy 1916–2000
American lawyer

9 When you want to get to the suites, start in the streets.
   her rule for political activism
   attributed; in *Los Angeles Times* 28 December 2000 (obituary)

John F. Kennedy 1917–63
American Democratic statesman, 35th President of the US, 1961–3. On Kennedy: see **Bentsen 29:1**, **Hope 147:7, Kennedy 168:3, Stevenson 301:8**

10 Don't buy a single vote more than necessary. I'll be damned if I'm going to pay for a landslide.
   telegraphed message from his father, read at a Gridiron dinner in Washington, 15 March 1958, and almost certainly JFK's invention
   J. F. Cutler *Honey Fitz* (1962)

11 We stand today on the edge of a new frontier…But the New Frontier of which I speak is not a set of promises—it is a set of challenges. It sums up not what I intend to offer the American people, but what I intend to ask of them.
   accepting the Democratic nomination
   speech in Los Angeles, 15 July 1960; see **Schlossberg 275:2**

12 Let the word go forth from this time and place, to friend and foe alike, that the torch has been passed to a new generation of Americans—born in this century, tempered by war, disciplined by a hard and bitter peace, proud of our ancient heritage—and unwilling to witness or permit the slow undoing of those human rights to which this nation has always been committed, and to which we are committed today at home and around the world.
   inaugural address, 20 January 1961

13 Let every nation know, whether it wishes us well or ill, that we shall pay any price, bear any burden, meet any hardship, support any friend, oppose any foe to assure the

survival and the success of liberty.
inaugural address, 20 January 1961

1 If a free society cannot help the many who are poor, it cannot save the few who are rich.
inaugural address, 20 January 1961

2 Let us never negotiate out of fear. But let us never fear to negotiate.
inaugural address, 20 January 1961

3 All this will not be finished in the first 100 days. Nor will it be finished in the first 1,000 days, nor in the life of this Administration, nor even perhaps in our lifetime on this planet. But let us begin.
inaugural address, 20 January 1961

4 And so, my fellow Americans: ask not what your country can do for you—ask what you can do for your country. My fellow citizens of the world: ask not what America will do for you, but what together we can do for the freedom of man.
inaugural address, 20 January 1961; Oliver Wendell **Holmes** Jr., speaking at Keene, New Hampshire, 30 May 1884 said: 'We pause to... recall what our country has done for each of us and to ask ourselves what we can do for our country in return' (see also **Gibran 123:8**)

5 I believe that this Nation should commit itself to achieving the goal, before this decade is out, of landing a man on the Moon and returning him safely to earth.
supplementary State of the Union message to Congress, 25 May 1961

6 When we got into office, the thing that surprised me most was to find that things were just as bad as we'd been saying they were.
speech at the White House, 27 May 1961

7 Mankind must put an end to war or war will put an end to mankind.
speech to United Nations General Assembly, 25 September 1961

8 Those who make peaceful revolution impossible will make violent revolution inevitable.
speech at the White House, 13 March 1962

9 Probably the greatest concentration of talent and genius in this house except for perhaps those times when Thomas Jefferson ate alone.
of a dinner for the Nobel prizewinners at the White House
in *New York Times* 30 April 1962

10 If we cannot end now our differences, at least we can help make the world safe for diversity.
address at American University, Washington, DC, 10 June 1963

11 No one has been barred on account of his race from fighting or dying for America—there are no 'white' or 'coloured' signs on the foxholes or graveyards of battle.
message to Congress on proposed Civil Rights Bill, 19 June 1963

12 All free men, wherever they may live, are citizens of Berlin, and therefore, as a free man, I take pride in the words *Ich bin ein Berliner* [I am a Berliner].
speaking in the newly divided city of Berlin, and expressing the USA's commitment to the support and defence of West Berlin
speech in West Berlin, 26 June 1963

13 When power leads man toward arrogance, poetry reminds him of his limitations. When power narrows the areas of man's concern, poetry reminds him of the richness and diversity of his existence. When power corrupts, poetry cleanses. For art establishes the basic human truths which must serve as the touchstone of our judgement.
speech at Amherst College, Massachusetts, 26 October 1963

14 In free society art is not a weapon... Artists are not engineers of the soul.
speech at Amherst College, Massachusetts, 26 October 1963; see **Gorky 128:6**, **Stalin 299:4**

15 *on being asked how he became a war hero:*
It was involuntary. They sank my boat.
Arthur M. Schlesinger Jr. *A Thousand Days* (1965)

16 Washington is a city of southern efficiency and northern charm.
Arthur M. Schlesinger Jr. *A Thousand Days* (1965)

1 I'm an idealist without illusions.
  attributed; see **Macleod 198:11**

Joseph P. Kennedy 1888–1969
American financier and diplomat; father of John F.
Kennedy. See also **Proverbs 252:10**

2 This is a hell of a long way from East
  Boston.
  *to his wife Rose, on a visit to Windsor Castle two
  weeks after his arrival as Ambassador*
  in *Times* 24 January 1995 (obituary of Rose
  Kennedy)

3 We're going to sell Jack like
  soapflakes.
  *when his son John F. **Kennedy** made his bid for
  the Presidency*
  John H. Davis *The Kennedy Clan* (1984)

Robert F. Kennedy 1925–68
American democratic politician; son of Joseph
Kennedy and brother of John F. **Kennedy**

4 About one-fifth of the people are
  against everything all the time.
  speech at University of Pennsylvania, 6 May
  1964

5 Each time a man stands up for an
  ideal, or acts to improve the lot
  of others, or strikes out against
  injustice, he sends forth a tiny
  ripple of hope, and crossing each
  other from a million different
  centres of energy and daring those
  ripples build a current which can
  sweep down the mightiest walls of
  oppression and resistance.
  speech, Cape Town, 6 June 1966

6 What is objectionable, what is
  dangerous about extremists is not
  that they are extreme but that they
  are intolerant.
  The Pursuit of Justice (1964)

7 Every society gets the kind
  of criminal it deserves. What
  is equally true is that every
  community gets the kind of law
  enforcement it insists on.
  The Pursuit of Justice (1964)

Jomo Kenyatta 1891–1978
Kenyan statesman, Prime Minister of Kenya 1963 and
President 1964–78

8 The African is conditioned, by the

cultural and social institutions of
centuries, to a freedom of which
Europe has little conception, and
it is not in his nature to accept
serfdom forever. He realizes that he
must fight unceasingly for his own
emancipation; for without this he is
doomed to remain the prey of rival
imperialisms.
  Facing Mount Kenya (1938); conclusion

John Kerry 1943–
American Democratic politician, presidential candidate
in 2004

9 How do you ask a man to be the last
  man to die in Vietnam? How do you
  ask a man to be the last man to die
  for a mistake?
  speech to Senate Committee, 23 April 1971

10 It's the wrong war, in the wrong
  place, at the wrong time.
  *of the war in Iraq, echoing the words of Omar
  Bradley on the Korean War in 1951*
  campaigning in Canonsburg, Pennsylvania,
  6 September 2004; Reuters 6 September
  2004 (electronic edition)

11 It's one thing to be certain, but
  you can be certain and you can be
  wrong.
  televised presidential debate with George W.
  Bush, 30 September 2004; in *New York Times*
  1 October 2004 (electronic edition)

Francis Scott Key 1779–1843
American lawyer and verse-writer

12 'Tis the star-spangled banner; O
  long may it wave
  O'er the land of the free, and the
  home of the brave!
  'The Star-Spangled Banner' (1814)

John Maynard Keynes 1883–1946
English economist

13 I work for a Government I despise
  for ends I think criminal.
  letter to Duncan Grant, 15 December 1917

14 A 'sound' banker, alas! is not one
  who foresees danger and avoids it,
  but one who, when he is ruined,
  is ruined in a conventional and
  orthodox way along with his
  fellows, so that no one can really

blame him.
'The Consequences to the Banks of the Collapse of Money Values' (1931)

1 of **Clemenceau**:
He felt about France what Pericles felt of Athens—unique value in her, nothing else mattering; but his theory of politics was Bismarck's. He had one illusion—France; and one disillusion—mankind, including Frenchmen, and his colleagues not least.
The Economic Consequences of the Peace (1919)

2 Like Odysseus, the President looked wiser when he was seated.
of Woodrow **Wilson**
The Economic Consequences of the Peace (1919)

3 Lenin was right. There is no subtler, no surer means of overturning the existing basis of society than to debauch the currency. The process engages all the hidden forces of economic law on the side of destruction, and does it in a manner which not one man in a million is able to diagnose.
The Economic Consequences of the Peace (1919)

4 Capitalism, wisely managed, can probably be made more efficient for attaining economic ends than any alternative system yet in sight, but…in itself it is in many ways extremely objectionable.
The End of Laissez-Faire (1926)

5 Marxian Socialism must always remain a portent to the historians of Opinion—how a doctrine so illogical and so dull can have exercised so powerful and enduring an influence over the minds of men, and, through them, the events of history.
The End of Laissez-Faire (1926)

6 I do not know which makes a man more conservative—to know nothing but the present, or nothing but the past.
The End of Laissez-Faire (1926)

7 The important thing for Government is not to do things which individuals are doing already, and to do them a little better or a little worse; but to do those things which at present are not done at all.
The End of Laissez-Faire (1926)

8 of **Lloyd George**:
This extraordinary figure of our time, this syren, this goat-footed bard, this half-human visitor to our age from the hag-ridden magic and enchanted woods of Celtic antiquity.
Essays in Biography (1933) 'Mr Lloyd George'

9 of **Lloyd George**:
Who shall paint the chameleon, who can tether a broomstick?
Essays in Biography (1933) 'Mr Lloyd George'

10 Speculators may do no harm as bubbles on a steady stream of enterprise. But the position is serious when enterprise becomes the bubble on a whirlpool of speculation.
General Theory (1936)

11 It is better that a man should tyrannize over his bank balance than over his fellow-citizens.
General Theory (1936)

12 We take it as a fundamental psychological rule of any modern community that, when its real income is increased, it will not increase its consumption by an equal *absolute* amount.
General Theory (1936)

13 The ideas of economists and political philosophers, both when they are right and when they are wrong, are more powerful than is commonly understood…Practical men, who believe themselves to be quite exempt from any intellectual influences, are usually the slaves of some defunct economist. Madmen in authority, who hear voices in the air, are distilling their frenzy from some academic scribbler of a few years back.
General Theory (1947 ed.)

14 But this *long run* is a misleading guide to current affairs. *In the long*

run we are all dead.
A Tract on Monetary Reform (1923)

1 I evidently knew more about economics than my examiners.
explaining why he performed badly in the Civil Service examinations
Roy Harrod *Life of John Maynard Keynes* (1951)

2 We threw good housekeeping to the winds. But we saved ourselves and helped save the world.
of Britain in the Second World War
A. J. P. Taylor *English History, 1914–1945* (1965)

3 LADY VIOLET BONHAM CARTER: What do you think happens to Mr Lloyd George when he is alone in the room?
MAYNARD KEYNES: When he is alone in the room there is nobody there.
Lady Violet Bonham Carter *The Impact of Personality in Politics* (Romanes Lecture, 1963)

Reg Keys 1952–
British father of a serviceman killed in Iraq

4 Fighting this campaign has not been an easy task for me but I had to do it for my son…I hope…the Prime Minister one day will say sorry.
having fought the election in Tony **Blair**'s *Sedgefield constituency, 6 May 2005*

Ayatollah Ruhollah Khomeini
1900–89
Iranian Shiite Muslim leader, who returned to Iran from exile in 1979 to lead an Islamic revolution which overthrew the Shah

5 The regime occupying Jerusalem must vanish from the page of time.
quoted annually on Jerusalem Day in Iran, instituted by Khomeini in 1979; see **Ahmadinejad 5:7**

6 If laws are needed, Islam has established them all. There is no need…after establishing a government, to sit down and draw up laws.
Islam and Revolution: Writings and Declarations of Imam Khomeini (1981) 'Islamic Government'

Nikita Khrushchev 1894–1971
Soviet statesman; Premier, 1958–64

7 If anyone believes that our smiles

involve abandonment of the teaching of Marx, Engels and Lenin he deceives himself. Those who wait for that must wait until a shrimp learns to whistle.
speech in Moscow, 17 September 1955

8 We must abolish the cult of the individual decisively, once and for all.
speech to secret session of the 20th Congress of the Communist Party, 25 February 1956

9 We say this not only for the socialist states, who are more akin to us. We base ourselves on the idea that we must peacefully co-exist. About the capitalist States, it doesn't depend on you whether or not we exist. If you don't like us, don't accept our invitations and don't invite us to come to see you. Whether you like it or not, history is on our side. We will bury you.
speech to Western diplomats at reception in Moscow for Polish leader Mr Gomulka, 18 November 1956; 'We will bury you' in this context means 'we will outlive you'
in *Times* 19 November 1956

10 If one cannot catch the bird of paradise, better take a wet hen.
in *Time* 6 January 1958

11 Politicians are the same all over. They promise to build a bridge where there is no river.
at a press conference in New York, October 1960

12 We are going to make the imperialists dance like fishes in a saucepan, even without war.
in Vienna, 2 July 1960

13 If you start throwing hedgehogs under me, I shall throw a couple of porcupines under you.
in *New York Times* 7 November 1963

14 Anyone who believes that the worker can be lulled by fine revolutionary phrases is mistaken… If no concern is shown for the growth of material and spiritual riches, the people will listen today, they will listen tomorrow, and then they may say: 'Why do you promise us everything for the future? You are talking, so to speak, about life

beyond the grave. The priest has already told us about this.'
speech at World Youth Forum, 19 September 1964

David Maxwell Fyfe, Lord Kilmuir 1900–67
British Conservative politician and lawyer

1 Gratitude is not a normal feature of political life.
Political Adventure (1964)

2 Loyalty is the Tory's secret weapon.
Anthony Sampson *Anatomy of Britain* (1962); see **Critchley 82:4**

Martin Luther King 1929–68
American civil rights leader. See also **Epitaphs 106:1**

3 I want to be the white man's brother, not his brother-in-law.
in *New York Journal-American* 10 September 1962

4 Injustice anywhere is a threat to justice everywhere.
letter from Birmingham Jail, Alabama, 16 April 1963

5 Freedom is never voluntarily given by the oppressor; it must be demanded by the oppressed.
letter from Birmingham Jail, Alabama, 16 April 1963

6 We will have to repent in this generation not merely for the hateful words and actions of the bad people, but for the appalling silence of the good people.
letter from Birmingham Jail, Alabama, 16 April 1963

7 I submit to you that if a man hasn't discovered something he will die for, he isn't fit to live.
speech in Detroit, 23 June 1963

8 I have a dream that one day on the red hills of Georgia the sons of former slaves and the sons of former slave owners will be able to sit down together at the table of brotherhood...
I have a dream that my four little children will one day live in a nation where they will not be judged by the colour of their skin but by the content of their character.
speech at Civil Rights March in Washington, 28 August 1963

9 When we let freedom ring, when we let it ring from every village and every hamlet, from every state and every city, we will be able to speed up that day when all of God's children, black men and white men, Jews and Gentiles, Protestants and Catholics, will be able to join hands and sing in the words of the old Negro spiritual, 'Free at last! Free at last! Thank God Almighty, we are free at last!'
speech at Civil Rights March in Washington, 28 August 1963

10 We must learn to live together as brothers or perish together as fools.
speech at St Louis, 22 March 1964

11 Cowardice asks the question, 'Is it safe?' Expediency asks the question, 'Is it politic?' Vanity asks the question, 'Is it popular?' But Conscience asks the question, 'Is it right?'
in 1967; in *Autobiography of Martin Luther King Jr.* (1999)

12 We shall overcome because the arc of a moral universe is long, but it bends toward justice.
sermon at the National Cathedral, Washington, 31 March 1968, in James Melvin Washington *A Testament of Hope* (1991); see **Obama 230:10, Parker 239:14**

13 I just want to do God's will. And he's allowed me to go up to the mountain. And I've looked over, and I've seen the promised land... So I'm happy tonight. I'm not worried about anything. I'm not fearing any man.
speech in Memphis, 3 April 1968, the day before his assassination
in *New York Times* 4 April 1968

14 If we assume that mankind has a right to survive, then we must find an alternative to war and destruction. In our day of space vehicles and guided ballistic missiles, the choice is either nonviolence or nonexistence.
Strength to Love (1963)

1 Nothing in all the world is more dangerous than sincere ignorance and conscientious stupidity.
    Strength to Love (1963)

2 The ultimate measure of a man is not where he stands in moments of comfort and convenience, but where he stands at times of challenge and controversy.
    Strength to Love (1963)

3 The means by which we live have outdistanced the ends for which we live. Our scientific power has outrun our spiritual power. We have guided missiles and misguided men.
    Strength to Love (1963)

4 A riot is at bottom the language of the unheard.
    Where Do We Go From Here? (1967)

5 What is needed is a realization that power without love is reckless and abusive, and love without power is sentimental and anaemic.
    Where Do We Go From Here? (1967)

6 Ultimately a genuine leader is not a searcher for consensus, but a moulder of consensus.
    Where Do We Go From Here? (1967)

William Lyon Mackenzie King

1874–1950
Canadian Liberal statesman, Prime Minister 1921–6, 1926–30, and 1935–48

7 If some countries have too much history, we have too much geography.
    speech on Canada as an international power, 18 June 1936

8 Not necessarily conscription, but conscription if necessary.
    speech, Canadian House of Commons, 7 July 1942

Hugh Kingsmill 1889–1949
English man of letters

9 A nation is only at peace when it's at war.
    attributed

Neil Kinnock 1942–
British Labour politician. See also **Newspaper headlines 225:9**

10 Loyalty is a fine quality but in excess it fills political graveyards.
    in June 1976, in opposition to Conference decisions on devolution
    G. M. F. Drower *Neil Kinnock* (1984)

11 *of servicemen in the Falklands War, when replying to a heckler who said that Margaret Thatcher 'showed guts':*
    It's a pity others had to leave theirs on the ground at Goose Green to prove it.
    television interview, 6 June 1983

12 If Margaret Thatcher wins on Thursday, I warn you not to be ordinary, I warn you not to be young, I warn you not to fall ill, and I warn you not to grow old.
    on the prospect of a Conservative re-election
    speech at Bridgend, 7 June 1983

13 The grotesque chaos of a Labour council hiring taxis to scuttle round the city handing out redundancy notices to its own workers.
    of the actions of the Labour city council in Liverpool
    speech at the Labour Party Conference, 1 October 1985

14 I would die for my country but I could never let my country die for me.
    speech at Labour Party Conference, 30 September 1986

15 Why am I the first Kinnock in a thousand generations to be able to get to university?
    later plagiarized by the American politician Joe Biden
    speech at Llandudno, 15 May 1987

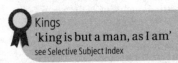

Kings
'king is but a man, as I am'
see Selective Subject Index

1 There are lots of ways to get socialism, but I think trying to fracture the Labour party by incessant contest cannot be one of them.
in *Guardian* 29 January 1988

2 I don't think anyone could accuse someone who has been leader of the Labour party for more than seven years of being impulsive.
in *Sunday Times* 5 August 1990

3 Referendums produce results and results have got to be listened to.
on the French rejection of the European Constitution
in *Guardian* 1 June 2005 (online edition)

Rudyard Kipling 1865–1936
English writer and poet

4 Oh, East is East, and West is West, and never the twain shall meet.
'The Ballad of East and West' (1892)

5 All Power, each Tyrant, every Mob Whose head has grown too large, Ends by destroying its own job And works its own discharge.
'The Benefactors' (1919)

6 Winds of the World, give answer! They are whimpering to and fro— And what should they know of England who only England know?—
The poor little street-bred people that vapour and fume and brag.
'The English Flag' (1892)

7 I could not dig: I dared not rob: Therefore I lied to please the mob. Now all my lies are proved untrue And I must face the men I slew. What tale shall serve me here among Mine angry and defrauded young?
'Epitaphs of the War: A Dead Statesman' (1919)

8 As it will be in the future, it was at the birth of Man—
There are only four things certain since Social Progress began:—
That the Dog returns to his Vomit and the Sow returns to her Mire,
And the burnt Fool's bandaged finger goes wabbling back to the Fire.
'The Gods of the Copybook Headings' (1927)

9 And that after this is accomplished, and the brave new world begins When all men are paid for existing, and no man must pay for his sins, As surely as Water will wet us, as surely as Fire will burn, The Gods of the Copybook Headings with terror and slaughter return!
'The Gods of the Copybook Headings' (1927)

10 If you can keep your head when all about you Are losing theirs and blaming it on you; If you can trust yourself when all men doubt you, But make allowance for their doubting too; If you can wait and not be tired by waiting, Or being lied about, don't deal in lies, Or being hated, don't give way to hating, And yet don't look too good, nor talk too wise; If you can dream—and not make dreams your master; If you can think—and not make thoughts your aim, If you can meet with triumph and disaster And treat those two impostors just the same...
'If—' (1910)

11 If you can talk with crowds and keep your virtue, Or walk with Kings—nor lose the common touch.
'If—' (1910)

12 Now this is the Law of the Jungle— as old and as true as the sky; And the Wolf that shall keep it may prosper, but the Wolf that shall break it must die.
'The Law of the Jungle' (1895)

13 Let us admit it fairly, as a business people should, We have had no end of a lesson: it will do us no end of good.
of the Boer Wars
'The Lesson' (1902)

14 Ship me somewheres east of Suez, where the best is like the worst,

Where there aren't no Ten
Commandments an' a man can
raise a thirst.
'Mandalay' (1892)

1 A Nation spoke to a Nation,
A Throne sent word to a Throne:
'Daughter am I in my mother's house,
But mistress in my own.
The gates are mine to open,
As the gates are mine to close,
And I abide by my Mother's House.'
Said our Lady of the Snows.
'Our Lady of the Snows' (1898)

2 God of our fathers, known of old,
Lord of our far-flung battle-line,
Beneath whose awful Hand we hold
Dominion over palm and pine—
Lord God of Hosts, be with us yet,
Lest we forget—lest we forget!
The tumult and the shouting dies—
The captains and the kings depart—
Still stands Thine ancient Sacrifice,
An humble and a contrite heart.
'Recessional' (1897)

3 Far-called our navies melt away—
On dune and headland sinks the
fire—
Lo, all our pomp of yesterday
Is one with Nineveh, and Tyre!
'Recessional' (1897)

4 Such boasting as the Gentiles use,
Or lesser breeds without the Law.
'Recessional' (1897)

5 For frantic boast and foolish
word—
Thy mercy on Thy People, Lord.
'Recessional' (1897)

6 If blood be the price of admiralty,
Lord God, we ha' paid in full!
'The Song of the Dead' (1896)

7 It is always a temptation to a rich
and lazy nation,
To puff and look important and to
say:-
'Though we know we should defeat
you, we have not the time to meet
you,
We will therefore pay you cash to go
away.'
And that is called paying the Dane-
geld;
But we've proved it again and again,

That if once you have paid him the
Dane-geld
You never get rid of the Dane.
'What Dane-geld means' (1911)

8 Take up the White Man's burden—
Send forth the best ye breed—
Go, bind your sons to exile
To serve your captives' need.
'The White Man's Burden' (1899)

9 Take up the White Man's burden—
And reap his old reward—
The blame of those ye better,
The hate of those ye guard.
'The White Man's Burden' (1899)

10 He was the greatest, as he
was the hugest, of the war
correspondents...and he always
opened his conversation with the
news that there would be trouble in
the Balkans in the spring.
The Light that Failed (1891) ch. 4

11 Power without responsibility:
the prerogative of the harlot
throughout the ages.
summing up Lord **Beaverbrook**'s political
standpoint vis-à-vis the Daily Express, after
he had said to Kipling, 'What I want is power.
Kiss 'em one day and kick 'em the next'; Stanley
Baldwin, Kipling's cousin, subsequently obtained
permission to use the phrase in a speech in
London on 18 March 1931
in Kipling Journal December 1971

Henry Kissinger 1923–
German-born American politician, US Secretary of
State 1973–7

12 There cannot be a crisis next week.
My schedule is already full.
in New York Times Magazine 1 June 1969

13 Power is the great aphrodisiac.
in New York Times 19 January 1971

14 The illegal we do immediately.
The unconstitutional takes a little
longer.
in Washington Post 20 January 1977;
attributed

15 If I want to talk to Europe who do
I call?
c. 1977, attributed saying; quoted by Crispin
Blunt in Minutes of the House of Commons
Select Committee on Defence, 16 February
2002

16 Ninety percent of the politicians

give the other ten percent a bad name.
in 1978, attributed

1 The pity in this war is that only one side can lose.
of the Iran-Iraq war 1980–8, often quoted as 'A pity they can't both lose'
c. 1980, attributed; Steven Greffenius The Logic of Conflict (1993)

2 History has so far shown us only two roads to international stability: domination and equilibrium.
in Times 12 March 1991

3 The management of a balance of power is a permanent undertaking, not an exertion that has a foreseeable end.
White House Years (1979)

4 We are the President's men and we must behave accordingly.
M. and B. Kalb Kissinger (1974)

5 For other nations, Utopia is a blessed past never to be recovered; for Americans it is just beyond the horizon.
attributed

6 The main advantage of being famous is that when you bore people at dinner parties they think it is their fault.
James Naughtie in Spectator 1 April 1995; attributed

Lord Kitchener 1850–1916
British soldier and statesman. On Kitchener: see
Asquith 13:12

7 You are ordered abroad as a soldier of the King to help our French comrades against the invasion of a common enemy… In this new experience you may find temptations both in wine and women. You must entirely resist both temptations, and, while treating all women with perfect courtesy, you should avoid any intimacy. Do your duty bravely. Fear God. Honour the King.
message to soldiers of the British Expeditionary Force (1914)
in Times 19 August 1914

8 I don't mind your being killed, but I

object to your being taken prisoner.
to the Prince of Wales (later Edward VIII) on his asking to be allowed to the Front during the First World War
in Journals and Letters of Reginald Viscount Esher vol. 3 (1938) 18 December 1914

Frank Knox –
American publisher and Secretary of the Navy

9 Whatever happens, the US Navy is not going to be caught napping.
on 4 December 1941, three days before the Japanese attack on Pearl Harbor, Bruce Catton The Warlords of Washington (1948)

John Knox c. 1505–72
Scottish Protestant reformer. On Knox: see
Epitaphs 106:6

10 The first blast of the trumpet against the monstrous regiment of women.
here, regiment means 'rule'
title of pamphlet (1558)

11 Un homme avec Dieu est toujours dans la majorité.
A man with God is always in the majority.
inscription on the Reformation Monument, Geneva; see Proverbs 252:2

Philander C. Knox 1853–1921
American lawyer and Republican politician, US Attorney-General 1901–4

12 Theodore Roosevelt had requested a legal justification for his acquisition of the Panama Canal:
Oh, Mr. President, do not let so great an achievement suffer from any taint of legality.
Tyler Dennett John Hay: From Poetry to Politics (1933)

Helmut Kohl 1930–
German statesman, Chancellor of West Germany (1982–90) and first postwar Chancellor of united Germany (1990–8)

13 I have been underestimated for decades. I have done very well that way.
in New York Times 25 January 1987

14 My goal, when the historical hour

allows it, is the unity of the nation.
to crowds in Dresden on the occasion of his first official visit to East Germany, 19 December 1989
in *Times* 20 December 1989

1 We Germans now have the historic chance to realize the unity of our fatherland.
in *Guardian* 15 February 1990

2 The policy of European integration is in reality a question of war and peace in the 21st century.
speech at Louvain University, 2 February 1996

The Koran

3 Then, when the sacred months are drawn away, slay the idolaters wherever you find them, and take them, and confine them, and lie in wait for them at every place of ambush.
known as the 'Sword Verse'
sura 9

Karl Kraus 1874–1936
Austrian satirist

4 How is the world ruled and how do wars start? Diplomats tell lies to journalists and then believe what they read.
Aphorisms and More Aphorisms (1909)

Paul Kruger 1825–1904
South African soldier and statesman

5 A bill of indemnity...for raid by Dr Jameson and the British South Africa Company's troops. The amount falls under two heads—first, material damage, total of claim, £677,938 3s. 3d.—second, moral or intellectual damage, total of claim, £1,000,000.
telegram from the South African Republic, communicated to the House of Commons by Joseph **Chamberlain**
in the House of Commons 18 February 1897

Stanley Kubrick 1928–99
American film director

6 The great nations have always acted like gangsters, and the small nations like prostitutes.
in *Guardian* 5 June 1963

Henry Labouchere 1831–1912
British politician

7 I do not object to the old man always having a card up his sleeve, but I do object to his insinuating that the Almighty has placed it there.
on **Gladstone**'s 'frequent appeals to a higher power'
Earl Curzon *Modern Parliamentary Eloquence* (1913)

Jean de la Bruyère 1645–96
French satiric moralist

8 When the populace is excited, one cannot conceive how calm can be restored; and when it is peaceful, one cannot see how calm can be disturbed.
Characters (1688) 'Of the Sovereign and the State'

Fiorello La Guardia 1882–1947
American politician, Republican Mayor of New York 1933–45

9 When I make a mistake, it's a beaut!
on the appointment of Herbert O'Brien as a judge in 1936
William Manners *Patience and Fortitude* (1976)

10 There is no Democratic or Republican way of cleaning the streets.
Charles Garrett *The La Guardia Years, Machine and Reform Politics in New York City* (1961)

John Lambert 1619–83
English soldier and Parliamentary supporter

1 The quarrel is now between light and darkness, not who shall rule, but whether we shall live or be preserved or no. Good words will not do with the cavaliers.
speech in the Parliament of 1656 supporting the rule of the major-generals
in *Dictionary of National Biography*

John George Lambton see Lord Durham

Norman Lamont 1942–
British Conservative politician, Chancellor 1990–3

2 Rising unemployment and the recession have been the price that we've had to pay to get inflation down. [Labour shouts] That is a price well worth paying.
in the House of Commons, 16 May 1991

3 The turn of the tide is sometimes difficult to discern. What we are seeing is the return of that vital ingredient—confidence. The green shoots of economic spring are appearing once again.
speech at the Conservative Party Conference, 9 October 1991; see **Misquotations 215:10**

4 My wife said she had never heard me sing in the bath before.
of the aftermath of sterling's exit from the ERM (Exchange Rate Mechanism)
quoted in *Financial Times* 23 September 1992

5 We give the impression of being in office but not in power.
*'in office, but not in power' had earlier been used by A. J. P. **Taylor** of Ramsay **MacDonald**'s minority government of 1924*
speech in House of Commons, 9 June 1993

Giuseppe di Lampedusa
1896–1957
Italian writer

6 If we want things to stay as they are, things will have to change.
The Leopard (1957)

Bert Lance 1931–
American government official

7 If it ain't broke, don't fix it.
in *Nation's Business* May 1977

Walter Savage Landor 1775–1864
English poet

8 The wise become as the unwise in the enchanted chambers of Power, whose lamps make every face the same colour.
Imaginary Conversations (1824–9)

9 George the First was always reckoned
Vile, but viler George the Second;
And what mortal ever heard
Any good of George the Third?
When from earth the Fourth descended
God be praised the Georges ended!
epigram in *The Atlas*, 28 April 1855

Andrew Lang 1844–1912
Scottish man of letters

10 He uses statistics as a drunken man uses lampposts—for support rather than illumination.
Alan L. Mackay *Harvest of a Quiet Eye* (1977); attributed

David Lange 1942–2005
New Zealand statesman, Prime Minister 1984–89

11 We ended up being run very similarly to a Polish shipyard.
on the Muldoon government
attributed; in *New Zealand Herald* 15 August 2005

William Langland c. 1330–c. 1400
English poet

12 Brewesters and baksters, bochiers and cokes—
For thise are men on this molde that moost harm wercheth
To the povere peple.
in an alternative text, 'As bakeres and breweres, bocheres and cokes; / For thyse men don most harm to the mene peple'
The Vision of Piers Plowman

Last words

1 All my possessions for a moment
of time.
*Queen **Elizabeth I** (1533–1603)*
attributed, but almost certainly apocryphal

2 Be of good comfort Master Ridley,
and play the man. We shall this day
light such a candle by God's grace
in England, as (I trust) shall never
be put out.
*Hugh Latimer (1485–1555), prior to being
burned for heresy, 16 October 1555*
John Foxe *Actes and Monuments* (1570 ed.)

3 Come closer, boys. It will be easier
for you.
*Erskine Childers (1870–1922), British writer
and Irish nationalist, to the firing squad at his
execution*
Burke Wilkinson *The Zeal of the Convert* (1976)
ch. 26

4 Die, my dear Doctor, that's the last
thing I shall do!
*Lord **Palmerston** (1784–1865)*
E. Latham *Famous Sayings and their Authors*
(1904)

5 An emperor ought to die standing.
***Vespasian** (AD 9–79)*
Suetonius *Lives of the Caesars* 'Vespasian'

6 For my name and memory, I leave it
to men's charitable speeches, and
to foreign nations, and the next
ages.
*Francis **Bacon** (1561–1626)*
his last will, 19 December 1625

7 God save Ireland!
*called out from the dock by the Manchester
Martyrs, William Allen (d. 1867), Michael Larkin
(d. 1867), and William O'Brien (d. 1867)*
Robert Kee *The Bold Fenian Men* (1989); see
Sullivan 303:1

8 How's the Empire?
*said by King **George V** (1865–1936) to his
private secretary on the morning of his death,
probably prompted by an article in* The Times,
*which he held open at the imperial and foreign
page; Lord Wigram in a memorandum of
20 January 1936 also recorded that the King had
said, 'Gentlemen, I am so sorry for keeping you
waiting like this. I am unable to concentrate.'
The (probably apocryphal) response 'Bugger
Bognor' to the suggestion, 'Cheer up, your
Majesty, you will soon be at Bognor again', has*

*also been attributed to an earlier illness in 1929
letter from Lord Wigram, 31 January 1936, in*
J. E. Wrench *Geoffrey Dawson and Our Times*
(1955).

9 I die happy.
*Charles James **Fox** (1749–1806)*
Lord John Russell *Life and Times of C. J. Fox*
vol. 3 (1860) ch. 69

10 I find, then, I am but a bad
anatomist.
*Wolfe Tone (1763–98), who in trying to cut his
throat in prison severed his windpipe instead of
his jugular, and lingered for several days*
Oliver Knox *Rebels and Informers* (1998)

11 I have loved justice and hated
iniquity: therefore I die in exile.
*Pope Gregory VII (1020–85) at Salerno,
following his conflict with the Emperor Henry IV*
J. W. Bowden *The Life and Pontificate of
Gregory VII* (1840) vol. 2

12 I only regret that I have but one life
to lose for my country.
*Nathan Hale (1755–76), prior to his execution by
the British for spying, 22 September 1776*
Henry Phelps Johnston *Nathan Hale,
1776* (1914)

13 It is a bad cause which cannot bear
the words of a dying man.
*Sir Henry Vane (1613–62) as drums and
trumpets were ordered to sound at his execution
to drown anything he might say*
Charles Dickens *A Child's History of England*
(1853) ch. 35

14 It is well, I die hard, but I am not
afraid to go.
*George **Washington** (1732–99)*
on 14 December 1799

15 I will die like a true-blue
rebel. Don't waste any time in
mourning—organize.
*Joe **Hill** (1879–1915) before his death by firing
squad*
farewell telegram to Bill Haywood,
18 November 1915, in *Salt Lake Tribune*
19 November 1915

16 Let's roll.
*Todd Beamer (1968–2001), American
businessman*
heard by telephone operator as Beamer and
other passengers were planning to storm the
cockpit of the hijacked United Airlines Flight 93,

Last words *continued*

11 September 2001; the plane crashed in Pennsylvania minutes later; in *Washington Post* 17 September 2001

1 Lord have mercy on my poor country that is so barbarously oppressed.
*Andrew **Fletcher** of Saltoun, Scottish patriot and anti-Unionist*
September 1716

2 Lord, open the King of England's eyes!
*William **Tyndale** (1494–1536), at the stake*
John Foxe *Actes and Monuments* (1570)

3 My design is to make what haste I can to be gone.
*Oliver **Cromwell** (1599–1658)*
John Morley *Oliver Cromwell* (1900)

4 *on his death-bed, declining a proposed visit from Queen Victoria:*
No it is better not. She would only ask me to take a message to Albert.
*Benjamin **Disraeli** (1804–81)*
Robert Blake *Disraeli* (1966)

5 Oh, my country! how I leave my country!
*William **Pitt** (1759–1806); also variously reported as 'How I love my country'; and 'My country! oh, my country!'; oral tradition reports 'I think I could eat one of Bellamy's veal pies'*
Earl Stanhope *Life of the Rt. Hon. William Pitt* vol. 3 (1879); Earl Stanhope *Life of the Rt. Hon. William Pitt* (1st ed.), vol. 4 (1862); and G. Rose *Diaries and Correspondence* (1860) 23 January 1806

6 Ô liberté! Ô liberté! que de crimes on commet en ton nom!
O liberty! O liberty! what crimes are committed in thy name!
Mme Roland (1754–93), French revolutionary, before being guillotined
A. de Lamartine *Histoire des Girondins* (1847)

7 Put out the light.
*Theodore **Roosevelt** (1858–1919)*
on 6 January 1919

8 Remember—.
***Charles I** (1600–49), giving his George (insignia of the Order of the Garter) to Bishop Juxon*
speech on the scaffold, 30 January 1649

9 So little done, so much to do.
*Cecil **Rhodes** (1853–1902), on the day of his death*
Lewis Michell *Life of Rhodes* (1910)

10 Strike the tent.
*Robert E. **Lee** (1807–70), 12 October 1870*
attributed

11 This hath not offended the king.
*Thomas **More** (1478–1535), lifting his beard aside after laying his head on the block*
Francis Bacon *Apophthegms New and Old* (1625) no. 22

12 This *is* a beautiful country!
*John **Brown** (1800–59) as he rode to the gallows, seated on his coffin*
at his execution on 2 December 1859

13 This is the Fourth?
*Thomas **Jefferson** (1743–1826)*
on 4 July 1826

14 This, this is the end of earth. I am content.
*John Quincy **Adams** (1767–1848) on collapsing in the Senate, 21 February 1848 (he died two days later)*
William H. Seward *Eulogy of John Quincy Adams to Legislature of New York* 1848

15 Thomas—Jefferson—still surv—
*in fact Thomas **Jefferson** died on the same day*
John **Adams**, 4 July 1826

16 Useless! Useless!
*John Wilkes **Booth** (1838–65)*
Philip van Doren Stern *The Man Who Killed Lincoln* (1939)

17 Would to God this wound had been for Ireland.
Patrick Sarsfield (1655–93) on being mortally wounded at the battle of Landen, 19 August 1693, while fighting for France
attributed

Lao-tzu c. 604–c. 531 BC
Chinese philosopher; founder of Taoism

1 The best [rulers] are those whose
  existence is [merely] known by
  the people.
  The next best are those who are loved
  and praised.
  The next are those who are feared.
  And the next are those who are
  reviled...
  [The great rulers] accomplish their
  task; they complete their work.
  Nevertheless their people say that
  they simply follow Nature.
  *often quoted as, 'A leader is best when people
  barely know he exists...He acts without
  unnecessary speech, and when the work is done
  the people say "We did it ourselves"'*
  Tao-te Ching

James Larkin 1867–1947
Irish labour leader

2 Our fathers died that we might be
  free men. Are we going to allow
  their sacrifices to be as naught?
  Or are we going to follow in their
  footsteps at the Rising of the Moon?
  in Irish Worker July 1914

3 Hell has no terror for me. I have
  lived there. Thirty six years of
  hunger and poverty have been my
  portion. They cannot terrify me
  with hell. Better to be in hell with
  Dante and Davitt than to be in
  heaven with Carson and Murphy.
  *in 1913, during the 'Dublin lockout' labour dispute
  Ulick O'Connor The Troubles (rev. ed., 1996)*

**Duc de la Rochefoucauld-
Liancourt** 1747–1827
French social reformer

4 LOUIS XVI: It is a big revolt.
  LA ROCHEFOUCAULD-LIANCOURT: No,
  Sire, a big revolution.
  *on a report reaching Versailles of the Fall of the
  Bastille, 1789*
  F. Dreyfus La Rochefoucauld-Liancourt (1903)

Harold Laski 1893–1950
British Labour politician. See also **Crossman 83:10**

5 I respect fidelity to colleagues
  even though they are fit for the
  hangman.
  *letter to Oliver Wendell Holmes Jr.,
  4 December 1926*

6 He searched always to end a
  sentence with a climax. He looked
  for antithesis like a monkey looking
  for fleas.
  *of Winston Churchill at a dinner at the London
  School of Economics*
  *letter to Oliver Wendell Holmes Jr., 7 May
  1927*

Hugh Latimer see **Last words 178:2**

William L. Laurence 1888–1977
American journalist

7 At first it was a giant column
  that soon took the shape of a
  supramundane mushroom.
  *on the first atomic explosion in New Mexico,
  16 July 1945*

Wilfrid Laurier 1841–1919
Canadian Liberal statesman, Prime Minister
1896–1911

8 Had I been born on the banks of
  the Saskatchewan, I would myself
  have shouldered a musket to fight
  against the neglect of governments
  and the shameless greed of
  speculators.
  *addressing meeting in the Champ de Mars,
  Montreal, 22 November 1885; O.D. Skelton Life
  and Letters of Sir Wilfrid Laurier (1921)*

9 The nineteenth century was the
  century of the United States. I think
  we can claim that it is Canada that
  shall fill the twentieth century.
  *speech in Ottawa, 18 January 1904; see
  Trudeau 316:17*

10 Quebec does not have opinions,

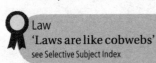

Law
'Laws are like cobwebs'
see Selective Subject Index

only sentiments.
Mason Wade *The French Canadians:1760–1967* (1968)

T. E. Lawrence 1888–1935
English soldier and writer

1 The trouble with Communism is that it accepts too much of today's furniture. I hate furniture.
letter to Cecil Day Lewis, 20 December 1934

Mark Lawson 1962–
British writer and journalist

2 Office tends to confer a dreadful plausibility on even the most negligible of those who hold it.
Joe Queenan *Imperial Caddy* (1992); introduction

Nigel Lawson 1932–
British Conservative politician

3 The Conservative Party has never believed that the business of government is the government of business.
in the House of Commons, 10 November 1981

4 Teenage scribblers.
of the financial press
in *Financial Times* 28 September 1985

5 It represented the tip of a singularly ill-concealed iceberg, with all the destructive potential that icebergs possess.
of an article by Alan Walters, the Prime Minister's economic adviser, criticizing the Exchange Rate Mechanism
in the House of Commons following his resignation as Chancellor, 31 October 1989

6 When I was a minister I always looked forward to the Cabinet meeting immensely because it was, apart from the summer holidays, the only period of real rest I got in what was a very heavy job.
'Cabinet Government in the Thatcher Years' (1994)

7 All the current talk of no return

to 'boom and bust' is somewhat premature to say the least.
lecture, London School of Economics, 20 June 1994; see **Brown 43:4**, **Clarke 73:9**

8 I went to live in France to get away from the European Community.
on the French ability to ignore EC regulations
In conversation with Antony Jay, 2006

Kenneth L. Lay 1942–2006
American businessman, former CEO of Enron

9 I am deeply troubled about asserting these rights, because it may be perceived by some that I have something to hide.
invoking his Fifth Amendment protection and declining to answer Congress's questions on the Enron collapse
in *Newsweek* 25 February 2002

Emma Lazarus 1849–87
American poet

10 Give me your tired, your poor,
Your huddled masses yearning to breathe free,
The wretched refuse of your teeming shore,
Send these, the homeless, tempest-tossed, to me:
I lift my lamp beside the golden door.
inscription on the Statue of Liberty, New York
'The New Colossus' (1883)

Alexandre Auguste Ledru-Rollin 1807–74
French politician

11 Ah well! I am their leader, I really had to follow them!
E. de Mirecourt *Les Contemporains* vol. 14 (1857) 'Ledru-Rollin'

Charles Lee 1731–82
American soldier

12 Beware that your Northern laurels do not change to Southern willows.
to General Horatio Gates after the surrender of Burgoyne at Saratoga, on 17 October 1777

Leaders
'desiccated calculating machine'
see Selective Subject Index

Henry ('Light-Horse Harry') Lee 1756–1818
American soldier and politician

1 A citizen, first in war, first in peace, and first in the hearts of his countrymen.
*of George **Washington***
Funeral Oration on the death of General Washington (1800)

Richard Henry Lee 1732–94
American politician

2 That these united colonies are, and of right ought to be, free and independent states; that they are absolved from all allegiance to the British crown; and that all political connection between them and the State of Great Britain is, and ought to be, totally dissolved.
resolution moved at the Continental Congress on 7 June 1776; adopted 2 July 1776

Robert E. Lee 1807–70
American Confederate general. See also **Last words 179:10**

3 It is well that war is so terrible. We should grow too fond of it.
after the battle of Fredericksburg, December 1862, attributed

4 There is nothing left for me to do but to go and see General Grant and I would rather die a thousand deaths.
just before the Confederate surrender at Appomattox in 1865; Geoffrey C. Ward *The Civil War* (1991)

5 I have fought against the people of the North because I believed they were seeking to wrest from the South its dearest rights. But I have never cherished toward them bitter or vindictive feelings, and I have never seen the day when I did not pray for them.
Geoffrey C. Ward *The Civil War* (1991)

Curtis E. LeMay 1906–90
American air-force officer

6 They've got to draw in their horns and stop their aggression, or we're going to bomb them back into the Stone Age.
on the North Vietnamese Mission with LeMay (1965)

Lenin 1870–1924
Russian revolutionary. See also **Misquotations 215:4**

7 Imperialism is the monopoly stage of capitalism.
Imperialism as the Last Stage of Capitalism (1916) 'Briefest possible definition of imperialism'

8 One step forward two steps back
title of book 1904

9 No, Democracy is *not* identical with majority rule. Democracy is a *State* which recognizes the subjection of the minority to the majority, that is, an organization for the systematic use of *force* by one class against the other, by one part of the population against another.
State and Revolution (1919)

10 While the State exists, there can be no freedom. When there is freedom there will be no State.
State and Revolution (1919)

11 What is to be done?
title of pamphlet (1902); originally the title of a novel (1863) by N. G. Chernyshevsky

12 We must now set about building a proletarian socialist state in Russia.
speech in Petrograd, 7 November 1917

13 Communism equals Soviet power plus the electrification of the whole country.
report to 8th Congress, 1920

14 Who? Whom?
definition of political science, meaning 'Who will outstrip whom?'
in *Polnoe Sobranie Sochinenii* (1970) 17 October 1921

15 A good man fallen among Fabians.
*of George Bernard **Shaw***
Arthur Ransome *Six Weeks in Russia in 1919* (1919) 'Notes of Conversations with Lenin'

16 Liberty is precious—so precious that it must be rationed.
Sidney and Beatrice Webb *Soviet Communism* (1935) vol. 2

William Lenthall 1591–1662
English politician, Speaker of the House of Commons

1 I have neither eye to see, nor tongue to speak here, but as the House is pleased to direct me.
to **Charles I**, *4 January 1642, on being asked if he had seen any of the five MPs whom the King had ordered to be arrested*
   John Rushworth *Historical Collections. The Third Part* vol. 2 (1692)

Alan Jay Lerner 1918–86
American songwriter

2 Don't let it be forgot
   That once there was a spot
   For one brief shining moment that was known
   As Camelot.
particularly associated with the Kennedy White House
   'Camelot' (1960 song); see **Onassis 232:2**

Doris Lessing 1919–
English writer

3 When old settlers say 'One has to understand the country,' what they mean is, 'You have to get used to our ideas about the native.'
   The Grass is Singing (1950)

4 When a white man in Africa by accident looks into the eyes of a native and sees the human being (which it is his chief preoccupation to avoid), his sense of guilt, which he denies, fumes up in resentment and he brings down the whip.
   The Grass is Singing (1950)

Leslie Lever 1905–77
British Labour politician

5 Generosity is part of my character, and I therefore hasten to assure this Government that I will never make an allegation of dishonesty against it wherever a simple explanation of stupidity will suffice.
   Leon Harris *The Fine Art of Political Wit* (1964)

René Lévesque 1922–87
Canadian politician, founder of Parti Québécois

6 Outside Quebec, I don't find two great cultures. I feel like a foreigner. First and foremost, I am a Québecois, and second—with a rather growing sense of doubt—a Canadian.
   in *Toronto Star* 1 June 1963

7 A nation is judged by how it treats its minorities.
   attributed, 1978; John Robert Colombo *Colombo's New Canadian Quotations* (1987)

Primo Levi 1919–87
Italian novelist and poet

8 Our language lacks words to express this offence, the demolition of a man.
of a year spent in Auschwitz
   If This is a Man (1958)

Bernard Levin 1928–2004
British journalist

9 Since when was fastidiousness a quality useful for political advancement?
   If You Want My Opinion (1992)

10 Harold Macmillan, whose elevation was achieved by a brutality, cunning and greed for power normally met only in the conclaves of Mafia *capi*, said, after he had climbed the greasy pole and pushed all his rivals off (*takes out handkerchief containing concealed onion*) that the whole thing was Dead Sea Fruit.
   If You Want My Opinion (1992); see **Macmillan 199:16**

11 *of Harold **Macmillan** and Harold **Wilson***: Between them, then, Walrus and Carpenter, they divided up the Sixties.
   The Pendulum Years (1970)

12 Whom the mad would destroy, they first make gods.
*of **Mao** Zedong in 1967*
   in *Times* 21 September 1987

13 Once, when a British Minister sneezed, men half a world away would blow their noses. Now when a British Prime Minister sneezes nobody else will even say, 'Bless You.'
   in *Times* 1976

1 The less the power, the greater the desire to exercise it.
in *Times* 21 September 1993

2 I have more than once pointed out that no organization with 'Liberation' in its title has ever, or ever will, liberate anyone or anything.
in *Times* 14 April 1995

Duc de Lévis 1764–1830
French soldier and writer

3 *Gouverner, c'est choisir.*
To govern is to choose.
Maximes et Réflexions (1812 ed.) 'Politique: Maximes de Politique'

David Lewis 1909–81
Canadian politician

4 Louder voices: the corporate welfare bums.
title of book, 1972

5 Welfare is for the needy, not big and wealthy multinational corporations.
Louder Voices: the Corporate Welfare Bums (1972)

Willmott Lewis 1877–1950
British journalist

6 Every government will do as much harm as it can and as much good as it must.
to Claud **Cockburn**, Claud Cockburn *In Time of Trouble* (1957)

Joseph Lieberman 1942–
American Democratic politician and vice-presidential candidate in 2000

7 His wrongdoing in this sordid saga does not justify making him the first president to be ousted from office in our history.
voting to acquit President **Clinton**
at the trial for impeachment, 11 February 1999

8 *to the suggestion that he and George W.* **Bush** *share a stance on issues:*
That's like saying the veterinarian and the taxidermist are in the same business because either way you get your dog back.
speech in Nashville, Tennessee, 8 August 2000

Abbott Joseph Liebling 1904–63

9 Freedom of the press is guaranteed only to those who own one.
in *New Yorker* 14 May 1960

Charles-Joseph, Prince de Ligne 1735–1814
Belgian soldier

10 *Le congrès ne marche pas, il danse.*
The Congress makes no progress; it dances.
of the Congress of Vienna
Auguste de la Garde-Chambonas *Souvenirs du Congrès de Vienne* (1820)

Abraham Lincoln 1809–65
American statesman, 16th President of the US. On Lincoln: see **Stanton 299:9, Whitman 331:13**

11 Prohibition…goes beyond the bounds of reason in that it attempts to control a man's appetite by legislation, and makes a crime out of things that are not crimes. A Prohibition law strikes a blow at the very principles upon which our government was founded.
speech in the Illinois House of Representatives, 18 December 1840

12 Any people anywhere, being inclined and having the power, have the *right* to rise up, and shake off the existing government, and form a new one that suits them better.
in the House of Representatives, 12 January 1848

13 No man is good enough to govern another man without that

Liberty
'Let freedom reign'
see Selective Subject Index

other's consent.
speech at Peoria, Illinois, 16 October 1854

1 To give victory to the right, not
bloody bullets, but peaceful ballots
only, are necessary.
speech, 18 May 1858; see **Misquotations 215:2**

2 'A house divided against itself
cannot stand.' I believe this
government cannot endure
permanently, half slave and half
free.
speech, 16 June 1858

3 As I would not be a *slave*, so I would
not be a *master*. This expresses my
idea of democracy. Whatever differs
from this, to the extent of the
difference, is no democracy.
fragment, 1 August 1858?

4 I have no purpose to introduce
political and social equality
between the white and black races.
There is a physical difference
between the two which, in my
judgement, will probably for ever
forbid their living together upon
the footing of perfect equality; and
inasmuch as it becomes a necessity
that there must be a difference,
I…am in favour of the race to
which I belong having the superior
position.
speech, 21 August 1858

5 When…you have succeeded in
dehumanizing the Negro, when
you have put him down and made
it forever impossible for him to be
but as the beasts of the field; when
you have extinguished his soul and
placed him where the ray of hope
is blown out in darkness like that
which broods over the spirits of the
damned, are you quite sure that
the demon you have roused will not
turn and rend you?
speech at Edwardsville, Illinois, 11 September
1858

6 What is conservatism? Is it not
adherence to the old and tried,
against the new and untried?
speech, 27 February 1860

7 If we do not make common cause to
save the good old ship of the Union

on this voyage, nobody will have
a chance to pilot her on another
voyage.
address at Cleveland, Ohio, 15 February 1861

8 It is safe to assert that no
government proper ever had a
provision in its organic law for its
own termination.
first inaugural address, 4 March 1861

9 I take the official oath to-day
with no mental reservations,
and with no purpose to construe
the Constitution or laws by any
hypercritical rules.
first inaugural address, 4 March 1861

10 This country, with its institutions,
belongs to the people who inhabit
it. Whenever they shall grow weary
of the existing government, they
can exercise their constitutional
right of amending it, or their
revolutionary right to dismember
or overthrow it.
first inaugural address, 4 March 1861

11 The mystic chords of memory,
stretching from every battlefield
and patriot grave to every living
heart and hearthstone all over this
broad land, will yet swell the chorus
of the Union when again touched,
as surely they will be, by the better
angels of our nature.
first inaugural address, 4 March 1861

12 I think the necessity of being *ready*
increases. Look to it.
the whole of a letter to Governor Andrew
Curtin of Pennsylvania, 8 April 1861

13 *on his suspension of habeas corpus:*
The whole of the laws which were
required to be faithfully executed,
were being resisted, and failing of
execution in nearly one-third of
the states. Must they be allowed to
finally fail of execution, even had
it been perfectly clear, that by the
means necessary to their execution,
some single law, made in such
extreme tenderness of the citizen's
liberty, that practically, it relieves
more of the guilty, than of the
innocent, should, to a very limited
extent, be violated? To state the

question more directly, are all the laws, *but one* [the right to habeas corpus], to go unexecuted and the government itself go to pieces, lest that one be violated?
message to Congress, 4 July 1861

1 My paramount object in this struggle is to save the Union... If I could save the Union without freeing any slave, I would do it; and if I could save it by freeing all the slaves, I would do it; and if I could save it by freeing some and leaving others alone, I would also do that...I have here stated my purpose according to my views of official duty and I intend no modification of my oft-expressed personal wish that all men everywhere could be free.
letter to Horace **Greeley**, 22 August 1862

2 On the first day of January in the year of our Lord, one thousand eight hundred and sixty-three, all persons held as slaves within any state, or designated part of a state, the people whereof shall then be in rebellion against the United States shall be then, thenceforward, and forever free.
Preliminary Emancipation Proclamation, 22 September 1862

3 *when asked how he felt about the New York elections:*
Somewhat like the boy in Kentucky who stubbed his toe while running to see his sweetheart. The boy said he was too big to cry, and far too badly hurt to laugh.
in *Frank Leslie's Illustrated Weekly* 22 November 1862

4 Fellow citizens, we cannot escape history...No personal significance or insignificance can spare one or another of us. The fiery trial through which we pass will light us down in honour or dishonour to the last generation.
annual message to Congress, 1 December 1862

5 In giving freedom to the slave, we assure freedom to the free— honourable alike in what we give

and what we preserve. We shall nobly save, or meanly lose, the last, best hope of earth.
annual message to Congress, 1 December 1862

6 Fourscore and seven years ago our fathers brought forth upon this continent a new nation, conceived in liberty, and dedicated to the proposition that all men are created equal...In a larger sense we cannot dedicate, we cannot consecrate, we cannot hallow this ground. The brave men, living and these dead, who struggled here, have consecrated it far above our power to add or detract. The world will little note, nor long remember, what we say here, but it can never forget what they did here. It is for us, the living, rather to be dedicated here to the unfinished work which they who fought here have thus far so nobly advanced...we here highly resolve that the dead shall not have died in vain, that this nation, under God, shall have a new birth of freedom; and that government of the people, by the people, and for the people, shall not perish from the earth.
address at the Dedication of the National Cemetery at Gettysburg, 19 November 1863, as reported the following day; the Lincoln Memorial inscription reads 'by the people, for the people'; see **Anonymous 9:14**, **Everett 108:1**, **Webster 327:12**

7 The President tonight has a dream:—He was in a party of plain people, and, as it became known who he was, they began to comment on his appearance. One of them said:—'He is a very common-looking man.' The President replied:—'The Lord prefers common-looking people. That is the reason he makes so many of them.'
John Hay *Letters of John Hay and Extracts from Diary* (1908) vol 1, 23 December 1863

8 Only those generals who gain success can set up dictators. What I ask of you is military success, and I

will risk the dictatorship.
*letter appointing Joseph Hooker to command of
the Army of the Potomac in 1863*
  Shelby Foote *The Civil War: Fredericksburg to
  Meridian* (1991)

1 I claim not to have controlled
events, but confess plainly that
events have controlled me.
  letter to A. G. Hodges, 4 April 1864

2 It is not best to swap horses when
crossing streams.
  reply to National Union League, 9 June 1864

3 I desire so to conduct the affairs of
this administration that if at the
end, when I come to lay down the
reins of power, I have lost every
other friend on earth, I shall at least
have one friend left, and that friend
shall be down inside me.
  reply to the Missouri Committee of Seventy,
  1864

4 Fondly do we hope, fervently do
we pray, that this mighty scourge
of war may speedily pass away.
Yet, if God wills that it continue
until all the wealth piled by the
bond-man's two hundred and fifty
years of unrequited toil shall be
sunk, and until every drop of blood
drawn with the lash shall be paid
by another drawn with the sword,
as was said three thousand years
ago, so still it must be said, 'The
judgements of the Lord are true and
righteous altogether.'
  second inaugural address, 4 March 1865

5 With malice toward none; with
charity for all; with firmness
in the right, as God gives us to
see the right, let us strive on to
finish the work we are in: to bind
up the nation's wounds; to care
for him who shall have borne
the battle, and for his widow and
his orphan, to do all which may
achieve and cherish a just and
lasting peace among ourselves, and
with all nations.
  second inaugural address, 4 March 1865

6 Whenever I hear anyone arguing
for slavery, I feel a strong impulse to
see it tried on him personally.
  address to an Indiana Regiment, 17 March
  1865

7 As President, I have no eyes but
constitutional eyes; I cannot see
you.
  reply to the South Carolina Commissioners
  attributed

8 People who like this sort of thing
will find this the sort of thing they
like.
  judgement of a book
    G. W. E. Russell *Collections and Recollections*
    (1898)

9 So you're the little woman who
wrote the book that made this great
war!
  on meeting Harriet Beecher Stowe, author of
  Uncle Tom's Cabin *(1852)*
    Carl Sandburg *Abraham Lincoln: The War Years*
    (1936) vol. 2

10 You cannot help the poor by
destroying the rich. You cannot lift
the wage earner by pulling down
the wage payer.
  attributed, but probably apocryphal

11 You may fool all the people some of
the time; you can even fool some
of the people all the time; but you
can't fool all of the people all the
time.
  Alexander K. McClure *Lincoln's Yarns and
  Stories* (1904); also attributed to Phineas
  Barnum; see **Thurber 312:8**

Eric Linklater 1899–1974
Scottish novelist

12 'There won't be any revolution
in America,' said Isadore. Nikitin
agreed. 'The people are all too
clean. They spend all their time
changing their shirts and washing
themselves. You can't feel fierce and
revolutionary in a bathroom.'
  Juan in America (1931)

Walter Lippmann 1889–1974
American journalist

13 Private property was the original
source of freedom. It still is its main
bulwark.
  The Good Society (1937)

14 Mr Coolidge's genius for inactivity

is developed to a very high point.
It is far from being an indolent
activity. It is a grim, determined,
alert inactivity which keeps Mr
Coolidge occupied constantly.
Nobody has ever worked harder
at inactivity, with such force of
character, with such unremitting
attention to detail, with such
conscientious devotion to the task.
Men of Destiny (1927)

1 The final test of a leader is that he
leaves behind him in other men the
conviction and the will to carry on.
Franklin D. Roosevelt died on 12 June 1945
in *New York Herald Tribune* 14 April 1945

2 A free press is not a privilege but an
organic necessity in a great society.
address at the International Press Institute
Assembly in London, 27 May 1965

Maxim Litvinov 1876–1951
Soviet diplomat

3 Peace is indivisible.
note to the Allies, 25 February 1920; A. U.
Pope *Maxim Litvinoff* (1943)

Ken Livingstone 1945–
British Labour politician

4 If voting changed anything, they'd
abolish it.
title of book, 1987; recorded earlier as a saying

5 The problem is that many MPs
never see the London that exists
beyond the wine bars and brothels
of Westminster.
in *Times* 19 February 1987

6 Politics is a marathon, not a sprint.
in *New Statesman* 10 October 1997

7 Every year the international
finance system kills more people
than the Second World War. But at
least Hitler was mad, you know.
in *Sunday Times* 16 April 2000 'Talking Heads'

Livy 59 BC–AD 17
Roman historian

8 *Vae victis.*
Down with the defeated!
cry (already proverbial) of the Gallic King, Brennus,
on capturing Rome in 390 BC
Ab Urbe Condita

9 *Pugna magna victi sumus.*
We have been defeated in a great
battle.
the announcement of disaster for the Romans in
Hannibal's ambush at Lake Trasimene in 217 BC
Ab Urbe Condita

David Lloyd George 1863–1945
British Liberal statesman; Prime Minister, 1916–22.
On Lloyd George: see **Asquith 14:1**, **Baldwin 22:14**,
Baldwin 23:3, **Bennett 28:3**, **Churchill 69:15**,
Clemenceau 75:1, **Grigg 131:1**, **Keynes 169:8**,
Keynes 169:9, **Taylor 306:4**

10 You cannot feed the hungry on
statistics.
speech in the House of Commons, 1904

11 The leal and trusty mastiff which
is to watch over our interests, but
which runs away at the first snarl
of the trade unions…A mastiff? It is
the right hon. Gentleman's poodle.
*on the House of Lords and Arthur **Balfour***
respectively
in the House of Commons, 26 June 1907

12 I have no nest-eggs. I am looking
for someone else's hen-roost to rob
next year.
in 1908, as Chancellor
Frank Owen *Tempestuous Journey* (1954)

13 A fully-equipped duke costs
as much to keep up as two
Dreadnoughts; and dukes are
just as great a terror and they last
longer.
speech at Newcastle, 9 October 1909

14 A body of five hundred men chosen
at random from amongst the
unemployed.
of the House of Lords
speech at Newcastle, 9 October 1909

15 The great peaks of honour we had
forgotten—Duty, Patriotism, and—
clad in glittering white—the great
pinnacle of Sacrifice, pointing like a
rugged finger to Heaven.
speech at Queen's Hall, London, 19 September
1914

16 At eleven o'clock this morning
came to an end the cruellest and
most terrible war that has ever
scourged mankind. I hope we may
say that thus, this fateful morning,

came to an end all wars.
in the House of Commons, 11 November 1918;
see **Wells 330:4**

1 What is our task? To make Britain a
fit country for heroes to live in.
speech at Wolverhampton, 23 November 1918

2 Wild men screaming through the
keyholes.
of the Versailles Peace Conference
in the House of Commons, 16 April 1919

3 If you want to succeed in politics,
you must keep your conscience well
under control.
Lord Riddell diary, 23 April 1919

4 M. Clemenceau…is one of the
greatest living orators, but he
knows that the finest eloquence is
that which gets things done and the
worst is that which delays them.
*speech at Paris Peace Conference, 18 January
1919*
in *Times* 20 January 1919

5 Unless I am mistaken, by the steps
we have taken [in Ireland] we have
murder by the throat.
speech at the Mansion House, 9 November
1920

6 *of Arthur **Balfour**'s impact on history:*
No more than the whiff of scent on
a lady's pocket handkerchief.
Thomas Jones, diary, 9 June 1922

7 The world is becoming like a
lunatic asylum run by lunatics.
in *Observer* 8 January 1933

8 A politician was a person with
whose politics you did not agree.
When you did agree, he was a
statesman.
speech at Central Hall, Westminster, 2 July
1935

9 Neville has a retail mind in a
wholesale business.
*of Neville **Chamberlain***
in 1935; David Dilks *Neville Chamberlain*
(1984)

10 *after meeting **Hitler** in 1936:*
Führer is the proper name for him.
He is a great and wonderful leader.
Frank Owen *Tempestuous Journey* (1954)

11 Winston would go up to his Creator
and say that he would very much
like to meet His Son, of Whom
he had heard a great deal and, if

possible, would like to call on the
Holy Ghost. Winston *loves* meeting
people.
*of Winston **Churchill***
A. J. Sylvester diary, 2 January 1937

12 The Prime Minister should give an
example of sacrifice, because there
is nothing which can contribute
more to victory than that he should
sacrifice the seals of office.
*of Neville **Chamberlain***
in the House of Commons, 7 May 1940

13 Truth against the world.
*Welsh proverb; motto taken on becoming Earl
Lloyd-George of Dwyfor, January 1945*
Donald McCormick *The Mask of Merlin* (1963)

14 Of all the bigotries that savage the
human temper there is none so
stupid as the anti-Semitic.
Is It Peace? (1923)

15 *on being told by Lord **Beaverbrook**'s butler
that, 'The Lord is out walking':*
Ah, on the water, I presume.
Lord Cudlipp letter in *Daily Telegraph*
13 September 1993

16 Brilliant—to the top of his boots.
of Earl Haig
attributed

17 Death is the most convenient time
to tax rich people.
in *Lord Riddell's Intimate Diary of the Peace
Conference and After, 1918–23* (1933)

18 He has sat on the fence so long the
iron has entered into his soul.
of John Simon
attributed

19 He would make a drum out of the
skin of his mother in order to sound
his own praises.
*of Winston **Churchill***
Peter Rowland *Lloyd George* (1975)

20 Negotiating with de Valera…is like
trying to pick up mercury with a
fork.
*to which **de Valera** replied, 'Why doesn't he use
a spoon?'*
M. J. MacManus *Eamon de Valera* (1944)

21 Sufficient conscience to bother
him, but not sufficient to keep him
straight.
*of Ramsay **MacDonald***
A. J. Sylvester *Life with Lloyd George* (1975)

1 There is no friendship at the top.
 habitual remark, said to be quoting
 Gladstone; A. J. P. Taylor *Lloyd George, Rise
 and Fall* (1961)

2 *of the 1905 Tory Government:*
 They died with their drawn salaries
 in their hands.
 attributed

John Locke 1632–1704
English philosopher

3 Man…hath by nature a power…to
 preserve his property—that is, his
 life, liberty, and estate—against the
 injuries and attempts of other men.
 Second Treatise of Civil Government (1690)

4 Man being…by nature all free,
 equal, and independent, no one
 can be put out of this estate, and
 subjected to the political power of
 another, without his own consent.
 Second Treatise of Civil Government (1690)

5 The great and chief end,
 therefore, of men's uniting into
 commonwealths, and putting
 themselves under government, is
 the preservation of their property.
 Second Treatise of Civil Government (1690)

6 The only way by which any one
 divests himself of his natural
 liberty and puts on the bonds of
 civil society is by agreeing with
 other men to join and unite into a
 community.
 Second Treatise of Civil Government (1690)

7 This power to act according to
 discretion for the public good,
 without the prescription of the law,
 and sometimes even against it, is
 that which is called prerogative.
 Second Treatise of Civil Government (1690)

Huey Long 1893–1935
American Democratic politician

8 For the present you can just call me
 the Kingfish.
 Every Man a King (1933)

9 *answering his opponent's supporters, who
 said their candidate had gone barefoot as
 a boy:*
 I can go Mr Wilson one better; I was

born barefoot.
 T. Harry Williams *Huey Long* (1969)

10 Oh hell, say that I am *sui generis*
 and let it go at that.
 *to journalists attempting to analyse his political
 personality*
 T. Harry Williams *Huey Long* (1969)

11 The time has come for all good men
 to rise above principle.
 attributed

Henry Wadsworth Longfellow
1807–82
American poet

12 Thou, too, sail on, O Ship of State!
 Sail on, O Union, strong and great!
 Humanity with all its fears,
 With all the hopes of future years,
 Is hanging breathless on thy fate!
 'The Building of the Ship' (1849)

Alice Roosevelt Longworth
1884–1980
American daughter of Theodore **Roosevelt**

13 Harding was not a bad man. He was
 just a slob.
 *of US President Warren G. **Harding***
 Crowded Hours (1933)

Louis XIV 1638–1715
French monarch, King from 1643

14 *L'État c'est moi.*
 I am the State.
 before the Parlement de Paris, 13 April
 1655 (probably apocryphal); J. A. Dulaure
 Histoire de Paris (1834) vol. 6

15 *Il n'y a plus de Pyrénées.*
 The Pyrenees are no more.
 *on the accession of his grandson to the throne of
 Spain, 1700*
 attributed to Louis by Voltaire in *Siècle de Louis
 XIV* (1753), but to the Spanish Ambassador to
 France in the *Mercure Galant* (Paris) November
 1700

16 I was nearly kept waiting.
 attribution queried, among others, by E.
 Fournier in *L'Esprit dans l'Histoire* (1857)

17 Every time I create an appointment,
 I create a hundred malcontents and
 one ingrate.
 Voltaire *Siècle de Louis XIV* (1768 ed.) vol. 2

Louis XV 1710–74
French monarch, King from 1715

1 Are the streets being paved with gold over there? I fully expect to awake one morning in Versailles to see the walls of the fortress rising above the horizon.
on the costs of fortifying Louisbourg on Cape Breton Island, Canada, 1745
attributed

Louis XVI 1754–93
French monarch, King from 1774; deposed in 1789 on the outbreak of the French Revolution and executed in 1793

2 *Rien.*
Nothing.
diary, 14 July 1789

Louis XVIII 1755–1824
French monarch, King from 1814; titular king from 1795

3 Remember that there is not one of you who does not carry in his cartridge-pouch the marshal's baton of the duke of Reggio; it is up to you to bring it forth.
speech to Saint-Cyr cadets, 9 August 1819
in *Moniteur Universel* 10 August 1819

4 *L'exactitude est la politesse des rois.*
Punctuality is the politeness of kings.
in *Souvenirs de J. Lafitte* (1844), attributed

Louis Philippe 1773–1850
French monarch, King 1830–48

5 Died, has he? Now I wonder what he meant by that?
*of **Talleyrand***
attributed, perhaps apocryphal

David Low 1891–1963
British political cartoonist

6 I have never met anyone who wasn't against war. Even Hitler and Mussolini were, according to themselves.
in *New York Times Magazine* 10 February 1946

Robert Lowe 1811–92
British Liberal politician

7 I believe it will be absolutely

necessary that you should prevail on our future masters to learn their letters.
on the passing of the 2nd Reform Bill
in the House of Commons, 15 July 1867; see **Misquotations 216:8**

8 The Chancellor of the Exchequer is a man whose duties make him more or less of a taxing machine. He is intrusted with a certain amount of misery which it is his duty to distribute as fairly as he can.
in the House of Commons, 11 April 1870

James Russell Lowell 1819–91
American poet

9 We've a war, an' a debt, an' a flag; an' ef this
Ain't to be interpendunt, why, wut on airth is?
The Biglow Papers (Second Series, 1867) no. 4 'A Message of Jeff. Davis in Secret Session'

10 Once to every man and nation comes the moment to decide,
In the strife of Truth with Falsehood, for the good or evil side.
'The Present Crisis' (1845)

11 Truth forever on the scaffold, Wrong forever on the throne,—
Yet that scaffold sways the future, and, behind the dim unknown,
Standeth God within the shadow, keeping watch above his own.
'The Present Crisis' (1845)

Lucan AD 39–65
Roman poet

12 It is not granted to know which man took up arms with more right on his side. Each pleads his cause before a great judge: the winning cause pleased the gods, but the losing one pleased Cato.
Pharsalia

13 *Stat magni nominis umbra.*
There stands the ghost of a great name.
of Pompey
Pharsalia

14 *Nil actum credens, dum quid superesset agendum.*
Thinking nothing done while

anything remained to be done.
Pharsalia

Clare Booth Luce 1903–87
American diplomat, Republican politician, and writer

1 But much of what Mr Wallace calls his global thinking is, no matter how you slice it, still 'globaloney.' Mr Wallace's warp of sense and his woof of nonsense is very tricky cloth out of which to cut the pattern of a post-war world.
on Vice-President Henry Wallace's post-war theories
maiden speech to the House of Representatives, 9 February 1943

Lucretius (Titus Lucretius Carus) c. 94–55 BC
Roman poet

2 *Tantum religio potuit suadere malorum.*
So much wrong could religion induce.
De Rerum Natura bk. 1, l. 101

Luiz Inácio Lula da Silva 1945–
Brazilian statesman, President 2003–

3 A war can perhaps be won single-handedly. But peace—lasting peace—cannot be secured without the support of all.
speech, United Nations, 23 September 2003; in *Guardian* (online edition) 24 September 2003

Martin Luther 1483–1546
German Protestant theologian

4 Here stand I. I can do no other. God help me. Amen.
speech at the Diet of Worms, 18 April 1521; attributed

5 If I had heard that as many devils would set on me in Worms as there are tiles on the roofs, I should none the less have ridden there.
to the Princes of Saxony, 21 August 1524

Rosa Luxemburg 1871–1919
German revolutionary

6 Freedom is always and exclusively freedom for the one who thinks

differently.
Die Russische Revolution (1918)

Jack Lynch 1917–99
Irish statesman, Taoiseach 1966–73, 1977–9

7 I have never and never will accept the right of a minority who happen to be a majority in a small part of the country to opt out of a nation.
in *Irish Times* 14 November 1970 'This Week They Said'

Robert Lynd 1879–1949
Anglo-Irish essayist and journalist

8 The belief in the possibility of a short decisive war appears to be one of the most ancient and dangerous of human illusions.
attributed

Jonathan Lynn 1943– and Antony Jay 1930–

9 'Opposition's about asking awkward questions.' 'Yes…and government's about not answering them.'
Yes Minister vol. 1 (1981)

10 The PM—whose motto is…'In Defeat, Malice—in Victory, Revenge!'
Yes Minister vol. 1 (1981)

11 If you wish to describe a proposal in a way that guarantees that a Minister will reject it, describe it as *courageous.*
Yes Minister vol. 1 (1981)

12 The Official Secrets Act is not to protect secrets but to protect officials.
Yes Minister vol. 1 (1981)

13 Diplomacy is about surviving till the next century—politics is about surviving till Friday afternoon.
Yes Prime Minister vol. 1 (1986)

14 *what is known to the Civil Service as the* Politicians' Syllogism*:*
Step One: We must do something.
Step Two: This is something.
Step Three: Therefore we must do it.
Yes Prime Minister vol. 2 (1987)

Mary McAleese 1951–
Irish stateswoman; President from 1997

1 Apart from the shamrock, the
President should not wear emblems
or symbols of any kind.
*deciding not to wear a poppy at her inauguration
on 11 November 1997*
in *Guardian* 6 November 1997

Douglas MacArthur 1880–1964
American general

2 I came through and I shall return.
*on reaching Australia, 20 March 1942, having
broken through Japanese lines en route from
Corregidor*
in *New York Times* 21 March 1942

3 In war, indeed, there can be no
substitute for victory.
in *Congressional Record* 19 April 1951, vol. 97

4 I still remember the refrain of
one of the most popular barracks
ballads of that day, which
proclaimed most proudly that old
soldiers never die; they just fade
away. I now close my military
career and just fade away.
address to a Joint Meeting of Congress,
19 April 1951

Lord Macaulay 1800–59
English Whig politician, historian, and poet. On
Macaulay: see **Melbourne 209:13, Smith 294:12**

5 In order that he might rob a
neighbour whom he had promised
to defend, black men fought on the
coast of Coromandel, and red men
scalped each other by the Great
Lakes of North America.
Biographical Essays (1857) 'Frederic the Great'

6 The gallery in which the reporters
sit has become a fourth estate of
the realm.
Essays Contributed to the Edinburgh Review
(1843) vol. 1 'Hallam'

7 He knew that the essence of war is
violence, and that moderation in
war is imbecility.
Essays Contributed to the Edinburgh Review
(1843) vol. 1 'John Hampden'

8 *of Niccolò* **Machiavelli**:
Out of his surname they have
coined an epithet for a knave,
and out of his Christian name a
synonym for the Devil.
Essays Contributed to the Edinburgh Review
(1843) vol. 1 'Machiavelli'

9 Many politicians of our time are
in the habit of laying it down as a
self-evident proposition, that no
people ought to be free till they are
fit to use their freedom. The maxim
is worthy of the fool in the old story,
who resolved not to go into the
water till he had learnt to swim. If
men are to wait for liberty till they
become wise and good in slavery,
they may indeed wait for ever.
Essays Contributed to the Edinburgh Review
(1843) vol. 1 'Milton'

10 On the rich and the eloquent,
on nobles and priests, they [the
Puritans] looked down with
contempt: for they esteemed
themselves rich in a more precious
treasure, and eloquent in a more
sublime language, nobles by the
right of an earlier creation, and
priests by the imposition of a
mightier hand.
Essays Contributed to the Edinburgh Review
(1843) vol. 1 'Milton'

11 We know no spectacle so ridiculous
as the British public in one of its

periodical fits of morality.
Essays Contributed to the Edinburgh Review (1843) vol. 1 'Moore's *Life of Lord Byron*'

1 We have heard it said that five per cent is the natural interest of money.
Essays Contributed to the Edinburgh Review (1843) vol. 1 'Southey's Colloquies'

2 With the dead there is no rivalry. In the dead there is no change. Plato is never sullen. Cervantes is never petulant. Demosthenes never comes unseasonably. Dante never stays too long. No difference of political opinion can alienate Cicero. No heresy can excite the horror of Bossuet.
Essays Contributed to the Edinburgh Review (1843) vol. 2 'Lord Bacon'

3 An acre in Middlesex is better than a principality in Utopia.
Essays Contributed to the Edinburgh Review (1843) vol. 2 'Lord Bacon'

4 The rising hope of those stern and unbending Tories.
*of **Gladstone***
Essays Contributed to the Edinburgh Review (1843) vol. 2 'Gladstone on Church and State'

5 The history of England is emphatically the history of progress.
Essays Contributed to the Edinburgh Review (1843) vol. 2 'Sir James Mackintosh'

6 On the day of the accession of George the Third, the ascendancy of the Whig party terminated; and on that day the purification of the Whig party began.
Essays Contributed to the Edinburgh Review (1843) vol. 2 'William Pitt, Earl of Chatham'

7 The reluctant obedience of distant provinces generally costs more than it [the territory] is worth.
Essays Contributed to the Edinburgh Review (1843) vol. 2 'The War of Succession in Spain'

8 Every schoolboy knows who imprisoned Montezuma, and who strangled Atahualpa.
Essays Contributed to the Edinburgh Review (1843) vol. 3 'Lord Clive'

9 The Chief Justice was rich, quiet, and infamous.
Essays Contributed to the Edinburgh Review (1843) vol. 3 'Warren Hastings'

10 Thus our democracy was, from an early period, the most aristocratic, and our aristocracy the most democratic in the world.
History of England vol. 1 (1849)

11 Persecution produced its natural effect on them [Puritans and Calvinists]. It found them a sect; it made them a faction.
History of England vol. 1 (1849)

12 [Louis XIV] had shown, in an eminent degree, two talents invaluable to a prince, the talent of choosing his servants well, and the talent of appropriating to himself the chief part of the credit of their acts.
History of England vol. 1 (1849)

13 No man is fit to govern great societies who hesitates about disobliging the few who have access to him for the sake of the many he will never see.
History of England vol. 1 (1849)

14 It was a crime in a child to read by the bedside of a sick parent one of those beautiful collects which had soothed the griefs of forty generations of Christians.
History of England vol. 1 (1849)

15 The Puritan hated bear-baiting, not because it gave pain to the bear, but because it gave pleasure to the spectators.
History of England vol. 1 (1849)

16 It has often been found that profuse expenditure, heavy taxation, absurd commercial restrictions, corrupt tribunals, disastrous wars, seditions, persecutions, conflagrations, inundations, have not been able to destroy capital so fast as the exertions of private citizens have been able to create it.
History of England vol. 1 (1849)

17 Obadiah Bind-their-kings-in-chains-and-their-nobles-with-links-of-iron.
'The Battle of Naseby' (1824) fictitious author's name

18 Oh, wherefore come ye forth in triumph from the north,

With your hands, and your feet, and
your raiment all red?
'The Battle of Naseby' (1824)

1 And the Man of Blood was there,
with his long essenced hair,
And Astley, and Sir Marmaduke, and
Rupert of the Rhine.
'The Battle of Naseby' (1824)

2 To my true king I offered free from
stain
Courage and faith; vain faith, and
courage vain.
'A Jacobite's Epitaph' (1845)

3 By those white cliffs I never more
must see,
By that dear language which I spake
like thee,
Forget all feuds, and shed one
English tear
O'er English dust. A broken heart lies
here.
'A Jacobite's Epitaph' (1845)

4 Then none was for a party;
Then all were for the state;
Then the great man helped the poor,
And the poor man loved the great:
Then lands were fairly portioned;
Then spoils were fairly sold:
The Romans were like brothers
In the brave days of old.
Lays of Ancient Rome (1842) 'Horatius'

5 Thank you, madam, the agony is
abated.
aged four, having had hot coffee spilt over his legs
G. O. Trevelyan Life and Letters of Lord
Macaulay (1876)

6 The object of oratory alone is not
truth, but persuasion.
'Essay on Athenian Orators' in Knight's
Quarterly Magazine August 1824

7 Nothing is so galling to a people
not broken in from the birth as
a paternal, or in other words
a meddling government, a
government which tells them what
to read and say and eat and drink
and wear.
in Edinburgh Review January 1830

8 I detest him more than cold
boiled veal.
of the Tory essayist and politician John Wilson
Croker
letter, 5 August 1831

9 We must at present do our best
to form a class who may be
interpreters between us and
the millions whom we govern; a
class of persons, Indian in blood
and colour, but English in taste,
in opinions, in morals, and in
intellect.
minute, as Member of Supreme Council of
India, 2 February 1835

John McCain 1936–
American Republican politician

10 I will not take the low road to the
highest office in the land. I want the
presidency in the best way, not the
worst way.
conceding victory in the South Carolina
presidential primary to George W. **Bush**
in Guardian 24 February 2000

11 I fell in love with my country when I
was a prisoner in someone else's.
speech at Republican National Convention,
Minneapolis-St Paul, 4 September 2008

Eugene McCarthy 1916–
American Democratic politician

12 Being in politics is like being a
football coach. You have to be
smart enough to understand the
game, and dumb enough to think
it's important.
while campaigning for the presidency
in an interview, 1968

Joseph McCarthy 1908–57
American Republican politician and anti-Communist
agitator. On McCarthy: see **Welch 328:15**

13 I have here in my hand a list of two
hundred and five [people] that were
known to the Secretary of State as
being members of the Communist
Party and who nevertheless are still
working and shaping the policy of
the State Department.
speech at Wheeling, West Virginia, 9 February
1950

14 McCarthyism is Americanism with
its sleeves rolled.
speech in Wisconsin, 1952; Richard Rovere
Senator Joe McCarthy (1973)

Mary McCarthy 1912–89
American novelist

1 Bureaucracy, the rule of no one, has become the modern form of despotism.
in *New Yorker* 18 October 1958

George B. McClellan 1826–85
American soldier and politician

2 All quiet along the Potomac.
said at the time of the American Civil War
attributed

John McCrae 1872–1918
Canadian poet and military physician

3 To you from failing hands we throw
The torch; be yours to hold it high.
If ye break faith with us who die
We shall not sleep, though poppies grow
In Flanders Fields.
'In Flanders Fields' (1915)

Hugh MacDiarmid 1892–1978
Scottish poet and nationalist

4 The rose of all the world is not for me.
I want for my part
Only the little white rose of Scotland
That smells sharp and sweet—and breaks the heart.
'The Little White Rose' (1934)

5 Scotland small? Our multiform, our infinite Scotland *small*?
Only as a patch of hillside may be a cliché corner
To a fool who cries 'Nothing but heather!'...
Direadh 1 (1974)

Dwight Macdonald 1906–82
American writer and film critic

6 Götterdämmerung without the gods.
of the use of atomic bombs against the Japanese
in *Politics* September 1945 'The Bomb'

John A. Macdonald 1815–91
Scottish-born Canadian Liberal-Conservative statesman, Prime Minister 1867–73 and 1878–91

7 When fortune empties her chamberpot on your head, smile—

and say 'we are going to have a summer shower'.
spoken 1875 when Leader of the Opposition

8 A British subject I was born, and a British subject I will die.
speech, 17 February 1891, in Toronto *Empire* 18 February 1891

Ramsay MacDonald 1866–1937
British Labour statesman; Prime Minister, 1924, 1929–31, 1931–5. On MacDonald: see **Churchill 66:7, George V 121:4, Lloyd George 189:21, Nicolson 227:3**; see also **Lamont 177:5**

9 Wars are popular. Contractors make profits; the aristocracy glean honour.
in *Labour Leader* 11 March 1915

10 A terror decreed by a Secret Committee is child's play compared with a terror instituted by 'lawful authority'.
in *Socialist Review* January–March 1921

11 We hear war called murder. It is not: it is suicide.
in *Observer* 4 May 1930

12 Tomorrow every Duchess in London will be wanting to kiss me!
after forming the National Government, 25 August 1931
Viscount Snowden *An Autobiography* (1934) vol. 2

13 A body representing the citizenship of the whole nation is charged with so much that it can do nothing swiftly and well.
Carl Cohen *Parliament and Democracy* (1962)

Ian McEwan 1948–
English novelist

14 No human society, from the hunter-gatherer to the postindustrial, has come to the attention of anthropologists that did not have its leaders and the led; and no emergency was ever dealt with effectively by democratic process.
Enduring Love (1987)

George McGovern 1922–
American Democratic politician, presidential candidate in 1972

15 Sometimes, when they say you're

ahead of your time, it's just a polite way of saying you have a real bad sense of timing.
in *Observer* 18 March 1990 'Sayings of the Week'

Lord McGregor 1921–
British sociologist

1 An odious exhibition of journalists dabbling their fingers in the stuff of other people's souls.
on press coverage of the marriage of the Prince and Princess of Wales, speaking as Chairman of the Press Complaints Commission
in *Times* 9 June 1992

Martin McGuinness 1950–
Northern Irish politician

2 My war is over. My job as a political leader is to prevent war.
in *Daily Telegraph* 30 October 2002

Niccolò Machiavelli 1469–1527
Italian political philosopher and Florentine statesman.
On Machiavelli: see **Macaulay 193:8**

3 And if, to be sure, sometimes you need to conceal a fact with words, do it in such a way that it does not become known, or, if it does become known, that you have a ready and quick defence.
'Advice to Raffaello Girolami when he went as Ambassador to the Emperor' (October 1522)

4 It is necessary for him who lays out a state and arranges laws for it to presuppose that all men are evil and that they are always going to act according to the wickedness of their spirits whenever they have free scope.
Discourses on the First Ten Books of Livy (1513–17)

5 Success or failure lies in conforming to the times.
Discourses on the First Ten Books of Livy (1513–17)

6 Wars begin when you will, but they do not end when you please.
History of Florence (1521–4)

7 Men should be either treated generously or destroyed, because they take revenge for slight injuries—for heavy ones they cannot.
The Prince (1513)

8 In seizing a state, the usurper ought to examine closely into all those injuries which it is necessary for him to inflict, and to do them all at one stroke, so as not to have to repeat them daily; and thus by not unsettling men he will be able to reassure them, and win them to himself by benefits. He who does otherwise, either from timidity or evil advice, is always compelled to keep the knife in his hand.
The Prince (1513)

9 Let no one oppose this belief of mine with that well-worn proverb: 'He who builds on the people builds on mud.'
The Prince (1513)

10 If a prince holds on to his state by means of mercenary armies, he will never be stable or secure.
The Prince (1513)

11 This leads to a debate: is it better to be loved than feared, or the reverse? The answer is that it is desirable to be both, but because it is difficult to join them together, it is much safer for a prince to be feared than loved, if he is to fail in one of the two.
The Prince (1513)

12 Since, then, a prince is necessitated to play the animal well, he chooses among the beasts the fox and the lion, because the lion does not protect himself from traps; the fox does not protect himself from wolves. The prince must be a fox, therefore, to recognize the traps and a lion to frighten the wolves.
The Prince (1513)

13 A wise ruler cannot and should not keep his word when such an observance would be against his interests.
The Prince (1513)

14 A prince never lacks legitimate reasons to excuse his failure to keep his word.
The Prince (1513)

1 Princes ought to leave affairs of reproach to the management of others, and keep those of grace in their own hands.
The Prince (1513)

2 So long as the great majority of men are not deprived of either property or honour, they are satisfied.
The Prince (1513)

3 The first method for estimating the intelligence of a ruler is to look at the men he has around him.
The Prince (1513)

4 There is no other way for securing yourself against flatteries except that men understand that they do not offend you by telling you the truth; but when everybody can tell you the truth, you fail to get respect.
The Prince (1513)

Peter MacKay 1965–
Canadian Conservative politician

5 My head's clear. My heart's a little banged up, but that will heal.
*after the decision by his former Conservative colleague Belinda **Stronach**, with whom he had had a romantic relationship, to join the Liberal Party just before a key budget vote*
in an interview with CBC News, 18 May 2005

James Mackintosh 1765–1832
Scottish philosopher and historian

6 Men are never so good or so bad as their opinions.
Dissertation on the Progress of Ethical Philosophy (1830) 'Jeremy Bentham'

7 The Commons, faithful to their system, remained in a wise and masterly inactivity.
of the French Commons
Vindiciae Gallicae (1791)

Iain Macleod 1913–70
British Conservative politician. On Macleod: see **Salisbury 273:8**

8 To have a debate on the National Health Service without the right hon. Gentleman [Aneurin Bevan] would be like putting on Hamlet with no one in the part of the First Gravedigger.
in the House of Commons, 27 March 1952

9 It is some measure of the tightness of the magic circle on this occasion that neither the Chancellor of the Exchequer nor the Leader of the House of Commons had any inkling of what was happening.
*of the 'evolvement' of Lord **Home** as Conservative leader after the resignation of Harold **Macmillan***
in *The Spectator* 17 January 1964

10 The Conservative Party always in time forgives those who were wrong. Indeed often, in time, they forgive those who were right.
in *The Spectator* 21 February 1964

11 John Fitzgerald Kennedy described himself, in a brilliant phrase, as an idealist without illusions. I would describe the Prime Minister as an illusionist without ideals.
in the House of Commons, 1 March 1966; see **Kennedy 168:1**

12 In Parliament it should not only be the duty but the pleasure of the Opposition to oppose whenever they reasonably can.
in *The Spectator* 26 August 1966

13 I cannot help it if every time the Opposition are asked to name their weapons they pick boomerangs.
in *Dictionary of National Biography* (1917–)

Marshall McLuhan 1911–80
Canadian communications scholar

14 Television brought the brutality of war into the comfort of the living room. Vietnam was lost in the living rooms of America—not the battlefields of Vietnam.
in *Montreal Gazette* 16 May 1975

Comte de Macmahon 1808–93
French military commander and statesman; President of the Third Republic, 1873–9

15 *J'y suis, j'y reste.*
Here I am, and here I stay.
at the taking of the Malakoff fortress during the Crimean War, 8 September 1855
G. Hanotaux *Histoire de la France Contemporaine* (1903–8) vol. 2

Harold Macmillan 1894–1986
British Conservative statesman; Prime Minister, 1957–63. On Macmillan: see **Bevan 31:3**, **Hennessy 141:4**, **Levin 183:10**, **Levin 183:11**, **Macleod 198:9**, **Thorpe 312:7**

1 Toryism has always been a form of paternal socialism.
   in 1936; Anthony Sampson *Macmillan* (1967)

2 We...are Greeks in this American empire...We must run the Allied Forces HQ as the Greeks ran the operations of the Emperor Claudius.
   *to Richard **Crossman** in 1944, after French North Africa had become an American sphere of influence, with **Eisenhower** as Supreme Allied Commander*
   in *Sunday Telegraph* 9 February 1964

3 The Whips want the safe men...I reminded Winston again that it took Hitler to make him PM and me an under-secretary. The Tory Party would do neither.
   diary, 13 October 1954

4 There ain't gonna be no war.
   at a London press conference, 24 July 1955, following the Geneva summit
   in *News Chronicle* 25 July 1955

5 Forever poised between a cliché and an indiscretion.
   on the life of a Foreign Secretary
   in *Newsweek* 30 April 1956

6 Let us be frank about it: most of our people have never had it so good. Go around the country, go to the industrial towns, go to the farms, and you'll see a state of prosperity such as we have never had in my lifetime—nor indeed ever in the history of this country. What is beginning to worry some of us is 'Is it too good to be true?' or perhaps I should say 'Is it too good to last?'
   speech at Bedford, 20 July 1957; see **Slogans 292:7**

7 I thought the best thing to do was to settle up these little local difficulties, and then turn to the wider vision of the Commonwealth.
   statement at London airport on leaving for a Commonwealth tour, 7 January 1958, following the resignation of the Chancellor of the Exchequer and others
   in *Times* 8 January 1958

8 The wind of change is blowing through this continent, and, whether we like it or not, this growth of [African] national consciousness is a political fact.
   speech at Cape Town, 3 February 1960

9 Can we say that with fifteen representatives, Ambassadors or Ministers, in Nato acting in unanimity, the deterrent would continue to be credible? There might be one finger on the trigger. There would be fifteen fingers on the safety catch.
   attributed, 1960

10 As usual the Liberals offer a mixture of sound and original ideas. Unfortunately none of the sound ideas is original and none of the original ideas is sound.
   speech to London Conservatives, 7 March 1961

11 I do not intend to live 'after my flame lacks oil, to be the snuff of younger spirits'.
   to Conservative Party conference, October 1961, Randolph Spencer Churchill *The Fight for the Tory Leadership* (1964); see **Shakespeare 277:7**

12 He [Aneurin Bevan] enjoys prophesying the imminent fall of the capitalist system and is prepared to play a part, any part, in its burial, except that of mute.
   Michael Foot *Aneurin Bevan* (1962)

13 I was determined that no British government should be brought down by the action of two tarts.
   comment on the Profumo affair, July 1963
   Anthony Sampson *Macmillan* (1967)

14 I have never found, in a long experience of politics, that criticism is ever inhibited by ignorance.
   in *Wall Street Journal* 13 August 1963

15 It is thinking about themselves that is really the curse of the younger generation—they appear to have no other subject which interests them at all.
   the 'Tuesday memorandum', a draft of a letter to the Queen, advising on his successor but not sent, 1963; D. R. Thorpe *Alec Douglas-Home* (1996)

16 Power? It's like a Dead Sea fruit.

When you achieve it, there is
nothing there.
Anthony Sampson *The New Anatomy of Britain*
(1971); see **Levin 183:10**

1 Churchill was fundamentally
what the English call unstable—by
which they mean anybody who
has that touch of genius which is
inconvenient in normal times.
attributed, 1975

2 There are three bodies no sensible
man directly challenges: the
Roman Catholic Church, the
Brigade of Guards and the National
Union of Mineworkers.
in *Observer* 22 February 1981; see
Baldwin 23:2

3 First of all the Georgian silver goes,
and then all that nice furniture that
used to be in the saloon. Then the
Canalettos go.
on privatization
speech to the Tory Reform Group, 8 November
1985, in *Times* 9 November 1985; see
Misquotations 216:2

4 It has always seemed to me more
artistic, when the curtain falls on
the last performance, to accept the
inevitable *E finita la commedia*.
It is tempting, perhaps, but
unrewarding to hang about the
greenroom after final retirement
from the stage.
At the End of the Day (1973)

5 The opposition of events.
on his biggest problem (see also **Misquotations**)
David Dilks *The Office of Prime Minister in
Twentieth Century Britain* (1993)

6 *of the office of Prime Minister:*
Sometimes the strain is awful, you
have to resort to Jane Austen.
in the Butler Papers; Peter Hennessy *The
Hidden Wiring* (1995)

Robert McNamara 1916–2009
American Democratic politician, Secretary of Defense
during the Vietnam War

7 I don't object to it's being called
'McNamara's War'...It is a very
important war and I am pleased
to be identified with it and do
whatever I can to win it.
in *New York Times* 25 April 1964

8 We...acted according to what we
thought were the principles and
traditions of this nation. We were
wrong. We were terribly wrong.
of the conduct of the Vietnam War by the
Kennedy *and* **Johnson** *administrations*
speaking in Washington, just before the
twentieth anniversary of the American
withdrawal from Vietnam; in *Daily Telegraph*
(electronic edition) 10 April 1995

Eoin MacNeill 1867–1945
Irish nationalist

9 What we call our country is not
a poetical abstraction...There
is no such person as Caitlin Ni
Uallachain or Roisin Dubh or the
Sean-bhean Bhocht, who is calling
on us to save her.
in February, 1916; Robert Kee *The Bold Fenian
Men* (1989)

10 I wish it then to be clearly
understood that under present
conditions I am definitely opposed
to any proposal that may come
forward involving insurrection.
memorandum to Irish Volunteers, February
1916

William Macpherson of Cluny
1926–
Scottish lawyer

11 For the purposes of our Inquiry
the concept of institutional racism
which we apply consists of:
The collective failure of an
organisation to provide an
appropriate and professional service
to people because of their colour,
culture, or ethnic origin. It can
be seen or detected in processes,
attitudes and behaviour which
amount to discrimination through
unwitting prejudice, ignorance,
thoughtlessness and racist
stereotyping which disadvantage
minority ethnic people.
The Stephen Lawrence Inquiry: Report (February
1999) ch. 6

Denis MacShane 1948–
British Labour politician

12 I liken the French/British

relationship to a very old married couple who often think of killing each other but would never dream of divorce.
on the revelation that in 1956 the French Prime Minister Guy Mollet suggested to Anthony Eden a union between the United Kingdom and France in *Times* (online edition) 15 January 2007

Salvador de Madariaga 1886–1978
Spanish writer and diplomat

1 Since, in the main, it is not armaments that cause wars but wars (or the fears thereof) that cause armaments, it follows that every nation will at every moment strive to keep its armament in an efficient state as required by its fear, otherwise styled security.
Morning Without Noon (1974) pt. 1, ch. 9

James Madison 1751–1836
American Democratic Republican statesman; 4th President of the US, 1809–17

2 Liberty is to faction what air is to fire, an aliment without which it instantly expires. But it could not be less folly to abolish liberty, which is essential to political life, because it nourishes faction than it would be to wish the annihilation of air, which is essential to animal life, because it imparts to fire its destructive agency.
The Federalist (1787)

3 The diversity in the faculties of men, from which the rights of property originate, is not less an insuperable obstacle to a uniformity of interests. The protection of these faculties is the first object of government. From the protection of different and unequal faculties of acquiring property, the possession of different degrees and kinds of property immediately results.
The Federalist (1787)

4 The accumulation of all powers, legislative, executive, and judiciary, in the same hands, whether of one, a few, or many, and whether hereditary, self-appointed, or elective, may justly be pronounced the very definition of tyranny.
The Federalist (1787)

5 In framing a government, which is to be administered by men over men, the great difficulty lies in this: you must first enable the government to control the governed, and in the next place, oblige it to control itself.
The Federalist (1787)

6 I believe there are more instances of the abridgement of freedom of the people by gradual and silent encroachments of those in power than by violent and sudden usurpations.
speech in Virginia Convention, 16 June 1788

7 No nation could preserve its freedom in the midst of continual warfare.
Political Observations [pamphlet published in Philadelphia] 20 April 1795

8 The advancement and diffusion of knowledge…is the only guardian of true liberty.
letter to George Thomson, 30 June 1825

Bernard Madoff 1938–
American businessman

9 It's all just one big lie.
on his investment business after it collapsed in *Washington Post* 13 December 2008 online ed.

Magna Carta
Political charter signed by King John at Runnymede, 1215

10 That the English Church shall be free.
Clause 1

11 No free man shall be taken or imprisoned or dispossessed, or outlawed or exiled, or in any way destroyed, nor will we go upon him, nor will we send against him except by the lawful judgement of his peers or by the law of the land.
Clause 39

12 To no man will we sell, or deny, or delay, right or justice.
Clause 40

Alfred T. Mahan 1840–1914
American naval officer and historian

1 Those far distant, storm-beaten
ships, upon which the Grand Army
never looked, stood between it and
the dominion of the world.
*The Influence of Sea Power upon the French
Revolution and Empire 1793–1812* (1892) vol. 2

Norman Mailer 1923–2007
American novelist and essayist

2 The world stood like a playing
card on edge...One looked at the
buildings one passed and wondered
if one was to see them again.
*looking back at the week of the Cuban Missile
Crisis*
The Presidential Papers (1964)

3 All the security around the
American President is just to make
sure the man who shoots him gets
caught.
in *Sunday Telegraph* 4 March 1990

Henry Sumner Maine 1822–88
British jurist

4 War appears to be as old as
mankind, but peace is a modern
invention.
International Law (Whewell Lectures, 1887)

Joseph de Maistre 1753–1821
French writer and diplomat

5 Every country has the government
it deserves.
letter, 15 August 1811

John Major 1943–
British Conservative statesman; Prime Minister,
1990–7. On Major: see **Thatcher 311:2**

6 The first requirement of politics
is not intellect or stamina but
patience. Politics is a very long-run
game and the tortoise will usually
beat the hare.
in *Daily Express* 25 July 1989

7 If the policy isn't hurting, it isn't
working.
speech in Northampton, 27 October 1989; see
Slogans 292:4

8 Society needs to condemn a little
more and understand a little less.
interview with *Mail on Sunday* 21 February
1993

9 Fifty years on from now, Britain will
still be the country of long shadows
on county [cricket] grounds, warm
beer, invincible green suburbs,
dog lovers, and—as George Orwell
said—old maids bicycling to Holy
Communion through the morning
mist.
speech to the Conservative Group for Europe,
22 April 1993; see **Orwell 233:4**

10 It is time to get back to basics: to
self-discipline and respect for the
law, to consideration for others,
to accepting responsibility for
yourself and your family, and not
shuffling it off on the state.
speech to the Conservative Party Conference,
8 October 1993

11 When the final curtain comes
down, it's time to get off the stage.
*outside 10 Downing Street on 2 May, leaving
office as Prime Minister and announcing that he
would resign as Party Leader*
in *Guardian* 3 May 1997

12 Margaret had been at her happiest
confronting political dragons: I
chose consensus.
*contrasting himself with Margaret **Thatcher***
John Major *The Autobiography* (1999)

Bernard Malamud 1914–86
American novelist and short-story writer

13 There's no such thing as an
unpolitical man, especially a Jew.
The Fixer (1966)

Malcolm X 1925–65
American civil rights campaigner

14 The white man was *created* a devil,
to bring chaos upon this earth.
speech, 1953; Malcolm X with Alex Haley
The Autobiography of Malcolm X (1965); see
Fard 109:4

15 If you're born in America with a
black skin, you're born in prison.
in an interview, June 1963

16 We are not fighting for integration,
nor are we fighting for separation.
We are fighting for recognition as

human beings. We are fighting for...
human rights.
Black Revolution, speech in New York, 1964

1 You can't separate peace from
freedom because no one can be at
peace unless he has his freedom.
speech in New York, 7 January 1965

2 We are not speaking of any
individual white man. We are
speaking of the *collective* white
man's *historical* record. We are
speaking of the collective white
man's cruelties, and evils, and
greeds, that have seen him *act* like a
devil toward the non-white man.
Malcolm X with Alex Haley *The Autobiography
of Malcolm X* (1965)

Seamus Mallon 1936–
Northern Irish politician

3 Sunningdale for slow learners.
*comparing the earlier stages of the Northern
Irish talks with the 1973 negotiations towards
a power-sharing executive held at Sunningdale
College, Berkshire*
in *Daily Telegraph* 6 April 1998

Thomas Robert Malthus
1766–1834
English political economist

4 Population, when unchecked,
increases in a geometrical ratio.
Subsistence only increases in an
arithmetical ratio.
Essay on the Principle of Population (1798)

5 The perpetual struggle for room
and food.
Essay on the Principle of Population (1798)

6 A man who is born into a world
already possessed, if he cannot get
subsistence from his parents on
whom he has a just demand, and if
the society do not want his labour,
has no claim of *right* to the smallest
portion of food, and, in fact, has
no business to be where he is. At
Nature's mighty feast there is no
vacant cover for him.
Essay on the Principle of Population (1803 ed.)

Earl of Manchester 1602–71
English politician and Parliamentary commander in
the Civil War

7 If we beat the King ninety-nine
times, yet he is king still and so will
his posterity be after him; but if
the king beat us once we shall all
be hanged, and our posterity made
slaves.
at a Parliamentary Council-of-War,
10 November 1644, in *Calendar of State
Papers, Domestic* 1644–5

Nelson Mandela 1918–
South African statesman, President of South Africa
1994–9

8 I have dedicated my life to this
struggle of the African people.
I have fought against white
domination, and I have fought
against black domination. I have
cherished the ideal of a democratic
and free society in which all
persons live together in harmony
with equal opportunities. It is an
ideal which I hope to live for and
to achieve. But if needs be, it is an
ideal for which I am prepared to
die.
speech at his trial in Pretoria, 20 April 1964

9 I stand here before you not as a
prophet but as a humble servant
of you, the people. Your tireless
and heroic sacrifices have made it
possible for me to be here today. I
therefore place the remaining years
of my life in your hands.
speech in Cape Town, 11 February 1990

10 Through its imperialist system
Britain brought about untold
suffering of millions of people. And
this is an historical fact. To be able
to admit this would increase the
respect, you know, which we have
for British institutions.
in *Guardian* 2 April 1990

11 Let freedom reign. The sun shall
never set on so glorious a human
achievement.
inaugural address as President of South Africa,
10 May 1994; see also **Bush 51:6**

1 True reconciliation does not consist in merely forgetting the past.
on healing the bitterness caused by apartheid
speech, 7 January 1996

2 No one is born hating another person because of the colour of his skin, or his background, or his religion. People must learn to hate, and if they can learn to hate, they can be taught to love, for love comes more naturally to the human heart than its opposite.
Long Walk to Freedom (1994)

3 We close the century with most people still languishing in poverty, subjected to hunger, preventable disease, illiteracy and insufficient shelter.
speaking at a ceremony at his former prison cell on Robben Island; in *Observer* on 2 January 2000

4 One of the things I learnt when I was negotiating was that until I changed myself I could not change others.
in *Sunday Times* 16 April 2000

5 *of Yasser* **Arafat**:
He was like a surrealistic painting. He was complex, deep, superficial, rational, irrational, cold, warm.
in *Independent* 14 November 2004

Winnie Madikizela-Mandela
1934–
South African political activist, former wife of Nelson **Mandela**

6 With that stick of matches, with our necklace, we shall liberate this country.
a 'necklace' was a tyre soaked or filled with petrol, placed around a victim's neck, and set alight
speech in black townships, 14 April 1986; in *Guardian* 15 April 1986

Peter Mandelson 1953–
British Labour politician. On Mandelson: see **Blair 36:2, Parris 241:3**

7 [New Labour] is intensely relaxed about people getting filthy rich.
speech to executives in Silicon Valley, California, October 1999; Andrew Rawnsley *Servants of the People* (2000)

8 Before this campaign started, it was said that I was facing political oblivion, my career in tatters...They underestimated me, because I am a fighter and not a quitter.
on winning back his Hartlepool seat in the General Election
speech, 8 June 2001

9 I don't really see myself as a big beast. More as a kindly pussycat.
in *Guardian* 10 August 2009

John Manners 1818–1906
English Tory politician and writer

10 Let wealth and commerce, laws and learning die,
But leave us still our old nobility!
England's Trust (1841)

Lord Mansfield 1705–93
Scottish lawyer and politician

11 The constitution does not allow reasons of state to influence our judgements: God forbid it should! We must not regard political consequences; however formidable soever they might be: if rebellion was the certain consequence, we are bound to say '*fiat justitia, ruat caelum*'.
Rex v. Wilkes, 8 June 1768, in *The English Reports* (1909) vol. 98; see **Adams 3:15**

12 Consider what you think justice requires, and decide accordingly. But never give your reasons; for your judgement will probably be right, but your reasons will certainly be wrong.
advice to a newly appointed colonial governor ignorant in the law
Lord Campbell *The Lives of the Chief Justices of England* (1849) vol. 2

Mao Zedong 1893–1976
Chinese statesman, chairman of the Communist Party of the Chinese People's Republic 1949–76 and head of state 1949–59

13 Politics is war without bloodshed while war is politics with bloodshed.
lecture, 1938

1 Every Communist must grasp the truth, 'Political power grows out of the barrel of a gun'.
   speech, 6 November 1938

2 The atom bomb is a paper tiger which the United States reactionaries use to scare people. It looks terrible, but in fact it isn't... All reactionaries are paper tigers.
   interview, 1946

3 Letting a hundred flowers blossom and a hundred schools of thought contend is the policy for promoting progress in the arts and the sciences and a flourishing socialist culture in our land.
   speech in Peking, 27 February 1957

4 People of the world, unite and defeat the US aggressors and all their running dogs!
   'Statement Supporting the People of the Congo against US Aggression' 28 November 1964

John Marchi 1921–2009
American Republican politician

5 We ought not to permit a cottage industry in the God business.
   on hearing that British scientists had successfully cloned a lamb (Dolly)
   in Guardian 28 February 1997

Ferdinand Marcos 1917–89
Filipino statesman

6 It is easier to run a revolution than a government.
   in Time 6 June 1977

Princess Margaret 1930–2002
British princess, sister of **Elizabeth II**

7 Mindful of the Church's teaching that Christian marriage is indissoluble, and conscious of my duty to the Commonwealth, I have resolved to put these considerations before any others.
   announcing her decision not to marry a divorced man, Group Captain Peter Townsend
   statement from Clarence House, 31 October 1955; in Times 1 November 1955

Marie-Antoinette 1755–93
French Queen consort of **Louis XVI**

8 Qu'ils mangent de la brioche.
   Let them eat cake.
   on being told that her people had no bread
   attributed; in Confessions (1740) Rousseau refers to a similar remark being a well-known saying; in Relation d'un Voyage à Bruxelles et à Coblentz en 1791 (1823), Louis XVIII attributes 'Why don't they eat pastry?' to Marie-Thérèse (1638–83), wife of Louis XIV

Constance Markievicz 1868–1927
Irish nationalist. On Markievicz: see **de Valera 90:3**

9 I wish you had the decency to shoot me.
   on hearing of the commutation of her death sentence
   Diana Norman Terrible Beauty (1987)

10 I have seen the stars, and I am not going to follow a flickering will o' the wisp.
   rejecting the Treaty in the Dáil debate, 1921
   Diana Norman Terrible Beauty (1987)

George C. Marshall 1880–1959
American general and statesman, who as US Secretary of State (1947–9) initiated the programme of economic aid to European countries known as the Marshall Plan

11 If man does find the solution for world peace it will be the most revolutionary reversal of his record we have ever known.
   biennial report of the Chief of Staff, United States Army, 1 September 1945

12 Our policy is directed not against any country or doctrine but against hunger, poverty, desperation and chaos. Its purpose should be the revival of a working economy in the world so as to permit the emergence of political and social conditions in which free institutions can exist.
   announcing the Marshall Plan, address at Harvard, 5 June 1947

John Marshall 1755–1835
American jurist

13 The power to tax involves the power to destroy.
   in McCulloch v. Maryland (1819)

1 The people made the Constitution, and the people can unmake it. It is the creature of their own will, and lives only by their will.
in *Cohens v. Virginia* (1821)

Thomas R. Marshall 1854–1925
American politician

2 What this country needs is a really good 5-cent cigar.
in *New York Tribune* 4 January 1920

Thurgood Marshall 1908–93
American Supreme Court judge

3 We must never forget that the only real source of power that we as judges can tap is the respect of the people.
in *Chicago Tribune* 15 August 1981

William McChesney Martin Jr.
1906–98
American economist, Chairman of the Federal Reserve, 1951–70

4 The job of the Federal Reserve is to take away the punch bowl just when the party is getting good.
attributed; Paul Volcker interview on PBS, 26 September 2000

Andrew Marvell 1621–78
English poet

5 Choosing each stone, and poising every weight,
Trying the measures of the breadth and height;
Here pulling down, and there erecting new,
Founding a firm state by proportions true.
'The First Anniversary of the Government under His Highness the Lord Protector, 1655'

6 *He* nothing common did or mean
Upon that memorable scene:
But with his keener eye
The axe's edge did try:
Nor called the gods with vulgar spite
To vindicate his helpless right,
But bowed his comely head,
Down as upon a bed.
*on the execution of **Charles I***
'An Horatian Ode upon Cromwell's Return from Ireland' (written 1650)

7 And now the Irish are ashamed
To see themselves in one year tamed:
So much one man can do,
That does both act and know.
'An Horatian Ode upon Cromwell's Return from Ireland' (written 1650)

Karl Marx 1818–83
German socialist and political philosopher; co-founder (with Friedrich **Engels**) of modern Communism

8 Religion…is the opium of the people.
A Contribution to the Critique of Hegel's Philosophy of Right (1843–4) introduction

9 Mankind always sets itself only such problems as it can solve; since, looking at the matter more closely, it will always be found that the task itself arises only when the material conditions for its solution already exist or are at least in the process of formation.
A Contribution to the Critique of Political Economy (1859) preface

10 It is not the consciousness of men that determines their being, but, on the contrary, their social being that determines their consciousness.
A Contribution to the Critique of Political Economy (1859) preface

11 From each according to his abilities, to each according to his needs.
Critique of the Gotha Programme (written 1875, but of earlier origin); see Morelly *Code de la nature* (1755) , and J. J. L. Blanc *Organisation du travail* (1839) (who, in quoting Saint-Simon, rejects the notion) for possible sources

12 Hegel says somewhere that all great events and personalities in world history reappear in one fashion or another. He forgot to add: the first time as tragedy, the second as farce.
The Eighteenth Brumaire of Louis Bonaparte (1852); the origin of the Hegel reference is uncertain, but see **Hegel 140:11**

13 It is the ultimate aim of this work, to lay bare the economic law of motion of modern society.
Das Kapital (1st German ed., 1867) preface (25 July 1865)

1 The philosophers have only interpreted the world in various ways; the point is to change it.
Theses on Feuerbach (written 1845)

2 What I did that was new was to prove...that the class struggle necessarily leads to the dictatorship of the proletariat.
the phrase 'dictatorship of the proletariat' had been used earlier in the Constitution of the World Society of Revolutionary Communists (1850), signed by Marx and others
letter to Georg Weydemeyer 5 March 1852; Marx claimed that the phrase had been coined by Auguste Blanqui (1805–81), but it has not been found in this form in Blanqui's work

3 All I know is that I am not a Marxist.
attributed in a letter from Friedrich Engels to Conrad Schmidt, 5 August 1890

Karl Marx 1818–83 and Friedrich Engels 1820–95

4 A spectre is haunting Europe—the spectre of Communism.
The Communist Manifesto (1848) opening words

5 The history of all hitherto existing society is the history of class struggles.
The Communist Manifesto (1848)

6 In place of the old bourgeois society, with its classes and class antagonists, we shall have an association, in which the free development of each is the free development of all.
The Communist Manifesto (1848)

7 The proletarians have nothing to lose but their chains. They have a world to win. WORKING MEN OF ALL COUNTRIES, UNITE!
often quoted as 'Workers of the world, unite!'
The Communist Manifesto (1848) closing words

Mary I 1516–58
Queen of England from 1553

8 When I am dead and opened, you shall find 'Calais' lying in my heart.
in *Holinshed's Chronicles* vol. 4 (1808)

Queen Mary 1867–1953
British princess, Queen Consort of **George V**

9 *This* is a pretty kettle of fish!
to the Prime Minister, Stanley **Baldwin**, after **Edward VIII** had told her that he was prepared to give up the throne to marry Mrs Simpson
James Pope-Hennessy *Life of Queen Mary* (1959)

10 All *this* thrown away for *that*.
on returning home to Marlborough House, London after the abdication of her son, King **Edward VIII**, December 1936
David Duff *George and Elizabeth* (1983)

11 I do not think you have ever realised the shock, which the attitude you took up caused your family and the whole nation. It seemed inconceivable to those who had made such sacrifices during the war that you, as their King, refused a lesser sacrifice.
letter to the Duke of Windsor, the former **Edward VIII**, July 1938

Mary, Queen of Scots 1542–87
Scottish monarch, Queen 1542–67

12 Look to your consciences and remember that the theatre of the world is wider than the realm of England.
to the commissioners appointed to try her at Fotheringhay, 13 October 1586
Antonia Fraser *Mary Queen of Scots* (1969) ch. 25

13 *En ma fin git mon commencement.* In my end is my beginning.
motto embroidered with an emblem of her mother, Mary of Guise, quoted in a letter from William Drummond of Hawthornden to Ben Jonson in 1619

Philip Massinger 1583–1640
English dramatist

14 Ambition, in a private man a vice, Is in a prince the virtue.
The Bashful Lover (licensed 1636, published 1655)

15 Greatness, with private men Esteemed a blessing, is to me a curse; And we, whom, for our high births, they conclude The only freemen, are the only slaves.

Happy the golden mean!
The Great Duke of Florence (licensed 1627, printed 1635)

Reginald Maudling 1917–79
British Conservative politician

1 Sorry, old cock, to leave it in this shape.
*to **Callaghan** when he arrived at the Treasury in 1964*
James Callaghan *Time and Chance* (1987)

Richard Mawrey 1942–
British judge

2 *commenting on the government's refusal to revise the rules for postal voting:*
Anyone who has sat through the case I have just tried and listened to evidence of electoral fraud that would disgrace a banana republic would find this statement surprising.
in *Guardian* 4 April 2005

James Maxton 1885–1946
British Labour politician

3 All I say is, if you cannot ride two horses you have no right in the circus.
opposing disaffiliation of the Scottish Independent Labour Party from the Labour Party, often quoted as 'no right in the bloody circus'
in *Daily Herald* 12 January 1931

Theresa May 1956–
British Conservative politician

4 You know what some people call us: the nasty party.
speech to the Conservative Conference, 7 October 2002

Horace Maybray-King 1901–86
British Labour politician; Speaker of the House of Commons

5 One of the myths of the British Parliament is that there are three parties there. I can assure you from bitter personal experience there are 629.
in *Observer* 9 October 1966 'Sayings of the Week'

Jonathan Mayhew 1720–66
American divine

6 Rulers have no authority from God to do mischief.
A Discourse Concerning Unlimited Submission and Non-Resistance to the Higher Powers (1750)

7 As soon as the prince sets himself up above the law, he loses the king in the tyrant; he does to all intents and purpose unking himself…And in such cases, has no more right to be obeyed, than any inferior officer who acts beyond his commission.
A Discourse Concerning Unlimited Submission and Non-Resistance to the Higher Powers (1750)

Cardinal Mazarin 1602–61
Italian-born French statesman

8 Is he lucky?
*first question on being requested to take anyone into his service, later associated with **Napoleon I***
attributed; Elizabeth Charlotte, Duchess of Orleans *Secret Memoirs of the Court of Louis XIV, and of the Regency* (1824)

Giuseppe Mazzini 1805–72
Italian nationalist leader

9 Insurrection—by means of guerrilla bands—is the true method of warfare for all nations desirous of emancipating themselves from a foreign yoke.
General Instructions for the Members of Young Italy (1833) sect. 4

10 A nation is the universality of citizens speaking the same tongue.
in *La Giovine Italia*, 1832

Thabo Mbeki 1942–
South African statesman, President of South Africa 1999–2008. On Mbeki: see **Sexwale 277:4**

11 I know that none dare challenge me when I say: I am an African.
statement on behalf of the African National Congress, 8 May 1996, on the occasion of the adoption by the Constitutional Assembly of the Republic of South Africa Constitution Bill

Margaret Mead 1901–78
American anthropologist

1 Never doubt that a small group of thoughtful committed citizens can change the world. In fact, it's the only thing that ever has.
attributed; Mary Bowman-Kruhm *Margaret Mead: a biography* (2003)

Catherine de' Medici 1518–89
Italian-born queen consort of Henri II of France

2 A false report, if believed during three days, may be of great service to a government.
Isaac D'Israeli *Curiosities of Literature* 2nd series (1849) vol. 2; perhaps apocryphal

Cosimo de' Medici 1389–1464
Italian statesman and patron of the arts

3 We read that we ought to forgive our enemies; but we do not read that we ought to forgive our friends.
speaking of what Bacon refers to as 'perfidious friends'
Francis Bacon *Apophthegms* (1625) no. 206

Robert Megarry 1910–2006
English judge

4 Whereas in England all is permitted that is not expressly prohibited, it has been said that in Germany all is prohibited unless expressly permitted and in France all is permitted that is expressly prohibited. In the European Common Market (as it then was) no-one knows what is permitted and it all costs more.
'Law and Lawyers in a Permissive Society' (5th Riddell Lecture delivered in Lincoln's Inn Hall 22 March 1972)

Golda Meir 1898–1978
Israeli stateswoman, Prime Minister 1969–74

5 Those that perished in Hitler's gas chambers were the last Jews to die without standing up to defend themselves.
speech to United Jewish Appeal Rally, New York, 11 June 1967

Lord Melbourne 1779–1848
British Whig statesman; Prime Minister 1834, 1835–41

6 I have always thought complaints of ill-usage contemptible, whether from a seduced disappointed girl or a turned-out Prime Minister.
on being dismissed by William IV
Emily Eden, letter to Mrs Lister, 23 November 1834

7 If left out he would be dangerous, but if taken in, he would be simply destructive.
*when forming his second administration in 1835, Melbourne omitted the former Lord Chancellor, Lord **Brougham***
Lord David Cecil *Lord M* (1954)

8 You domineered too much, you interfered too much with other departments, you encroached upon the provinces of the Prime Minister, you worked, as I believe, with the Press in a manner unbecoming to the dignity of your station.
*letter to the former Lord Chancellor, Lord **Brougham**, explaining why he had been omitted from Melbourne's second administration, 1835*
Lord David Cecil *Lord M* (1954)

9 Universities never reform themselves; everyone knows that.
speech, House of Lords, 11 April 1837

10 If we really are in that situation that we must do something, it is only another proof of the fatal necessity by which a nation that once begins to colonize is led step by step over the whole globe.
of intervention in New Zealand
to Lord Howick, 16 December 1837

11 Damn it! Another Bishop dead! I believe they die to vex me.
Lord David Cecil *Lord M* (1954)

12 God help the Minister that meddles with art!
Lord David Cecil *Lord M* (1954)

13 I wish I was as cocksure of anything as Tom Macaulay is of everything.
Earl Cowper *Preface to Lord Melbourne's Papers* (1889)

14 Nobody ever did anything very foolish except from some strong principle.
Lord David Cecil *The Young Melbourne* (1939)

1 Now, is it to lower the price of corn, or isn't it? It is not much matter which we say, but mind, we must all say *the same*.
   at the end of a Cabinet meeting to agree a fixed tariff for corn; Melbourne is said to have put his back to the door and opened it only when they agreed
   Walter Bagehot *The English Constitution* (1867)

2 Things have come to a pretty pass when religion is allowed to invade the sphere of private life.
   on hearing an evangelical sermon
   G. W. E. Russell *Collections and Recollections* (1898)

3 This damned morality will undo us all.
   of Prince Albert's wish to establish the Royal Family as a national icon of domestic life
   Samuel Weintraub *Albert* (1997)

4 What all the wise men promised has not happened, and what all the d—d fools said would happen has come to pass.
   of the Catholic Emancipation Act (1829)
   H. Dunckley *Lord Melbourne* (1890)

5 What I like about the Order of the Garter is that there is no damned merit about it.
   Lord David Cecil *The Young Melbourne* (1939)

6 What I want is men who will support me when I am in the wrong.
   replying to a politician who said 'I will support you as long as you are in the right'
   Lord David Cecil *Lord M* (1954)

7 When in doubt what should be done, do nothing.
   Lord David Cecil *Lord M* (1954)

8 The whole duty of government is to prevent crime and to preserve contracts.
   Lord David Cecil *Lord M* (1954)

David Mellor 1949–
British Conservative politician and broadcaster

9 I do believe the popular press is drinking in the last chance saloon.
   interview on *Hard News* (Channel 4), 21 December 1989

H. L. Mencken 1880–1956
American journalist and literary critic

10 Nothing is so abject and pathetic as a politician who has lost his job, save only a retired stud-horse.
   Chrestomathy (1949)

11 Puritanism. The haunting fear that someone, somewhere, may be happy.
   Chrestomathy (1949)

12 The whole aim of practical politics is to keep the populace alarmed (and hence clamorous to be led to safety) by menacing it with an endless series of hobgoblins, all of them imaginary.
   In Defence of Women (1923)

13 Democracy is the theory that the common people know what they want, and deserve to get it good and hard.
   A Little Book in C major (1916)

14 A government can never be the impersonal thing described in text-books. It is simply a group of men like any other. In every 100 of the men composing it there are two who are honest and intelligent, ten obvious scoundrels, and 88 poor fish.
   Minority Report (1956)

15 Under democracy one party always devotes its chief energies to trying to prove that the other party is unfit to rule—and both commonly succeed, and are right.
   Minority Report (1956)

16 The worst government is often the most moral. One composed of cynics is often very tolerant and humane. But when fanatics are on top there is no limit to oppression.
   Minority Report (1956)

17 The urge to save humanity is almost always only a false-face for the urge to rule it.
   Minority Report (1956)

18 A good politician is quite as unthinkable as an honest burglar.
   Prejudices 4th series (1925)

19 No one in this world, so far as I know—and I have searched the records for years, and employed agents to help me—has ever lost money by underestimating the

intelligence of the great masses of the plain people.
in *Chicago Tribune* 19 September 1926

1 The saddest life is that of a political aspirant under democracy. His failure is ignominious and his success is disgraceful.
in *Baltimore Evening Sun* 9 December 1929

2 He [Calvin Coolidge] slept more than any other President, whether by day or by night. Nero fiddled, but Coolidge only snored.
in *American Mercury* April 1933

3 If there had been any formidable body of cannibals in the country he would have promised to provide them with free missionaries fattened at the taxpayer's expense.
of Harry **Truman**'s success in the 1948 presidential campaign
in *Baltimore Sun* 7 November 1948

Robert Gordon Menzies 1894–1978
Australian Liberal statesman, Prime Minister 1939–41 and 1949–66

4 What Great Britain calls the Far East is to us the near north.
in *Sydney Morning Herald* 27 April 1939

Jean Meslier c. 1664–1733
French priest

5 I remember, on this matter, the wish made once by an ignorant, uneducated man…He said he wished…that all the great men in the world and all the nobility could be hanged, and strangled with the guts of priests. For myself…I wish I could have the strength of Hercules to purge the world of all vice and sin, and to have the pleasure of destroying all those monsters of error and sin [priests] who make all the peoples of the world groan

so pitiably.
often quoted as, 'I should like…the last king to be strangled with the guts of the last priest'
Testament (1864); see **Diderot 91:10**, **Nairn 223:2**

Prince Metternich 1773–1859
Austrian statesman

6 Italy is a geographical expression.
discussing the Italian question with Lord **Palmerston** in 1847
Mémoires, Documents, etc. de Metternich publiés par son fils (1883) vol. 7; see **Bismarck 34:8**

7 of his own downfall:
I feel obliged to call to the supporters of the social uprising: Citizens of a dream-world, nothing is altered. On 14 March 1848, there was merely one man fewer.
Aus Metternich's Nachgelassenen Papieren (ed. A. von Klinkowström, 1880) vol. 8

8 Error has never approached my spirit.
addressed to Guizot in 1848; François Pierre G. Guizot *Mémoires* (1858–67) vol. 4

9 The Emperor is everything, Vienna is nothing.
letter to Count Bombelles, 5 June 1848

10 The greatest gift of any statesman rests not in knowing what concessions to make, but recognising when to make them.
Concessionen und Nichtconcessionen (1852)

11 The word 'freedom' means for me not a point of departure but a genuine point of arrival. The point of departure is defined by the word 'order'. Freedom cannot exist without the concept of order.
Mein Politisches Testament

Anthony Meyer 1920–2004
British Conservative politician

12 I question the right of that great Moloch, national sovereignty, to

Middle East
'enough of blood and tears'
see Selective Subject Index

burn its children to save its pride.
speaking against the Falklands War, 1982
in *Listener* 27 September 1990

Jules Michelet 1798–1874
French historian

1 What is the first part of politics?
Education. The second? Education.
And the third? Education.
Le Peuple (1846); see **Blair 36:3**

William Porcher Miles 1822–96

2 'Vote early and vote often,' the
advice openly displayed on the
election banners in one of our
northern cities.
in the House of Representatives, 31 March
1858

John Stuart Mill 1806–73
English philosopher and economist

3 No great improvements in the lot
of mankind are possible, until a
great change takes place in the
fundamental constitution of their
modes of thought.
Autobiography (1873)

4 The working classes, though
differing from those in some other
countries in being ashamed of
lying, are yet generally liars.
Autobiography (1873)

5 The Conservatives…being by the
law of their existence the stupidest
party.
Considerations on Representative Government
(1861)

6 It is but a small portion of the public
business of a country which can be
well done, or safely attempted, by
the central authorities.
Considerations on Representative Government
(1861)

7 When society requires to be rebuilt,
there is no use in attempting to
rebuild it on the old plan.
Dissertations and Discussions vol. 1 (1859)
'Essay on Coleridge'

8 The sole end for which mankind
are warranted, individually or
collectively, in interfering with
the liberty of action of any of their

number, is self-protection.
On Liberty (1859)

9 The only freedom which deserves
the name, is that of pursuing our
own good in our own way.
On Liberty (1859)

10 The only purpose for which power
can be rightfully exercised over any
member of a civilized community,
against his will, is to prevent harm
to others. His own good, either
physical or moral, is not a sufficient
warrant.
On Liberty (1859)

11 If all mankind minus one were
of one opinion, and only one
person were of the contrary
opinion, mankind would be no
more justified in silencing that
one person, than he, if he had
the power, would be justified in
silencing mankind.
On Liberty (1859)

12 A party of order or stability, and
a party of progress or reform,
are both necessary elements of a
healthy state of political life.
On Liberty (1859)

13 The liberty of the individual must
be thus far limited; he must not
make himself a nuisance to other
people.
On Liberty (1859)

14 I am not aware that any community
has a right to force another to be
civilized.
On Liberty (1859)

15 Liberty consists in doing what one
desires.
On Liberty (1859)

16 A State which dwarfs its men, in
order that they may be more docile
instruments in its hands even for
beneficial purposes, will find that
with small men no great thing can
really be accomplished.
On Liberty (1859)

17 The principle which regulates
the existing social relations
between the two sexes—the legal
subordination of one sex to the
other—is wrong in itself, and now

one of the chief hindrances to
human improvement.
The Subjection of Women (1869)

1 Everyone who desires power,
desires it most over those who are
nearest to him, with whom his life
is passed, with whom he has most
concerns in common, and in whom
any independence of his authority
is oftenest likely to interfere with
his individual preferences.
The Subjection of Women (1869)

Edna St Vincent Millay 1892–1950
American poet

2 Justice denied in Massachusetts.
*relating to the trial of Sacco and **Vanzetti** and
their execution on 22 August 1927*
title of poem (1928)

3 The sun that warmed our stooping
backs and withered the weed
uprooted—
We shall not feel it again.
We shall die in darkness, and be
buried in the rain.
'Justice Denied in Massachusetts' (1928)

Alice Duer Miller 1874–1942
American writer

4 I am American bred,
I have seen much to hate here—much
to forgive,
But in a world where England is
finished and dead,
I do not wish to live.
The White Cliffs (1940)

Arthur Miller 1915–2005
American dramatist

5 The ultimate human mystery may
not be anything more than the
claims on us of clan and race, which
may yet turn out to have the power,
because they defy the rational
mind, to kill the world.
Timebends (1987)

6 A good newspaper, I suppose, is a
nation talking to itself.
in *Observer* 26 November 1961

7 A theatre where no-one is allowed
to walk out and everyone is forced

to applause.
describing Eastern Europe
Omnibus (BBC TV) 30 October 1987; in
Independent 31 October 1987

Charles Wright Mills 1916–62
American sociologist

8 By the power elite, we refer to those
political, economic, and military
circles which as an intricate set
of overlapping cliques share
decisions having at least national
conseqences. In so far as national
events are decided, the power elite
are those who decide them.
The Power Elite (1956)

Lord Milner 1854–1925
British colonial administrator

9 If we believe a thing to be bad, and
if we have a right to prevent it, it is
our duty to try to prevent it and to
damn the consequences.
speech in Glasgow, 26 November 1909

John Milton 1608–74
English poet

10 Cromwell, our chief of men.
'To the Lord General Cromwell' (written 1652)

11 …Peace hath her victories
No less renowned than war.
'To the Lord General Cromwell' (written 1652)

12 They also serve who only stand and
wait.
'When I consider how my light is spent' (1673)

13 I cannot praise a fugitive and
cloistered virtue, unexercised and
unbreathed, that never sallies
out and sees her adversary, but
slinks out of the race, where that
immortal garland is to be run for,
not without dust and heat.
Areopagitica (1644)

14 Here the great art lies, to discern
in what the law is to be to restraint
and punishment, and in what
things persuasion only is to work.
Areopagitica (1644)

15 Let not England forget her
precedence of teaching nations

how to live.
The Doctrine and Discipline of Divorce (1643)
'To the Parliament of England'

1 What I have spoken, is the language
of that which is not called amiss
The good old Cause.
*The Ready and Easy Way to Establish a Free
Commonwealth* (2nd ed., 1660)

2 The land had once
enfranchised herself from this
impertinent yoke of prelaty,
under whose inquisitorious and
tyrannical duncery no free and
splendid wit can flourish.
The Reason of Church Government (1642) bk.
2, introduction

3 None can love freedom
heartily, but good men; the rest love
not freedom, but licence.
The Tenure of Kings and Magistrates (1649)

4 No man who knows aught,
can be so stupid to deny that all
men naturally were born free.
The Tenure of Kings and Magistrates (1649)

Comte de Mirabeau 1749–91
French revolutionary

5 War is the national industry
of Prussia.
attributed to Mirabeau by Albert Sorel (1842–
1906), based on Mirabeau's introduction to
*De la monarchie prussienne sous Frédéric le
Grand* (1788)

John Mitchel 1815–75
Irish nationalist

6 Families, when all was eaten
and no hope left, took their last look
at the sun, built up their cottage
doors, that none might see them
die nor hear their groans, and were
found weeks afterwards, skeletons
on their own hearth.
of the Irish Famine
Jail Journal (1854)

7 Next to the British government, the
worst enemy Ireland ever had—or

rather the most fatal friend.
of Daniel **O'Connell**
The Last Conquest of Ireland (Perhaps) (1861)

George Mitchell 1933–
American Democratic politician, chairman of the
Northern Ireland peace talks

8 Although he is regularly asked to
do so, God does not take sides in
American politics.
comment during the hearing of the Senate
Select Committee on the Iran-Contra affair,
July 1987

9 I am pleased to announce that the
two governments and the political
parties in Northern Ireland have
reached agreement.
announcing the Good Friday agreement
in *Times* 11 April 1998

John Mitchell 1913–88
lawyer, US Attorney-General to the Nixon administration

10 Katie Graham's gonna get her tit
caught in a big fat wringer if that's
published.
on hearing that Katherine Graham's Washington
Post *was to reveal the connection between
Watergate and the campaign funding for the
Committee to Re-Elect the President*
in 1973; Katherine Graham *Personal History*
(1997)

Joni Mitchell 1945–
Canadian singer and songwriter

11 Lord, there's danger in this land.
You get witch-hunts and wars when
church and state hold hands.
attributed; Peter McWilliams *Ain't Nobody's
Business If You Do* (1993)

François Mitterrand 1916–96
French socialist statesman; President of France
1981–95

12 She has the eyes of Caligula, but the
mouth of Marilyn Monroe.
of Margaret **Thatcher**, briefing his new European
Minister Roland Dumas
in *Observer* 25 November 1990

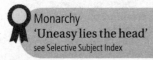
Monarchy
'Uneasy lies the head'
see Selective Subject Index

Misquotations

1 All is lost save honour.
popular summary of the words of **Francis I** of France in a letter to his mother following his defeat at Pavia, 1525; see **Francis I 113:12**

2 The ballot is stronger than the bullet.
popular version of a speech by **Lincoln**, 18 May 1858; see **Lincoln 185:1**

3 The budget should be balanced, the treasury should be refilled, public debt should be reduced, the arrogance of officialdom should be tempered and controlled, assistance to foreign lands should be curtailed lest Rome should become bankrupt, the mobs should be forced to work and not depend on government for subsistence.
attributed to **Cicero** in *Congressional Record* 25 April 1968, but not traced in his works

4 The capitalists will sell us the rope with which to hang them.
attributed to **Lenin**, but not found in his published works; I. U. Annenkov, in 'Remembrances of Lenin' includes a manuscript note attributed to Lenin: 'They [capitalists] will furnish credits which will serve us for the support of the Communist Party in their countries and, by supplying us materials and technical equipment which we lack, will restore our military industry necessary for our future attacks against our suppliers. To put it in other words, they will work on the preparation of their own suicide', in *Novyi Zhurnal/New Review* September 1961

5 Crisis? What Crisis?
Sun headline, 11 January 1979, summarizing James **Callaghan**'s remark: 'I don't think other people in the world would share the view there is mounting chaos', interview at London Airport, 10 January 1979; see **Newspaper headlines 225:3**

6 England and America are two countries divided by a common language.
attributed in this and other forms to George Bernard **Shaw**, but not found in Shaw's published writings; see **Wilde 333:1**

7 Events, dear boy. Events.
popular version of Harold Macmillan's summary of a politician's biggest problem (see **Macmillan 200:5**)

8 Few die and none resign.
popular summary of a letter of Thomas **Jefferson**, 1801; see **Jefferson 156:4**

9 A good day to bury bad news.
popular misquotation of Jo **Moore**'s email of 11 September 2001; see **Moore 218:13**

10 The green shoots of recovery.
popular misquotation of Norman **Lamont**'s upbeat assessment of the economic situation, 9 October 1991; see **Lamont 177:3**

11 Hawking his conscience round the Chancelleries of Europe.
popular version of Ernest **Bevin**'s description of Lansbury, 1935; see **Bevin 31:13**

12 I disapprove of what you say, but I will defend to the death your right to say it.
to the French philosopher Helvétius (1715–71), following the burning of Helvétius's book De l'esprit *in 1759*
attributed to **Voltaire**, but in fact a later summary of his attitude by S. G. Tallentyre in *The Friends of Voltaire* (1907); see **Voltaire 323:11**

13 I fear we have only awakened a sleeping giant, and his reaction will be terrible.
of the attack on Pearl Harbor, 1941
attributed to the Japanese admiral Isoruko Yamamoto, but not found earlier than in *Tora! Tora! Tora!* (1970 film), written by Larry Forrester, Hideo Oguni, and Ryuzo Kikushima; see **Yamamoto 339:1**

14 In trust I have found treason.
traditional concluding words of a speech by **Elizabeth I** to a Parliamentary deputation at Richmond, 12 November 1586; see **Elizabeth 103:13**

15 It is necessary only for the good man to do nothing for evil to triumph.
attributed (in a number of forms) to **Burke**, but not found in his writings; see **Burke 48:14**

16 Just a heart-beat away from the Presidency of the United States.
popular version of Adlai **Stevenson**'s description of the Vice-Presidency, 23 October 1952; see **Stevenson 301:3**

17 Laws are like sausages. It's better not to see them being made.
attributed to **Bismarck**, but not traced and probably apocryphal

Misquotations *continued*

1 My lips are sealed.
popular version of **Baldwin**'s speech on the Abyssinian crisis, 10 December 1935; see **Baldwin 22:9**

2 Selling off the family silver.
popular summary of Harold **Macmillan**'s attack on privatization, 8 November 1985; see **Macmillan 200:3**

3 The soft underbelly of Europe.
popular version of **Churchill**'s words in the House of Commons, 11 November 1942; see **Churchill 68:3**

4 Something must be done.
popular version of **Edward VIII**'s words at the derelict Dowlais Iron and Steel Works, 18 November 1936; see **Edward VIII 101:11**

5 Take away these baubles.
popular version of **Cromwell**'s words at the dismissal of the Rump Parliament, 20 April 1653; see **Cromwell 82:13**

6 Warts and all.
popular summary of **Cromwell**'s *instructions to the court painter Lely: 'Mr Lely, I desire you would use all your skill to paint my picture truly like me, and not flatter me at all; but remark all these roughnesses, pimples, warts, and everything as you see me; otherwise I will never pay a farthing for it'*
Horace Walpole *Anecdotes of Painting in England* vol. 3 (1763) ch. 1

7 We are the masters now.
popular misquotation of Hartley **Shawcross**'s speech in the House of Commons, 2 April 1946; see **Shawcross 286:17**

8 We must educate our masters.
popular version of Robert **Lowe**'s comment on the passing of the Reform Bill, 1867; see **Lowe 191:7**

9 We must guard even our enemies against injustice.
Graham Greene's version of Thomas **Paine**'s *Dissertation on the First Principles of Government*; see **Paine 236:16**

10 What a glorious morning for America.
popular version of the words of Samuel **Adams** on hearing gunfire at Lexington, 19 April 1775; see **Adams 4:3**

11 What are you going to do about it?
supposed reply of 'Boss' **Tweed** to those protesting at the political corruption of New York under the control of the Tweed Ring; see **Nast 224:9**

12 The white heat of technology.
popular version of Harold **Wilson**'s speech at the Labour Party Conference, 1 October 1963; see **Wilson 334:5**

Walter Mondale 1928–
American Democratic politician

13 When I hear your new ideas I'm reminded of that ad, 'Where's the beef?'
alluding to an advertising slogan which made an unfavourable comparison between the relative sizes of a small hamburger and a large bun
in a televised debate with Gary Hart, 11 March 1984

14 Political image is like mixing cement. When it's wet, you can move it around and shape it, but at some point it hardens and there's almost nothing you can do to reshape it.
in *Independent on Sunday* 12 May 1991

Duke of Monmouth 1649–85
British peer, illegitimate son of Charles II; focus of the supporters of the Protestant succession in the Exclusion crisis of 1681 (see **Dryden**) and leader of the failed Monmouth rebellion against James II

15 Do not hack me as you did my Lord Russell.
words addressed to his executioner; according to a contemporary account five blows were needed
T. B. Macaulay *History of England* vol. 1 (1849)

Jean Monnet 1888–1979
French economist and diplomat; founder of the European Community

16 Europe has never existed. It is not the addition of national sovereignties in a conclave which creates an entity. One must

genuinely *create* Europe.
Anthony Sampson *The New Europeans* (1968)

1 The common market is a process, not a product.
Anthony Sampson *The New Europeans* (1968)

2 I did not understand the politics of Versailles, only the economics.
of the Treaty of Versailles
in an interview in 1971; François Duchêne *Jean Monnet* (1994)

3 A great statesman is one who can work for long-term goals which eventually suit situations as yet unforeseen.
Memoirs (1978)

4 Each man begins the world afresh. Only institutions grow wiser; they store up the collective experience; and, from this experience and wisdom, men subject to the same laws will gradually find, not that their natures change but that their experience does.
a favourite sentiment ascribed by Monnet to the nineteenth-century Genevese diarist Henri Frédéric Amiel
François Duchêne *Jean Monnet* (1994)

5 Institutions govern relationships between people. They are the real pillars of civilization.
François Duchêne *Jean Monnet* (1994)

6 We should not create a nation Europe instead of a nation France.
François Duchêne *Jean Monnet* (1994)

James Monroe 1758–1831
American Democratic Republican statesman, 5th President of the US 1817–25

7 We owe it...to the amicable relations existing between the United States and those [European] powers to declare that we should consider any attempt on their part to extend their system to any portion of this hemisphere as dangerous to our peace and safety.
principle that became known as the 'Monroe Doctrine'
annual message to Congress, 2 December 1823

8 The American continents...are henceforth not to be considered as subjects for future colonization by

any European powers.
annual message to Congress, 2 December 1823

Montaigne 1533–92
French moralist and essayist

9 There is scarcely any less bother in the running of a family than in that of an entire state. And domestic business is no less importunate for being less important.
Essays (1580)

10 Fame and tranquillity can never be bedfellows.
Essays (1580)

11 Tortures are a dangerous invention, and seem to be a test of endurance rather than of truth.
Essays (1580)

12 On the highest throne in the world, we still sit only on our own bottom.
Essays (1580)

Montesquieu 1689–1755
French political philosopher

13 That huge distemper'd body does not support itself by a mild and temperate regimen; but by violent remedies, which are incessantly corroding and exhausting its strength.
*of the Ottoman empire; see **Nicholas I***
Lettres Persanes (1721)

14 Thou knowest that ever since the invention of gunpowder...I continually tremble lest men should, in the end, uncover some secret which would provide a short way of abolishing mankind, of annihilating peoples and nations in their entirety.
Lettres Persanes (1721)

15 Republics end in luxury; monarchies, in poverty.
The Spirit of the Laws (1748)

16 The corruption of each government almost always begins with that of its principles.
The Spirit of the Laws (1748)

17 The principle of democracy is corrupted not only when the spirit of equality is lost but also when the

spirit of extreme equality is taken up and each one wants to be the equal of those chosen to command.
The Spirit of the Laws (1748)

1 If a republic is small, it is destroyed by a foreign force; if it is large, it is destroyed by an internal vice.
The Spirit of the Laws (1748)

2 Liberty is the right to do everything the laws permit.
The Spirit of the Laws (1748)

3 It has eternally been observed that any man who has power is led to abuse it.
The Spirit of the Laws (1748)

4 The English have taken their idea of political government from the Germans. This fine system was found in the forests.
The Spirit of the Laws (1748)

5 This state [England] will perish when legislative power is more corrupt than executive power.
The Spirit of the Laws (1748)

6 Royal authority is a great spring that should move easily and noiselessly.
The Spirit of the Laws (1748)

7 In moderate states, there is a compensation for heavy taxes; it is liberty. In despotic states, there is an equivalent for liberty; it is the modest taxes.
The Spirit of the Laws (1748)

8 Lands produce less by reason of their fertility than by reason of the liberty of their inhabitants.
Alexis de Tocqueville *The Ancien Régime* (1856); attributed

Lord Montgomery 1887–1976
British field marshal

9 War is a very rough game, but I think that politics is worse.
attributed, 1956

10 Rule 1, on page 1 of the book of war, is: 'Do not march on Moscow'... [Rule 2] is: 'Do not go fighting with your land armies in China.'
in the House of Lords, 30 May 1962

James Graham, Marquess of Montrose 1612–50
Scottish royalist general and poet

11 Great, Good and Just, could I but rate
My grief to thy too rigid fate!
'Epitaph on King Charles I'

12 Let them bestow on every airth a limb;
Then open all my veins, that I may swim
To thee, my Maker! in that crimson lake;
Then place my parboiled head upon a stake—
Scatter my ashes—strew them in the air;—
Lord! since thou know'st where all these atoms are,
I'm hopeful thou'lt recover once my dust,
And confident thou'lt raise me with the just.
'Lines written on the Window of his Jail the Night before his Execution'

Jo Moore
British government adviser

13 It is now a very good day to get out anything we want to bury.
email sent in the aftermath of the terrorist action in America, 11 September 2001
in *Daily Telegraph* 10 October 2001; see also **Misquotations 215:9**

Thomas More 1478–1535
English scholar and saint; Lord Chancellor of England, 1529–32. On More: see **Whittington 332:8**; see also **Last words 179:11**

14 Your sheep, that were wont to be so meek and tame, and so small eaters, now, as I hear say, be become so great devourers, and so wild, that they eat up and swallow down the very men themselves.
Utopia (1516); following the marginal précis 'The Disaster Produced by Standing Military Garrisons'

15 Anyone who campaigns for public office becomes disqualified for holding any office at all.
Utopia (1516)

1 If the parties will at my hands call for justice, then, all were it my father stood on the one side, and the Devil on the other, his cause being good, the Devil should have right.
William Roper *Life of Sir Thomas More*

2 'By god's body, master More, *Indignatio principis mors est* [The anger of the sovereign is death].' 'Is that all, my Lord?' quoth he [to the Duke of Norfolk]. 'Then in good faith is there no more difference between your grace and me, but that I shall die to-day, and you tomorrow.'
William Roper *Life of Sir Thomas More*

3 Is not this house [the Tower of London] as nigh heaven as my own?
William Roper *Life of Sir Thomas More*

4 I pray you, master Lieutenant, see me safe up, and my coming down let me shift for my self.
on mounting the scaffold
William Roper *Life of Sir Thomas More*

Rhodri Morgan 1939–
British Labour politician

5 I thought you were the original professor of rotational medicine.
*to Bernard **Ingham**, who was appearing before the Commons public administration select committee*
in *Mail on Sunday* 7 June 1998 'Quotes of the Week'

6 We cannot allow the culling of First Secretaries to become Wales's own annual blood sport. My number one target as First Secretary is to survive until the half-term recess at the end of this week.
on succeeding Alun Michael as First Secretary for Wales
in *Observer* 20 February 2000 'They Said What…?'

John Morley 1838–1923
British Liberal politician and writer

7 The golden Gospel of Silence is effectively compressed in thirty fine volumes.
*on **Carlyle**'s History of Frederick the Great (1858–65), Carlyle having written of his subject as 'that strong, silent man'*
Critical Miscellanies (1886) 'Carlyle'

8 Simplicity of character is no hindrance to subtlety of intellect.
Life of Gladstone (1903)

9 You have not converted a man, because you have silenced him.
On Compromise (1874)

10 *of parliamentary life:*
Having the singular peculiarity of being neither business nor rest.
Recollections (1917) vol. 1

11 The proper memory for a politician is one that knows what to remember and what to forget.
Recollections (1917)

12 Although in Cabinet all its members stand on an equal footing, speak with equal voices and, on the rare occasions when a division is taken, are counted on the fraternal principle of one man, one vote, yet the head of the Cabinet is *primus inter pares*, and occupies a position which, so long as it lasts, is one of exceptional and peculiar authority.
Walpole (1889)

Estelle Morris 1952–
British Labour politician

13 I am not good at dealing with the modern media…I have not felt I have been as effective as I should be, or as effective as you need me to be.
resignation letter to Tony Blair, 23 October 2002; in *Guardian* 24 October 2002 (electronic edition)

William Morris 1834–96
English writer, artist, and designer

14 What is this, the sound and rumour? What is this that all men hear,
Like the wind in hollow valleys when the storm is drawing near,
Like the rolling on of ocean in the eventide of fear?

'Tis the people marching on.
Chants for Socialists (1885) 'The March of the Workers'

Herbert Morrison 1888–1965
British Labour politician, grandfather of Peter **Mandelson**

1 Work is the call. Work at war speed. Good-night—and go to it.
broadcast as Minister of Supply, 22 May 1940

2 It is no good, we cannot do it, the Durham miners won't wear it.
on the plan for a European Coal and Steel Community
in 1950; B. Donoghue and G. Jones *Herbert Morrison* (1973)

3 Socialism is what the Labour Government does.
attributed

Dwight D. Morrow 1873–1931
American lawyer, banker, and diplomat

4 Any party which takes credit for the rain must not be surprised if its opponents blame it for the drought.
attributed; William Safire *Safire's New Political Dictionary* (1993)

Wayne Lyman Morse 1900–74
American Democratic politician

5 I believe that history will record that we have made a great mistake.
in the Senate debate on the Tonkin Gulf Resolution, which committed the United States to intervention in Vietnam; Morse was the only Senator to vote against the resolution
in *Congressional Record* 6–7 August 1964

Owen Morshead 1893–1977
English librarian

6 The House of Hanover, like ducks, produce bad parents—they trample on their young.
*in conversation with Harold **Nicolson**, biographer of **George V***
Harold Nicolson, letter to Vita Sackville-West, 7 January 1949

Rogers Morton 1914–79
American public relations officer

7 I'm not going to rearrange the

furniture on the deck of the Titanic.
*having lost five of the last six primaries as President **Ford**'s campaign manager*
in *Washington Post* 16 May 1976

Nicholas Mosley 1923–
British writer

8 While the right hand dealt with grandiose ideas and glory, the left hand let the rat out of the sewer.
of his father, Oswald Mosley, as leader of the British Union of Fascists
Robert Skidelsky *Oswald Mosley* (1975)

Oswald Mosley 1896–1980
British politician and Fascist leader

9 I am not, and never have been, a man of the right. My position was on the left and is now in the centre of politics.
letter to *Times* 26 April 1968

John Lothrop Motley 1814–77
American historian

10 As long as he lived, he was the guiding-star of a whole brave nation, and when he died the little children cried in the streets.
of William the Silent, Prince of Orange (1533–84)
The Rise of the Dutch Republic (1856); see **Auden 15:9**

Lord Mountbatten 1900–79
British sailor, soldier, and statesman. On Mountbatten: see **Templer 308:4**

11 Right, now I understand people think you're the Forgotten Army on the Forgotten Front. I've come here to tell you you're quite wrong. You're not the Forgotten Army on the Forgotten Front. No, make no mistake about it. Nobody's ever *heard* of you.
encouragement to troops when taking over as Supreme Allied Commander South-East Asia in late 1943
R. Hough *Mountbatten* (1980)

12 The nuclear arms race has no military purpose. Wars cannot be fought with nuclear weapons. Their existence only adds to our perils.
speech at Strasbourg, 11 May 1979

Mottoes

1 *Aut Caesar, aut nihil.*
Caesar or nothing.
motto inscribed on the sword of Cesare Borgia
(1476–1507)

2 The buck stops here.
motto on the desk of Harry S **Truman**

3 *Fiat justitia et pereat mundus.*
Let justice be done, though the
world perish.
motto of Ferdinand I (1503–64), Holy
Roman Emperor; Johannes Manlius *Locorum
Communium Collectanea* (1563) vol. 2 'De
Lege: Octatum Praeceptum'; see **Adams 3:15**,
Watson 326:11

4 *Honi soit qui mal y pense.*
Evil be to him who evil thinks.
motto of the Order of the Garter, originated by

Edward III (1312–77), probably on 23 April of
1348 or 1349

5 *Nemo me impune lacessit.*
No one provokes me with impunity.
motto of the Crown of Scotland and of all
Scottish regiments

6 Rebellion to tyrants is
obedience to God.
motto of Thomas **Jefferson**, from John
Bradshaw; see **Bradshaw 40:8**

7 *Semper eadem.*
Ever the same.
motto of **Elizabeth I**

8 *Sic semper tyrannis.*
Thus always to tyrants.
motto of the State of Virginia; see **Booth 39:4**

Marjorie ('Mo') Mowlam
1949–2005
British Labour politician

9 It takes courage to push things
forward.
*on her decision to visit Loyalist prisoners in The
Maze*
in *Guardian* 8 January 1998

10 You can't switch on peace like a
light.
in *Independent* 6 September 1999

Hosni Mubarak 1928–
Egyptian statesman, President since 1981

11 Instead of having one [Osama] bin
Laden, we will have 100 bin Ladens.
*on the probable result of a western invasion of
Iraq*
in *Newsweek* 14 April 2003

Robert Mugabe 1924–
African statesman; Prime Minister of Zimbabwe,
1980–7, President 1987–

12 Cricket civilizes people and creates
good gentlemen. I want everyone
to play cricket in Zimbabwe; I want
ours to be a nation of gentlemen.
in *Sunday Times* 26 February 1984

13 Our present state of mind is that

you are now our enemies.
to white farmers in Zimbabwe
television broadcast, 18 April 2000

14 Blair, keep your England and let me
keep my Zimbabwe.
at the Earth Summit in Johannesburg,
2 September 2002

15 We are not going to give up our
country for a mere X on a ballot.
How can a ballpoint pen fight with
a gun?
*refusing to cede power regardless of the results of
the forthcoming election*
in *Herald* [Zimbabwe] 16 June 2008, reported
in *Guardian* 17 June 2008

Malcolm Muggeridge 1903–90
British journalist

16 To succeed pre-eminently in
English public life it is necessary
to conform either to the popular
image of a bookie or of a clergyman;
Churchill being a perfect example
of the former, Halifax of the latter.
The Infernal Grove (1973)

17 He was not only a bore; he bored for
England.
*of Anthony **Eden***
Tread Softly (1966)

Robert Muldoon 1921–92
New Zealand statesman, Prime Minister 1975–84

1 When New Zealanders emigrate to
Australia, it raises the average IQ of
both countries.
   attributed

Brian Mulroney 1939–
Canadian Conservative statesman, Prime Minister
1984–93

2 *challenging the Prime Minister, John
Turner, for his approval of the patronage
appointments made by the retiring Prime
Minister, Pierre Trudeau:*
You had an option, sir. You could
have said, 'I am not going to do it.
This is wrong for Canada. And I am
not going to ask Canadians to pay
the price.' You had an option, sir,
to say no, and you chose to say yes,
yes to the old attitudes and the old
stories of the Liberal Party.
   televised debate between national leaders,
   25 July 1984

Rupert Murdoch 1931–
Australian-born American publisher and media
entrepreneur

3 I have heard cynics who say he's a
very political old monk shuffling
around in Gucci shoes.
   on the Dalai Lama
   in *Daily Telegraph* 7 September 1999

Ed Murrow 1908–65
American broadcaster and journalist

4 I admired your history, doubted
your future.
   of Britain in the 1930s
   radio broadcast; in *Listener* 28 February 1946

5 Future generations who bother
to read the official record of
proceedings in the House of
Commons will discover that British
armies retreated from many places,
but that there was no retreat from
the principles for which your
ancestors fought.
   radio broadcast; in *Listener* 28 February 1946

6 No one can terrorize a whole
nation, unless we are all his
accomplices.
   of Joseph McCarthy
   'See It Now', broadcast, 7 March 1954

7 *of Winston Churchill:*
He mobilized the English language
and sent it into battle to steady his
fellow countrymen and hearten
those Europeans upon whom the
long dark night of tyranny had
descended.
   broadcast, 30 November 1954; *In Search of
   Light* (1967)

8 When the politicians complain that
TV turns their proceedings into a
circus, it should be made plain that
the circus was already there, and
that TV has merely demonstrated
that not all the performers are well
trained.
   attributed, 1959

9 Anyone who isn't confused doesn't
really understand the situation.
   on the Vietnam War
   Walter Bryan *The Improbable Irish* (1969)

Benito Mussolini 1883–1945
Italian Fascist dictator

10 We must leave exactly on time…
From now on everything must
function to perfection.
   to a stationmaster
   Giorgio Pini *Mussolini* (1939) vol. 2

Sarojini Naidu 1879–1949
Indian politician

1 If only Bapu [Gandhi] knew the cost of setting him up in poverty!
   A. Campbell-Johnson *Mission with Mountbatten* (1951)

Tom Nairn
Scottish writer

2 As far as I am concerned, Scotland will be reborn when the last minister is strangled with the last copy of the *Sunday Post*.
   'The Dreams of Scottish Nationalism'; Karl Miller (ed.) *Memoirs of a Modern Scotland* (1970); see **Meslier 211:5**

Lewis Namier 1888–1960
Polish-born British historian

3 What matters most about political ideas is the underlying emotions, the music, to which ideas are a mere libretto, often of very inferior quality.
   Personalities and Powers (1955)

4 No number of atrocities however horrible can deprive a nation of its right to independence, nor justify its being put under the heel of its worst enemies and persecutors.
   in 1919; Julia Namier *Lewis Namier* (1971)

Napoleon I 1769–1821
French monarch, Emperor 1804–15. See also
Mazarin 208:8

5 What I have done so far is nothing. I am only at the beginning of the career that lies before me.
   in May 1796; F. Furcet *The French Revolution 1770–1814* (1996)

6 Think of it, soldiers; from the summit of these pyramids, forty centuries look down upon you.
   speech to the Army of Egypt on 21 July 1798, before the Battle of the Pyramids
   Gaspard Gourgaud *Mémoires* (1823) vol. 2 'Égypte—Bataille des Pyramides'

7 It [the Channel] is a mere ditch, and will be crossed as soon as someone has the courage to attempt it.
   letter to Consul Cambacérès, 16 November 1803

8 Let us be masters of the Channel for six hours, and we are masters of the world.
   1803; J. R. Green *History of the English People* (1880) vol. 4, ch. 9

9 A prince who gets a reputation for good nature in the first year of his reign, is laughed at in the second.
   letter to the King of Holland, 4 April 1807

10 It is easier to put up with unpleasantness from a man of one's own way of thinking than from one who takes an entirely different point of view.
   letter to J. Finckenstein, 14 April 1807

11 I want the whole of Europe to have one currency; it will make trading much easier.
   letter to his brother Louis, 6 May 1807

12 It is a matter of great interest what sovereigns are doing; but as to what Grand Duchesses are doing—Who cares?
   letter, 17 December 1811

13 There is only one step from the sublime to the ridiculous.
   to De Pradt, Polish ambassador, after the retreat from Moscow in 1812
   D. G. De Pradt *Histoire de l'Ambassade dans le grand-duché de Varsovie en 1812* (1815)

14 France has more need of me than I

have need of France.
speech to the Corps Législatif, Paris,
31 December 1813

1 As to moral courage, I have very
rarely met with two o'clock in
the morning courage: I mean
instantaneous courage.
E. A. de Las Cases *Mémorial de Ste-Hélène*
(1823) vol. 1, 4–5 December 1815

2 An army marches on its stomach.
attributed, but probably condensed from a
long passage in E. A. de Las Cases *Mémorial de
Ste-Hélène* (1823) vol. 4, 14 November 1816;
also attributed to **Frederick the Great**

3 *when asked how to deal with the Pope:*
As though he had 200,000 men.
J. M. Robinson *Cardinal Consalvi* (1987); see
Stalin 299:5

4 The career open to the talents.
Barry E. O'Meara *Napoleon in Exile* (1822)
vol. 1

5 England is a nation of shopkeepers.
Barry E. O'Meara *Napoleon in Exile* (1822)
vol. 2; see **Adams 4:4, Smith 293:4**

6 Nothing is more contrary to the
organization of the mind, of the
memory, and of the imagination...
The new system of weights and
measures will be a stumbling
block and the source of difficulties
for several generations...It's just
tormenting the people with trivia!!!
on the introduction of the metric system
Mémoires...écrits à Ste-Hélène (1823–5)

7 Not tonight, Josephine.
attributed, but probably apocryphal; R. H.
Horne *The History of Napoleon* (1841) vol. 2
describes the circumstances in which the
affront may have occurred

8 *of **Talleyrand**:*
A pile of shit in a silk stocking.
attributed

Thomas Nast 1840–1902
German-born American cartoonist, whose work
was highly damaging to 'Boss' **Tweed**'s Tammany
domination of New York

9 The Boss. 'Well, what are you going
to do about it?'
*caption to a cartoon entitled 'Under the
Thumb' showing a giant hand, with **Tweed**'s
name on the cufflink, putting its thumb down*

over Manhattan
in *Harper's Weekly* 10 June 1871; a later cartoon
of 11 November 1871 depicted 'The Tammany
Tiger Loose: "What are you going to do about
it?"' (see also **Misquotations 216:11**)

Jawaharlal Nehru 1889–1964
Indian statesman. On Nehru: see **Patil 241:6**

10 At the stroke of the midnight hour,
while the world sleeps, India will
awake to life and freedom.
immediately prior to Independence
speech to the Indian Constituent Assembly,
14 August 1947

11 The light has gone out of our lives
and there is darkness everywhere.
*broadcast, 30 January 1948, following **Gandhi**'s
assassination*
Richard J. Walsh *Nehru on Gandhi* (1948)

12 I may lose many things including
my temper, but I do not lose my
nerve.
at a press conference in Delhi, 4 June 1958

13 Democracy and socialism are
means to an end, not the end itself.
'Basic Approach'; written for private circulation
and reprinted in Vincent Shean *Nehru: the
Years of Power* (1960)

14 Normally speaking, it may be
said that the forces of a capitalist
society, if left unchecked, tend to
make the rich richer and the poor
poorer and thus increase the gap
between them.
'Basic Approach' in Vincent Shean *Nehru...*
(1960)

15 History is almost always written
by the victors and conquerors and
gives their viewpoint.
The Discovery of India (1946)

16 There is no easy walk-over to
freedom anywhere, and many of us
will have to pass through the valley
of the shadow again and again
before we reach the mountain-tops
of our desire.
'From Lucknow to Tripuri' (1939)

17 After every other Viceroy has
been forgotten, Curzon will be
remembered because he restored
all that was beautiful in India.
in conversation with Lord Swinton; Kenneth
Rose *Superior Person* (1969)

Newspaper headlines and leaders

1 Bush Wins It.
original headline in the Miami Herald *for 8 November 2000; changed in final edition to 'It's Not Over Yet'*
in *Daily Telegraph* 9 November 2000

2 *on the suggestion that* **Edward VIII** *could marry Wallis Simpson without her becoming Queen:*
The constitution is to be amended in order that she [Mrs Simpson] may carry in solitary prominence the brand of unfitness for the Queen's Throne.
leader in *Times* 8 December 1936

3 Crisis? What crisis?
summarizing an interview with James **Callaghan**
headline in *Sun*, 11 January 1979; see **Misquotations 215:5**

4 Dewey defeats Truman.
anticipating the result of the Presidential election, which **Truman** *won against expectation*
in *Chicago Tribune* 3 November 1948

5 Downing Street's dodgy dossier of 'intelligence' about Iraq.
referring to a briefing document on Iraqi weaponry which was later withdrawn
leading article, *Observer* 9 February 2003

6 45 Minutes from Attack.
Evening Standard 24 September 2002

7 GOTCHA!
on the sinking of the General Belgrano
headline in *Sun* 4 May 1982

8 Go West, young man, go West!
editorial in *Terre Haute* [Indiana] *Express* (1851), by John L. B. Soule (1815–91)

9 If Kinnock wins today will the last person to leave Britain please turn out the lights.
on election day, showing Neil Kinnock's head inside a light bulb
headline in *Sun* 9 April 1992

10 In that case, it might be worthwhile for the Czechoslovak government to consider whether they should exclude altogether the project, which has found favour in some quarters, of making Czechoslovakia a more homogeneous State, by the secession of that fringe of alien populations who are contiguous to the nation with which they are united by race.
referring to the Sudeten Germans
leader in *Times* 7 September 1938

11 IS THIS the most dangerous man in Britain?
headline beside a picture of Tony **Blair**, *attacking his perceived sympathy for the euro*
in *Sun* 25 June 1998

12 It *is* a moral issue.
leader following the resignation of Profumo
in *Times* 11 June 1963, written by William Haley (1901–87)

13 It's that man again…! At the head of a cavalcade of seven black motor cars Hitler swept out of his Berlin Chancellery last night on a mystery journey.
headline in *Daily Express* 2 May 1939; the acronym ITMA became the title of a BBC radio show, from September 1939

14 It's The Sun wot won it.
following the 1992 general election
headline in *Sun* 11 April 1992

15 King's Moll Reno'd in Wolsey's Home Town.
US newspaper headline on the divorce proceedings of Wallis Simpson (later Duchess of Windsor) in Ipswich
Frances Donaldson *Edward VIII* (1974)

16 Most Conservatives, and almost certainly some of the wiser Trade Union leaders, are waiting to feel the *smack of firm government.*
on the government of Anthony Eden
editorial comment in *Sunday Telegraph* 3 January 1956, written by Donald McLachlan

17 Only a sentence, but what a sentence!
on Prince Charles' speech referring to the Falklands
in *La Nación* (Buenos Aires) 11 March 1999

18 Outside the G.O.P.'s big tent, hoping he's let back in.
of the former Republican Robert C. Smith, whose independent campaign for the presidential nomination had failed; G.O.P. = 'Grand Old Party'
headline in *New York Times* 1 November 1999; see **Slogans 290:8**

Newspaper headlines and leaders *continued*

1 Splendid isolation.
   headline in *Times* 22 January 1896, referring to George **Foster**'s speech in the Canadian House of Commons; see **Foster 112:8**

2 The Sun backs Blair.
   the day after the announcement of the general election
   headline in *Sun* 18 March 1997

3 Unless the people—the people everywhere—come forward and petition, ay, thunder for reform.
   leader on the Reform Bill, possibly written by Edward Sterling (1773–1847), resulting in the nickname 'The Thunderer'
   in *Times* 29 January 1831; the phrase 'we thundered out' had been used earlier, 11 February 1829

4 Wall St. lays an egg.
   crash headline, *Variety* 30 October 1929

5 We shall not pretend that there is nothing in his long career which those who respect and admire him would wish otherwise.
   on Edward VII's accession to the throne
   in *Times* 23 January 1901, leading article

6 Whose finger do you want on the trigger?
   headline alluding to the atom bomb, apropos the failure of both the Labour and Conservative parties to purge their leaders of proven failures
   in *Daily Mirror* 21 September 1951

7 Winter of discontent.
   headline in *Sun* 30 April 1979, after Shakespeare; see **Callaghan 53:11**, **Shakespeare 284:11**

8 I shall be the last Englishman to rule in India.
   J. K. Galbraith *A Life in Our Times* (1981)

Horatio, Lord Nelson 1758–1805
British admiral

9 In case signals cannot be seen, or perfectly understood, no captain can do very wrong if he places his ship alongside that of an enemy.
   memorandum to commanders of ships before the battle of Trafalgar, 10 October 1805, in *The Naval Chronicle* vol. 14 (1805)

10 England expects that every man will do his duty.
   signal at the battle of Trafalgar, 21 October 1805; Robert Southey *Life of Nelson* (1813) ch. 9

Huey Newton 1942–89
American political activist

11 I suggested [in 1966] that we use the panther as our symbol and call our political vehicle the Black Panther Party. The panther is a fierce animal, but he will not attack until he is backed into a corner; then he will strike out.
   Revolutionary Suicide (1973)

Nicholas I 1796–1855
Russian monarch, emperor from 1825

12 Turkey is a dying man. We may endeavour to keep him alive, but we shall not succeed. He will, he must die.
   origin of the expression 'the sick man of Europe' referring to Ottoman Turkey
   F. Max Müller (ed.) *Memoirs of Baron Stockmar* (1873)

13 Russia has two generals in whom she can confide—Generals Janvier [January] and Février [February].
   attributed; in *Punch* 10 March 1855

Nicias c. 470–413 BC
Greek politician and Athenian general

14 For a city consists in men, and not

New Zealand
'When New Zealanders emigrate'
see Selective Subject Index

in walls nor in ships empty of men.
speech to the defeated Athenian army at Syracuse, 413 BC
Thucydides *History of the Peloponnesian Wars*

Harold Nicolson 1886–1968
English diplomat, politician, and writer

1 Ponderous and uncertain is that relation between pressure and resistance which constitutes the balance of power. The arch of peace is morticed by no iron tendons... One night a handful of dust will patter from the vaulting: the bats will squeak and wheel in sudden panic: nor can the fragile fingers of man then stay the rush and rumble of destruction.
Public Faces (1932); see **Strafford 302:11**

2 We shall have to walk and live a Woolworth life hereafter.
anticipating the aftermath of the Second World War
diary, 4 June 1941

3 I am haunted by mental decay such as I saw creeping over Ramsay MacDonald. A gradual dimming of the lights.
diary, 28 April 1947

4 *comparing* **Attlee** *as a public speaker with Winston* **Churchill**:
Like a village fiddler after Paganini.
diary, 10 November 1947

5 I do not think it is quite fair to say that the British businessman has trampled on the faces of the poor. But he has sometimes not been very careful where he put his feet.
replying to a heckler in the North Croydon by-election, 1948
Nigel Nicolson (ed.) *Diaries and Letters of Harold Nicolson 1945–1962* vol. 3 (1968)

6 For seventeen years he did nothing at all but kill animals and stick in stamps.
of **George V** *as a subject for biography*
letter to Vita Sackville-West, 17 August 1949

7 Suez—a smash and grab raid that was all smash and no grab.
in conversation with Antony Jay, November 1956; see also letter to Vita Sackville-West, 8 November 1956, 'Our smash-and-grab raid got stuck at the smash'

Nigel Nicolson 1917–2004
British Conservative politician and writer; son of Harold **Nicolson**

8 There is no place where a man can occupy himself more intensively or usefully, and no place where he can hold down his job by doing so little.
of the House of Commons
People and Parliament (1958)

Reinhold Niebuhr 1892–1971
American theologian

9 Man's capacity for justice makes democracy possible, but man's inclination to injustice makes democracy necessary.
Children of Light and Children of Darkness (1944) foreword

Martin Niemöller 1892–1984
German theologian

10 When Hitler attacked the Jews I was not a Jew, therefore, I was not concerned. And when Hitler attacked the Catholics, I was not a Catholic, and therefore, I was not concerned. And when Hitler attacked the unions and the industrialists, I was not a member of the unions and I was not concerned. Then, Hitler attacked me and the Protestant church— and there was nobody left to be concerned.
often quoted in the form 'In Germany they came first for the Communists, and I didn't speak up because I wasn't a Communist...' and so on
in *Congressional Record* 14 October 1968

Friedrich Nietzsche 1844–1900
German philosopher and writer

11 I teach you the superman. Man is something to be surpassed.
Also Sprach Zarathustra (1883) prologue

12 Morality is the herd-instinct in the individual.
Die fröhliche Wissenschaft (1882)

13 Master-morality and slave-morality.
Jenseits von Gut und Böse (1886)

14 At the base of all these aristocratic

races the predator is not to be mistaken, the splendorous *blond beast*, avidly rampant for plunder and victory.
Zur Genealogie der Moral (1887)

Richard Milhous Nixon 1913–94
American Republican statesman, 37th President of the US. On Nixon: see **Abzug 1:3, Anonymous 7:9, Conable 78:6, Johnson 159:4, Roosevelt 261:10, Slogans 292:3, Stevenson 301:12, Ziegler 341:1**

1 She's pink right down to her underwear.
in 1950, accusing Helen Gahagan Douglas, his opponent for a Senate seat, of Communist sympathies
Stephen E. Ambrose *Nixon: The Education of a Politician* (1987); see **Roosevelt 261:10**

2 Pat and I have the satisfaction that every dime that we've got is honestly ours...Pat doesn't have a mink coat. But she does have a respectable Republican cloth coat. And I always tell her that she'd look good in anything.
having been elected as Vice-President in 1952, in response to criticisms of his electoral campaign
speech on television, 23 September 1952

3 *of the post-election gift of a cocker spaniel, named Checkers by his small daughter:*
One other thing I probably should tell you, because if I don't they'll probably be saying this about me too, we did get something—a gift—after the election...It was a little cocker-spaniel dog...The kids love that dog and I just want to say this right now, that regardless of what they say about it, we're going to keep it.
speech on television, 23 September 1952

4 There is no such thing as a nonpolitical speech by a politician.
address to Radio-Television Executives Society, New York City, 14 September 1955

5 You won't have Nixon to kick around any more.
press conference after losing the election for Governor of California, 5 November 1962, in *New York Times* 8 November 1962

6 There is nothing wrong with this country which a good election

can't fix.
at a campaign meeting during the Presidential election, in Syracuse, New York, 29 October 1968

7 Let us begin by committing ourselves to the truth, to see it like it is and tell it like it is, to find the truth, to speak the truth and to live the truth. That's what we will do.
nomination acceptance speech in Miami, 1968, in *New York Times* 9 August 1968

8 This is the greatest week in the history of the world since the Creation.
welcoming the return of the first men to land on the moon
speech, 24 July 1969

9 The great silent majority.
broadcast, 3 November 1969

10 In our own lives, let each of us ask—not just what government will do for me, but what can I do for myself?
second inaugural address, 20 January 1973; see **Kennedy 167:4**

11 There can be no whitewash at the White House.
television speech on Watergate, 30 April 1973

12 I made my mistakes, but in all my years of public life, I have never profited, never profited from public service. I've earned every cent. And in all of my years in public life I have never obstructed justice...I welcome this kind of examination because people have got to know whether or not their President is a crook. Well, I'm not a crook.
speech at press conference, 17 November 1973

13 This country needs good farmers, good businessmen, good plumbers, good carpenters.
farewell address at White House, 9 August 1974, in *New York Times* 10 August 1974

14 My own view is that taping of conversations for historical purposes was a bad decision.
attributed, 1974

15 I brought myself down. I gave them a sword. And they stuck it in.
television interview, 19 May 1977; David Frost *I Gave Them a Sword* (1978)

16 Foreign aid is the most unpopular

damn thing in the world. It is a loser politically.
in *Observer* 21 April 1985 'Sayings of the Week'

1 I played by the rules of politics as I found them. Not taking a higher road than my predecessors and my adversaries was my central mistake.
In the Arena (1990)

2 Defeat doesn't finish a man—quit does. A man is not finished when he's defeated. He's finished when he quits.
on Edward Kennedy and Chappaquiddick
William Safire *Before the Fall* (1975)

3 When the President does it, that means that it is not illegal.
in conversation; David Frost *I Gave Them a Sword* (1978)

Kwame Nkrumah 1900–72
Ghanaian statesman, Prime Minister 1957–60, President 1960–6

4 Forward ever, backward never.
motto of his Convention People's Party, *Autobiography* (1959)

5 Freedom is not something that one people can bestow on another as a gift. They claim it as their own and none can keep it from them.
speech in Accra, 10 July 1953

6 We face neither East nor West: we face forward.
conference speech, Accra, 7 April 1960; *Axioms of Kwame Nkrumah* (1967)

Peggy Noonan 1950–
American writer, speechwriter for Ronald Reagan

7 The battle for the mind of Ronald Reagan was like the trench warfare of World War I. Never have so many fought so hard for such barren terrain.
What I Saw at the Revolution (1990)

Oodgeroo Noonuccal (Kath Walker) 1920–93
Australian poet

8 My son, your troubled eyes search mine,
Puzzled and hurt by colour line.

Your black skin as soft as velvet shine;
What can I tell you, son of mine?
'Son of Mine (To Denis)' (1960)

Grover Norquist 1956–
American lobbyist

9 I don't want to abolish government. I simply want to reduce it to the size where I can drag it into the bathroom and drown it in the bathtub.
interview on National Public Radio, Morning Edition, 25 May 2001

Steven Norris 1945–
British Conservative politician

10 You have your own company, your own temperature control, your own music—and don't have to put up with dreadful human beings sitting alongside you.
on cars compared to public transport
comment to Commons Environment Select Committee, in *Daily Telegraph* 9 February 1995

Christopher North 1785–1854
Scottish literary critic

11 His Majesty's dominions, on which the sun never sets.
in *Blackwood's Magazine* (April 1829) 'Noctes Ambrosianae'

12 Laws were made to be broken.
in *Blackwood's Magazine* (May 1830) 'Noctes Ambrosianae'

13 I cannot sit still, James, and hear you abuse the shopocracy.
in *Blackwood's Magazine* (February 1835) 'Noctes Ambrosianae'

Lord North 1732–92
British statesman, Prime Minister 1770–82

14 His Majesty has thought proper to order a new Commission of the Treasury to be made out, in which I do not see your name.
letter dismissing Charles James **Fox** from office, 1774

15 Oh God! It is all over!
on receiving the news of Cornwallis's surrender at Yorktown, 19 October 1781
in *Dictionary of National Biography* (1917–)

1 Those persons who have for some time conducted the public affairs are no longer His Majesty's Ministers.
announcing the fall of his government to the House of Commons
in the House of Commons, 20 March 1782

Lord Northcliffe 1865–1922
British newspaper proprietor

2 The power of the press is very great, but not so great as the power of suppress.
office message, *Daily Mail* 1918; Reginald Rose and Geoffrey Harmsworth *Northcliffe* (1959)

3 When I want a peerage, I shall buy it like an honest man.
Tom Driberg *Swaff* (1974)

Sam Nunn 1938–
American Democratic politician

4 Don't ask, don't tell.
*summary of the **Clinton** administration's compromise policy on homosexuals serving in the armed forces*
in *New York Times* 12 May 1993

Julius Nyerere 1922–99
Tanzanian statesman, President of Tanganyika 1962–4 and of Tanzania 1964–85

5 Should we really let our people starve so we can pay our debts?
in *Guardian* 21 March 1985

6 We are a poor country and we opted for socialist policies, but to build a socialist society you have to have a developed society.
in *Observer* 28 July 1985 'Sayings of the Week'

Michael Oakeshott 1901–91
British academic

7 A plan to resist all planning may be better than its opposite, but it belongs to the same style of politics.
*of **Hayek**'s The Road to Serfdom*
Rationalism in Politics (1962)

Barack Obama 1961–
American Democratic statesman; 44th President of the US from 2009. See also **Slogans 292:6**

8 There is not a black America and a white America and Latino America and Asian America; there's the United States of America... We worship an awesome God in the blue states, and we don't like federal agents poking around our libraries in the red states.
on the view of a red and blue America divided by party
Democratic National Convention keynote address, 27 July 2004

9 The hope of a skinny kid with a funny name who believes that America has a place for him, too... The audacity of hope!
Democratic National Convention keynote address, 27 July 2004

10 The arc of history is long but it bends towards justice.
speech, George Mason University, 2 February 2007, in *Guardian* 10 February 2007; see **King 171:12**, **Parker 239:14**

11 While we breathe, we hope, and where we are met with cynicism, and doubt, and those who tell us that we can't, we will respond with that timeless creed that sums up the spirit of a people: yes we can.
speech on winning the Presidency, Chicago, 4 November 2008; see **Slogans 292:6**

12 We reject as false the choice between our safety and our ideals.
inaugural address, 20 January 2009

13 We will extend a hand if you are

Official advice

1 Careless talk costs lives.
Second World War security poster

2 Dig for Victory.
Second World War slogan, from a radio broadcast by Reginald Dorman-Smith (1899–1977), 3 October 1939: 'Let "Dig for Victory" be the motto of every one with a garden and of every able-bodied man and woman capable of digging an allotment in their spare time'

3 Don't die of ignorance.
Aids publicity campaign, 1987

4 Duck and cover.
US advice in the event of a missile attack, 1950; associated particularly with children's cartoon character 'Bert the Turtle'

5 Is your journey *really* necessary?
slogan coined to discourage Civil Servants from going home for Christmas, 1939

6 Keep calm and carry on.
poster designed by the Ministry of Information in 1939 but not used in World War II; rediscovered and popularized in the early 21st century

7 Make do and mend.
wartime slogan, 1940s

8 Smoking can seriously damage your health.
government health warning required by British law to be printed on cigarette packets from early 1970s, in form 'Smoking can damage your health'

9 *Taisez-vous! Méfiez-vous! Les oreilles ennemies vous écoutent.* Keep your mouth shut! Be on your guard! Enemy ears are listening to you.
official notice in France, 1915

willing to unclench your fist.
inaugural address, 20 January 2009

10 A man whose father less than sixty years ago might not have been served at a local restaurant can now stand before you to take a most sacred oath.
inaugural address, 20 January 2009

11 I—like every politician at the federal level—am almost entirely dependent on the media to reach my constituents…I am who the media says I am. I say what they say I say. I become who they say I've become.
The Audacity of Hope (2006)

Conor Cruise O'Brien 1917–2008
Irish politician, writer, and journalist

12 The first great act of intellectual resistance to the first great experiment in totalitarian innovation.
*of **Burke**'s writings on the French Revolution* *The Great Melody* (1992)

13 If I saw Mr Haughey buried at midnight at a crossroads, with a stake driven through his heart— politically speaking—I should

continue to wear a clove of garlic round my neck, just in case.
in *Observer* 10 October 1982

Daniel O'Connell 1775–1847
Irish nationalist leader and social reformer, elected to Parliament in 1828

14 I shall be as brief as I can upon this subject, for it is quite clear, that no man ever yet rose to address a more unwilling audience.
introducing a motion for the Repeal of the Union speech in the House of Commons, 22 April 1834

15 A NATION is starving.
in 1846; Charles Chevenix Trench *The Great Dan* (1984)

16 There is a moral electricity in the continuous expression of public opinion concentrated on a single point.
R. F. Foster *Modern Ireland* (1988)

James Ogilvy, Lord Seafield
1664–1730
Scottish lawyer, Lord Chancellor of Scotland

17 Now there's ane end of ane old song.
as he signed the engrossed exemplification of the Act of Union, 1706
in *The Lockhart Papers* (1817)

Jacqueline Kennedy Onassis
1929–94
American wife of John F. **Kennedy**, First Lady of the US 1961–3

1 The one thing I do not want to be called is First Lady. It sounds like a saddle horse.
Peter Colier and David Horowitz *The Kennedys* (1984)

2 There'll be great Presidents again—and the Johnsons are wonderful, they've been wonderful to me—but there'll never be another Camelot again.
in *Life* 6 December 1963; see **Lerner 183:2**

Paul O'Neill 1935–
American businessman and Republican politician, US Treasury Secretary 2001–3

3 Like a blind man in a roomful of deaf people.
*of George W. **Bush** in cabinet meetings*
in *Independent* 12 January 2004

Thomas ('Tip') O'Neill 1912–94
American Democratic politician; Speaker of the House of Representatives 1977–87

4 All politics is local.
in *New York Review of Books* 13 March 1989

James Oppenheim 1882–1932
American poet

5 Hearts starve as well as bodies: Give us Bread, but give us Roses.
'Bread and Roses' (1911)

J. Robert Oppenheimer 1904–67
American physicist

6 I remembered the line from the Hindu scripture, the *Bhagavad Gita*...'I am become death, the destroyer of worlds.'
on the explosion of the first atomic bomb near Alamogordo, New Mexico, 16 July 1945
Len Giovannitti and Fred Freed *The Decision to Drop the Bomb* (1965)

7 When you see something that is technically sweet, you go ahead and do it and you argue about what to do about it only after you have had your technical success. That is the way it was with the atomic bomb.
in *In the Matter of J. Robert Oppenheimer, USAEC Transcript of Hearing Before Personnel Security Board* (1954)

P. J. O'Rourke 1947–
American humorous writer and journalist

8 Giving money and power to government is like giving whisky and car keys to teenage boys.
Parliament of Whores (1991)

9 Whatever it is that the government does, sensible Americans would prefer that the government does it to somebody else. This is the idea behind foreign policy.
Parliament of Whores (1991)

10 When buying and selling are controlled by legislation, the first things to be bought and sold are legislators.
Parliament of Whores (1991)

11 Every government is a parliament of whores. The trouble is, in a democracy the whores are us.
Parliament of Whores (1991)

George Orwell 1903–50
English novelist

12 Man is the only creature that consumes without producing.
Animal Farm (1945)

13 Four legs good, two legs bad.
Animal Farm (1945)

14 All animals are equal but some animals are more equal than others.
Animal Farm (1945)

15 The Indian Empire is a despotism— benevolent, no doubt, but still a despotism with theft as its final object.
Burmese Days (1934)

16 Down here it was still the England I had known in my childhood: the railway cuttings smothered in wild flowers...the red buses, the blue policemen—all sleeping the deep, deep sleep of England, from which I

sometimes fear that we shall never wake till we are jerked out of it by the roar of bombs.
Homage to Catalonia (1938)

1 Most revolutionaries are potential Tories, because they imagine that everything can be put right by altering the *shape* of society; once that change is effected, as it sometimes is, they see no need for any other.
Inside the Whale (1940) 'Charles Dickens'

2 England...resembles a family, a rather stuffy Victorian family, with not many black sheep in it but with all its cupboards bursting with skeletons. It has rich relations who have to be kowtowed to and poor relations who are horribly sat upon, and there is a deep conspiracy of silence about the source of the family income. It is a family in which the young are generally thwarted and most of the power is in the hands of irresponsible uncles and bed-ridden aunts. Still, it is a family. It has its private language and its common memories, and at the approach of an enemy it closes its ranks. A family with the wrong members in control.
The Lion and the Unicorn (1941) pt. 1 'England Your England'

3 Probably the battle of Waterloo *was* won on the playing-fields of Eton, but the opening battles of all subsequent wars have been lost there.
The Lion and the Unicorn (1941) pt. 1 'England Your England'; see **Wellington 329:13**

4 Old maids biking to Holy Communion through the mists of the autumn mornings...these are not only fragments, but *characteristic* fragments, of the English scene.
The Lion and the Unicorn (1941) pt. 1 'England Your England'; see **Major 202:9**

5 BIG BROTHER IS WATCHING YOU.
Nineteen Eighty-Four (1949)

6 War is peace. Freedom is slavery. Ignorance is strength.
Nineteen Eighty-Four (1949)

7 Who controls the past controls the future: who controls the present controls the past.
Nineteen Eighty-Four (1949)

8 Don't you see that the whole aim of Newspeak is to narrow the range of thought? In the end we shall make thoughtcrime literally impossible, because there will be no words in which to express it.
Nineteen Eighty-Four (1949)

9 Freedom is the freedom to say that two plus two make four. If that is granted, all else follows.
Nineteen Eighty-Four (1949)

10 Syme was not only dead, he was abolished, an un-person.
Nineteen Eighty-Four (1949)

11 *Doublethink* means the power of holding two contradictory beliefs in one's mind simultaneously, and accepting both of them.
Nineteen Eighty-Four (1949)

12 Power is not a means, it is an end. One does not establish a dictatorship in order to safeguard a revolution; one makes the revolution in order to establish the dictatorship.
Nineteen Eighty-Four (1949)

13 If you want a picture of the future, imagine a boot stamping on a human face—for ever.
Nineteen Eighty-Four (1949)

14 It is only because miners sweat their guts out that superior persons can remain superior.
The Road to Wigan Pier (1937)

15 In a Lancashire cotton-town you could probably go for months on end without once hearing an 'educated' accent, whereas there can hardly be a town in the South of England where you could throw a brick without hitting the niece of a bishop.
The Road to Wigan Pier (1937)

16 The typical Socialist is...a prim little man with a white-collar job, usually a secret teetotaller and often with vegetarian leanings, with a history of Nonconformity

behind him, and, above all, with a social position which he has no intention of forfeiting.
The Road to Wigan Pier (1937)

1 To the ordinary working man, the sort you would meet in any pub on Saturday night, Socialism does not mean much more than better wages and shorter hours and nobody bossing you about.
The Road to Wigan Pier (1937)

2 We of the sinking middle class... may sink without further struggles into the working class where we belong, and probably when we get there it will not be so dreadful as we feared, for, after all, we have nothing to lose but our aitches.
The Road to Wigan Pier (1937)

3 The great enemy of clear language is insincerity. When there is a gap between one's real and one's declared aims, one turns as it were instinctively to long words and exhausted idioms, like a cuttlefish squirting out ink.
Shooting an Elephant (1950) 'Politics and the English Language'

4 In our time, political speech and writing are largely the defence of the indefensible.
Shooting an Elephant (1950) 'Politics and the English Language'

5 Political language...is designed to make lies sound truthful and murder respectable, and to give an appearance of solidity to pure wind.
Shooting an Elephant (1950) 'Politics and the English Language'

6 If liberty means anything at all it means the right to tell people what they do not want to hear.
'The Freedom of the Press' (written 1944), in *Times Literary Supplement* 15 September 1972

7 The Catholic and the Communist are alike in assuming that an opponent cannot be both honest and intelligent.
in *Polemic* January 1946 'The Prevention of Literature'

8 The quickest way of ending a war is to lose it.
in *Polemic* May 1946 'Second Thoughts on James Burnham'

John Osborne 1929–94
English dramatist

9 There aren't any good, brave causes left. If the big bang does come, and we all get killed off, it won't be in aid of the old-fashioned, grand design. It'll just be for the Brave New-nothing-very-much-thank-you. About as pointless and inglorious as stepping in front of a bus.
Look Back in Anger (1956)

10 Royalty...is the gold filling in a mouthful of decay.
'They call it cricket'; T. Maschler (ed.) *Declaration* (1957)

11 This is a letter of hate. It is for you my countrymen, I mean those men of my country who have defiled it. The men with manic fingers leading the sightless, feeble, betrayed body of my country to its death...damn you England.
in *Tribune* 18 August 1961

Arthur O'Shaughnessy 1844–81
English poet

12 One man with a dream, at pleasure
Shall go forth and conquer a crown;
And three with a new song's measure
Can trample an empire down.
'Ode' (1874)

13 For each age is a dream that is dying,
Or one that is coming to birth.
'Ode' (1874)

John L. O'Sullivan 1813–95
American journalist and diplomat

14 Understood as a central consolidated power, managing and directing the various general interests of the society, all government is evil, and the parent of evil...The best government is that which governs least.
in *United States Magazine and Democratic Review* (1837) introduction; see **Thoreau 312:2**

1 A spirit of hostile interference against us...checking the fulfilment of our manifest destiny to overspread the continent allotted by Providence for the free development of our yearly multiplying millions.
on opposition to the annexation of Texas in *United States Magazine and Democratic Review* (1845) vol. 17

James Otis 1725–83
American politician

2 Taxation without representation is tyranny.
watchword (1761) of the American Revolution in *Dictionary of American Biography*

3 Where liberty is, there is my country.
motto used by James Otis; also attributed to Benjamin **Franklin**; see **Paine 238:4**

Ovid 43 BC–C. AD 17
Roman poet

4 *Video meliora, proboque;*
Deteriora sequor.
I see the better things, and approve;
I follow the worse.
Metamorphoses

5 How you, rebellious Germany, laid your wretched head beneath the feet of the great general.
Tristia

David Owen 1938–
British Social Democratic politician

6 The price of championing human rights is a little inconsistency at times.
speech, House of Commons, 30 March 1977

7 We are fed up with fudging and mudging, with mush and slush. We need courage, conviction, and hard work.
speech to his supporters at Labour Party Conference in Blackpool, 2 October 1980

Robert Owen 1771–1858
Welsh-born socialist and philanthropist

8 All the world is queer save thee and me, and even thou art a little queer.
to his partner W. Allen, on severing business relations at New Lanark, 1828
attributed

Count Oxenstierna 1583–1654
Swedish statesman

9 Dost thou not know, my son, with how little wisdom the world is governed?
letter to his son, 1648; John Selden, in *Table Talk* (1689) 'Pope', quotes 'a certain Pope' (possibly Julius III) saying 'Thou little thinkest what *a little foolery governs the whole world!*'

John Page 1743–1808
American politician

10 We know the race is not to the swift nor the battle to the strong. Do you not think an angel rides in the whirlwind and directs this storm?
*quoted by George W. **Bush** in his first inaugural address, 20 January 2001*
letter to Thomas Jefferson, 20 July 1776; see **Addison 4:7, Bible 32:19**

William Tyler Page 1868–1942
American public servant and writer

11 I therefore believe it is my duty to my country to love it, to support its Constitution, to obey its laws, to respect its flag, and to defend it against all enemies.
American's Creed (prize-winning competition entry, 1918) in *Congressional Record* vol. 56

Thomas Paine 1737–1809
English political theorist

1 It is necessary to the happiness of man that he be mentally faithful to himself. Infidelity does not consist in believing, or in disbelieving, it consists in professing to believe what one does not believe.
The Age of Reason pt. 1 (1794)

2 Though we have been wise enough to shut and lock a door against absolute Monarchy, we at the same time have been foolish enough to put the crown in possession of the key.
Common Sense (1776)

3 Government, even in its best state, is but a necessary evil; in its worst state, an intolerable one. Government, like dress, is the badge of lost innocence; the palaces of kings are built upon the ruins of the bowers of paradise.
Common Sense (1776)

4 Monarchy and succession have laid…the world in blood and ashes.
Common Sense (1776)

5 Of more worth is one honest man to society, and in the sight of God, than all the crowned ruffians that ever lived.
Common Sense (1776)

6 'Tis not the affair of a city, a county, a province, or a kingdom; but of a continent—of at least one eighth part of the habitable globe. 'Tis not the concern of a day, a year, or an age; posterity are virtually involved in the contest. Now is the seed-time of continental union.
Common Sense (1776)

7 Any submission to, or dependence on, Great Britain, tends directly to involve this continent in European wars and quarrels, and set us at variance with nations who would otherwise seek our friendship, and against whom we have neither anger nor complaint.
Common Sense (1776)

8 *to America:*
Freedom hath been hunted round the globe. Asia and Africa have long expelled her. Europe regards her like a stranger, and England hath given her warning to depart. O! receive the fugitive, and prepare in time an asylum for mankind.
Common Sense (1776)

9 We have it in our power to begin the world over again.
Common Sense (1776)

10 As to religion, I hold it to be the indispensable duty of government to protect all conscientious professors thereof, and I know of no other business which government hath to do therewith.
Common Sense (1776)

11 These are the times that try men's souls. The summer soldier and the sunshine patriot will, in this crisis, shrink from the service of their country; but he that stands it *now*, deserves the love and thanks of men and women.
The Crisis (December 1776) introduction

12 The harder the conflict, the more glorious the triumph. What we obtain too cheap, we esteem too lightly: it is dearness only that gives everything its value.
The Crisis (December 1776) introduction

13 If there must be trouble, let it be in my day, that my child may have peace.
The Crisis (December 1776)

14 Wisdom is not the purchase of a day.
The Crisis (December 1776)

15 I love the man that can smile in trouble, that can gather strength from distress and grow brave by reflection.
The Crisis (December 1776)

16 He that would make his own liberty secure must guard even his enemy from oppression; for if he violates this duty he establishes a precedent that will reach to himself.
Dissertation on First Principles of Government (1795); see **Misquotations 216:9**

1 The religion of humanity.
Letter...on the Invasion of England (1804)

2 As he rose like a rocket, he fell like the stick.
*on Edmund **Burke**'s losing the parliamentary debate on the French Revolution to Charles James **Fox***
Letter to the Addressers on the late Proclamation (1792)

3 [Edmund Burke] is not affected by the reality of distress touching his heart, but by the showy resemblance of it striking his imagination. He pities the plumage, but forgets the dying bird.
*on **Burke**'s Reflections on the Revolution in France, 1790*
The Rights of Man (1791)

4 Lay then the axe to the root, and teach governments humanity. It is their sanguinary punishments which corrupt mankind.
The Rights of Man (1791)

5 [In France] all that class of equivocal generation, which in some countries is called *aristocracy*, and in others *nobility*, is done away, and the peer is exalted into MAN.
The Rights of Man (1791)

6 Titles are but nick-names, and every nick-name is a title.
The Rights of Man (1791)

7 The idea of hereditary legislators is as inconsistent as that of hereditary judges, or hereditary juries; and as absurd as an hereditary mathematician, or an hereditary wise man; and as ridiculous as an hereditary poet laureate.
The Rights of Man (1791)

8 Persecution is not an original feature of *any* religion; but it is always the strongly marked feature of all law-religions, or religions established by law.
The Rights of Man (1791)

9 All hereditary government is in its nature tyranny...To inherit a government, is to inherit the people, as if they were flocks and herds.
The Rights of Man pt. 2 (1792)

10 With respect to the two Houses,

of which the English Parliament is composed, they appear to be effectually influenced into one, and as a legislature, to have no temper of its own. The Minister, whoever he at any time may be, touches it as with an opium wand, and it sleeps obedience.
The Rights of Man pt. 2 (1792)

11 The candidates were not men but principles.
The Rights of Man (1791)

12 What were formerly called revolutions were little more than a change of persons...what we now see in the world, from the revolutions of America and France, is a renovation of the natural order of things.
The Rights of Man (1791)

13 The instant formal government is abolished, society begins to act. A general association takes place, and common interest produces common security.
The Rights of Man pt. 2 (1792)

14 *of monarchy:*
I compare it to something kept behind a curtain, about which there is a great deal of bustle and fuss, and a wonderful air of seeming solemnity; but when, by any accident, the curtain happens to be open, and the company see what it is, they burst into laughter.
The Rights of Man pt. 2 (1792)

15 When, in countries that are called civilized, we see age going to the workhouse and youth to the gallows, something must be wrong in the system of government.
The Rights of Man pt. 2 (1792)

16 My country is the world, and my religion is to do good.
The Rights of Man pt. 2 (1792)

17 I do not believe that any two men, on what are called doctrinal points, think alike who think at all. It is only those who have not thought that appear to agree.
The Rights of Man pt. 2 (1792)

18 To elect, and to reject, is the

prerogative of a free people.
in *National Intelligencer* 29 November 1802

1 When moral principles, rather than persons, are candidates for power, to vote is to perform a moral duty, and not to vote is to neglect a duty.
in *Trenton True-American* April 1803

2 A share in two revolutions is living to some purpose.
Eric Foner *Tom Paine and Revolutionary America* (1976)

3 When it shall be said in any country in the world, 'My poor are happy; neither ignorance nor distress is to be found among them; my jails are empty of prisoners, my streets of beggars; the aged are not in want, the taxes are not oppressive; the rational world is my friend, because I am the friend of its happiness': when these things can be said, then may that country boast of its constitution and its government.
John Keane *Tom Paine* (1995)

4 Where Liberty is not, there is my country.
John Keane *Tom Paine* (1995); see **Otis 235:3**

Ian Paisley 1926–
Northern Irish politician and Presbyterian minister

5 Trusting in the God of our fathers and confident that our cause is just, we will never surrender our heritage.
in *Guardian* 21 August 1968

6 The mother of all treachery.
on the Good Friday agreement
in *Times* 16 April 1998

Sarah Palin 1964–
American Republican politician

7 What's the difference between a hockey mom and a pitbull? Lipstick.
speech to Republican Party convention, 3 September 2008

8 You can actually see Russia from land here in Alaska.
interview, ABC News, 11 September 2008

9 The America I know and love is not one in which my parents or my baby with Down Syndrome will have to stand in front of Obama's

'death panel' so his bureaucrats can decide, based on a subjective judgement of their 'level of productivity in society,' whether they are worthy of health care. Such a system is downright evil.
Facebook page, 7 August 2009

Lord Palmerston 1784–1865
British Whig statesman, Prime Minister 1855–8 and 1859–65. See also **Last words 178:4**

10 We have no eternal allies, and we have no perpetual enemies. Our interests are eternal and perpetual, and those interests it is our duty to follow.
in the House of Commons, 1 March 1848

11 I therefore fearlessly challenge the verdict which this House…is to give…whether, as the Roman, in days of old, held himself free from indignity, when he could say *Civis Romanus sum*; so also a British subject, in whatever land he may be, shall feel confident that the watchful eye and the strong arm of England will protect him against injustice and wrong.
speech in the debate on the protection afforded to the Greek trader David Pacifico (1784–1854), who had been born a British subject at Gibraltar
in the House of Commons, 25 June 1850

12 I do not believe that a majority of Englishmen would consent to give their votes in secret even if the law permitted them to do so…I say that for men who are charged with the high and important duty of choosing the best men to represent the country in Parliament to go sneaking to the ballot-box, and, poking in a piece of paper, looking round to see that no one could read it, is a course which is unconstitutional and unworthy of the character of straightforward and honest Englishmen.
address to his electors,1852; Evelyn Ashley *The Life of Henry John Temple, Viscount Palmerston* (1876)

13 You may call it combination, you may call it the accidental and

fortuitous concurrence of atoms.
*on a projected coalition with **Disraeli***
in the House of Commons, 5 March 1857

1 The function of a government
is to calm, rather than to excite
agitation.
P. Guedalla *Gladstone and Palmerston* (1928)

2 Lord Palmerston, with
characteristic levity had once said
that only three men in Europe had
ever understood [the Schleswig-
Holstein question], and of these
the Prince Consort was dead, a
Danish statesman (unnamed) was
in an asylum, and he himself had
forgotten it.
R. W. Seton-Watson *Britain in Europe
1789–1914* (1937)

3 What is merit? The opinion one
man entertains of another.
T. Carlyle *Shooting Niagara: and After?* (1867)

4 *on being told that English has no word
equivalent to* sensibilité:
Yes we have. Humbug.
attributed

Orhan Pamuk 1952–
Turkish novelist

5 The biggest deception of the past
thousand years is this: to confuse
poverty with stupidity.
Snow (2004)

Christabel Pankhurst 1880–1958
English suffragette; daughter of Emmeline Pankhurst

6 We are here to claim our right as
women, not only to be free, but to
fight for freedom. That it is our right
as well as our duty.
in *Votes for Women* 31 March 1911

7 Never lose your temper with the
Press or the public is a major rule of
political life.
Unshackled (1959)

Emmeline Pankhurst 1858–1928
English suffragette leader; founder of the Women's
Social and Political Union, 1903

8 There is something that
Governments care far more for
than human life, and that is the
security of property, and so it is

through property that we shall
strike the enemy…I say to the
Government: You have not dared to
take the leaders of Ulster for their
incitement to rebellion. Take me if
you dare.
speech at Albert Hall, 17 October 1912

9 The way to reform has always led
through prison.
My Own Story (1914)

10 The argument of the broken
window pane is the most valuable
argument in modern politics.
George Dangerfield *The Strange Death of
Liberal England* (1936)

Boris Pankin 1931–
Russian diplomat

11 Recession is when you have to
tighten the belt. Depression is
when there is no belt to tighten. We
are probably in the next degree of
collapse when there are no trousers
as such.
of Russia
in *Independent* 25 July 1992

Dorothy Parker 1893–1967
American critic and humorist

12 *on being told that Calvin **Coolidge** was
dead:*
How do they know?
Malcolm Cowley *Writers at Work* 1st Series
(1958)

Martin Parker d. c. 1656
English balladmonger

13 But all's to no end, for the times will
not mend
Till the King enjoys his own again.
'Upon Defacing of Whitehall' (1671)

Theodore Parker 1810–60
American Unitarian preacher

14 I do not pretend to understand
the moral universe; the arc is a
long one, my eye reaches but little
ways; I cannot calculate the curve
and complete the figure by the
experience of sight; I can divine it
by conscience. And from what I see

I am sure it bends toward justice.
Ten Sermons on Religion (1853) 'Justice and the conscience'; see **King 171:12**, **Obama 230:10**

Henry Parkes 1815–95
English-born Australian statesman

1 The crimson thread of kinship runs through us all.
on Australian federation
speech at banquet in Melbourne 6 February 1890; *The Federal Government of Australasia* (1890)

C. Northcote Parkinson 1909–93
English writer

2 Expenditure rises to meet income.
Parkinson's Law (1958)

3 Work expands so as to fill the time available for its completion.
Parkinson's Law (1958)

4 A committee is organic rather than mechanical in its nature: it is not a structure but a plant. It takes root and grows, it flowers, wilts, and dies, scattering the seed from which other committees will bloom in their turn.
Parkinson's Law (1958)

5 Time spent on any item of the agenda will be in inverse proportion to the sum involved.
Parkinson's Law (1958)

6 The man who is denied the opportunity of taking decisions of importance begins to regard as important the decisions he is allowed to take.
Parkinson's Law (1958)

7 Men enter local politics solely as a result of being unhappily married.
Parkinson's Law (1958)

Rosa Parks 1913–2005
American civil rights activist. On Parks: see **Jackson 154:3**

8 Our mistreatment was just not right, and I was tired of it.
of her refusal, in December 1955, to surrender her seat on a segregated bus in Alabama to a white man
Quiet Strength (1994)

Charles Stewart Parnell 1846–91
Irish nationalist leader. On Parnell: see **Joyce 163:10**, **Yeats 339:11**

9 Why should Ireland be treated as a geographical fragment of England…Ireland is not a geographical fragment, but a nation.
in the House of Commons, 26 April 1875

10 I do not believe, and I never shall believe, that any murder was committed at Manchester.
objecting to the expression 'the Manchester murders' in alluding to the escape of the Fenians, Kelly and Deasy, in 1867
in the House of Commons, June 1876

11 My policy is not a policy of conciliation, but a policy of retaliation.
in 1877, on his parliamentary tactics in the House of Commons as leader of the Irish party
in *Dictionary of National Biography* (1917–)

12 None of us, whether we are in America or Ireland, or wherever we may be, will be satisfied until we have destroyed the last link which keeps Ireland bound to England.
speech at Cincinnati, 20 February 1880

13 No man has a right to fix the boundary of the march of a nation; no man has a right to say to his country—thus far shalt thou go and no further.
speech at Cork, 21 January 1885

14 Get the advice of everybody whose advice is worth having—they are very few—and then do what you think best yourself.
Conor Cruise O'Brien *Parnell* (1957)

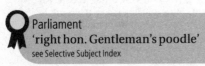

Parliament
'right hon. Gentleman's poodle'
see Selective Subject Index

Matthew Parris 1949–
British journalist and former politician

1 *of Lady **Thatcher** in the House of Lords:*
A big cat detained briefly in a
poodle parlour, sharpening her
claws on the velvet.
Look Behind You! (1993)

2 Being an MP feeds your vanity and
starves your self-respect.
in *Times* 9 February 1994

3 My name is Mandy: Peter B.,
I'm back in charge—don't mess with
me.
My cheeks are drawn, my face is
bony,
The line I take comes straight from
Tony.
*on Peter **Mandelson**'s return to government*
in *Times* 21 October 1999; see
Anonymous 8:17

Carolyn Parrish 1946–
Canadian Independent politician

4 Come hell or high water, there's no
frigging way I'm going to let one
ovary bring the government down.
*on her determination to be present for the critical
budget vote, despite suffering stomach pains*
quoted in *GlobeandMail.com* 20 May
2005 (online edition)

Blaise Pascal 1623–62
French mathematician, physicist, and moralist

5 Had Cleopatra's nose been shorter,
the whole face of the world would
have changed.
Pensées (1670)

Sadashiv Kanoji Patil
Indian politician

6 The Prime Minister is like the great
banyan tree. Thousands shelter
beneath it, but nothing grows.
*when asked in an interview who would be
Nehru's successor*
J. K. Galbraith *A Life in Our Times* (1981)

Chris Patten 1944–
British Conservative politician

7 Attacking the Liberals is a difficult
business, involving all the hazards
of wrestling with a greased pig at a
village fair, and then insulting the
vicar.
attributed, 1996

Jeremy Paxman 1950–
British journalist and broadcaster

8 Did you threaten to overrule him?
*question asked 14 times of Michael **Howard**,
referring to the sacking of a prison governor by
Derek Lewis, Director of the Prison Service*
interview, BBC2 *Newsnight* 13 May 1997

9 Labour's attack dog.
*description of the Labour politician John Reid, to
which Reid took great exception (see **Reid** 257:5)*
on *Newsnight* programme, 8 March 2005

Patrick Pearse 1879–1916
Irish nationalist leader; executed after the Easter
Rising. On Pearse: see **Yeats 339:4**

10 The fools, the fools, the fools, they
have left us our Fenian dead, and
while Ireland holds these graves
Ireland unfree shall never be at
peace.
*oration over the grave of the Fenian Jeremiah
O'Donovan Rossa, 1 August 1915*

11 Here be ghosts that I have raised
this Christmastide, ghosts of
dead men that have bequeathed a
trust to us living men. Ghosts are
troublesome things in a house or
in a family, as we knew even before
Ibsen taught us. There is only one
way to appease a ghost. You must
do the thing it asks you. The ghosts
of a nation sometimes ask very big
things and they must be appeased,
whatever the cost.
*on Christmas Day, 1915; Conor Cruise O'Brien
Ancestral Voices (1994)*

Patriotism
'our country, right or wrong'
see Selective Subject Index

Lester Pearson 1897–1972
Canadian diplomat and Liberal statesman, Prime Minister 1963–8

1 The grim fact is that we prepare for war like precocious giants and for peace like retarded pygmies.
speech in Toronto, 14 March 1955

2 This is the flag of the future, but it does not dishonour the past.
on Canada obtaining a flag of its own, a project Pearson successfully achieved
speech in the House of Commons, Ottawa, 15 December 1964

3 To be Prime Minister of Canada, you need the hide of a rhinoceros, the morals of St. Francis, the patience of Job, the wisdom of Solomon, the strength of Hercules, the leadership of Napoleon, the magnetism of a Beatle and the subtlety of Machiavelli.
in 1964, attributed; see **Hennessy 141:4**

4 Not only did he not suffer fools gladly, he did not suffer them at all.
*of Dean **Acheson***
in *Time* 25 October 1971

5 The chief distinction of a diplomat is that he can say no in such a way that it sounds like yes.
Geoffrey Pearson *Seize the Day* (1993)

Robert Peel 1788–1850
British Conservative statesman; Prime Minister, 1834–5, 1841–6. On Peel: see **Curran 83:14**, **Disraeli 92:8**, **Disraeli 92:11**, **Disraeli 95:8**, **Hennessy 141:4**, **Wellington 329:15**

6 What is right must unavoidably be politic.
to Goulburn, 23 September 1822

7 There is no appetite for truth in Ireland.
to Leveson Gower in 1828

8 As minister of the Crown…I reserve to myself, distinctly and unequivocally, the right of adapting my conduct to the exigency of the moment, and to the wants of the country.
in the House of Commons, 30 March 1829

9 All my experience in public life is in favour of the employment of what the world would call young men instead of old ones.
to Wellington in 1829

10 The longer I live, the more clearly do I see the folly of yielding a rash and precipitate assent to any political measure.
in the House of Commons, 1830

11 We are here to consult the interests and not to obey the will of the people, if we honestly believe that that will conflicts with those interests.
in the House of Commons, 1831

12 No man attached to his country could always acquiesce in the opinions of the majority.
in the House of Commons, 1831

13 No government can exist which does not control and restrain the popular sentiments.
in the House of Commons, 1832

14 There will always be found a permanent fund of discontent and dissatisfaction in every country.
in the House of Commons, 1832

15 The hasty inordinate demand for peace might be just as dangerous as the clamour for war.
in the House of Commons, 1832

16 I see no dignity in persevering in error.
in the House of Commons, 1833

17 *of Robert **Walpole**:*
So far as the great majority of his audience was concerned, he had blocks to cut, and he chose a fitter instrument than a razor to cut them with.
to Mahon in 1833

18 I am not sure that those who

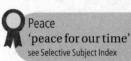

Peace
'peace for our time'
see Selective Subject Index

clamour most, suffer most.
in the House of Commons, 1834

1 Of all vulgar arts of government, that of solving every difficulty which might arise by thrusting the hand into the public purse is the most delusory and contemptible.
in the House of Commons, 1834

2 The distinction of being without an honour is becoming a rare and valuable one and should not become extinct.
to Graham in 1841

3 A cordial and good understanding between France and England is essential to the peace and welfare of Europe.
in the House of Commons, 1841

4 Speaking with that caution with which I am sometimes taunted but which I find a great convenience.
in the House of Commons, 1842

5 There are those who seem to have nothing else to do but to suggest modes of taxation to men in office.
in the House of Commons, 1842

6 The great art of government is to work by such instruments as the world supplies.
in Cabinet, 1844

7 There are many parties in Ireland who desire to have a grievance and prefer the grievance to the remedy.
to the Queen, 1844

8 Philosophers are very regardless of expense when the public has to bear it.
to Haddington in 1844

9 Priests are not above sublunary considerations. Priests have nephews.
to Graham, 13 August 1845

10 An Irishman has no sense of the ridiculous when office is in question.
to Graham, 28 December 1845

11 There seem to me very few facts, at least ascertainable facts, in politics.
to Lord **Brougham** in 1846

12 Great public measures cannot be carried by the influence of mere reason.
to Lord Radnor in 1846

Charles Péguy 1873–1914
French poet and essayist

13 Tyranny is always better organized than freedom.
Basic Verities (1943) 'War and Peace'

Henry Herbert, Lord Pembroke c. 1534–1601

14 A parliament can do any thing but make a man a woman, and a woman a man.
quoted by his son, the 4th Earl, in a speech on 11 April 1648, proving himself Chancellor of Oxford

William Penn 1644–1718
English Quaker; founder of Pennsylvania

15 It is a reproach to religion and government to suffer so much poverty and excess.
Some Fruits of Solitude (1693)

16 The taking of a bribe or gratuity, should be punished with as severe penalties as the defrauding of the State.
Some Fruits of Solitude (1693)

Samuel Pepys 1633–1703
English diarist

17 I went out to Charing Cross, to see Major-general Harrison hanged, drawn, and quartered; which was done there, he looking as cheerful as any man could do in that condition.
diary, 13 October 1660

18 But methought it lessened my esteem of a king, that he should not be able to command the rain.
diary, 19 July 1662

19 I see it is impossible for the King to have things done as cheap as other men.
diary, 21 July 1662

20 While we were talking came by several poor creatures carried by, by constables, for being at a conventicle...I would to God they would either conform, or be more wise, and not be catched!
diary, 7 August 1664

1 Pretty witty Nell.
of Nell Gwyn
diary, 3 April 1665

Shimon Peres 1923–
Israeli statesman

2 Television has made dictatorship impossible, but democracy unbearable.
at a Davos meeting, in *Financial Times* 31 January 1995

Pericles *c.* 495–429 BC
Greek statesman and Athenian general

3 For famous men have the whole earth as their memorial.
Thucydides *History of the Peloponnesian War*

4 Happiness depends on being free, and freedom depends on being courageous.
Thucydides *History of the Peloponnesian War*

Eva Perón 1919–52
Argentinian wife of Juan Perón. On Perón: see
Epitaphs 106:7

5 Keeping books on charity is capitalist nonsense! I just use the money for the poor. I can't stop to count it.
Fleur Cowles *Bloody Precedent: the Peron Story* (1952)

Juan Perón 1895–1974
Argentinian soldier and statesman, President 1946–55 and 1973–4

6 If I had not been born Perón, I would have liked to be Perón.
in *Observer* 21 February 1960

Henri Philippe Pétain 1856–1951
French soldier and statesman

7 To write one's memoirs is to speak ill of everybody except oneself.
in *Observer* 26 May 1946

Jamie Petrie and Peter Cunnah

8 Things can only get better.
title of song (1994); see **Slogans 291:14**

Roger Peyrefitte 1907–2000
French writer

9 The ideal civil servant should always be colourless, odourless and tasteless.
Diplomatic Diversions (1953)

Edward John Phelps 1822–1900
American lawyer and diplomat

10 The man who makes no mistakes does not usually make anything.
speech at the Mansion House, London, 24 January 1889

Kim Philby 1912–88
British intelligence officer and Soviet spy

11 To betray, you must first belong.
in *Sunday Times* 17 December 1967

Prince Philip 1921–
British prince, husband of **Elizabeth II**

12 Just at this moment we are suffering a national defeat comparable to any lost military campaign, and what is more it is self-inflicted…I think it is about time we pulled our finger out.
speech to businessmen, 17 October 1961

Morgan Phillips 1902–63
British Labour politician

13 The Labour Party owes more to Methodism than to Marxism.
James Callaghan *Time and Chance* (1987); coined by Denis **Healey** as speechwriter for Phillips at the Socialist International Conference, Copenhagen, 1953

Wendell Phillips 1811–84
American abolitionist and orator

14 Revolutions are not made; they come. A revolution is as natural a growth as an oak. It comes out of the past. Its foundations are laid far back.
speech, 8 January 1852

15 The best use of laws is to teach men to trample bad laws under their feet.
speech, 12 April 1852

16 Truth is one forever absolute, but opinion is truth filtered through the moods, the blood, the disposition of the spectator.
in *Idols* 4 October 1859

1 One on God's side is a majority.
  speech, 1 November 1859

Phocion c. 402–317 BC
Athenian soldier

2 Have I inadvertently said
  something foolish?
  upon his opinion being cheered by the populace
  Plutarch *Parallel Lives* 'Phocion'

3 DEMOSTHENES: The Athenians will
  kill thee, Phocion, should they go
  crazy.
  PHOCION: But they will kill thee,
  should they come to their senses.
  Plutarch *Parallel Lives* 'Phocion'

John Pilger 1939–
Australian journalist

4 It was all too easy for journalists to
  see Vietnam as a war, rather than a
  country.
  comment, 1995

William Pitt, Earl of Chatham
1708–78
British Whig statesman; Prime Minister, 1766–8. On
Pitt: see **Walpole 325:6**

5 The atrocious crime of being a
  young man...I shall neither attempt
  to palliate nor deny.
  in the House of Commons, 2 March 1741

6 I must now address a few words to
  the Solicitor; they shall be few, but
  they shall be daggers.
  to William Murray, the Attorney-General, in the
  House of Commons, 1755

7 My Lord, I am sure I can save this
  country, and nobody else can.
  said to the Duke of Devonshire in 1757; Horace
  Walpole *Memoirs of the Reign of King George II*
  (1846)

8 The poorest man may in his cottage
  bid defiance to all the forces of the
  Crown. It may be frail—its roof may
  shake—the wind may blow through
  it—the storm may enter—the rain
  may enter—but the King of England
  cannot enter!
  speech, March 1763

9 Confidence is a plant of slow
  growth in an aged bosom: youth is
  the season of credulity.
  in the House of Commons, 14 January 1766

10 Unlimited power is apt to corrupt
  the minds of those who possess it.
  in the House of Lords, 9 January 1770; see
  Acton 1:10

11 There is something behind the
  throne greater than the King
  himself.
  in the House of Lords, 2 March 1770

12 We have a Calvinistic creed, a
  Popish liturgy, and an Arminian
  clergy.
  in the House of Lords, 19 May 1772

13 You cannot conquer America.
  in the House of Lords, 18 November 1777

14 I invoke the genius of the
  Constitution!
  in the House of Lords, 18 November 1777

15 Shall a people that fifteen years
  ago was the terror of the world now
  stoop so low as to tell its ancient
  inveterate enemy, 'Take all we have,
  only give us peace?'
  *in his last speech in the Lords, shortly before his
  death, opposing a surrender to the American
  colonists and their ally France*
  Basil Williams *William Pitt, Earl of Chatham*
  (1913)

16 Our watchword is security.
  attributed

17 The parks are the lungs of London.
  quoted in the House of Commons by William
  Windham, 30 June 1808

William Pitt 1759–1806
British Tory statesman; Prime Minister, 1783–1801,
1804–6. On Pitt: see **Burke 49:10**, **Fox 113:2**,
Fox 113:4, **Scott 276:2**, **Wraxall 337:12**;
see also **Last words 179:5**

18 Lord North will, I hope, in a very
  little time make room for me in
  Downing Street, which is the best
  summer Town House possible.
  as newly appointed Chancellor of the
  Exchequer, 16 July 1782

19 Necessity is the plea for every
  infringement of human freedom: it
  is the argument of tyrants; it is the
  creed of slaves.
  in the House of Commons, 18 November 1783

20 We must anew commence the
  salvation of Europe.
  in 1795; in *Dictionary of National Biography*
  (1917–)

1 All wars depend now on the finances of the nations engaged in them.
   speech in the House of Commons, 30 December 1796

2 We must recollect...what it is we have at stake, what it is we have to contend for. It is for our property, it is for our liberty, it is for our independence, nay, for our existence as a nation; it is for our character, it is for our very name as Englishmen, it is for everything dear and valuable to man on this side of the grave.
   on the rupture of the Peace of Amiens and the resumption of war with Napoleon, 22 July 1803
   Speeches of the Rt. Hon. William Pitt (1806)

3 England has saved herself by her exertions, and will, as I trust, save Europe by her example.
   replying to a toast in which he had been described as the saviour of his country in the wars with France
   R. Coupland War Speeches of William Pitt (1915)

4 Roll up that map; it will not be wanted these ten years.
   of a map of Europe, on hearing of Napoleon I's victory at Austerlitz, December 1805
   Earl Stanhope Life of the Rt. Hon. William Pitt (1862)

Pius VII 1742–1823
Italian cleric, Pope from 1800

5 We are prepared to go to the gates of Hell—but no further.
   attempting to reach an agreement with Napoleon I, 1800–1
   J. M. Robinson Cardinal Consalvi (1987)

Pius XII 1876–1958
Italian cleric; Pope from 1939

6 One Galileo in two thousand years is enough.
   on being asked to proscribe the works of Teilhard de Chardin
   attributed; Stafford Beer Platform for Change (1975)

Plato 429–347 BC
Greek philosopher

7 What I say is that 'just' or 'right' means nothing but what is in the interest of the stronger party.
   spoken by Thrasymachus in The Republic

8 One of the penalties for refusing to participate in politics is that you end up being governed by your inferiors.
   The Republic

9 When the tyrant has disposed of foreign enemies by conquest or treaty, and there is nothing to fear from them, then he is always stirring up some war or other, in order that the people may require a leader.
   'foreign enemies' here means 'exiled opponents'
   The Republic

10 The city in which those who are to rule are least eager to hold office must needs be the best governed and freest from strife.
   The Republic

Pliny the Elder AD 23–79
Roman statesman and scholar

11 Ex Africa semper aliquid novi. Always something new out of Africa.
   traditional form of Semper aliquid novi Africam adferre; Historia Naturalis

George Washington Plunkitt
1842–1924
American Tammany politician

12 There's an honest graft, and I'm an example of how it works. I might sum up the whole thing by sayin': 'I seen my opportunities and I took 'em.'
   'Honest Graft and Dishonest Graft' in William L. Riordon Plunkitt of Tammany Hall (1905)

13 The politician who steals is worse than a thief. He is a fool. With the

Politics
'Politics is the art of the possible'
see Selective Subject Index

grand opportunities all around for a man with a political pull, there's no excuse for stealin' a cent.
'On the Shame of Cities' in William L. Riordon *Plunkitt of Tammany Hall* (1905)

Plutarch c. AD 46–c. 120
Greek philosopher and biographer

1 To break a treaty is contempt for the gods. But to outwit an enemy is not only just and glorious—but profitable and sweet.
often quoted in the form 'To deceive a friend is impious. But…'
Parallel Lives 'Agesilaus'

2 For we are told that when a certain man was accusing both of them to him, he [Caesar] said that he had no fear of those fat and long-haired fellows, but rather of those pale and thin ones.
Parallel Lives 'Anthony'; see **Shakespeare 280:6**

3 The man who is thought to have been the first to see beneath the surface of Caesar's public policy and to fear it, as one might fear the smiling surface of the sea.
of **Cicero**
Parallel Lives 'Julius Caesar'

Harry Pollitt 1890–1960
British Communist politician

4 *on being asked by Stephen Spender (1909–95) in the 1930s how best a poet could serve the Communist cause:*
Go to Spain and get killed. The movement needs a Byron.
attributed, perhaps apocryphal

Polybius c. 200–c. 118 BC
Greek historian

5 Those who know how to win are much more numerous than those who know how to make proper use of their victories.
History

Madame de Pompadour (Antoinette Poisson, Marquise de Pompadour) 1721–64
French favourite of Louis XV of France

6 *Après nous le déluge.*
After us the deluge.
Madame du Hausset *Mémoires* (1824)

Georges Pompidou 1911–74
French statesman; President of France from 1969

7 A statesman is a politician who places himself at the service of the nation. A politician is a statesman who places the nation at his service.
in 1973, attributed

Alexander Pope 1688–1744
English poet

8 Lo! thy dread empire, Chaos! is restored;
Light dies before thy uncreating word:
Thy hand, great Anarch! lets the curtain fall;
And universal darkness buries all.
The Dunciad (1742)

9 Old politicians chew on wisdom past,
And totter on in business to the last.
Epistles to Several Persons 'To Lord Cobham' (1734)

10 Statesman, yet friend to Truth! of soul sincere,
In action faithful, and in honour clear;
Who broke no promise, served no private end,
Who gained no title, and who lost no friend.
Epistles to Several Persons 'To Mr Addison' (1720)

11 For forms of government let fools contest;
Whate'er is best administered is best.
An Essay on Man Epistle 3 (1733)

12 If parts allure thee, think how

Poverty
'Let them eat cake'
see Selective Subject Index

Bacon shined,
The wisest, brightest, meanest of
mankind:
Or ravished with the whistling of a
name,
See Cromwell, damned to everlasting
fame!
An Essay on Man Epistle 4 (1734)

1 Get place and wealth, if possible,
with grace;
If not, by any means get wealth and
place.
Imitations of Horace Horace bk. 1, Epistle
1 (1738); see **Horace 147:9**

2 Here thou, great Anna! whom three
realms obey,
Dost sometimes counsel take—and
sometimes tea.
The Rape of the Lock (1714)

Karl Popper 1902–94
Austrian-born philosopher

3 We may become the makers of our
fate when we have ceased to pose as
its prophets.
The Open Society and its Enemies (1945)
introduction

4 We must plan for freedom, and not
only for security, if for no other
reason than that only freedom can
make security secure.
The Open Society and its Enemies (1945)

5 There is no history of mankind,
there are only many histories of
all kinds of aspects of human life.
And one of these is the history of
political power. This is elevated
into the history of the world.
The Open Society and its Enemies (1945)

6 Marxism is only an episode—one of
the many mistakes we have made
in the perennial and dangerous
struggle for building a better and a
freer world.
The Open Society and its Enemies (rev. ed., 1952)

7 Piecemeal social engineering
resembles physical engineering in

regarding the *ends* as beyond the
province of technology.
The Poverty of Historicism (1957)

Michael Portillo 1953–
British Conservative politician and broadcaster

8 A truly terrible night for the
Conservatives.
*after losing Enfield South to Labour in the General
Election of 1997*
comment, 2 May 1997; Brian Cathcart *Were
You Still Up for Portillo?* (1997)

9 You don't look tall if you surround
yourself by short grasses.
on Iain Duncan **Smith**
in *Independent* 22 February 2003

Eugène Pottier see Songs 296:5

Enoch Powell 1912–98
British Conservative politician

10 History is littered with the wars
which everybody knew would never
happen.
speech to the Conservative Party Conference,
19 October 1967

11 Those whom the gods wish to
destroy, they first make mad. We
must be mad, literally mad, as a
nation to be permitting the annual
inflow of some 50,000 dependents,
who are for the most part the
material of the future growth of the
immigrant descended population.
It is like watching a nation busily
engaged in heaping up its own
funeral pyre.
speech at Birmingham, 20 April 1968

12 As I look ahead, I am filled with
foreboding. Like the Roman, I seem
to see 'the River Tiber foaming with
much blood'.
speech at Birmingham, 20 April 1968; see
Virgil 322:10

13 No one is forced to be a politician. It
can only compare with fox-hunting
and writing poetry. These are

Power
'Dead Sea fruit'
see Selective Subject Index

two things that men do for sheer enjoyment too.
attributed, 1973

1 Judas was paid! I am sacrificing my whole political life.
response to a heckler's call of 'Judas', having advised Conservatives to vote Labour at the coming general election
speech at Bull Ring, Birmingham, 23 February 1974

2 For a politician to complain about the press is like a ship's captain complaining about the sea.
in *Guardian* 3 December 1984

3 A Tory is someone who thinks institutions are wiser than those who operate them.
in *Daily Telegraph* 31 March 1986

4 ANNE BROWN: How would you like to be remembered?
ENOCH POWELL: I should like to have been killed in the war.
in a radio interview, 13 April 1986

5 To pretend that you cannot exchange goods and services freely with a Frenchman or an Italian, unless there is an identical standard of bathing beaches or tap water in the different countries is not logic. It is naked aggression.
in *Guardian* 22 May 1990

6 All political lives, unless they are cut off in midstream at a happy juncture, end in failure, because that is the nature of politics and of human affairs.
Joseph Chamberlain (1977); epilogue

7 To be and to remain a member of the House of Commons was the overriding and undiscussable motivation of my life as a politician.
'Theory and Practice' 1990

8 Lift the curtain and 'the State' reveals itself as a little group of fallible men in Whitehall, making guesses about the future, influenced by political prejudices and partisan prejudices, and working on projections drawn from the past by a staff of economists.
attributed

John O'Connor Power 1848–1919
Irish lawyer and politician

9 *of the Liberal Unionists:*
The mules of politics: without pride of ancestry, or hope of posterity.
H. H. Asquith *Memories and Reflections* (1928); see **Disraeli 94:16**, **Donnelly 97:3**

John Prescott 1938–
British Labour politician

10 We did it! Let's wallow in our victory!
*on Tony **Blair**'s warning that the Labour Party should not be triumphalist in victory*
speech to the Labour Party Conference, 29 September 1997

11 When plates appear to be moving, everyone positions themselves for it.
in *Times* 15 May 2004

Richard Price 1723–91
English nonconformist minister

12 Now, methinks, I see the ardour for liberty catching and spreading; a general amendment beginning in human affairs; the dominion of kings changed for the dominion of laws, and the dominion of priests giving way to the dominion of reason and conscience.
A Discourse on the Love of our Country (1790)

Matthew Prior 1664–1721
English poet

13 What is a King?—a man condemned to bear
The public burden of the nation's care.
Solomon (1718)

The Presidency
'no whitewash at the White House'
see Selective Subject Index

Romano Prodi 1939–
Italian statesman, President of the European
Commission 1999–2004

1 The pillars of the nation state are
the sword and the currency, and we
changed that. The euro-decision
changed the concept of the nation
state.
in *Daily Telegraph* 7 April 1999

2 I know very well that the stability
pact is stupid, like all decisions that
are rigid.
on the rules underpinning the single currency
interview in *Le Monde* (electronic edition)
17 October 2002

Pierre-Joseph Proudhon 1809–65
French social reformer

3 Property is theft.
Qu'est-ce que la propriété? (1840)

Joseph Pulitzer 1847–1911
Hungarian-born American newspaper proprietor and
editor

4 Our Republic and its press will rise
or fall together.
referring to the importance of media independence
in *North American Review* May 1904

5 A cynical, mercenary, demagogic,
corrupt press will produce in time a
people as base as itself.
*inscribed on the gateway to the Columbia School
of Journalism in New York*
W. J. Granberg *The World of Joseph Pulitzer*
(1965)

Vladimir Putin 1952–
Russian statesman, President of the Russian
Federation 2000–2008, Prime Minister 2008–

6 Anyone who doesn't regret the

passing of the Soviet Union has
no heart. Anyone who wants it
restored has no brains.
in *New York Times* 20 February 2000; a similar
remark was attributed to General Alexander
Lebed in *St Petersburg Times* (Florida) 28 June
1996

7 Please forgive us. We shall win
this fight against international
terrorism.
*addressing the nation and apologising for failing
to save all the hostages in the Moscow theatre
siege*
in *Sunday Telegraph* 27 October 2002

Mario Puzo 1920–99 and **Francis
Ford Coppola** 1939–
American novelist and American film director

8 Keep your friends close, but your
enemies closer.
*often wrongly attributed to **Sun Tzu***
The Godfather: Part II (1974 film), spoken by Al
Pacino as Michael Corleone

John Pym 1584–1643
English Parliamentary leader

9 To have granted liberties, and not to
have liberties in truth and realities,
is but to mock the kingdom.
*after the battle of Edgehill, 1642, in a speech at
Guildhall to the citizens of London pointing out
the illusory nature of **Charles I**'s promises*
in *Dictionary of National Biography* (1917–)

Pyrrhus 319–272 BC
Greek monarch, King of Epirus from 306 BC

10 One more such victory and we are
lost.
*on defeating the Romans at Asculum, 279 BC;
origin of the phrase 'Pyrrhic victory'*
Plutarch *Parallel Lives* 'Pyrrhus'

Prime Ministers
'top of the greasy pole'
see Selective Subject Index

Proverbs and sayings

1 **Action this day.**
annotation as used by Winston Churchill at the Admiralty in 1940

2 **Are you now, or have you ever been, a member of the Communist Party?**
from 1947, the question habitually put by the House Un-American Activities Committee (HUAC) to those appearing before it, now particularly associated with the McCarthy period of the 1950s

3 **As Maine goes, so goes the nation.**
American political saying, 1840; see **Farley 109:5**

4 **Bad money drives out good.**
proverbial expression of a principle attributed to Sir Thomas Gresham (1519–79), founder of the Royal Exchange

5 **A conservative is a liberal who's been mugged.**
American saying, 1980s; see **Wolfe 336:11**

6 **Daddy, what did you do in the Great War?**
daughter to father in First World War recruiting poster

7 **Don't sell America short.**
popular version of saying attributed, 1890s, to John Pierpont Morgan (1837–1913)

8 **The enemy of my enemy is my friend.**
late 20th century, said to be 'an old Arab proverb'

9 **England's difficulty is Ireland's opportunity.**
proverbial from mid 19th century

10 **An Englishman's home is his castle.**
proverbial from late 16th century

11 **Every bullet has its billet.**
proverbial from late 16th century; attributed to **William III** in John Wesley *Journal* (1827) 6 June 1765

12 **The higher the monkey climbs the more he shows his tail.**
proverbial from late 14th century

13 **If you don't like the heat, get out of the kitchen.**
associated with Harry S. **Truman**, but attributed by him to Harry Vaughan, his 'military jester' mid 20th century saying; in *Time* 28 April 1952

14 *Il ne faut pas être plus royaliste que le roi.*
You mustn't be more of a royalist than the king.
noted as a current catch-phrase which was not in fact new; 'it was coined under Louis XVI: it chained up the hands of the loyal, leaving free only the arm of the hangman'
François René, Vicomte de Chateaubriand *De la monarchie selon la charte* (1816)

15 *Ils ne passeront pas.*
They shall not pass.
slogan used by French army defence at Verdun in 1916
variously attributed to Marshal Pétain and to General Robert Nivelle; see **Ibarruri 151:7**

16 **In matters of principle, stand like a rock; in matters of taste, swim with the current.**
from the mid 20th century associated with **Jefferson**, in the form 'In matters of style, swim with the current; in matters of principle, stand like a rock'
late 19th century saying

17 **It'll play in Peoria.**
catchphrase of the **Nixon** administration (early 1970s) meaning 'it will be acceptable to middle America'
originating in a standard music hall joke of the 1930s

18 **Let's run it up the flagpole and see if anyone salutes it.**
Reginald Rose *Twelve Angry Men* (1955); recorded as an established advertising expression in the 1960s

19 **Lions led by donkeys.**
associated with British soldiers during the First World War
attributed to Max Hoffman (1869–1927) in Alan Clark *The Donkeys* (1961); this attribution has not been traced elsewhere, and the phrase is of much earlier origin: 'Unceasingly they had drummed into them the utterance of *The Times*: "You are lions led by packasses"' was said of French troops defeated by Prussians, in Francisque Sarcey *Paris during the Siege* (1871)

20 **Members rise from CMG (known sometimes in Whitehall as 'Call Me God') to the KCMG ('Kindly Call Me God') to—for a select few governors**

Proverbs and sayings *continued*

and super-ambassadors—the GCMG ('God Calls Me God').
of civil service orders
Anthony Sampson *Anatomy of Britain* (1962)

1 Not to be a republican at twenty is proof of want of heart; to be one at thirty is proof of want of head.
often used in the form 'Not to be a socialist...'
adopted by **Clemenceau**, and attributed by him to the French historian and politician François Guizot (1787–1874)

2 One man plus the truth makes a majority.
traditional saying; see **Knox 175:11**

3 Politics makes strange bedfellows.
proverbial from mid 19th century

4 Revolutions are not made with rose-water.
proverbial from early 19th century

5 A rising tide lifts all boats.
mid 20th century saying; principally known in the United States and associated with the Kennedy family

6 There's no such thing as a free lunch.
colloquial axiom in US economics from the 1960s, much associated with Milton **Friedman**
first found in printed form in Robert Heinlein *The Moon is a Harsh Mistress* (1966)

7 To succeed in public life you have

to be sincere. Once you can fake that, you've got it made.
traditional saying

8 War is God's way of teaching Americans geography.
widely attributed to Ambrose **Bierce**, but not found before the early 1990s

9 What Manchester says today, the rest of England says tomorrow.
late 19th century saying

10 When the going gets tough, the tough get going.
proverbial from mid 20th century; widely associated with Joseph P. **Kennedy**, J. H. Cutler *Honey Fitz* (1962); also attributed to Knute Rockne

11 When war is declared, Truth is the first casualty.
attributed to Hiram Johnson, speaking in the US Senate, 1918, but not recorded in his speech; the first recorded use is as epigraph to Arthur Ponsonby's *Falsehood in Wartime* (1928); see **Johnson 160:11**

12 You have the watches, but we have the time.
early 21st century, said to be an Afghan saying addressed to ISAF/NATO forces

13 Your King and Country need you.
recruitment slogan for First World War, coined by Eric Field, July 1914; *Advertising* (1959); see **Songs 297:4**

Qianlong 1711–99
Chinese monarch, Emperor of China 1735–95

1 As your ambassador can see for himself we possess all things. I set no value on objects strange or ingenious, and have no use for your country's manufactures.
*writing to **George III** after the first British trade mission had reached Beijing*
'The First Edict' September 1793, in Pei-Kai Cheng, Michael Lestz, and Jonathan D. Spence (eds.) *The Search for Modern China: A Documentary Collection* (1999)

François Quesnay 1694–1774
French political economist

2 *Vous ne connaissez qu'une seule règle du commerce; c'est (pour me servir de vos propres termes) de laisser passer et de laisser faire tous les acheteurs et tous les vendeurs quelconques.*
You recognize but one rule of commerce; that is (to avail myself of your own terms) to allow free passage and freedom of action to all buyers and sellers whoever they may be.
letter from M. Alpha to de Quesnay, 1767, in L. Salleron *François Quesnay et la Physiocratie* (1958) vol. 2, but not found in de Quesnay's writings; see **Argenson 11:14**

Josiah Quincy 1772–1864
American Federalist politician

3 As it will be the right of all, so it will be the duty of some, definitely to prepare for a separation, amicably if they can, violently if they must.
in *Abridgement of Debates of Congress* 14 January 1811

The Qur'an see The Koran

Yitzhak Rabin 1922–95
Israeli statesman and military leader, Prime Minister 1974–7 and 1992–5

4 We say to you today in a loud and a clear voice: enough of blood and tears. Enough.
to the Palestinians, at the signing of the Israel–Palestine Declaration, Washington, 13 September 1993

Lord Radcliffe 1899–1977
British lawyer and public servant

5 Society has become used to the standing armies of power—the permanent Civil Service, the police force, the tax-gatherer—organized on a scale which was unknown to earlier centuries.
Power and the State (BBC Reith Lectures, 1951)

6 Governments always tend to want not really a free press but a

managed or well-conducted one.
in 1967; Peter Hennessy *What the Papers Never Said* (1985)

Jean-Pierre Raffarin 1948–
French statesman, Prime Minister 2002–5

1 We have a country which loves ideology, and we need pragmatism.
in *Independent* 11 May 2002

Thomas Rainborowe d. 1648
English soldier and parliamentarian

2 The poorest he that is in England hath a life to live as the greatest he; and therefore truly, Sir, I think it's clear, that every man that is to live under a government ought to first by his own consent to put himself under that government; and I do think that the poorest man in England is not at all bound in a strict sense to that government that he hath not had a voice to put himself under.
during the Army debates at Putney, 29 October 1647
C. H. Firth (ed.) *The Clarke Papers* vol. 1 (1891)

Milton Rakove 1918–83

3 The second law, Rakove's law of principle and politics, states that the citizen is influenced by principle in direct proportion to his distance from the political situation.
in *Virginia Quarterly Review* (1965)

Walter Ralegh c. 1552–1618
English explorer and courtier

4 Say to the court, it glows
And shines like rotten wood;
Say to the church, it shows
What's good, and doth no good:
If church and court reply,
Then give them both the lie.
'The Lie' (1608)

5 Fain would I climb, yet fear I to fall.
line written on a window-pane; see **Elizabeth I**
Thomas Fuller *History of the Worthies of England* (1662) 'Devonshire'

6 Whoso taketh in hand to frame any state or government ought to presuppose that all men are evil, and at occasions will show themselves so to be.
The Cabinet-Council (1658) ch. 26

7 Whosoever commands the sea commands the trade; whosoever commands the trade of the world commands the riches of the world, and consequently the world itself.
'A Discourse of the Invention of Ships, Anchors, Compass, &c.'

8 'Tis a sharp remedy, but a sure one for all ills.
on feeling the edge of the axe prior to his execution
D. Hume *History of Great Britain* (1754)

9 So the heart be right, it is no matter which way the head lies.
at his execution, on being asked which way he preferred to lay his head
W. Stebbing *Sir Walter Raleigh* (1891)

Ayn Rand 1905–82
American writer

10 When money ceases to become the means by which men deal with one another, then men become the tools of other men. Blood, whips and guns—or dollars. Take your choice—there is no other.
Atlas Shrugged (1957)

11 A statist system—whether of a communist, fascist, Nazi, socialist or 'welfare' type—is based on the… government's unlimited power, which means: on the rule of brute force. The differences among statist systems are only a matter of time

Racism
'I have a dream'
see Selective Subject Index

and degree.
often quoted as 'The difference between a welfare state and a totalitarian state is merely a matter of time'
    in *The Objectivist* October 1962

John Randolph 1773–1833
American politician

1 God has given us Missouri, and the devil shall not take it from us.
in the debate in the US Senate in 1820 on the admission of Missouri to the Union as a slave state
    Robert V. Remini *Henry Clay* (1991)

2 Never were abilities so much below mediocrity so well rewarded; no, not when Caligula's horse was made Consul.
*on John Quincy **Adams**'s appointment of Richard Rush as Secretary of the Treasury*
    speech, 1 February 1828

3 He is a man of splendid abilities but utterly corrupt. He shines and stinks like rotten mackerel by moonlight.
of Edward Livingston
    W. Cabell Bruce *John Randolph of Roanoke* (1923) vol. 2

4 He rowed to his object with muffled oars.
of Martin Van Buren
    W. Cabell Bruce *John Randolph of Roanoke* (1923) vol. 2

5 That most delicious of all privileges—spending other people's money.
    William Cabell Bruce *John Randolph of Roanoke* (1923) vol. 2

Dan Rather 1931–
American journalist

6 I worry that patriotism run amok will trample the very values that the country seeks to defend.
    in *Independent* 18 May 2002

Irina Ratushinskaya 1954–
Russian poet

7 Russian literature saved my soul. When I was a young girl in school and I asked what is good and what is evil, no one in that corrupt system could show me.
    in *Observer* 15 October 1989 'Sayings of the Week'

Sam Rayburn 1882–1961
American Democratic politician, Speaker of the US House of Representatives

8 If you want to get along, go along.
    Neil MacNeil *Forge of Democracy* (1963)

Nancy Reagan 1923–
American actress and wife of Ronald **Reagan**, First Lady of the US, 1981–9

9 If the President has a bully pulpit, then the First Lady has a white glove pulpit…more refined, restricted, ceremonial, but it's a pulpit all the same.
    in *New York Times* 10 March 1988; see **Roosevelt 264:10**

Ronald Reagan 1911–2004
American Republican statesman; 40th President of the US, 1981–9. On Reagan: see **Keillor 166:2**, **Noonan 229:7**, **Schroeder 275:4**, **Vidal 322:5**; see also **Dempsey 88:15**, **Gipp 124:3**

10 Government is like a big baby— an alimentary canal with a big appetite at one end and no responsibility at the other.
campaigning for the governorship of California, 1965
    attributed

11 Politics is just like show business, you have a hell of an opening, coast for a while and then have a hell of a close.
    in 1966; Mark Green and Gail MacColl (eds.) *There He Goes Again* (1983)

12 Politics is supposed to be the second oldest profession. I have come to realize that it bears a very close resemblance to the first.
    at a conference in Los Angeles, 2 March 1977

13 I've noticed that everybody who is for abortion has already been born.
    presidential campaign debate, 21 September 1980

14 I paid for this microphone.
*in 1980, debating for the Republican nomination against George **Bush**; the moderator had ordered Reagan's microphone turned off when he asked for the participation of other candidates, and the refusal to allow this was held to be very damaging to Bush*
    Lou Cannon *Ronald Reagan* (1982)

1 *President **Carter** had described a proposal for a national health insurance plan*
JIMMY CARTER: Governor Reagan, again, typically is against such a proposal.
RONALD REAGAN: There you go again!
as Republican challenger debating with President Carter in the 1980 presidential campaign; in *Times* 30 October 1980

2 You can tell a lot about a fellow's character by his way of eating jellybeans.
in *New York Times* 15 January 1981

3 We're the party that wants to see an America in which people can still get rich.
at a Republican congressional dinner, 4 May 1982

4 So in your discussions of the nuclear freeze proposals, I urge you to beware the temptation of pride—the temptation blithely to declare yourselves above it all and label both sides equally at fault, to ignore the facts of history and the aggressive impulses of an evil empire.
speech to the National Association of Evangelicals, 8 March 1983

5 My fellow Americans, I am pleased to tell you I just signed legislation which outlaws Russia forever. The bombing begins in five minutes.
said during radio microphone test, 11 August 1984
in *New York Times* 13 August 1984

6 If we ever forget that we are one nation under God, then we will be a nation gone under.
speech to ecumenical prayer breakfast in Dallas, Texas, August 1984

7 I've laid down the law, though, to everyone from now on about anything that happens: no matter what time it is, wake me, even if it's in the middle of a Cabinet meeting.
speech to the White House Correspondents Association, 1984

8 The taxpayer—that's someone who works for the federal government but doesn't have to take a Civil Service examination.
attributed, 1985

9 We are especially not going to tolerate these attacks from outlaw states run by the strangest collection of misfits, Looney Tunes, and squalid criminals since the advent of the Third Reich.
speech following the hijack of a US plane, 8 July 1985
in *New York Times* 9 July 1985

10 We will never forget them, nor the last time we saw them this morning, as they prepared for the journey and waved goodbye and 'slipped the surly bonds of earth' to 'touch the face of God.'
after the loss of the space shuttle Challenger *with all its crew*
broadcast from the Oval Office, 28 January 1986, quoting from 'High Flight' by the American airman John Gillespie Magee (1922–41)

11 The nine most terrifying words in the English language are, 'I'm from the government and I'm here to help.'
on assistance to farmers
at a press conference in Chicago, 2 August 1986

12 Government's view of the economy could be summed up in a few short phrases: If it moves, tax it. If it keeps moving, regulate it. And if it stops moving, subsidize it.
National White House Conference on Small Business, 15 August 1986

13 Mr Gorbachev, tear down this wall!
at the Brandenburg Gate in West Berlin, 12 June 1987

14 We have listened to the wisdom in an old Russian maxim. And I'm sure you're familiar with it, Mr General Secretary. The maxim is...'trust, but verify'.
at the signing of the INF treaty on arms limitation, 8 December 1987, and used frequently thereafter

15 To grasp and hold a vision, that is the very essence of successful leadership—not only on the movie set where I learned it, but everywhere.
in *The Wilson Quarterly* Winter 1994; attributed

16 I now begin the journey that will

lead me into the sunset of my life.
statement to the American people revealing that he had Alzheimer's disease, 1994
in *Daily Telegraph* 5 January 1995

Red Cloud (Mahpiua Luta)

1822–1909
American Sioux chief

1 You have heard the sound of the white soldier's axe upon the Little Piney. His presence here is...an insult to the spirits of our ancestors. Are we then to give up their sacred graves to be ploughed for corn? Dakotas, I am for war!
speech at council at Fort Laramie, 1866

John Redmond 1856–1918

Irish politician and nationalist leader

2 *in the Spring of 1914 Redmond was asked by a friend, a priest from Tipperary, if anything could now rob them of Home Rule:*
A European war might do it.
in *Dictionary of National Biography* (1917–)

Joseph Reed 1741–85

American Revolutionary politician

3 I am not worth purchasing, but such as I am, the King of Great Britain is not rich enough to do it.
replying to an offer from Governor George Johnstone of £10,000, and any office in the Colonies in the King's gift, if he were able successfully to promote a Union between the United Kingdom and the American Colonies
W. B. Read *Life and Correspondence of Joseph Reed* (1847)

John Reid 1947–

British Labour politician

4 What enjoyment does a single mother of three living in a council estate get? The only enjoyment sometimes is having a cigarette.
in *Sunday Times* 13 June 2004

5 If you have a PhD and a posh accent from a school like yours, you are regarded as a sophisticate...You called me an attack dog because I've got a Glasgow accent.
*to Jeremy Paxman (see **Paxman** 241:9)*
on *Newsnight* progamme, 8 March 2005

6 Our system is not fit for purpose.
on the Home Office Immigration and Nationality Directorate (IND)
speaking to the Commons Home Affairs Committee, 23 May 2006; see **Anonymous 9:10**

Ernest Renan 1823–92

French philologist and historian

7 *L'oubli et je dirai même l'erreur historique, sont un facteur essentiel de la formation d'une nation.*
Forgetting and even mistakes in history are an essential part of becoming a nation.
usually quoted as 'Getting its history wrong is part of being a nation'
What is a Nation? (1882)

Montague John Rendall 1862–1950

British member of the first BBC Board of Governors

8 Nation shall speak peace unto nation.
motto of the BBC; see **Bible 32:21**

Jean-François Paul de Gondi, Cardinal de Retz 1613–79

French cardinal

9 There is nothing in the world which does not have its decisive moment, and the masterpiece of good management is to recognize and grasp this moment.
Mémoires (1717) bk. 2

10 There are no small steps in great affairs.
Mémoires (1717) bk. 2

11 Nothing is so uneasy as to be the minister of a prince, of whom one is not the favourite.
Mémoires (1717) bk. 3

12 Fear is, of all passions, that which weakens the judgment most.
Mémoires (1717) bk. 3

13 A man who does not trust himself will never really trust anybody.
Mémoires (1717) bk. 3

14 Every numerous assembly is a mob, influenced by their passions, humours, and affections, which nothing but eloquence ever did or

ever can engage.
attributed; Lord Chesterfield *Letters to his Son* 5 December 1749 (1901) vol. 1

1 The head of a party may do what he pleases; as long as he retains the confidence of his own friends, he can never do wrong.
attributed (not found in de Retz's writings); Adam Smith *The Theory of Moral Sentiments* (1759)

Walter Reuther 1907–70
American labour leader

2 Injustice was as common as streetcars. When men walked into their jobs, they left their dignity, their citizenship and their humanity outside.
on working life in America before the Wagner Act of 1935
attributed

Paul Revere 1735–1818
American patriot

3 To the memory of the glorious Ninety-two: members of the Honorable House of Representatives of the Massachusetts Bay who, undaunted by the insolent menaces of villains in power, from a strict regard to conscience and the liberties of their constituents on the 30th June 1768 voted NOT TO RESCIND.
inscription on Revere's silver 'Liberty' bowl, 1768
attributed

4 [We agreed] that if the British went out by water, we would show two lanterns in the North Church steeple; and if by land, one as a signal; for we were apprehensive it would be difficult to cross the Charles River or get over Boston Neck.
signals to be used if the British troops moved out of Boston
arrangements agreed with the Charlestown Committee of Safety on 16 April, 1775

Cecil Rhodes 1853–1902
South African statesman. See also **Last words 179:**

5 Being an Englishman is the greates prize in the lottery of life.
A. W. Jarvis *Jottings from an Active Life* (1928)

David Ricardo 1772–1823
British economist

6 Rent is that portion of the earth, which is paid to the landlord for the use of the original and indestructible powers of the soil.
On the Principles of Political Economy and Taxation (1817)

Condoleezza Rice 1954–
American Republican politician, National Security Advisor 2001–5, Secretary of State 2005–9

7 We don't want the smoking gun to be a mushroom cloud.
interviewed by Wolf Blitzer for CNN, 8 September 2002; quoted on CNN.com 10 January 2003

8 When the Founding Fathers said 'we the people', they did not mean me. My ancestors were three-fifths of a man.
in *Independent* 3 April 2004 (see **Constitution 79:8, Constitution 79:9**)

Grantland Rice 1880–1954
American sports writer

9 All wars are planned by old men In council rooms apart.
'The Two Sides of War' (1955)

Stephen Rice 1637–1715
Irish lawyer

10 I will drive a coach and six horses through the Act of Settlement.
W. King *State of the Protestants of Ireland* (1672)

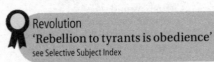

Revolution
'Rebellion to tyrants is obedience'
see Selective Subject Index

Tim Rice 1944–
English songwriter

1 Don't cry for me, Argentina.
from the musical Evita, *based on the life of Eva Perón*
title of song (1976)

Mandy Rice-Davies 1944–
English model and showgirl

2 *at the trial of Stephen Ward, 29 June 1963, on being told that Lord Astor claimed that her allegations, concerning himself and his house parties at Cliveden, were untrue:*
He would, wouldn't he?
in *Guardian* 1 July 1963

Ann Richards 1933–2006
American Democratic politician

3 That dog won't hunt.
of Republican policies
keynote speech at the Democratic convention, 1988

4 Poor George, he can't help it—he was born with a silver foot in his mouth.
of George **Bush**
keynote speech at the Democratic convention, 1988

Johann Paul Friedrich Richter
1763–1825
German novelist

5 Providence has given to the French the empire of the land, to the English that of the sea, and to the Germans that of—the air!
Thomas Carlyle 'Jean Paul Friedrich Richter' in *Edinburgh Review* no. 91 (1827)

Adam Ridley 1942–
British economist, former Director of the Conservative Research Department

6 Parties come to power with silly, inconsistent and impossible policies because they have spent their whole period in opposition forgetting about the real world, destroying the lessons they learnt in government and clambering slowly back on to the ideological plain where they feel happiest.
in *RIPA Report* Winter 1985

Nicholas Ridley 1929–93
British Conservative politician

7 *of the European monetary union:*
This is all a German racket designed to take over the whole of Europe.
in an interview with Dominic Lawson, in the aftermath of which Ridley resigned from the Government
in *Spectator* 14 July 1990

Louis Riel 1844–85
Canadian Métis political leader

8 People say the native stands on the edge of a chasm. It is not he who stands on the edge of a chasm; his claims are not false. They are just… Every step the Indian takes is based on a profound sense of fairness.
diary, 6 May 1885

9 I have been hunted as an elk for fifteen years.
speaking at the end of his trial, 1 August 1885; *The Queen vs. Louis Riel* (1886)

10 Every day in which I have neglected to prepare myself to die was a day of mental alienation.
interview published in the *Regina Leader* shortly before his execution by hanging on 16 November 1885

George Robertson 1946–
British Labour politician

11 Serbs out, Nato in, refugees back.
summing up the Nato objective in Kosovo, 7 June 1999

Maximilien Robespierre 1758–94
French revolutionary. On Robespierre: see **Carlyle 57:1**

12 I am no courtier, nor moderator, nor Tribune, nor defender of the people: I am myself the people.
speech at the Jacobin Club, 27 April 1792

13 *Citoyens, vouliez-vous une revolution sans revolution?*
Citizens, would you want a revolution without revolution?
speech to the Convention, 5 November 1792

14 The general will rules in society as the private will governs each

separate individual.
Lettres à ses commettans (2nd series) 5 January 1793

1 Any law which violates the inalienable rights of man is essentially unjust and tyrannical; it is not a law at all.
Déclaration des droits de l'homme 24 April 1793, article 6; this article, in slightly different form, is recorded as having figured in Robespierre's *Projet* of 21 April 1793

2 Any institution which does not suppose the people good, and the magistrate corruptible, is evil.
Déclaration des droits de l'homme 24 April 1793, article 25

3 Avoid the ancient insanity of governments: the mania of wishing to govern too much.
speech, 10 May 1793; F.-A. Aulard *The French Revolution* (1910)

4 The revolutionary government is the despotism of liberty against tyranny.
speech, 5 February 1794

5 Wickedness is the root of despotism as virtue is the essence of the Republic.
in the Convention, 7 May 1794

6 One single will is necessary.
private note; S. A. Berville and J. F. Barrière *Papiers inédits trouvés chez Robespierre* vol. 2 (1828)

7 Intimidation without virtue is disastrous; virtue without intimidation is powerless.
J. M. Thompson *The French Revolution*; attributed

Mary Robinson 1944–
Irish Labour stateswoman; President 1990–97

8 Instead of rocking the cradle, they rocked the system.
in her victory speech, paying tribute to the women of Ireland
in *Times* 10 November 1990

9 There are 70 million people living on this globe who claim Irish descent. I will be proud to represent them.
inaugural speech as President, 1990

10 May it be a presidency where I the President can sing to you, citizens of Ireland, the joyous refrain of the 14th century Irish poet as recalled by W. B. Yeats: 'I am of Ireland... come dance with me in Ireland.'
inaugural speech as President, 1990

11 As a native of Ballina, one of the most western towns in the most western province of the most western nation in Europe, I want to say—'the West's awake.'
inaugural speech as President, 1990; see **Davis 86:6**

Boyle Roche 1743–1807
Irish politician

12 Mr Speaker, I smell a rat; I see him forming in the air and darkening the sky; but I'll nip him in the bud.
attributed

Lord Rochester 1647–80
English poet. See also **Epitaphs 106:3**

13 A merry monarch, scandalous and poor.
'A Satire on King Charles II' (1697)

Almiro Rodrigues 1932–
Portuguese judge, presiding at the War Crimes Tribunal in The Hague

14 Individually you agreed to evil.
sentencing the Bosnian Serb General Radislav Krstic for his part in the massacre of Bosnian Muslims at Srebenica in July 1995
at The Hague, 2 August 2001

Sue Rodriguez 1951–94
Canadian activist for the legalization of assisted suicide

15 If I cannot give consent to my own death, then whose body is this? Who owns my life?
appealing to a subcommittee of the Canadian Commons, November 1992, as the victim of a terminal illness
in *Globe and Mail* 5 December 1992

Will Rogers 1879–1935
American actor and humorist

16 The more you read and observe about this Politics thing, you got to admit that each party is worse than the other. The one that's out alway

looks the best.
Illiterate Digest (1924)

1 A conservative is a man who has plenty of money and doesn't see why he shouldn't always have plenty of money...A Democrat is a fellow who never had any money but doesn't see why he shouldn't have some money.
Alex Ayres (ed.) *The Wit and Wisdom of Will Rogers* (1993)

2 I am not a member of any organized political party—I am a Democrat.
P. J. O'Brien *Will Rogers* (1935)

3 I don't know jokes—I just watch the government and report the facts.
'A Rogers Thesaurus' in *Saturday Review* 25 August 1962

4 Communism is like prohibition, it's a good idea but it won't work.
in 1927; *Weekly Articles* (1981) vol. 3

Mme Roland see **Last words 179:6**

Oscar Romero 1917–80
Salvadorean Roman Catholic priest, Archbishop of San Salvador

5 When a dictatorship seriously violates human rights and attacks the common good of the nation, when it becomes unbearable and closes all channels of dialogue, of understanding, of rationality, when this happens, the Church speaks of the legitimate right of insurrectional violence.
Alan Riding 'The Cross and the Sword in Latin America' (1981)

Erwin Rommel 1891–1944
German field marshal

6 The first twenty-four hours of the invasion will be decisive...for the Allies, as well as Germany, it will be the longest day.
to his aide, 22 April 1944; Cornelius Ryan *The Longest Day: June 6, 1944* (1959)

Eleanor Roosevelt 1884–1962
American humanitarian and diplomat. On Roosevelt: see **Stevenson 301:9**

7 Always be on time...Do as little talking as humanly possible... Remember to lean back in the parade car so everybody can see the president.
campaign rules for wives
in 1936; Beth Furman *Washington Byline* (1949)

8 Is there anything we can do for you? For you are the one in trouble now.
*to Harry **Truman**, who became President on the death of Franklin D. **Roosevelt***
in conversation, 12 April 1945

9 I cannot believe that war is the best solution. No one won the last war, and no one will win the next war.
letter to Harry Truman, 22 March 1948

10 I have always felt that anyone who wanted an election so much that they would use those methods did not have the character that I really admired in public life.
*on the tactics used by Richard **Nixon** in his 1950 Senatorial campaign against the actress and politician Helen Gahagan Douglas*
on 'Meet the Press' (NBC TV), 16 September 1956

11 No one can make you feel inferior without your consent.
in *Catholic Digest* August 1960

Franklin D. Roosevelt 1882–1945
American Democratic statesman, 32nd President of the US 1933–45. On Roosevelt: see **Churchill 68:12, Holmes 146:6, Truman 317:1**

12 These unhappy times call for the building of plans that...build from the bottom up and not from the top down, that put their faith once more in the forgotten man at the bottom of the economic pyramid.
radio address, 7 April 1932

13 I pledge you, I pledge myself, to a

Rome
'Carthage must be destroyed'
see Selective Subject Index

new deal for the American people.
accepting the presidential nomination
speech to the Democratic Convention in Chicago, 2 July 1932

1 The only thing we have to fear is fear itself.
inaugural address, 4 March 1933

2 In the field of world policy I would dedicate this Nation to the policy of the good neighbour.
inaugural address, 4 March 1933

3 We face the arduous days that lie before us in the warm courage of national unity.
inaugural address, 4 March 1933; see **Bush 51:3**

4 This generation of Americans has a rendezvous with destiny.
speech accepting renomination as President, 27 June 1936

5 I have seen war. I have seen war on land and sea. I have seen blood running from the wounded. I have seen men coughing out their gassed lungs. I have seen the dead in the mud. I have seen cities destroyed. I have seen 200 limping, exhausted men come out of line—the survivors of a regiment of 1,000 that went forward 48 hours before. I have seen children starving. I have seen the agony of mothers and wives. I hate war.
speech at Chautauqua, NY, 14 August 1936

6 I see one-third of a nation ill-housed, ill-clad, ill-nourished.
second inaugural address, 20 January 1937

7 The only sure bulwark of continuing liberty is a government strong enough to protect the interests of the people, and a people strong enough and well enough informed to maintain its sovereign control over its government.
'Fireside Chat' radio broadcast, 14 April 1938

8 When peace has been broken anywhere, the peace of all countries everywhere is in danger.
'Fireside Chat' radio broadcast, 3 September 1939

9 I am reminded of four definitions: A Radical is a man with both feet firmly planted—in the air. A

Conservative is a man with two perfectly good legs who, however, has never learned to walk forward. A Reactionary is a somnambulist walking backwards. A Liberal is a man who uses his legs and his hands at the behest—at the command—of his head.
radio address to *New York Herald Tribune* Forum, 26 October 1939

10 On this tenth day of June 1940 the hand that held the dagger has struck it into the back of its neighbour.
on hearing that Italy had declared war on France
address at the University of Virginia, Charlottesville, 10 June 1940

11 I have said this before, but I shall say it again and again and again: Your boys are not going to be sent into any foreign wars.
speech in Boston, 30 October 1940

12 We have the men—the skill—the wealth—and above all, the will... We must be the great arsenal of democracy.
'Fireside Chat' radio broadcast, 29 December 1940

13 We, too, born to freedom, and believing in freedom, are willing to fight to maintain freedom. We, and all others who believe as deeply as we do, would rather die on our feet than live on our knees.
on receiving the degree of Doctor of Civil Law from Oxford
on 19 June 1941; see **Ibarruri 151:8**

14 We look forward to a world founded upon four essential human freedoms. The first is freedom of speech and expression—everywhere in the world. The second is freedom of every person to worship God in his own way—everywhere in the world. The third is freedom from want...everywhere in the world. The fourth is freedom from fear...anywhere in the world.
message to Congress, 6 January 1941

15 I can't believe that we can fight a war against fascist slavery, and at the same time not work to free people all over the world from a

backward colonial policy.
*drawing up the Atlantic Charter with **Churchill*** *on board the Augusta, August 1941; Elliott Roosevelt As He Saw It (1946)*

1 Yesterday, December 7, 1941—a date which will live in infamy— the United States of America was suddenly and deliberately attacked by naval and air forces of the Empire of Japan.
address to Congress, 8 December 1941

2 Books can not be killed by fire. People die, but books never die. No man and no force can abolish memory...In this war, we know, books are weapons. And it is a part of your dedication always to make them weapons for man's freedom.
'Message to the Booksellers of America' 6 May 1942

3 The American people are quite competent to judge a political party that works both sides of the street.
campaign speech in Boston, 4 November 1944

4 We have learned that we cannot live alone, at peace; that our own well-being is dependent on the well-being of other nations, far away. We have learned that we must live as men, and not as ostriches, nor as dogs in the manger. We have learned to be citizens of the world, members of the human community.
fourth inaugural address, 20 January 1945

5 Oh Lord, give us faith. Give us faith in Thee; faith in our sons; faith in each other; faith in our united crusade.
address to the nation, D-Day, 6 June 1944

6 It is fun to be in the same decade with you.
cabled reply to Winston Churchill, acknowledging congratulations on his 60th birthday in 1942. Churchill was then 67
W. S. Churchill *The Hinge of Fate* (1950)

7 You've convinced me. Now go out and put pressure on me.
attributed; Peter Hennessy *Whitehall* (1990)

8 The work, my friend, is peace. More than an end of this war—an end to the beginnings of all wars.
undelivered address for Jefferson Day, 13 April 1945, the day after Roosevelt died
Public Papers (1950) vol. 13

9 The only limit to our realization of tomorrow will be our doubts of today. Let us move forward with strong and active faith.
undelivered address for Jefferson Day, 13 April 1945, final lines
Public Papers (1950) vol. 13

Theodore Roosevelt 1858–1919
American Republican statesman, 26th President of the US 1901–9. On Roosevelt: see **Hanna 135:3, Knox 175:12**; see also **Last words 179:7**

10 I wish to preach, not the doctrine of ignoble ease, but the doctrine of the strenuous life.
speech to the Hamilton Club, Chicago, 10 April 1899

11 I am as strong as a bull moose and you can use me to the limit.
'Bull Moose' subsequently became the popular name of the Progressive Party
letter to Mark **Hanna**, 27 June 1900

12 McKinley has no more backbone than a chocolate éclair!
of William McKinley (1843–1901), Republican statesman and 25th President of the US, whose assassination brought about the accession of Roosevelt
H. T. Peck *Twenty Years of the Republic* (1906)

13 The first requisite of a good citizen in this Republic of ours is that he shall be able and willing to pull his weight.
speech in New York, 11 November 1902

14 There is a homely old adage which runs: 'Speak softly and carry a big stick; you will go far.' If the American nation will speak softly, and yet build and keep at a pitch of the highest training a thoroughly efficient navy, the Monroe Doctrine will go far.
speech in Chicago, 3 April 1903

15 A man who is good enough to shed his blood for the country is good enough to be given a square deal afterwards. More than that no man is entitled to, and less than that no

man shall have.
speech at the Lincoln Monument, Springfield,
Illinois, 4 June 1903; see **Slogans 292:1**

1 Far and away the best prize that life
offers is the chance to work hard at
work worth doing.
address at the State Fair, Syracuse, New York
Labour Day, 7 September 1903

2 You can no more make an
agreement with those leaders of
Colombia than you can nail currant
jelly to the wall. And the failure
to nail currant jelly to the wall is
not due to the nail. It's due to the
currant jelly.
at the time of the Panama revolution, 1903
attributed by Edmund Morris, John F. Kennedy
Presidential Historians Forum, 5 March 2002

3 The men with the muckrakes
are often indispensable to the
well-being of society; but only if
they know when to stop raking the
muck.
speech in Washington, 14 April 1906

4 [My ability] to put into words what
is in their hearts and minds but not
in their mouths.
*when asked by Douglas MacArthur in 1906 to
what he attributed his popularity*
William Safire *New Political Dictionary* (1978)

5 It is not the critic who counts; not
the man who points out how the
strong man stumbles, or where
the doer of deeds could have done
better. The credit belongs to the
man who is actually in the arena.
'Citizenship in a Republic', speech at the
Sorbonne, Paris, 23 April 1910

6 We stand at Armageddon and we
battle for the Lord.
speech at Progressive Party Convention,
Chicago, 17 June 1912

7 There is no room in this country
for hyphenated Americanism...
The one absolutely certain way
of bringing this nation to ruin,
of preventing all possibility of its
continuing to be a nation at all,
would be to permit it to become a
tangle of squabbling nationalities.
speech in New York, 12 October 1915

8 One of our defects as a nation
is a tendency to use what have

been called 'weasel words'. When
a weasel sucks eggs the meat is
sucked out of the egg. If you use a
'weasel word' after another, there is
nothing left of the other.
speech in St Louis, 31 May 1916

9 Foolish fanatics...the men who
form the lunatic fringe in all reform
movements.
Autobiography (1913)

10 I have got such a bully pulpit!
his personal view of the presidency
in *Outlook* (New York) 27 February 1909; see
Reagan 255:9

11 To announce that there must
be no criticism of the president,
or that we are to stand by the
president, right or wrong, is not
only unpatriotic and servile, but
is morally treasonable to the
American public.
in *Kansas City Star* 7 May 1918

12 No man is justified in doing evil on
the ground of expediency.
Works (1925) vol. 15 'Latitude and Longitude
among Reformers'

Lord Rosebery 1847–1929
British Liberal statesman; Prime Minister, 1894–5

13 There is no need for any nation,
however great, leaving the
Empire, because the Empire is a
commonwealth of nations.
speech in Adelaide, Australia, 18 January 1884

14 I have never known the sweets
of place with power, but of place
without power, of place with the
minimum of power—that is a
purgatory, and if not a purgatory it
is a hell.
in *The Spectator* 6 July 1895

15 Imperialism, sane Imperialism, as
distinguished from what I may call
wild-cat Imperialism, is nothing
but this—a larger patriotism.
speech, City of London Liberal Club, 5 May
1899

16 It is beginning to be hinted that we
are a nation of amateurs.
Rectorial address at Glasgow University,
16 November 1900

17 No one outside an asylum wishes to

be rid of it.
of the British Empire
Rectorial address at Glasgow University,
16 November 1900

1 I must plough my furrow alone.
*speech on remaining outside the Liberal Party
leadership, 19 July 1901*
in *Times* 20 July 1901

2 There are two supreme pleasures in
life. One is ideal, the other real. The
ideal is when a man receives the
seals of office from his Sovereign.
The real pleasure comes when he
hands them back.
Sir Robert Peel (1899)

Ethel Rosenberg 1916–53 and Julius Rosenberg 1918–53

3 We are innocent...To forsake this
truth is to pay too high a price even
for the priceless gift of life.
petition for executive clemency, filed 9 January
1953; Ethel Rosenberg *Death House Letters*
(1953)

4 We are the first victims of American
Fascism.
letter from Julius to Emanuel Bloch before
the Rosenbergs' execution, 19 June 1953;
Testament of Ethel and Julius Rosenberg (1954)

Lord Rothschild 1910–90
British administrator and scientist. On Rothschild: see
Hurd 150:5

5 Politicians often believe that their
world is the real one. Officials
sometimes take a different view.
*on resigning as Director of the Central Policy
Review Staff*
in *Times* 13 October 1974

6 The promises and panaceas that
gleam like false teeth in the party
manifestoes.
Meditations of a Broomstick (1977)

Jean-Jacques Rousseau 1712–78
French philosopher and novelist

7 The social contract
title of book, 1762

8 Man was born free, and everywhere
he is in chains.
The Social Contract (1762)

9 Slaves become so debased by their

chains as to lose even the desire of
breaking from them.
The Social Contract (1762)

Maude Royden 1876–1956
English religious writer

10 The Church should go forward
along the path of progress and be
no longer satisfied only to represent
the Conservative Party at prayer.
address at Queen's Hall, London, 16 July 1917

Kevin Rudd 1957–
Australian statesman, Prime Minister 2007–10

11 My name is Kevin, I'm from
Queensland and I'm here to help.
speech to Australian Labor Party conference,
27 April 2007

Richard Rumbold c. 1622–85
English republican conspirator

12 I never could believe that
Providence had sent a few men
into the world, ready booted and
spurred to ride, and millions ready
saddled and bridled to be ridden.
on the scaffold
T. B. Macaulay *History of England* vol. 1 (1849)

Donald Rumsfeld 1932–
American Republican politician and businessman,
Defense Secretary 2001–6

13 When they are being moved
from place to place, will they be
restrained in a way so that they
are less likely to be able to kill an
American soldier? You bet. Is it
inhumane to do that? No. Would it
be stupid to do anything else? Yes.
on al-Qaeda prisoners being held in Cuba
in *Times* 26 January 2002

14 Reports that say that something
hasn't happened are always
interesting to me, because as we
know, there are known knowns;
there are things we know we know.
We also know there are known
unknowns; that is to say we know
there are some things we do not
know. But there are also unknown
unknowns—the ones we don't

know we don't know.
to a Defense Department meeting, 12 February 2002

1 You're thinking of Europe as Germany and France. I don't. I think that's old Europe. If you look at the entire Nato Europe today, the centre of gravity is shifting to the east.
to journalists who asked him about European hostility to a possible war, 22 January 2003
in *Independent* 21 February 2003

2 Stuff happens.
on looting in Iraq
press conference, 11 April 2003

3 You go to war with the Army you have. They're not the Army you might want or wish to have at a later time.
briefing to troops at a Town Hall Meeting in Kuwait, 8 December 2004

Robert Runcie 1921–2000
English Protestant clergyman; Archbishop of Canterbury

4 People are mourning on both sides of this conflict. In our prayers we shall quite rightly remember those who are bereaved in our own country and the relations of the young Argentinian soldiers who were killed. Common sorrow could do something to reunite those who were engaged in this struggle. A shared anguish can be a bridge of reconciliation. Our neighbours are indeed like us.
service of thanksgiving at the end of the Falklands war, St Paul's Cathedral, London, 26 July 1982

Dean Rusk 1909–94
American politician; Secretary of State, 1961–9

5 We're eyeball to eyeball, and I think the other fellow just blinked.
on the Cuban missile crisis, 24 October 1962
in *Saturday Evening Post* 8 December 1962

6 Only one-third of human beings are asleep at one time, and the other two-thirds are awake and up to some mischief somewhere.
attributed, 1966

7 Scratch any American and

underneath you'll find an isolationist.
to the British Foreign Secretary, George Brown; Tony Benn diary 12 January 1968

8 It has been said that power tends to corrupt, but that loss of power tends to corrupt absolutely.
attributed, 1968; see **Acton 1:10**

John Ruskin 1819–1900
English art and social critic

9 We Communists of the old school think that our property belongs to everybody, and everybody's property to us; so of course I thought the Louvre belonged to me as much as to the Parisians, and expected they would have sent word over to me, being an Art Professor, to ask whether I wanted it burnt down. But no message or intimation to that effect ever reached me.
Fors Clavigera (1871)

10 You have founded an entire Science of Political Economy, on what you have stated to be the constant instinct of man—the desire to defraud his neighbour.
Fors Clavigera (1871)

11 Visible governments are the toys of some nations, the diseases of others, the harness of some, the burdens of more, the necessity of all.
Fors Clavigera (1871)

12 I am, and my father was before me, a violent Tory of the old school; Walter Scott's school, that is to say, and Homer's.
Praeterita (1885)

13 The first duty of a State is to see that every child born therein shall be well housed, clothed, fed and educated, till it attain years of discretion.
Time and Tide (1867)

14 All mastership is not alike in principle; there are just and unjust masterships.
Time and Tide (1867)

15 You want to have voices in

Parliament! Your voices are not worth a rat's squeak, either in Parliament or out of it, till you have some ideas to utter with them.
Time and Tide (1867)

1 It ought to be quite as natural and straightforward a matter for a labourer to take his pension from his parish, because he has deserved well of his parish, as for a man in higher rank to take his pension from his country, because he has deserved well of his country.
Unto this Last (1862) preface

2 The force of the guinea you have in your pocket depends wholly on the default of a guinea in your neighbour's pocket. If he did not want it, it would be of no use to you.
Unto this Last (1862)

3 Government and co-operation are in all things the laws of life; anarchy and competition the laws of death.
Unto this Last (1862)

4 Whereas it has long been known and declared that the poor have no right to the property of the rich, I wish it also to be known and declared that the rich have no right to the property of the poor.
Unto this Last (1862)

Bertrand Russell 1872–1970
British philosopher and mathematician

5 Envy is the basis of democracy.
The Conquest of Happiness (1930)

6 One should as a rule respect public opinion in so far as is necessary to avoid starvation and to keep out of prison, but anything that goes beyond this is voluntary submission to an unnecessary tyranny.
The Conquest of Happiness (1930)

7 Next to enjoying ourselves, the next greatest pleasure consists in preventing others from enjoying themselves, or, more generally, in the acquisition of power.
Sceptical Essays (1928)

8 The opinions that are held with passion are always those for which no good ground exists; indeed the passion is the measure of the holder's lack of rational conviction.
Sceptical Essays (1928)

9 If the Communists conquered the world it would be very unpleasant for a while, but not for ever.
attributed, 1958

10 Few people can be happy unless they hate some other person, nation, or creed.
attributed

11 Religion may in most of its forms be defined as the belief that the gods are on the side of the Government.
attributed

12 The trouble with the world is that the stupid are cocksure and the intelligent are full of doubt.
attributed

Lord John Russell 1792–1878
British Whig statesman; Prime Minister 1846–52, 1865–6. On Russell: see **Derby 89:7**, **Smith 294:10**

13 It is impossible that the whisper of a faction should prevail against the voice of a nation.
reply to an Address from a meeting of 150,000 persons at Birmingham on the defeat of the second Reform Bill, October 1831
S. Walpole *Life of Lord John Russell* (1889)

14 If peace cannot be maintained with honour, it is no longer peace.
speech at Greenock, 19 September 1853; see **Disraeli 94:3**

15 Among the defects of the Bill, which were numerous, one provision was conspicuous by its presence and another by its absence.
speech to the electors of the City of London, April 1859

Russia
'riddle wrapped in a mystery'
see Selective Subject Index

Anwar al-Sadat 1918–81
Egyptian statesman, President 1970–81

1 Peace is much more precious than a piece of land.
   speech in Cairo, 8 March 1978

Mohammed al-Sahhaf 1940–
Iraqi politician, Minister of Information in Saddam **Hussein**'s government, nicknamed 'Comical Ali'

2 Baghdad is safe, protected. There are no American infidels in Baghdad.
   press briefing during the war in Iraq
   in *Sunday Telegraph* 13 April 2003

3 I now inform you that you are too far from reality.
   final briefing to the press in Baghdad
   in *Sunday Telegraph* 13 April 2003

Andrei Sakharov 1921–89
Russian nuclear physicist

4 Every day I saw the huge material, intellectual and nervous resources of thousands of people being poured into the creation of a means of total destruction, something capable of annihilating all human civilization. I noticed that the control levers were in the hands of people who, though talented in their own ways, were cynical.
   Sakharov Speaks (1974)

Saki (Hector Hugh Munro)
1870–1916
Scottish writer

5 We all know that Prime Ministers are wedded to the truth, but like other married couples they sometimes live apart.
   The Unbearable Bassington (1912)

Lord Salisbury (Robert Arthur Talbot Gascoyne-Cecil, third Marquess of Salisbury) 1830–1903
British Conservative statesman; Prime Minister 1855–6, 1886–92, 1895–1902. On Salisbury: see **Bismarck 34:11, Disraeli 93:23, Goschen 128:7, Hennessy 141:4**

6 She has given us foreign invasions, domestic rebellions; and in quieter times the manly sport of landlord shooting.
   on Ireland
   in *Saturday Review,* 1857

7 The witness of history is uniform to this, that Nemesis may spare the sagacious criminal, but never fails to overtake the weak, the undecided and the over-charitable fool.
   in *Saturday Review* 10 March 1860

8 They believe intensely in amiable theories, they loved the sympathy and applause of their fellow men, they were kind-hearted, and charitably fancied everybody as well meaning as themselves; and therefore—so far as it can be said of any single man—they were the proximate causes of a civil convulsion which, for the horror of its calamities, stands alone in the history of the world.
   of those he regarded as weak-willed liberals
   in *Saturday Review* 10 March 1860

9 The distribution of property and the distribution of political power are inseparably connected. If power is not made to go with property, property will, in the long run, infallibly follow power.
   in *Quarterly Review* April 1860

10 We do not care to scrutinise too

closely, the moral boundary which separates a reckless hustings pledge from premeditated fraud.
in *Saturday Review* February 1861

1 The axioms of the last age are the fallacies of the present, the principles which save one generation may be the ruin of the next. There is nothing abiding in political science but the necessity of truth, purity and justice.
on Salisbury's ultimate political hero, William **Pitt** the Younger
in *Quarterly Review* April 1861

2 No man was ever so yielding without ever being weak, or so stern without being obstinate.
of William **Pitt** the Younger
in *Quarterly Review* April 1861

3 There is nothing dramatic in the success of a diplomatist. His victories are made up of a series of microscopic advantages: of a judicious suggestion here, or an opportune civility there: of a wise concession at one moment, and a farsighted persistence at another; of sleepless tact, immovable calmness, and patience that no folly, no provocation, no blunders can shake.
on Lord Castlereagh
in *Quarterly Review* January 1862

4 *of intervention in the domestic quarrels of other countries:*
There is no practice which the experience of nations more uniformly condemns, and none which governments more consistently pursue.
in *Quarterly Review* April 1862

5 No one is fit to be trusted with a secret who is not prepared, if necessary, to tell an untruth to defend it.
in *Saturday Review* 15 November 1862

6 The just Nemesis which generally decrees that partisans shall be forced to do in office precisely that which they most loudly decried in opposition.
in *Quarterly Review* January 1862

7 In a carefully balanced structure like the European system of nations, each State has a vested right in the complete and real independence of its neighbour.
in *Quarterly Review* 1862

8 It is the same with all efforts to root up any evil by the expenditure of money. To attach a money value to the existence of an evil, even for the purpose of extirpating it, can have no other end than that of multiplying the evil.
in *Saturday Review* 10 January 1863

9 Directly man has satisfied his most elementary material wants, the first aspiration of his amiable heart is for the privilege of being able to look down upon his neighbours.
in *Saturday Review* 1864

10 First rate men will not canvas mobs: and mobs will not elect first rate men.
in 1866; Andrew Roberts *Salisbury: Victorian Titan* (1999)

11 To expect political support as a consequence of good Government is an optimist's dream. Good government avoids one of the causes of hate: but it does not inspire love.
of imperial rather than domestic government
in 1867; Andrew Roberts *Salisbury: Victorian Titan* (1999)

12 Too clever by half.
of **Disraeli**'s amendment on Disestablishment speech, House of Commons, 30 March 1868; see **Salisbury 273:8**

13 [The] perils of change are so great, the promise of the most hopeful theories is so often deceptive, that it is frequently the wiser part to uphold the existing state of things, if it can be done, even though in point of argument it should be utterly indefensible.
in *Quarterly Review* October 1871

14 I have a profound distrust of government inspectors, and I am generally disposed to find them wrong.
to the Rev. Nathaniel Woodard, 1871; Andrew Roberts *Salisbury: Victorian Titan* (1999)

1 Horny-handed sons of toil.
in *Quarterly Review* October 1873; later popularized in the US by Denis Kearney (1847–1907)

2 English policy is to float lazily downstream, occasionally putting out a diplomatic boathook to avoid collisions.
letter to Lord Lytton, 9 March 1877

3 The commonest error in politics sticking to the carcasses of dead policies. When a mast falls overboard, you do not try to save a rope here and a spar there, in memory of its former utility; you can cut away the hamper altogether.
letter to Lord Lytton, 23 April 1877

4 No lesson seems to be so deeply inculcated by the experience of life as that you never should trust experts. If you believe the doctors, nothing is wholesome: if you believe the theologians, nothing is innocent: if you believe the soldiers, nothing is safe. They all require to have their strong wine diluted by a very large admixture of insipid common sense.
letter to Lord Lytton, 15 June 1877

5 One of the nuisances of the ballot is that when the oracle has spoken you never know what it means.
to G. M. Sandford, October 1877

6 If our ancestors had cared for the rights of other people, the British Empire would not have been made.
in J. Vincent (ed.) *Derby Diaries 1869–1878* (1994) 8 March 1878

7 The agonies of a man who has to finish a difficult negotiation, and at the same time to entertain four royalties at a country house can be better imagined than described.
letter to Lord Lyons, 5 June 1878

8 What with deafness, ignorance of French, and Bismarck's extraordinary mode of speech, Beaconsfield has the dimmest idea of what is going on—understands everything crossways—and imagines a perpetual conspiracy.
on the Congress of Berlin
letter to Lady Salisbury, 23 June 1878; Lady Gwendolen Cecil *Life of Robert, Marquis of Salisbury* (1921–32)

9 Whatever happens will be for the worse, and therefore it is in our interest that as little should happen as possible.
said to Lord Dufferin about events in Persia, December 1879; Andrew Roberts *Salisbury: Victorian Titan* (1999)

10 There are marks of hurry which in so old a man are inexplicable. I suppose he still cherishes his belief in an early monastic retreat from this wicked world—and is feverishly anxious to annihilate all his enemies before he takes it.
on **Gladstone**
letter to Arthur Balfour, 16 June 1880; compare **Churchill**

11 The duty was to represent the permanent as opposed to the passing feeling of the English nation.
on the House of Lords
speech to Hackney Conservative Club, November 1880

12 I wish the English army may be equal to all the work his peace-loving policy has given it.
of **Gladstone**
letter to the Rev. Charles Conybeare, February 1881

13 As a rule I observe that the places where we win seats are the places where no Tory Leader has spoken.
letter to Arthur Balfour, 22 September 1881

14 To those who have found breakfast with difficulty and do not know where to find dinner, intricate questions of politics are a matter of comparatively secondary interest.
in 1881; Andrew Roberts *Salisbury: Victorian Titan* (1999)

15 A party whose mission it is to live entirely upon the discovery of grievances are apt to manufacture the element upon which they subsist.
speech at Edinburgh, 24 November 1882

16 By a free country, I mean a country

where people are allowed, so long as they do not hurt their neighbours, to do as they like. I do not mean a country where six men may make five men do exactly as they like.

speech to the Kingston and District Working Men's Conservative Association, June 1883

1 Possession of Ireland is our peculiar punishment, our unique affliction, among the family of nations. What crime have we committed, with what particular vice is our national character chargeable, that this chastisement should have befallen us?

in *Quarterly Review* October 1883

2 They who have the absolute power of preventing lamentable events, and knowing what is taking place, refuse to exercise that power, are responsible for what happens.

in the House of Lords, 12 February 1884

3 People imagine that where an evil exists, the Queen, the Lords and the Commons should stop it. I wonder they have not brought in an Act of Parliament to stop unfavourable weather on the occasion of political demonstrations.

speech at Newport, 7 October 1885

4 Nobody argues now. They give you an opinion neatly expressed in a single sentence, and that does the work of argument. My belief is that a fallacy in two lines will carry you further that a mathematical demonstration in two pages.

speech to Conservative Conference, St James's Hall Piccadilly, 15 May 1886

5 Upon those points upon which they are precise they are not agreed, and upon those points upon which they are agreed they are not precise.

challenging the Fair Traders to produce a detailed programme

speech to the National Unionist and Conservative Constituency Association Conference at Derby, 19 December 1887

6 We are part of the community of Europe and we must do our duty as such.

speech at Caernarvon, 10 April 1888

7 I do believe politicians would be far more ready to resign office if they did not feel that their doing so would give such infinite pleasure to their adversaries.

letter to the Duchess of Rutland, 8 March 1889

8 We have been engaged in drawing lines upon maps where no white man's foot has ever trod. We have been giving away mountains and rivers and lakes to each other, only hindered by the small impediment that we never knew exactly where the mountains and rivers and lakes were.

speech at the Mansion House, August 1890

9 Parliament is a potent engine, and its enactments must always do something, but they very seldom do what the originators of these enactments meant. [Therefore most legislation] will have the effect of surrounding the industry which it touches with precautions and investigations, inspections and regulations, in which it will be slowly enveloped and stifled.

in *Times* March 1891

10 There is not such thing as a fixed policy, because policy like all organic entities is always in the making.

in 1896; Andrew Roberts *Salisbury: Victorian Titan* (1999)

11 Where property is in question I am guilty...of erecting individual liberty as an idol, and of resenting all attempts to destroy or fetter it; but when you pass from liberty to life, in no well-governed State, in no State governed according to the principles of common humanity, are the claims of mere liberty allowed to endanger the lives of the citizens.

in the House of Lords, 29 July 1897

12 If you consider the position of the Russians ethically, it is as bad as can be. Negotiating with them is like catching soaped eels.

to Joseph Chamberlain, 1899; Andrew Roberts *Salisbury: Victorian Titan* (1999)

1 I had secretly indulged the hope that we should be beaten in this election. A spell in Opposition is so good for bracing up the Conservative fibre of our party.
letter to Lord Granby, 6 October 1900

2 In making appointments I can count on a Scotchman not falling below a certain level, they may not be very clever, but they are safe not to be stupid. There is a strong resemblance between the Scotch and the Jews. They both begin as fighters, then become very religious and finally are devoted to money-making.
in Lady Rayleigh diary, 1900; Andrew Roberts *Salisbury: Victorian Titan* (1999)

3 It is a Party shackled by tradition; all the cautious people, all the timid, all the unimaginative, belong to it. It stumbles slowly and painfully from precedent to precedent with its eyes fixed on the ground.
of the Conservative Party
letter to Lord Milner, 1901; Milner Papers

4 [The Admiralty would always] follow the progress of science at a respectful distance, always arriving at an appreciation of each successive invention just soon enough to find that it is obsolete, and never yielding their adhesion to anything new until the time has come to defend it against the claims of something newer.
Andrew Roberts *Salisbury: Victorian Titan* (1999)

5 By office boys for office boys.
of the Daily Mail
H. Hamilton Fyfe *Northcliffe, an Intimate Biography* (1930)

6 Dizzy intends to pursue the old game of talking Green in the House and Orange in the Lobby.
Andrew Roberts *Salisbury: Victorian Titan* (1999)

7 An emotion will shoot electrically through a crowd which might have appealed to each man by himself in vain.
Andrew Roberts *Salisbury: Victorian Titan* (1999)

8 A highly-paid chairman is a luxury which should be reserved for the return of a good shareholders' dividend.
Andrew Roberts *Salisbury: Victorian Titan* (1999)

9 I am an utter unbeliever that anything that is violent will have permanent results.
Andrew Roberts *Salisbury: Victorian Titan* (1999)

10 If these gentlemen had their way, they would soon be asking me to defend the moon against a possible attack from Mars.
of his senior military advisers, and their tendency to see threats which did not exist
Robert Taylor *Lord Salisbury* (1975)

11 An indiscreet admirer is a far more intolerable nuisance than an acrimonious enemy.
Andrew Roberts *Salisbury: Victorian Titan* (1999)

12 In this country we have got to look upon Budget promises as made of the same stuff as lovers' oaths.
Andrew Roberts *Salisbury: Victorian Titan* (1999)

13 I rank myself no higher in the scheme of things than a policeman—whose utility would disappear if there were no criminals.
comparing his role in the Conservative Party with that of **Gladstone**
Lady Gwendolen Cecil *Biographical Studies...of Robert, Third Marquess of Salisbury* (1962)

14 It's difficult enough to go around doing what is right without going around trying to do good.
Andrew Roberts *Salisbury: Victorian Titan* (1999)

15 I wish party government was at the bottom of the sea. It is only insincerity codified.
Arthur Hardinge *Life of Henry Herbert, 4th Earl of Carnarvon* (1925) vol. 2

16 One of the difficulties about great thinkers is that they so often

think wrong.
Andrew Roberts *Salisbury: Victorian Titan*
(1999)

1 A parapet which gives way when
you lean upon it is more dangerous
than no parapet at all.
*on his private uncertainty of the degree to which
he could rely on colleagues' support for the
Reform Bill*
Andrew Roberts *Salisbury: Victorian Titan*
(1999)

2 The result of recent experience is
that 'if you wish to keep a secret
you must say nothing 1. To Cabinet
Ministers. 2. To Foreign Diplomats.
3. To the War Office'.
in minutes to Lord Bertie; Andrew Roberts
Salisbury: Victorian Titan (1999)

3 To defend a bad policy as an 'error
of judgement' does not excuse
it—the right functioning of a man's
judgement is his most fundamental
responsibility.
Gwendolen Cecil *Life of Robert, Marquis of
Salisbury* (1921–32) vol. 3

4 A very useful institution. It fosters a
wholesome taste for bright colours,
and gives old men who have good
legs an excuse for showing them.
*of the Order of the Garter, which had been
awarded to both his father and grandfather as
well as the early Cecils*
in Houghton Papers; Andrew Roberts *Salisbury:
Victorian Titan* (1999)

5 When a man says that he agrees
with me in principle, I am quite
certain that he does not agree with
me in practice.
Andrew Roberts *Salisbury: Victorian Titan*
(1999)

6 When great men get drunk with a
theory, it is the little men who have
the headache.
on political theorists
Andrew Roberts *Salisbury: Victorian Titan*
(1899)

7 [Whitehall] will create business for
itself surely as a new railway will
create traffic.
Andrew Roberts *Salisbury: Victorian Titan*
(1999)

Lord Salisbury (Robert Arthur James Gascoyne-Cecil, fifth Marquess of Salisbury) 1893–1972
British Conservative politician

8 Too clever by half.
of Iain **Macleod**, *Colonial Secretary, 'in his
relationship to the white communities of Africa'*
in the House of Lords, 7 March 1961; see
Salisbury 269:12

Sallust 86–35 BC
Roman historian

9 *Alieni appetens, sui profusus.*
Greedy for the property of others,
extravagant with his own.
Catiline

10 *Quieta movere magna merces
videbatur.*
To stir up undisputed matters
seemed a great reward in itself.
Catiline

11 *Esse quam videri bonus malebat.*
He preferred to be rather than to
seem good.
of Cato
Catiline

12 *Urbem venalem et mature
perituram, si emptorem invenerit.*
A venal city ripe to perish, if a buyer
can be found.
of Rome
Jugurtha

13 *Punica fide.*
With Carthaginian
trustworthiness.
meaning treachery
Jugurtha

Alex Salmond 1954–
Scottish Nationalist politician

14 Nobody ever celebrated Devolution
Day.
asserting his belief in full independence
in *Independent* 2 April 1992

15 The Scottish parliament is our
passport to independence.
*outgoing speech as party leader to the Scottish
Nationalist Party Conference,* in *Guardian*
23 September 2000

Anthony Sampson 1926–2004
British author and journalist

1 A secret tome of *The Great and the Good* is kept, listing everyone who has the right, safe qualifications of worthiness, soundness and discretion; and from this tome came the stage army of committee people.
Anatomy of Britain Today (1965)

Paul A. Samuelson 1915–2009
American economist

2 Wall Street indexes predicted nine out of the last five recessions.
in *Newsweek* 19 September 1966

Lord Sandwich 1718–92
British politician and diplomat; First Lord of the Admiralty

3 If any man will draw up his case, and put his name at the foot of the first page, I will give him an immediate reply. Where he compels me to turn over the sheet, he must wait my leisure.
on appeals made by officers to the Navy Board
N. W. Wraxall *Memoirs* (1884) vol. 1

George Santayana 1863–1952
Spanish-born philosopher and critic

4 Fanaticism consists in redoubling your effort when you have forgotten your aim.
The Life of Reason (1905); introduction

5 Those who cannot remember the past are condemned to repeat it.
The Life of Reason (1905)

Jacques Santer 1937–
Luxembourgeois politician, former head of the European Commission

6 I note with considerable satisfaction that I am whiter than white.
of the inquiry into fraud at the European Commission
at a news conference, 16 March 1999

Nicolas Sarkozy 1955–
French statesman; President from 2007

7 The referendum? It'll be a small no...or a big no.
attributed in Guardian 27 May 2005 (online edition)

Patrick Sarsfield c. 1655–93
Irish Jacobite. See also **Last words 179:17**

8 As low as we now are, change kings with us, and we will fight it over again with you.
to English officers during negotiations for the Treaty of Limerick, 1690
in *Dictionary of National Biography* (1917–)

Jean-Paul Sartre 1905–80
French philosopher, novelist, dramatist, and critic

9 When the rich wage war it's the poor who die.
Le Diable et le bon Dieu (1951)

Sayings see **Proverbs**

Hugh Scanlon 1913–2004
British trade union leader. On Scanlon: see **Wilson 334:12**

10 Of course liberty is not licence. Liberty in my view is conforming to majority opinion.
television interview, 9 August 1977

Lord Scarman 1911–2004
British judge

11 A government above the law is a menace to be defeated.
Why Britain Needs a Written Constitution (1992)

12 When times are abnormally alive with fear and prejudice, the common law is at a disadvantage: it cannot resist the will, however frightened and prejudiced it may be, of parliament.
after delivering a lecture advocating the establishment of a Bill of Rights
in conversation, 20 July 1992; Anthony Sampson *The Essential Anatomy of Britain* (1992)

Arthur M. Schlesinger Jr.
1917–2007
American historian

13 The answer to the runaway Presidency is not the messenger-

boy Presidency. The American democracy must discover a middle way between making the President a czar and making him a puppet.
The Imperial Presidency (1973) preface

1 Suppose...that Lenin had died of typhus in Siberia in 1895 and Hitler had been killed on the western front in 1916. What would the twentieth century have looked like now?
The Cycles of American History (1986)

Caroline Kennedy Schlossberg
1958–
American writer, daughter of John F. **Kennedy**

2 Now it is our turn to prove that the New Frontier was not a place in time, but a timeless call.
speech at the Democratic Convention, 15 August 2000; see **Kennedy 166:11**

Arthur Schopenhauer 1788–1860
German philosopher

3 There is no opinion, however absurd, which men will not readily embrace as soon as they can be brought to the conviction that it is generally adopted.
The Art of Controversy (1896)

Patricia Schroeder 1940–
American Democratic politician

4 Ronald Reagan...is attempting a great breakthrough in political technology—he has been perfecting the Teflon-coated Presidency. He sees to it that nothing sticks to him.
speech in the US House of Representatives, 2 August 1983

E. F. Schumacher 1911–77
German-born economist

5 It was not the power of the Spaniards that destroyed the Aztec

Empire but the disbelief of the Aztecs in themselves.
Roots of Economic Growth (1962)

6 Small is beautiful. A study of economics as if people mattered.
title of book, 1973

J. A. Schumpeter 1883–1950
Austrian-born American economist

7 Bureaucracy is not an obstacle to democracy but an inevitable complement to it.
Capitalism, Socialism, and Democracy (1942)

Carl Schurz 1829–1906
American soldier and politician

8 My country, right or wrong; if right, to be kept right; and if wrong, to be set right!
speech, US Senate, 29 February 1872

Claud Schuster 1869–1956
British civil servant

9 *of the relationship between the Prime Minister and the Cabinet:*
Like the procreation of eels, [it] is slippery and mysterious.
G. H. L. Le May *The Victorian Constitution* (1979)

Arnold Schwarzenegger 1947–
Austrian-born American actor and Republican politician

10 To those critics who are so pessimistic about our economy, I say, don't be economic girlie men!
speech to Republican National Convention, New York, 31 August 2004

C. P. Scott 1846–1932
British journalist; editor of the *Manchester Guardian*, 1872–1929

11 Comment is free, but facts are sacred.
in *Manchester Guardian* 5 May 1921; see **Stoppard 302:5**

Scotland
'O flower of Scotland'
see Selective Subject Index

Sir Walter Scott 1771–1832
Scottish novelist and poet

1 Breathes there the man, with soul
   so dead,
   Who never to himself hath said,
   This is my own, my native land!
   Whose heart hath ne'er within him
   burned,
   As home his footsteps he hath turned
   From wandering on a foreign strand!
   The Lay of the Last Minstrel (1805)

2 Now is the stately column broke,
   The beacon-light is quench'd in
   smoke,
   The trumpet's silver sound is still,
   The warder silent on the hill!
   on the death of Pitt
   Marmion (1808); introduction to canto 1

3 Civil war is a species of misery
   which introduces men to strange
   bedfellows.
   Rob Roy (1817) introduction

John Seeley 1834–95
English historian

4 We [the English] seem, as it were,
   to have conquered and peopled
   half the world in a fit of absence of
   mind.
   The Expansion of England (1883); see
   Hailsham 132:7

John Selden 1584–1654
English historian and antiquary

5 Ignorance of the law excuses no
   man; not that all men know the law,
   but because 'tis an excuse every
   man will plead, and no man can tell
   how to confute him.
   Table Talk (1689) 'Law'

6 A king is a thing men have made
   for their own sakes, for quietness'
   sake. Just as in a family one man is
   appointed to buy the meat.
   Table Talk (1689) 'Of a King'

7 There is not anything in the world
   so much abused as this sentence,
   Salus populi suprema lex esto.
   Table Talk (1689) 'People'; see **Cicero 72:7**

Arthur Seldon 1916–2005
British economist

8 Government of the busy by the
   bossy for the bully.
   subheading on over-government
   Capitalism (1990)

W. C. Sellar 1898–1951 and
R. J. Yeatman 1898–1968

9 The Cavaliers (Wrong but
   Wromantic) and the Roundheads
   (Right but Repulsive).
   1066 and All That (1930)

10 The Rump Parliament—so called
   because it had been sitting for such
   a long time.
   1066 and All That (1930)

11 Charles II was always very merry
   and was therefore not so much a
   king as a Monarch.
   1066 and All That (1930)

12 The National Debt is a very Good
   Thing and it would be dangerous
   to pay it off, for fear of Political
   Economy.
   1066 and All That (1930)

13 Most memorable…was the
   discovery (made by all the rich men
   in England at once) that women
   and children could work twenty-
   five hours a day in factories without
   many of them dying or becoming
   excessively deformed. This was
   known as the Industrial Revelation.
   1066 and All That (1930)

14 Gladstone…spent his declining
   years trying to guess the answer to
   the Irish Question; unfortunately
   whenever he was getting warm,
   the Irish secretly changed the
   Question.
   1066 and All That (1930)

15 AMERICA was thus clearly top
   nation, and History came to a.
   1066 and All That (1930)

Amartya Sen 1933–
Indian economist

16 No famine has ever taken place
   in the history of the world in a

functioning democracy.
Development as Freedom (1999)

Seneca ('the Younger') c. 4 BC–AD 65
Roman philosopher and poet

1 *Non habemus illos hostes, sed facimus.*
They are not enemies when we acquire them; we make them so.
on slaves
Epistulae Morales no. 47, sect. 5

William Seward 1801–72
American politician

2 I know, and all the world knows, that revolutions never go backward.
speech at Rochester, 25 October 1858

Edward Sexby d. 1658
English conspirator

3 Killing no murder briefly discourst in three questions.
title of pamphlet (an apology for tyrannicide, 1657)

Tokyo Sexwale 1953–
South African politician and businessman

4 The president's shoes are huge and Thabo has tiny feet.
*of Thabo **Mbeki** as President of South Africa*
quoted on *BBC News Online* website, 7 August 2001

5 If blacks get hurt, I get hurt. If whites get hurt, that's my wife, and if you harm coloured people, you're looking for my children. Your unity embodies who I am.
quoted in *Biographies of Special South Africans* (website www.zar.co.za)

Anthony Ashley Cooper, Lord Shaftesbury 1621–83
English peer, in the English Civil War, adherent first of the royalist and then (from 1644) of the Parliamentary cause; in the reign of **Charles II**, supporter of **Monmouth**'s claim to the succession. On Shaftesbury: see **Cromwell 83:2, Dryden 98:7**

6 *refusing the claims of Cromwell's House of Lords:*
Admit lords, and you admit all.
in *Dictionary of National Biography* (1917–)

William Shakespeare 1564–1616
English dramatist

7 'Let me not live', quoth he, 'After my flame lacks oil, to be the snuff Of younger spirits.'
All's Well That Ends Well (1603–4); see **Macmillan 199:11**

8 What's the matter, you dissentious rogues, That, rubbing the poor itch of your opinion, Make yourselves scabs?
Coriolanus (1608)

9 He that depends Upon your favours swims with fins of lead, And hews down oaks with rushes.
Coriolanus (1608)

10 Hear you this Triton of the minnows? mark you His absolute 'shall'?
Coriolanus (1608)

11 What is the city but the people?
Coriolanus (1608)

12 You common cry of curs! whose breath I hate As reek o' the rotten fens, whose loves I prize As the dead carcases of unburied men That do corrupt my air,—I banish you.
Coriolanus (1608)

13 Despising, For you, the city, thus I turn my back: There is a world elsewhere.
Coriolanus (1608)

14 The beast With many heads butts me away.
Coriolanus (1608)

15 Let me have war, say I; it exceeds peace as far as day does night; it's spritely, waking, audible, and full of vent. Peace is a very apoplexy, lethargy: mulled, deaf, sleepy, insensible; a getter of more bastard children than war's a destroyer of men.
Coriolanus (1608); some editions prefer 'spritely walking'

16 I think he'll be to Rome As is the osprey to the fish, who

takes it
By sovereignty of nature.
Coriolanus (1608)

1 Why should we pay tribute? If
Caesar can hide the sun from us
with a blanket, or put the moon in
his pocket, we will pay him tribute
for light; else, sir, no more tribute.
Cymbeline (1609–10)

2   The art o' th' court,
As hard to leave as keep, whose top
to climb
Is certain falling, or so slipp'ry that
The fear's as bad as falling.
Cymbeline (1609–10)

3 But in the gross and scope of my
opinion,
This bodes some strange eruption to
our state.
Hamlet (1601)

4 His greatness weighed, his will is
not his own,
For he himself is subject to his birth.
He may not, as unvalued persons do,
Carve for himself, for on his choice
depends
The sanity and health of the whole
state.
Hamlet (1601)

5 Something is rotten in the state of
Denmark.
Hamlet (1601)

6 The time is out of joint; O cursèd
spite,
That ever I was born to set it right!
Hamlet (1601)

7 For who would bear the whips and
scorns of time,
The oppressor's wrong, the proud
man's contumely,
The pangs of disprized love, the law's
delay,
The insolence of office, and the
spurns
That patient merit of the unworthy
takes,
When he himself might his quietus
make
With a bare bodkin?...
Thus conscience doth make cowards
of us all.
Hamlet (1601)

8 Madness in great ones must not
unwatched go.
Hamlet (1601)

9   Indeed this counsellor
Is now most still, most secret, and
most grave,
Who was in life a foolish prating
knave.
Hamlet (1601)

10 And where the offence is let the
great axe fall.
Hamlet (1601)

11 The great man down, you mark his
favourite flies;
The poor advanced makes friends of
enemies.
Hamlet (1601)

12   Diseases desperate grown,
By desperate appliances are relieved,
Or not at all.
Hamlet (1601)

13 We go to gain a little patch of
ground,
That hath in it no profit but the name.
Hamlet (1601)

14   Rightly to be great
Is not to stir without great argument,
But greatly to find quarrel in a straw
When honour's at the stake.
Hamlet (1601)

15 There's such divinity doth hedge a
king,
That treason can but peep to what it
would.
Hamlet (1601)

16 Rebellion lay in his way, and he
found it.
Henry IV, Part 1 (1597)

17 It was always yet the trick of our
English nation, if they have a good
thing, to make it too common.
Henry IV, Part 2 (1597)

18 Uneasy lies the head that wears a
crown.
Henry IV, Part 2 (1597)

19 O England! model to thy inward
greatness,
Like little body with a mighty heart,
What might'st thou do, that honour
would thee do,
Were all thy children kind and
natural!

But see thy fault!
Henry V (1599)

1 A little touch of Harry in the night.
Henry V (1599)

2 Discuss unto me; art thou officer?
Or art thou base, common and
popular?
Henry V (1599)

3 I think the king is but a man, as I
am: the violet smells to him as it
doth to me.
Henry V (1599)

4 I am afeard there are few die well
that die in a battle; for how can
they charitably dispose of any thing
when blood is their argument?
Henry V (1599)

5 Every subject's duty is the king's;
but every subject's soul is his own.
Henry V (1599)

6 Upon the king! let us our lives, our
souls,
Our debts, our careful wives,
Our children, and our sins lay on the
king!
We must bear all. O hard condition!
Henry V (1599)

7   What infinite heart's ease
Must kings neglect, that private men
enjoy!
And what have kings that privates
have not too,
Save ceremony, save general
ceremony?
Henry V (1599)

8 I say it was never merry world in
England since gentlemen came up.
Henry VI, Part 2 (1592)

9 The first thing we do, let's kill all
the lawyers.
Henry VI, Part 2 (1592)

10 Is not this a lamentable thing, that
of the skin of an innocent lamb
should be made parchment? that
parchment, being scribbled o'er,
should undo a man?
Henry VI, Part 2 (1592)

11 Thou hast most traitorously
corrupted the youth of the realm
in erecting a grammar school: and
whereas, before, our forefathers
had no other books but the score

and the tally, thou hast caused
printing to be used; and, contrary
to the king, his crown and dignity,
thou hast built a paper-mill.
Henry VI, Part 2 (1592)

12 Peace! impudent and shameless
Warwick, peace;
Proud setter up and puller down of
kings.
Henry VI, Part 3 (1592)

13   You know his nature,
That he's revengeful; and I know, his
sword
Hath a sharp edge; it's long, and 't
may be said,
It reaches far, and where 'twill not
extend,
Thither he darts it.
the Duke of Norfolk of Cardinal Wolsey
Henry VIII (1613)

14 Farewell! a long farewell, to all my
greatness!
Henry VIII (1613)

15   I have ventured,
Like little wanton boys that swim on
bladders,
This many summers in a sea of glory,
But far beyond my depth.
Henry VIII (1613)

16 And when he falls, he falls like
Lucifer,
Never to hope again.
Henry VIII (1613)

17 Cromwell, I charge thee, fling away
ambition:
By that sin fell the angels.
Henry VIII (1613)

18 Had I but served my God with half
the zeal
I served my king, he would not in
mine age
Have left me naked to mine enemies.
Henry VIII (1613)

19 In her days every man shall eat in
safety
Under his own vine what he plants;
and sing
The merry songs of peace to all his
neighbours.
Henry VIII (1613)

20 You blocks, you stones, you worse
than senseless things!

O you hard hearts, you cruel men of
Rome,
Knew you not Pompey?
Julius Caesar (1599)

1 CAESAR: Speak; Caesar is turned to
hear.
SOOTHSAYER: Beware the ides of
March.
Julius Caesar (1599)

2 Ye gods, it doth amaze me,
A man of such a feeble temper should
So get the start of the majestic world,
And bear the palm alone.
Julius Caesar (1599)

3 Why, man, he doth bestride the
narrow world
Like a Colossus; and we petty men
Walk under his huge legs, and peep
about
To find ourselves dishonourable
graves.
Men at some time are masters of their
fates:
The fault, dear Brutus, is not in our
stars,
But in ourselves, that we are
underlings.
Julius Caesar (1599)

4 'Brutus' will start a spirit as soon as
'Caesar'.
Now in the names of all the gods at
once,
Upon what meat doth this our Caesar
feed,
That he is grown so great?
Julius Caesar (1599)

5 When could they say, till now, that
talked of Rome,
That her wide walls encompassed but
one man?
Now is it Rome indeed and room
enough,
When there is in it but one only man.
Julius Caesar (1599)

6 Let me have men about me that
are fat;
Sleek-headed men and such as sleep
o' nights;
Yond' Cassius has a lean and hungry
look;
He thinks too much: such men are

dangerous.
Julius Caesar (1599); see **Plutarch 247:2**

7 Such men as he be never at heart's
ease,
Whiles they behold a greater than
themselves,
And therefore are they very
dangerous.
Julius Caesar (1599)

8 Th' abuse of greatness is, when it
disjoins
Remorse from power.
Julius Caesar (1599)

9 'Tis a common proof,
That lowliness is young ambition's
ladder,
Whereto the climber-upward turns
his face;
But when he once attains the upmost
round,
He then unto the ladder turns his
back,
Looks in the clouds, scorning the
base degrees
By which he did ascend.
Julius Caesar (1599)

10 O conspiracy!
Sham'st thou to show thy dangerous
brow by night,
When evils are most free?
Julius Caesar (1599)

11 Let us be sacrificers, but not
butchers, Caius.
Julius Caesar (1599)

12 But when I tell him he hates
flatterers,
He says he does, being then most
flattered.
Julius Caesar (1599)

13 CAESAR: The ides of March are
come.
SOOTHSAYER: Ay, Caesar; but not gone.
Julius Caesar (1599)

14 If I could pray to move, prayers
would move me;
But I am constant as the northern
star,
Of whose true-fixed and resting
quality
There is no fellow in the firmament.
The skies are painted with
unnumbered sparks,

They are all fire and every one
doth shine,
But there's but one in all doth hold
his place:
So, in the world; 'tis furnished well
with men,
And men are flesh and blood, and
apprehensive;
Yet in the number I do know but one
That unassailable holds on his rank,
Unshaked of motion: and that I am
he.
Julius Caesar (1599)

1 *Et tu, Brute?* Then fall, Caesar!
Julius Caesar (1599); see **Caesar 53:2**

2 Ambition's debt is paid.
Julius Caesar (1599)

3 CASSIUS: How many ages hence
Shall this our lofty scene be acted
o'er,
In states unborn, and accents yet
unknown!
BRUTUS: How many times shall
Caesar bleed in sport.
Julius Caesar (1599)

4 Waving our red weapons o'er our
heads
Let's all cry 'Peace, freedom, and
liberty!'
Julius Caesar (1599)

5 O mighty Caesar! dost thou lie so
low?
Are all thy conquests, glories,
triumphs, spoils,
Shrunk to this little measure?
Julius Caesar (1599)

6 Caesar's spirit, ranging for
revenge,
With Ate by his side, come hot from
hell,
Shall in these confines, with a
monarch's voice
Cry, 'Havoc!' and let slip the dogs of
war;
That this foul deed shall smell above
the earth
With carrion men, groaning for
burial.
Julius Caesar (1599)

7 Not that I loved Caesar less, but that
I loved Rome more.
Julius Caesar (1599)

8 As he was valiant, I honour him:
but, as he was ambitious, I slew
him.
Julius Caesar (1599)

9 Friends, Romans, countrymen, lend
me your ears;
I come to bury Caesar, not to praise
him.
The evil that men do lives after them,
The good is oft interrèd with their
bones;
So let it be with Caesar. The noble
Brutus
Hath told you Caesar was ambitious;
If it were so, it was a grievous fault;
And grievously hath Caesar
answered it.
Julius Caesar (1599)

10 He was my friend, faithful and just
to me:
But Brutus says he was ambitious;
And Brutus is an honourable man.
Julius Caesar (1599)

11 When that the poor have cried,
Caesar hath wept;
Ambition should be made of sterner
stuff.
Julius Caesar (1599)

12 You all did love him once, not
without cause.
Julius Caesar (1599)

13 But yesterday the word of Caesar
might
Have stood against the world; now
lies he there,
And none so poor to do him
reverence.
Julius Caesar (1599)

14 This was the most unkindest cut
of all.
Julius Caesar (1599)

15 O! what a fall was there, my
countrymen;
Then I, and you, and all of us fell
down,
Whilst bloody treason flourished
over us.
Julius Caesar (1599)

16 I come not, friends, to steal away
your hearts:
I am no orator, as Brutus is;
But, as you know me all, a plain, blunt

man,
That love my friend.
Julius Caesar (1599)

1 For I have neither wit, nor words,
   nor worth,
Action, nor utterance, nor power of
   speech,
To stir men's blood; I only speak right
   on;
I tell you that which you yourselves
   do know.
Julius Caesar (1599)

2   But were I Brutus,
And Brutus Antony, there were an
   Antony
Would ruffle up your spirits, and put
   a tongue
In every wound of Caesar, that should
   move
The stones of Rome to rise and
   mutiny.
Julius Caesar (1599)

3 Now let it work; mischief, thou art
   afoot,
Take thou what course thou wilt!
Julius Caesar (1599)

4 He shall not live; look, with a spot I
   damn him.
Julius Caesar (1599)

5 This is a slight unmeritable man,
Meet to be sent on errands.
Julius Caesar (1599)

6 There is a tide in the affairs of men,
Which, taken at the flood, leads on to
   fortune;
Omitted, all the voyage of their life
Is bound in shallows and in miseries.
Julius Caesar (1599)

7 O Julius Caesar! thou art mighty
   yet!
Thy spirit walks abroad, and turns
   our swords
In our own proper entrails.
Julius Caesar (1599)

8 This was the noblest Roman of
   them all;
All the conspirators save only he
Did that they did in envy of great
   Caesar;
He, only, in a general honest thought
And common good to all, made one
   of them.

His life was gentle, and the elements
So mixed in him that Nature might
   stand up
And say to all the world, 'This was a
   man!'
Julius Caesar (1599)

9 This England never did, nor never
   shall,
Lie at the proud foot of a conqueror,
But when it first did help to wound
   itself.
Now these her princes are come
   home again,
Come the three corners of the world
   in arms,
And we shall shock them: nought
   shall make us rue,
If England to itself do rest but true.
King John (1591–8)

10 A dog's obeyed in office.
King Lear (1605–6)

11   Get thee glass eyes;
And, like a scurvy politician, seem
To see the things thou dost not.
King Lear (1605–6)

12   Nothing in his life
Became him like the leaving it.
Macbeth (1606)

13   There's no art
To find the mind's construction in
   the face;
He was a gentleman on whom I built
An absolute trust.
Macbeth (1606)

14   Thou wouldst be great;
Art not without ambition, but
   without
The illness should attend it. What
   thou wouldst highly,
That wouldst thou holily; wouldst not
   play false,
And yet wouldst wrongly win.
Macbeth (1606)

15   Besides, this Duncan
Hath borne his faculties so meek,
   hath been
So clear in his great office, that his
   virtues
Will plead like angels trumpet-
   tongued, against
The deep damnation of his taking-off.
Macbeth (1606)

1   I have no spur
To prick the sides of my intent, but
   only
Vaulting ambition, which o'erleaps
   itself,
And falls on the other.
Macbeth (1606)

2 Confusion now hath made his
   masterpiece!
Macbeth (1606)

3 Thou hast it now: King, Cawdor,
   Glamis, all,
As the weird women promised; and,
   I fear,
Thou play'dst most foully for't.
Macbeth (1606)

4 LADY MACBETH: Things without all
   remedy
Should be without regard: what's
   done is done.
MACBETH: We have scotched the
   snake, not killed it:
She'll close and be herself.
Macbeth (1606)

5   Duncan is in his grave;
After life's fitful fever he sleeps well;
Treason has done his worst: nor steel,
   nor poison,
Malice domestic, foreign levy,
   nothing,
Can touch him further.
Macbeth (1606)

6 Stands Scotland where it did?
Macbeth (1606)

7   Liberty plucks justice by the nose;
The baby beats the nurse, and quite
   athwart
Goes all decorum.
Measure for Measure (1604)

8 We must not make a scarecrow of
   the law,
Setting it up to fear the birds of prey,
And let it keep one shape, till custom
   make it
Their perch and not their terror.
Measure for Measure (1604)

9 'Tis one thing to be tempted,
   Escalus,
Another thing to fall. I not deny,
The jury, passing on the prisoner's
   life,

May in the sworn twelve have a
   thief or two
Guiltier than him they try.
Measure for Measure (1604)

10 No ceremony that to great ones
   'longs,
Not the king's crown, nor the deputed
   sword,
The marshal's truncheon, nor the
   judge's robe,
Become them with one half so good
   a grace
As mercy does.
Measure for Measure (1604)

11   O! it is excellent
To have a giant's strength, but it is
   tyrannous
To use it like a giant.
Measure for Measure (1604)

12   Man, proud man,
Drest in a little brief authority,
Most ignorant of what he's most
   assured,
His glassy essence, like an angry ape,
Plays such fantastic tricks before
   high heaven,
As make the angels weep.
Measure for Measure (1604)

13 The quality of mercy is not strained,
It droppeth as the gentle rain from
   heaven
Upon the place beneath.
The Merchant of Venice (1596–8)

14 A substitute shines brightly as a
   king
Until a king be by, and then his state
Empties itself, as doth an inland
   brook
Into the main of waters.
The Merchant of Venice (1596–8)

15 We were not born to sue, but to
   command.
Richard II (1595)

16 How long a time lies in one little
   word!
Four lagging winters and four
   wanton springs
End in a word; such is the breath of
   kings.
Richard II (1595)

17 This royal throne of kings, this
   sceptred isle,

This earth of majesty, this seat
    of Mars,
This other Eden, demi-paradise,
This fortress built by Nature for
    herself
Against infection and the hand of
    war,
This happy breed of men, this little
    world,
This precious stone set in the silver
    sea,
Which serves it in the office of a wall,
Or as a moat defensive to a house,
Against the envy of less happier
    lands,
This blessèd plot, this earth, this
    realm, this England.
    Richard II (1595)

1 The caterpillars of the
    commonwealth.
    Richard II (1595)

2 Not all the water in the rough rude
    sea
    Can wash the balm from an anointed
    king;
    The breath of worldly men cannot
    depose
    The deputy elected by the Lord.
    Richard II (1595)

3 Is not the king's name twenty
    thousand names?
    Arm, arm, my name! A puny subject
    strikes
    At thy great glory.
    Richard II (1595)

4 For God's sake, let us sit upon the
    ground
    And tell sad stories of the death of
    kings.
    Richard II (1595)

5   For within the hollow crown
    That rounds the mortal temples of
    a king
    Keeps Death his court, and there the
    antick sits,
    Scoffing his state and grinning at his
    pomp.
    Richard II (1595)

6 What must the king do now? Must
    he submit?
    The king shall do it: must he be
    deposed?

The king shall be contented: must
    he lose
    The name of king? o' God's name, let
    it go.
    Richard II (1595)

7 You may my glories and my state
    depose,
    But not my griefs; still am I king of
    those.
    Richard II (1595)

8 Now mark me how I will undo
    myself.
    Richard II (1595)

9 With mine own tears I wash away
    my balm,
    With mine own hands I give away my
    crown.
    Richard II (1595)

10 Mine eyes are full of tears, I cannot
    see:
    And yet salt water blinds them not
    so much
    But they can see a sort of traitors
    here.
    Nay, if I turn my eyes upon myself,
    I find myself a traitor with the rest.
    Richard II (1595)

11 Now is the winter of our discontent
    Made glorious summer by this sun
    of York.
    Richard III (1591); some editions prefer 'son
    of York'

12 Since every Jack became a
    gentleman
    There's many a gentle person made
    a Jack.
    Richard III (1591)

13 Woe to the land that's governed by
    a child!
    Richard III (1591); see **Bible 32:20**

14 Talk'st thou to me of 'ifs'? Thou art
    a traitor:
    Off with his head!
    Richard III (1591)

15 I am not in the giving vein to-day.
    Richard III (1591)

16 Men shut their doors against a
    setting sun.
    Timon of Athens (1607)

17 A stone is soft as wax, tribunes
    more hard than stones.
    A stone is silent and offendeth not,

And tribunes with their tongues
doom men to death.
Titus Andronicus (1590)

1 Rome is but a wilderness of tigers.
Titus Andronicus (1590)

2 The heavens themselves, the
planets, and this centre
Observe degree, priority, and place.
Troilus and Cressida (1602)

3 O! when degree is shaked,
Which is the ladder to all high
designs,
The enterprise is sick.
Troilus and Cressida (1602)

4 Take but degree away, untune that
string,
And, hark! what discord follows.
Troilus and Cressida (1602)

5 A plague of opinion! a man may
wear it on both sides, like a leather
jerkin.
Troilus and Cressida (1602)

6 How my achievements mock me!
Troilus and Cressida (1602)

Robert Shapiro 1942–
American lawyer

7 *of the change of strategy embraced after
Johnnie Cochran took over from him the
leadership of the defence team at the trial of
O. J. Simpson:*
Not only did we play the race card,
we played it from the bottom of the
deck.
*to which Cochran responded, 'We didn't play the
race card, we played the credibility card'*
in *Times* 5 October 1995; see **Churchill 65:2**

Ariel Sharon 1928–
Israeli Likud statesman, Prime Minister 2001–6

8 I'm not going to make any
compromise whatsoever.
on relations with the Palestinians
in *Sunday Times* 12 August 2001

George Bernard Shaw 1856–1950
Irish dramatist. See also **Misquotations 215:6**

9 All great truths begin as
blasphemies.
Annajanska (1919)

10 What Englishman will give his
mind to politics as long as he can

afford to keep a motor car?
The Apple Cart (1930)

11 Life is not meant to be easy, my
child; but take courage: it can be
delightful.
Back to Methuselah (rev. ed., 1930); see also
Fraser 115:2

12 You see things; and you say 'Why?'
But I dream things that never were;
and I say 'Why not?'
Back to Methuselah (1921)

13 He [the Briton] is a barbarian, and
thinks that the customs of his tribe
and island are the laws of nature.
Caesar and Cleopatra (1901)

14 SWINDON: What will history say?
BURGOYNE: History, sir, will tell lies
as usual.
The Devil's Disciple (1901)

15 Your friend the British soldier can
stand up to anything except the
British War Office.
The Devil's Disciple (1901)

16 A government which robs Peter to
pay Paul can always depend on the
support of Paul.
Everybody's Political What's What? (1944)

17 Go anywhere in England where
there are natural, wholesome,
contented, and really nice English
people; and what do you always
find? That the stables are the real
centre of the household.
Heartbreak House (1919)

18 The captain is in his bunk, drinking
bottled ditch-water; and the crew
is gambling in the forecastle. She
will strike and sink and split. Do
you think the laws of God will be
suspended in favour of England
because you were born in it?
Heartbreak House (1919)

19 It is evident that if the incomes of
the rich were taken from them and
divided among the poor as we stand
at present, the poor would be very
little less poor; the supply of capital
would cease because nobody could
afford to save; the country houses
would fall into ruins; and learning
and science and art and literature
and all the rest of what we call

culture would perish.
The Intelligent Woman's Guide to Socialism and Capitalism (1928)

1 You have to choose (as a voter) between trusting to the natural stability of gold and the natural stability of the honesty and intelligence of the members of the Government. And, with due respect for these gentlemen, I advise you, as long as the Capitalist system lasts, to vote for gold.
The Intelligent Woman's Guide to Socialism and Capitalism (1928)

2 Money is indeed the most important thing in the world; and all sound and successful personal and national morality should have this fact for its basis.
The Irrational Knot (1905) preface

3 An Irishman's heart is nothing but his imagination.
John Bull's Other Island (1907)

4 He knows nothing; and he thinks he knows everything. That points clearly to a political career.
Major Barbara (1907)

5 Nothing is ever done in this world until men are prepared to kill one another if it is not done.
Major Barbara (1907)

6 Englishmen never will be slaves: they are free to do whatever the Government and public opinion allow them to do.
Man and Superman (1903)

7 In the arts of peace Man is a bungler.
Man and Superman (1903)

8 Revolutions have never lightened the burden of tyranny: they have only shifted it to another shoulder.
Man and Superman (1903) 'The Revolutionist's Handbook' foreword

9 Democracy substitutes election by the incompetent many for appointment by the corrupt few.
Man and Superman (1903) 'Maxims: Democracy'

10 Liberty means responsibility. That is why most men dread it.
Man and Superman (1903) 'Maxims: Liberty and Equality'

11 The art of government is the organization of idolatry.
Man and Superman (1903) 'Maxims: Idolatry'

12 The reasonable man adapts himself to the world: the unreasonable one persists in trying to adapt the world to himself. Therefore all progress depends on the unreasonable man.
Man and Superman (1903) 'Maxims: Reason'

13 Titles distinguish the mediocre, embarrass the superior, and are disgraced by the inferior.
Man and Superman (1903) 'Maxims for Revolutionists: Titles'

14 Anarchism is a game at which the police can beat you.
Misalliance (1914)

15 You'll never have a quiet world till you knock the patriotism out of the human race.
O'Flaherty V.C. (1919)

16 Assassination is the extreme form of censorship.
The Showing-Up of Blanco Posnet (1911) 'Limits to Toleration'

Hartley Shawcross 1902–2003
British Labour politician

17 'But,' said Alice, 'the question is whether you can make a word mean different things.' 'Not so,' said Humpty-Dumpty, 'the question is which is to be the master. That's all.' We are the masters at the moment, and not only at the moment, but for a very long time to come.
in the House of Commons, 2 April 1946; see **Carroll 57:16, Misquotations 216:7**

Charles Shaw-Lefevre 1794–1888

18 What is that fat gentleman in such a passion about?
*as a child, on hearing Charles James **Fox** speak in Parliament*
G. W. E. Russell *Collections and Recollections* (1898)

Francis Sheehy-Skeffington
1878–1916
Irish nationalist

19 A crank is a small engine that

causes revolutions.
on being described as a crank
Owen Dudley Edwards and Fergus Pyle *1916: the Easter Rising* (1968)

Lord Shelburne 1737–1805
British Whig statesman; Prime Minister 1782–3

1 The country will neither be united at home nor respected abroad, till the reins of government are lodged with men who have some little pretensions to common sense and common honesty.
in the House of Lords, 22 November 1770

2 *of the defence of the king's speech at the opening of the parliamentary session:*
Nothing more than a string of sophisms, no less wretched in their texture than insolent in their tenor.
in the House of Lords, 31 October 1776

3 The sun of Great Britain will set whenever she acknowledges the independence of America…the independence of America would end in the ruin of England.
in the House of Lords, October 1782

Percy Bysshe Shelley 1792–1822
English poet

4 Let there be light! said Liberty,
And like sunrise from the sea,
Athens arose!
Hellas (1822)

5 I met Murder on the way—
He had a mask like Castlereagh.
'The Mask of Anarchy' (1819)

6 'My name is Ozymandias, king of kings:
Look on my works, ye Mighty, and despair!'
'Ozymandias' (1819)

7 Kingly conclaves stern and cold
Where blood with guilt is bought and sold.
Prometheus Unbound (1820)

8 Men of England, wherefore plough
For the lords who lay ye low?
'Song to the Men of England' (written 1819)

9 The seed ye sow, another reaps;
The wealth ye find, another keeps;
The robes ye weave, another wears;

The arms ye forge, another bears.
'Song to the Men of England' (written 1819)

10 An old, mad, blind, despised, and dying king.
'Sonnet: England in 1819' (written 1819)

11 The accident of her birth neither made her life more virtuous nor her death more worthy of grief.
An Address to the People on the Death of the Princess Charlotte (1817)

12 Tyranny entrenches itself within the existing interests of the most refined citizens of a nation and says 'If you dare trample upon these, be free.'
A Philosophical View of Reform (written 1819–20)

13 Monarchy is only the string that ties the robber's bundle.
A Philosophical View of Reform (written 1819–20)

William Shenstone 1714–63
English poet and essayist

14 Laws are generally found to be nets of such a texture, as the little creep through, the great break through, and the middle-sized are alone entangled in.
Works in Verse and Prose (1764) vol. 2 'On Politics'; see **Anacharsis 6:10**, **Swift 303:10**

Philip Henry Sheridan 1831–88
American Union cavalry commander in the Civil War

15 The only good Indian is a dead Indian.
at Fort Cobb, January 1869
attributed; perhaps already proverbial

Richard Brinsley Sheridan
1751–1816
Irish dramatist and Whig politician

16 The newspapers! Sir, they are the most villainous—licentious—abominable—infernal—Not that I ever read them—No—I make it a rule never to look into a newspaper.
The Critic (1779)

17 The throne *we* honour is the *people's choice.*
Pizarro (1799)

18 The Right Honourable gentleman is

indebted to his memory for his jests, and to his imagination for his facts.
in reply to Mr Dundas, in the House of Commons; T. Moore *Life of Sheridan* (1825) vol. 2

William Tecumseh Sherman
1820–91
American general; from 1864 chief Union commander in the west in succession to Ulysses S. **Grant**

1 I will never again command an army in America if we must carry along paid spies. I will banish myself to some foreign country first.
a reference to war correspondents
letter to his wife, February 1863

2 War is the remedy our *enemies* have chosen, and I say let us give them all they want.
in 1864; Geoffrey C. Ward *The Civil War* (1991)

3 [Grant] stood by me when I was crazy, and I stood by him when he was drunk; and now we stand by each other always.
of his relationship with his fellow Union commander, Ulysses S. **Grant**
in 1864; Geoffrey C. Ward *The Civil War* (1991)

4 I will not accept if nominated, and will not serve if elected.
on being urged to stand as Republican candidate in the 1884 presidential election
telegram to General Henderson; *Memoirs* (4th ed., 1891)

Emanuel Shinwell 1884–1986
British Labour politician

5 We know that the organised workers of the country are our friends. As for the rest, they don't matter a tinker's cuss.
speech to the Electrical Trades Union conference at Margate, 7 May 1947

Jonathan Shipley 1714–88
English clergyman, Bishop of St Asaph

6 I look upon North America as the only great nursery of freemen left on the face of the earth.
in 1774, after voting against the alteration of the constitution of Massachusetts, proposed as a punishment for the tea-ship riots at Boston
in *Dictionary of National Biography*

William Shippen 1673–1743
English Jacobite politician

7 Robin and I are two honest men: he is for King George and I for King James, but those men in long cravats [Sandys, Rushout, Pulteney, and their following] only desire places under one or the other.
view of his relationship with his political opponent Robert **Walpole**
in *Dictionary of National Biography* (1917–)

Clare Short 1946–
British Labour politician

8 *contrasting Tony Blair's political advisers with elected politicians:*
I sometimes call them the people who live in the dark. Everything they do is in hiding…Everything we do is in the light. They live in the dark.
in *New Statesman* 9 August 1996

9 It will be golden elephants next.
suggesting that the government of Montserrat was 'talking mad money' in claiming assistance for evacuating the island
in *Observer* 24 August 1997

10 Reckless with our government; reckless with his own future, position and place in history. It's extraordinarily reckless.
when asked if she thought that Tony **Blair** *was acting recklessly on Iraq*
in an interview on *Westminster Hour* (BBC Radio 4), 9 March 2003

Algernon Sidney 1622–83
English conspirator, executed for his alleged part in the Rye House Plot, 1683

11 Liars ought to have good memories.
Discourses concerning Government (1698)

12 Men lived like fishes; the great ones devoured the small.
Discourses concerning Government (1698)

13 'Tis not necessary to light a candle to the sun.
Discourses concerning Government (1698)

14 The law is established, which no passion can disturb. 'Tis void of desire and fear, lust and anger…'Tis

deaf, inexorable, inflexible.
Discourses concerning Government (1698) ch. 3, sect. 15; see **Adams 2:12**

Emmanuel Joseph Sieyès
1748–1836
French abbot and statesman

1 *La mort, sans phrases.*
Death, without rhetoric.
on voting in the French Convention for the death of **Louis XVI**, *16 January 1793*
attributed to Sieyès, but afterwards repudiated by him (*Le Moniteur* 20 January 1793 records his vote as 'La mort')

2 *when asked what he had done during the French Revolution:*
J'ai vécu.
I survived.
F. A. M. Mignet *Notice historique sur la vie et les travaux de M. le Comte de Sieyès* (1836)

Jim Sillars 1937–
Scottish Nationalist politician

3 I think the greatest problem we have is that we will sing Flower of Scotland at Hampden or Murrayfield, and that we have too many 90-minute patriots.
interview on Scottish Television, 23 April 1992

Simonides see Epitaphs 106:2

Kirke Simpson
American journalist

4 [Warren] Harding of Ohio was chosen by a group of men in a smoke-filled room early today as Republican candidate for President.
news report, 12 June 1920; see **Simpson 289:4**

C. H. Sisson 1914–2003
English poet

5 Here lies a civil servant. He was civil
To everyone, and servant to the devil.
The London Zoo (1961)

Sitting Bull (Tatanka Iyotake)
c. 1831–90
American Sioux chief

6 The Black Hills belong to me. If the whites try to take them, I will fight.
Dee Brown *Bury My Heart at Wounded Knee* (1970) ch. 12

Noel Skelton 1880–1935
British Conservative politician

7 To state as clearly as may be what means lie ready to develop a property-owning democracy, to bring the industrial and economic status of the wage-earner abreast of his political and educational, to make democracy stable and four-square.
in *The Spectator* 19 May 1923

Gillian Slovo 1952–
South African writer

8 In most families it is the children who leave home. In mine it was the parents.
of her anti-apartheid activist parents, Joe Slovo and Ruth First
Every Secret Thing (1997)

Joseph Roberts Smallwood
1900–91
Canadian journalist and politician, Premier of Newfoundland 1949–70

9 I am king of my own little island, and that's all I've ever wanted to be.
Richard Gwyn *Smallwood: The Unlikely Revolutionary* (1968)

Adam Smith 1723–90
Scottish philosopher and economist

10 Little else is requisite to carry a state to the highest degree of opulence from the lowest barbarism, but peace, easy taxes, and a tolerable administration of justice; all the rest being brought
(*continued*)

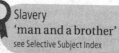

Slavery
'man and a brother'
see Selective Subject Index

Slogans

1 All power to the Soviets.
workers in Petrograd, 1917

2 All the way with LBJ.
*US Democratic Party campaign slogan supporting Lyndon Baines **Johnson***
in *Washington Post* 4 June 1960

3 *Arbeit macht frei.*
Work makes free.
on the gates of Dachau concentration camp, and subsequently on those of Auschwitz
inscription, 1933

4 Ban the bomb.
US anti-nuclear slogan, 1953 onwards
adopted by the Campaign for Nuclear Disarmament

5 A bayonet is a weapon with a worker at each end.
British pacifist slogan (1940)

6 Better red than dead.
slogan of nuclear disarmament campaigners, late 1950s

7 A bigger bang for a buck.
Charles E. **Wilson**'s defence policy, in *Newsweek* 22 March 1954

8 The big tent.
slogan used by the Republican Party to denote a policy of inclusiveness
recorded from 1990; see also **Newspaper headlines 225:18**

9 Black is beautiful.
slogan of American civil rights campaigners, mid-1960s

10 Burn, baby, burn.
Black extremist slogan in use during the Los Angeles riots, August 1965

11 Can't pay, won't pay.
anti-Poll Tax slogan, 1990; see **Fo 111:4**

12 *Ein Reich, ein Volk, ein Führer.*
One realm, one people, one leader.
Nazi Party slogan
early 1930s

13 Fair shares for all, is Labour's call.
*slogan for the North Battersea by-election, 1946, coined by Douglas **Jay***
Douglas Jay *Change and Fortune* (1980)

14 Fifty-four forty, or fight!
slogan of expansionist Democrats in the presidential campaign of 1844, in which the Oregon boundary definition was an issue (in

1846 the new Democratic president, James K. Polk, compromised on the 49th parallel with Great Britain)
William Allen (1803–79), American Democratic politician, speech in the US Senate, 1844

15 Free by '93.
Scottish National Party, general election campaign, 1992

16 Give us back our eleven days.
protesting against the adoption of the Gregorian Calendar in 1752, and in this form associated with Hogarth's cartoon showing a rowdy Oxfordshire election of 1754
David Ewing Duncan *The Calendar* (1998)

17 Hey, hey, LBJ, how many kids have you killed today?
*anti-Vietnam War marching slogan during the presidency of Lyndon **Johnson***
Jacquin Sanders *The Draft and the Vietnam War* (1966)

18 I like Ike.
*used when General **Eisenhower** was first seen as a potential presidential nominee*
US button badge, 1947; coined by Henry D. Spalding (d. 1990)

19 I'm backing Britain.
slogan coined by workers at the Colt factory, Surbiton, Surrey, and subsequently used in a national campaign
in *Times* 1 January 1968

20 It's morning again in America.
slogan for Ronald **Reagan**'s election campaign, 1984; coined by Hal Riney (1932–); in *Newsweek* 6 August 1984

21 It's Scotland's oil.
Scottish National Party, 1972

22 It's the economy, stupid.
on a sign put up at the 1992 **Clinton** presidential campaign headquarters by campaign manager James Carville

23 Keep the bastards honest.
coined by the Australian politician Don Chipp (1925–), on leaving the Liberal Party to form the Australian Democrats, from 1980

24 *Kraft durch Freude.*
Strength through joy.
German Labour Front slogan, from 1933; coined by Robert Ley (1890–1945)

25 Labour isn't working.
caption to Conservative Party poster,

Slogans *continued*

1978–9, showing a long queue outside an unemployment office
Philip Kleinman *The Saatchi and Saatchi Story* (1987)

1 Labour's double whammy.
Conservative Party election slogan 1992

2 The land for the people.
Communist slogan, 1917

3 Let Reagan be Reagan.
Republican campaign slogan, 1980s

4 *Liberté! Égalité! Fraternité!*
Freedom! Equality! Brotherhood!
motto of the French Revolution (though of earlier origin)
the Club des Cordeliers passed a motion, 30 June 1793, 'that owners should be urged to paint on the front of their houses, in large letters, the words: Unity, indivisibility of the Republic, Liberty, Equality, Fraternity or death'; in *Journal de Paris* no. 182 (from 1795 the words 'or death' were dropped)

5 Life's better with the Conservatives.
Don't let Labour ruin it.
Conservative Party election slogan, 1959

6 Lousy but loyal.
London East End slogan at George V's Jubilee (1935)

7 Make love not war.
student slogan, 1960s

8 New Labour, new danger.
Conservative slogan, 1996

9 No crown of thorns, no cross of gold.
American Democratic party, 1900; see **Bryan 44:10**

10 *the defenders of the besieged city of Derry to the Jacobite army of James II, April 1689:*
No surrender!
adopted as a slogan of Protestant Ulster
Jonathan Bardon *A History of Ulster* (1992)

11 Not in my name.
protesters against the war in Iraq, 2003

12 The personal is political.
1970s feminist slogan, attributed to Carol Hanisch (1945–)

13 Power to the people.
slogan of the Black Panther movement, from 1968 onwards

14 Things can only get better.
Labour campaign slogan, 1997; see **Petrie and Cunnah 244:8**

15 Think globally, act locally.
Friends of the Earth slogan, 1985

16 *in response to a Republican slogan, 'Thinking feller, vote for McKellar':*
Think some more and vote for Gore.
American Democratic slogan in Senate campaign, Tennessee, 1952; coinage is attributed to Pauline LaFon Gore on behalf of her husband Albert Gore Sr.

17 Thirteen years of Tory misrule.
unofficial Labour party election slogan, also in the form 'Thirteen wasted years', 1964

18 Three acres and a cow.
regarded as the requirement for self-sufficiency; associated with the radical politician Jesse Collings (1831–1920) and his land reform campaign begun in 1885
Jesse Collings in the House of Commons, 26 January 1886, although used earlier by Joseph **Chamberlain** in a speech at Evesham (in *Times* 17 November 1885), by which time it was already proverbial

19 Tippecanoe and Tyler, too.
presidential campaign song for William Henry **Harrison***, 1840*
attributed to A. C. Ross (fl. 1840); see **Songs 296:12**

20 Ulster says no.
slogan coined in response to the Anglo-Irish Agreement of 15 November 1985
in *Irish Times* 25 November 1985

21 Vote Blair, get Brown.
reflecting the rivalry of Tony **Blair** and Gordon **Brown**, and suggested variously as a threat and a promise to floating voters

22 Votes for women.
adopted when it proved impossible to use a banner with the longer slogan 'Will the Liberal Party Give Votes for Women?' made by Emmeline **Pankhurst** *(1858–1928), Christabel* **Pankhurst** *(1880–1958), and Annie Kenney (1879–1953)*
slogan of the women's suffrage movement, from 13 October 1905; Emmeline Pankhurst *My Own Story* (1914)

23 War will cease when men refuse

Slogans *continued*

to fight.
pacifist slogan (often quoted as 'Wars will cease...')
from 1936

1 We demand that big business give people a square deal.
Theodore Roosevelt, 1901; see **Roosevelt 263:15**

2 We want eight, and we won't wait.
on the construction of Dreadnoughts
quoted in George Wyndham's speech in *Times* 29 March 1909

3 Would you buy a used car from this man?
campaign slogan directed against Richard **Nixon**, 1968

4 Yes it hurt, yes it worked.
Conservative Party slogan, 1996; see **Major 202:7**

5 Yesterday's men (they failed before!).
Labour Party slogan, referring to the Conservatives, 1970; coined by David Kingsley, Dennis Lyons, and Peter Lovell-Davis

6 Yes, we can.
Barack **Obama** presidential campaign slogan, 2007–8; the slogan is also associated with the children's television character Bob the Builder (1999–)

7 You never had it so good.
Democratic Party slogan during the 1952 US election campaign; see **Macmillan 199:6**

---

about by the natural course of things.
in 1755; *Essays on Philosophical Subjects* (1795)

8 And thus, *Place*, that great object which divides the wives of aldermen, is the end of half the labours of human life; and is the cause of all the tumult and bustle, all the rapine and injustice, which avarice and ambition have introduced into this world.
Theory of Moral Sentiments (1759)

9 [The man of system] seems to imagine that he can arrange the different members of a great society with as much ease as the hand arranges the different pieces upon a chessboard; he does not consider that the pieces upon the chessboard have no other principle of motion besides that which the hand impresses upon them; but that, in the great chessboard of human society, every single piece has a principle of motion of its own, altogether different from that which the legislator might choose to impress upon it.
Theory of Moral Sentiments (1759)

10 It is not from the benevolence of the butcher, the brewer, or the baker, that we expect our dinner, but from

their regard to their own interest. We address ourselves not to their humanity but their self love, and never talk to them of our necessities but of their advantages.
Wealth of Nations (1776)

11 People of the same trade seldom meet together, even for merriment and diversion, but the conversation ends in a conspiracy against the public, or in some contrivance to raise prices.
Wealth of Nations (1776)

12 Great nations are never impoverished by private, though they sometimes are by public prodigality and misconduct. The whole, or almost the whole public revenue, is in most countries employed in maintaining unproductive hands.
Wealth of Nations (1776)

13 I have never known much good done by those who affected to trade for the public good.
Wealth of Nations (1776)

14 What is prudence in the conduct of every private family, can scarce be folly in that of a great kingdom. If a foreign country can supply us with a commodity cheaper than we ourselves can make it, better buy it of them with some part of

the produce of our own industry, employed in a way in which we have some advantage.
Wealth of Nations (1776)

1 Every individual necessarily labours to render the annual revenue of society as great as he can. He generally, indeed, neither intends to promote the public interest, nor knows how much he is promoting it. By preferring the support of domestic to that of foreign industry, he intends only his own security; and by directing that industry in such a manner as its produce may be of the greatest value, and he is in this, as in many other cases, led by an invisible hand to promote an end which was no part of his intention.
Wealth of Nations (1776)

2 That insidious and crafty animal, vulgarly called a statesman or politician, whose councils are directed by the momentary fluctuations of affairs.
Wealth of Nations (1776)

3 The natural effort of every individual to better his own condition…is so powerful, that it is alone, and without any assistance, not only capable of carrying on the society to wealth and prosperity, but of surmounting a hundred impertinent obstructions with which the folly of human laws too often encumbers its operations.
Wealth of Nations (1776)

4 To found a great empire for the sole purpose of raising up a people of customers, may at first sight appear a project fit only for a nation of shopkeepers. It is, however, a project altogether unfit for a nation of shopkeepers; but extremely fit for a nation whose government is influenced by shopkeepers.
Wealth of Nations (1776); see **Adams 4:4**, **Napoleon I 224:5**

5 Consumption is the sole end and purpose of all production; and the interest of the producer ought to be attended to only so far as it may be necessary for promoting that of the consumer.
Wealth of Nations (1776)

6 Those parts of education, it is to be observed, for the teaching of which there are no public institutions, are generally the best taught.
Wealth of Nations (1776)

7 There is no art which one government sooner learns of another than that of draining money from the pockets of the people.
Wealth of Nations (1776)

Alfred Emanuel Smith 1873–1944
American politician

8 The crowning climax to the whole situation is the undisputed fact that William Randolph Hearst gave him the kiss of death.
*on **Hearst**'s support for Ogden Mills, Smith's unsuccessful opponent for the governorship of New York State*
in *New York Times* 25 October 1926

9 All the ills of democracy can be cured by more democracy.
speech in Albany, 27 June 1933

10 No sane local official who has hung up an empty stocking over the municipal fireplace, is going to shoot Santa Claus just before a hard Christmas.
comment on the New Deal
in *New Outlook* December 1933

F. E. Smith, Lord Birkenhead
1872–1930
British Conservative politician and lawyer. On Smith: see **Asquith 13:15**

11 The world continues to offer glittering prizes to those who have stout hearts and sharp swords.
Rectorial address, Glasgow University, 7 November 1923

12 We have the highest authority for believing that the meek shall inherit the earth; though I have never found any particular corroboration of this aphorism in

the records of Somerset House.
Contemporary Personalities (1924) 'Marquess Curzon'

1 Nature has no cure for this sort of madness [Bolshevism], though I have known a legacy from a rich relative work wonders.
Law, Life and Letters (1927)

2 Austen [Chamberlain] always played the game, and he always lost it.
Lord Beaverbrook *Men and Power* (1956)

Iain Duncan Smith 1954–
British Conservative politician, Leader of the Conservative Party 2001–3. On Smith: see **Portillo 248:9**

3 Do not underestimate the determination of a quiet man.
speech to the Conservative Party Conference, 10 October 2002

Ian Smith 1919–2007
Rhodesian statesman; Prime Minister of Rhodesia (now Zimbabwe), 1964–79

4 I don't believe in black majority rule in Rhodesia—not in a thousand years.
broadcast speech, 20 March 1976

John Smith 1938–94
Scottish-born Labour politician, Leader of the Labour Party from 1992

5 I am a doer and I want to do things, but there exists the terrible possibility in politics that you might never win.
in *You* 22 March 1992

6 The settled will of the Scottish people.
of the creation of a Scottish parliament
speech at the Scottish Labour Conference, 11 March 1994

Samuel Francis Smith 1808–95
American poet and divine

7 My country, 'tis of thee,
Sweet land of liberty,
Of thee I sing:
Land where my fathers died,
Land of the pilgrims' pride,
From every mountain-side

Let freedom ring.
'America' (1831)

Sydney Smith 1771–1845
English clergyman and essayist

8 The moment the very name of Ireland is mentioned, the English seem to bid adieu to common feeling, common prudence, and common sense, and to act with the barbarity of tyrants, and the fatuity of idiots.
Letters of Peter Plymley (1807)

9 Tory and Whig in turns shall be my host,
I taste no politics in boiled and roast.
letter to John Murray, November 1834

10 Lord John...would perform the operation for the stone—build St Peter's or assume—(with or without ten minutes notice) the command of the Channel Fleet; and no one would discover by his manner that the patient had died, the church tumbled down, and the Channel Fleet been knocked to atoms.
of Lord John **Russell**
Letters to Archdeacon Singleton (1837–40) vol. 2

11 Daniel Webster struck me much like a steam-engine in trousers.
Lady Holland *Memoir* (1855)

12 He [Macaulay] has occasional flashes of silence, that make his conversation perfectly delightful.
Lady Holland *Memoir* (1855)

13 Minorities...are almost always in the right.
H. Pearson *The Smith of Smiths* (1934)

Tobias Smollett 1721–71
Scottish novelist

14 I think for my part one half of the nation is mad—and the other not very sound.
The Adventures of Sir Launcelot Greaves (1762)

15 Mourn, hapless Caledonia, mourn
Thy banished peace, thy laurels torn.
'The Tears of Scotland' (1746)

Jan Christiaan Smuts 1870–1950
South African soldier and statesman, Prime Minister 1919–24 and 1939–48

1 There is no doubt that mankind is once more on the move. The very foundations have been shaken and loosened, and things are again fluid. The tents have been struck, and the great caravan of humanity is once more on the march.
on the League of Nations
W. K. Hancock *Smuts* (1968)

C. P. Snow 1905–80
English novelist and scientist

2 The official world, the corridors of power.
Homecomings (1956)

Philip Snowden 1864–1937
British Labour politician

3 This is not Socialism. It is Bolshevism run mad.
on the Labour Party's 1931 election programme
radio broadcast, 17 October 1931

4 It would be desirable if every Government, when it comes to power, should have its old speeches burnt.
C. E. Bechofer Roberts ('Ephesian') *Philip Snowden* (1929)

Socrates 469–399 BC
Greek philosopher

5 Most excellent man, are you who are a citizen of Athens, the greatest of cities and the most famous for wisdom and power, not ashamed to care for the acquisition of wealth and for reputation and honour, when you neither care nor take thought for wisdom and truth and the perfection of your soul?
Plato *Apology*

6 And I tell you that virtue does not come from money, but from virtue comes money and all other good things to man, both to the individual and to the state.
Plato *Apology*

7 I am not Athenian or Greek but a citizen of the world.
Plutarch *Moralia* bk. 7 'On Exile'

Alexander Solzhenitsyn
1918–2008
Russian novelist

8 You only have power over people as long as you don't take *everything* away from them. But when you've robbed a man of *everything* he's no longer in your power—he's free again.
The First Circle (1968)

9 The Gulag Archipelago.
referring to the political prison camps dotted around the Soviet Union
title of book (1973–5)

10 The thoughts of a prisoner—they're not free either. They keep returning to the same things.
One Day in the Life of Ivan Denisovich (1962)

11 Mankind's salvation lies exclusively in everyone's making everything his business, in the people of the East being anything but indifferent to what is thought in the West, and in the people of the West being anything but indifferent to what happens in the East.
Nobel Prize Lecture, 1970

12 In our country the lie has become not just a moral category but a pillar of the State.
interview in 1974; in appendix to *The Oak and the Calf* (1975)

13 Yes, we are still the prisoners of communism, and yet, for us in Russia, Communism is a dead dog, while for many people in the West it is still a living lion.
broadcast on BBC Russian Service, in *Listener* 15 February 1979

Anastasio Somoza 1925–80
Nicaraguan dictator

14 *replying to an accusation of ballot-rigging:*
You won the elections, but I won the count.
in *Guardian* 17 June 1977; see **Stalin 299:1**, **Stoppard 302:3**

Songs See also Benson 28:5

1 *Allons, enfants de la patrie,*
Le jour de gloire est arrivé...
Aux armes, citoyens!
Formez vos battaillons!
Come, children of our country, the
day of glory has arrived...To arms,
citizens! Form your battalions!
'La Marseillaise' (25 April 1792), written by
Claude-Joseph Rouget de Lisle (1760–1836)

2 Among our ancient mountains,
And from our lovely vales,
Oh, let the prayer re-echo:
'God bless the Prince of Wales!'
'God Bless the Prince of Wales' (1862 song),
written by George Linley (1798–1865)

3 Ara! but why does King James stay
 behind?
Lilli burlero bullen a la
Ho! by my shoul 'tis a Protestant
 wind
Lilli burlero bullen a la.
a Williamite song in mockery of Richard Talbot,
newly created Earl of Tyrconnell by the Catholic
James II in Dublin in 1688; the refrain parodies
the Irish language
'A New Song' (1687), written by Thomas, Lord
Wharton; Thomas Kinsella *The New Oxford*
Book of Irish Verse (1986); attribution to
Wharton has been disputed

4 Belgium put the kibosh on the
Kaiser.
title of song (1914), written by Alf Ellerton

5 *Debout! les damnés de la terre!*
Debout! les forçats de la faim!
On your feet, you damned souls of
the earth! On your feet, inmates of
hunger's prison!
'L'Internationale' (1871) by the French politician
Eugène Pottier (1818–87)

6 *C'est la lutte finale*
Groupons-nous, et, demain,
L'Internationale
Sera le genre humain.
This is the final conflict: let us
form up and, tomorrow, the
International will encompass the
human race.
'L'Internationale' (1871) by the French politician
Eugène Pottier (1818–87)

7 From the halls of Montezuma,
To the shores of Tripoli,
We fight our country's battles,
On the land as on the sea.
'The Marines' Hymn' (1847)

8 God save our gracious king!
Long live our noble king!
God save the king!
Send him victorious,
Happy, and glorious,
Long to reign over us:
God save the king!
'God save the King', attributed to various
authors of the mid eighteenth century,
including Henry Carey (1687–1743); Jacobite
variants, such as James Hogg 'The King's
Anthem' in *Jacobite Relics of Scotland* Second
Series (1821) also exist

9 Confound their politics,
Frustrate their knavish tricks.
'God save the King', attributed to various
authors; see **Songs 296:8**

10 I met wid Napper Tandy, and he
 took me by the hand,
And he said, 'How's poor ould
 Ireland, and how does she stand?'
She's the most disthressful country
 that iver yet was seen,
For they're hangin' men an' women
 for the wearin' o' the Green.
'The Wearin' o' the Green' (1795 ballad)

11 In good King Charles's golden days,
When loyalty no harm meant;
A furious High-Churchman I was,
And so I gained preferment.
Unto my flock I daily preached,
Kings are by God appointed,
And damned are those who dare
 resist,
Or touch the Lord's Anointed.
And this is law, I will maintain,
Unto my dying day, Sir,
That whatsoever King shall reign,
I will be the Vicar of Bray, sir!
'The Vicar of Bray' in *British Musical Miscellany*
(1734) vol. 1

12 The iron-armed soldier, the true-
 hearted soldier,

Songs *continued*

The gallant old soldier of
  Tippecanoe.
presidential campaign song for William Henry
Harrison, *1840*
attributed to George Pope Morris (1802–64);
see **Slogans 291:19**

1 John Brown's body lies a
    mould'ring in the grave,
  His soul is marching on.
  inspired by the execution of the abolitionist
  John **Brown**, *after the raid on Harper's Ferry, on*
  2 December 1859
  song (1861), variously attributed to Charles
  Sprague Hall, Henry Howard Brownell, and
  Thomas Brigham Bishop

2 Keep the Home-fires burning,
  While your hearts are yearning,
  Though your lads are far away
  They dream of Home.
  There's a silver lining
  Through the dark cloud shining;
  Turn the dark cloud inside out,
  Till the boys come Home.
  'Till the Boys Come Home!' (1914 song by Lena
  Guilbert Ford); music by Ivor Novello

3 Lloyd George knew my father,
  My father knew Lloyd George.
  two-line comic song, sung to the tune of
  'Onward, Christian Soldiers' and possibly by
  Tommy Rhys Roberts (1910–75)

4 Oh! we don't want to lose you but
    we think you ought to go
  For your King and your Country
    both need you so;
  'Your King and Country Want You' (1914 song),
  written by Paul Alfred Rubens (1875–1917)

5 The people's flag is deepest red;
  It shrouded oft our martyred dead.
  'The Red Flag' (1889), written by the Irish

socialist songwriter James M. Connell
(1852–1929)

6 Tho' cowards flinch and traitors
    sneer,
  We'll keep the red flag flying here.
  'The Red Flag' (1889), written by the Irish
  socialist songwriter James M. Connell
  (1852–1929)

7 So on the Twelfth I proudly wear
    the sash my father wore.
  'The Sash My Father Wore', traditional Orange
  song

8 We don't want to fight, but, by
    jingo if we do,
  We've got the ships, we've got the
    men, we've got the money too.
  We've fought the Bear before, and
    while Britons shall be true,
  The Russians shall not have
    Constantinople.
  We Don't Want to Fight (music hall song by
  G. W. Hunt, 1878)

9 We're gonna hang out the
    washing on the Siegfried Line.
  title of song (1939) by Jimmy Kennedy and
  Michael Carr

10 We shall not be moved.
  title of labour and civil rights song (1931)
  adapted from an earlier gospel hymn

11 We shall overcome.
  revived in 1946 as a protest song by Black
  tobacco workers, and in 1963 during the Black
  Civil Rights Campaign
  title of song, originating from before the
  American Civil War, adapted as a Baptist hymn
  ('I'll Overcome Some Day', 1901) by C. Albert
  Tindley

Susan Sontag 1933–2004
American writer

12 The white race *is* the cancer of
  human history, it is the white race,
  and it alone—its ideologies and
  inventions—which eradicates
  autonomous civilizations wherever
  it spreads, which has upset the
  ecological balance of the planet,

which now threatens the very
existence of life itself.
  in *Partisan Review* Winter 1967

Lord Soper 1903–98
British peer and Methodist minister

13 *of the quality of debate in the House of Lords:*
  It is, I think, good evidence of life
  after death.
  in *Listener* 17 August 1978

Robert Southey 1774–1843
English poet and writer

1 Now tell us all about the war,
   And what they fought each other for.
   'The Battle of Blenheim' (1800)

2 'And everybody praised the Duke,
   Who this great fight did win.'
   'But what good came of it at last?'
   Quoth little Peterkin.
   'Why that I cannot tell,' said he,
   'But 'twas a famous victory.'
   'The Battle of Blenheim' (1800)

3 The death of Nelson was felt in
   England as something more than a
   public calamity; men started at the
   intelligence, and turned pale, as if
   they had heard of the loss of a dear
   friend.
   The Life of Nelson (1813)

Edward Spears 1886–1974
British soldier and diplomat

4 Of all the crosses I have had to bear
   during this war, the heaviest has
   been the Cross of Lorraine.
   in the Second World War the Cross of Lorraine
   was the symbol of the Free French forces, led by
   General **de Gaulle**
      attributed in Times 1 June 2006, and often
      attributed to Winston **Churchill** who
      subsequently used it; Martin Gilbert Churchill:
      A Life (1991)

Lord Spencer 1964–
English peer

5 She needed no royal title to
   continue to generate her particular
   brand of magic.
   tribute at the funeral of his sister, **Diana**, Princess
   of Wales, 7 September 1997
      in Guardian 8 September 1997

6 We, your blood family, will do all
   we can to continue the imaginative
   way in which you were steering
   these two exceptional young men
   so that their souls are not simply
   immersed by duty and tradition but

can sing openly as you planned.
referring to his nephews, Prince William and
Prince Harry
   in Guardian 8 September 1997

Oswald Spengler 1880–1936
German historian

7 Socialism is nothing but the
   capitalism of the working class.
   The Hour of Decision (1933)

Edmund Spenser c. 1552–99
English poet

8 Ill can he rule the great, that cannot
   reach the small.
   The Faerie Queen (1596)

Benjamin Spock 1903–98
American paediatrician

9 To win in Vietnam, we will have to
   exterminate a nation.
   Dr Spock on Vietnam (1968)

Cecil Spring-Rice 1859–1918
British diplomat; Ambassador to Washington from
1912

10 I vow to thee, my country—all
    earthly things above—
    Entire and whole and perfect, the
    service of my love,
    The love that asks no question: the
    love that stands the test,
    That lays upon the altar the dearest
    and the best:
    The love that never falters, the love
    that pays the price,
    The love that makes undaunted the
    final sacrifice.
    'I Vow to Thee, My Country' (written on
    the eve of his departure from Washington,
    12 January 1918)

11 Wilson is the nation's shepherd and

Speeches
'being savaged by a dead sheep'
see Selective Subject Index

McAdoo his crook.
*of President Woodrow **Wilson** and his secretary of the treasury, a remark considered unfortunate in the light of British attempts to draw the US into the First World War*
　Robert Skidelsky *John Maynard Keynes* vol. 1 (1983)

Joseph Stalin 1879–1953
Soviet dictator

1 I consider it completely unimportant who in the party will vote, or how; but what is extraordinarily important is this— who will count the votes, and how.
　said in 1923; Boris Bazhanov The Memoirs of Stalin's Former Secretary (1992); see **Somoza 295:14, Stoppard 302:3**

2 The State is an instrument in the hands of the ruling class, used to break the resistance of the adversaries of that class.
　Foundations of Leninism (1924)

3 There is the question: Can Socialism *possibly* be established in one country alone by that country's unaided strength? The question must be answered in the affirmative.
　Problems of Leninism (1926)

4 There are various forms of production: artillery, automobiles, lorries. You also produce 'commodities', 'works', 'products'. Such things are highly necessary. Engineering things. For people's souls. 'Products' are highly necessary too. 'Products' are very important for people's souls. You are engineers of human souls.
　speech to writers at **Gorky**'s house, 26 October 1932; A. Kemp-Welch *Stalin and the Literary Intelligentsia, 1928–39* (1991); see **Gorky 128:6, Kennedy 167:14**

5 The Pope! How many divisions has *he* got?
　on being asked to encourage Catholicism in Russia by way of conciliating the Pope
　on 13 May 1935; W. S. Churchill *The Gathering Storm* (1948); see **Napoleon I 224:3**

6 There is one eternally true legend— that of Judas.
　at the trial of Radek in 1937
　Robert Payne *The Rise and Fall of Stalin* (1966)

7 One death is a tragedy, one million is a statistic.
　attributed

Charles E. Stanton 1859–1933
American soldier

8 *Lafayette, nous voilà!*
Lafayette, we are here.
　at the tomb of Lafayette in Paris, 4 July 1917
　in *New York Tribune* 6 September 1917

Edwin McMasters Stanton
1814–69
American lawyer

9 Now he belongs to the ages.
　*of Abraham **Lincoln**, following his assassination, 15 April 1865*
　I. M. Tarbell *Life of Abraham Lincoln* (1900)

David Steel 1938–
British Liberal politician; Leader of the Liberal Party 1976–88. On Steel: see **Foot 111:9**

10 I have the good fortune to be the first Liberal leader for over half a century who is able to say to you at the end of our annual assembly: go back to your constituencies and prepare for government.
　speech to the Liberal Party Assembly, 18 September 1981

11 It is the settled will of the majority of people in Scotland that they want not just the symbol, but the substance of the return of democratic control over

Statesmen
'hears the step of God'
see Selective Subject Index

internal affairs.
*on the announcement that the Stone of Destiny
would be returned to Scotland*
in *Scotsman* 4 July 1996

Anthony Steen 1939–
British Conservative politician

1 Do you know what it's about?
Jealousy. I've got a very, very large
house. Some people say it looks like
Balmoral.
*responding to criticism of his claims for
parliamentary expenses*
interview, BBC Radio 4 *The World at One*
21 May 2009

2 What right does the public have to
interfere with my private life? None.
on his parliamentary expenses
interview, BBC Radio 4 *The World at One*
21 May 2009

Lincoln Steffens 1866–1936
American journalist

3 I have seen the future; and it works.
following a visit to the Soviet Union
letter to Marie Howe, 3 April 1919; see J.
M. Thompson *Russia, Bolshevism and the
Versailles Treaty* (1954), where it is recalled
that Steffens had composed the expression
before he had even arrived in Russia

Gertrude Stein 1874–1946
American writer

4 In the United States there is more
space where nobody is than where
anybody is. That is what makes
America what it is.
The Geographical History of America (1936)

James Fitzjames Stephen 1829–94
English lawyer

5 The sentence of the law is to the
moral sentiment of the public in
relation to any offence what a seal
is to hot wax.
A History of the Criminal Law of England (1883)

6 The way in which the man of genius
rules is by persuading an efficient
minority to coerce an indifferent
and self-indulgent majority.
Liberty, Equality and Fraternity (1873)

James Stephens 1882–1950
Irish poet and nationalist

7 People say: 'Of course, they will be
beaten.' The statement is almost
a query, and they continue, 'but
they are putting up a decent fight.'
For being beaten does not matter
greatly in Ireland, but not fighting
does matter.
The Insurrection in Dublin (1916)

8 In my definition they were good
men—men, that is, who willed no
evil. No person living is the worse
off for having known Thomas
MacDonagh.
The Insurrection in Dublin (1916)

Adlai Stevenson 1900–65
American Democratic politician

9 We must be patient—making peace
is harder than making war.
speech to Chicago Council on Foreign
Relations, 21 March 1946

10 I am not a politician, I am a citizen.
speech during the 1948 election campaign;
Bert Cochran *Adlai Stevenson* (1969)

11 I suppose flattery hurts no one, that
is, if he doesn't inhale.
television broadcast, 30 March 1952

12 Better we lose the election than
mislead the people.
on accepting the Democratic nomination in
1952; Herbert Muller *Adlai Stevenson* (1968)

13 Let's talk sense to the American
people. Let's tell them the truth,
that there are no gains without
pains.
speech at the Democratic National Convention,
accepting the Democratic nomination, Chicago
Illinois, 26 July 1952

14 If they [the Republicans] will stop
telling lies about the Democrats,
we will stop telling the truth about
them.
speech during 1952 Presidential campaign; J.
B. Martin *Adlai Stevenson and Illinois* (1976)

15 A hungry man is not a free man.
speech at Kasson, Minnesota, 6 September
1952

16 There is no evil in the atom; only in

men's souls.
speech at Hartford, Connecticut, 18 September 1952

1 In America any boy may become President and I suppose it's just one of the risks he takes.
speech in Indianapolis, 26 September 1952

2 A free society is a society where it is safe to be unpopular.
speech in Detroit, 7 October 1952

3 The Republican party did not have to…encourage the excesses of its Vice-Presidential nominee [Richard Nixon]—the young man who asks you to set him one heart-beat from the Presidency of the United States.
speech at Cleveland, Ohio, 23 October 1952; see **Misquotations 215:16**

4 A funny thing happened to me on the way to the White House.
speech in Washington, 13 December 1952, following his defeat in the Presidential election
Alden Whitman *Portrait: Adlai E. Stevenson* (1965)

5 We hear the Secretary of State [John Foster Dulles] boasting of his brinkmanship—the art of bringing us to the edge of the abyss.
speech in Hartford, Connecticut, 25 February 1956; see **Dulles 99:16**

6 The idea that you can merchandize candidates for high office like breakfast cereal—that you can gather votes like box tops—is, I think, the ultimate indignity to the democratic process.
speech at the Democratic National Convention, 18 August 1956

7 You have taught me a lesson I should have learned long ago—to take counsel always of your courage and never of your fears.
on losing the Presidential nomination in 1960;
Herbert J. Muller *Adlai Stevenson* (1968)

8 Do you remember that in classical times when Cicero had finished speaking, the people said, 'How well he spoke', but when Demosthenes had finished speaking, they said, 'Let us march.'
*introducing John F. **Kennedy** in 1960*
Bert Cochran *Adlai Stevenson* (1969)

9 She would rather light a candle

than curse the darkness, and her glow has warmed the world.
*on learning of Eleanor **Roosevelt**'s death*
in *New York Times* 8 November 1962

10 Eggheads of the world unite; you have nothing to lose but your yolks.
perhaps a reworking of 'Eggheads of the world, arise—I was even going to add that you have nothing to lose but your yolks', speech at Oakland, 1 February 1956
attributed

11 If I had any epitaph that I would rather have more than another, it would be to say that I had disturbed the sleep of my generation.
epigraph to Jack W. Germand and Jules Witcover *Wake Us When It's Over* (1985)

12 The kind of politician who would cut down a redwood tree, and then mount the stump and make a speech on conservation.
*of Richard **Nixon***
Fawn M. Brodie *Richard Nixon* (1983)

13 A politician is a person who approaches every subject with an open mouth.
attributed

14 The sound of tireless voices is the price we pay for the right to hear the music of our own opinions.
in *The Guide to American Law* (1984)

Robert Louis Stevenson 1850–94
Scottish novelist

15 Politics is perhaps the only profession for which no preparation is thought necessary.
Familiar Studies of Men and Books (1882)

Sting 1951–
English rock singer, songwriter, and actor

16 If I were a Brazilian without land or money or the means to feed my children, I would be burning the rain forest too.
in *International Herald Tribune* 14 April 1989

Caskie Stinnett 1911–
American writer

17 A diplomat…is a person who can tell you to go to hell in such a way that you actually look forward

to the trip.
Out of the Red (1960)

Baroness Stocks 1891–1975
British educationist

1 The House of Lords is a perfect
eventide home.
My Commonplace Book (1970)

I. F. Stone 1907–89
American journalist

2 The difference between burlesque
and the newspapers is that the
former never pretended to be
performing a public service by
exposure.
I. F. Stone's Weekly 7 September 1952

Tom Stoppard 1937–
British dramatist

3 It's not the voting that's democracy,
it's the counting.
Jumpers (1972); see **Somoza 295:14**,
Stalin 299:1

4 The House of Lords, an illusion to
which I have never been able to
subscribe—responsibility without
power, the prerogative of the
eunuch throughout the ages.
Lord Malquist and Mr Moon (1966); see
Kipling 174:11

5 Comment is free but facts are on
expenses.
Night and Day (1978); see **Scott 275:11**

6 I'm with you on the free press. It's
the newspapers I can't stand.
Night and Day (1978)

7 War is capitalism with the gloves
off and many who go to war know
it but they go to war because they
don't want to be a hero.
Travesties (1975)

William Stoughton 1631–1701
American clergyman

8 God hath sifted a nation that he
might send choice grain into this
wilderness.
election sermon in Boston, 29 April 1669

Lord Stowell 1745–1836
English jurist

9 The elegant simplicity of the three
per cents.
Lord Campbell *Lives of the Lord Chancellors*
(1857); see **Disraeli 95:4**

10 A precedent embalms a principle.
an opinion, while Advocate-General, 1788,
quoted by Disraeli in the House of Commons,
22 February 1848

Thomas Wentworth, Lord Strafford 1593–1641
English statesman

11 The authority of a King is the
keystone which closeth up the arch
of order and government which,
once shaken, all the frame falls
together in a confused heap of
foundation and battlement.
Hugh Trevor-Roper *Historical Essays* (1952); see
Nicolson 227:1

John Whitaker ('Jack') Straw 1946–
British Labour politician

12 There is no list, and Syria isn't on it.
on the US description of Syria as a rogue state
speech, Qatar; in *Guardian* 15 April
2003 (online edition)

Barbra Streisand 1942–
American singer and actress

13 We elected a President, not a Pope.
to journalists at the White House, 5 February
1998; reported by James Naughtie, BBC Radio
4, Today programme, 6 February 1998

Belinda Stronach 1966–
Canadian politician

14 I do not believe that the party
leader [Stephen Harper] is truly
sensitive to the needs of each part
of the country and just how big and
complex Canada is.
at a news conference announcing her defection
from the Conservative Party to the Liberals,
17 May 2005 (see **Harper 136:7**)

Simeon Strunsky 1879–1948
American journalist

15 People who want to understand

democracy should spend less time in the library with Aristotle and more time on buses and in the subway.
No Mean City (1944)

Timothy Daniel Sullivan 1827–1914
Irish writer and politician

1 'God save Ireland!' said the heroes;
'God save Ireland', say they all:
Whether on the scaffold high
Or the battlefield we die,
Oh, what matter when for Erin dear we fall.
'God Save Ireland' (1867); see
Last words 178:7

Maximilien de Béthune, Duc de Sully 1559–1641
French statesman

2 Tilling and grazing are the two breasts by which France is fed.
Mémoires (1638)

3 The English take their pleasures sadly after the fashion of their country.
attributed

Arthur Hays Sulzberger 1891–1968
American newspaper proprietor

4 We tell the public which way the cat is jumping. The public will take care of the cat.
on journalism
in *Time* 8 May 1950

Charles Sumner 1811–74
American politician and orator. On Sumner: see
Adams 2:9

5 Where Slavery is, there Liberty cannot be; and where Liberty is, there Slavery cannot be.
'Slavery and the Rebellion'; speech at Cooper Institute 5 November 1864

6 There is the National flag. He must be cold, indeed, who can look upon its folds rippling in the breeze without pride of country. If in a foreign land, the flag is companionship, and country itself, with all its endearments.
Are We a Nation? 19 November 1867

Sun Tzu fl. c. 400–320 BC
Chinese general and military theorist. See also **Puzo and Coppola 250:8**

7 To win one hundred victories in one hundred battles is not the acme of skill. To subdue the enemy without fighting is the acme of skill.
The Art of War

Hannen Swaffer 1879–1962
British journalist

8 Freedom of the press in Britain means freedom to print such of the proprietor's prejudices as the advertisers don't object to.
said to Tom Driberg 1928; Tom Driberg *Swaff* (1974)

Jonathan Swift 1667–1745
Irish poet and satirist

9 It is the folly of too many, to mistake the echo of a London coffee-house for the voice of the kingdom.
The Conduct of the Allies (1711)

10 Laws are like cobwebs, which may catch small flies, but let wasps and hornets break through.
A Critical Essay upon the Faculties of the Mind (1709); see **Anacharsis 6:10**, **Shenstone 287:14**

11 I cannot but conclude the bulk of your natives to be the most pernicious race of little odious vermin that nature ever suffered to crawl upon the surface of the earth.
Gulliver's Travels (1726) 'A Voyage to Brobdingnag'

12 And he gave it for his opinion, that whoever could make two ears of corn or two blades of grass to grow upon a spot of ground where only one grew before, would deserve better of mankind, and do more essential service to his country than the whole race of politicians put together.
Gulliver's Travels (1726) 'A Voyage to Brobdingnag'

13 I have been assured by a very knowing American of my acquaintance in London, that a young healthy child well nursed

is at a year old a most delicious, nourishing, and wholesome food, whether stewed, roasted, baked, or boiled, and I make no doubt that it will equally serve in a fricassee, or a ragout.

A Modest Proposal for Preventing the Children of Ireland from being a Burden to their Parents or Country (1729)

1 Party is the madness of many for the gain of a few.
Thoughts on Various Subjects (1711)

2 It is useless to attempt to reason a man out of a thing he was never reasoned into.
attributed from the mid nineteenth century, but probably apocryphal

Tacitus c. AD 56–after 117
Roman senator and historian

3 *Res olim dissociabiles miscuerit, principatum ac libertatem.*
He [Nerva] has united things long incompatible, the principate and liberty.
Agricola; see **Disraeli 94:7**

4 *Nunc terminus Britanniae patet, atque omne ignotum pro magnifico est.*
Now the boundary of Britain is revealed, and everything unknown is held to be glorious.
reporting the speech of a British leader, Calgacus Agricola

5 They make a wilderness and call it peace.
Agricola

6 You were indeed fortunate, Agricola, not only in the distinction of your life, but also in the lucky timing of your death.
Agricola

7 *Sine ira et studio.*
With neither anger nor partiality.
Annals

8 The more corrupt the republic, the more numerous the laws.
Annals

9 These times having the rare good fortune that you may think what you like and say what you think.
Histories

10 *Maior privato visus dum privatus fuit, et omnium consensu capax imperii nisi imperasset.*
He seemed much greater than a private citizen while he still was a private citizen, and by everyone's consent capable of reigning if only he had not reigned.
of the Emperor Galba Histories

11 The gods are on the side of the stronger.
Histories; see **Voltaire 323:5**

William Howard Taft 1857–1930
American Republican statesman, 27th President of the US, 1909–13

12 Next to the right of liberty, the right of property is the most important individual right guaranteed by the Constitution and the one which, united with that of personal liberty, has contributed more to the growth of civilization than any other institution established by the human race.
Popular Government (1913)

Charles-Maurice de Talleyrand
1754–1838
French statesman. On Talleyrand: see **Louis Philippe 191:5, Napoleon I 224:8**

13 *of the Bourbons after returning from exile:*
They have learnt nothing, and

forgotten nothing.
*a similar comment on the courtiers of **Louis XVI**, attributed to the French general Dumouriez, was quoted by **Napoleon I** in his Declaration to the French on his return from Elba*
oral tradition, attributed to Talleyrand by the Chevalier de Panat, January 1796

1 *on hearing of **Napoleon I**'s costly victory at Borodino, 1812:*
This is the beginning of the end.
Sainte-Beuve *M. de Talleyrand* (1870); attributed

2 It is not an event, it is an item of news.
*on hearing of the death of **Napoleon I** in 1821*
Philip Henry Stanhope *Notes of Conversations with the Duke of Wellington* (1888) 1 November 1831

3 Above all, gentlemen, not the slightest zeal.
P. Chasles *Voyages d'un critique à travers la vie et les livres* (1868) vol. 2

4 That, Sire, is a question of dates.
often quoted as, 'treason is a matter of dates'; replying to the Tsar's criticism of those who 'betrayed the cause of Europe'
Duff Cooper *Talleyrand* (1932)

5 What a sad old age you are preparing for yourself.
to a young diplomat who boasted of his ignorance of whist
J. Amédée Pichot *Souvenirs Intimes sur M. de Talleyrand* (1870) 'Le Pour et le Contre'

Wilbert Joseph ('Billy') Tauzin
1943–
American Republican politician

6 In many respects, this case appears to be eerily similar to the accounting hocus-pocus that occurred at Enron.
on the WorldCom collapse
in *BBC News* 28 June 2002 (electronic edition)

R. H. Tawney 1880–1962
British economic historian

7 The characteristic virtue of Englishmen is power of sustained practical activity and their characteristic vice a reluctance to test the quality of that activity by reference to principles.
The Acquisitive Society (1921)

8 Militarism…is fetish worship. It is the prostration of men's souls and the laceration of their bodies to appease an idol.
The Acquisitive Society (1921)

9 That seductive border region where politics grease the wheels of business and polite society smiles hopefully on both.
Business and Politics under James I (1958)

10 Those who dread a dead-level of income or wealth…do not dread, it seems, a dead-level of law and order, and of security for life and property.
Equality (1931)

11 Freedom for the pike is death for the minnows.
Equality (ed. 3 1938)

12 Private property is a necessary institution, at least in a fallen world; men work more and dispute less when goods are private than when they are common. But it is to be tolerated as a concession to human frailty, not applauded as desirable in itself.
Religion and the Rise of Capitalism (1926) ch. 1, sect. 1

13 Both the existing economic order, and too many of the projects advanced for reconstructing it, break down through their neglect of the truism that, since even quite common men have souls, no increase in material wealth will compensate them for arrangements which insult their self-respect and impair their freedom. A reasonable estimate of economic organisation must allow for the fact that, unless industry is to be paralysed by recurrent revolts on the part of outraged human nature, it must satisfy criteria which are not purely economic.
Religion and the Rise of Capitalism (1926) conclusion

14 Democracy a society where ordinary men exercise initiative. Dreadful respect for superiors. Mental enlargement…Real foe

to be overcome…fact that large section of the public *like* plutocratic government, and are easily gullible. How shake them!
unpublished fragment of Chicago lecture (1939), read at Tawney's funeral

1 *declining the offer of a peerage:*
What harm have I ever done to the Labour Party?
in *Evening Standard* 18 January 1962

A. J. P. Taylor 1906–90
British historian

2 History gets thicker as it approaches recent times.
English History 1914–45 (1965) Bibliography

3 In the Second World War the British people came of age. This was a people's war…Few now sang *Land of Hope and Glory*. Few even sang *England Arise*. England had risen all the same.
English History, 1914–1945 (1965)

4 He aroused every feeling except trust.
*of **Lloyd George***
English History 1914–1945 (1965)

5 The politician performs upon the stage; the historian looks behind the scenery.
Englishmen and Others (1956)

6 The First World War had begun—imposed on the statesmen of Europe by railway timetables. It was an unexpected climax to the railway age.
The First World War (1963)

7 *of the period after the First World War:*
Civilization was held together by the civilized behaviour of ordinary people…In reality the masses were calmer and more sensible than those who ruled over them.
From Sarajevo to Potsdam (1966)

8 A racing tipster who only reached Hitler's level of accuracy would not

do well for his clients.
The Origins of the Second World War (1961)

9 Human blunders, however, usually do more to shape history than human wickedness.
The Origins of the Second World War (1961)

10 If men are to respect each other for what they are, they must cease to respect each other for what they own.
Politicians, Socialism and Historians (1980)

11 Crimea: The War That Would Not Boil.
Rumours of Wars (1952); originally the title of an essay in *History Today* 2 February 1951

12 Conformity may give you a quiet life; it may even bring you a University Chair. But all change in history, all advance, comes from the nonconformist. If there had been no trouble makers, no Dissenters, we should still be living in caves.
The Troublemakers (1957)

13 Without democracy socialism would be worth nothing, but democracy is worth a great deal even when it is not socialist.
in *Manchester Guardian* 7 March 1941

14 Bismarck was a political genius of the highest rank, but he lacked one essential quality of the constructive statesman: he had no faith in the future.
in *Encyclopedia Britannica* (1954)

15 Appeasement was a sensible course, even though it was tried with the wrong man; and it remains the noblest word in the diplomatist's vocabulary.
in *Manchester Guardian* 30 September 1958

16 Like Johnson's friend Edwards, I, too have tried to be a Marxist but common sense kept breaking in.
'Accident Prone' in *Journal of Modern History* 1977

Taxation
'shear his flock, not skin it'
see Selective Subject Index

Henry Taylor 1800–86
British civil servant

1 It is of far greater importance to a statesman to make one friend who will hold out with him for twenty years, than to find twenty followers in each year, losing as many.
The Statesman (1836)

2 No statesman, be he as discreet as he may, will escape having ascribed to him, as the result of interviews, promises and understandings which it was not his purpose to convey; and yet in a short time he will be unable to recollect what was said with sufficient distinctness to enable him to give a confident contradiction.
The Statesman (1836)

3 The conscience of a statesman should be rather a strong conscience than a tender conscience.
The Statesman (1836)

4 It is very certain that there may be met with, in public life, a species of conscience which is all bridle and no spurs.
The Statesman (1836)

5 The hand which executes a measure should belong to the head which propounds it.
The Statesman (1836)

6 One who would thrive by seeking favours from the great, should never trouble them for small ones.
The Statesman (1836)

7 [A statesman] should steer by the compass, but he must lie with the wind.
The Statesman (1836)

8 A secret may be sometimes best kept by keeping the secret of its being a secret.
The Statesman (1836)

9 To choose that which will bring him the most credit with the least trouble, has hitherto been the sole care of the statesman in office.
The Statesman (1836)

10 Good nature and kindness towards those with whom they come in personal contact, at the expense of public interests, that is of those whom they never see, is the besetting sin of public men.
The Statesman (1836)

11 He who has once advanced by a stride will not be content to advance afterwards by steps. Public servants, therefore, like racehorses, should be well fed with reward, but not to fatness.
The Statesman (1836)

12 Men in high places, from having less personal interest in the characters of others—being safe from them—are commonly less acute observers, and with their progressive elevation in life become, as more and more indifferent to what other men are, so more and more ignorant of them.
The Statesman (1836)

Norman Tebbit 1931–
British Conservative politician. On Tebbit: see **Foot 111:8**

13 I grew up in the Thirties with our unemployed father. He did not riot, he got on his bike and looked for work.
speech at Conservative Party Conference, 15 October 1981

14 The cricket test—which side do they cheer for?…Are you still looking back to where you came from or where you are?
on the loyalties of Britain's immigrant population interview in *Los Angeles Times*, reported in *Daily Telegraph* 20 April 1990

15 At first I thought it [blogging] was quite unlike anything else I'd done in my political life, but after a while I realised that it is really rather like an old-fashioned political public meeting of the kind that has melted away since television took politics away from the grass roots in the constituencies and concentrated it into the TV studios. It is a pity we can't have real-time heckling.
blog, http://blogs.telegraph.co.uk/news, 13 January 2010

Tecumseh 1768–1813
American Shawnee chief

1 Where today are the Pequot? Where
are the Narragansett, the Mohican,
the Pokanoket, and many other
once powerful tribes of our people?
They have vanished before the
avarice and oppression of the white
man, as snow before the summer
sun.
Dee Brown *Bury My Heart at Wounded Knee*
(1970) ch. 1

**Richard Grenville, 2nd Earl
Temple** 1711–79
English aristocrat and politician

2 A dead minister, the most
respectable that ever existed,
weighs very light in the scale
against any living one.
*to his nephew, William **Pitt** the Younger*
letter, 18 July 1779

William Temple 1881–1944
English theologian; Archbishop of Canterbury from
1942

3 In place of the conception of the
power-state we are led to that of the
welfare-state.
Citizen and Churchman (1941)

Gerald Templer 1898–1979
British general

4 Dickie, you're so crooked that if
you swallowed a nail you'd shit a
corkscrew.
*to Lord **Mountbatten***
Philip Ziegler *Mountbatten* (1985)

John Tenniel 1820–1914
English draughtsman

5 Dropping the pilot.
*cartoon caption, and title of poem, on
Bismarck's dismissal from office by Kaiser
Wilhelm II*
in *Punch* 29 March 1890

Lord Tennyson 1809–92
English poet

6 Kind hearts are more than
coronets,

And simple faith than Norman blood
'Lady Clara Vere de Vere' (1842) st. 7

7 Forward, forward let us range,
Let the great world spin for ever down
the ringing grooves of change.
'Locksley Hall' (1842)

8 The last great Englishman is low.
'Ode on the Death of the Duke of Wellington'
(1852)

9 O good grey head which all men
knew!
'Ode on the Death of the Duke of Wellington'
(1852)

10 O fall'n at length that tower of
strength
Which stood four-square to all the
winds that blew!
'Ode on the Death of the Duke of Wellington'
(1852)

11 That world-earthquake, Waterloo!
'Ode on the Death of the Duke of Wellington'
(1852)

12 Who never sold the truth to serve
the hour,
Nor paltered with Eternal God for
power.
'Ode on the Death of the Duke of Wellington'
(1852)

13 Not once or twice in our rough
island-story,
The path of duty was the way to glory
'Ode on the Death of the Duke of Wellington'
(1852)

14 Authority forgets a dying king.
'The Passing of Arthur' (1869)

15 The old order changeth, yielding
place to new,
And God fulfils himself in many
ways,
Lest one good custom should corrupt
the world.
'The Passing of Arthur' 1869

16 A land of settled government,
A land of just and old renown,
Where Freedom slowly broadens
down
From precedent to precedent.
'You ask me, why, though ill at ease' (1842)

Terence *c.* 190–159 BC
Roman comic dramatist

17 *Quot homines tot sententiae: suus*

cuique mos.
There are as many opinions as there are people: each has his own correct way.
Phormio

Margaret Thatcher 1925–
British Conservative stateswoman; Prime Minister, 1979–90. On Thatcher: see **Anonymous 8:6, Biffen 33:19, Callaghan 53:14, Critchley 82:3, Healey 139:3, Healey 139:6, Healey 139:8, Hennessy 141:4, Kinnock 172:12, Mitterrand 214:12, Parris 241:1, West 330:10**; see also **Francis 114:1**

1 No woman in my time will be Prime Minister or Chancellor or Foreign Secretary—not the top jobs. Anyway I wouldn't want to be Prime Minister. You have to give yourself 100%.
on her appointment as Shadow Education Spokesman
in *Sunday Telegraph* 26 October 1969

2 In politics if you want anything said, ask a man. If you want anything done, ask a woman.
in *People* (New York) 15 September 1975

3 I'll always be fond of dear Ted, but there's no sympathy in politics.
*of her predecessor, Edward **Heath***
attributed, 1975

4 I stand before you tonight in my red chiffon evening gown, my face softly made up, my fair hair gently waved...the Iron Lady of the Western World! Me? A cold war warrior? Well, yes—if that is how they wish to interpret my defence of values and freedoms fundamental to our way of life.
referring to 'the iron lady' as the name given to her by the Soviet defence ministry newspaper Red Star, which accused her of trying to revive the cold war
speech at Finchley, 31 January 1976

5 Socialist governments

traditionally do make a financial mess. They always run out of other people's money.
often quoted as 'the problem with socialism is that eventually you run out of other people's money'
interview, *This Week* Thames TV, 5 February 1976

6 Pennies don't fall from heaven. They have to be earned on earth.
in *Observer* 18 November 1979 'Sayings of the Week'

7 I don't mind how much my Ministers talk, as long as they do what I say.
in *Observer* 27 January 1980

8 We have to get our production and our earnings in balance. There's no easy popularity in what we are proposing, but it is fundamentally sound. Yet I believe people accept there is no real alternative.
popularly encapsulated in the acronym TINA
speech at Conservative Women's Conference, 21 May 1980

9 To those waiting with bated breath for that favourite media catch-phrase, the U-turn, I have only this to say. 'You turn if you want to; the lady's not for turning.'
speech at Conservative Party Conference in Brighton, 10 October 1980

10 Economics are the method; the object is to change the soul.
in *Sunday Times* 3 May 1981

11 We have to see that the spirit of the South Atlantic—the real spirit of Britain—is kindled not only by war but can now be fired by peace. We have the first prerequisite. We know that we can do it—we haven't lost the ability. That is the Falklands Factor.
speech in Cheltenham, 3 July 1982

12 Let me make one thing absolutely

Terrorism
'oxygen of publicity'
see Selective Subject Index

clear. The National Health Service is safe with us.
speech at Conservative Party Conference, 8 October 1982

1 Just rejoice at that news and congratulate our armed forces and the Marines. Rejoice!
on the recapture of South Georgia, usually quoted as, 'Rejoice, rejoice!'
to newsmen outside 10 Downing Street, 25 April 1982; see **Heath 140:9**

2 It is exciting to have a real crisis on your hands, when you have spent half your political life dealing with humdrum issues like the environment.
on the Falklands campaign, 1982
speech to Scottish Conservative Party conference, 14 May 1982

3 I was asked whether I was trying to restore Victorian values. I said straight out I was. And I am.
speech to the British Jewish Community, 21 July 1983, referring to an interview with Brian Walden on 17 January 1983

4 Now it must be business as usual.
on the steps of Brighton police station a few hours after the bombing of the Grand Hotel, Brighton; often quoted as 'We shall carry on as usual'
in Times 13 October 1984

5 In church on Sunday morning—it was a lovely morning and we haven't had many lovely days—the sun was coming through a stained glass window and falling on some flowers, falling right across the church. It just occurred to me that this was the day I was meant not to see. Then all of a sudden I thought, 'there are some of my dearest friends who are not seeing this day.'
after the Brighton bombing
television interview, 15 October 1984

6 of Mikhail **Gorbachev**:
We can do business together.
in Times 18 December 1984

7 We got a really good consensus during the last election. Consensus behind my convictions.
attributed, 1984

8 We must try to find ways to starve the terrorist and the hijacker of the oxygen of publicity on which they depend.
speech to American Bar Association in London, 15 July 1985

9 I don't spend a lifetime watching which way the cat jumps. I know really which way I want the cats to go.
interview with Michael Charlton on BBC radio, 17 December 1985

10 No one would remember the Good Samaritan if he'd only had good intentions. He had money as well.
television interview, 6 January 1986

11 There is no such thing as Society. There are individual men and women, and there are families.
in Woman's Own 31 October 1987; see **Cameron 54:7**

12 No generation has a freehold on this earth. All we have is a life tenancy—with a full repairing lease.
speech to the Conservative Party Conference, 14 October 1988

13 We have become a grandmother.
in Times 4 March 1989

14 Advisers advise and ministers decide.
on the respective roles of her personal economic adviser, Alan Walters, and her Chancellor, Nigel **Lawson** (who resigned the following day)
in the House of Commons, 26 October 1989

15 I am naturally very sorry to see you go, but understand…your wish to be able to spend more time with your family.
reply to Norman **Fowler**'s resignation letter
in Guardian 4 January 1990; see **Fowler 113:1**

16 Others bring me problems, David brings me solutions.
of Lord Young
in Observer 1 July 1990

17 No! No! No!
making clear her opposition to a single European currency, and more centralized controls from Brussels
in the House of Commons, 30 October 1990

18 I fight on, I fight to win.
having failed to win outright in the first ballot for party leader
comment, 21 November 1990

1 It's a funny old world.
on withdrawing from the contest for leadership of the Conservative party
comment, 22 November 1990

2 I shan't be pulling the levers there but I shall be a very good back-seat driver.
on the appointment of John Major as the next Prime Minister
in *Independent* 27 November 1990

3 Home is where you come to when you have nothing better to do.
in *Vanity Fair* May 1991

4 Every Prime Minister needs a Willie.
at the farewell dinner for William Whitelaw
in *Guardian* 7 August 1991

5 In my lifetime all our problems have come from mainland Europe and all the solutions have come from the English-speaking nations of the world.
in *Times* 6 October 1999

William Roscoe Thayer 1859–1923
American biographer and historian

6 From log-cabin to White House.
title of biography (1910) of James **Garfield**

Themistocles *c.* 528–*c.* 462 BC
Greek historian and Athenian statesman

7 The wooden wall is your ships.
interpreting the words of the Delphic oracle to the Athenians, before the battle of Salamis in 480 BC
Plutarch *Parallel Lives* 'Themistocles' bk. 2, ch. 1; according to Herodotus *Histories* bk. 7, sect. 141, the words of the prophetess at Delphi were: 'Yet Zeus the all-seeing grants to Athene's prayer / That the wooden wall only shall not fall, but help you and your children'

Louis Adolphe Thiers 1797–1877
French statesman and historian

8 The king reigns, and the people govern themselves.
unsigned article in *Le National*, 20 January 1830; a signed article, 4 February 1830, reads: 'The king neither administers nor governs, he reigns'

Dylan Thomas 1914–53
Welsh poet

9 The hand that signed the paper felled a city;

Five sovereign fingers taxed the breath,
Doubled the globe of death and halved a country;
These five kings did a king to death.
'The Hand That Signed the Paper Felled a City'

10 The hand that signed the treaty bred a fever,
And famine grew, and locusts came;
Great is the hand that holds dominion over
Man by a scribbled name.
'The Hand That Signed the Paper Felled a City'

J. H. Thomas 1874–1949
British Socialist politician

11 And now 'ere we 'ave this obstinate little man with 'is Mrs Simpson. Hit won't do, 'arold, I tell you that straight.
to Harold Nicolson on Edward VIII and the Abdication crisis
Harold Nicolson letter, 26 February 1936

12 They 'ate 'aving no family life at Court.
of the British people and the Abdication crisis
Harold Nicolson letter, 26 February 1936

Norman Thomas 1884–1968
American Presbyterian minister and writer

13 I'd rather see America save her soul than her face.
protesting against the Vietnam War
speech in Washington, DC, 27 November 1965

Julian Thompson 1934–
British soldier, second-in-command of the land forces during the Falklands campaign.

14 You don't mind dying for Queen and country, but you certainly don't want to die for politicians.
'The Falklands War— the Untold Story' (Yorkshire Television) 1 April 1987

Robert Norman Thompson
1914–97
American-born Canadian mission worker, politician, and academic

15 The Americans are our best friends whether we like it or not.
Peter C. Newman *Home Country: People, Places, and Power Politics* (1973)

Lord Thomson 1894–1976
Canadian-born British newspaper and television proprietor

1 *on owning a commercial television station:*
Like having a licence to print your own money.
R. Braddon *Roy Thomson* (1965)

Henry David Thoreau 1817–62
American writer

2 I heartily accept the motto, 'That government is best which governs least'…Carried out, it finally amounts to this, which I also believe,— 'That government is best which governs not at all.'
Civil Disobedience (1849); see **O'Sullivan 234:14**

3 Under a government which imprisons any unjustly, the true place for a just man is also a prison.
Civil Disobedience (1849)

4 The oldest, wisest politician grows not more human so, but is merely a grey wharf-rat at last.
Journal 1853

5 The government of the world I live in was not framed, like that of Britain, in after-dinner conversations over the wine.
Walden (1854) 'Conclusion'

6 It takes two to speak the truth,— one to speak, and another to hear.
A Week on the Concord and Merrimack Rivers (1849) 'Wednesday'

Jeremy Thorpe 1929–
British Liberal politician

7 *of Harold **Macmillan**'s sacking seven of his Cabinet on 13 July 1962*
Greater love hath no man than this, that he lay down his friends for his life.
D. E. Butler and Anthony King *The General Election of 1964* (1965)

James Thurber 1894–1961
American humorist

8 You can fool too many of the people too much of the time.
Fables for our Time (1940); see **Lincoln 187:11**

Lord Thurlow 1731–1806
English jurist; Lord Chancellor, 1778–83, 1783–92

9 Corporations have neither bodies to be punished, nor souls to be condemned, they therefore do as they like.
usually quoted as 'Did you ever expect a corporation to have a conscience, when it has no soul to be damned, and no body to be kicked?'
John Poynder *Literary Extracts* (1844) vol. 1

Tiberius 42 BC–AD 37
Roman emperor from AD 14

10 It is the part of the good shepherd to shear his flock, not skin it.
to governors who recommended burdensome taxes
Suetonius *Lives of the Caesars* 'Tiberius'

Kahn Tineta-Horn 1940–
American-born Canadian political activist, fashion model, and civil servant

11 Why don't you all go back to where you came from? We own this land; we're your landlords. And the rent is due.
on white Canadians occupying land belonging to Native Canadians
Myrna Kostash *Long Way From Home* (1980)

Tipu Sultan c. 1750–99
Indian ruler

12 In this world I would rather live two days like a tiger, than two hundred years like a sheep.
Alexander Beatson *A View of the Origin and Conduct of the War with Tippoo Sultan* (1800) ch. 10

Alexis de Tocqueville 1805–59
French historian and politician

13 Where is the man of soul so base that he would prefer to depend on the caprices of one of his fellow men rather than obey the laws which he has himself contributed to establish?
The Ancien Régime (1856)

14 Despots themselves do not deny that freedom is excellent; only they desire it for themselves alone, and they maintain that everyone else is

altogether unworthy of it.
The Ancien Régime (1856)

1 History is a gallery of pictures in which there are few originals and many copies.
The Ancien Régime (1856)

2 When a nation abolishes aristocracy, centralization follows as a matter of course.
The Ancien Régime (1856)

3 The only substantial difference between the custom of those days and our own resides in the price paid for office. Then they were sold by government, now they are bestowed; it is no longer necessary to pay money; the object can be attained by selling one's soul.
The Ancien Régime (1856)

4 Centralization and socialism are native of the same soil: one is the wild herb, the other the garden plant.
The Ancien Régime (1856)

5 What do men need in order to remain free? A taste for freedom. Do not ask me to analyze that sublime taste; it can only be felt. It has a place in every great heart which God has prepared to receive it; it fills and inflames it. To try to explain it to those inferior minds who have never felt it is to waste time.
The Ancien Régime (1856)

6 No example is so dangerous as that of violence employed by well-meaning people for beneficial objects.
The Ancien Régime (1856)

7 He who desires in liberty anything other than itself is born to be a servant.
The Ancien Régime (1856)

8 It is not always by going from bad to worse that a society falls into revolution...The social order destroyed by a revolution is almost always better than that which immediately preceded it, and experience shows that the most dangerous moment for a bad

government is generally that in which it sets about reform.
The Ancien Régime (1856)

9 It is impossible to destroy men with more respect for the laws of humanity.
of the treatment of the American Indians
Democracy in America (1835–40) vol. 1

10 The surface of American society is covered with a layer of democratic paint, but from time to time one can see the old aristocratic colours breaking through.
Democracy in America (1835–40) vol. 1

11 Americans rightly think their patriotism is a sort of religion strengthened by practical service.
Democracy in America (1835–40) vol. 1

12 The President may slip without the state suffering, for his duties are limited. Congress may slip without the Union perishing, for above Congress there is the electoral body which can change its spirit by changing its membership. But if ever the Supreme Court came to be composed of rash or corrupt men, the confederation would be threatened by anarchy or civil war.
Democracy in America (1835–40) vol. 1

13 Providence has not created mankind entirely independent or entirely free. It is true that around every man a fatal circle is traced, beyond which he cannot pass; but within the wide verge of that circle he is powerful and free.
Democracy in America (1835–40) vol. 1

14 Of all nations, those submit to civilization with the most difficulty which habitually live by the chase.
Democracy in America (1835–40) vol. 1

15 What is understood by republican government in the United States is the slow and quiet action of society upon itself.
Democracy in America (1835–40) vol. 1

16 On my arrival in the United States I was struck by the degree of ability among the governed and the lack of it among the governing.
Democracy in America (1835–40) vol. 2

1 The French want no-one to be their *superior*. The English want *inferiors*. The Frenchman constantly raises his eyes above him with anxiety. The Englishman lowers his beneath him with satisfaction. On either side it is pride, but understood in a different way.
Voyage en Angleterre et en Irlande de 1835 (1958) 8 May 1835

Wolfe Tone 1763–98
Irish nationalist. See also **Last words 178:10**

2 I am sorry it was necessary.
on the execution of Louis XVI, 21 January 1793
Oliver Knox *Rebels and Informers* (1997)

3 To unite the whole people of Ireland, to abolish the memory of all past dissension and to substitute the common name of Irishman in place of the denominations of Protestant, Catholic and Dissenter.
in August 1796; Marianne Elliott *Wolfe Tone* (1989)

Robert Torrens 1780–1864
British economist

4 In the first stone which he [the savage] flings at the wild animals he pursues, in the first stick that he seizes to strike down the fruit which hangs above his reach, we see the appropriation of one article for the purpose of aiding in the acquisition of another, and thus discover the origin of capital.
An Essay on the Production of Wealth (1821) ch. 2

Arnold Toynbee 1889–1975
English historian

5 Civilization is a movement and not a condition, a voyage and not a harbour.
in *Readers Digest* October 1958

6 America is a large, friendly dog in a very small room. Every time it wags its tail it knocks over a chair.
attributed

7 The twentieth century will be remembered chiefly, not as an age of political conflicts and technical inventions, but as an age in which human society dared to think of the health of the whole human race as a practical objective.
attributed

Joseph Trapp 1679–1747
English poet and pamphleteer

8 The King, observing with judicious eyes
The state of both his universities,
To Oxford sent a troop of horse, and why?
That learned body wanted loyalty;
To Cambridge books, as very well discerning
How much that loyal body wanted learning.
lines written on George I's donation of the Bishop of Ely's Library to Cambridge University
John Nichols *Literary Anecdotes* (1812–16) vol. 3; see **Browne 44:2**

Lord Trend 1914–87
British civil servant; Cabinet Secretary 1963–73

9 The acid test of any political decision is, 'What is the alternative?'
attributed, 1975

Charles Trevelyan 1807–86
British civil servant

10 *on the organization of a new system of admission into the civil service:*
It is proposed to invite the flower of our youth to the aid of public service.
to John Thadeus Delane, Editor of *The Times*, in 1853

G. M. Trevelyan 1876–1962
English historian

11 If the French noblesse had been

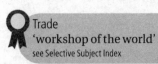

Trade
'workshop of the world'
see Selective Subject Index

capable of playing cricket with their peasants, their chateaux would never have been burnt.
English Social History (1942)

1 In a world of voluble hates, he plotted to make men like, or at least tolerate one another.
of Stanley **Baldwin**
in *Dictionary of National Biography 1941–50* (1959)

William Trevor 1928–
Irish novelist and short story writer

2 *of the troubles in Northern Ireland:*
A disease in the family that is never mentioned.
in *Observer* 18 November 1990

Hugh Trevor-Roper 1914–2003
British historian

3 Those who exercise power and determine policy are generally men whose minds have been formed by events twenty or thirty years before.
From Counter-Reformation to Glorious Revolution (1992); introduction

4 Historians in general are great toadies of power.
History and Imagination (1981)

5 Any reaction which is to be successful over a long period must have radical origins...A reaction which is to last, which is to be accepted as orthodoxy over several generations, must spring out of the same social circumstances as the progress which it resists.
The Rise of Christian Europe (1965)

David Trimble 1944–
Northern Irish politician, leader of the Ulster Unionist Party 1995–2005

6 The fundamental Act of Union is there, intact.
of the Northern Ireland settlement
in *Daily Telegraph* 11 April 1998

7 Mr Adams, it is over to you. We have jumped, you follow.
after the Ulster Unionist Council had voted to accept the setting up of the Northern Irish executive
in *Sunday Telegraph* 28 November 1999

Tommy Trinder 1909–89
British comedian

8 *of American troops in Britain during the Second World War:*
Overpaid, overfed, oversexed, and over here.
associated with Trinder, but probably not his invention

Anthony Trollope 1815–82
English novelist

9 A man who entertains in his mind any political doctrine, except as a means of improving the condition of his fellows, I regard as a political intriguer, a charlatan, and a conjuror.
Autobiography (1883)

10 When taken in the refreshing waters of office any...pill can be swallowed.
The Bertrams (1859)

11 To me it seems that no form of existing government—no form of government that ever did exist, gives or has given so large a measure of individual freedom to all who live under it as a constitutional monarchy.
North America (1862)

12 There is nothing more tyrannical than a strong popular feeling among a democratic people.
North America (1862)

13 I have sometimes thought that there is no being so venomous, so bloodthirsty as a professed philanthropist.
North America (1862)

14 [Equality] is a doctrine to be

Treason
'In trust I have found treason'
see Selective Subject Index

forgiven when he who preaches it is...striving to raise others to his own level.
North America (1862)

1 A fainéant government is not the worst government that England can have. It has been the great fault of our politicians that they have all wanted to do something.
Phineas Finn (1869)

2 *of the radical politician:*
It was his work to cut down forest-trees, and he had nothing to do with the subsequent cultivation of the land.
Phineas Finn (1869)

3 The first necessity for good speaking is a large audience.
Phineas Finn (1869)

4 Newspaper editors sport daily with the names of men of whom they do not hesitate to publish almost the severest words that can be uttered; but let an editor be himself attacked, even without his name, and he thinks that the thunderbolt of heaven should fall upon the offender.
Phineas Redux (1874) ch. 27

5 A man destined to sit conspicuously on our Treasury Bench, or on the seat opposite to it, should ask the Gods for a thick skin as a first gift.
Phineas Redux (1874)

6 Equality would be a heaven, if we could attain it.
The Prime Minister (1876)

7 What Good Government ever was not stingy?
South Africa (1878)

8 How seldom is it that theories stand the wear and tear of practice!
Thackeray (1879)

9 Let the Toryism of the Tory be ever so strong, it is his destiny to carry out the purposes of his opponents.
Why Frau Frohmann Raised Her Prices (1882)

Leon Trotsky 1879–1940
Russian revolutionary

10 Old age is the most unexpected of

all things that happen to a man.
Diary in Exile (1959) 8 May 1935

11 Civilization has made the peasantry its pack animal. The bourgeoisie in the long run only changed the form of the pack.
History of the Russian Revolution (1933) vol. 3

12 You [the Mensheviks] are pitiful isolated individuals; you are bankrupts; your role is played out. Go where you belong from now on—into the dustbin of history!
History of the Russian Revolution (1933) vol. 3

13 Where force is necessary, there it must be applied boldly, decisively and completely. But one must know the limitations of force; one must know when to blend force with a manoeuvre, a blow with an agreement.
What Next? (1932)

14 Not believing in force is the same thing as not believing in gravitation.
G. Maximov *The Guillotine at Work* (1940)

15 In a country where the sole employer is the State, opposition means death by slow starvation. The old principle: who does not work shall not eat, has been replaced by a new one: who does not obey shall not eat.
attributed

Pierre Trudeau 1919–2000
Canadian Liberal statesman, Prime Minister, 1968–79 and 1980–4

16 The state has no place in the nation's bedrooms.
interview, Ottawa, 22 December 1967

17 The twentieth century really belongs to those who will build it. The future can be promised to no one.
in 1968; see **Laurier 180:9**

18 Living next to you is in some ways like sleeping with an elephant. No matter how friendly and even-tempered the beast, one is affected by every twitch and grunt.
on relations between Canada and the US
speech at National Press Club, Washington D. C., 25 March 1969

Harry S. Truman 1884–1972

American Democratic statesman, 33rd President of the US 1945–53. On Truman: see **Mencken 211:3**, **Newspaper headlines 225:4**; see also **Mottoes 221:2, Proverbs 251:13**

1 *to reporters the day after his accession to the Presidency on the death of Franklin* ***Roosevelt***:
When they told me yesterday what had happened, I felt like the moon, the stars and all the planets had fallen on me.
on 13 April 1945

2 Sixteen hours ago an American airplane dropped one bomb on Hiroshima…The force from which the sun draws its power has been loosed against those who brought war to the Far East.
first announcement of the dropping of the atomic bomb
on 6 August 1945

3 Effective, reciprocal, and enforceable safeguards acceptable to all nations.
Declaration on Atomic Energy by President Truman, Clement **Attlee**, and W. L. Mackenzie **King**, 15 November 1945

4 All the President is, is a glorified public relations man who spends his time flattering, kissing and kicking people to get them to do what they are supposed to do anyway.
letter to his sister, 14 November 1947

5 What we are doing in Korea is this: we are trying to prevent a third world war.
*after the recall of General **MacArthur***
address to the nation, 16 April 1951

6 Those who want the Government to regulate matters of the mind and spirit are like men who are so afraid of being murdered that they commit suicide to avoid assassination.
address at the National Archives, Washington, DC, 15 December 1952

7 He'll sit right here and he'll say do this, do that! And nothing will happen. Poor Ike—it won't be a bit like the Army.
*of his successor **Eisenhower***
Harry S. Truman (1973) vol. 2

8 Once a decision was made, I did not worry about it afterward.
Memoirs (1955) vol. 2

9 I never give them [the public] hell. I just tell the truth, and they think it is hell.
in *Look* 3 April 1956

10 A politician is a man who understands government, and it takes a politician to run a government. A statesman is a politician who's been dead 10 or 15 years.
in *New York World Telegram and Sun* 12 April 1958

11 It's a recession when your neighbour loses his job; it's a depression when you lose yours.
in *Observer* 13 April 1958

12 Wherever you have an efficient government you have a dictatorship.
lecture at Columbia University, 28 April 1959

13 To me, party platforms are contracts with the people.
Memoirs (1955) vol. 2

14 If there is one basic element in our Constitution, it is civilian control of the military.
Memoirs (1955) vol. 2

15 I didn't fire him [General MacArthur] because he was a dumb son of a bitch, although he was, but that's not against the law for generals. If it was, half to three-quarters of them would be in jail.
Merle Miller *Plain Speaking* (1974)

16 Secrecy and a free, democratic government don't mix.
Merle Miller *Plain Speaking* (1974)

17 Always be sincere, even if you don't mean it.
attributed

18 If you want a friend in Washington, get a dog.
attributed; popularized by the Reagan administration, *c.* 1988

Sojourner Truth c. 1797–1883
American evangelist and reformer

1 That man…says that women need to be helped into carriages, and lifted over ditches, and to have the best place everywhere. Nobody ever helps me into carriages, or over mud puddles, or gives me any best place, and aren't I a woman?…I have ploughed, and planted, and gathered into barns, and no man could head me—and aren't I a woman? I could work as much and eat as much as a man (when I could get it), and bear the lash as well—and aren't I a woman? I have borne thirteen children and seen them most all sold off into slavery, and when I cried out with a mother's grief, none but Jesus heard—and aren't I a woman?
   speech at Women's Rights Convention, Akron, Ohio, 1851

Harriet Tubman c. 1820–1913
American abolitionist

2 Children, if you are tired, keep going; if you are scared, keep going; if you are hungry, keep going; if you want to taste freedom, keep going.
   attributed, but apparently a modern paraphrase of her views

Barbara W. Tuchman 1912–89
American writer

3 Dead battles, like dead generals, hold the military mind in their dead grip and Germans, no less than other peoples, prepare for the last war.
   August 1914 (1962)

4 No more distressing moment can ever face a British government than that which requires it to come to a hard, fast and specific decision.
   August 1914 (1962)

Dick Tuck 1924–
American Democratic politician

5 The people have spoke—the bastards.
   after being defeated in the California Senate primary c.1962; usually quoted as 'The people have spoken—the bastards'
   in Time 13 August 1973

A. R. J. Turgot 1727–81
French economist and statesman

6 Eripuit coelo fulmen, sceptrumque tyrannis.
   He snatched the lightning shaft from heaven, and the sceptre from tyrants.
   for a bust of Benjamin Franklin, inventor of the lightning conductor and one of those who drafted the Declaration of Independence
   inscription

Mark Twain 1835–1910
American writer

7 It could probably be shown by facts and figures that there is no distinctly native American criminal class except Congress.
   Following the Equator (1897)

8 It is by the goodness of God in our country that we have those three unspeakably precious things: freedom of speech, freedom of conscience, and the prudence never to practise either of them.
   Following the Equator (1897)

9 Get your facts first, and then you can distort them as much as you please.
   Rudyard Kipling From Sea to Sea (1899)

10 Suppose you were an idiot. And suppose you were a member of Congress. But I repeat myself.
   A. B. Paine Mark Twain (1912)

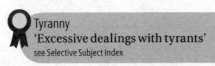

Tyranny
'Excessive dealings with tyrants'
see Selective Subject Index

William Magear ('Boss') Tweed
1823–78

American Democratic politician, Tammany 'boss' of New York City. On Tweed: see Misquotations 216:11

1 New York politics were always dishonest—long before my time…A politician coming forward takes things as they are.
interviewed in prison a few months before his death
Richard Ackerman *Boss Tweed* (2005)

William Tyndale c. 1494–1536

English translator of the Bible and Protestant martyr. See also Last words 179:2

2 If God spare my life, ere many years I will cause a boy that driveth the plough shall know more of the scripture than thou doest!
to an opponent; in *Dictionary of National Biography* (1917–)

Harlan K. Ullman and James P. Wade

3 The basis for rapid dominance rests in the ability to affect the will, perception, and understanding of the adversary through imposing sufficient Shock and Awe to achieve the necessary political, strategic, and operational goals of the conflict or crisis that led to the use of force.
Shock and Awe: Achieving Rapid Dominance (1996) ch. 2

Universal Declaration of Human Rights 1948

4 All human beings are born free and equal in dignity and rights.
article 1

5 Everyone has the right to freedom of movement and residence within the borders of each State. Everyone has the right to leave any country, including his own, and to return to his country.
article 13

6 Everyone has the right to seek and to enjoy in other countries asylum from persecution.
article 14

John Updike 1932–2009
American novelist and short-story writer

7 Without the cold war, what's the point of being an American?
Rabbit at Rest (1990) pt. 3

United States
'Fourscore and seven years ago'
see Selective Subject Index

Paul Valéry 1871–1945
French poet, critic, and man of letters

1 An attitude of permanent indignation signfies great mental poverty. Politics compels its votaries to take that line and you can see their minds growing more and more impoverished every day, from one burst of righteous anger to the next.
   Tel Quel (1941–3)

2 Politics is the art of preventing people from taking part in affairs which properly concern them.
   Tel Quel (1941–3)

William Henry Vanderbilt
1821–85
American railway magnate

3 The public be damned!
   on whether the public should be consulted about luxury trains
   A. W. Cole letter to *New York Times* 25 August 1918

Laurens van der Post 1906–96
South African explorer and writer

4 Human beings are perhaps never more frightening than when they are convinced beyond doubt that they are right.
   The Lost World of the Kalahari (1958)

Raoul Vaneigem 1934–
Belgian philosopher

5 Never before has a civilization reached such a degree of a contempt for life; never before has a generation, drowned in mortification, felt such a rage to live.
   of the 1960s
   The Revolution of Everyday Life (1967) ch. 5

Herman Van Rompuy 1947–
Belgian statesman, President of the European Council from 2009

6 Hair blows in the wind.
   After years there is still wind.
   Sadly no more hair.
   haiku, in *Sunday Times* 8 November 2009

Robert Vansittart 1881–1957
British diplomat

7 The soul of our service is the loyalty with which we execute ordained error.
   attributed; David Butler et al. *Failure in British Government* (1994)

Mordechai Vanunu 1954–
Moroccan-born Israeli nuclear technician, who made public Israel's nuclear progamme and was convicted of espionage

8 For all those calling me a traitor, I am proud of what I did and I'm glad I succeeded in what I did.
   in *Independent* 22 April 2004

Bartolomeo Vanzetti 1888–1927
American anarchist, born in Italy

9 Sacco's name will live in the hearts of the people and in their gratitude when Katzmann's and yours bones will be dispersed by time, when your name, his name, your laws, institutions, and your false god are but a deem rememoring of a cursed past in which man was wolf to the man.
   statement disallowed at his trial, with Nicola Sacco, for murder and robbery; both were sentenced to death on 9 April 1927, and executed on 23 August 1927
   M. D. Frankfurter and G. Jackson *Letters of Sacco and Vanzetti* (1928)

Thorstein Veblen 1857–1929
American economist and social scientist

1 Conspicuous consumption of valuable goods is a means of reputability to the gentleman of leisure.
Theory of the Leisure Class (1899)

2 From the foregoing survey of conspicuous leisure and consumption, it appears that the utility of both alike for the purposes of reputability lies in the element of waste that is common to both. In the one case it is a waste of time and effort, in the other it is a waste of goods.
Theory of the Leisure Class (1899)

Vegetius fl. AD 379–395
Roman military writer

3 Let him who desires peace, prepare for war.
usually quoted as 'If you want peace, prepare for war'
Epitoma Rei Militaris

Pierre Vergniaud 1753–93
French revolutionary; executed with other Girondists

4 There was reason to fear that the Revolution, like Saturn, might devour in turn each one of her children.
Alphonse de Lamartine *Histoire des Girondins* (1847)

Hendrik Frensch Verwoerd
1901–66
South African statesman; Prime Minister from 1958

5 Up till now he [the Bantu] has been subjected to a school system which drew him away from his own community and practically misled him by showing him the green pastures of the European but still did not allow him to graze there...It is abundantly clear that unplanned education creates many problems, disrupts the communal life of the Bantu and endangers the communal life of the European.
speech in South African Senate, 7 June 1954

Vespasian AD 9–79
Roman emperor from AD 69. See also
Last words 178:5

6 *Pecunia non olet.*
Money has no smell.
replying to Titus's objection to his tax on public lavatories; holding a coin to Titus's nose and being told it didn't smell, he replied, 'Atque e lotio est [Yes, that's made from urine]'
traditional summary of Suetonius *Lives of the Caesars* 'Vespasian'

7 Woe is me, I think I am becoming a god.
when fatally ill
Suetonius *Lives of the Caesars* 'Vespasian'

Queen Victoria 1819–1901
British monarch, Queen of the United Kingdom from 1837. On Victoria: see **Gladstone 125:15**; see also **Anonymous 10:14**

8 I will be good.
on being shown a chart of the line of succession, 11 March 1830
Theodore Martin *The Prince Consort* (1875)

9 The Queen is most anxious to enlist every one who can speak or write to join in checking this mad, wicked folly of 'Woman's Rights', with all its attendant horrors, on which her poor feeble sex is bent, forgetting every sense of womanly feeling and propriety.
letter to Theodore Martin, 29 May 1870

10 *on **Gladstone**'s last appointment as Prime Minister:*
The danger to the country, to Europe, to her vast Empire, which is involved in having all these great interests entrusted to the shaking hand of an old, wild, and incomprehensible man of 82, is

Vietnam
'destroy the town to save it'
see Selective Subject Index

very great!
letter to Lord Lansdowne, 12 August 1892

1 The future Viceroy must...not be guided by the *snobbish* and vulgar, over-bearing and offensive behaviour of our Civil and Political Agents, if we are to go on peaceably and happily in India...not trying to trample on the people and continuously reminding them and making them feel they are a conquered people.
letter to Lord **Salisbury**, 27 May 1898

2 We are not interested in the possibilities of defeat; they do not exist.
on the Boer War during 'Black Week', December 1899
Lady Gwendolen Cecil *Life of Robert, Marquis of Salisbury* (1931)

3 He speaks to Me as if I was a public meeting.
of **Gladstone**
G. W. E. Russell *Collections and Recollections* (1898)

4 We are not amused.
attributed; Caroline Holland *Notebooks of a Spinster Lady* (1919), 2 January 1900

Gore Vidal 1925–
American novelist and critic

5 *of Ronald* **Reagan***:*
A triumph of the embalmer's art.
in *Observer* 26 April 1981

José Antonio Viera Gallo 1943–
Chilean politician

6 Socialism can only arrive by bicycle.
Ivan Illich *Energy and Equity* (1974) epigraph

Peter Viggers 1938–
British Conservative politician

7 I paid for it myself and in fact it was

never liked by the ducks.
on his claim for a duck house, not allowed by the Commons Fees Office
statement, 23 May 2009; in *Times* 24 May 2009

Virgil 70–19 BC
Roman poet

8 *Tantae molis erat Romanam condere gentem.*
So massive was the effort to found the Roman nation.
Aeneid

9 *Equo ne credite, Teucri. Quidquid id est, timeo Danaos et dona ferentes.*
Do not trust the horse, Trojans. Whatever it is, I fear the Greeks even when they bring gifts.
Aeneid

10 *Bella, horrida bella, Et Thybrim multo spumantem sanguine cerno.*
I see wars, horrible wars, and the Tiber foaming with much blood.
Aeneid; see **Powell 248:12**

Voltaire 1694–1778
French writer and philosopher. See also **Misquotations 215:12**

11 These two nations have been at war over a few acres of snow near Canada, and...they are spending on this fine struggle more than Canada itself is worth.
of the struggle between the French and the British for the control of colonial north Canada
Candide (1759)

12 *Dans ce pays-ci il est bon de tuer de temps en temps un amiral pour encourager les autres.*
In this country [England] it is thought well to kill an admiral from time to time to encourage the others.
Candide (1759)

13 The art of government consists in

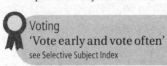

Voting
'Vote early and vote often'
see Selective Subject Index

taking as much money as possible from one class of citizens to give to the other.
Dictionnaire philosophique (1764) 'Money'

1 Superstition sets the whole world in flames; philosophy quenches them.
Dictionnaire philosophique (1764) 'Superstition'

2 This agglomeration which was called and which still calls itself the Holy Roman Empire was neither holy, nor Roman, nor an empire.
Essai sur l'histoire générale et sur les moeurs et l'esprit des nations (1756)

3 Indeed, history is nothing more than a tableau of crimes and misfortunes.
L'Ingénu (1767); see **Gibbon 122:9**

4 Governments need both shepherds and butchers.
'The Piccini Notebooks' (1735–50)

5 God is on the side not of the heavy battalions, but of the best shots.
'The Piccini Notebooks' (1735–50); see **Tacitus 304:11**

6 Truly, whoever is able to make you absurd is able to make you unjust.
commonly quoted as 'Those who can make you believe in absurdities can make you commit atrocities'
Questions sur les miracles (1765)

7 Whatever you do, stamp out abuses, and love those who love you.
letter to M. d'Alembert, 28 November 1762

8 The froth at top, dregs at bottom, but the middle excellent.
comparing the English to their own beer attributed; in *Edinburgh Magazine* (1786)

9 If one must serve, I hold it better to serve a well-bred lion, who is naturally stronger than I am, than two hundred rats of my own breed.
letter to a friend; Alexis de Tocqueville *The Ancien Régime* (1856)

10 To succeed in chaining the crowd you must seem to wear the same fetters.
attributed

11 *what Voltaire apparently said on the burning of* De l'esprit:
What a fuss about an omelette!
James Parton *Life of Voltaire* (1881) vol. 2; see **Misquotations 215:12**

William Waldegrave 1946–
British Conservative politician

12 In exceptional circumstances it is necessary to say something that is untrue in the House of Commons.
to a House of Commons select committee, in *Guardian* 9 March 1994

Lech Wałęsa 1943–
Polish trade unionist and statesman, President 1990–5

13 You have riches and freedom here but I feel no sense of faith or direction. You have so many computers, why don't you use them in the search for love?
in Paris, on his first journey outside the Soviet area, in *Daily Telegraph* 14 December 1988

Felix Walker fl. 1820
American politician

14 *excusing a long, dull, irrelevant speech in the House of Representatives, 1820 (Buncombe being his constituency):*
I'm talking to Buncombe ['bunkum'].
W. Safire *New Language of Politics* (2nd ed., 1972); see **Carlyle 57:4**

George Wallace 1919–98
American Democratic politician

15 Segregation now, segregation

tomorrow and segregation forever!
inaugural speech as Governor of Alabama, January 1963

Henry Wallace 1888–1965
American Democratic politician

1 The century on which we are entering—the century which will come out of this war—can be and must be the century of the common man.
speech, 8 May 1942

William Wallace
American general

2 The enemy we're fighting is a bit different than the one we war-gamed against.
of the campaign in Iraq
in *New York Times* 28 March 2003

William Wallace c. 1270–1305
Scottish national hero

3 I hae brocht ye to the ring, now see gif ye can dance.
before the battle of Falkirk, 1298; attributed in varying forms, including '…hop if ye can'; James MacKay William Wallace: Brave Heart *(1996)*

Edmund Waller 1606–87
English poet

4 Others may use the ocean as their road,
Only the English make it their abode.
'Of a War with Spain' (1658)

5 Rome, though her eagle through the world had flown,
Could never make this island all her own.
'Panegyric to My Lord Protector' (1655)

6 Under the tropic is our language spoke,
And part of Flanders hath received our yoke.
'Upon the Late Storm, and of the Death of His Highness Ensuing the Same' (1659)

William Waller 1598–1668
English Parliamentary general

7 With what a perfect hatred I detest this war without an enemy.
letter to the Royalist Ralph Hopton, 16 June 1643; Samuel R. Gardiner History of the Great Civil War *(1894)*

Horace Walpole 1717–97
English writer and connoisseur, son of Robert **Walpole**

8 His speeches were fine, but as much laboured as his extempore sayings.
*of Lord **Chesterfield**, 1751*
Memoirs of the Reign of King George II *(1846) vol. 1*

9 While he felt like a victim, he acted like a hero.
of Admiral Byng, on the day of his execution, 1757
Memoirs of the Reign of King George II *(1846) vol. 2*

10 Perhaps those, who, trembling most, maintain a dignity in their fate, are the bravest: resolution on reflection is real courage.
in 1757; Memoirs of the Reign of King George II *(1846) vol. 2*

11 They seem to know no medium between a mitre and a crown of martyrdom. If the clergy are not called to the latter, they never deviate from the pursuit of the former. One would think their motto was, *Canterbury or Smithfield*.
in 1758; Memoirs of the Reign of King George II *(1846) vol. 3*

12 All his passions were expressed by one livid smile.
*of George **Grenville**, 1763*
Memoirs of the Reign of King George III *(1845) vol. 1*

13 He lost his dominions in America, his authority over Ireland, and all influence in Europe, by aiming at despotism in England; and exposed himself to more mortifications and

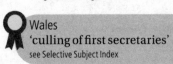

Wales
'culling of first secretaries'
see Selective Subject Index

humiliations than can happen to a quiet Doge of Venice.
of George III
Memoirs of the Reign of King George III (1845) vol. 4

1 Our supreme governors, the mob.
letter to Horace Mann, 7 September 1743

2 Everybody talks of the constitution, but all sides forget that the constitution is extremely well, and would do very well, if they would but let it alone.
letter to Horace Mann, 18–19 January 1770

3 It was easier to conquer it [the East] than to know what to do with it.
letter to Horace Mann, 27 March 1772

4 By the waters of Babylon we sit down and weep, when we think of thee, O America!
letter to Revd William Mason, 12 June 1775

Robert Walpole 1676–1745
English Whig statesman; first British Prime Minister, 1721–42; father of Horace **Walpole**. On Walpole: see **Peel 242:17, Shippen 288:7**

5 Madam, there are fifty thousand men slain this year in Europe, and not one Englishman.
to Queen Caroline, 1734, on the war of the Polish succession, in which the English had refused to participate
John Hervey *Memoirs* (written 1734–43, published 1848) vol. 1

6 We must muzzle this terrible young cornet of horse.
*of the elder William **Pitt**, who had held a cornetcy before his election to Parliament, but whose speech in support of the congratulatory address on the Prince of Wales's marriage in 1736 was regarded as so offensive through its covert satire that he was shortly afterwards dismissed from the army*
in *Dictionary of National Biography* (1917–)

7 They now *ring* the bells, but they will soon *wring* their hands.
on the declaration of war with Spain, 1739
W. Coxe *Memoirs of Sir Robert Walpole* (1798) vol. 1

8 All those men have their price.
of fellow parliamentarians
W. Coxe *Memoirs of Sir Robert Walpole* (1798) vol. 1

9 [Gratitude of place-expectants] is a lively sense of future favours.
W. Hazlitt *Lectures on the English Comic Writers* (1819) 'On Wit and Humour'

10 *the normally imperturbable Walpole, having lost his temper at a Council, broke up the meeting:*
No man is fit for business with a ruffled temper.
Edmund Fitzmaurice *Life of Shelburne* (1875)

11 There is enough pasture for all the sheep.
on his ability to spread round patronage satisfactorily
attributed

12 *on seeing Henry Fox (Lord **Holland**) reading in the library at Houghton:*
You can read. It is a great happiness. I totally neglected it while I was in business, which has been the whole of my life, and to such a degree that I cannot now read a page—a warning to all Ministers.
Edmund Fitzmaurice *Life of Shelburne* (1875) vol. 1

Charles Dudley Warner 1829–1900
American writer and editor

13 Politics makes strange bedfellows.
My Summer in a Garden (1871); see **Clay 74:7**

Earl Warren 1891–1974
American Chief Justice

14 In civilized life, law floats in a sea of ethics.
in *New York Times* 12 November 1962

15 The freedom to marry has long been recognized as one of the vital personal rights essential to the orderly pursuit of happiness by free men.
judgement in *Loving v. Virginia* 1967

War
'army marches on its stomach'
see Selective Subject Index

Booker T. Washington 1856–1915
American educationist and emancipated slave

1 No race can prosper till it learns that there is as much dignity in tilling a field as in writing a poem.
Up from Slavery (1901)

2 You can't hold a man down without staying down with him.
attributed

George Washington 1732–99
American statesman, 1st President of the US. On Washington: see **Byron 52:6**, **Franklin 114:10**, **Lee 182:1**; see also **Last words 178:14**

3 I can't tell a lie, Pa; you know I can't tell a lie. I did cut it with my hatchet.
M. L. Weems *Life of George Washington* (10th ed., 1810)

4 Discipline is the soul of an army. It makes small numbers formidable; procures success to the weak and esteem to all.
letter to the captains of the Virginia Regiments, July 1759

5 The time is now near at hand which must probably determine whether Americans are to be freemen or slaves; whether they are to have any property they can call their own...The fate of unborn millions will now depend, under God, on the courage and conduct of this army. Our cruel and unrelenting enemy leaves us only the choice of brave resistance, or the most abject submission. We have, therefore, to resolve to conquer or die.
General orders, 2 July 1776, in J. C. Fitzpatrick (ed.) *Writings of George Washington* vol. 5 (1932)

6 Few men have virtue to withstand the highest bidder.
letter, 17 August 1779

7 'Tis our true policy to steer clear of permanent alliances, with any portion of the foreign world.
President's Address... (17 September 1796)

8 Let me...warn you in the most solemn manner against the baneful effects of the spirit of party.
President's Address... (17 September 1796)

9 The nation which indulges toward another an habitual hatred or an habitual fondness is in some degree a slave. It is a slave to its animosity or to its affection, either of which is sufficient to lead it astray from its duty and its interest.
President's Address... (17 September 1796)

10 Liberty, when it begins to take root, is a plant of rapid growth.
attributed

William Watson c. 1559–1603
English Roman Catholic conspirator

11 *Fiat justitia et ruant coeli.*
Let justice be done even though the heavens fall.
A Decacordon of Ten Quodlibeticall Questions Concerning Religion and State (1602), being the first citation in an English work of a famous maxim; see **Adams 3:15**, **Mottoes 221:3**

Evelyn Waugh 1903–66
English novelist

12 'In a democracy,' said Mr Pinfold, with more weight than originality, 'Men do not seek authority so that they may impose a policy. They seek a policy so that they may achieve authority.'
The Ordeal of Gilbert Pinfold (1957)

13 *The Beast* stands for strong mutually antagonistic governments everywhere...Self-sufficiency at home, self-assertion abroad.
Scoop (1938)

14 Remember that the Patriots are in the right and are going to win...But they must win quickly. The British public has no interest in a war that drags on indecisively. A few sharp victories, some conspicuous acts of personal bravery on the Patriot side and a colourful entry into the capital. That is *The Beast* Policy for the war.
Scoop (1938)

15 Other nations use 'force'; we Britons alone use 'Might'.
Scoop (1938)

16 I do not aspire to advise my

sovereign in her choice of servants.
on why he did not vote
in *Spectator* 2 October 1959

1 *it had been announced after an operation on Randolph Churchill that the trouble was 'not malignant':*
It was a typical triumph of modern science to find the only part of Randolph that was not malignant and remove it.
Michael Davie (ed.) *Diaries of Evelyn Waugh* (1976) 'Irregular Notes 1960–65', March 1964

2 The Conservative Party have never put the clock back a single second.
Frances Donaldson *Evelyn Waugh* (1967)

Beatrice Webb 1858–1943
English socialist

3 Restless, almost intolerably so, without capacity for sustained and unexcited labour, egotistical, bumptious, shallow-minded and reactionary, but with a certain personal magnetism, great pluck and some originality, not of intellect but of character.
*of Winston **Churchill***
in 1903, Martin Gilbert *In Search of Churchill* (1994)

Sidney Webb 1859–1947
English socialist

4 Once we face the necessity of putting our principles first into Bills, to be fought through committee clause by clause; and then into the appropriate machinery for carrying them into execution from one end of the kingdom to the other...the inevitability of gradualness cannot fail to be appreciated.
presidential address to the annual conference of the Labour Party, 26 June 1923

5 Nobody told us we could do this.
when the new National Government came off the Gold Standard in 1931, the outgoing Labour Government not having resorted to this tactic
Nigel Rees *Brewer's Quotations* (1994)

Max Weber 1864–1920
German sociologist

6 The Protestant ethic and the spirit

of capitalism.
Archiv für Sozialwissenschaft Sozialpolitik vol. 20 (1904–5) (title of article)

7 In Baxter's view the care for external goods should only lie on the shoulders of the saint like 'a light cloak, which can be thrown aside at any moment.' But fate decreed that the cloak should become an iron cage.
Gesammelte Aufsätze zur Religionssoziologie (1920) vol. 1

8 The State is a relation of men dominating men, a relation supported by means of legitimate (i.e. considered to be legitimate) violence.
'*Politik als Beruf*' (1919)

9 The authority of the 'eternal yesterday'.
'*Politik als Beruf*' (1919)

10 The experience of the irrationality of the world has been the driving force of all religious revolution.
'*Politik als Beruf*' (1919)

11 The concept of the 'official secret' is its [bureaucracy's] specific invention.
'*Politik als Beruf*' (1919)

Daniel Webster 1782–1852
American politician. On Webster: see **Smith 294:11**

12 The people's government, made for the people, made by the people, and answerable to the people.
second speech in the Senate on Foote's Resolution, 26 January 1830; see **Lincoln 186:6**

13 Liberty *and* Union, now and forever, one and inseparable!
second speech in the Senate on Foote's Resolution, 26 January 1830

14 When my eyes shall be turned to behold for the last time the sun in heaven, may I not see him shining on the broken and dishonored fragments of a once glorious Union; on States dissevered, discordant, belligerent; on a land rent with civil feuds, or drenched, it may be, in fraternal blood.
second speech in the Senate on Foote's Resolution, 26 January 1830

1 Fearful concatenation of
circumstances.
argument on the murder of Captain Joseph White
speech on 6 April 1830

2 He smote the rock of the national
resources, and abundant streams of
revenue gushed forth. He touched
the dead corpse of the Public
Credit, and it sprung upon its feet.
*of Alexander **Hamilton***
speech 10 March 1831

3 Whatever government is not a
government of laws, is a despotism,
let it be called what it may.
at a reception in Bangor, Maine, 25 August
1835

4 One country, one constitution, one
destiny.
speech 15 March 1837

5 Thank God, I—I also—am an
American!
speech on the completion of Bunker Hill
Monument, 17 June 1843

6 The Law: It has honoured us, may
we honour it.
speech at the Charleston Bar Dinner, 10 May
1847

7 I was born an American; I will
live an American; I shall die an
American.
speech in the Senate on 'The Compromise Bill',
17 July 1850

8 There is always room at the top.
*on being advised against joining the overcrowded
legal profession*
attributed

Josiah Wedgwood 1730–95
English potter

9 Am I not a man and a brother.
*legend on Wedgwood cameo, depicting a
kneeling Negro slave in chains*
reproduced in facsimile in E. Darwin *The
Botanic Garden* pt. 1 (1791)

Simone Weil 1909–43
French essayist and philosopher

10 I would suggest that barbarism be
considered as a permanent and
universal human characteristic
which becomes more or less
pronounced according to the play

of circumstances.
Écrits Historiques et politiques (1960)
'Réflexions sur la barbarie' (written 1939)

11 A right is not effectual by itself, but
only in relation to the obligation
to which it corresponds...
An obligation which goes
unrecognized by anybody
loses none of the full force of its
existence. A right which goes
unrecognized by anybody is not
worth very much.
L'Enracinement (1949) 'Les Besoins de l'âme'

12 What a country calls its vital
economic interests are not the
things which enable its citizens to
live, but the things which enable it
to make war.
W. H. Auden *A Certain World* (1971)

Stanley Weiser 1946– and Oliver Stone

13 Greed—for lack of a better word—is
good. Greed is right. Greed works.
Wall Street (1987 film); see **Boesky 38:1**

Chaim Weizmann 1874–1952
Russian-born Israeli statesman, President 1949–52

14 Something had been done for us
which, after two thousand years
of hope and yearning, would at
last give us a resting-place in this
terrible world.
of the Balfour declaration
speech in Jerusalem, 25 November 1936; see
Balfour 23:6

Joseph Welch 1890–1960
American lawyer

15 Until this moment, Senator, I think
I never really gauged your cruelty
or your recklessness...Have you no
sense of decency, sir? At long last,
have you left no sense of decency?
*to Joseph **McCarthy**, 9 June 1954, defending
the US Army against allegations of harbouring
subversive activities; the televised confrontation
was deeply damaging to McCarthy*
in *American National Biography* (online edition)
'Joseph McCarthy'

Orson Welles 1915–85
American actor and film director

1 In Italy for thirty years under the Borgias they had warfare, terror, murder, bloodshed — they produced Michelangelo, Leonardo da Vinci and the Renaissance. In Switzerland they had brotherly love, five hundred years of democracy and peace and what did that produce…? The cuckoo clock.
The Third Man (1949 film); words added by Welles to Graham Greene's script

Duke of Wellington 1769–1852
British soldier and statesman, Prime Minister 1828–30, 1834. On Wellington: see **Tennyson 308:8**, **Tennyson 308:9**, **Tennyson 308:10**

2 As Lord Chesterfield said of the generals of his day, 'I only hope that when the enemy reads the list of their names, he trembles as I do.'
usually quoted as 'I don't know what effect these men will have upon the enemy, but, by God, they frighten me'
letter, 29 August 1810

3 Trust nothing to the enthusiasm of the people. Give them a strong and a just, and, if possible, a good, government; but, above all, a strong one.
letter to Lord William Bentinck, 24 December 1811

4 Up Guards and at them!
letter from an officer in the Guards, 22 June 1815, in *The Battle of Waterloo* by a Near Observer [J. Booth] (1815); later denied by Wellington

5 Hard pounding this, gentlemen; let's see who will pound longest.
at the Battle of Waterloo, 1815
Sir Walter Scott *Paul's Letters* (1816)

6 Publish and be damned.
replying to Harriette Wilson's blackmail threat, 1825
attributed; Elizabeth Longford *Wellington: The Years of the Sword* (1969)

7 *of his first Cabinet meeting as Prime Minister:*
An extraordinary affair. I gave them their orders and they wanted to stay and discuss them.
Peter Hennessy *Whitehall* (1990)

8 I used to say of him [Napoleon] that his presence on the field made the difference of forty thousand men.
Philip Henry Stanhope *Notes of Conversations with the Duke of Wellington* (1888)
2 November 1831

9 Ours [our army] is composed of the scum of the earth—the mere scum of the earth.
Philip Henry Stanhope *Notes of Conversations with the Duke of Wellington* (1888)
4 November 1831

10 I never saw so many shocking bad hats in my life.
on seeing the first Reformed Parliament
William Fraser *Words on Wellington* (1889)

11 Nothing the people of this country like so much as to see their great men take part in their amusements. The aristocracy will commit a great error if they ever fail to mix freely with their neighbours.
on foxhunting
in 1836; Philip Henry Stanhope *Notes of Conversations with the Duke of Wellington* (1888)

12 All the business of war, and indeed all the business of life, is to endeavour to find out what you don't know by what you do; that's what I called 'guessing what was at the other side of the hill'.
in *The Croker Papers* (1885) vol. 3

13 The battle of Waterloo was won on the playing fields of Eton.
oral tradition, but not found in this form of words; C. F. R. Montalembert *De l'avenir politique de l'Angleterre* (1856); see **Orwell 233:3**

14 *to a gentleman who had accosted him in the street saying, 'Mr Jones, I believe?'*
If you believe that, you'll believe anything.
George Jones RA (1786–1869), painter of military subjects, bore a striking resemblance to Wellington
Elizabeth Longford *Pillar of State* (1972)

15 I have no small talk and Peel has no manners.
G. W. E. Russell *Collections and Recollections* (1898)

16 Next to a battle lost, the greatest misery is a battle gained.
in *Diary of Frances, Lady Shelley 1787–1817* (ed. R. Edgcumbe); see S. Rogers *Recollections* (1859) for variations on the theme

1 There is no such thing as a little war
for a great nation.
to Fitzroy Somerset, urging military preparedness
attributed

2 You must build your House of
Parliament upon the river...
the populace cannot exact their
demands by sitting down round
you.
William Fraser *Words on Wellington* (1889)

H. G. Wells 1866–1946
English novelist

3 The Social Contract is nothing
more or less than a vast conspiracy
of human beings to lie to and
humbug themselves and one
another for the general Good. Lies
are the mortar that bind the savage
individual man into the social
masonry.
Love and Mr Lewisham (1900)

4 The war that will end war.
title of book (1914); see **Lloyd George 188:16**

5 We fight not to destroy a nation, but
a nest of evil ideas...Our business is
to kill ideas. The ultimate purpose
of this war is propaganda, the
destruction of certain beliefs, and
the creation of others.
The War That Will End War (1914) ch. 11

6 In England we have come to rely
upon a comfortable time-lag of
fifty years or a century intervening
between the perception that
something ought to be done and a
serious attempt to do it.
The Work, Wealth and Happiness of Mankind
(1931)

Rebecca West 1892–1983
English novelist and journalist

7 Having watched the form of our
traitors for a number of years, I
cannot think that espionage can be
recommended as a technique for
building an impressive civilization.
It's a lout's game.
The Meaning of Treason (1982 ed.)

8 I myself have never been able to
find out precisely what feminism
is: I only know that people call

me a feminist whenever I express
sentiments that differentiate me
from a doormat or a prostitute.
in *The Clarion* 14 November 1913

9 It was in dealing with the early
feminist that the Government
acquired the tact and skilfulness
with which it is now handling
Ireland.
in 1916; *The Young Rebecca* (1982)

10 Whatever happens, never forget
that people would rather be lead to
perdition by a man, than to *victory*
by a woman.
in conversation in 1979, just before Margaret
Thatcher's *first election victory*
in *Sunday Telegraph* 17 January 1988

William C. Westmoreland 1914–
American general

11 Vietnam was the first war ever
fought without censorship. Without
censorship, things can get terribly
confused in the public mind.
attributed, 1982

John Fane, Lord Westmorland
1759–1841
English peer

12 *Merit*, indeed!...We are come to a
pretty pass if they talk of *merit* for a
bishopric.
noted in Lady Salisbury's diary, 9 December
1835

Charles Wetherell 1770–1846
English lawyer and politician

13 Then there is my noble and
biographical friend who has added
a new terror to death.
of Lord Campbell
Lord St Leonards *Misrepresentations in
Campbell's Lives of Lyndhurst and Brougham*
(1869); also attributed to Lord Lyndhurst

Grover A. Whalen 1886–1962

14 There's a lot of law at the end of a
nightstick.
Quentin Reynolds *Courtroom* (1950)

Thomas, Lord Wharton 1648–1715
English Whig politician

1 I sang a king out of three kingdoms.
said to have been Wharton's boast after 'A New Song' became a propaganda weapon against James II
in *Dictionary of National Biography* (1917–); see **Songs 296:3**

Richard Whately 1787–1863
English philosopher and theologian

2 It is not that pearls fetch a high price *because* men have dived for them; but on the contrary, men dive for them because they fetch a high price.
Introductory Lectures on Political Economy (1832) p. 253

E. B. White 1899–1985
American humorist

3 Democracy is the recurrent suspicion that more than half of the people are right more than half of the time.
in *New Yorker* 3 July 1944

4 The so-called science of poll-taking is not a science at all but a mere necromancy. People are unpredictable by nature, and although you can take a nation's pulse, you can't be sure that the nation hasn't just run up a flight of stairs.
in *New Yorker* 13 November 1948

Theodore H. White 1915–86
American writer and journalist

5 Johnson's instinct for power is as primordial as a salmon's going upstream to spawn.
of Lyndon **Johnson**
The Making of the President (1964)

6 The flood of money that gushes into politics today is a pollution of democracy.
in *Time* 19 November 1984

William Allen White 1868–1944
American journalist and editor

7 Tinhorn politicians.
in *Emporia Gazette* 25 October 1901

8 Liberty is the only thing you cannot have unless you are willing to give it to others.
attributed

William Whitelaw 1918–99
British Conservative politician. On Whitelaw: see **Thatcher 311:4**

9 They are going about the country stirring up complacency.
commonly quoted as '...stirring up apathy'
of the Labour Party in the October 1974 election campaign; in *Independent* 13 June 1999

10 It is never wise to appear to be more clever than you are. It is sometimes wise to appear slightly less so.
attributed, 1975

Gough Whitlam 1916–
Australian Labor statesman, Prime Minister 1972–5

11 *of the part played by the new Prime Minister, William McMahon, in the resignation of his predecessor John Grey Gorton:*
He sat there on the Isle of Capri [at Surfers Paradise] plotting his destruction—Tiberius with a telephone.
in the House of Representatives, 1971

12 *the Governor-General, Sir John Kerr, had dismissed the Labor government headed by Gough Whitlam in November 1975:*
Well may he say 'God Save the Queen'. But after this nothing will save the Governor-General... Maintain your rage and your enthusiasm through the campaign for the election now to be held and until polling day.
speech in Canberra, 11 November 1975

Walt Whitman 1819–92
American poet

13 O Captain! my Captain! our fearful trip is done,
The ship has weathered every rack, the prize we sought is won,
The port is near, the bells I hear, the people all exulting.
allegorical poem on the death of Abraham **Lincoln**
'O Captain! My Captain!' (1871)

1 The ship is anchored safe and
  sound, its voyage closed and done.
  From fearful trip the victor ship
  comes in with object won;
  Exult O shores, and ring O bells! But I
  with mournful tread
  Walk the deck my Captain lies, Fallen
  cold and dead.
  'O Captain! My Captain!' (1871)

2 Where the populace rise at once
  against the never-ending audacity
  of elected persons.
  'Song of the Broad Axe' (1881)

3 Where the city of the healthiest
  fathers stands,
  Where the city of the best-bodied
  mothers stands,
  There the great city stands.
  'Song of the Broad Axe' (1881)

4 This dust was once the man,
  Gentle, plain, just and resolute,
  under whose cautious hand,
  Against the foulest crime in history
  known in any land or age,
  Was saved the Union of these States.
  'This dust was once the man' (1881)

5 The United States themselves are
  essentially the greatest poem.
  Leaves of Grass (1855) preface

6 Strange, (is it not?) that battles,
  martyrs, blood, even assassination,
  should so condense—perhaps
  only really, lastingly condense—a
  Nationality.
  of the American Civil War
  Geoffrey C. Ward The Civil War (1991)

John Greenleaf Whittier 1807–92
American poet

7 'Shoot, if you must, this old grey
  head,
  But spare your country's flag,' she
  said.
  A shade of sadness, a blush of shame,
  Over the face of the leader came.
  'Barbara Frietchie' (1863)

Robert Whittington c. 1480–1553?
English grammarian

8 As time requireth, a man of
  marvellous mirth and pastimes,
  and sometime of as sad gravity, as

who say: a man for all seasons.
  of Thomas **More**
    in Vulgaria (1521) pt. 2; Erasmus famously
    applied the idea to More, writing in his
    prefatory letter to In Praise of Folly (1509) that
    he played 'omnium horarum hominem [a man
    of all hours]'

Ann Widdecombe 1947–
British Conservative politician

9 He has something of the night in
  him.
  of **Howard** as a contender for the Conservative
  leadership
    in Sunday Times 11 May 1997 (electronic
    edition)

Elie Wiesel 1928–
Romanian-born American writer and Nobel Prize
winner; Auschwitz survivor

10 Take sides. Neutrality helps the
   oppressor, never the victim. Silence
   encourages the tormentor, never
   the tormented.
   accepting the Nobel Peace Prize
     in New York Times 11 December 1986

11 God of forgiveness, do not forgive
   those murderers of Jewish children
   here.
   at Auschwitz
     in Times 27 January 1995

William Wilberforce 1759–1833
British politician, philanthropist, and abolitionist

12 As soon as ever I had arrived
   thus far in my investigation of
   the slave trade, I confess to you,
   so enormous, so dreadful, so
   irremediable did its wickedness
   appear that my own mind was
   completely made up for the
   abolition.
   speech, 12 May 1789; in W. Cobbett et al.
   (eds.) The Parliamentary History of England
   (1806–20) vol. 28

13 If to be feelingly alive to the
   sufferings of my fellow-creatures…
   is to be a fanatic, I am one of the
   most incurable fanatics ever
   permitted to be at large.
   in 1816, Robert Wilberforce The Life of William
   Wilberforce (1838)

Oscar Wilde 1854–1900
Irish dramatist and poet

1 We have really everything in
common with America nowadays
except, of course, language.
The Canterville Ghost (1887); see
Misquotations 215:6

2 If the country doesn't go to the dogs
or the Radicals, we shall have you
Prime Minister, some day.
An Ideal Husband (1895)

3 The English country gentleman
galloping after a fox—the
unspeakable in full pursuit of the
uneatable.
A Woman of No Importance (1893) act 1; see
Zobel 341:3

Wilhelm II 1859–1941
German monarch, emperor 1888–1918

4 We have…fought for our place in
the sun and have won it. It will be
my business to see that we retain
this place in the sun unchallenged,
so that the rays of that sun may
exert a fructifying influence upon
our foreign trade and traffic.
speech in Hamburg, 18 June 1901; see
Bülow 45:5

John Wilkes 1727–97
English parliamentary reformer

5 EARL OF SANDWICH: 'Pon my soul,
Wilkes, I don't know whether
you'll die upon the gallows or of
the pox.
WILKES: That depends, my Lord,
whether I first embrace your
Lordship's principles, or your
Lordship's mistresses.
Charles Petrie *The Four Georges* (1935);
probably apocryphal

6 Give me a grain of truth and I
will mix it up with a great mass of
falsehood so that no chemist will
ever be able to separate them.
Adrian Hamilton *The Infamous Essay on
Women, or John Wilkes seated between Vice
and Virtue* (1972)

William III 1650–1702
British monarch, King of Great Britain and Ireland from
1688. See also **Proverbs 251:11**

7 'Do you not see your country
is lost?' asked the Duke of
Buckingham. 'There is one way
never to see it lost' replied William,
'and that is to die in the last ditch.'
Bishop Gilbert Burnet *History of My Own Time*
(1838 ed.)

Roy Williamson 1936–90
Scottish folksinger and musician

8 O flower of Scotland, when will we
see your like again,
that fought and died for your wee bit
hill and glen
and stood against him, proud
Edward's army,
and sent him homeward tae think
again.
unofficial Scottish Nationalist anthem
'O Flower of Scotland' (1968)

Wendell Willkie 1892–1944
American lawyer and Republican politician

9 Freedom is an indivisible word. If
we want to enjoy it, and fight for it,
we must be prepared to extend it to
everyone, whether they are rich or
poor, whether they agree with us
or not, no matter what their race or
the colour of their skin.
One World (1943)

10 The constitution does not provide
for first and second class citizens.
An American Programme (1944)

Charles E. Wilson 1890–1961
American industrialist; President of General Motors,
1941–53. See also **Slogans 290:7**

11 For years I thought what was
good for our country was good for
General Motors and vice versa.
The difference did not exist. Our
company is too big. It goes with the
welfare of the country.
testimony to the Senate Armed Services
Committee on his proposed nomination to be
Secretary of Defence, 15 January 1953

Harold Wilson 1916–95
British Labour statesman; Prime Minister, 1964–70,
1974–6. On Wilson: see **Benn 27:10**, **Bulmer-
Thomas 45:4**, **Home 146:10**, **Junor 164:10**

1 All these financiers, all the little
gnomes in Zurich and the other
financial centres about whom we
keep on hearing.
in the House of Commons, 12 November 1956

2 I think it's a trap, but I suppose
you can always walk into a trap
provided you are packing a Luger.
*in 1961, when pressed by Hugh Gaitskell to
exchange his successful shadow Treasury portfolio
for Foreign Affairs*
recalled by Anthony Howard; in *Times*
8 February 2005

3 I myself have always deprecated…
in crisis after crisis, appeals to the
Dunkirk spirit as an answer to our
problems.
in the House of Commons, 26 July 1961; see
Wilson 334:7

4 This party is a moral crusade or it is
nothing.
speech at the Labour Party Conference,
1 October 1962

5 We are restating our socialism in
terms of the scientific revolution…
the Britain that is going to be forged
in the white heat of this revolution
will be no place for restrictive
practices or outdated methods on
either side of industry.
speech at the Labour Party Conference,
1 October 1963; see **Misquotations 216:12**

6 What I think we are going to need
is something like what President
Kennedy had when he came in after
years of stagnation in the United
States. He had a programme of a
hundred days—a hundred days of
dynamic action.
in a party political broadcast, 15 July 1964

7 I believe that the spirit of Dunkirk
will carry us through…to success.
speech to the Labour Party Conference,
12 December 1964; see **Wilson 334:3**

8 The Smethwick Conservatives can
have the satisfaction of having
topped the poll, and of having sent
here as their Member one who,

until a further General Election
restores him to oblivion, will serve
his term here as a Parliamentary
leper.
*on the outcome of a by-election with racist
overtones*
in the House of Commons, 3 November 1964

9 A week is a long time in politics.
*probably first said at a lobby briefing at the time
of the 1964 sterling crisis*
Nigel Rees *Sayings of the Century* (1984); see
Chamberlain 60:3

10 [Labour is] the natural party of
government.
in 1965; Anthony Sampson *The Changing
Anatomy of Britain*

11 From now the pound abroad is
worth 14 per cent or so less in terms
of other currencies. It does not
mean, of course, that the pound
here in Britain, in your pocket or
purse or in your bank, has been
devalued.
ministerial broadcast, 19 November 1967

12 Get your tanks off my lawn, Hughie.
to the trade union leader Hugh **Scanlon**, at
Chequers in June 1969, Peter Jenkins *The
Battle of Downing Street* (1970)

13 I know what is going on. I am going
on.
*commenting on rumours of conspiracies against
his leadership*
at a May Day rally, 4 May 1969; Ben Pimlott
Harold Wilson (1992)

14 One man's wage increase is another
man's price increase.
speech at Blackburn, 8 January 1970

15 This party is a bit like an old
stagecoach. If you drive along
at a rapid rate, everyone aboard
is either so exhilarated or so
seasick that you don't have a lot of
difficulty.
of the Labour Party, 1974
Anthony Sampson *The Changing Anatomy of
Britain* (1982)

16 Whichever party is in office, the
Treasury is in power.
while in opposition, 1974; Anthony Sampson
The Changing Anatomy of Britain (1982)

17 I've buried all the hatchets. But I
know where I've buried them and I

can dig them up if necessary.
of the Cabinet in 1974
Lord Hunt in *Secret History. Harold Wilson: The Final Years* (Channel 4 TV) 15 August 1996

1 The trouble is when the old problems reappear I reach for the old solutions.
to his Press Secretary Joe Haines, July 1975; Peter Hennessy *The Prime Minister: the Office and its Holders since 1945* (2000)

2 The Monarchy is a labour-intensive industry.
in *Observer* 13 February 1977

3 In the 1964 Government…I had to occupy almost every position on the field, goalkeeper, defence, attack—I had to take the corner-kicks and penalties, administer to the wounded and bring on the lemons at half-time.
Final Term: The Labour Government 1974–76 (1979)

4 The one thing we need to nationalize in this country is the Treasury, but no one has ever succeeded.
in 1984; Peter Hennessy *Whitehall* (1990)

Joe Wilson 1947–
American Republican politician

5 You lie!
*shouted at President **Obama** during his speech on reforming health care*
joint session of Congress, 9 September 2009

Woodrow Wilson 1856–1924
American Democratic statesman, 28th President of the US. On Wilson: see **Clemenceau 75:1**, **Keynes 169:2**

6 Prosperity is necessarily the first theme of a political campaign.
speech, 4 September, 1912; see **Slogans 290:22**

7 Liberty has never come from the government. Liberty has always come from the subjects of government. The history of liberty is the history of resistance. The history of liberty is a history of the limitation of governmental power, not the increase of it.
speech to the New York Press Club, 9 September 1912

8 The United States must be neutral

in fact as well as in name.
at the outbreak of the First World War
message to the Senate, 19 August 1914

9 It is like writing history with lightning. And my only regret is that it is all so terribly true.
on seeing D. W. Griffith's film The Birth of a Nation *at the White House, 18 February 1915*

10 No nation is fit to sit in judgement upon any other nation.
speech in New York, 20 April 1915

11 There is such a thing as a man being too proud to fight; there is such a thing as a nation being so right that it does not need to convince others by force that it is right.
speech in Philadelphia, 10 May 1915

12 We have stood apart, studiously neutral.
speech to Congress, 7 December 1915

13 America can not be an ostrich with its head in the sand.
speech at Des Moines, 1 February 1916

14 It must be a peace without victory… Only a peace between equals can last.
speech to US Senate, 22 January 1917

15 Armed neutrality is ineffectual enough at best.
speech to Congress, 2 April 1917

16 The day has come when America is privileged to spend her blood and her might for the principles that gave her birth and happiness and the peace which she has treasured.
speech to Congress, 2 April 1917

17 The world must be made safe for democracy.
speech to Congress, 2 April 1917; see **Wolfe 336:10**

18 The right is more precious than peace.
speech to Congress, 2 April 1917

19 Once lead this people into war and they will forget there ever was such a thing as tolerance.
John Dos Passos *Mr Wilson's War* (1917)

20 The programme of the world's peace…is this:
1. Open covenants of peace, openly arrived at.
speech to Congress, 8 January 1918

1 A general association of nations must be formed...for the purpose of affording mutual guarantees of political independence and territorial integrity to great and small states alike.
speech to Congress, 8 January 1918

2 America is the only idealistic nation in the world.
speech at Sioux Falls, South Dakota, 8 September 1919

3 If I am to speak for ten minutes, I need a week for preparation; if fifteen minutes, three days; if half an hour, two days; if an hour, I am ready now.
Josephus Daniels *The Wilson Era* (1946)

William Windham 1750–1810
English politician

4 Those entrusted with arms...should be persons of some substance and stake in the country.
in the House of Commons, 22 July 1807

David Winnick 1933–
British Labour politician

5 Your early retirement would help the reputation of the House.
often quoted as 'Your early retirement, Sir...'
to the Speaker Michael Martin, in House of Commons, 18 May 2009

John Winthrop 1588–1649
American settler

6 We must consider that we shall be a city upon a hill, the eyes of all people are on us; so that if we shall deal falsely with our God in this work we have undertaken, and so cause Him to withdraw His present help from us, we shall be made a story and a byword through the world.
Christian Charity, A Model Hereof (sermon, 1630)

Robert Charles Winthrop 1809–94
American politician

7 A Star for every State, and a State for every Star.
speech on Boston Common, 27 August 1862

Humbert Wolfe 1886–1940
British poet

8 You cannot hope
to bribe or twist,
thank God! the
British journalist.
But, seeing what
the man will do
unbribed, there's
no occasion to.
'Over the Fire' (1930)

James Wolfe 1727–59
British general; captor of Quebec

9 The General...repeated nearly the whole of Gray's Elegy...adding, as he concluded, that he would prefer being the author of that poem to the glory of beating the French to-morrow.
J. Playfair *Biographical Account of J. Robinson* in *Transactions of the Royal Society of Edinburgh* vol. 7 (1815)

Thomas Wolfe 1900–38
American novelist

10 'Where they got you stationed now, Luke?' said Harry Tugman peering up snoutily from a mug of coffee. 'At the p-p-p-present time in Norfolk at the Navy base,' Luke answered, 'm-m-making the world safe for hypocrisy.'
Look Homeward, Angel (1929); see **Wilson 335:17**

Tom Wolfe 1931–
American writer

11 A liberal is a conservative who's

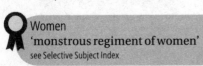

Women
'monstrous regiment of women'
see Selective Subject Index

been arrested.
The Bonfire of the Vanities (1987); see **Proverbs 251:5**

1 A cult is a religion with no political power.
In Our Time (1980)

Mary Wollstonecraft 1759–97
English feminist

2 It is justice, not charity, that is wanting in the world.
A Vindication of the Rights of Woman (1792)

Thomas Wolsey c. 1475–1530
English cardinal; Lord Chancellor, 1515–29

3 Father Abbot, I am come to lay my bones amongst you.
George Cavendish *Negotiations of Thomas Wolsey* (1641)

4 Had I but served God as diligently as I have served the King, he would not have given me over in my grey hairs.
George Cavendish *Negotiations of Thomas Wolsey* (1641); see **Shakespeare 279:18**

Lord Woolf 1933–
British judge, Lord Chief Justice

5 What is the difference between a Lord Chancellor and a Secretary of State, the man on Clapham Omnibus could, with reason, ask. After all, that engagingly friendly and cheerful chappie, Lord Falconer, seems to be quite happy playing both roles.
in *Guardian Unlimited* 4 March 2004. Quote from Lord Woolf's Squire Centenary Lecture 'The Rule of Law and a Change in the Constitution'

Alexander Woollcott 1887–1943
American writer

6 I think your slogan 'Liberty or Death' is splendid, and whichever one you decide on will be all

right with me.
attributed

William Wordsworth 1770–1850
English poet

7 Bliss was it in that dawn to be alive, But to be young was very heaven!
'The French Revolution, as it Appeared to Enthusiasts' (1809); also *The Prelude* (1850)

8   In our halls is hung
Armoury of the invincible Knights of old:
We must be free or die, who speak the tongue
That Shakespeare spake; the faith and morals hold
Which Milton held. In every thing we are sprung
Of Earth's first blood, have titles manifold.
'It is not to be thought of that the Flood' (1807)

9 Once did she hold the gorgeous East in fee,
And was the safeguard of the West.
'On the Extinction of the Venetian Republic' (1807)

Henry Wotton 1568–1639
English poet and diplomat

10 Dazzled thus with height of place, Whilst our hopes our wits beguile, No man marks the narrow space 'Twixt a prison and a smile.
'Upon the sudden restraint of the Earl of Somerset' (1651)

11 An ambassador is an honest man sent to lie abroad for the good of his country.
written in the album of Christopher Fleckmore in 1604

Nathaniel Wraxall 1751–1831
English traveller and memoirist

12 Eloquence, transcendent eloquence, formed the foundation and the key-stone of Pitt's

World Wars
'blood, toil, tears and sweat'
see Selective Subject Index

Ministerial greatness. Every other quality in him was accessory.
*of William **Pitt** the Younger*
Historical and Posthumous Memoirs (1884) vol. 4

Kenyon Wright 1932–

Scottish Methodist minister, Chairman of the Scottish Constitutional Convention

1 What if that other single voice we know so well responds by saying, 'We say No and we are the State.' Well, we say Yes and we are the People!
*of Margaret **Thatcher** as Prime Minister*
speech at the inaugural meeting of the Scottish Constitutional Convention, 30 March 1989

Harry Wu 1937–

Chinese-born American political activist

2 I want to see the word *laogai* in every dictionary in every language in the world. I want to see the laogai ended. Before 1974, the word 'gulag' did not appear in any dictionary. Today, this single word conveys the meaning of Soviet political violence and its labour camp system. 'Laogai' also deserves a place in our dictionaries.
the laogai *are Chinese labour camps*
in *Washington Post* 26 May 1996

Augustin, Marquis de Ximénèz

1726–1817
French poet

3 *Attaquons dans ses eaux*
La perfide Albion!
Let us attack in her own waters perfidious Albion!
'L'Ère des Français' (October 1793)

Isoroku Yamamoto 1884–1943
Japanese admiral, Commander-in-Chief responsible
for planning the Japanese attack on Pearl Harbor

1 A military man can scarcely pride
himself on having 'smitten a
sleeping enemy'; in fact, to have
it pointed out is more a matter of
shame.
letter, 9 January 1942; Hirosuki Asawa *The
Reluctant Admiral* (1979, tr. John Bester); see
Misquotations 215:13

William Yancey 1814–63
American Confederate politician

2 *of Jefferson* **Davis**, *President-elect of the
Confederacy, in 1861:*
The man and the hour have met.
Shelby Foote *The Civil War: Fort Sumter to
Perryville* (1991)

W. B. Yeats 1865–1939
Irish poet

3 Too long a sacrifice
Can make a stone of the heart.
O when may it suffice?
'Easter, 1916' (1921)

4 I write it out in a verse—
MacDonagh and MacBride
And Connolly and Pearse
Now and in time to be,
Wherever green is worn,
Are changed, changed utterly:
A terrible beauty is born.
'Easter, 1916' (1921)

5 Those that I fight I do not hate,
Those that I guard I do not love.
'An Irish Airman Foresees his Death' (1919)

6 I think it better that at times like
these
We poets keep our mouths shut, for
in truth

We have no gift to set a statesman
right.
'A Reason for Keeping Silent' (1916)

7 Out of Ireland have we come.
Great hatred, little room,
Maimed us at the start.
I carry from my mother's womb
A fanatic heart.
'Remorse for Intemperate Speech' (1933)

8 Turning and turning in the
widening gyre
The falcon cannot hear the falconer;
Things fall apart; the centre cannot
hold;
Mere anarchy is loosed upon the
world,
The blood-dimmed tide is loosed,
and everywhere
The ceremony of innocence is
drowned;
The best lack all conviction, while
the worst
Are full of passionate intensity.
'The Second Coming' (1920)

9 Romantic Ireland's dead and gone,
It's with O'Leary in the grave.
'September, 1913' (1914)

10 Cast your mind on other days
That we in coming days may be
Still the indomitable Irishry.
'Under Ben Bulben' (1939)

11 *of the Anglo-Irish:*
We…are no petty people. We are
one of the great stocks of Europe.
We are the people of Burke; we are
the people of Swift, the people of
Emmet, the people of Parnell. We
have created most of the modern
literature of this country. We have
created the best of its political
intelligence.
speech in the Irish Senate, 11 June 1925, in the
debate on divorce

Boris Yeltsin 1931–2007
Russian statesman, President of the Russian
Federation 1991–2000

1 Today is the last day of an era past.
   at a Berlin ceremony to end the Soviet military
   presence in Germany
   in *Guardian* 1 September 1994

2 Europe is in danger of plunging into
   a cold peace.
   at the summit meeting of the Conference on
   Security and Co-operation in Europe, December
   1994; in Newsweek *19 December 1994*

Shoichi Yokoi 1915–97
Japanese soldier

3 It is a terrible shame for me—I
   came back, still alive, without
   having won the war.
   on returning to Japan after surviving for 28 years
   in the jungles of Guam before surrendering to the
   Americans in 1972
   in *Independent* 26 September 1997

Andrew Young 1932–
American clergyman and diplomat

4 Nothing is illegal if one hundred
   well-placed business men decide
   to do it.
   Morris K. Udall *Too Funny to be President*
   (1988)

Michael Young 1915–2002
British writer

5 Today we frankly recognize
   that democracy can be no more
   than aspiration, and have rule
   not so much by the people as
   by the cleverest people; not
   an aristocracy of birth, not a
   plutocracy of wealth, but a true
   meritocracy of talent.
   The Rise of the Meritocracy (1958)

Israel Zangwill 1864–1926
Jewish spokesman and writer

6 America is God's Crucible, the
   great Melting-Pot where all the
   races of Europe are melting and
   re-forming!
   The Melting Pot (1908)

Emiliano Zapata 1879–1919
Mexican revolutionary

7 Many of them, so as to curry favour
   with tyrants, for a fistful of coins,
   or through bribery or corruption,
   are shedding the blood of their
   brothers.
   on the maderistas *who, in Zapata's view, had*
   betrayed the revolutionary cause
   Plan de Ayala 28 November 1911

José Luis Rodriguez Zapatero
1960–
Spanish Socialist statesman, Prime Minister from 2004

8 You can't lead a war with lies.
   in *Independent* 16 March 2004

Muntadar al-Zeidi 1979–
Iraqi journalist

9 It is the farewell kiss, you dog.
   hurling his shoes at George W. Bush
   press conference, Baghdad, 14 December 2008

Mikhail Zhvanetsky 1934–
Russian writer

10 We enjoyed…his slyness. He
   mastered the art of walking
   backward into the future. He would
   say 'After me'. And some people
   went ahead, and some went behind,

and he would go backward.
*of Mikhail **Gorbachev***
in *Time* 12 September 1994; attributed

Ronald L. Ziegler 1939–
American government spokesman

1 *reminded of the President's previous statements that the White House was not involved in the Watergate affair:*
[Mr Nixon's latest statement] is the Operative White House Position… and all previous statements are inoperative.
in *Boston Globe* 18 April 1973

Grigori Zinoviev 1883–1936
Soviet politician

2 Armed warfare must be preceded by a struggle against the inclinations to compromise which are embedded among the majority of British workmen, against the ideas of evolution and peaceful extermination of capitalism. Only then will it be possible to count upon complete success of an armed insurrection.
letter to the British Communist Party, 15 September 1924, in *Times* 25 October 1924 (the 'Zinoviev Letter', said by some to be a forgery)

Hiller B. Zobel 1932–
American judge

3 Asking the ignorant to use the incomprehensible to decide the unknowable.
'The Jury on Trial' in *American Heritage* July–August 1995; see **Wilde 333:3**

4 Judges must follow their oaths and do their duty, heedless of editorials, letters, telegrams, threats, petitions, panellists and talk shows.
judicial ruling reducing the conviction of Louise Woodward from murder to manslaughter, 10 November 1997

Émile Zola 1840–1902
French novelist

5 *La vérité est en marche, et rien ne l'arrêtera.*
Truth is on the march, and nothing will stop it.
on the Dreyfus affair
in *Le Figaro* 25 November 1897

6 *J'accuse.*
I accuse.
title of an open letter to the President of the French Republic, in connection with the Dreyfus affair
in *L'Aurore* 13 January 1898

Keyword Index

A. friends	Blai 36:11	anguish howls of a.	Heal 138:12
A. government	Jeff 157:12	animal by nature a political a.	Aris 12:4
A. people have spoken	Clin 76:8	insidious and crafty a.	Smit 293:2
A., this new man	Crèv 81:6	animals All a. are equal	Orwe 232:14
bad news to the A. people	Keil 166:2	ankle chain about the a.	Doug 97:11
chief business of the A. people	Cool 80:9	Anna Here thou, great A.	Pope 248:2
free man, an A.	John 159:5	annihilating a. all civilization	Sakh 268:4
Greeks in this A. empire	Macm 199:2	a. nations	Mont 217:14
I also—am an A.	Webs 328:5	annus a. horribilis	Eliz 105:3
I am A. bred	Mill 213:4	anointed balm from an a. king	Shak 284:2
in A. politics	Mitc 214:8	answer a. to the Irish Question	Sell 276:14
I shall die an A.	Webs 328:7	answering about not a.	Lynn 192:9
knocking the A. system	Capo 56:4	antiblack a. laws	Frie 116:3
no A. infidels	Sahh 268:2	Antichrist A. of Communism	Buch 45:1
not a Virginian, but an A.	Henr 142:2	anticipate What we a.	Disr 95:6
point of being an A.	Updi 319:7	anti-Semitic stupid as the a.	Lloy 189:14
Scratch any A.	Rusk 266:7	anvil will be the a.	Hitl 144:9
send A. boys	John 159:13	anybody no one's a.	Gilb 123:10
voodoo about A. foreign policy	Fulb 116:15	anywhere a. I damn well please	Bevi 32:2
welfare of the A. people	Hear 140:3	apart have stood a.	Wils 335:12
Americanism A. with its sleeves rolled	McCa 195:14	apathy stirring up a.	Whit 331:9
hyphenated A.	Roos 264:7	ape Is man an a.	Disr 93:8
Americans A. are our best friends	Thom 311:15	aphrodisiac Power is the great a.	Kiss 174:13
A. are to be freemen	Wash 326:5	apologize Never a.	Fish 110:6
A. in and the Germans down	Isma 152:15	apology defence or a.	Char 61:6
for A. it is just beyond	Kiss 175:5	equated with an a.	Brow 44:1
let A. disdain	Hami 134:12	apostles A. of freedom	Conn 79:2
my fellow A.	Kenn 167:4	true a. of equality	Arno 12:14
passed to new generation of A.	Kenn 166:12	appeasement A. was a sensible	Tayl 306:15
teaching A. geography	Prov 252:8	appeaser a. is one who	Chur 66:14
amiable in a. theories	Sali 268:8	appeasers A. believe	Brou 43:3
amicably a. if they can	Quin 253:3	appetite no a. for truth	Peel 242:7
ammunition pass the a.	Forg 112:2	appetites chains upon their own a.	Burk 46:3
amok patriotism run a.	Rath 255:6	applause everyone is forced to a.	Mill 213:7
amused We are not a.	Vict 322:4	appointment a. by the corrupt few	Shaw 286:9
amusements part in their a.	Well 329:11	create an a.	Loui 190:17
anarch Thy hand, great A.	Pope 247:8	appointments In making a.	Sali 272:2
anarchism A. is a game	Shaw 286:14	apprenticeship a. for freedom	Bara 24:4
A. stands for the liberation	Gold 126:13	approbation a. of all their actions	Hobb 145:6
anarchy a. and competition	Rusk 267:3	appropriate that was not a.	Clin 76:6
cure of a.	Burk 46:21	Arab A. world together	Araf 11:9
democracy, call it *a.*	Hobb 145:7	Arabs seven hundred thousand A.	Balf 23:7
Mere a. is loosed	Yeat 339:8	Arbeicht A. macht frei	Slog 290:3
anatomist am but a bad a.	Last 178:10	arbiter a. of others' fate	Byro 52:7
ancestors If our a. had cared	Sali 270:6	arbitrary a. government	Char 62:6
look backward to their a.	Burk 47:9	*supreme power must be a.*	Hali 133:8
ancestry delusion about its a.	Inge 152:5	arc a. of a moral universe	King 171:12
pride of a.	Powe 249:9	a. of history is long	Obam 230:10
anchor firm a. in nonsense	Galb 117:8	arch a. of order	Stra 302:11
angel a. of death	Brig 42:1	like a triumphal a.	Dunn 100:3
a. rides in the whirlwind	Page 235:10	triumphant a.	Comm 78:5
ape or an a.	Disr 93:8	archipelago Gulag a.	Solz 295:9
angels better a. of our nature	Linc 185:11	are A. you now	Prov 251:2
By that sin fell the a.	Shak 279:17	arena actually in the a.	Roos 264:5
make the a. weep	Shak 283:12	Argentina Don't cry for me, A.	Rice 259:1
plead like a.	Shak 282:15	Argentinian young A. soldiers	Runc 266:4
anger a. of the sovereign	More 219:2	argues Nobody a. now	Sali 271:4
neither a. nor partiality	Taci 304:7	argument a. for fisticuffs	Chur 69:14
Anglicization demon of A.	Hyde 151:5	no force but a.	Brow 44:2
Anglo-Irishman He was an A.	Beha 26:5	once in the use of an a.	Benn 28:3
Anglo-Saxon natural idol of the A.	Bage 19:9	stir without great a.	Shak 278:14

civil c. to everyone	Siss 289:5
C. war is a species of misery	Scot 276:3
dire effects from c. discord	Addi 4:9
If this is not c. war	Alla 6:2
civilian c. control	Trum 317:14
civilization annihilating all c.	Sakh 268:4
C. a movement	Toyn 314:5
C. and profits	Cool 80:8
C. was held together	Tayl 306:7
in a state of c.	Jeff 156:12
pillars of c.	Monn 217:5
submit to c.	Tocq 313:14
test of c.	John 161:2
thought of modern c.	Gand 119:5
civilized c. society	Holm 146:5
force another to be c.	Mill 212:14
that are called c.	Pain 237:15
civilizers two c. of man	Disr 93:18
civilizes Cricket c. people	Muga 221:12
civil servant c. doesn't make jokes	Ione 152:14
Give a c. a good case	Clar 73:2
Here lies a c.	Siss 289:5
ideal c.	Peyr 244:9
civil servants conviction c.	Banc 24:2
Civil Service business of the C.	Arms 12:12
C. is a bit like	Butl 51:13
C. is deferential	Cros 83:8
Reorganizing the C.	Anon 9:11
civis C. Romanus sum	Cice 72:12
C. Romanus sum	Palm 238:11
claim last territorial c.	Hitl 144:7
claims c. are not false	Riel 259:8
clamour those who c. most	Peel 242:18
clan c. and race	Mill 213:5
Clapham man on the C. omnibus	Bowe 40:2
clapped-out c., post-imperial	Drab 97:12
class first and second c. citizens	Will 333:10
hands of the ruling c.	Stal 299:2
history of c. struggles	Marx 207:5
use of *force* by one c.	Leni 182:9
While there is a lower c.	Debs 86:13
classes All c. of society	Jevo 158:7
c. and class antagonists	Marx 207:6
lower c. had such white	Curz 84:5
masses against the c.	Glad 125:11
cleaning c. the streets	La G 176:10
clearing c.-house of the world	Cham 60:5
Cleopatra C.'s nose been shorter	Pasc 241:5
clergy Arminian c.	Pitt 245:12
c. are not called	Walp 324:11
Established C.	Glad 125:6
clergyman bookie or a c.	Mugg 221:16
clerks statesmen or of c.	Disr 94:11
clever become the c. country	Hawk 137:7
more c. than you are	Whit 331:10
to appear c.	Hill 143:12
Too c. by half	Sali 269:12
Too c. by half	Sali 273:8
cleverest c. woman in England	Anon 10:14
cliché c. and an indiscretion	Macm 199:5
used every c.	Chur 67:7

clichés wreck it with c.	Clar 73:2
cliffs white c. I never more must see	Maca 195:3
climax end a sentence with a c.	Lask 180:6
climb c. not at all	Eliz 104:8
Fain would I c.	Rale 254:5
climbs None c. so high	Crom 83:1
cloak c. become an iron cage	Webe 327:7
clock never put the c. back	Waug 327:2
cloistered fugitive and c. virtue	Milt 213:13
cloned successfully c. a lamb	Marc 205:5
close Keep your friends c.	Puzo 250:8
peacefully towards its c.	Daws 86:8
will not c. my politics	Fox 113:9
closed greatest c. shop	Hosk 147:12
closer Come c., boys	Last 178:3
cloth Republican c. coat	Nixo 228:2
cloud c. in the west	Glad 124:7
in C.-cuckoo-land	Heal 139:5
cloudcuckooland How about 'C.'	Aris 11:15
clunking big c. fist	Blai 36:18
CMG C. (Call Me God)	Prov 251:20
coach c. and six horses	Rice 258:10
like being a football c.	McCa 195:12
coal shortage of c. and fish	Beva 30:4
coalition rainbow c.	Jack 154:1
coalitions England does not love c.	Disr 93:1
coals c. to Newcastle	Geor 121:7
coat doesn't have a mink c.	Nixo 228:2
stick in his c.	Brow 44:4
cobwebs Laws are like c.	Swif 303:10
cock Our c. won't fight	Beav 25:8
cocksure c. of anything	Melb 209:13
stupid are c.	Russ 267:12
codified insincerity c.	Sali 272:15
coercion effect of c.	Jeff 157:7
coexistence peaceful c.	Fulb 116:12
coffee C. house babble	Disr 94:1
echo of a London c.-house	Swif 303:9
put poison in your c.	Asto 14:3
coffin silver plate on a c.	Curr 83:14
coins for a fistful of c.	Zapa 340:7
cold c. relation	Burk 48:3
c. war warrior	That 309:4
Fallen c. and dead	Whit 332:1
midst of a c. war	Baru 24:11
plunging into a c. peace	Yelt 340:2
Without the c. war	Updi 319:7
colleagues fidelity to c.	Lask 180:5
collects beautiful c.	Maca 194:14
collision avoid foreign c.	Clay 73:3
colonial backward c. policy	Roos 262:15
colonies commerce with our c.	Burk 46:16
New c. seek	Free 115:10
not cease to be c.	Disr 93:4
These wretched c.	Disr 92:14
united c.	Lee 182:2
colonization subjects for future c.	Monr 217:8
colony fuzzy wuzzy c.	Cair 53:3
colossus Like a C.	Shak 280:3
colour by the c. of their skin	King 171:8
c. of their skin	Will 333:9

matches have a box of m.	Home 146:9	M. lived like fishes	Sidn 288:12
with that stick of m.	Mand 204:6	m. with the muck-rakes	Roos 264:3
material elementary m. wants	Sali 269:9	*Not m., but measures*	Burk 48:15
mateship as dearly as m.	Anon 10:12	State is a relation of m.	Webe 327:8
matter not fighting does m.	Step 300:7	twelve good m.	Brou 42:12
matters Nothing m. very much	Balf 23:14	**menace** m. to be defeated	Scar 274:11
maxim just political m.	Hume 149:10	**mend** Make do and m.	Offi 231:7
mayor tart who has married the M.	Baxt 25:6	**mental** Freedom and slavery are m.	Gand 119:3
maypole organ and the m.	Jord 162:11	m. decay	Nico 227:3
McCarthyism M. is Americanism with	McCa 195:14	**mercenary** by means of m. armies	Mach 197:10
McNamara M.'s War	McNa 200:7	m. calling	Hous 147:14
me save thee and m.	Owen 235:8	**merchandise** mechanical arts and m.	Baco 17:15
mean nothing common did or m.	Marv 206:6	**merchandize** m. candidates	Stev 301:6
meanest m. of mankind	Pope 247:12	**merchants** M. have no country	Jeff 156:11
means Increased m.	Disr 93:18	**mercury** pick up m. with a fork	Lloy 189:20
m. just what I choose	Carr 57:16	**mercy** crowning m.	Crom 82:11
politics by other m.	Clau 74:1	m. on my poor country	Last 179:1
meant damned dots m.	Chur 65:6	m. to forgive	Dryd 99:2
what he m. by that	Loui 191:5	quality of m.	Shak 283:13
measles m. of the human race	Eins 102:5	so good a grace As m.	Shak 283:10
measure m. becomes a target	Good 127:10	Thy m. on Thy People	Kipl 174:5
Shrunk to this little m.	Shak 281:5	**merit** *m.* for a bishopric	West 330:12
measures Great public m.	Peel 243:12	no damned m. about it	Melb 210:5
M. not men	Cann 55:15	What is m.	Palm 239:3
Not men, but m.	Burk 48:15	**meritocracy** m. of talent	Youn 340:5
weights and m.	Napo 224:6	**merry** always very m.	Sell 276:11
meat appointed to buy the m.	Seld 276:6	m. monarch	Roch 260:13
flies off the m.	Chur 67:8	never m. world in England	Shak 279:8
Upon what m.	Shak 280:4	**message** ask me to take a m.	Last 179:4
mechanical m. arts and merchandise	Baco 17:15	**messenger** m.-boy Presidency	Schl 274:13
medal m. glitters	Chur 67:15	**met** m. Saddam Hussein	Gall 118:15
meddle I m. not	Crom 82:9	**Methodism** more to M. than to Marxism	Phil 244:13
M. and muddle	Derb 89:7	**Mexico** M., so far from God	Diaz 90:11
meddles Minister that m. with art	Melb 209:12	**MI5** M. is a job creation	Henn 141:5
meddling m. government	Maca 195:7	**Micawbers** like inverted M.	Gued 131:5
Medes law of the M. and Persians	Bibl 32:23	**mice** as long as it catches m.	Deng 88:16
media m. like an oil painting	Ingh 152:12	**microphone** paid for this m.	Reag 255:14
who the m. says I am	Obam 231:11	**microscopic** m. advantages	Sali 269:3
medicine rotational m.	Morg 219:5	**middle** m. excellent	Volt 323:8
mediocre Titles distinguish the m.	Shaw 286:13	m. of the road	High 143:11
meek borne his faculties so m.	Shak 282:15	m. way is none at all	Adam 3:2
m. shall inherit	Smit 293:12	**middle class** dregs of the m.	Beaz 26:2
meet to m. my Maker	Chur 70:3	m. is in control	Aris 12:9
meeting *loves* m. people	Lloy 189:11	M. was quite prepared	Bell 26:10
old-fashioned political public m.	Tebb 307:15	Philistines proper, or m.	Arno 12:15
Mehmets Johnnies and the M.	Atat 14:4	sinking m.	Orwe 234:2
melted soft centre has always m.	Hail 132:5	**Middlesex** acre in M.	Maca 194:3
melting M.-Pot where all the races	Zang 340:6	**midnight** fire-bell at m.	Burk 49:4
memoirs write one's m. is to speak ill	Péta 244:7	stroke of the m. hour	Nehr 224:10
memorandum m. is written	Ache 1:8	**might** Britons alone use 'M.'	Waug 326:15
memorial whole earth as their m.	Peri 244:3	**mighty** Look on my works, ye M.	Shel 287:6
memories ought to have good m.	Sidn 288:11	thou art m. yet	Shak 282:7
memory m. for a politician	Morl 219:11	**migration** M....is the oldest action	Galb 118:7
my name and m.	Last 178:6	**militarism** M....is fetish worship	Tawn 305:8
mystic chords of m.	Linc 185:11	**military** control of the m.	Trum 317:14
no force can abolish m.	Roos 263:2	entrust to m. men	Clem 75:5
to his m. for his jests	Sher 287:18	m.-industrial complex	Eise 103:4
men 200,000 m.	Napo 224:3	**milk** putting m. into babies	Chur 68:5
economic girlie m.	Schw 275:10	**million** m. is a statistic	Stal 299:7
government of laws, and not of m.	Adam 3:1	promise a m. light bulbs	Harp 136:8
Measures not m.	Cann 55:15	**millionaire** m. has just as good	Hope 147:7

Selective Subject Index

UK General Election 2010

1 I am not the kingmaker. The 45 million voters of Britain are the kingmakers. They give the politicians their marching orders, not the other way round.
Nick **Clegg**, Liberal Democrat pre-election conference, Birmingham, 14 March 2010

2 Our nation deserves more, much more, than a decade of dismal cuts from Tory and Labour.
Alex **Salmond**, launching Scottish National Party manifesto, 12 April 2010

3 I agree with Nick.
Gordon **Brown**, in the first televised Party Leaders' debate, ITV, 15 April 2010

4 The more they attack each other, the more they sound exactly the same.
Nick **Clegg**, in the first televised Party Leaders' debate, ITV, 15 April 2010

5 The Big Society is our big idea.
David **Cameron**, speech to voters, Swindon 18 April 2010; the Big Society formed part of the Conservative Party manifesto launched on 13 April 2010

6 These two guys remind me of my two young boys squabbling at bathtime.
*on David **Cameron** and Nick **Clegg***
Gordon **Brown**, in the second televised Party Leaders' debate, Sky News, 22 April 2010

7 She's just a sort of bigoted woman that said she used to be Labour.
after speaking to a voter, Gillian Duffy, who had questioned him on issues including immigration
Gordon **Brown**, aside to an aide (overheard on a microphone) in Rochdale, 28 April 2010

8 Whoever wins this election will be out of power for a whole generation because of how tough the fiscal austerity will have to be.
Mervyn King (1948–) English economist, Governor of the Bank of England, quoted by American economist David Hale on *Lateline* (Australian Broadcasting Corporation) 28 April 2010

9 I believe Gordon Brown has been the worst prime minister we have had in this country.
Manish Sood, British Labour politician, candidate for Norfolk North-West, in *Lynn News* 4 May 2010

10 I'm of course sorry for the cameras that they didn't quite get the moment they were looking for, but I have to say, it was quite close.
on being re-elected as MP for Morley & Outwood despite predictions that he would lose
Ed Balls (1967–) British Labour politician, 7 May 2010

11 My instinct is that, regrettably, we have lost the election.
David **Blunkett**, 7 May 2010

12 Shameful scenes of hundreds of voters turned away from polling stations are unworthy of a mature democracy like ours.
Shami Chakrabarti (1969–) British lawyer, Director of Liberty, 7 May 2010

13 I want to make a big, open and comprehensive offer to the Liberal Democrats. I want us to work together in tackling our country's big and urgent problems—the debt crisis, our deep social problems and our broken political system.
David **Cameron**, speech, Westminster, 7 May 2010

14 Whatever type of Wall's sausage is contrived by this great experiment, the dominant ingredient has got to be Conservative, the meat in the sausage has got to be Conservative.
Boris **Johnson**, interviewed by Jeremy **Paxman**, 7 May 2010

15 Your system is a recipe for corruption; it was a massive shock when I saw you didn't need any identification to vote.
Marie Marilyn Jalloh, Sierra Leonean politician, Commonwealth electoral observer, in *Sunday Times* 9 May 2010

UK General Election 2010 *continued*

1 I said the other day that I thought the British electorate had invented a deliciously painful torture mechanism for the Liberal Democrats because our instincts go one way but the mathematics go the other.
   Lord Ashdown (1941–) British Liberal Democrat politician, *The Andrew Marr Show* BBC TV 9 May 2010

2 Above all, it was a privilege to serve. And yes, I loved the job not for its prestige, its titles and its ceremony—which I do not love at all. No, I loved the job for its potential to make this country I love fairer, more tolerant, more green, more democratic, more prosperous and more just—truly a greater Britain.
   Gordon **Brown**, speech announcing his resignation, Downing Street, London, 10 May 2010

3 This is going to be hard and difficult work. A coalition will throw up all sorts of challenges, but I believe together we can provide that strong and stable government that our country needs, based on those values, rebuilding family, rebuilding community—and above all— rebuilding responsibility in our country.
   David **Cameron**, speech, Downing Street, London, 11 May 2010

4 We are now going to form a new government. More importantly we are going to get a new kind of government. I hope that this is the start of the new politics I always believed in.
   Nick **Clegg**, speech following a meeting with Liberal Democrat MPs and the party federal executive, shortly after midnight, 12 May 2010

5 Dear chief secretary, I'm afraid to tell you there's no money left.
   Liam Byrne (1970–) British Labour politician, letter left for his successor as Chief Secretary to the Treasury, David Laws, as quoted by Laws, 17 May 2010